VOLUME I
TO 1877

OUT OF MANY

A HISTORY
OF THE
AMERICAN PEOPLE

THIRD EDITION

JOHN MACK FARAGHER
Yale University

MARI JO BUHLE
Brown University

DANIEL CZITROM
Mount Holyoke College

SUSAN H. ARMITAGE
Washington State University

Prentice Hall, Upper Saddle River, New Jersey 07458

Library of Congress Cataloging–in–Publication Data

Out of many: a history of the American people / John Mack Faragher
   . . . [et al.]. — 3rd ed., Combined ed.
     p. cm.
   Includes bibliographical references and index.
   ISBN 0-13-949760-9
   1. United States—History.   I. Faragher, John Mack
E178.1.0935 2000   98–34110
973—dc21   CIP

Editorial Director: Charlyce Jones Owen
Executive Editor: Todd R. Armstrong
Development Editor: David Chodoff
Production Editor: Louise Rothman
Creative Director: Leslie Osher
Art Director: Anne Bonanno Nieglos
Editor-in-Chief of Development: Susanna Lesan
Marketing Manager: Sheryl Adams
Interior and Cover Designer: Thomas Nery
Cover Art: John L. Krimmel, Painting, (1786–1821), oil on
     on canvas, H. 16¾" x 25⅝". (AN:59.131)
     Courtesy, Winterthur Museum, *Election Day*
     in Philadelphia (1815)—detail.

AVP, Director of Production and Manufacturing: Barbara Kittle
Manufacturing Manager: Nick Sklitsis
Manufacturing Buyer: Lynn Pearlman
Photo Researcher: Barbara Salz
Photo Editor: Lorinda Morris-Nantz
Copy Editor: Sylvia Moore
Editorial Assistant: Holly Jo Brown
Line Art Coordinator: Guy Ruggiero
Cartographers: Alice and William Thiede/
     CARTO-GRAPHICS
Electronic Page Layout: Scott Garrison and Rosemary Ross

Credits and acknowledgments for materials borrowed from other sources and reproduced,
with permission, in this textbook appear on pages C–1 – C–3.

This book was set in 11/12 Weiss by the HSS in-house formatting
and production services groups and was printed and bound by RR Donnelley & Sons Company.
The cover was printed by Phoenix Color Corp.

Printed in the United States of America
10 9 8 7 6 5 4 3 2 1

ISBN 0-13-949306-9

Prentice-Hall International (UK) Limited, *London*
Prentice-Hall of Australia Pty. Limited, *Sydney*
Prentice-Hall Canada Inc., *Toronto*
Prentice-Hall Hispanoamericana, S.A., *Mexico*
Prentice-Hall of India Private Limited, *New Delhi*
Prentice-Hall of Japan, Inc., *Tokyo*
Pearson Education Asia Pte. Ltd., *Singapore*
Editora Prentice-Hall do Brasil, Ltda., *Rio de Janeiro*

TO OUR STUDENTS,
OUR SISTERS,
AND OUR BROTHERS

BRIEF CONTENTS

CONTENTS

MAPS

CHARTS, GRAPHS, AND TABLES

PREFACE

Out of Many, A History of the American People, third edition, offers a distinctive and timely approach to American history, highlighting the experiences of diverse communities of Americans in the unfolding story of our country. These communities offer a way of examining the complex historical forces shaping people's lives at various moments in our past. The debates and conflicts surrounding the most momentous issues in our national life—independence, emerging democracy, slavery, westward settlement, imperial expansion, economic depression, war, technological change—were largely worked out in the context of local communities. Through communities we focus on the persistent tensions between everyday life and those larger decisions and events that continually reshape the circumstances of local life. Each chapter opens with a description of a representative community. Some of these portraits feature American communities struggling with one another: African slaves and English masters on the rice plantations of colonial Georgia, or Tejanos and Americans during the Texas war of independence. Other chapters feature portraits of communities facing social change: the feminists of Seneca Falls, New York, in 1848; the sitdown strikers of Flint, Michigan, in 1934; and the African Americans of Montgomery, Alabama, in 1955. As the story unfolds we find communities growing to include ever larger groups of Americans: The soldiers from every colony who forged the Continental Army into a patriotic national force at Valley Forge during the American Revolution; the movie-goers who dreamed a collective dream of material prosperity and upward mobility during the 1920s; and the Americans linked in ever-growing numbers in the virtual communities of cyberspace as the twenty-first century begins.

Out of Many is also the only American history text with a truly continental perspective. With community vignettes from New England to the South, the Midwest to the far West, we encourage students to appreciate the great expanse of our nation. For example, a vignette of seventeenth-century Santa Fé, New Mexico illustrates the founding of the first European settlements in the New World. We present territorial expansion into the American West from the point of view of the Mandan villagers of the upper Missouri River of North Dakota. We introduce the policies of the Reconstruction era through the experience of African Americans in the Sea Island of South Carolina. This continental perspective drives home to students that American history has never been the preserve of any particular region.

In these ways *Out of Many* breaks new ground, but without compromising its coverage of the traditional turning points that we believe are critically important to an understanding of the American past. Among these watershed events are the Revolution and the struggle over the Constitution, the Civil War and Reconstruction, and the Great Depression and World War II. In *Out of Many*, however, we seek to *integrate* the narrative of national history with the story of the nation's many diverse communities. The Revolutionary and Constitutional period tried the ability of local communities to forge a new unity, and success depended on their ability to build a nation without compromising local identity. The Civil War and Reconstruction formed a second great test of the balance between the national ideas of the revolution and the power of local and sectional communities. The Depression and the New Deal demonstrated the impotence of local communities and the growing power of national institutions during the greatest economic challenge in our history. *Out of Many* also looks back in a new and comprehensive way—from the vantage point of the beginning of a new century and the end of the Cold War—at the salient events of the last fifty years and their impact on American communities. The community focus of *Out of Many* weaves the stories of the people and of the nation into a single compelling narrative.

SPECIAL FEATURES

With each edition of *Out of Many* we have sought to strengthen its unique integration of the best of traditional American history with its innovative community-based focus and strong continental perspective. A wealth of special features and pedagogical aids reinforces our narrative and helps students grasp key issues.

- ◆ **Community and Diversity.** *Out of Many*, third edition, opens with an introduction, titled "Community and Diversity," that acquaints students with the major themes of the book, providing them with a framework for understanding American history.

- ◆ **Immigration and Community: The Changing Face of Ethnicity in America.** This feature, new to this edition, highlights the impact of the immigrant experience on the formation of American communities. There are four Immigration and Community features in the book. The first covers the colonial period through 1800, the second covers from 1800 to 1860, the third covers from 1860 to 1930, and the last covers the period since 1930. Each is six pages long and opens with an overview of the character of immigration during the period in question. This overview is followed by a section called "In Their Own Words" that consists of extracts from primary sources written by immigrants themselves and by native-born Americans in response to the new arrivals. Study questions at the end of each Immigration and Community feature ask students to relate issues raised in the overview and documents to broader issues in American history.

- ◆ **History and the Land.** These features focus on the geographical dimension of historical change to give students an appreciation of the relationship between geography and history. Each elucidates an important historical trend or process with a map and a brief explanatory essay.

- ◆ **American Communities.** Each chapter opens with an American Communities vignette that relates the experience of a particular community to the broader issues discussed in the chapter.

- ◆ **Maps.** *Out of Many*, third edition, has more maps than any other American history textbook. Many maps include topographical detail that helps students appreciate the impact of geography on history.

- ◆ **Overview tables.** Overview tables, also new to this edition, provide students with a summary of complex issues.

- ◆ **Graphs, charts and tables.** Every chapter includes one or more graphs, charts, or tables that help students understand important events and trends.

- ◆ **Photos and illustrations.** The abundant illustrations in *Out of Many*, third edition, include many images that have never before been used in an American history text. None of the images is anachronistic—each one dates from the historical period under discussion. Extensive captions treat the

images as visual primary source documents from the American past, describing their source and explaining their significance.

- ◆ **Chapter-opening outlines and key topics lists.** These pedagogical aids provide students with a succinct preview of the material covered in each chapter.

- ◆ **Chronologies.** A chronology at the end of each chapter helps students build a framework of key events.

- ◆ **Review Questions.** Review questions help students review, reinforce, and retain the material in each chapter and encourage them to relate the material to broader issues in American history.

- ◆ **Recommended Reading and Additional Bibliography.** The works on the short, annotated Recommended Reading list at the end of each chapter have been selected with the interested introductory student in mind. The extensive Additional Bibliography provides a comprehensive overview of current scholarship on the subject of the chapter.

CLASSROOM ASSISTANCE PACKAGE

In classrooms across the country, many instructors encounter students who perceive history as merely a jumble of names, dates, and events. *Out of Many*, third edition, brings our dynamic past alive for these students with a text and accompanying print and multimedia classroom assistance package that combine sound scholarship, engaging narrative, and a rich array of pedagogical tools.

PRINT SUPPLEMENTS

Instructor's Resource Manual

A true time-saver in developing and preparing lecture presentations, the *Instructor's Resource Manual* contains chapter outlines, detailed chapter overviews, lecture topics, discussion questions, readings, and information on audio-visual resources.

Test Item File

Prepared by Gisela Ables, Mike McCormick, and David Aldstadt, Houston Community College

The *Test Item File* offers a menu of more than 1,500 multiple-choice, identification, matching, true-false, and essay test questions and 10–15 questions per chapter on maps found in each chapter. The guide includes a collection of blank maps that can be photocopied and used for map testing purposes or for other class exercises.

Prentice Hall Custom Test

This commercial-quality computerized test management program, available for Windows, DOS, and Macintosh environments, allows instructors to select items from the Test Item File and design their own exams.

Transparency Pack

Prepared by Robert Tomes, St. John's University

This collection of more than 160 full-color transparency acetates provides instructors with all the maps, charts, and graphs in the text for use in the classroom. Each transparency is accompanied by a page of descriptive material and discussion questions.

Study Guide, Volumes I and II

Prepared by Elizabeth Neumeyer, Kellogg Community College, and S. Ross Doughty, Ursinus College

Each chapter in the *Study Guide* includes a chapter commentary and outline, identification terms, multiple-choice questions, short essay questions, map questions, and questions based on primary source extracts.

Documents Set, Volumes I and II

Prepared by John Mack Faragher, Yale University, and Daniel Czitrom, Mount Holyoke College

The authors have selected and carefully edited more than 300 documents that relate directly to the themes and content of the text and organized them into five general categories: community, social history, government, culture, and politics. Each document is approximately two pages long and includes a brief introduction and study questions intended to encourage students to analyze the document critically and relate it to the content of the text. The Documents Set is available at a substantial discount when packaged with *Out of Many*.

Retrieving the American Past:
A Customized U.S. History Reader

Written and developed by leading historians and educators, this reader is an on-demand history database that offers 52 compelling modules on topics in American History, such as: Women on the Frontier, The Salem Witchcraft Scare, The Age of Industrial Violence, and Native American Societies, 1870–1995. Approximately 35 pages in length, each module includes an introduction, several primary documents and secondary sources, follow-up questions, and

recommendations for further reading. By deciding which modules to include and the order in which they will appear, instructors can compile the reader they want to use. Instructor-originated material—other readings, exercises—can be included. Contact your local Prentice Hall Representative for more information about this exciting custom publishing option.

Understanding and Answering Essay Questions

Prepared by Mary L. Kelley, San Antonio College

This brief guide suggests helpful study techniques as well as specific analytical tools for understanding different types of essay questions and provides precise guidelines for preparing well-crafted essay answers. The guide is available free to students when packaged with *Out of Many*.

Reading Critically About History

Prepared by Rose Wassman and Lee Rinsky, both of DeAnza College

This brief guide provides students with helpful strategies for reading a history textbook. It is available free when packaged with *Out of Many*.

Themes of the Times

Themes of the Times is a newspaper supplement prepared jointly by Prentice Hall and the premier news publication, *The New York Times*. Issued twice a year, it contains recent articles pertinent to American history. These articles connect the classroom to the world. For information about a reduced-rate subscription to *The New York Times*, call toll-free: (800) 631–1222.

MULTIMEDIA SUPPLEMENTS

History on the Internet

This brief guide introduces students to the origin and innovations behind the Internet and World Wide Web and provides clear strategies for navigating the web to find historical materials. Exercises within and at the end of the chapters allow students to practice searching the wealth of resources available to the student of history. This 48-page supplementary book is free to students when packaged with *Out of Many*.

Out of Many CD-ROM

This innovative electronic supplement takes advantage of the interactive capabilities of multimedia technology to enrich students' understanding of the geographic dimension of history with animated maps, timelines, and related on-screen activities tied to key issues in each chapter of *Out of Many*.

Out of Many Companion Website
Address: http://www.prenhall.com/faragher

With the *Out of Many* Companion Website, students can now take full advantage of the World Wide Web and use it in tandem with the text to enrich their study of American history. The Companion Website ties the text to related material available on the Internet. Its instructional features include chapter objectives, study questions, news updates, and labeling exercises.

The American History CD-ROM
This vast library of more than 2500 images was compiled by Instructional Resources Corporation for instructors for creating slide shows and supplementing lectures. Among its resources are 68 film sequences, 200 works of art, and more than 100 maps. It also includes an overview of historical periods narrated by Charles Kuralt.

ACKNOWLEDGMENTS

In the years it has taken to bring *Out of Many* from idea to reality and to improve it in successive editions, we have often been reminded that although writing history sometimes feels like isolated work, it actually involves a collective effort. We want to thank the dozens of people whose efforts have made the publication of this book possible.

At Prentice Hall, Todd Armstrong, Executive Editor, gave us his full support and oversaw the entire publication process. David Chodoff, Senior Development Editor, greatly helped to strengthen the book's most distinctive features with his careful attention to detail and clarity. Susanna Lesan, now Editor-in-Chief of Development, worked with us on the first edition of the text; without her efforts this book would never have been published. Louise Rothman, Production Editor, oversaw the entire complicated production process in an exemplary fashion. Barbara Salz, our photo researcher, expertly tracked down the many pertinent new images that appear in this edition.

Among our many other friends at Prentice Hall we also want to thank: Phil Miller, President; Charlyce Jones Owen, Editorial Director; Sheryl Adams, Marketing Manager; Leslie Osher, Creative Design Director; Anne Nieglos, Art Director; Patterson Lamb, Copy Editor; and Holly Jo Brown, Editorial Assistant.

Although we share joint responsibility for the entire book, the chapters were individually authored: John Mack Faragher wrote chapters 1–8; Mari Jo Buhle wrote chapters 18–20, 25–26, 29–30; Daniel Czitrom wrote chapters 17, 21–24, 27–28, 31; and Susan Armitage wrote chapters 9–16.

Historians around the country greatly assisted us by reading and commenting on our chapters for this and previous editions. We want to thank each of them for the commitment of their valuable time.

Donald Abbe, Texas Tech University, TX
Richard H. Abbott, Eastern Michigan University, MI
Guy Alchon, University of Delaware, DE
Don Barlow, Prestonsburg Community College, KY
William Barney, University of North Carolina, NC
Alwyn Barr, Texas Tech University, TX
Debra Barth, San Jose City College, CA
Peter V. Bergstrom, Illinois State University, IL
William C. Billingsley, South Plains College, TX
Peter H. Buckingham, Linfield College, OR
Bill Cecil-Fronsman, Washburn University of Topeka, KS
Victor W. Chen, Chabot College, CA
Jonathan M. Chu, University of Massachusetts, MA
P. Scott Corbett, Oxnard College, CA
Matther Coulter, Collin Country Community College, TX
Virginia Crane, University of Wisconsin, Oshkosh, WI
Jim Cullen, Harvard University, MA
Thomas J. Curran, St. John's University, NY
Richard V. Damms, Ohio State University, OH
Elizabeth Dunn, Baylor University, TX
Emmett G. Essin, Eastern Tennessee State Unversity, TN
Mark F. Fernandez, Loyola University, IL
Leon Fink, University of North Carolina, Chapel Hill, NC
Michael James Foret, University of Wisconsin, Stevens Point, WI
Joshua B. Freeman, Columbia University, NY
Glenda E. Gilmore, Yale University, CT
Don C. Glenn, Diablo Valley College, CA
Lawrence Glickman, University of South Carolina, SC
Kenneth Goings, Florida Atlantic University, FL
Mark Goldman, Tallahassee Community College, FL
Gregory L. Goodwin, Bakersfield College, CA
Gretchen Green, University of Missouri, Kansas City, MO
Emily Greenwald, University of Nebraska at Lincoln, NE
Mark W. T. Harvey, North Dakota State University, ND
James A. Hijiya, University of Massachusetts at Dartmouth, MA
Raymond M. Hyser, James Madison University, VA
John Inscoe, University of Georgia, GA

John C. Kesler, Lakeland Community College, OH
Peter N. Kirstein, Saint Xavier University, IL
Frank Lambert, Purdue University, IN
Susan Rimby Leighow, Millersville University, PA
Janice M. Leone, Middle Tennessee University, TN
Glenn Linden, Southern Methodist University, Dallas, TX
George Lipsitz, University of California, San Diego, CA
Judy Barrett Litoff, Bryant College, RI
Jesus Luna, California State University, CA
Larry Madaras, Howard Community College, MD
Lynn Mapes, Grand Valley State University, MI
John F. Marszalek, Mississippi State University, MS
Scott C. Martin, Bowling Green State University, OH
Robert L. Matheny, Eastern New Mexico University, NM
Thomas Matijasic, Prestonsburg Community College, KY
M. Delores McBroome, Humboldt State University, CA
Gerald McFarland, University of Massachusetts, Amherst, MA
Sam McSeveney, Vanderbilt University, TN
Warren Metcalf, Arizona State University, AZ
M. Catherine Miller, Texas State University, TX
Norman H. Murdoch, University of Cincinnati, OH
Gregory H. Nobles, Georgia Institute of Technology, GA
Dale Odom, University of Texas at Denton, TX
Sean O'Neill, Grand Valley State University, MI
Edward Opper, Greenville Technical College, Greenville, SC
Charles K. Piehl, Mankato State University, MN
Carolyn Garrett Pool, University of Central Oklahoma, OK
Christie Farnham Pope, Iowa State University, IA
Susan Porter-Benson, University of Missouri, MO
Russell Posner, City College of San Francisco, CA
John Powell, Penn State University, Erie, PA
Sarah Purcell, Central Michigan University, MI
Joseph P. Reidy, Howard University, DC
Marilyn D. Rhinehart, North Harris College, TX

Leo P. Ribuffo, George Washington University, DC
Judy Ridner, California State University at Northridge, CA
Neal Salisbury, Smith College, MA
Roberto Salmon, University of Texas-Pan American, TX
Steven Schuster, Brookhaven Community College, TX
Megan Seaholm, University of Texas, Austin, TX
Nigel Sellars, University of Oklahoma, Norman, OK
John David Smith, North Carolina State University, NC
Patrick Smith, Broward Community College, FL
Mark W. Summers, University of Kentucky, KY
John D. Tanner, Jr., Palomar College, CA
Robert R. Tomes, St. John's University, NY
Michael Miller Topp, University of Texas at El Paso, TX
John Trickel, Richland Community College, IL
Steve Tripp, Grand Valley State University, MI
Fred R. Van Hartesveldt, Fort Valley State University, GA
Philip H. Vaughan, Rose State College, OK
Robert C. Vitz, Northern Kentucky University, KY
F. Michael Williams, Brevard Community College, FL
Charles Regan Wilson, University of Mississippi, MS
Harold Wilson, Old Dominion University, VA
William Woodward, Seattle Pacific University, WA
Loretta E. Zimmerman, University of Florida, FL

Each of us depended on a great deal of support and assistance with the research and writing that went into this book. We want to thank: Kathryn Abbott, Nan Boyd, Krista Comer, Crista DeLuzio, Keith Edgerton, Carol Frost, Jesse Hoffnung Garskof, Jane Gerhard, Todd Gernes, Melani McAlister, Cristiane Mitchell, J. C. Mutchler, Tricia Rose, Gina Rourke, and Jessica Shubow.

Our families and close friends have been supportive and ever so patient over the many years we have devoted to this project. But we want especially to thank Paul Buhle, Meryl Fingrutd, Bob Greene, and Michele Hoffnung.

ABOUT THE AUTHORS

Chris Freitag

JOHN MACK FARAGHER

John Mack Faragher is Arthur Unobskey Professor of American History at Yale University. Born in Arizona and raised in southern California, he received his B.A. at the University of California, Riverside, and his Ph.D. at Yale University. He is the author of *Women and Men on the Overland Trail* (1979), which won the Frederick Jackson Turner Award of the Organization of American Historians, *Sugar Creek: Life on the Illinois Prairie* (1986), and *Daniel Boone: The Life and Legend of an American Pioneer* (1992). He is also the editor of *The American Heritage Encyclopedia* (1988).

DANIEL CZITROM

Daniel Czitrom is Professor and Chair of History at Mount Holyoke College. He received his B.A. from the State University of New York at Binghamton and his M.A. and Ph.D. from the University of Wisconsin, Madison. He is the author of *Media and the American Mind: From Morse to McLuhan* (1982), which won the First Books Award of the American Historical Association. His scholarly articles and essays have appeared in the *Journal of American History, American Quarterly, The Massachusetts Review,* and *The Atlantic.* He is currently completing *Mysteries of the City: Culture, Politics, and the Underworld in New York, 1870–1920.*

MARI JO BUHLE

Mari Jo Buhle is Professor of American Civilization and History at Brown University, specializing in American women's history. She is the author of *Women and American Socialism, 1870–1920* (1981) and *Feminism and its Discontents: A Century of Struggle with Psychoanalysis* (1998). She is also coeditor of *Encyclopedia of the American Left,* second edition (1998). She currently serves as an editor of a series of books on women and American history for the University of Illinois Press. Professor Buhle held a fellowship (1991–1996) from the John D. and Catherine T. MacArthur Foundation.

SUSAN H. ARMITAGE

Susan H. Armitage is Professor of History at Washington State University. She earned her Ph.D. from the London School of Economics and Political Science. Among her many publications on western women's history are three coedited books, *The Women's West* (1987), *So Much To Be Done: Women on the Mining and Ranching Frontier* (1991), and *Writing the Range: Race, Class, and Culture in the Women's West* (1997). She is the editor of *Frontiers: A Journal of Women's Studies.*

COMMUNITY & DIVERSITY

One of the most characteristic features of our country has always been its astounding variety. The American people include the descendants of native Indians, colonial Europeans, Africans, and migrants from virtually every country and continent. Indeed, as we enter the new century the nation is absorbing a tide of immigrants from Latin America and Asia that rivals the great tide of immigrants from eastern and southern Europe that arrived at the beginning of the twentieth century. Moreover, the United States is one of the world's largest nations, incorporating more than 3.6 million square miles of territory. The struggle to make a nation out of our many communities is what much of American history is all about. That is the story told in this book.

Every human society is made up of communities. A community is a set of relationships that link men, women, and their families into a coherent social whole, more than the sum of its parts. In a community people develop the capacity for unified action. In a community people learn, often through trial and error, how to transform and adapt to their environment. The sentiment that binds the members of a community together is the origin of group identity and ethnic pride. In the making of history, communities are far more important than even the greatest of leaders, for the community is the institution most capable of passing a distinctive historical tradition to future generations.

Communities bind people together in multiple ways. They can be as small as the local neighborhood, in which people maintain face-to-face relations, or as large as the imagined entity of the nation. This book examines American history from the perspective of community life—an ever widening frame that has included larger and larger groups of Americans.

Networks of kinship and friendship, and connections across generations and among families, establish the bonds essential to community life. Shared feelings about values and history establish the basis for common identity. In communities, people find the power to act collectively in their own interest. But American communities frequently took shape as a result of serious conflicts among groups, and within communities there often has been significant fighting among competing groups or classes. Thus the term community,

John L. Krimmel, Election Day in Philadelphia (1815).

John L. Krimmel, Painting, (1786–1821), oil on canvas. H. 16½″ x W. 25¾″. (AN-59.131) Courtesy, Winterthur Museum. *Election Day in Philadelphia* (1815).

as we employ it here, includes tension and discord as well as harmony and agreement.

For years there have been persistent laments about the "loss of community" in modern America. But community has not disappeared—it is continually being reinvented. Until the late eighteenth century, community was defined primarily by space and local geography. The closer one gets to the present, the more community is reshaped by new and powerful historical forces such as the nation state, the marketplace, industrialization, the corporation, mass immigration, and electronic media.

The American Communities vignettes that open each chapter of *Out of Many* reflect this shift. Most of the vignettes in the pre–Civil War chapters focus on geographically-defined communities, such as the ancient Indian city at Cahokia, or the experiment in industrial urban planning in early nineteenth-century Lowell, Massachusetts. In the post–Civil War chapters different and more modern kinds of communities make their appearance—the community of Holly-

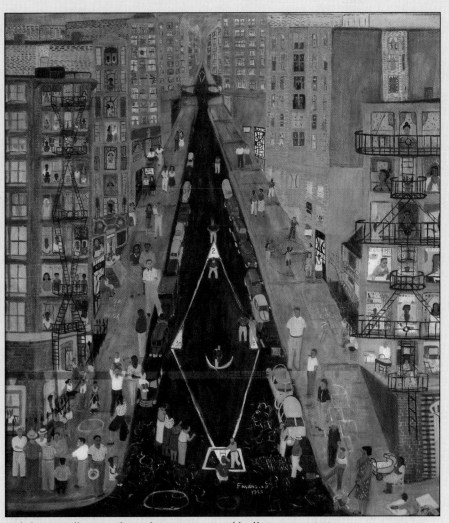

Ralph Fasanella, Sunday Afternoon—Stickball Game, 1953

wood movie audiences in the 1920s, or the "virtual communities" made possible by new computer technologies. Also, the nearer we get to the present, the more we find Americans struggling to balance their membership in several communities simultaneously. These are defined not simply by local spatial arrangements, but by categories as varied as racial and ethnic groups, occupations, political affiliations, and consumer preferences.

The title for our book was suggested by the Latin phrase selected by John Adams, Benjamin Franklin, and Thomas Jefferson for the Great Seal of the United States: *E Pluribus Unum*—"Out of Many Comes Unity." These men understood that unity could not be imposed by a powerful central authority but had to develop out of mutual respect among Americans of different backgrounds. The revolutionary leadership expressed the hope that such respect could grow on the basis of a remarkable proposition: "We hold these truths to be self-evident, that all men are created equal; that they are endowed by their Creator with certain unalienable rights; that among these are life, liberty, and the pursuit of happiness." The national government of the United States would preserve local and state authority but would guarantee individual rights. The nation would be strengthened by guarantees of difference.

Out of Many—that is the promise of America, and the premise of this book. The underlying dialectic of American history, we believe, is that as a people

William Hahn, Market Scene, Sansome Street, San Francisco.

we need to locate our national *unity* in the celebration of the *differences* that exist among us; these differences can be our strength, as long as we affirm the promise of the Declaration. Protecting the "right to be different," in other words, is absolutely fundamental to the continued existence of democracy, and that right is best protected by the existence of strong and vital communities. We are bound together as a nation by the ideal of local and cultural differences protected by our common commitment to the values of our revolution.

Today—with the many social and cultural conflicts that abound in the United States—some Americans have lost faith in that vision. But our history shows that the promise of American unity has always been problematic. Centrifugal forces have been powerful in the American past, and at times the country has seemed about to fracture into its component parts. Our transformation from a collection of groups and regions into a nation has been marked by painful and often violent struggles. Our past is filled with conflicts between Indians and colonists, masters and slaves,

Patriots and Loyalists, Northerners and Southerners, Easterners and Westerners, capitalists and workers, and sometimes the government and the people. Americans often appear to be little more than a contentious collection of peoples with conflicting interests, divided by region and background, race and class.

Our most influential leaders also sometimes suffered a crisis of faith in the American project of "liberty and justice for all." Thomas Jefferson not only believed in the inferiority of African Americans, but he feared that immigrants from outside the Anglo-American tradition might "warp and bias" the development of the nation "and render it a heterogeneous, incoherent, distracted mass." We have not always lived up to the American promise, and there is a dark side to our history. It took the bloodiest war in American history to secure the human rights of African Americans, and the struggle for full equality continues nearly a century and a half later. During the great influx of immigrants in the early twentieth century, fears much like Jefferson's led to movements to *Americanize* the foreign born by forcing them, in the words of one leader, "to give up the languages, customs, and methods of life which they have brought with them across the ocean, and adopt instead the language, habits, and customs of this country, and the general standards and ways of American living." Similar thinking motivated Congress at various times to bar the immigration of Asians and other ethnic groups into the country, and to force assimilation on American Indians by denying them the freedom to practice their religion or even to speak their own language. Such calls for restrictive unity resound in our own day.

But other Americans have argued for a more idealistic version of *Americanization*. "What is the American, this new man?" asked the French immigrant Michel Crévecoeur in 1782. "A strange mixture of blood which you will find in no other country," he answered; in America, "individuals of all nations are melted into a new race of men." A century later Crévecoeur was echoed by historian Frederick Jackson Turner, who believed that "in the crucible of the frontier, the immigrants were Americanized, liberated, and fused into a mixed race, English in neither nationality nor characteristics. The process has gone on from the early days to our own."

The process by which diverse communities have come to share a set of common American values is one of the most fundamental aspects of our history. It did not occur, however, because of compulsory *Americanization* programs, but because of free public education, popular participation in democratic politics, and the impact of popular culture. Contemporary America does have a common culture: we laugh at the same television sitcoms and share the same aspirations to own a home and send our children to college—all unique American traits.

To a degree that too few Americans appreciate, this common culture resulted from a complicated process of mutual discovery that took place when different ethnic and regional groups encountered one another. Consider just one small and unique aspect of our culture, the barbecue. Americans have been barbecuing since before the beginning of written history. Early settlers adopted this technique of cooking from the Indians—the word itself comes from a native term for a framework of sticks over a fire on which meat was slowly cooked. Colonists typically barbecued pork, fed on Indian corn. African slaves lent their own touch by introducing the use of hot sauces. Thus the ritual that is a part of nearly every American family's Fourth of July silently celebrates the heritage of diversity that went into making our common culture.

The American educator John Dewey recognized this diversity early in this century. "The genuine American, the typical American is himself a hyphenated character," he declared, "international and interracial in his make-up." The point about our "hyphenated character," Dewey believed, "is to see to it that the hyphen connects instead of separates." We, the authors of *Out of Many*, share Dewey's perspective on American history. "Creation comes from the impact of diversity," wrote the American philosopher Horace Kallen. We also endorse Kallen's vision of the American promise: "A democracy of nationalities, cooperating voluntarily and autonomously through common institutions, . . . a multiplicity in a unity, an orchestration of mankind." And now, let the music begin.

CHAPTER ONE

A CONTINENT OF VILLAGES
TO 1500

AMERICAN COMMUNITIES
Cahokia: Thirteenth-Century Life on the Mississippi

As the sun rose over the rich floodplain, the people of the riverbank city set about their daily tasks. Some went to shops where they manufactured tools, crafted pottery, worked metal, or fashioned ornamental jewelry—goods destined to be exchanged in the far corners of the continent. Others left their densely populated neighborhoods for the outlying countryside, where in the summer heat they worked the seemingly endless fields that fed the city. From almost any point people could see the great temple that rose from the center of their city—the temple where priests in splendid costumes acted out public rituals of death and renewal.

This thirteenth-century city was not in preindustrial Europe but in North America. It flourished long before the first European explorer arrived. Its residents lived and worked on the alluvial soil of the Mississippi River, across from present-day St. Louis, at a place archaeologists have named Cahokia. In its heyday, in the mid-1200s, Cahokia was an urban cluster of perhaps 30,000 people. Its farm fields were abundant with corn, beans, and pumpkins, crops no European had ever seen. The temple, a huge earthwork pyramid, covered fifteen acres at its base and rose as high as a ten-story building. On top were the sacred residences of chiefs and priests, who dressed in elaborate headdresses made from the plumage of American birds.

By the fourteenth century, Cahokia had been abandoned, but its great central temple mound and dozens of smaller ones in the surrounding area, as well as hundreds more throughout the Mississippi Valley, remained to puzzle the European immigrants who resettled the valley in the eighteenth and nineteenth centuries. Treasure seekers plundered the mounds, and most were eventually dynamited and plowed under for farmland. Only a few were saved, inside parks or estates. Cahokia's central mound survived because in the nineteenth century its summit became the site of a monastery, now long gone.

The Europeans who first explored and excavated these mounds were convinced they were the ruins of a vanished civilization, but could not believe they were the work of Native Americans. The first comprehensive study of Cahokia, published in 1848 under the sponsorship of the Smithsonian Institution, noted that "the mound-builders were an agricultural people, considerably advanced in arts, manners, habits, and religion." But because "Indians were hunters averse to labor, and not known to have constructed any works approaching [the] skillfulness of design or [the] magnitude" of Cahokia, surely these wonders must have been constructed by a "lost race."

The Smithsonian scientists were wrong. Thanks to modern archaeology and anthropology we now know that it was the ancestors

1

of contemporary Native Americans who began to construct massive earthworks in the Mississippi Valley as early as 1300 B.C.E. (Before the Common Era) at a place called Poverty Point in Louisiana. The vast urban complex of Cahokia flourished from the tenth to the fourteenth century and at its height stretched six miles along the Mississippi. Its residents were not nomadic hunters but farmers, members of an agricultural society—which archaeologists call the Mississippian—that had developed highly productive techniques of cultivation. Hundreds of acres of crops fed the people of Cahokia, which was the most populated urban community north of the Valley of Mexico. Mississippian farmers constructed ingenious raised plots of land on which they heaped compost in wide ridges for improved drainage and protection from unseasonable frosts. To their square houses of wood and mud they attached pens in which they kept flocks of domesticated turkeys and, perhaps, small herds of young deer that they slaughtered for meat and hides. Cahokia was at the center of a long-distance trading system that linked it to Indian towns over a vast area. Cahokia's specialized artisans were renowned for the manufacture of high-quality flint hoes, exported throughout the Mississippi Valley. Copper came to the city from Lake Superior, mica from the southern Appalachians, conch shells from the Atlantic coast.

The archaeological evidence suggests that Cahokia was emerging as a state supported by tribute and taxation. Like the awe-inspiring public works of early urban societies in other parts of the world—the pyramids of ancient Egypt, the

Cahokia

acropolis of Athens—the great temple mound of Cahokia reflected the city's wealth and power. The great mound and other colossal public works at Cahokia were monuments of a society dominated by an elite class of priests and rulers. From their residences and temples atop the mound the city's elite could look down on their awe-struck subjects. There is no indication, however, that the Mississippian peoples had developed a system of writing that would permit us to glimpse their own version of their history.

As the words of the 1848 Smithsonian report on Cahokia make clear, the stereotypical view of Indians that emerged in the nineteenth and twentieth centuries was that they all lived in isolated hunting bands. But the great variety of lifeways Indian peoples developed in their long occupation of North America belies this stereotype. All Native Americans lived in strong vibrant communities that ranged from small hunting bands to large agricultural cities like Cahokia and splendid imperial capitals like that of the Aztecs of Mexico. Before the coming of the Europeans, North America was, as one historian phrases it, "a continent of villages," a land with thousands of local communities. Over many centuries the Indian peoples of North America developed a variety of community types, each with its own system of family and social organization, each integrated with its natural surroundings. The wonders of Cahokia are but one aspect of the little-understood history of the Indians of the Americas.

KEY TOPICS

- The peopling of the Americas by migrants from Asia
- The adaptation of native cultures to the distinctive regions of North America
- The increase in complexity of many native societies following the development of farming
- The nature of Indian cultures in the three major regions of European invasion and settlement

SETTLING THE CONTINENT

"Why do you call us Indians?" a Massachusetts native complained to Puritan missionary John Eliot in 1646. More than a hundred years earlier, Christopher Columbus had mistaken the Arawaks of the Caribbean for the people of the East Indies and called them *Indios*. By the middle of the sixteenth century this Spanish word had passed into English as "Indians" and was widely used to refer to all the native peoples of the Americas. Today anthropologists often use the term "Amerindians," and many people prefer "Native Americans." But most indigenous Americans refer to themselves as "Indian people."

Who Are the Indian People?

At the time of their first contacts with Europeans, near the close of the fifteenth century, the native inhabitants of the Western Hemisphere represented more than 2,000 distinct cultures, spoke hundreds of different languages, and lived and worked in scores of different environments. Just as the term "European" includes such different peoples as the English, French, and Spanish, so "Indian" covers an enormous diversity of peoples. For example, the people of the mid-Atlantic coast called themselves *Lenni Lenape*, meaning "true men"; those of the northern Great Plains were *Lakota*, or "the allies"; and the hunters of the Southwest used the name *Dine* (pronounced "dee-nay"), meaning simply "the people." Interestingly, Europeans came to know these three groups by rather different names: the *Delawares* (from the principal river of the mid-Atlantic region), the *Sioux*, and the *Apaches* (both of which meant "enemy" in the language of a neighboring tribe).

Once Europeans realized that the Americas were in fact a "New World" rather than part of the Asian continent, they began debating how people might have moved there from Europe and Asia, where the Judeo-Christian Bible indicated human life had begun. Over the succeeding centuries writers proposed elaborate theories of transoceanic migrations that linked native Americans variously to ancient Greeks, Carthaginians, Tartars, Chinese, and Welsh; one theory even held they were the survivors of the mythical Atlantis. Common to all these theories was a belief that the Americas had been populated for a few thousand years at most and that native American societies were the degenerate offspring of a far superior Old World culture.

A number of Spanish observers thought more deeply about the question of Indian origins. In 1590 Joseph de Acosta reasoned that because Old World animals were present in the Americas, they must have crossed by a land bridge that could have been used by humans as well. A few years later, Enrico Martín speculated that since no such land passage had been found between the Americas and Europe, it must exist in the unexplored far northwest of the continent, and thus the people using it must have been Asian. In the 1650s Bernabé Cobo, who had lived most of his life in the Caribbean, argued that the great variety of native American languages showed that Indian peoples must have lived on the continent for centuries. But, he continued, their physical similarities suggested that "it was doubtless one nation or family of men which passed to people this land." Here were the principal elements of the migration hypothesis: Indian peoples were descended from a common stock of Asian migrants, they arrived by way of a northwestern land passage, and they had experienced a long and independent history in the Americas.

Certainly no single physical type characterized all the native peoples of the Americas. Although most had straight, black hair and dark, almond-shaped eyes, their skin ranged in color from mahogany to light brown and few fit the "yellow men" or "redskin" descriptions given them by colonists and settlers of the eighteenth and nineteenth centuries. Indeed, it was only when Europeans compared Indian peoples with natives of other continents, such as Africans, that they seemed similar enough to be classified as a group.

Migration from Asia

The theory most widely held today is that the native American peoples moved to this hemisphere from Asia some 25,000 to 30,000 years ago—about the

OVERVIEW

ORIGINS OF SOME INDIAN TRIBAL NAMES

Cherokee	A corruption of the Choctaw *chiluk-ki*, meaning "cave people," an allusion to the many caves in the Cherokee homeland. The Cherokees called themselves *Ani-Yun-Wiya*, or "real people."
Cheyenne	From the Sioux *Sha-hiyena*, "people of strange speech." The Cheyennes called themselves *Dzi-tsistas*, meaning "our people."
Hopi	A shortening of the Hopis' own name for themselves, *Hópitu*, which means "peaceful ones."
Mohawk	From the Algonquian *Mohawaúuck*, meaning "man-eaters." The Mohawks called themselves *Kaniengehaga*, "people of the place of the flint."
Pawnee	From the Pawnee term *paríki*, which describes a distinctive style of dressing the hair with paint and fat to make it stand erect like a horn. The Pawnees called themselves *Chahik-sichahiks*, "men of men."

time that Japan and the countries of Scandinavia were being settled. Evidence supporting this view includes a common dental pattern found among the most ancient human fossils in the Americas and those in northeastern Asia. The most distinctive marker of modern native American peoples is blood type, for although the vast majority have type O blood and a few have type A, almost none have type B. Because modern Asian populations exhibit all three blood types, scientists have postulated that migrations to the New World took place before the evolution of type B, which they believe occurred about 30,000 years ago. Studies of genetic evolution suggest that it took at least 20,000 years to evolve the variety of physical traits found among native American populations today. And modern linguists, agreeing essentially with Cobo's observation, cited earlier, estimate that it would require about 25,000 years to develop, from a common base, the nearly 500 distinct languages of the Americas.

At the time of the proposed migration from Asia to the Americas, the Northern Hemisphere was experiencing the Ice Age that characterized the geological epoch known as the Pleistocene. Huge glaciers locked up massive volumes of water, and sea levels were as much as 300 feet lower than they are today. Asia and North America were joined by a huge subcontinent of ice-free, treeless grassland, 750 miles wide from north to south. Geologists have named this area Beringia, from the Bering Straits. Summers there were warm, winters were cold, dry, and almost snowfree. This was a perfect environment for large mammals—mammoth and mastodon, bison, horse, reindeer, camel, and saiga (a goatlike antelope).

Beringia also attracted Stone Age hunter-gatherers who lived in small, nomadic bands and subsisted almost entirely on these animals. The animals provided them not only with food but with hides for clothing and shelter, dung for fuel, and bones for tools and weapons. Hunting bands were driven to expand their territories by the powerful force of their own population growth and the pressure it placed on local resources. Today's few remaining hunting-and-gathering peoples have an annual population growth rate of 0.5 percent, which would double their populations only every 140 years. Ancient Asian hunters, with seemingly limitless open country into which they could move, likely had growth rates that were much higher, and their expansion into new territory was correspondingly rapid. Following the big game, and accompanied by a husky-like species of dog, hunting bands gradually penetrated Beringia, moving as far east as the Yukon River basin of northern Canada.

Until recently most scientists dated the first migrations at about 15,000 years ago, but there is growing evidence that people were moving from Asia considerably earlier. Because much of Beringia was later submerged beneath rising seas, definitive archaeological evidence of migration from Asia is difficult to find. No fossil human bones have yet been uncovered there. But in 1966, field excavations in the Yukon basin uncovered what appeared to be fossilized bone tools estimated to be 27,000 years old. Fieldworkers found that these tools fit perfectly into their hands and had worn edges exactly where one would expect them to be. Later digs in the area produced the jawbones of several dogs estimated to be at least 30,000 years old. The most persuasive evidence for an earlier migration,

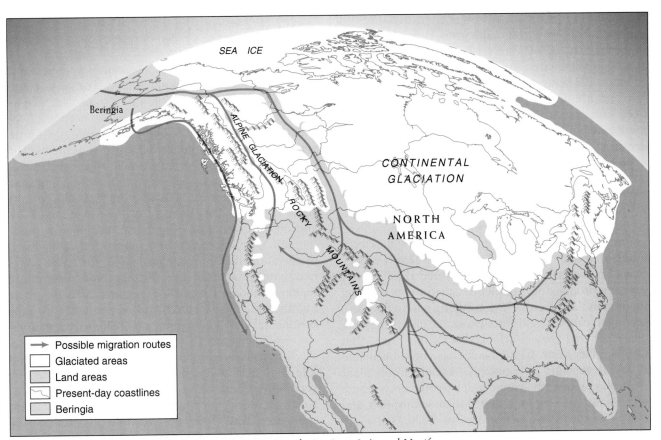

Migration Routes from Asia to America   *During the Ice Age, Asia and North America were joined where the Bering Straits are today, forming a migration route for hunting peoples. Either by boat along the coast, or through a narrow corridor between the huge northern glaciers, these migrants began making their way to the heartland of the continent as much as 30,000 years ago.*

however, comes from the other end of the hemisphere, in South America. Archaeologists working at separate sites in the Amazon basin and in southern Chile in the early 1990s found striking evidence of human tool-making, house-building, and rock painting that date from at least 12,000 years ago. The ancestors of those peoples must have crossed Beringia many thousands of years before. The consensus today is that the migration from Asia probably began about 30,000 years ago.

Huge glaciers to the south of Beringia blocked passage during most of the last Ice Age, but occasionally a narrow land corridor opened up along the eastern base of the Rocky Mountains. As early as 25,000 years ago, hunting bands following this corridor south could have emerged onto the northern Great Plains— a hunter's paradise teeming with animals of great variety. Migrants probably also moved south in boats, following the Pacific coastline. Rapid population growth would have permitted these groups to populate the entire Western Hemisphere in a few thousand years. Remarkably, the oral traditions of many Indian peoples depict a long journey from a distant place of

origin to a new homeland. Europeans have recorded the Pima people of the Southwest singing this "Emergence Song":

> *This is the White Land; we arrive singing,*
> *Headdresses waving in the breeze.*
> *We have come! We have come!*
> *The land trembles with our dancing and singing.*

Clovis: The First American Technology

The earliest tools found at North American archaeological sites, crude choppers and scrapers made of stone or bone, are similar to artifacts from the same period found in Europe or Asia. About 12,000 years ago, however, a much more sophisticated style of tool-making seems to have developed. Named after the site of its discovery in 1932, near Clovis, New Mexico, the Clovis tradition was a powerful new and more sophisticated technology, unlike anything found in the archaeology of the Old World. In the years since the initial discovery, archaeologists have unearthed Clovis artifacts at sites ranging from Montana to Mexico,

Nova Scotia to Arizona. All these finds date back to within one or two thousand years of one another, suggesting that Clovis spread quickly throughout the continent. This discovery has led, in turn, to speculation that the settlement of North America might then have been entering its final phase, as the continent filled with people. Scientists theorize that it was to feed their expanding populations that communities were driven to find a more efficient way to hunt and developed this greatly improved technology.

The evidence suggests that Clovis users were mobile peoples who traveled in communities numbering perhaps thirty to fifty individuals from several interrelated families. They returned to the same hunting camps year after year, migrating seasonally within territories of several hundred square miles. Near Delbert, Nova Scotia, archaeologists discovered the floors of ten tents arranged in a semicircle, their doors opening south to avoid the prevailing northerly winds. Both this camp and others found throughout the continent were placed so that they overlooked watering places that would attract game. Clovis blades have been excavated amid the remains of mammoth, camel, horse, giant armadillo, and sloth. Hunters apparently drove these animals into shallow bogs, killed them with spears, and butchered them on the spot.

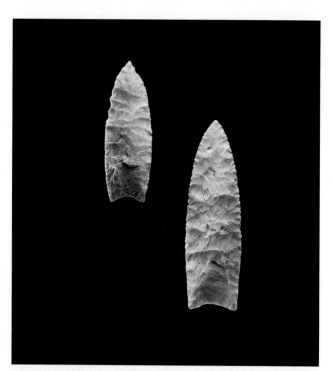

These Clovis points are typical of thousands that archaeologists have found at sites all over the continent, dating from a period about 12,000 years ago. When inserted in a spear shaft, these three- to six-inch fluted points made effective weapons for hunting mammoth and other big game.

THE BEGINNING OF REGIONAL CULTURES

About 15,000 years ago a global warming trend began to alter the North American climate. The giant continental glaciers began to melt, a shift so pronounced by 8000 B.C.E. that it is used to mark the passing of the Pleistocene epoch. As the glaciers retreated, the northern latitudes were colonized by plants, animals, and humans. Meltwater created the lake and river systems of today and raised the level of the surrounding seas, flooding Beringia as well as vast stretches of the Atlantic and Gulf coasts and creating fertile tidal pools and offshore fishing banks. These monumental transformations produced new patterns of wind, rainfall, and temperature, reshaping the ecology of the entire continent and producing the distinct North American regions of today. The great integrating force of a single continental climate faded, and, with its passing, the continental Clovis culture fragmented into many different regional patterns.

Regions have ever since played an important role in American history. Variations in climate and geography combine to form the distinct regions of North America: the Arctic and Subarctic, the Northwest, the Great Plains, the Northeast, California, the Great Basin, the Southwest, the South, the Caribbean, and Mexico. Within these regions, human communities have had to adapt to nature, evolving their own ways of life. Indian peoples were the first in North America to embark on the long journey toward regionally distinct cultures, developing a wide variety of food sources to support their growing populations.

Hunting Traditions of the Plains and Forests

One of the most important effects of this massive climatological shift was the stress it placed on the big-game animals best suited to an Ice Age environment. The archaeological record details the extinction of thirty-two classes of large New World animals, including not only the mammoth and mastodon but the horse and camel, both of which evolved in America and then migrated to Asia across Beringia. It seems likely that lowered reproduction and survival rates of large animals forced hunting bands to intensify their efforts, and the combined effects of warmer climate and increased hunting eventually led to what some archaeologists have called the "Pleistocene Overkill."

As the other large-mammal populations declined, hunters on the Great Plains concentrated on the herds of American bison, more commonly called buffalo. To hunt these animals people needed a weapon they could throw quickly with great accuracy and velocity at fast-moving targets over distances of as much as a hundred yards. The Folsom technology, a refinement of the Clovis tradition, featured points that were more delicate and lighter in weight, but deadlier.

Folsom points were named for the site of their first major excavation, at Folsom, New Mexico, where the tools uncovered were judged to be about 10,000 years old. In one dramatic find, a Folsom point was discovered embedded between the fossilized ribs of an ancient species of bison. Hunters probably hurled the lances to which these points were attached with wooden spear-throwers, achieving far greater velocity than they could with their arms alone. By 7000 B.C.E., Folsom had evolved into a technology that archaeologists call Plano, and the points are often found with grinding tools suitable for processing vegetable foods. This association indicates that peoples of the Great Plains were in the process of developing a varied diet.

Archaeological finds also suggest the growing complexity of early Indian communities. Folsom and Plano hunters frequently stampeded herds of bison or other animals into canyon traps or over cliffs. At one such kill site in southeastern Colorado, estimated to be 8,500 years old, archaeologists uncovered the remains of nearly 200 bison that had been slaughtered and then systematically butchered on a single occasion. This job would have required at least 150 men and women and a sophisticated division of labor, which in turn probably involved the cooperation of a number of communities. Taking food in such quantities indicates a knowledge of basic preservation techniques: these people must have been among the first to make jerky, or dried strips of meat, and pemmican, a mixture of dried meat, animal fat, and berries that can keep into the winter when stored in hide containers. These characteristic products of the Great Plains later became the staple foods of European fur traders in the North American West.

The passing of the Pleistocene epoch and the submergence of Beringia were preceded by a second wave of Beringia migrants—the Athapascans, or Na-Dene people. After entering North America they moved southeast from Alaska, following the melting glacier that had formerly blocked passage. From 7,000 to 4,000 years ago, they settled the forests of the continent's Northwest. Although they eventually adopted a technology for making weapons and tools similar to that of neighboring peoples, the Na-Dene maintained a separate cultural and linguistic identity. The ancestors of the Athapascan-speaking Navajos and Apaches later migrated from this northern country, journeying across the Great Plains to the Southwest.

In a final migration from Asia that took place about 5,000 years ago, the Inupiat—more commonly known as Eskimos—and the Aleuts, other hunting peoples, crossed the flooded Bering Straits by boat.

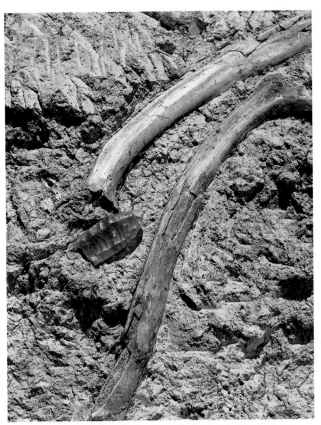

When in 1927 archaeologists at Folsom, New Mexico, uncovered this dramatic example of a projectile point embedded in the ribs of a long-extinct species of bison it was the first proof that Indians had been in North America for many thousands of years.

The Eskimos colonized the polar coasts of the Arctic, the Aleuts the Aleutian Islands (later named for them) and the southern coast of Alaska.

Desert Culture in Western America

As the glaciers began to retreat, people developed new ways of finding food. During what archaeologists call the Archaic period (which corresponds to the late phases of the Stone Age in Eurasia and Africa), varying modes of subsistence evolved in different regions of North America. Between about 10,000 and 2,500 years ago, desert foraging began in the arid Great Basin, fishing along the Northwest coast of the Pacific, and hunting and gathering in the forests of the humid eastern half of the continent.

In the Great Basin of present-day Utah and Nevada the warming trend associated with the end of the Ice Age created a desert where once there had been enormous inland seas. Here, Indian people developed Desert Culture, a way of life based on the pursuit of small game and intensified foraging for plant foods. Small communities or bands of desert foragers migrated seasonally within a small range. They collected seeds,

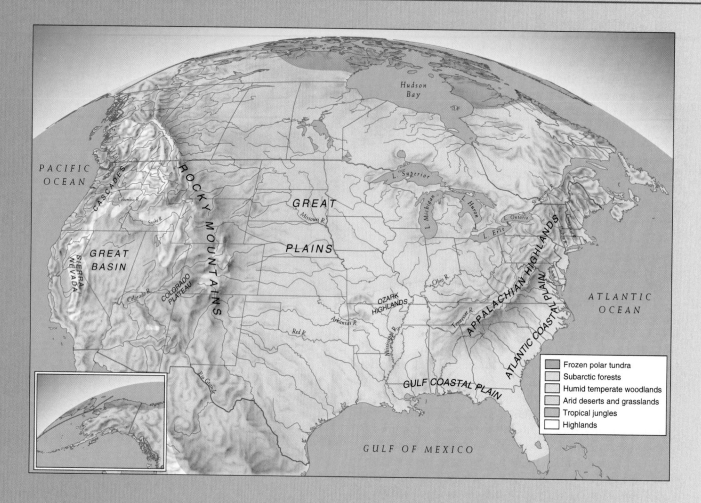

The Regions of Native North America

Occupying more than a third of the continent, the United States is alone among the world's nations in encompassing all five general classes of global climate: tropical jungles, arid deserts and grasslands, temperate woodlands, subarctic forests, and frozen polar tundra.

The country also contains some of the world's largest lakes, most extensive grasslands, and mightiest rivers.

All peoples must adjust their diet, shelter, and other material aspects of their lives to the physical conditions of the world around them; thus a knowledge of the way in which geography and

fiber, and prickly pear from the yucca one season, then moved to highland mesas to gather grass seed, acorns, juniper berries, and piñon nuts, and next to mountain streams to spear and net fish. This strategy required considerable skill in handicrafts: fiber baskets for collecting, pitch-lined baskets for cooking, nets and traps, and stone grinders for processing seeds and nuts, as well as stone knives, hammers, and mauls.

Archaeologists know that desert foragers lived in caves and rock shelters, for their artifacts are found there today. In addition to stone tools these artifacts include objects of wood, hide, and fiber, wonderfully preserved for thousands of years in the dry climate. The Desert Culture persisted into the nineteenth century among modern Shoshoni and Ute communi-

ties. Although these people were once scornfully labeled "Diggers" because of their practice of gathering edible roots and were ridiculed for their "primitive" life ways, we now appreciate the very sophisticated adjustments they made to a harsh environment.

Descriptions of the culture of the modern Shoshonis suggest that the force of community was strong among the people of the desert. An emphasis on sharing and gift giving, the condemnation of hoarding, and the limitations posed by a nomadic lifestyle on the accumulation of material goods prevented individuals or families from acquiring excessive wealth. Thus, desert communities were characterized by general social equality. Decisions were made by consensus among the adults, and lead-climate combine to form regions is a prerequisite to understanding the cultures of the peoples of America. Using the concept of "culture areas," anthropologists divide the continent into several fundamental regions, which have played an important role in the history of the continent for the past 10,000 years.

The Indian peoples of North America were first to develop distinct cultures suited to the regions in which they lived. Just as regions shaped the life-ways and history of Indian peoples, after the coming of the Europeans they nurtured the development of regional American cultures.

ership tended to be informal, based on achievement and reputation. The men of one band generally married women from another, and wives came to live with the people of their husbands, creating important linkages between groups that contributed to the sense of shared ethnic identity.

The innovative practices of the Desert Culture gradually spread from the Great Basin to the Great Plains and the Southwest, where foraging techniques began to supplement intensive hunting. About 6,000 years ago, archaeologists estimate, colonists from the Great Basin carried Desert Culture farther west to California. There, in the natural abundance of the valleys and coasts, Indian peoples developed an economy capable of supporting some of the densest popu-

lations and the first permanently settled communities in North America. Another dynamic center in the West developed along the Northwest Pacific coast, where native American communities developed a way of life based on the exploitation of abundant fish and sea mammals. This Old Cordilleran Culture became the basis for the historic cultures of the Plateau and Northwest, which also included densely populated sedentary communities.

Forest Efficiency

Similar trends were at work east of the Mississippi. Before European settlers destroyed countless acres of forest during the eighteenth and nineteenth centuries, the whole of eastern North America was a vast woodland. Hardwoods grew in the north, southern pine in the south. The Winnebagos of the Great Lakes region sang of these forests:

Pleasant it looked,
this newly created world.
Along the entire length and breadth
of the earth, our grandmother
extended the green reflection
of her covering
and the escaping odors
were pleasant to inhale.

Archaic forest communities achieved a comfortable and secure life based on what archaeologists call "forest efficiency"—a sophisticated exploitation of their rich and diverse resources. Archaic Indian communities of the forest hunted small game and gathered seeds, nuts, roots, and other wild plant foods. They also developed the practice of burning the woodlands and prairies to stimulate the growth of berries, fruits, and edible roots. The resulting meadows and forest edge produced harvestable foods and attracted grazing animals, which were then hunted for their meat and hides. Another important resource was the abundant fish of the rivers.

Archaeological sites in the East suggest that during the late Archaic period community populations grew and settlements became increasingly permanent, providing convincing evidence of the viability of forest efficiency. The artifacts these people buried with their dead—axes, fishhooks, and animal bones with males, nut-cracking stones, beads, and pestles with females—reflect the different roles of men and women in their society.

THE DEVELOPMENT OF FARMING

The exploitation of a wide variety of food sources during the Archaic period eventually led many Indian people to develop and adopt the practice of farming. The dynamic center of this development in North America was the highlands of Mexico, from which the new technology spread north and east.

Mexico

At the end of the Stone Age, people in four different parts of the world developed farming systems, each based on a different crop: rice in Southeast Asia, wheat in West Asia, maize (or Indian corn) in Mexico, and potatoes in the Andean highlands of South America. In Mexico a great variety of other crops—most importantly beans and squash, but also tomatoes, peppers, avocados, cocoa (chocolate), and vanilla—supplemented maize. Today the two American staples—maize and potatoes—contribute more to the world's

food supply than do wheat and rice. These "miracle crops" fueled the expansion of European human and livestock populations in the three centuries after 1650. Without these and other New World crops such as tobacco, American cotton, and rubber—each the basis of important new industries and markets—the history of the modern world would have been far different.

Archaeological evidence suggests that plant cultivation in the highlands of central Mexico began about 5,000 years ago. Ancient Mexicans developed crops that responded well to human care and produced larger quantities of food in a limited space than did plants occurring naturally. Maize was particularly productive; over time it was adapted to a wide range of American climates, and farming spread throughout the temperate regions of North America.

As farming became increasingly important, it radically reshaped social life. Where a foraging society might require 100 square miles to support 100 people, a farming society required only one square mile. Population growth and the need for people to remain near their fields throughout the year led to the appearance of villages and permanent architecture and eventually to the emergence of large, densely settled communities like Cahokia. Autumn harvests had to be stored during winter months, and the storage and distribution of food had to be managed. The division of labor increased with the appearance of specialists like toolmakers, craftsworkers, administrators, priests, and rulers as well as farmers and food processors. Ultimately, unequal access to wealth and power resulted in the emergence of classes.

By 1000 B.C.E., urban communities governed by permanent bureaucracies had begun to form in Mesoamerica, the region stretching from central Mexico to Central America. By the beginning of the first millenium C.E. (Common Era) highly productive farming was supporting complex urban civilizations in the Valley of Mexico (the location of present-day Mexico City), the Yucatan Peninsula, and other parts of Mesoamerica. Like many of the ancient civilizations of Asia and the Mediterranean, these Mesoamerican civilizations were characterized by the concentration of wealth and power in the hands of an elite class of priests and rulers, the construction of impressive temples and other public structures, and the development of systems of mathematics and astronomy, and several forms of hieroglyphic writing. The civilizations of Mesomerica were also marked by warfare between states and by terrifying public rituals of human sacrifice.

The great city of Teotihuacan in the Valley of Mexico, which emerged about 100 B.C.E., had a population of as many as 200,000 at the height of its power around C.E. 500. Teotihuacan's elite class of religious and political leaders controlled an elaborate state-sponsored trading system that stretched from present-

Mesoamerican maize cultivation, as illustrated by an Aztec artist for the Florentine Codex, *a book prepared a few years after the Spanish conquest. The peoples of Mesoamerica developed a greater variety of cultivated crops than those of any other region in the world, and their agricultural productivity helped sustain one of the world's great civilizations.*

Arizona south to Central America and may have included coastal shipping connections with the pre-Inca civilizations of Peru. The city had a highly specialized division of labor. Artisans manufactured tools and produced textiles, stoneware, pottery, and obsidian blades; the bureaucratic elite collected taxes and tribute; farmers left the city every day to work the fields that fed its people; and armies of workers constructed such monumental edifices as the Pyramids of the Sun and Moon, which still dominate the city's ruins.

Teotihuacan began to decline in the sixth century, and by the eighth century it was mostly abandoned. A new empire, that of the Toltecs, dominated central Mexico from the tenth to the twelfth century. By the fourteenth century a people known as the Aztecs, migrants from the north, had settled in the Valley of Mexico and begun a dramatic expansion into a formidable imperial power (see Chapter 2).

The Mayan peoples of the Yucatan peninsula developed a group of competing city-states that flourished from about 300 B.C.E. until about C.E. 900. The achievements of the Mayans included Mesoamerica's most advanced writing and calendrical systems and a sophisticated knowledge of mathematics that included the concept of zero.

The Resisted Revolution

Historians once described the development of farming as the "Neolithic Revolution" (*neolithic* means "New, or Later, Stone Age"). They believed that agricultural communities offered such obvious advantages that neighboring peoples must have rushed to adopt this way of life. Societies that remained without a farming tradition must simply have been too "primitive" to achieve this breakthrough; vulnerability to fickle nature was the penalty for their ignorance. This interpretation was based on a scheme of social evolution that viewed human history as the story of technological progress, in which savage hunters gradually developed into civilized farmers.

But there is very little evidence to support the notion that such a "revolution" occurred during a short, critical period. The adoption of farming was a gradual process, one that required hundreds, even thousands of years. Moreover, ignorance of cultivation was never the reason that cultures failed to take up farming, for all hunter-gatherer peoples understand a great deal about plant reproduction. When the Menomini Indians of the northern forests of Wisconsin gathered wild rice, for example, they purposely allowed some of it to fall back into the water to ensure a crop for the next season, and Desert Paiutes of the Great Basin systematically irrigated stands of their favorite wild food sources.

The way today's remaining hunter-gatherers view the farming way of life is instructive. Foragers generally look upon their own method of getting food as vastly superior to any other. The food sources of desert gatherers, for example, are considerably more varied and higher in protein than those of desert farmers, whose diets concentrate almost exclusively on grains. Because foragers took advantage of natural diversity, they were also less vulnerable to climatological stress; although gathering communities frequently experienced periods of scarcity and hunger, unlike farming societies they were rarely devastated by famine. Foragers also point out that farming requires much more work. Why sweat all day in the fields producing tasteless corn, they argue, when in an hour or two one can gather enough sweet prickly pear to last a week? Indeed, rather than freeing men and women from the tyranny of nature, farming tied people to a work discipline unlike anything previously known in human history. Finally, foragers consider their migratory ways far more interesting than village life, which they claim is dull and monotonous, preferred only by those whose possessions are too cumbersome to move.

As the techniques of large-scale agriculture became available, cultures in different regions assessed its advantages and limitations. In California and the Pacific Northwest, acorn gathering or salmon fishing made the cultivation of food crops seem a waste of time. In the Great Basin, several peoples attempted to farm, but without success. Before the invention of modern irrigation systems, which require sophisticated engineering, only the Archaic Desert Culture could prevail in this harsh environment. In the neighboring Southwest, however, farming resolved certain ecological dilemmas and transformed the way of life. Like the development of more sophisticated traditions of tool manufacture, farming represented another stage in the economic intensifications that kept populations and available resources in balance. It seems that where climate favored cultivation, people tended to adopt farming as a way of increasing the production of food, thus continuing the Archaic tradition of squeezing as much productivity as they could from their environment. But in a few areas farming resulted in a truly revolutionary transformation, pushing in the direction of an urban civilization like that of central Mexico or Cahokia on the banks of the Mississippi.

Increasing Social Complexity

Farming created the basis for much greater social complexity within Indian communities. Most important were elaborate systems of kinship. Greater population density prompted families to group themselves into clans responsible for different social, political, or ritual functions. These clans became an important mechanism for binding together the people of several communities into a tribe. A tribe, based on ethnic, linguistic, and territorial unity, was led by a leader or chief from an honored clan, who was often advised by councils of elders, all of whom were also clan leaders. In all likelihood, the city of Cahokia was governed by such a system. The tribal council sometimes arbitrated disputes between individuals or families, but most crimes—theft, adultery, rape, murder—were avenged by the aggrieved kinship group itself.

The primary function of the ruling council was to supervise the economy—to see that the harvest was collected and stored and that the food stores were distributed to the clans. Differences in wealth—small by the standards of modern societies—could develop between the families of a farming tribe, but these inequalities were kept in check by a system of redistribution that followed the principles of sharing characteristic of foraging communities. Nowhere in North America did Indian cultures develop a concept of the private ownership of land. Invariably, land was a common resource of the people and thus worked collectively.

Indian communities practiced a rather strict division of labor by gender that in its details varied greatly from culture to culture. Among foraging peoples, hunting was generally the work of men,

whereas the gathering of food and the maintenance of home-base camps were the responsibility of women. This pattern probably originated during the early years of the Archaic period. But the development of farming disrupted these patterns. In Mexico, where communities became almost totally dependent on crops, both men and women worked in the fields. Where hunting remained important, the older division of labor continued, with women responsible for field work. In general, however, Indian patterns contrasted in important ways with the norms of colonizing Europeans, prompting much misunderstanding. When English colonists saw Indian women working in the cornfields, for example, they thought them greatly oppressed; Indians, on the other hand, thought colonial men who labored in the fields were performing "women's work."

In most North American Indian farming communities, women and men belonged to separate social groupings, each with its own rituals and lore. Membership in these societies was one of the most important elements of a person's identity. Marriage ties, on the other hand, were relatively weak, and in most Indian communities divorce was easy. The couple simply separated, the children almost always remaining with the mother. Indian women were free to determine the timing of reproduction as well as to use herbs to prevent pregnancy, induce abortion, or ease the pain of childbirth. The status and role of Indian women were strikingly different from European patterns, in which the rule of men over women and fathers over households was the norm.

Farming communities were far more complex than foraging communities, but they were also less stable. Growing populations demanded increasingly large surpluses of food, and this need frequently led to social conflict and warfare among farming communities. Moreover, farming systems were especially vulnerable to climatological disruptions such as drought, as well as to ecological crises of their own creation, such as soil depletion or erosion.

The Religions of Foragers and Farmers

The religions of Indian peoples were shaped primarily by the two great traditions of foraging and farming. The first, rooted deep in the Archaic past, is sometimes called the Hunting Tradition. This complex of beliefs centered in the relationship of hunters and prey and celebrated the existence of a "Master of Animals," often portrayed as the sacred bear. Associated with this tradition was the vision quest, a practice in which young men and women sought out personal protective spirits by going alone into the wilderness, exposing themselves to the elements, fasting, and inducing hallucinations and dreams. An individual who developed a special sensitivity to spiritual forces might

The creation of man and woman depicted on a pot (dated about C.E. 1000) from the ancient villages of the Mimbres River of southwestern New Mexico, the area of Mogollon culture. Mimbres pottery is renowned for its spirited artistry. Such artifacts were usually intended as grave goods, to honor the dead.

Human figures dance on this characteristic piece of red-on-buff pottery of the Hohokams (dated about C.E. 1000). The Hohokams, located on the floodplain of the Gila River near present-day Phoenix, Arizona, were the first irrigation farmers of North America. The Pima and Papago people of Arizona may be descended from them.

become a shaman—a "medicine" man or woman of the community. The Hunting Tradition was important throughout the continent but was strongest in the northern latitudes, where hunting played a prominent role in the economy.

With the northward spread of maize farming came a second religious complex, known as the Agrarian Tradition, which emphasized and celebrated the notion of fertility in ritual festivals marking the annual change of seasons. At Cahokia, archaeological evidence of posts used to mark the summer and winter solstices suggests that the Agrarian Tradition was honored there. Because this tradition was associated with the greater social complexity of the farming way of life, it was generally characterized by organized cults and priesthoods rather than by individualistic shamans. At its most elaborate, it featured a war-sacrifice-cannibalism ideology that glorified violence and included the ritual consumption of enemy flesh, a tradition whose origins may be related to those of the awe-inspiring sacrificial rituals performed by the priests and leaders of the Mesoamerican city-states.

Although religious beliefs were probably as distinctive as the local communities that held them, some combination of the Hunting and Agrarian traditions characterized most of the Indian cultures of North America. Natural and supernatural forces were thought to be inseparable, a system of belief called *pantheism;* people were thought to share a basic kinship

with animals, plants, inanimate objects, and natural forces. Although many native religions recognized the existence of a paramount spiritual force, they were also generally polytheistic, with numerous gods and spirits.

The Earliest Farmers of the Southwest

Farming communities began to emerge in the arid Southwest during the first millenium B.C.E. Among the first to develop a settled farming way of life were the Mogollon people, who lived along what is today the southern Arizona–New Mexico border from around 250 B.C.E. to around C.E. 1450. Living along mountain ridges and near streams in permanent villages of ingenious pit houses well suited to the region's temperature extremes, these people used digging sticks to cultivate maize, beans, and squash. Some of the Mogollon pit structures may have been what Southwestern peoples today call *kivas*, which are used for community religious rituals.

From about C.E. 300 to 1500 the people of the Hohokam ("those who are gone," in the language of the modern Pimas and Papagos of the area) culture flourished in the region along the floodplain of the Salt and Gila Rivers in southern Arizona. The Hohokams, who lived in agricultural villages, built and maintained the first irrigation system in America north of Mexico, channeling river water many miles to desert fields of maize, beans, squash, tobacco, and cotton. They made jewelry from shells and developed a process for etching shells with animal designs. They shared many traits with Mesoamerican civilization to the south, including platform mounds for religious ceremonies and large courts for ball playing. One thoroughly excavated Hohokam community site is a place the Pimas call Skoaquik, or Snaketown. Located near present-day Phoenix, Snaketown includes the

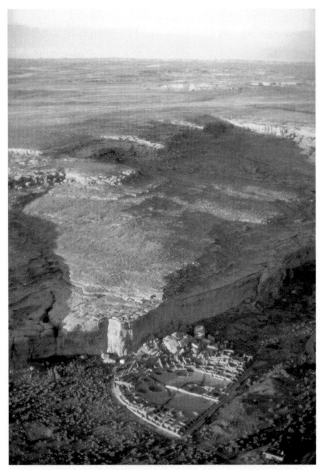

In Chaco Canyon, in northern New Mexico, lie the ruins of Pueblo Bonito, built in the twelfth century C.E. during the golden age of the Anasazis, an agricultural people who created a complex urban civilization amid the arid landscape of the Colorado Plateau. Until the invention of the modern construction techniques, Pueblo Bonito held the record as the world's largest apartment house.

remains of a hundred pit houses spread over 300 acres. The number and variety of goods from central Mexico uncovered at the site—rubber balls, mirrors of pyrite mosaics, copper bells, and fashionable ear ornaments—suggest that it may have housed a community of merchants who traded Mesoamerican manufactured goods for locally mined turquoise.

The Anasazis

The best-known farming culture of the Southwest is that of the Anasazis ("ancient outsiders," in the Navajo language), which developed around the first century C.E. several hundred miles to the north of the Hohokam communities in the Four Corners area, where today Arizona, New Mexico, Utah, and Colorado meet on the eastern portion of the great plateau of the Colorado River. Around 750, possibly in response to population pressure and an increasingly dry climate, the Anasazis

began a shift from pit-house villages to densely populated, multistoried apartment complexes called *pueblos* ("towns" in Spanish, for they were named by Spanish invaders). These complexes clustered around central plazas with circular underground *kivas*. The Anasazis grew high-yield varieties of maize in terraced fields irrigated by canals flowing from mountain catchment basins. To supplement this vegetable diet they hunted animals for their meat, using the bow and arrow that first appeared in the region about C.E. 500.

Anasazi culture extended over an area larger than California. The sites of more than 25,000 Anasazi communities are known in New Mexico alone. Only a few have been excavated, so there is much that archaeologists do not yet understand. The most prominent of the Anasazi centers was Pueblo Bonito in Chaco canyon. Completed in the twelfth century, this complex of 650 interconnected rooms is a monument to the golden age of the Anasazis. Hundreds of miles of arrow-straight roads and an interpueblo communication system consisting of mountaintop signaling stations connect Chaco Canyon to outlying sites, making it the center of a food distribution, trading, and ceremonial network.

During the thirteenth century, drought conditions in the Southwest worsened. Growing Anasazi populations redoubled their efforts to improve their production methods, building increasingly complex irrigation canals, dams, and terraced fields. Many large fields were mulched with small stones to retain moisture more effectively. But these measures were not sufficient. Scientific analysis of the varying size of the growth rings of ancient tree trunks reveals that between 1276 and 1293 there was a prolonged and devastating drought that must have resulted in repeated crop failures and eventual famine.

The Anasazis were confronted with an additional difficulty—the arrival of bands of Athapascan migrants who for a thousand years or more had been gradually moving south from Subarctic regions. If the Athapascans were anything like their immediate descendants, the Navajos and the Apaches, they must have been fierce fighters. By the fourteenth and fifteenth centuries, the Athapascans were raiding Anasazi farming communities, taking food, goods, and possibly slaves. The dramatic Anasazi cliff dwellings at Mesa Verde, Colorado, constructed about this time, may have been built as a defense against these raiders. Gradually the Anasazis abandoned the Four Corners area altogether. Their movements have not yet been fully traced, but most seem to have resettled in communities along the Rio Grande, joining with local residents to form the Pueblo people of modern times.

Farmers of the Eastern Woodlands

Archaeologists date the beginning of the farming culture of eastern North America, known as Woodland, from the first appearances of pottery in the region about 3,000 years ago. The Woodland culture was based on a sophisticated way of life that combined gathering and hunting with the cultivation of a few crops. People lived most of the year at permanent community sites but left them seasonally to take advantage of resources at different locations. Their crops included sunflowers and other locally domesticated plants. The discovery of clay pipes in archaeological excavations suggests that the early Woodlands people may also have cultivated tobacco, which was first domesticated in the Caribbean region.

Woodlands peoples began cultivating maize during the first millenium C.E., but even before then they had begun to adopt an increasingly settled existence and a more complex social organization in some regions. Between 1700 and 700 B.C.E. the people of the Poverty Point culture in the lower Mississippi Valley erected a remarkable site consisting of a series of concentric semicircular earth mounds covering an area about a mile square. The people of the Adena culture (the name is taken from a site on the upper Ohio River) occupied the Ohio River basin from present-day Indiana to Pennsylvania from before 1000 B.C.E. to about C.E. 250. They lived in permanent or semipermanent villages and built large burial mounds.

Between about 200 B.C.E. and fifth century C.E. the Hopewell people settled in the Mississippi-Ohio Valley. Hopewell communities were devoted to mortuary cults, in which the dead were honored through ceremony, display, and the construction of enormous and elaborate burial mounds. In support of this tradition, Hopewell chiefs mobilized an elaborate trade network that acquired obsidian from the Rocky Mountains, copper from the Great Lakes, mica from the Appalachians, and shells from the Gulf coast. Hopewell artisans converted these materials into distinctive and artistically sophisticated goods that played an important role in Hopewell trade and were buried with the dead in Hopewell graves.

Mississippian Society

The Hopewell culture collapsed in the fifth century, perhaps as a result of shifting climate patterns. Local communities continued to practice their late Archaic subsistence strategies, but abandoned the expensive cultural displays demanded by the Hopewell mortuary cult. Following the collapse of Hopewell, however, several important innovations were introduced in the East. The bow and arrow, developed on the Great Plains, appeared east of the Mississippi about the seventh century, greatly increasing the efficiency of hunting. Also between 450 and 800, maize farming spread widely in the east. Indian farmers had developed a new variety of maize called Northern Flint, with large cobs and plentiful kernels that matured in a short enough time to make it suitable for cultivation in temperate northern latitudes. Also about this time a shift from digging sticks to flint hoes took place, further increasing the productive potential of maize farming.

It was on the basis of these innovations that, in the seventh or eighth century, the powerful new Mississippian culture arose. The Mississippians were master maize farmers who lived in permanent villages along the floodplain of the Mississippi River. Cahokia, the most important of these, was the urban heart of Mississippian America. Cahokia's dense urban center with its monumental temple, its residential neighborhoods, and its surrounding farmlands were mirrored in many other regional centers, each with thousands of residents. There were cities on the Arkansas River near Spiro, Oklahoma; on the Black Warrior River at Moundville, Alabama; at Hiwassee Island on the Tennessee River; and along the Etowah and Ocmulgee Rivers in Georgia. Like Cahokia, these centers of civilization were probably characterized by a sophisticated division of labor that

The Great Serpent Mound in southern Ohio, the shape of an uncoiling snake more than 1,300 feet long, is the largest effigy earthwork in the world. Monumental public works like these suggest the high degree of social organization of the Mississippian people.

Native North American Trade Networks, ca. C.E. 1400   *By determining the places of origin of artifacts found at ancient sites, historians have devised a conjectural map of Indian trade networks. Among large regional centers and smaller local ones, trade connected Indian peoples of many different communities and regions.*

included artisans, priests, and an elite class of rulers. The Great Serpent Mound, the largest effigy earthwork in the world, was constructed by Mississippian peoples in southern Ohio.

Linked by the vast water transportation system of the Mississippi and its many tributaries, these communities became the earliest city-states north of Mexico, hierarchical chiefdoms that extended political control over the farmers of the surrounding countryside. With continued population growth, these cities engaged in vigorous and probably violent competition for the limited space along the rivers. It may have been the need for more orderly ways of allocating territories that stimulated the evolution of political hierarchies. The tasks of preventing local conflict, storing large food surpluses, and redistributing foodstuffs from farmers to artisans and elites required a leadership class with the power to command. Mound-building and the use of tribute labor in the construction of other public works testified to the power the chiefs wielded from their sumptuous quarters atop the commanding mounds. If politics is defined as the orga-

nized contest for power among people and groups, then the Mississippians and the Anasazis were the first truly political societies north of Mexico.

Mississippian culture reached its height between the eleventh and thirteenth centuries C.E., the same period in which the Anasazis were constructing their desert cities. Both groups adapted the technology that was spreading northward from Mexico to their particular environments, both developed impressive artistic traditions, and their feats of engineering reflect the beginnings of science and technology. These were complex societies characterized by urbanism, social stratification, craft specialization, and regional trade. Except for a formal system of writing, they had all the traits of European and Asian civilizations.

The Politics of Warfare and Violence

The late thirteenth century marked the end of several hundred years of climatological conditions that were very favorable to maize farming and the beginning of a century and a half of cool, dry conditions.

Although the changes in climate in the Mississippi Valley were not as severe as those that devastated the Anasazis of the Southwest, over the long term they significantly lowered the potential of farming to support growing urban populations. Some archaeologists have suggested that this extended drought sharpened political conflict in both areas and greatly increased violence and social disorder.

Warfare among Indian peoples certainly predated the colonial era. Organized violence was probably rare among hunting bands, which could seldom muster the manpower for more than a small raid against an enemy. Certain hunting peoples, though, such as the southward-moving Athapascans, undoubtedly engaged in systematic raiding of settled farming communities. Warfare was also common among farming societies fighting to gain additional lands for cultivation. The first Europeans in what is now the South of the United States described highly organized combat among large tribal armies. The bow and arrow was a deadly weapon of war, and the practice of scalping seems to have originated among warring tribes, who believed one could capture a warrior's spirit by taking his hair. (During the period of colonial warfare, the practice of scalping spread widely among both European colonists and the Indian tribes of other regions.) Sculpted images of human sacrifice found at Mississippian sites suggest that these peoples, like the inhabitants of Mexican city-states, not only waged war but practiced human sacrifice and cannibalism.

The archaeological remains of Cahokia reveal that during the thirteenth and fourteenth centuries the people of that great city surrounded its central sections with a heavy log stockade. This defensive structure suggests that there may have been a great deal of violent warfare with other nearby communities. Indeed, the fourteenth century may have been a period of intense conflict and war among competing city-states throughout the valleys of the Mississippi, each based on the domination of farming countrysides by metropolitan centers. Eventually conditions in the upper Mississippi Valley deteriorated so far that Cahokia and many other sites were abandoned altogether, and as the cities collapsed, people relocated in smaller, decentralized communities. Nevertheless, as we will see, among the peoples of the South, Mississippian patterns continued into the period of colonization.

NORTH AMERICA ON THE EVE OF COLONIZATION

The first Europeans to arrive in North America found a continent populated by more than 350 native societies speaking nearly as many distinct languages. Although anthropologists of the early twentieth century estimated that the population of the entire area north of Mexico was little more than a million, historians have now raised this estimate substantially.

The Indian Population of America

In determining the precolonial population of the Americas, today's historical demographers consider a number of factors—the population densities that different technological and economic systems could support, the archaeological evidence, the very earliest European accounts, and the estimated impact of epidemic diseases. (For a discussion of epidemics among Indian peoples, see Chapter 2.) Although estimates vary, most historians now believe that the population of America north of Mexico in the early sixteenth century numbered between 7 and 10 million. Moreover, probably another 25 million were concentrated in the complex societies of the Mexican highlands. Thus at the time of their first contact with European explorers and settlers, the peoples of the Western Hemisphere numbered some 60 to 70 million, about the same as Europe's population.

Population density in North America varied widely according to ways of life. Only scattered bands populated the Great Basin, the Great Plains, and Subarctic regions, but the Northwest and what is today California were densely settled because the foraging peoples of those areas maintained highly productive fishing and gathering economies. The Southwest, South, and Northeast contained the largest populations, and it was in these areas that European explorers, conquerors, and colonists first concentrated their efforts.

The Southwest

The single overwhelming fact of life in the Southwest is aridity. Summer rains average only ten to twenty inches annually, and on much of the dry desert cultivation is impossible. Several rivers, however, flow southward out of pine-covered mountain plateaus to the Gulf of Mexico and the Gulf of California. Narrow bands of green vegetation in parched sands of brown and red, they have made irrigation farming possible.

On the eve of European colonization, Indian farmers in the Southwest had been cultivating fields for nearly 3,000 years. In the floodplain of the Gila and Salt Rivers lived the Pimas and Papagos, descendants of the ancient Hohokams. Working small irrigated fields along the Colorado River and even on the floor of the Grand Canyon were the Yuman peoples. These desert farmers cultivated corn, beans, squash, sunflowers, and cotton, which they traded throughout the Southwest. They lived in dispersed

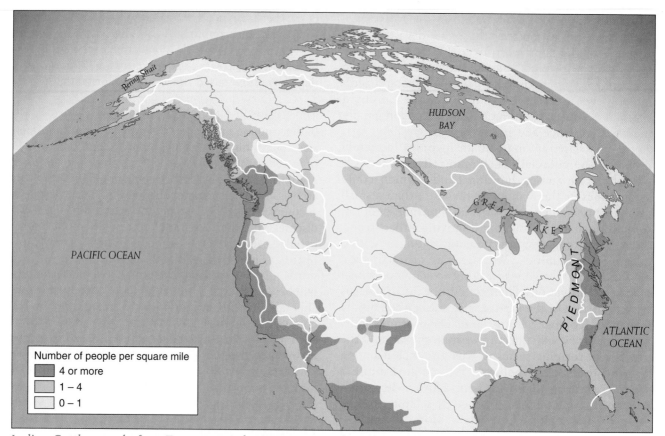

Indian Settlement before European Colonization   *Based on what is called the "carrying capacity" of different subsistence strategies—the population density they could support—historical demographers have mapped the hypothetical population density of Indian societies in the fifteenth century, before the era of European colonization. Populations were most dense in farming societies or in coastal areas with marine resources and least dense in extreme environments like the Great Basin.*

settlements that the Spanish called *rancherias* (meaning "settlements"), which were separated by as much as a mile. That way, say the Pimas, people avoid getting on each other's nerves. Rancherias were governed in general by councils of adult men whose decisions required unanimous consent, although a headman was chosen to manage the irrigation works. Ceremonies focused, appropriately, on rainmaking; one ritual required everyone to drink cactus wine until thoroughly drunk, a state of presumed purification that was thought to bring rain.

East of the Grand Canyon, in their unique dwellings of stacked, interconnected apartments, lived the Pueblo peoples, who inherited this architectural form, as well as their farming techniques and religious practices, from their Anasazi forebears. Although the many Pueblo peoples spoke several languages, as a group they shared a commitment to communal village life that differentiated them from the individualistic desert farmers. A strict communal code of behavior regulating personal conduct was enforced by the Pueblos through a maze of matrilin-

eal clans and secret religious societies; unique combinations of these clans and societies formed the governing systems of different Pueblo villages. Seasonal public ceremonies in the village squares featured colorful impersonations, with singing, chanting, and dancing, of ancestral sacred spirits called *kachinas.* "Clowns" mimicked in slapstick style those who did not conform to the communal ideal, pretending to drink urine or eat dirt, for example, in front of the home of a person who kept an unclean house.

The Pueblos inhabit the oldest continuously occupied towns in the United States. The village of Oraibi, Arizona, dates from the twelfth century, when the Hopis ("peaceful ones") founded it in the isolated central mesas of the Colorado Plateau. Using dry-farming methods and drought-resistant plants, these western Pueblo Indians produced rich harvests of corn and squash amid shifting sand dunes. On a mesa top about fifty miles southwest of present-day Albuquerque, New Mexico, Anasazi immigrants from Mesa Verde built Acoma, the "sky city," in the late thirteenth century. The Pueblo people established approximately

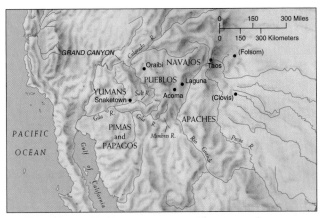

Southwestern Indian Groups on the Eve of Colonization   *The Southwest was populated by desert farmers like the Pimas, Papagos, Yumans, and Pueblos, as well as by nomadic hunters and raiders like the Apaches and Navajos.*

seventy other villages during the next two hundred years; fifty of these were still in existence in the seventeenth century when the Spanish founded Santa Fé, and two dozen survive today, including the large Indian towns of Laguna, Isleta, Santo Domingo, Jémez, San Felipe, and Taos (see the map on p. 52).

In the arid deserts and mountains surrounding these towns were bands of nomadic hunters, some of whom had lived in the region thousands of years. But there were also the Athapascans who, as we have seen, began arriving in the fourteenth and fifteenth centuries and who hunted and foraged, traded meat and medicinal herbs with farmers, and frequently raided and plundered these same villages and rancherias. Gradually, some of the Athapascan people surrounding the Pueblo villages adopted their neighbors' farming and handicraft skills; these people were the Navajos. Others, who came be known as the Apaches, were more heavily influenced by the hunting and gathering traditions of the Great Basin and Great Plains and remained nomadic.

The South

The South enjoys a mild, moist climate with short winters and long summers, ideal for farming. From the Atlantic and Gulf coasts, a broad fertile plain extends inland to the Piedmont, a plateau separating the coastal plains from the Appalachian Mountains. The transition between plateau and coastal plain is marked by the fall line, an area of rapids and waterfalls in the descending rivers. The upper courses of the waterways originating in the Appalachian highlands offered ample rich bottomland for farming, and the extensive forests, mostly of yellow pine, offered abundant animal resources. In the sixteenth century, large populations of Indian peoples farmed this rich land, fishing or hunting to supplement their diets. They lived in communities ranging from villages of

twenty or so dwellings to large towns of a thousand or more inhabitants.

Mississippian cultural patterns continued among the peoples of the South. They were organized into confederacies of farming towns, the most powerful living along the river floodplains. Because most of these groups were quickly decimated in the first years of European colonization, they are poorly documented. We know the most about the Natchez, farmers of the rich lands in the lower Mississippi delta who survived into the eighteenth century before being destroyed in a war with the French. Overseeing the Natchez was a ruler known as the Great Sun, who lived in royal splendor on a ceremonial mound in his village capital. When out among his subjects he was carried on a litter, the path before him swept by his retinue of servants and wives. Natchez society was class based. Noble families were represented on the Great Sun's council of advisers and appointed village peace and war chiefs. The majority of people, however, were a subordinate group known as the "Stinkards." Persistent territorial conflict with other confederacies elevated warfare to an honored status among the Natchez, and public torture and human sacrifice of enemies were commonplace. The Natchez give us our best glimpse at what life may have been like in ancient Cahokia.

The Indians of Florida also lived in sophisticated chiefdoms characterized by class systems, monarchs, and priests. Archaeological evidence implies that central towns dominated farmers in the countryside, demanding from them large quantities of maize, squash, and other cultivated plants grown on fields large enough to support populations numbering in the tens of thousands. As in the Natchez villages and the city of Cahokia, life in these Florida towns centered around the ceremonial mounds where the ruling families resided. Honored clans

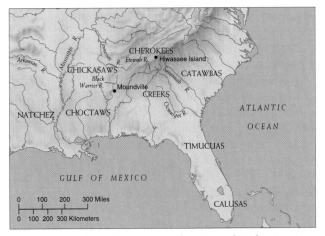

Southern Indian Groups on the Eve of Colonization
On the eve of colonization the Indian societies of the South shared many traits of the complex Mississippian farming culture.

The New Queen Being Taken to the King, *engraved by Theodor de Bry in the sixteenth century from a drawing by Jacques le Moyne, an early French colonist of Florida. The communities of Florida were hierarchical, with classes and hereditary chiefs, some of whom were women. Here le Moyne depicted a "queen" being carried on an ornamental litter by men of rank.*

lived in the plaza below, with ordinary people on the fringes of town and in the countryside.

Eventually, these chiefdoms proved highly vulnerable to conquest, but the looser confederacies of the interior were considerably more resilient. Among the latter the most prominent were the Choctaws of present-day Mississippi and Alabama, the Chickasaws in western Tennessee, and the Creeks of Georgia, each confederacy, including several dozen towns. On the mountain plateaus lived the Cherokees, who made up the single largest confederacy, of more than sixty towns. Farming was somewhat less important in the highlands than along the coast, hunting somewhat more so. There were no ruling classes or kings, and leaders were either women or men. Most peoples reckoned their descent matrilineally (that is, through their mothers, grandmothers, and so on), and at marriage husbands left the homes of their mothers to reside with the families of their wives. Women controlled household and village life and were influential as well in the

matrilineal clans that linked communities together. Councils of elderly men governed the confederacies but were joined by clan matrons for annual meetings at the central council house. These gatherings could last days or even weeks, since all clan members, male and female, were given the opportunity to speak.

All the peoples of the South farmed the same crops, hunted in the same kind of piney woods, and lived in similar villages. They celebrated a common round of agricultural festivals that brought clans together from surrounding communities. At the harvest festival, for example, people thoroughly cleaned their homes and villages. They fasted and purified themselves by consuming the "black drink," a vision-inducing libation made from roasted leaves of the cassina plant. They extinguished old fires, lit new ones, and then celebrated the new crop of sweet corn with dancing and other festivities. During the following days, villages, clans, and groups of men and women competed against each other in the ancient stick-and-ball game that the French named lacrosse; in the evenings men and women played chunkey, a gambling game.

The Northeast

The Northeast, the colder sector of the eastern woodlands, has a varied geography of coastal plains and mountain highlands, great rivers, lakes, and valleys. After C.E. 500, cultivation became the main support of the Indian economy in those places where the growing season was long enough to bring a crop of corn to maturity. In such areas of the Northeast—along the coasts and in the river valleys—Indian populations were large and dense.

The Iroquois of present-day Ontario and upstate New York, who have lived in these areas for at least 4,500 years, were among the first northeastern peoples to adopt cultivation. As they shifted from primary reliance on fishing and hunting to maize farming, they apparently relocated their villages from river floodplains to hilltops. There Iroquois women produced crops of corn, beans, squash, and sunflowers sufficient to support fifty longhouses, each occupied by a large matrilineal, extended family. Some of those houses were truly long; archaeologists have excavated the foundations of 400-foot-long dwellings that may have housed dozens of families. Typically, these villages were surrounded by substantial wooden walls, clear evidence of intergroup conflict and warfare.

Population growth and the resulting intensification of farming in Iroquois country stimulated the development of chiefdoms there as elsewhere. By the fifteenth century several centers of population, each in a separate river system, had coalesced from east to west across upstate New York. These were the five Iroquois chiefdoms or "nations": the Mohawks, Oneidas, Onondagas, Cayugas, and Senecas. Iroquois oral histories collected during the nineteenth century recall this as a period of persistent violence, possibly the consequence of conflicts over territory.

Historians believe that the Iroquois founded a confederacy to control this violence. The confederacy outlawed warfare among the member nations and established regulated forms of gift exchange and payment to replace revenge. According to Iroquois oral history, Chief Deganawida—known as the lawgiver—founded the confederacy. It is said that he "blocked out the sun" as a demonstration of his powers; it may be that these events took place during the full solar eclipse that was visible in the Northeast in 1451. Deganawida's message was proclaimed by his supporter, Hiawatha, a great orator, who convinced all the five Iroquois nations to join. As a model, the confederacy used the powerful metaphor of the longhouse; each nation, it was said, occupied

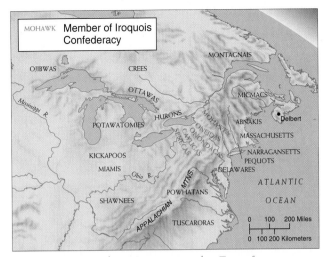

Northeastern Indian Groups on the Eve of Colonization   *The Indians of the Northeast were mostly village peoples. In the fifteenth century five Iroquois groups—the Mohawks, Oneidas, Onondagas, Cayugas, and Senecas—joined together to form the Iroquois Five Nation Confederacy.*

a separate hearth but acknowledged descent from a common mother. As in the longhouse, women played important roles in choosing the male leaders who would represent their lineages and chiefdom on the Iroquois council. The confederacy suppressed violence among its members but did not hesitate to encourage war against outside groups such as the neighboring Hurons or the Eries, who constructed defensive confederacies of their own at about the same time. The Iroquois Confederacy would become one of the most powerful contenders in the struggles among competing Indian and European forces during the colonial period.

The Iroquois spoke Iroquoian. The other major language group of the Northeast was Algonquian, whose speakers belonged to at least fifty distinct cultures. In contrast to the Iroquois, most Algonquian peoples were patrilineal. In general, they lived in less extensive dwellings and in smaller villages than the Iroquois, often without palisade fortifications. The Algonquian peoples north of the Great Lakes and in northern New England were hunters and foragers, organized into bands with loose ethnic affiliations. Several of these peoples, including the Micmacs, Crees, Montagnais, and Ojibwas (also known as Chippewas), were the first to become enmeshed in the early fur trade with European newcomers. Among the Algonquians of the Atlantic coast from present-day Massachusetts south to Virginia, as well as among those in the Ohio Valley, farming led to the development of settlements as densely populated as those of the Iroquois, although the abundance of coastal and riverine resources made

CHRONOLOGY

30,000–15,000 B.C.E.	First humans in the Americas	250 B.C.E.	Beginning of Mogollon culture in the Southwest
13,000 B.C.E.	Global warming trend begins	200 B.C.E.–C.E. 400	Hopewell culture flourishes
10,000 B.C.E.	Clovis technology	650	Bow and arrow, flint hoes, and Northern Flint corn in the Northeast
9000 B.C.E.	Extinction of big-game animals		
8000 B.C.E.	Beginning of the Archaic period	775–1150	Hohokam site of Snaketown reaches its greatest extent
7000 B.C.E.	First cultivation of plants in the Mexican highlands	1000	Tobacco in use throughout North America
5000 B.C.E.	Athapascan migrations to America begin	1150	Founding of Hopi village of Oraibi, oldest continuously occupied town in the United States
4000 B.C.E.	First settled communities along the Pacific coast		
3000 B.C.E.	Inupiat and Aleut migrations begin	1200	High point of Mississippian and Anasazi cultures
1500–1000 B.C.E.	Maize and other Mexican crops introduced into the Southwest	1276	Severe drought begins in the Southwest
1000 B.C.E.	Beginning of Adena culture	1300	Arrival of Athapascans in the Southwest
	First urban communities in Mexico	1451	Founding of Iroquois Confederacy

the bow and arrow and the fishing spear as important to these people as the hoe.

Algonquian communities, although relatively autonomous from one another, also began to form confederacies during the fifteenth and sixteenth centuries. Among these groupings were those of the Massachusetts, Narragansets, and Pequots of New England, the Delawares and the peoples of Powhatan's confederacy on the mid-Atlantic coast, and the Shawnees, Miamis, Kickapoos, and Potawatomis of the Ohio Valley.

CONCLUSION

Over the thousands of years that elapsed between the settlement of the North American continent and the invasion of Europeans at the end of the fifteenth century, Indian peoples developed hundreds of distinctive cultures that were fine-tuned to the geographic and climatological possibilities and limitations of their homelands. In the northern forests they hunted game and perfected the art of processing furs and hides. Along the coasts and rivers they harvested the abundant runs of fish and learned to navigate the waters with sleek and graceful boats. In the arid Southwest they mastered irrigation farming and made the deserts bloom, while in the humid Southeast they mastered the large-scale production of crops that could sustain large cities with sophisticated political systems. North America was not a "virgin" continent, as so many of the Europeans believed. Indians had transformed the natural world, making it over into a human landscape.

"Columbus did not discover a new world," writes the historian J. H. Perry. "He established contact between two worlds, both already old." North America had a rich history, one that Europeans did not understand and later generations of Americans have too frequently ignored. The European colonists who came to settle encountered thousands of Indian communities with deep roots and vibrant traditions. In the confrontation that followed, Indian communities viewed the colonists as invaders and called upon their traditions and their gods to help them defend their homelands.

REVIEW QUESTIONS

1. List the evidence for the hypothesis that the Americas were settled by migrants from Asia.
2. Discuss the impact of environmental change and human hunting on the big-game populations of North America.
3. Review the principal regions of the North American continent and the human adaptations that made social life possible in each of them.
4. Define the concept of "forest efficiency." How does it help to illuminate the major development of the Archaic period?
5. Why did the development of farming lead to increasing social complexity? Discuss the reasons why organized political activity began in farming societies.
6. What were the Hunting and Agrarian Traditions? In what ways did the religious beliefs of Indian peoples reflect their environmental adaptations?
7. What factors led to the organization of the Iroquois Confederacy?

RECOMMENDED READING

Tom D. Dillehay and David J. Miltzer, eds., *The First Americans: Search and Research* (1991). A summary of the most recent archaeological findings, suggesting a much earlier migration to the Americas. For the newest discoveries, see recent issues of *National Geographic* and *Scientific American.*

Thomas E. Emerson, *Cahokia and the Archaeology of Power* (1997). The fascinating story of North America's first metropolis.

Brian M. Fagan, *The Great Journey: The Peopling of Ancient America* (1987). An anthropologist's account of the Asian migration to the Americas.

Stuart J. Fiedel, *Prehistory of the Americas* (1987). The best introduction for the nonspecialist, covering the first migrations, the development of technologies, and the spread of farming.

Alvin M. Josephy Jr., ed., *America in 1492* (1992). Important essays by the leading scholars of the North American Indian experience. Includes beautiful illustrations and maps as well as an excellent bibliography.

Alvin M. Josephy Jr., *500 Nations: An Illustrated History of North American Indians* (1995). A magnificent volume that includes historic illustrations as well as fascinating computer re-creations of the pre-European human landscape of America.

Alice B. Kehoe, *North American Indians: A Comprehensive Account* (1992). The best general anthropological survey of the history and culture of the Indians of North America. Organized by culture areas, the new edition covers all the peoples of the continent and includes the most recent scholarship.

Robert Silverberg, *Mound Builders of Ancient America: The Archaeology of a Myth* (1968). A brilliant history of opinion and theory about the mound builders, combined with a review of the best archaeological evidence then available.

William C. Sturtevant, general editor, *Handbook of North American Indians*, 20 vols. proposed (1978–). The most comprehensive collection of the best current scholarship. The completed series will include a volume for each of the culture regions of North America; volumes on origins, Indian-white relations, languages, and art; a biographical dictionary; and a general index.

Russell Thornton, *American Indian Holocaust and Survival: A Population History since 1492* (1987). The best introduction to the historical demography of North America. In a field of great controversy, it provides a judicious review of all the evidence.

ADDITIONAL BIBLIOGRAPHY

Settling the Continent

Larry D. Agenbroad, et al., eds., *Megafauna and Man* (1990)

John Bierhorst, ed., *The Red Swan: Myths and Tales of the American Indians* (1976)

Warwick M. Bray, et al., *The New World: The Making of the Past* (1977)

Mark Nathan Cohen, *The Food Crisis in Prehistory: Overpopulation and the Origins of Agriculture* (1977)

E. James Dixon, *Quest for the Origins of the First Americans* (1993)

Henry F. Dobyns, *Native American Historical Demography: A Critical Bibliography* (1976)

Richard Erdoes and Alfonso Ortiz, eds., *American Indian Myths and Legends* (1984)

Jonathon E. Ericson, et al., eds., *Peopling of the New World* (1982)

Brian M. Fagan, *Ancient North America: The Archaeology of a Continent*, Second Edition (1995)

Jeffrey Goodman, *American Genesis: The American Indian and the Origins of Modern Man* (1981)

Ted Hirschfield, *Middle Mississippians: Encounters with the Prehistoric Amerindians* (1996).

Lee Eldridge Huddleston, *Origins of the American Indians: European Concepts, 1492–1729* (1967)

Jesse D. Jennings, ed., *Ancient North Americans* (1983)

George Kubler, *Esthetic Recognition of Ancient Amerindian Art* (1991)

William S. Laughlin and Albert B. Harper, eds., *The First Americans: Origins, Affinities, and Adaptations* (1979)

James L. Phillips and James A. Brown, eds., *Archaic Hunters and Gatherers in the American Midwest* (1983)

Hanns J. Prem, *The Ancient Americas: A Brief History and Guide to Research* (1997).

Heather Anne Pringle, *In Search of Ancient North America: An Archaeological Journey to Forgotten Cultures* (1996).

Paul Shao, *The Origin of Ancient American Cultures* (1983)

Richard Shutler Jr., ed., *Early Man in the New World* (1983)

Richard F. Townsend, ed., *The Ancient Americas: Art from Sacred Landscapes* (1992)

Waldo R. Wedel, *Prehistoric Man on the Great Plains* (1961)

Gordon R. Willey, *An Introduction to American Archaeology* (1966)

The Beginning of Regional Cultures

Michael A. Adler, ed., *The Prehistoric Pueblo World, A.D. 1150–1350* (1996).

Frances R. Berdan, *The Aztecs of Central Mexico* (1982)

David S. Brose, et al., *Ancient Art of the American Woodland Indians* (1985)

David S. Brose and N'omi Greber, eds., *Hopewell Archaeology* (1979)

Michael D. Coe, *Mexico* (1967)

Linda S. Cordell, *Prehistory of the Southwest* (1984)

Munro Edmondson, ed., *Sixteenth-Century Mexico: The Works of Sahagun* (1974)

Richard I. Ford, ed., *Prehistoric Food Production in North America* (1985)

Melvin L. Fowler, *Perspectives in Cahokia Archeology* (1975)

Emil W. Haury, *The Hohokam* (1976)

William F. Keegan, ed., *Emergent Horticultural Economies of the Eastern Woodlands* (1987)

A. L. Kroeber, *Cultural and Natural Areas of Native North America* (1939)

Barker H. Morrow and V. B. Price, eds., *Anasazi Architecture and American Design* (1997)

Timothy R. Pauketat and Thomas E. Emerson, eds., *Cahokia: Domination and Ideology in the Mississippian World* (1997)

W. H. Wills, *Early Prehistoric Agriculture* (1988)

Eric Wolf, *Sons of the Shaking Earth* (1959)

The Eve of Colonization

James Axtell, ed., *The Indian Peoples of Eastern America: A Documentary History of the Sexes* (1981)

Elizabeth M. Brunfiel and John W. Fox, *Factional Competition and Political Development in the New World* (1993)

Lyle Campbell and Marianne Mithun, eds., *The Languages of Native America* (1979)

Olive P. Dickason, *Canada's First Nations: A History of Founding Peoples* (1992)

Edward P. Dozier, *The Pueblo Indians of North America* (1970)

Harold E. Driver, *Indians of North America* (1961)

James A. Ford, *A Comparison of Formative Cultures in the Americas* (1969)

Charles Hudson, *The Southeastern Indians* (1976)

Mallory McCane O'Connor, *Lost Cities of the Ancient Southeast* (1995)

Alfonso Ortiz, ed., *New Perspectives on the Pueblos* (1972)

Howard S. Russell, *Indian New England before the Mayflower* (1980)

Bruce D. Smith, *The Mississippian Emergence* (1990)

Frank G. Speck, *Penobscot Man* (1940)

Robert F. Spencer and Jesse D. Jennings, et al., *The Native Americans: Ethnology and Backgrounds of the North American Indians* (1977)

John R. Swanton, *The Indians of the Southeastern United States* (1946)

Bruce Trigger, *The Children of Aaeaentsic: A History of the Huron People to 1660* (1976)

Wilcomb E. Washburn, *The Indian in America* (1975)

J. Leitch Wright Jr., *The Only Land They Knew* (1981)

CHAPTER TWO

WHEN WORLDS COLLIDE

1492–1590

F. Maij

AMERICAN COMMUNITIES
The English and the Algonquians at Roanoke

It was late August 1590 when English ships sailed through Hatteras Inlet into Pamlico Sound, off the coast of present-day North Carolina, and made their way north through rough seas to Roanoke Island, where Governor John White had left the first English community in North America three years before. Anxiously, White went ashore in search of the sixty-five single men and twenty families including that of his own daughter, son-in-law, and granddaughter Virginia Dare, the first English baby born in America. Finding the houses "taken down" and possessions "spoiled and scattered about," White suddenly noticed some writing on a tree trunk: "in fair capital letters was graven CROATOAN." Because this was the name of a friendly Indian village fifty miles south and because White found no sign of a cross, which he had instructed the colonists to leave if they were in trouble, he felt sure that his people awaited him at Croatoan, and he returned to his ship, anxious to speed to their rescue.

The Roanoke settlement had been sponsored by Walter Raleigh, a wealthy adventurer who sought profit and prestige by organizing an English colony in the New World. When his men returned from a reconnoitering expedition to the area in 1584, they reported that the coastal region was densely populated by a "very handsome and goodly people." These Indians, the most southerly of the Algonquian coastal peoples, enjoyed a prosperous livelihood farming, fishing, and hunting from their small villages of one or two dozen communal houses. At an island the Indians called Roanoke, the English had been "entertained with all love and kindness" by a chief named Wingina. The leader of several surrounding villages, Wingina welcomed the English as potential allies in his struggle to extend his authority over still others. So when Raleigh's adventurers asked the chief's permission to establish a settlement on the island, he readily granted it, even sending two of his men back to England to assist in preparations for the enterprise. Manteo and Wanchese, the Indian emissaries, worked with Thomas Harriot, an Oxford scholar, and John White, a trained artist. The four men learned one another's language, and there seems to have been a good deal of mutual respect among them.

But when an all-male force of Englishmen returned the subsequent year, 1585, to establish the colony of Virginia (christened in honor of England's virgin queen, Elizabeth I), the two Indian ambassadors offered Wingina conflicting reports. Although Manteo, from the village of Croatoan, argued that the English technology and weaponry would make these men powerful allies, Wanchese described the disturbing inequalities of English society and warned of potential brutality. Wanchese was right to suspect English intentions, for Raleigh's plans were based not on respect for the Indians but on the expectation of exploiting them. He had directed the mission's commander to "proceed with extremity" should the Indians prove difficult and "bring them all in subjection to civility," meaning that they should be made serfs to English colonial masters. Raleigh anticipated that his colony would return profits through a lucrative trade in furs, or a flourishing plantation agriculture, or, best of all, mines of gold or silver. In any case, the Indians would supply the labor.

A colony like this—some 100 soldiers and adventurers with plunder foremost in their minds—was incapable of supporting itself. After building a rough fort on the island, the English went to Wingina for supplies of food. With his harvest in the storage pits, with fish running in the streams and game in the woods, Wingina did the hospitable thing. It was, after all, the duty of a chief to distribute presents and thus to create obligations on the part of recipients. But as fall turned to winter and the stores declined, the constant English demands began to tax the Indians' resources. Rather than hunt or fish, the colonists were out exploring for precious metals. They attacked several outlying villages, burning Indian homes and cornfields and kidnapping Indian women. By spring—traditionally the "starving season" for the Indians, before the crops were up or the game fat—Wingina and his people had had enough. But before the Indians could act, the English caught wind of the rising hostility, and in May 1586 they surprised the Roanoke villagers, killing several of the leading men and beheading Wingina. With the plan of using Indian labor now clearly impossible, the colonists returned to England.

John White and Thomas Harriot, who had spent their time exploring the physical and human world of the coast and recording their findings in notes and sketches, were appalled by this turn of events. Back in England Harriot insisted to Raleigh that the attack on the villagers came "upon causes that on our part might easily enough have been borne" and argued that "through discreet dealing" the Indians might "honor, obey, fear and love us." White proposed a new plan for a colony of real settlers, a community of English families who might live in harmony with the Indians. Harriot and White clearly thought English civilization was superior to the civilization of the Indians, but their vision of colonization was considerably different from that of the plunderers.

In 1587 Raleigh arranged for White to return to America as governor of a new family colony. But despite good intentions, the colonists could not overcome the legacy of violence and hatred left by the former expedition. Within a month one of White's colonists had been shot full of arrows by attackers under the leadership of Wanchese, who after Wingina's death became the most militant opponent of the English among the Roanoke Indians. White retaliated by attacking Wanchese's village, but the Indians fled into the forest with few casualties. Knowing that their entire mission hung in the balance but lacking a vessel large enough to carry them all back to England, the colonists begged White to return home in their only seaworthy ship to press Raleigh for support. Reluctantly, White set sail but arrived in England to find war threatening between England and Spain. Three anxious years elapsed before White was able to return to Roanoke, only to find the settlement destroyed and the colonists gone.

As White and his crew set their sights for Croatoan that August morning in 1590, a great storm blew up. "We drove fast into the shore," White wrote, and all hands feared imminent shipwreck. Several times they dropped anchor, but each time the cable broke. Finally, White and the ship's captain agreed that they would have to leave the sound for deeper waters. It proved to be White's last glimpse of America. Tossed home to England on a stormy sea, he never returned. The English settlers of Roanoke became known as the Lost Colony, their disappearance and ultimate fate one of the enduring mysteries of colonial history.

The Roanoke experience is a reminder of the underlying assumptions of New World colonization. "The English would act just as the Spanish had done in creating their empire," writes the historian and geographer Carl Sauer; they had "naked imperial objectives." It also suggests the wasted opportunity of the Indians' initial welcome. But in an unexpected way, the Roanoke story also emphasizes the importance of community. Many historians believe that the lost colonists lived out the rest of their lives in an Algonquian village. Many years later an English settler reported that a group of coastal North Carolina Indians had told him that "several of their Ancestors were white People," that "the English were forced to cohabit with them for Relief and Conversation, and that in the process of Time, they conformed themselves to the Manners of their Indian Relations." Thus it may be that Virginia Dare and the other children married into Indian families, creating the first mixed community of English and Indians in North America.

Roanoke

KEY TOPICS

- The European background of American colonization

- Creation of the Spanish New World empire and its first extensions to North America

- The large-scale intercontinental exchange of peoples, crops, animals, and diseases

- The French role in the beginnings of the North American fur trade

- England's first overseas colonies in Ireland and America

THE EXPANSION OF EUROPE

There may have been numerous unrecorded contacts between the peoples of America and the Old World before the fifteenth century. Archaeological excavations at L'Anse aux Meadows on the fogbound Newfoundland coast provide evidence for a tenth- or eleventh-century landing in North America by the Norse people from Scandinavian countries. But earthshaking consequences were triggered by the contact with the Americas established in 1492 by Christopher Columbus. Within a generation of Columbus's first voyage, intercontinental exchanges of peoples, crops, animals, and germs had reshaped the Atlantic world. To appreciate these remarkable changes it is important to understand how Europe was transformed during the several centuries that preceded the voyage of Columbus.

European Communities

Western Europe was an agricultural society, the majority of its people peasant farmers. Farming and livestock raising had been practiced in Europe for thousands of years, but great advances in the technology of farming took place during the late Middle Ages. Water mills, iron plows, improved devices for harnessing ox and horse power, and systems of crop rotation greatly increased productivity. Over several centuries farmers more than doubled the quantity of European land in cultivation. The increased supply of food helped the population of western Europe nearly triple between the eleventh and fourteenth centuries.

Rural Europeans lived in family households clustered in farming villages. Men performed the basic field work; women were responsible for child care, livestock, and food preparation. In the European pattern, a daughter usually left the home and village of her family to take up residence among her husband's people. A woman's family gave her a dowry, or a gift of money at the time of marriage, but in general women were excluded from inheritance. Divorce was almost unknown.

This was a world of social contrasts. Europe was dominated by a social system historians have called "feudalism." The land was divided into hundreds of small territories, each ruled by a family of lords monopolizing wealth and power. From the peasants of their districts the noble lords commanded labor service and tribute in the form of crops. Thus the nobility was the main beneficiary of medieval economic expansion, accumulating great estates and building imposing castles. A relatively small class of freehold farmers prospered as well, but the majority of peasants experienced little improvement in their standard of living.

The majority of Europeans were Christians, united under the authority of the Roman Catholic Church, whose complex organization spanned thousands of local communities with a hierarchy that extended from parish priests all the way to the pope in Rome. At the core of Christian belief was a set of communal values: love of God the father, loving behavior toward other people, and the fellowship of all believers. Nevertheless, the Catholic Church itself was one of the most powerful landowners in Europe, devoting a large portion of its considerable resources to awe-inspiring display rather than the amelioration of poverty and suffering. Counseling the poor and downtrodden to place their hopes in heavenly rewards, the Church provided legitimization for the power relationships of Europe.

Europe was also home to numerous communities of Jews, a people who dispersed from their homeland in Palestine after a series of unsuccessful revolts against Roman rule in the first century C.E. Both church and civic authorities subjected the Jews to discriminatory treatment. Restricted to ghettos and forbidden from owing land, many Jews turned adversity to advantage, becoming merchants who specialized in long-distance trade. But Jewish success only seemed to stimulate Christian hostility, culminating in a series of expulsions in the thirteenth and fourteenth

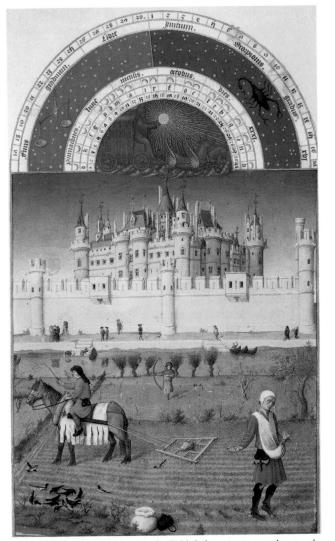

A French peasant labors in the field before a spectacular castle in a page taken from the illuminated manuscript Tres Riches Heures, *made in the fifteenth century for the duc de Berry. In 1580 the essayist Montaigne talked with several American Indians at the French court who "noticed among us some men gorged to the full with things of every sort while their other halves were beggars at their doors, emaciated with hunger and poverty" and "found it strange that these poverty-stricken halves should suffer such injustice, and that they did not take the others by the throat or set fire to their houses."*

centuries: the Jews were forced out of England in 1290, France in 1394, and Spain in 1492. Religious tolerance was unknown in early modern Europe.

For the great majority of Europeans, those were the bad old days. Most rural people survived on bread and porridge, supplemented with seasonal vegetables and an occasional piece of meat or fish. Infectious diseases abounded; perhaps a third of all children died before their fifth birthday, and only half the population reached adulthood. Famines periodically ravaged the countryside. In the fourteenth century a series of crop failures resulted in widespread starvation and death. Malnutrition paved the way for disease. Between 1347 and 1353 the widespread epidemic of bubonic plague known as the Black Death swept in from Asia and wiped out a third of Europe's population. In many places Jews were accused of spreading the plague by poisoning wells, and there were violent attacks on the ghettos.

By 1500, however, Europe's agricultural economy, strengthened by the technological breakthroughs of the Middle Ages, had recovered and its population had nearly returned to its former peak of about 30 million. Europe's social structure was hierarchical and authoritarian, but its agricultural system had the technological capacity for far greater growth than the farming economy of the Americas.

The Merchant Class and the Renaissance

The economic growth of the late Middle Ages was accompanied by the expansion of commerce, especially trade in basic goods such as minerals, salt, timber, fish, cereals, wool, and wine. Commercial expansion stimulated the growth of markets and towns: the heart of this dynamic European commercialism lay in the city-states of Italy.

During the late Middle Ages, the cities of Venice, Genoa, and Pisa launched armed, commercial fleets that seized control of Mediterranean trade. The merchants of these cities became the principal outfitters of the Crusades, a series of great military expeditions promoted by the Catholic Church to recover Palestine from the Muslims. When the Crusaders conquered the Holy Land at the end of the eleventh century they delivered the silk and spice trades of Asia into the hands of the Italian merchants. Tropical spices—cloves, cinnamon, nutmeg, and pepper—were in great demand, for they made the European diet far less monotonous for the lords who could afford them. Asian civilization also supplied a number of technical innovations that further propelled European economic growth. From China alone came the compass, gunpowder, and the art of printing with movable type. These were, according to the seventeenth-century English philosopher Francis Bacon, "the three greatest inventions known to man."

Contact with Muslim civilization provided Western scholars with access to important ancient Greek and Roman texts that had been lost to them during the Middle Ages but that had been preserved in the great Muslim libraries. The revived interest in classical antiquity that resulted triggered during the fourteenth and fifteenth centuries a period of intellectual and artistic flowering known as the Renaissance. The revolution in learning made possible by the printing press, the beginning of regular postal service,

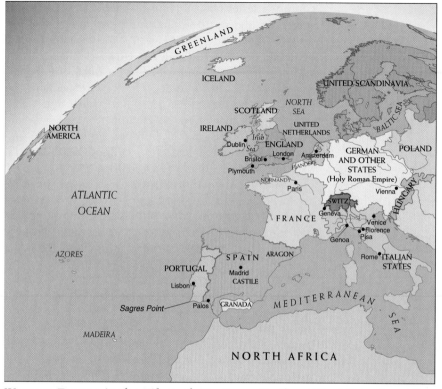

Western Europe in the Fifteenth Century   *By the middle of the century, the monarchs of western Europe had unified their realms and begun to build royal bureaucracies and standing armies and navies. These states, all with extensive Atlantic coastlines, sponsored the voyages that inaugurated the era of European colonization.*

violence, as groups fought for shares of a shrinking economy. In Flanders—a cultural and linguistic region now spread across portions of France, Belgium, and the Netherlands—during the 1320s, peasants rose against both the noble lords and the Church, beginning a series of rebellions that culminated in the great English Peasants' Revolt of 1381. "We are made men in the likeness of Christ," one rebel cried out, "but you treat us like savage beasts!" Meanwhile civil and international warfare among the nobility greatly reduced the power of the landed classes and the Catholic Church was seriously weakened by an internal struggle between French and Italian factions.

During this period of social and political chaos, the monarchs of western Europe began to replace the lords as the new centers of power, building their legitimacy by promising internal order as they unified their realms. They built royal bureaucracies and standing armies and navies. In many cases, these new monarchs found support among the increasingly wealthy merchants, who in return sought lucrative royal contracts and trading monopolies. This alliance between commerce and political power was another of the important developments that prepared the way for European expansion.

and the growth of universities helped spread the Renaissance throughout the elite circles of Europe.

The Renaissance celebrated human possibility. "The nature of all other beings is limited," the Italian intellectual Pico della Mirandola wrote in 1486; "but you, constrained by no limits, in accordance with your own free will, shall ordain for yourself the limits of your nature." This human-centered perspective was evident in architecture. The Gothic style of medieval cathedrals, whose soaring forms were intended to take human thoughts heavenward, gave way to styles borrowed from ancient Greece and Rome, which were thought to encourage rational reflection. In painting and sculpture there was a new focus on the human body. Artists modeled muscles with light and shadow to produce heroic images of men and women. These new artistic trends were aspects of what became known as *humanism*, a revolt against religious authority in which human life on earth took precedence over the afterlife of the soul. This outlook was a critical component of the inquisitive and acquisitive spirit that motivated the exploration of the Americas.

The New Monarchies

The Renaissance flowered amid the ruins that had been wrought by the plague. Famine and disease led to

Portuguese Explorations

Portugal, a narrow land along the western coast of the Iberian Peninsula with a long tradition of seafaring, became the first of these new kingdoms to explore distant lands. Lisbon, the principal port on the sea route between the Mediterranean and northwestern Europe, was a bustling, cosmopolitan city with large enclaves of Italian merchants. By 1385 local merchants had grown powerful enough to place their own favorite, João I, on the throne, and he laid ambitious plans to establish a Portuguese trading empire.

A central figure in this development was the son of the king, Prince Henry, known to later generations as "the Navigator." In the spirit of Renaissance learning, Henry established an institute of eminent geographers, instrument makers, shipbuilders, and seamen on Sagres Point, the southwestern tip of Portugal. By the mid-fifteenth century, principally as a result of their efforts, all educated Europeans knew the world was "round." (The idea that Europeans believed the world to be flat was invented in the nineteenth century.) The men of Sagres studied the seafaring techniques of Asia and the Muslim world. Incorporating these with European designs, they developed a new ship called the caravel, a faster, more maneuverable, and more seaworthy vessel than any previously known in Europe.

Using this new ship, the Portuguese plied the Atlantic coast of northwestern Africa, where gold mines and a long-established slave trade offered lucrative trading. By the time of Prince Henry's death in 1460, they had colonized the Atlantic islands of the Azores and the Madeiras and had founded bases along the West African Gold Coast. In 1488 the Portuguese captain Bartolomeu Días rounded the southern tip of Africa, known as the Cape of Good Hope, and ten years later Vasco da Gama, with the aid of Arab pilots, followed the same route to reach India. The Portuguese eventually erected strategic trading posts along the coasts of Africa, India, and China. Marrying native women and fitting into indigenous communities rather than trying to dominate them as the Roanoke colonists later would, Portuguese traders created the first and longest-lasting outposts of European world colonization, eventually gaining control of much of the Asian spice trade. Most important for the history of the Americas, however, was their establishment of the slave trade that spanned the Atlantic. (For a full discussion of slavery, see Chapter 4.)

Columbus Reaches the Americas

In 1476, Christopher Columbus, a young Genoan sailor, was shipwrecked off Sagres Point in Portugal. Making his way to Lisbon, he joined his brother, a chart maker in the Italian community there. Over the next ten years Columbus worked as a seafaring merchant seaman, visiting ports from Iceland in the North Atlantic to the Gold Coast in the south. He married and settled on the Portuguese island colony of Madeira in the Atlantic, and it was there that he developed the idea of opening a new route to Asia by sailing west across the

ocean. Such a venture would require royal backing, but when he approached the various monarchs of Europe with his idea, their advisers laughed at his geographic ignorance, pointing out that his calculation of the distance to Asia was much too short. They were right, Columbus was wrong, but it turned out to be an error of monumental good fortune.

Columbus finally sold his idea to the monarchs of Castile and Aragon, Isabella and Ferdinand. This royal couple, who through marriage had joined their kingdoms to form the state of Spain, had just conquered the southern Iberian province of Granada, formerly held by the Moors of North Africa. Their victory completed the *Reconquista* (Reconquest), the centuries-long struggle between Catholics and Muslims for the control of Iberia. Through these many generations of warfare, the Spanish had developed a military tradition that thrived on conquest and plunder. Military service was a popular means by which ordinary men could enrich themselves and rise into the ranks of the noble class. The Catholic monarchs of Spain were eager for new lands to conquer, and observing the successful Portuguese push to the south, they also became interested in opening lucrative trade routes of their own with Asia. Columbus's name for his under-

This ship, thought to be similar to Columbus's Niña, is a caravel, a type of vessel developed by the naval experts at Henry the Navigator's institute at Sagres Point, in Portugal. To the traditional square-rigged Mediterranean ship, they added the "lateen" sail of the Arabs, which permitted much greater maneuverability. Other Asian improvements, such as the stern-post rudder and multiple masting, allowed caravels to travel farther and faster than any earlier ships, and made possible the invasion of America.

taking, "the Enterprise of the Indies," suggested its commercial motive, but his expedition symbolized hopes of both trade and conquest. It did not envision the establishment of a colonial community. Like the adventurers who later peopled the first English colony of Roanoke, the Spanish had material gain in mind.

Columbus's ships left the port of Palos, Spain, in August 1492, pushed west across the Atlantic by the prevailing trade winds. By October flocks of birds and bits of driftwood announced the ships' approach to land, which turned out to be a small, flat island somewhere in the Bahamas. Although scholars disagree on the precise location, many believe it to be a spot now known as Samana Cay. Columbus, however, believed he was somewhere near the Asian mainland. He explored the northern island coasts of Cuba and Hispaniola (now Haiti and the Dominican Republic) before heading home, fortuitously catching the westerly winds that blow from the American coast toward Europe north of the tropics. One of Columbus's most important contributions was the discovery of the clockwise circulation of the Atlantic winds and currents that ultimately carried thousands of ships back and forth between Europe and the Americas.

Leading Columbus's triumphal procession to the royal court were a number of Taino Indians, dressed in bright feathers with ornaments of gold. The natives, Columbus noted, were "of a very acute intelligence" but had "no iron or steel weapons." "Should your majesties command it," Columbus announced to Ferdinand and Isabella, "all the inhabitants could be made slaves." Columbus also reported that "there are many spices and great mines of gold and of other metals." In fact, none of the spices familiar to Europeans grew in the Caribbean, and there were only small quantities of the precious metal in the riverbeds of the islands. But the sight of the little gold ornaments worn by the Indians had infected Columbus with a bad case of gold fever. He had left a small force behind in a rough fort on what is now the isolated northern coast of Haiti with instructions to continue the search for gold—the first European foothold in the Americas.

The Spanish monarchs, enthusiastic about Columbus's report, financed a convoy of 17 ships and 1,500 men that left in late 1493 to begin the colonization of the islands Columbus described as "rich for planting and sowing, for breeding cattle of every kind, for building towns and villages." As later at Roanoke, it was expected that Indians would provide the labor for these enterprises. But on his return to Hispaniola, Columbus found his fort in ruins, his men killed by Indians who, like the Algonquians at Roanoke, lost patience with the demands and brutality of the invading Europeans. Columbus destroyed the nearby native villages, enslaving the Tainos and demanding tribute from them in gold. He took slaves back to Spain, but most soon sickened and died, and the supply of gold quickly ran out. By the time of Columbus's third voyage the Spanish monarchs

This image accompanied Columbus's account of his voyage, which was published in Latin and reissued in many other languages and editions that circulated throughout Europe before 1500. The Spanish King Ferdinand is shown directing the voyage to a tropical island, where the natives flee in terror. Columbus's impression of native Americans as a people vulnerable to conquest shows clearly in this image.

had become so dissatisfied with these results that they ordered the admiral home in leg irons.

Columbus made a fourth and final trip to the Caribbean that was characterized by the same violent slave raiding and obsessive searching for gold. He died in Spain in 1506, still convinced that he had opened the way to Asia, a belief that persisted among many Europeans well into the sixteenth century. But others had already begun to see the discoveries from a different perspective. Amerigo Vespucci of Florence, who voyaged to the Caribbean in 1499, was the first European to describe the lands as *mundus novus*, a New World. When European geographers named these continents in the first decade of the sixteenth century, they called them America, after Vespucci.

THE SPANISH IN THE AMERICAS

A century after Columbus's death, before the English had

The Invasion of America   *In the sixteenth century the Spanish first invaded the Caribbean and used it to stage their successive wars of conquest in North and South America. In the seventeenth century, the French, English, and Dutch invaded the Atlantic coast. The Russians, sailing across the northern Pacific, mounted the last of the colonial invasions in the eighteenth century.*

planted a single New World colony of their own, the Spanish had created a huge and wealthy empire in the Americas. In theory, all law and policy for the empire came from Spain; in practice, the isolation of the settlements permitted a good deal of local autonomy. The Spanish created a caste system, in which a small minority of settlers and their offspring controlled the lives and labor of millions of Indian and African workers. At the same time, theirs was a society in which colonists, Indians, and Africans mixed to form a new people.

The Invasion of America

The first stages of the Spanish invasion of America included frightful violence. Armies led by conquistadors marched across the Caribbean islands, plundering villages, slaughtering men, and capturing women. The Spanish crown created a system known as *encomienda*, in which colonial lords were given the right to the labor of a community of Indians; it was supposed to be a reciprocal relationship, with the lord protecting the Indians as well as exploiting them, but in practice it amounted to simply another

form of slavery. Rather than work, one observer noted, many Indians took poison, "and others hanged themselves." Faced with labor shortages, slavers raided what King Ferdinand labeled the "useless islands" of the Bahamas and soon had entirely depopulated them. The depletion of gold on Hispaniola led to the invasion of the islands of Puerto Rico and Jamaica in 1508, and Cuba in 1511. Meanwhile, rumors of wealthy societies farther west led to scores of probing expeditions. The Spanish invasion of Central America began in 1511, and two years later Vasco Nuñez de Balboa crossed the Isthmus of Panama to what he called the "South Sea," the Pacific Ocean. In 1517 Spaniards landed on the coast of Mexico, and within a year they had made contact with the Aztec empire.

The warlike Aztecs had migrated to the high Valley of Mexico from the harsh deserts of the American Southwest during the thirteenth century in the wake of the collapse of the Toltec Empire (see Chapter 1). They settled the marshy lake district of the valley and built the city of Tenochtitlán. By the early fifteenth century the Aztecs had come to dominate

The Cruelties used by the Spaniards on the Indians, *from a 1599 English edition of* The Destruction of the Indies *by Bartolomé de las Casas. These scenes were copied from a series of engravings produced by Theodore de Bry that accompanied an earlier edition.*

the farming communities of the highlands, in the process building a powerful state. Tribute flowed into Tenochtitlán from all over Mexico and Central America. In public rituals designed to appease their gods, Aztec priests brutally sacrificed captives atop grand pyramids. By 1519, when Hernán Cortés, a veteran of the conquest of Cuba, landed on the Mexican coast, the population of the Aztec capital numbered as much as 300,000, five times the size of the largest city in Spain.

Within two years Cortés and his army had overthrown the Aztec empire, a spectacular military accomplishment that has no parallel in the annals of conquest. The Spanish had superior arms, and they also had horses, which the Indians found terrifying, mistaking mounted men for four-legged monsters. But these were not the principal causes of the Spanish success. Cortés skillfully exploited the resentments of the many native peoples who lived under Aztec domination, forging Spanish-Indian alliances that became a model for the subsequent European colonization of the Americas. Here, as at Roanoke and dozens of other sites of European invasion, colonists found Indians eager for allies to support them in their conflicts with their neighbors. Still, the Aztecs were militarily powerful, successfully driving the Spaniards from Tenochtitlán and putting up a bitter and prolonged defense when they returned to besiege the capital. But in the meantime the Aztecs were hit by a devastating smallpox epidemic that killed thousands and undermined their ability to resist. In the aftermath of conquest, the Spanish

unmercifully plundered Aztec society, providing the Catholic monarchs with wealth beyond their wildest imagining. Later, the discovery of rich silver mines and the exploitation of Mexican labor through the encomienda system turned Spain into the mightiest state in Europe.

The Destruction of the Indies

Like the Aztecs, the other Indian peoples of the Americas resisted Spanish conquest, but most proved a poor match for mounted warriors wielding steel swords and accompanied by vicious bloodhounds. The record of the conquest, however, includes many brave Indian leaders and thousands of martyrs. The Carib people (from whose name "Caribbean" is derived) successfully defended the outermost islands until the end of the sixteenth century, and in the arid lands of northern Mexico the nomadic tribes known collectively as the Chichimecs proved equally difficult to subdue.

Among the Europeans who protested the horrors of the conquest, the most famous may have been Bartolomé de las Casas, a Spanish Catholic priest who had participated in the plunder of Cuba in 1511 but who several years later suffered a crisis of conscience and began to denounce the conquest. The Christian mission in the New World was to convert the Indians, he argued, and "the means to effect this end are not to rob, to scandalize, to capture or destroy them, or to lay waste their lands." Long before the world recognized the concept of universal human rights, Las Casas was proclaiming that "the entire human race is one," a statement that has earned him a reputation as one of the towering moral figures in the early history of the Americas. Las Casas's powerful supporters at court made repeated but unsuccessful attempts to reform the treatment of Indians.

In his brilliant history of the conquest, *The Destruction of the Indies* (1552), Las Casas blamed the Spanish for millions of deaths—in effect, for genocide. Translated into several languages and widely circulated throughout Europe, Las Casas's book was used by other European powers to condemn Spain in an effort to cover up their own dismal colonial records. Later scholars, questioning the accuracy of Las Casas's estimates of huge population losses, condemned his work as contributing to a "Black Legend" of the Spanish conquest. But many of today's historians find Las Casas's figures more believable. Demographic studies suggest that the Tainos of Hispaniola numbered in the hundreds of thousands when Columbus arrived; fifty years later they were reduced to a few hundred, and soon they disappeared from the face of the earth. Over the sixteenth century, the approximately 25 million people thought to have inhabited the highlands of Mexico were reduced to only one million.

Las Casas was incorrect, however, in attributing most of these losses to warfare. To be sure, thousands of lives were lost in battle, but these deaths were but a small proportion of the overall population decline. Thousands more starved because their economies were destroyed or their food stores taken by conquering armies. Even more important, native birth rates fell drastically after the conquest. Indian women were so "worn out with work," one Spaniard wrote, that they avoided conception, induced abortion, and even "killed their children with their own hands so that they [should] not have to endure the same hardships."

But by far the greatest loss of life resulted from the introduction of Old World diseases. The people of the Americas, separated from Asia, Africa, and Europe by the rising oceans following the Ice Age, were isolated from the virulent epidemic diseases that developed along with civilization, diseases such as smallpox, measles, pneumonia, and malaria. Pre-Columbian America was blessed with a remarkably disease-free environment, but the Indian peoples also lacked the antibodies necessary to protect them from European bacteria and viruses. A shipload of colonists carried smallpox to Hispaniola in 1516, causing an epidemic in the Caribbean that by 1520 crossed into Mexico and eventually spread along the trading network through both North and South America. This was the epidemic that provided Cortés with the critical edge in overcoming the Aztecs. Such devastating outbreaks of disease, striking for the first time against a completely unprotected population, are known as "virgin soil epidemics." After the conquest, Mexicans sang of an earlier time:

> There was then no sickness.
> They had then no aching bones.
> They had then no high fever.
> They had then no smallpox.
> They had then no burning chest.
> They had then no abdominal pains.
> They had then no consumption.
> They had then no headache.
> At that time the course of humanity was orderly.
> The foreigners made it otherwise when they arrived here.

This drawing of victims of the smallpox epidemic that struck the Aztec capital of Tenochtitlán in 1520 is taken from the Florentine Codex, a postconquest history written and illustrated by Aztec scribes. "There came amongst us a great sickness, a general plague," reads the account, "killing vast numbers of people. It covered many all over with sores: on the face, on the head, on the chest, everywhere.... The sores were so terrible that the victims could not lie face down, nor on their backs, nor move from one side to the other. And when they tried to move even a little, they cried out in agony."

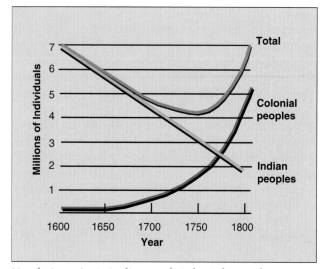

North America's Indian and Colonial Populations in the Seventeenth and Eighteenth Centuries *The primary factor in the decimation of native peoples was epidemic disease, brought to the New World from the Old. In the eighteenth century the colonial population overtook North America's Indian populations.*

Source: *Historical Statistics of the United States* (Washington, D.C.: Government Printing Office, 1976), 8, 1168; Russell Thornton, *American Indian Holocaust and Survival* (Norman: University of Oklahoma Press, 1987), 32.

Warfare, famine, lower birth rates, and epidemic disease knocked the population of Indian America into a downward spiral that did not swing upward until the twentieth century. By that time the native population had fallen by 90 percent. It was the greatest demographic disaster in world history. The outstanding difference between the European colonial experience in the Americas and elsewhere—Africa and Asia, for example—was this radical reduction in the native population.

It is possible that the New World sent one disease back across the Atlantic. On the basis of considerable evidence, archaeologists have concluded that syphilis was present in ancient America but not in the Old World before 1492. The first recorded epidemic of venereal syphilis in Europe took place in Spain in 1493, and many historians think it may have been carried home by the sailors on Columbus's ships. By 1495 the disease was spreading rapidly among Europe's armies, and by the sixteenth century it had found its way to Asia and Africa.

Intercontinental Exchange

The passage of diseases between the Old and New Worlds was just one part of the large-scale intercontinental exchange that marks the beginning of the modern era. The most obvious exchange was the vast influx into Europe of the precious metals plundered from the Aztec and Incan empires of the New World. "The best thing in the world is gold," wrote Columbus, and Cortés remarked, "We Spaniards suffer from a disease of the heart, the specific remedy for which is gold." Most of the booty was melted down, destroying forever thousands of priceless Indian artifacts. Even more important were the silver mines the Spanish discovered and operated in Mexico and Peru. Between 1500 and 1550 the amount of silver coin circulating in Europe tripled, then tripled again before 1600. The result was runaway inflation, which stimulated commerce and raised profits but lowered the standard of living for most people. During the sixteenth century, for example, rising prices depressed the value of European wages by more than 50 percent.

But of even greater long-term importance were the New World crops brought to Europe. Maize, or corn, from Mexico—the staff of life for most North Americans—became a staple human crop in Mediterranean countries, an important feed crop for livestock elsewhere in Europe, and the primary provision for the slave ships of Africa. Over the next few centuries, potatoes from Peru provided the margin between famine and subsistence for the peasant peoples of northern Europe and Ireland. And, of course, tomatoes transformed the cuisine of Italy. These "miracle crops" provided abundant food sources that went a long way toward ending the persistent problem of famine in Europe.

Although the Spanish failed to locate valuable spices such as black pepper or cloves in the New World, new tropical crops more than compensated. Tobacco, which was first prescribed as an antidote to disease when it appeared in Europe about 1550, soon became widely used as an intoxicant. American vanilla and chocolate both became highly valued commodities, and American cotton proved superior to Asian varieties for the production of cheap textiles. These native crops, together with crops brought from the Old World to the New, like sugar, rice, and coffee, supplied the basis for important new industries and markets that altered the course of world history.

Columbus introduced domesticated animals into Hispaniola and Cuba, and this breeding stock later supplied the conquistadors of Mexico. The movement of Spanish settlement into northern Mexico was greatly aided by an advancing wave of livestock, for not only did these animals supply the colonists with animal power and meat but they disturbed native fields and forests, disrupting Indian societies and preparing the way for conquest. Horses, used by Spanish stockmen to tend their cattle, also spread northward. Eventually they reached the Great

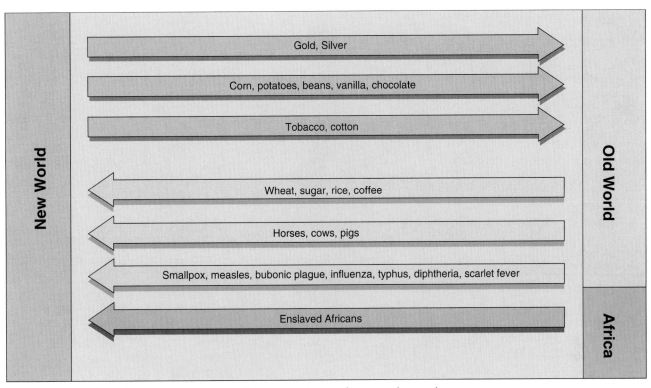

New World		Old World
	Gold, Silver →	
	Corn, potatoes, beans, vanilla, chocolate →	
	Tobacco, cotton →	
	← Wheat, sugar, rice, coffee	
	← Horses, cows, pigs	
	← Smallpox, measles, bubonic plague, influenza, typhus, diphtheria, scarlet fever	
	← Enslaved Africans	Africa

Intercontinental Exchange   *The exchange between continents of crops and animals, microbes and men, marks the beginning of the modern era of world history.*

Plains of North America, where they transformed the lives of the nomadic hunting Indians.

The First Europeans in North America

Juan Ponce de León, governor of Puerto Rico, was the first conquistador to attempt to extend the Spanish conquest to North America. In 1513 he landed on the southern Atlantic coast, which he named Florida in honor of the Easter season, in Spanish called *pascua florida*. Florida is thus the oldest European place-name in the continental United States. Warriors from some of the powerful Indian chiefdoms of the South beat back Ponce de León's attempts to take slaves and finally killed him in battle in 1521. Seven years later another Spanish attempt to colonize Florida, under the command of Pánfilo de Narváez, also ended in disaster. Most of Narváez's men were lost in a shipwreck, but a small group of them survived, living and wandering for several years among the Indian peoples of the Gulf coast and the Southwest until they were finally rescued in 1536 by Spanish slave hunters in northern Mexico. One of these castaways, Alvar Núñez Cabeza de Vaca, published an account of his adventures in which he told of a North American empire known as Cíbola, with golden cities "larger than the city of Mexico."

Cabeza de Vaca's report inspired two Spanish attempts to penetrate the mystery of North America.

Hernán de Soto, a veteran of the conquest of Peru, landed in Florida in 1539 with a Cuban army of more than 700 men and thousands of hogs and cattle. As he pushed hundreds of miles through the heavily populated South, he commandeered food and slaves from the Mississippian Indian towns in his path. De Soto failed, though, to locate another Aztec empire. In present-day Alabama, thousands of warriors of the powerful Alibamu chiefdom besieged his army, and a few months later the ancestors of the modern Chickasaws chewed the Spaniards apart. His army depleted by half, de Soto desperately drove his men westward, crossing the Mississippi and marching deep into present-day Arkansas before returning to the banks of the great river, where he died in 1542. Some 300 of de Soto's dispirited survivors eventually reached Mexico on rafts in 1543. They told of the great farming fields of the Mississippians but also emphasized the ferocity of the warriors. The native peoples of the South had successfully turned back Spanish invasion. If this were the end of the story, de Soto's expedition would be barely remembered, but his army also introduced epidemic diseases to the South that drastically undermined and depopulated the societies there. When Europeans finally returned to colonize the region in the seventeenth century, they found the descendants of the Mississippian chiefdoms living in much simpler tribal confederacies.

European Exploration, 1492–1591   By the mid-sixteenth century Europeans had
explored most of the Atlantic coast of North America and penetrated into the interior in the
disastrous expeditions of de Soto and Coronado.

The year following the beginning of the de Soto expedition, 1540, Spanish officials in Mexico launched a second attempt to find and conquer the cities of Cíbola, this one aimed at the North American Southwest. Francisco Vásquez de Coronado led 300 mounted men and infantry and 800 Indian porters north along well-marked Indian trading paths, passing through the settlements of Piman Indians near the present border of the United States and Mexico and finally reaching the Pueblo villages along the Rio Grande. The initial resistance of the Pueblo people was quickly quashed. But Coronado was deeply disappointed by these towns "of stone and mud, rudely fashioned." He led his army as far north as the Great Plains, where they observed great herds of "shaggy cows" (buffalo) and made contact with nomadic hunting peoples, but returned without gold. When Coronado and his men failed to find the "new Mexico" for which they had been looking, Spain lost all interest in the Southwest for the next fifty years.

The Spanish New World Empire

Despite these setbacks, by the late sixteenth century the Spanish had control of a powerful empire in the Americas. A century after Columbus, some 200,000 Europeans, most of them Spaniards, had settled in the Americas. Another 125,000 Africans had been forcibly resettled on the Spanish plantations of the Caribbean, as well as on the plantations of Brazil, which the Portuguese had colonized under the terms of the Treaty of Tordesillas, a 1494 agreement between Spain and Portugal setting a line of demarcation between their respective colonial domains. Most of the Spanish settlers resided in the more than 200 urban communities founded during the conquest, including cities such as Santo Domingo in Hispaniola; Havana, Cuba; Mexico City, built atop the ruins of Tenochtitlán; Quito, Peru (today in Ecuador), in the north of the conquered empire of the Incas; and Lima, Peru, near the empire's center. The few Spaniards who lived in the countryside supervised Indian or African workers in mining, ranching, or agriculture.

Because European women constituted only about 10 percent of the immigrants, from the beginning male colonists married or simply lived with African or Indian women. The result was the growth of large mixed-ancestry groups. The Spanish communities were characterized by what has been called a "frontier of inclusion," with a great deal of sexual mixing and marriage between male colonists and native women. Hundreds of thousands of Indians died, but Indian genes were passed on to generations of mestizo (European-Indian) and mulatto (European-African) peoples, who became the majority population in the mainland Spanish American empire.

Populated by Indians, Africans, Spanish colonists, and their mixed offspring, the New World colonies of Spain constituted one of the largest empires in the history of the world. In theory, the empire was a highly centralized and bureaucratic system, but in operation there was significant local autonomy. The Council of the Indies, composed of the king's principal advisers, formulated all the laws and regulations of the empire, but the Council was in Spain. In the colonies, halfway around the globe, passive resistance and sometimes outright defiance of central authority were commonplace.

FRENCH AND ENGLISH EXPLORATIONS AND ENCOUNTERS

With the Spanish empire at the height of its power in the sixteenth century, the merchants and monarchs of other important European seafaring states looked across the Atlantic for opportunities of their own. In the early sixteenth century France was first to sponsor intensive expeditions to the New World. At first the French attempted to plant settlements on the coasts of Brazil and Florida, but Spanish opposition ultimately persuaded them to concentrate on the northern regions. It was the second half of the

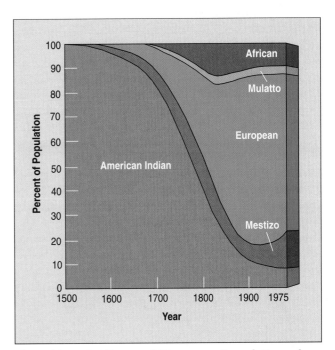

The African, Indian, and European Population of the Americas   *In the 500 years since the European invasion of the Americas, the population has included varying proportions of native, European, and African peoples, as well as large numbers of persons of mixed ancestry.*

Source: Colin McEvedy and Richard Jones, *Atlas of World Population History* (New York: Penguin, 1978), 280.

sixteenth century before England developed plans to colonize North America. With the Spanish in Florida and the French establishing close ties with coastal tribes as far south as present-day Maine, the English focused on the middle latitudes.

The Political Impact of the Reformation

The religious revolt against Catholicism known as the Reformation began in 1517 when the German priest Martin Luther publicized his differences with Rome. Luther declared that eternal salvation was a gift from God, not something earned by good works or service to the Roman Catholic Church. He also emphasized the importance of individual Bible study, underlining the impact of the revolution in printing and literacy and undercutting the authority of priests. As a result of his attacks on the Catholic hierarchy Luther was excommunicated in 1521. But his ideas reflected a growing climate of dissatisfaction throughout Europe with the power and prosperity of the Catholic Church. And when German princes who wished to strengthen their independence from Rome subscribed to Luther's views, the controversy became political, inaugurating a series of bloody religious wars that ravaged Europe for the next century.

Protestantism, as Luther's protest movement came to be called, aroused considerable enthusiasm in France. Catholic persecution of French Protestants in the 1520s, however, caused John Calvin, a prominent reformer even more radical than Luther, to flee to Switzerland. Calvin settled in Geneva, where he organized a model Christian community that by the 1530s was in control of the entire city-state. A former lawyer, Calvin was the most systematic of the early Protestant theologians. His doctrine of predestination proposed that God had chosen a small number of men and women for "election," or salvation, while condemning the vast majority to eternal damnation. Calvinists were encouraged to examine themselves closely for "signs of election," which were usually thought to be prominence and prosperity. The virtues of thrift, industry, sobriety, and personal responsibility, which Calvin argued were essential to the Christian life, likewise promoted material success. This conjunction of spiritual and secular values proved powerful in the growth of the spirit of enterprise that characterized early European capitalism.

Sixteenth-century England also became deeply involved in struggles to reform the Catholic Church. At first King Henry VIII of England (reigned 1509–47) supported the Church against the Protestants. But in England, too, there was great public resentment of the ostentatious display of the Church and the drain of tax money to Rome. When the pope refused to grant Henry an annulment of his marriage

to Catherine of Aragon, daughter of Isabella and Ferdinand of Spain, who had not produced a surviving male heir, the king exploited this popular mood. Taking up the cause of reform in 1534, he declared himself head of a separate Church of England. He later confiscated monastic property—the Catholic Church owned about a quarter of the country's land—and used the revenues to begin constructing a powerful English state system, including a standing army and navy. Working through Parliament, Henry carefully enlisted the support of the merchants and landed gentry for his program, parceling out a measure of royal prosperity in the form of titles, offices, lands, and commercial favors. By the mid-sixteenth century he had forged a solid alliance with the wealthy merchant class.

England and France moved in very different directions during the Reformation. Calvin's French followers—known as the Huguenots—were concentrated among merchants and the middle class, but they also included many of the nobility. In 1560 a group of Huguenot nobles tried to seize power, and their defeat initiated nearly forty years of religious struggle, during which France became known as the enemy of the new Protestant faith that was becoming so popular in England. One event that established France's fierce opposition to Protestantism was the St. Bartholomew's Day Massacre of August 24, 1572, in which some 6,000 Huguenots in Paris and thousands more throughout the country were slain at the direction of the French crown. Although in 1589 the Huguenot Henry IV became king of France, he found it impossible to govern until he converted to Catholicism. Henry's Edict of Nantes of 1598 guaranteed freedom of worship and the civil rights of Huguenots, but Henry's conversion, in effect, made Roman Catholicism the official religion of France.

The French Colony in Florida

Efforts by Huguenot leaders to establish a refuge for French Protestants in the New World led to the establishment of a French colony in Florida. In 1562 Jean Ribault and 150 Protestants from Normandy landed on Parris Island, near present-day Beaufort, South Carolina, and began constructing a fort and crude mud huts. Ribault soon returned to France for supplies, where he was caught up in the religious wars. The French colonists nearly starved, finally resorting to cannibalism before being rescued by a passing British ship. In 1564 another French expedition established the Huguenot colony of Fort Caroline on the St. Johns River in Florida, near the present-day city of Jacksonville. When Ribault arrived the next year, he reported that the people of the nearby Timucua villages were friendly and

This watercolor of Jacques le Moyne, painted in 1564, depicts the friendly relations between the Timucuas of coastal Florida and the colonists of the short-lived French colony of Fort Caroline. The Timucuas hoped that the French would help defend them against the Spanish, who plundered the coast in pursuit of Indian slaves.

hospitable, welcoming the French colonists into their homes and honoring them with food and drink. It seems possible that at Fort Caroline the Huguenots enjoyed the kinds of relations with the Indians that John White later hoped for at Roanoke.

The Spanish, however, saw Fort Caroline as a threat. Uninterested in settlement, the Spanish had established a foothold along the Atlantic coast of Florida simply to protect their fleets riding the offshore Gulf Stream home to Spain. Fort Caroline was manned not only by Frenchmen but by French Protestants—deadly enemies of the Catholic monarchs of Spain. "We are compelled to pass in front of their port," wrote one official of New Spain, "and with the greatest ease they can sally out with their armadas to seek us." In 1565 the Spanish crown sent Don Pedro Menéndez de Avilés, captain general of the Indies, to crush the Huguenots. He established the Spanish fort of St. Augustine on the coast, south of the French, then marched overland through the swamps to surprise them with an attack from the rear. "I put Jean Ribault and all the rest of them to the knife," Menéndez wrote triumphantly to the king, "judging it to be necessary to the service of the Lord Our God and of Your Majesty." More than 500 Frenchmen lay dead on the beaches of Florida; the French attempt to plant a colony along the South Atlantic coast had ended in disaster. Today, St. Augustine claims the distinction of being the oldest continuously occupied European city in North America.

Fish and Furs

For the French overseas empire, far more significant than these efforts at colonization was the entrance of French fishermen into the waters of the North Atlantic. It is possible that fishing ships from England, France, Spain, and Portugal had discovered the great fishing grounds off North America's northern coast long before Columbus's voyages. In the Grand Banks, the waters teemed with "so great multitudes of certain big fishes," in the words of one early seaman, "that they sometimes stayed my ships." By 1500, hundreds of ships and thousands of sailors were regularly fishing the coastal waters of the North Atlantic, many

In his sketch of this "Capitaine" of the Illinois nation (drawn about 1700), the French artist Charles Becard de Granville carefully noted the tattooing of the warrior's face and body, his distinctive costume and feather headdress, his spear and tobacco pipe.

making landfall to take on wood and fuel and to dry their catch. Fishermen were not particularly interested in conquest, and in their contacts with Indian people they established relationships based on the exchange of goods and ideas. Thus the pattern of colonial history in the early Northeast contrasted dramatically with that in the Spanish New World empire—and with later English colonization.

The first official voyages of exploration in the North Atlantic used the talents of experienced European sailors and fishermen. With a crew from Bristol, England, the Genoan navigator John Cabot reached Cape Breton Island or Newfoundland in 1497, and in 1524 the Tuscan captain Giovanni da Verrazano sailed with a crew from France, exploring the North American coast from Cape Fear (in today's North Carolina) to the Penobscot River (in Maine). Anxious to locate a passageway to the spice trade of Asia, the French king next commissioned the experienced captain

Jacques Cartier. In 1534 and 1535 Cartier reconnoitered the St. Lawrence River, which led deep into the continental interior, and established France's imperial claim to the lands of Canada.

The northern Indians found the Europeans odd—particularly their beards—but immediately appreciated the usefulness of the textiles, glass, copper, and ironware the Europeans possessed. Seeing Cartier's ship, the Micmacs waved him ashore. "The savages showed marvelous great pleasure in possessing and obtaining iron wares and other commodities," he noted in his report. For his part, Cartier was interested in the fur coats the Indians wore. Europeans, like Indians, used furs for winter clothing. But the growing population of the late Middle Ages had so depleted the wild game of Europe that the price of furs had risen beyond the reach of most people. The North American fur trade thus filled an important demand and produced high profits. Cartier attempted to found a French colony on the St. Lawrence in 1541, but the unremitting winter and the hostility of the Indians forced him to abandon the effort. For the rest of the sixteenth century relations between Europeans and Indians in the Northeast were dominated by commerce, not conquest.

By no means were Indians simply the victims of European traders. Indian traders had a sharp eye for quality, and because of the unbridled competition among the Europeans, they could demand good exchange rates. But the trade also had negative consequences for Indian people. Epidemic European diseases soon began to ravage their communities. Intense rivalry broke out between tribes over hunting territories, resulting in deadly warfare. By the 1580s, disease and violence had turned the St. Lawrence Valley into a virtual no-man's land. Moreover, as European manufactured goods, such as metal knives, kettles, and firearms, became essential to their way of life, the Indians became dependent upon European suppliers. Ultimately, the fur trade was stacked in favor of Europeans.

By the end of the sixteenth century over a thousand ships per year were trading for furs along the northern coast. The trade between Indians and Europeans of many nations grew increasingly important as the century progressed. The village of Tadoussac on the St. Lawrence, where a wide bay offered Europeans safe anchorage, became the customary place for several weeks of trading each summer, a forerunner of the western fur-trade rendezvous of the nineteenth century. Among European traders, the French were probably the most numerous, and later, in the early seventeenth century, they had to move to consolidate their hold by planting colonies along the St. Lawrence.

Social Change in Sixteenth-Century England

Henry VIII of England died in 1547. He was succeeded by his young and sickly son Edward VI, who six years later followed his father to the grave, then by his Catholic daughter Mary, who attempted to reverse her father's Reformation from the top. She added her own chapter to the century's many religious wars, martyring hundreds of English Protestants and gaining the title of "Bloody Mary." But upon Mary's death in 1558, her Protestant half-sister Elizabeth I (reigned 1558–1603) ascended to the throne. Although she outlawed Catholicism, Elizabeth sought to end the religious turmoil by tolerating a variety of views within the English church.

Criticized by radical Protestants for not going far enough and condemned by Catholics for her "pretended title to the kingdom," Elizabeth nevertheless gained popularity among the English people with her moderate approach. The Spanish monarchy, the head of the most powerful empire in the world, declared itself the defender of the Catholic faith and vowed to overthrow her. England and Spain now became the two principal rivals in the Catholic-Protestant confrontation.

In the 1570s several of Elizabeth's closest advisers began to argue that the time had come for England to enter the competition for American colonies. Their analysis linked colonization to social change at home.

Elizabeth I, Armada portrait, c. 1588 (oil on panel) by English School. Private collection/Bridgeman Art Library, London/New York

The Armada Portrait of Elizabeth I, *painted by an unknown artist in 1648. The queen places her hand on the globe, symbolizing the rising seapower of England. Through the open windows we see the battle against the Spanish Armada in 1588 and the destruction of the Spanish ships in a providential storm, interpreted by the queen as an act of divine intervention.*

Algonquian Indian village of Pomeiooc (North Carolina): watercolor, c. 1585, by John White; The Granger Collection.

In July 1585, John White sketched the Algonquian village of Pomeiooc, a palisaded enclosure with an easily guarded entrance. The eighteen longhouses would have made this a rather large community. Note the house with the pyramid-shaped roof. It is thought to have been a ceremonial or religious center.

As New World inflation caused the prices of European goods to rise steeply, English landlords, their rents fixed by custom, sought ways to increase their incomes. Seeking profits in the woolen trade, for example, many fenced off lands traditionally used as common pasture for villagers in order to provide grazing lands for their sheep. The result of this practice, called "enclosure" was the dislocation of farmers; between 1500 and 1650 a third of all the common lands in England were affected. Deprived of their traditional livelihoods, thousands of families left the countryside for the cities, and the roads were crowded with the homeless. In a state paper written for the queen, Richard Hakluyt argued that New World colonies could be populated by these "multitudes of loiterers and idle vagabonds." Such colonies, he said, could provide bases from which to raid the Spanish in the Caribbean, Indian markets for English goods, and plantations for growing tropical products, freeing England from a reliance on the long-distance trade with Asia. He urged Elizabeth to begin the planting of colonies "upon the mouths of the great navigable rivers" from Florida to the St. Lawrence.

England Turns toward Colonization

Elizabeth's first overseas priority, however, was Ireland, not America. Fearing Spanish subversion on that neighboring Catholic island, she urged enterprising supporters such as Walter Raleigh and his half-brother Humphrey Gilbert to subdue the Irish and settle English families on their land. During the 1560s both those men, and many other colonists as well, did precisely that, invading the island across the Irish Sea and viciously attacking the Irish defenders of their homeland, forcing them to retreat beyond the line of English settlement along the coast.

The English believed the Irish to be "savages," and indeed the Irish fought so ferociously in resisting the English invasions that an image of the "wild Irish" became fixed in the minds of English colonists. Gilbert retaliated with even greater brutality, ordering his soldiers to behead those they captured and line the walk to his quarters with their heads, "so that none should come into his tent for any cause but commonly he must pass through a lane of heads." Their own barbarism did not dissuade the English from considering the Irish an inferior race, and the notion that civilized people could not mix with such "savages" was an assumption that English colonists would carry with them to the Americas.

Like the invasion of Ireland, England's first ventures in the New World were made against the backdrop of its conflict with Spain. The goal of these ventures was to punish the Spanish, particularly to break the Spanish trading monopoly with tropical America. In 1562 John Hawkins inaugurated English participation in the slave trade, violating Spain's prohibition on foreign commerce with its colonies by transporting African slaves to the Caribbean and bringing back valuable tropical goods. In 1567 the Spanish attacked Hawkins, giving English privateers such as Francis Drake an excuse for launching devastating and lucrative raids against Spanish New World ports and fleets. The voyages of these English "Sea Dogs" greatly enriched their investors, including the queen herself. From a voyage that cost several thousand English pounds, Drake was said to have returned with booty valued in the millions. Thus, like the Spanish, the English began their American adventures by slaving and plundering.

It was not until the 1570s that Elizabeth finally authorized and invested in several private attempts at exploration and colonization in North America. In the late 1570s Martin Frobisher conducted three voyages of exploration in the North Atlantic, bringing back an Eskimo man, woman, and child and samples of worthless ores. Fresh from the Irish wars, Raleigh and Gilbert teamed up to plan their first American colonizing venture in 1578, but it failed to get off the ground. In 1583 Gilbert sailed with a flotilla of ships from Plymouth, England, and landed at St. John's Bay, Newfoundland, where he claimed the territory for his queen even though he found fishermen from several other nations there. But Gilbert's ship was lost on the return voyage.

Raleigh followed up Gilbert's efforts with plans to establish a colony to the south, in the more hospitable climate of the mid-Atlantic coast, but, as described in the opening of this chapter, the Roanoke enterprise of 1584–87 eventually failed as well. Nevertheless, it left as a considerable legacy the scientific work of Thomas Harriot and John White, who mapped the area, surveyed its commercial potential, and studied the Indian residents. Harriot's *Briefe and True*

Report of the Newfound Land of Virginia (1588) was addressed mainly to the problem of identifying the "merchantable commodities" that would support settlement, for without products a colonial system was impossible. A later edition of this book included engravings based on White's watercolors of the people and landscape of Virginia. Together Harriot and White provided the most accurate and sensitive description we have of North American Indians at the moment of their contact with Europeans.

King Philip II of Spain was outraged at these English incursions into territory that, in the Treaty of Tordesillas of 1493, the pope had reserved for Spain. Philip had previously authorized the destruction of the French colony in Florida, and England's expanding colonial interests turned the competition between Catholic Spain and Protestant England into war. In 1588 Philip sent the Spanish Armada, a fleet of 130 ships carrying 30,000 men, to invade the British Isles. Countered by men such as Drake and Hawkins, who commanded smaller and more maneuverable ships, and frustrated by an ill-timed storm that the English chose to interpret as an act of divine intervention, the Armada foundered. Half the ships were destroyed, their crews killed or captured. The war continued until 1604, but the Spanish monopoly of the New World was broken in the English Channel.

CONCLUSION

The European colonization of the Americas opened with Columbus's voyage in 1492. For Indian people, assaulted by invasion and disease, the consequences were disastrous. But first in the Caribbean, then most spectacularly in Mexico, the Spanish succeeded in constructing the world's most powerful empire on the backs of Indian and imported African laborers. The New World colonies of Spain were characterized by a great deal of mixing between the mostly male colonists and native women; in this sense they were communities of "inclusion."

Inspired by the Spanish success, in the second half of the sixteenth century both the French and the English attempted to colonize the coast of North America but by the century's end had not succeeded in establishing any lasting communities. Instead, a very different kind of colonial encounter was taking place in Northeast North America, one based on commerce rather than conquest. In the next century the French would turn this development to their advantage in Canada. Along the mid-Atlantic coast in Virginia, however, the English would put their Irish experience to use, pioneering an altogether new kind of American colonialism.

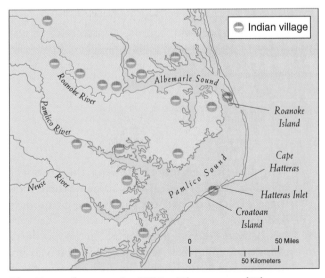

The Roanoke area in 1585   *The surveys of Thomas Harriot and John White revealed that the Roanoke area was densely settled with Indian villages. The information on this map is taken from their report.*

CHRONOLOGY

1000	Norse settlement at L'Anse aux Meadows
1347–53	Black Death in Europe
1381	English Peasants' Revolt
1488	Bartolomeu Días sails around the African continent
1492	Christopher Columbus first arrives in the Caribbean
1494	Treaty of Tordesillas
1497	John Cabot explores Newfoundland
1500	High point of the Renaissance
1508	Spanish invade Puerto Rico
1513	Juan Ponce de León lands in Florida
1514	Bartolomé de las Casas begins preaching against the conquest
1516	Smallpox introduced to the New World
1517	Martin Luther breaks with the Roman Catholic Church
1519	Hernán Cortés lands in Mexico
1534	Jacques Cartier first explores the St. Lawrence River
1539–40	Hernán de Soto and Francisco Vásquez de Coronado expeditions
1550	Tobacco introduced to Europe
1552	Bartolomé de Las Casas's *Destruction of the Indies* published
1558	Elizabeth I of England begins her reign
1562	Huguenot colony planted along the mid-Atlantic coast
1565	St. Augustine founded
1572	St. Bartholomew's Day Massacre in France
1583	Humphrey Gilbert attempts to plant a colony in Newfoundland
1584–87	Walter Raleigh's colony on Roanoke Island
1588	English defeat the Spanish Armada
1590	John White returns to find Roanoke colony abandoned

REVIEW QUESTIONS

1. Discuss the roles played by the rising merchant class, the new monarchies, Renaissance humanism, and the Reformation in the development of European colonialism.
2. Define a "frontier of inclusion." In what ways does this description apply to the Spanish empire in the Americas?
3. Make a list of the major exchanges that took place between the Old World and the New World in the centuries following the European invasion of America. Discuss some of the effects these exchanges had on the course of modern history.
4. In what ways did colonial contact in the Northeast differ from contacts in the Caribbean and Mexico?
5. In what ways might the English experience in Ireland have shaped expectations about American colonization?

RECOMMENDED READING

Cyclone Covey, translator and editor, *Cabeza de Vaca's Adventures in the Unknown Interior of America* (1983). The captivity narrative that lured the Spanish into North America. An eye-opening story of the peoples and places of the preconquest Southwest.

Alfred W. Crosby Jr., *The Columbian Exchange: Biological and Cultural Consequences of 1492* (1972). Pathbreaking account of the intersection of the biospheres of the Old and New Worlds.

David Ewing Duncan, *Hernando de Soto: A Savage Quest in the Americas* (1995). A well-written biography of the conquistador and the story of his brutal expedition through the Indian homelands of the Southeast.

Charles Gibson, *Spain in America* (1966). The best introductory history of Spain's American empire.

Lewis Hanke, *The Spanish Struggle for Justice in the Conquest of America* (1949; reprint, 1965). The classic account of Las Casas's attempts to rectify the wrongs committed by the Spanish against the Indians.

Miguel Leon-Portilla, *The Broken Spears: The Aztec Account of the Conquest of Mexico* (1962; expanded ed., 1992). The history of the Spanish conquest as told by the Aztecs, drawn from manuscripts dating as early as 1528, only seven years after the fall of Tenochtitlán.

Samuel Eliot Morison, *The European Discovery of America: The Northern Voyages*, A.D. 500–1600 (1971) and *The Southern Voyages*, A.D. 1492–1616 (1974). The most detailed treatment of all the important European explorations of the Americas.

Anthony Pagden, *Lords of All the Worlds: Ideologies of Empire in Spain, Britain and France c. 1500–c. 1850* (1995). An important comparative history of the European justifications for colonial conquest.

David Beers Quinn, *Set Fair for Roanoke: Voyages and Colonies, 1584–1606* (1985). The story of Roanoke—the Indian village, the English settlement, and the Lost Colony.

Kirkpatrick Sale, *The Conquest of Paradise: Christopher Columbus and the Columbian Legacy* (1990). A harsh view of Columbus, but important information on the world of the Caribbean and the disastrous effects of the encounter with Europeans.

Carl Ortwin Sauer, *Sixteenth Century North America: The Land and the People as Seen by the Europeans* (1971). An excellent source for the explorations of the continent, providing abundant descriptions of the Indians.

David E. Stannard, *American Holocaust: Columbus and the Conquest of the New World* (1992). A provocative argument that the Spanish inaugurated a genocidal policy against the Indians that has continued into the twentieth century.

Hugh Thomas, *Conquest: Montezuma, Cortés, and the Fall of Old Mexico* (1993). A fascinating account, written by a master of historical style, that incorporates the Aztec view as well as the words of the conquerors.

ADDITIONAL BIBLIOGRAPHY

The Expansion of Europe

James M. Blaut, *1492: The Debate on Colonialism, Eurocentrism, and History* (1992)

Fernand Braudel, *The Mediterranean and the Mediterranean World in the Age of Philip II* (1972)

———, *Civilization and Capitalism, 15th–18th Centuries*, 3 vols. (1981)

Carol Cipolla, *Before the Industrial Revolution: European Society and Economy, 1100–1700* (1976)

Patrick Collinson, *The Religion of Protestants: The Church in English Society, 1559–1625* (1982)

Ralph Davis, *The Rise of Atlantic Economies* (1973)

Andre Gunder Frank, *World Accumulation, 1492–1789* (1978)

Douglas North, *The Rise of the Western World: A New Economic History* (1973)

José Casas Pardo, ed., *Economic Effects of the European Expansion, 1492–1824* (1992)

J. H. Parry, *The Age of Reconnaissance* (1963)

———, *Europe and a Wider World: The Establishment of the European Hegemony: Trade and Expansion in the Age of the Renaissance* (1966)

Geoffrey Vaughn Scannell, *The First Imperial Age: European Overseas Expansion c. 1400–1715* (1989)

The Spanish in the Americas

Warner Bowden, *American Indians and Christian Missions: Studies in Cultural Conflict* (1982)

Fredi Chiapelli, ed., *First Images of America: The Impact of the New World on the Old* (1976)

Nobel David Cook and W. George Lovell, *Secret Judgments of God: Old World Disease in Colonial Spanish America* (1991)

Henry F. Dobyns, *Their Number Become Thinned: Native American Population Dynamics in Eastern North America* (1983)

J. H. Elliott, *The Old World and the New, 1492–1650* (1970)

Anthony Grafton, *New Worlds, Ancient Texts: The Power of Tradition and the Shock of Discovery* (1992)

Hugh Honour, *New Golden Land: European Images of America from the Discoveries to the Present Time* (1975)

Charles Hudson, *Knights of Spain, Warriors of the Sun: Hernando De Soto and the South's Ancient Chiefdoms* (1997)

Charles Hudson and Carmen Chaves Tesser, eds., *The Forgotten Centuries: Indians and Europeans in the American South, 1521–1704* (1994)

René Jara and Nicholas Spadaccini, eds., *Amerindian Images and the Legacy of Columbus* (1992)

Elizabeth A. H. John, *Storms Brewed in Other Men's Worlds: The Confrontation of Indians, Spanish, and French in the Southwest, 1540–1795* (1975)

James Lang, *Conquest and Commerce: Spain and England in the Americas* (1975)

James Lockhart and Stuart B. Schwartz, *Early Latin America: A History of Colonial Spanish America and Brazil* (1983)

Peter Mason, *Deconstructing America: Representations of the Other* (1990)

Jerald T. Milanich and Charles Hudson, *Hernando de Soto and the Indians of Florida* (1993)

James Howlett O'Donnell III, *Southeastern Frontiers: Europeans, Africans, and American Indians, 1513–1840: A Critical Bibliography* (1982)

Edmundo O'Gorman, *The Invention of America: An Inquiry into the Historical Nature of the New World and the Meaning of its History* (1961)

David M. Traboulay, *Columbus and Las Casas: The Conquest and Christianization of America, 1492–1566* (1994)

Ronald Wright, *Stolen Continents: The Americas through Indian Eyes since 1492* (1992)

Northern Explorations and Encounters

Alfred Goldsworthy Bailey, *The Conflict of European and Eastern Algonkian Cultures, 1504–1700* (1969)

Carl Bridenbaugh, *Vexed and Troubled Englishmen, 1590–1642* (1968)

Peter Clark and Paul Slack, *English Towns in Transition, 1500–1700* (1976)

Susan Danforth, *Encountering the New World, 1493–1800* (1991)

G. R. Elton, *England under the Tudors* (1974)

C. H. George and Katherine George, *The Protestant Mind of the English Reformation* (1961)

John Guy, *Tudor England* (1988)

Karen Ordahl Kupperman, *Roanoke: The Abandoned Colony* (1984)

Peter Laslett, *The World We Have Lost* (1965)

E. B. Leacock and N. O. Laurie, eds., *North American Indians in Historical Perspective* (1971)

Anthony McFarlane, *The British in the Americas, 1480-1815* (1994).

David B. Quinn, *North America from Earliest Discovery to First Settlements* (1977)

———, *The Roanoke Voyages, 1584–1590*, 2 vols. (1955)

Bernard W. Sheehan, *Savagism and Civility: Indians and Englishmen in Colonial Virginia* (1980)

Russell Thornton, *American Indian Holocaust and Survival* (1987)

Margo Todd, ed., *Reformation to Revolution: Politics and Religion in Early Modern England* (1995)

Marcel Trudel, *The Beginnings of New France, 1524–1663* (1973)

Keith Wrightson, *English Society, 1580–1680* (1982)

Biography

Joe Armstrong, *Champlain* (1987)

Carole Levin, *The Heart and Stomach of a King: Elizabeth I and the Politics of Sex and Power* (1994)

Richard Lee Marks, *Cortés: The Great Adventurer and the Fate of Aztec Mexico* (1993)

Samuel E. Morison, *Admiral of the Ocean Sea: A Life of Christopher Columbus* (1942)

A. L. Rowse, *Eminent Elizabethans* (1983)

John Ure, *Prince Henry the Navigator* (1977)

Henry Raup Wagner, *The Life and Writings of Bartolomé de las Casas* (1967)

CHAPTER THREE

PLANTING COLONIES IN NORTH AMERICA

1588–1701

Navajo painted "Mural" depicting Spanish horsemen, Canyon del Muerto at Canyon de Chelly National Monument, Arizona. Jerry Jacka Photography.

AMERICAN COMMUNITIES
Communities Struggle with Diversity in Seventeenth-Century Santa Fé

O n a hot August day in 1680, frantic messengers rode into the small mission outpost of El Paso with the news that the Pueblo Indians to the north had risen in revolt; corpses of more than 400 colonists lay bleeding in the dust. Two thousand Spanish survivors huddled inside the Palace of Governors in Santa Fé, surrounded by 3,000 angry Indian warriors. The Pueblo leaders had sent two crosses inside the palace—white for surrender, red for death. Which would the Spaniards choose?

Spanish colonists had been in New Mexico for nearly a century. Franciscan priests came first, followed by a military expedition from Mexico in search of precious metals. In 1609, in the picturesque foothills of the Sangre de Cristo Mountains, colonial authorities founded La Villa Real de la Santa Fé de San Francisco— "the royal town of the holy faith of St. Francis"—soon known simply as Santa Fé. Colonization efforts included converting the Pueblo Indians to Christianity, making them subjects of the king of Spain, and forcing them to work for the colonial elite who lived at the edges of the town.

In the face of overwhelming Spanish power—the military might that had retaken Spain from the Moors of North Africa and conquered the great Aztec and Incan civilizations farther south— the Pueblos adopted a flexible attitude. Although 20,000 converted to Christianity, most thought of the new religion as simply an appendage to their already complex culture. The Christian God was but one more of their numerous deities. They incorporated Church holidays into their own religious calendar and celebrated them with native dances and rituals.

Most ethnographers agree that the Pueblos were a sexually spirited people. Many of their public dances included erotic displays, and some ended in public lovemaking. Symbolizing the powerful force that brought the separate worlds of men and women together, sexual intercourse was emblematic of community. Indeed, the celibacy of the Franciscan priests not only astounded the Pueblos but horrified them; they saw the priests as only half-persons.

The Pueblos also found the Franciscan practice of subjecting themselves to prolonged fasts and tortures like self-flagellation completely inexplicable. "You Christians are crazy," one Pueblo chief told a priest. "You go through the streets in groups, flagellating yourselves, and it is not well that the people of this pueblo should be encouraged to commit such madness." The missionaries, for their part, were outraged by what they considered Pueblo sacrileges, and they invaded underground kivas, destroying sacred Indian artifacts, publicly humiliating holy men, and compelling whole villages to perform penance by working in irrigation ditches and fields. When the Spanish governor of New Mexico executed three Pueblo priests and publicly whipped dozens more for secretly practicing their religion, one of these priests, Popé of San Juan Pueblo, vowed to overthrow the Spanish regime and began organizing a conspiracy among more than twenty Indian towns.

Popé's job was not difficult, for there were plenty of local grievances. For example, the Hopis of northern Arizona still tell of a missionary who capped his ever-escalating demands on them with the order that all the young women of the village be brought to live with him. When the revolt of 1680 began throughout the entire colony, the Hopis surrounded the missionary's house. "I have come to kill you," the chief announced. "You can't kill me," the priest cried from behind his locked door. "I will come to life and wipe out your whole tribe." "My gods have more power than you have," the chief shouted back. He and his men broke down the door, hung the missionary from the beams, and lit a fire beneath his feet.

From within Santa Fé's Palace of Governors the Spanish sent back the red cross, signaling that they would fight to the death. But after a siege lasting five days the Pueblos agreed to allow most of them to flee south to El Paso, "the poor women and children on foot and unshod," in the words of one Spaniard's account, and "of such a hue that they looked like dead people." The Indians then ransacked the missions and churches, desecrating the holy furnishings with human excrement and leaving the mutilated bodies of priests lying upon their altars. They transformed the governor's chapel into a traditional kiva, his palace into a communal dwelling. On the elegant inlaid stone floors where the governor had held court, Pueblo women now ground their corn.

Santa Fé became the capital of a Pueblo confederacy led by Popé. Popé first forced Christian Indians to the river to scrub away the taint of baptism and then ordered the general population to destroy everything Spanish. But the latter command met with resistance. The colonists had introduced horses and sheep, fruit trees and wheat, new tools and new crafts—all things that the Indians found useful. In addition, the Pueblos sorely missed the support of the Spanish in their struggle against the Navajos and Apaches, the Pueblos' traditional enemies. Equipped with stolen horses and weapons, these nomadic tribespeople had become considerably more dangerous, and their raids on the unprotected Pueblo villages became much more destructive after the colonists fled. With chaos mounting, Popé was deposed in 1690, and many Indians found themselves thinking the unthinkable: If only the Spanish would come back!

Come back they did, beginning in 1692, and after six years of fighting succeeded in reestablishing Spanish authority. But both sides had learned a lesson, and over the next generation the colonists and the Indians reached an implicit understanding. Pueblos dutifully observed Catholicism in the missionary chapels, while missionaries tolerated the practice of traditional religion in the Indians' underground kivas. Royal officials guaranteed the inviolability of Indian lands, and Pueblos pledged loyalty to the Spanish monarch. Pueblos turned out for service on colonial lands, and colonists abandoned the system of forced labor. Together the Spanish and the Pueblos held off the nomadic tribes for the next 150 years. Colonist and Indian communities remained autonomous, but they were learning to live with one another.

Santa Fé

New France in the Seventeenth Century *By the late seventeenth century, French settlements were spread from the town of Port Royal in Acadia to the post and mission at Sault Ste. Marie, on the Great Lakes. But the heart of New France comprised the communities stretching along the St. Lawrence River between the towns of Quebec and Montreal.*

ENGLAND IN THE CHESAPEAKE

England first attempted to plant colonies in North America during the 1580s, in Newfoundland and on Roanoke Island in present-day North Carolina. Both attempts were failures. England's war with Spain, which lasted from 1588 to 1604, suspended colonization efforts, but at its close the English once again turned to the Americas.

Jamestown and the Powhatan Confederacy

Early in his reign, King James I (reigned 1603–25) issued royal charters for the colonization of the mid-Atlantic region, by then known as Virginia, to English joint-stock companies, which raised capital by selling shares. In 1607 a group of London investors known as the Virginia Company sent ships to the temperate latitudes of Chesapeake Bay, where a hundred men built a fort they named Jamestown, in honor of the king. It was destined to become the first permanent English settlement in North America.

The Chesapeake region was already home to an estimated 20,000 Algonquian people. The English colonists were immediately confronted by Powhatan, the powerful *werowance*, or leader, of a confederacy of Algonquian tribes. Powhatan had mixed feelings about the English. The Spanish had already attempted to plant a base nearby, bringing conflict and disease to his region. But he looked forward to valuable trade with the English as well as to their support for his struggle to extend his confederacy to outlying tribes. As was the case in Mexico and along the St. Lawrence, Indians tried to use Europeans to pursue ends of their own.

The English saw themselves as latter-day conquistadors. Abhorring the idea of physical labor, they survived the first year only with Powhatan's material assistance. Like the first Roanoke colonists (see Chapter 2), they were unable to support themselves. "In our extremity the Indians brought us corn," wrote John Smith, the colony's military leader, "when we rather expected they would destroy us." Jamestown grew so dependent on Algonquian stores that in 1609 Smith and his men began to plunder food from surrounding tribes. In retaliation, Powhatan decided to starve the colonists out. He now realized, as he said to Smith, that the

to the 1680s the French established outposts at strategic points on the lakes. By the 1670s French fur traders and missionaries were exploring the reaches of the upper Mississippi River. In 1681–82, fur trade commandant Robert Sieur de La Salle navigated the mighty river to its mouth on the Gulf of Mexico and claimed its entire watershed—a great inland empire—for France.

Thus although both the French and Spanish established societies of inclusion, in which settlers intermarried with native peoples, the early French colonial system differed from that of the Spanish. Whereas the French interest in the Indians was principally commercial, the Spanish organized Indian communities as a labor force for mines, plantations, and ranches. There were also important differences between Spanish and French missionary efforts. The Jesuits, arriving in 1625 and often accompanying French traders—and sometimes leading the way—introduced Christianity as a supplement to the Indian way of life. In contrast, the Franciscans of New Mexico insisted that Indian people accept European cultural norms.

The populations of Acadia and Canada grew throughout the seventeenth century but by 1700 still totaled only 15,000. Quebec City, the colony's administrative capital, was small by Spanish colonial standards, and Montreal, founded in 1642 as a missionary and trading center, remained little more than a frontier outpost. The real strength of New France lay in its extensive fur-trading system.

English had come "not for trade, but to invade my people and possess my country"—the approach not of the French but of the Spanish. During the winter of 1609–10 scores of colonists starved and a number resorted to cannibalism. By spring only 60 remained of the more than 900 colonists sent to Virginia.

Determined to prevail, the Virginia Company sent out a large additional force of men, women, and livestock, committing themselves to a protracted war against the Indians. By 1613 the colonists firmly controlled the territory between the James and York rivers. Worn down by warfare and disease, Powhatan accepted a treaty of peace in 1614. "I am old and ere long must die," he declared; "I know it is better to eat good meat, lie well, and sleep with my women and children, laugh and be merry than to be forced to flee and be hunted." He sent his daughter Pocahontas, fluent in English, on a diplomatic mission to Jamestown. She converted to Christianity and married John Rolfe, a leading settler. But Pocahontas died of disease while visiting England in 1617. Crushed by the news of her death, her father abdicated in favor of his brother Opechancanough and died the following year.

Tobacco, Expansion, and Warfare

Tobacco provided the Virginia colonists with the "merchantable commodity" for which Thomas Harriot, the scientist who accompanied the Roanoke expedition, had searched (see Chapter 2). In 1613 John Rolfe developed a hybrid of hearty North American and mild West Indian varieties, and soon the first commercial shipments of cured Virginia leaf reached England. The revenue from tobacco sales produced the first returns on the investment of the Virginia Company. Its cultivation quickly

The illustration on the left is a detail of John Smith's map of Virginia. It includes the names of many Indian villages, suggesting how densely settled was the Indian population of the coast of Chesapeake Bay. For the inset of Powhatan and his court in the upper left, the engraver borrowed images from John White's drawings of the Indians of the Roanoke area. The illustration on the right, from John Smith's memoirs (1624), was engraved by the artist Robert Vaughn. Seizing Chief Opechancanough, Powhatan's brother, by the scalplock, Smith attempts to obtain needed supplies from the Indians. Opechancanough later succeeded Powhatan and ruled the Chesapeake Algonquian Confederacy for a quarter century.

An eighteenth-century label for Virginia tobacco, featuring an African slave and a native American smoker. Tobacco was introduced to English consumers by Francis Drake in the 1580s, and despite King James's description of the habit as "loathsome to the eye, hateful to the nose, harmful to the brain, dangerous to the lungs," tobacco smoking developed into a craze that created strong consumer demand in the 1610s.

exhausted the soil, however, creating pressures for further expansion into Indian territory.

Because tobacco also required a great deal of hand labor, the company instituted what were called headright grants, or awards of large plantations on the condition that grant recipients transport workers from England at their own cost. Between 1619 and 1624 more than 4,500 English settlers arrived, many with families. But high rates of mortality—probably the result of epidemics of typhoid fever—kept the total population at just over a thousand. In populating their colony with families, the English had chosen a policy quite different from the Spanish practice of sending only male settlers. Moreover, the English emphasis on agriculture and lack of interest in trade with Indian peoples contrasted significantly with the French approach. With no need to incorporate Indians into the population, the English moved in the direction of exclusion, pushing Indian peoples to the periphery rather than incorporating them within colonial communities.

As the English pressed for additional lands, Opechancanough prepared the Chesapeake Algonquians for a final assault on the invaders. He encouraged a cultural revival under the guidance of the shaman Nemattanew, who instructed his followers to reject the English and their ways but to learn the use of firearms. The uprising, which began on Good Friday, March 22, 1622, completely surprised the English. Nearly 350 people, a quarter of the settlers, were killed before Jamestown could mobilize its forces. Yet the colony managed to hang on, and the attack stretched into a ten-year war of attrition. Horrors were committed by both sides, but English officials saw advantages in open warfare. As one wrote, "We may now by right of war, and law of nations, invade the country and destroy them who sought to destroy us, whereby we shall enjoy their cultivated places." Indian territory might now be obtained under the conventions of a "just war."

Long before it ended in 1632, the war bankrupted the Virginia Company. In 1624 the king converted Virginia into a royal colony, with civil authorities appointed by the crown, although the colony's House of Burgesses, created in 1619, continued to include representatives of Virginia's boroughs. Then, despite disease, famine, and warfare, the economy took off, and the English colonial population doubled every five years from 1625 to 1640, by which time it numbered approximately 10,000. Opechancanough emerged from the turmoil as undisputed leader of the still independent Chesapeake Algonquian Confederacy, but other smaller tribes, decimated by casualties and disease, were forced to accept English domination. By 1640 the native population of the Chesapeake had declined to about 10,000.

Numerical strength soon shifted in favor of the English. In 1644, Opechancanough organized a final desperate revolt, in which more than 500 colonists were killed. But the Virginians crushed the Algonquians in 1645, capturing and executing Opechancanough. The colonists then signed a formal treaty with the Indians, who were granted small reserved territories. By the 1670s, when the English population of Virginia numbered more than 40,000, only a dozen tribes and about 2,000 Algonquians remained from the 20,000 who inhabited the area when Jamestown was founded. Today, some 1,500 people who trace their roots to Powhatan's confederacy live in Chesapeake Indian communities near Richmond, Virginia, and Washington, D.C.

Maryland

In 1632, King Charles I (reigned 1625–49) granted 10 million acres at the northern end of Chesapeake Bay to the Calvert family, the Lords Baltimore, important supporters of the monarchy. The Calverts named their colony Maryland, in honor of the king's wife. The first party of colonists founded the settlement of St. Marys

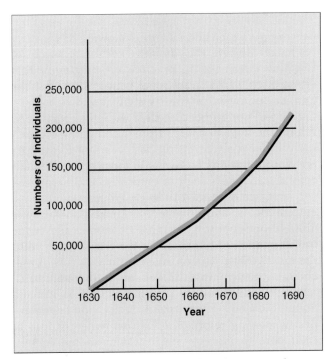

Population Growth of the British Colonies in the Seventeenth Century *The British colonial population grew steadily through the century, then increased sharply in the closing decade as a result of the new settlements of the Restoration colonies.*

near the mouth of the Potomac River in 1634. Two features distinguished Maryland from Virginia. First, it was a "proprietary" colony. The Calverts were sole owners of all the land, which they planned to carve into feudal manors that would provide them with annual rents, and they appointed all the civil officers. Second, because the proprietors were Catholics, they encouraged settlement by their coreligionists, a persecuted minority in seventeenth-century England. In fact, Maryland became the only English colony in North America with a substantial Catholic minority. Wealthy Catholic landlords were appointed to the governing council, and they came to dominate Maryland's House of Delegates, founded in 1635.

Despite these differences, Maryland quickly assumed the character of neighboring Virginia. Its tobacco plantation economy created pressures for labor and expansion that could not be met under the Calverts' original feudal plans. In 1640 the colony adopted the system of headright grants developed in Virginia, and settlements of independent planters quickly spread out on both sides of the bay. By the 1670s Maryland's English population numbered more than 15,000.

Indentured Servants

At least three-quarters of the English migrants to the Chesapeake came as indentured servants. In exchange for the cost of their transportation to the New World, men and women contracted to labor for a master for a fixed term. Most indentured servants were young, unskilled males, who served for two to seven years, but some were skilled craftsmen, and a few were women and children (the latter were expected to serve until they reached the age of twenty-one). A minority of these laborers were convicts or vagabonds bound into service by English courts for as long as fourteen years.

Masters were obliged to feed, clothe, and house these servants adequately. But work in the tobacco fields was backbreaking, and records include complaints of inadequate care. One Virginia ballad chronicled these complaints:

Come all you young fellows wherever you be,
Come listen awhile and I will tell thee,
Concerning the hardships that we undergo,
When we get lagg'd to Virginia
Now in Virginia I lay like a hog,
Our pillow at night is a brick or a log,
We dress and undress like some other sea dog,
How hard is my fate in Virginia.

Many servants tried to escape, but capture could mean a lengthening of their terms of service. On reaching the end of their service, servants were eligible for "freedom dues": clothing, tools, a gun, a spinning wheel, a little land, or perhaps food—something to help them get started on their own. Most former servants hoped to start farms in the backcountry and thus headed west, even though they thereby risked the danger of Indian attacks.

Reliance on indentured labor was unique to the English colonies. New France had little need for a systematic resort to servitude, for French colonists pretty much did their own labor. The Spanish, on the other hand, in places like Santa Fé, depended on the labor of Indians. African slaves were first introduced to the Chesapeake in 1619, but they were more expensive than servants, and as late as 1680 they made up less than 7 percent of the Chesapeake population. For many servants, however, the distinction between slavery and servitude may have seemed academic. Approximately two of every five servants died during their periods of indenture. In the hard-driving economy of the Chesapeake, many masters treated servants cruelly, and women especially were vulnerable to sexual exploitation. The harsh system of indentured labor prepared the tobacco masters of the Chesapeake for the transition to slavery that occurred during the second half of the seventeenth century. (Chapter 4 discusses the slave system and its implications for the economic and social aspects of American society as well as for slaves and masters themselves.)

Community Life in the Chesapeake

Most migrants were men, and male servants surviving their terms of indenture had a difficult time finding wives. Tobacco masters commonly received offers from men to pay off the indenture of a prospective wife, and free unmarried women often married as soon as they arrived. English men seemed to suffer a higher rate of mortality than English women in the disease-ridden environment of the early Chesapeake. Widows remarried quickly, sometimes within days. Their scarcity provided women with certain advantages. Shrewd widows bargained for remarriage agreements that gave them larger shares of the estate upon the death of their husband. So notable was the concentration of wealth in the hands of these widows that one historian has suggested that early Virginia was a "matriarchy." But because of high mortality rates, family size was smaller and kinship bonds—one of the most important components of community—were weaker than in England.

Visitors from England frequently remarked on the crude conditions of community life. Prosperous planters, investing everything in tobacco production, lived in rough wooden dwellings. Fifty miles inland, on the western edge of the settlements, freed servants lived with their families in shacks, huts, or even caves. Colonists spread across the countryside in search of new tobacco lands, creating dispersed settlements and few towns. Before 1650 there were relatively few community institutions such as schools and churches. The settlements of the Chesapeake, the site of England's premier colony in North America, looked temporary. Meanwhile, the Spanish in the Caribbean and Mexico were building communities that grew into great cities with permanent institutions.

In contrast to the colonists of New France, who were developing a distinctive American identity because of their commercial connections with native Americans, the population of the Chesapeake maintained close emotional ties to England. Colonial politics were shaped less by local developments than by a continuing relationship with the mother country. There was little movement toward a distinctively American point of view in the seventeenth-century Chesapeake.

THE NEW ENGLAND COLONIES

Both in climate and in geography, the northern coast of North America was far different from the Chesapeake. "Merchantable commodities" such as tobacco could not be produced there, and thus the region was far less favored for investment and settlement. Instead, it became a haven for Protestant dissenters from England, who gave the colonies of the North a distinctive character.

The Social and Political Values of Puritanism

Most English men and women, following to a greater or lesser degree the dictates of the Church of England, continued to practice a Christianity that differed little from traditional Catholicism. But the English followers of John Calvin (see Chapter 2), known as Puritans because they wished to purify and reform the English church from within, grew increasingly influential during the last years of Elizabeth's reign. Like Calvin's followers in Europe, the Puritans emphasized values such as enterprise and hard work and appealed especially to those groups—merchants, entrepreneurs, and commercial farmers—who were most responsible for the rapid economic and social transformation of England. But the Puritans were also the most vocal critics of the disruptive effects of that change, condemning the decline of the traditional rural community and the growing number of "idle and masterless men." They argued for reviving communities by placing reformed Christian congregations at their core to monitor the behavior of individuals. Puritanism was thus as much a set of social and political values as religious ones, a way of managing change in troubling times. By the early seventeenth century, Puritans controlled many congregations and had become an influential force at the universities in Oxford and Cambridge, training centers for the future political and religious leaders of England.

King James I, who assumed the throne after Elizabeth's death, abandoned her policy of religious tolerance. His persecution of the Puritans, however, merely stiffened their resolve and turned them toward overt political opposition. An increasingly vocal Puritan minority in Parliament complained that the Church of England was too "Catholic." These Puritans criticized King Charles I, James's son and successor, for supporting High Church policies—which emphasized the authority of the church and its traditional forms of worship—as well as for marrying a Catholic princess. In 1629, determined to rule without these troublesome opponents, Charles dissolved Parliament and launched a campaign of repression against the Puritans. "I am verily persuaded God will bring some heavy affliction upon this land," the Puritan leader John Winthrop despaired. This political turmoil provided the context for the migration of thousands of English Protestants to New England.

Early Contacts in New England

The northern Atlantic coast seemed an unlikely spot for English colonies, for the region was dominated by French and Dutch traders. In the early seventeenth century Samuel de Champlain established trading contacts with coastal Algonquians as far south as Cape Cod. The Dutch, following the explorations of Henry Hudson for the Netherlands, established settlements and a lucrative fur trade on the Hudson River. In 1613 the English, desperate to keep their colonial options open, dispatched a fleet from Jamestown that destroyed the French post at Port Royal on the Bay of Fundy and harassed the Dutch on the Hudson. The following year John Smith explored the northern coastline and christened the region "New England." The land was "so planted with Gardens and Corne fields," he wrote, that "I would rather live here than any where." But Smith's plans for a New England colony were aborted when he was captured and held captive by the French.

Then a twist of fate transformed English fortunes. From 1616 to 1618 a devastating plague ravaged the native peoples of the northern coast. Whole villages disappeared, and the trade system of the French and the Dutch was seriously disrupted. Indians perished so quickly and in such numbers that few remained to bury the dead. Modern estimates confirm the testimony of a surviving Indian that his people were "melted down by this disease, whereof nine-tenths of them have died." The native population of New England as a whole dropped from an estimated 120,000 to less than 70,000. So crippled were the surviving coastal societies that they could not provide effective resistance to the planting of English colonies.

Plymouth Colony and the Mayflower Compact

The first English colony in New England was founded by a group of religious dissenters known to later generations as the Pilgrims. The Pilgrims were English Separatists, people who believed the Anglican establishment so corrupt that they must establish their own independent church. One group of Separatists first moved to Holland in 1609, but, fearful that Dutch society was seducing their children, they soon began exploring the idea of emigrating to North America. Backed by the Virginia Company of London and led by Pilgrim William Bradford, 102 people embarked on the *Mayflower*, sailing from Plymouth, England, in September 1620.

The little group, mostly families but also a substantial number of single men hired by the investors, arrived in Massachusetts Bay at Plymouth, the site of the former Indian village of Patuxet. Soon the hired men began to grumble about Pilgrim authority, and to reassure them Bradford drafted a document known as the Mayflower Compact, in which all the men of the expedition did "covenant and combine [themselves] together into a civil body politic." Signed in November 1620, the Mayflower Compact was the first document of self-government in North America.

Weakened by scurvy and malnutrition, nearly half the Pilgrims perished over the first winter. Like the earlier settlers of Roanoke and Jamestown, however, the Pilgrims were rescued by Indians.

Massasoit, the sachem, or leader, of the local tribe of Wampanoags, offered food and advice in return for an alliance with the newcomers against his enemies, the Narragansets, a powerful neighboring tribe to his immediate west.

The interpreter in these negotiations was an Indian named Squanto who had been kidnapped in 1614 by the captain of one English ship and who had returned to New England five years later as guide on another vessel. Finding that plague had wiped out his village of Patuxet, and knowledgeable in the ways of the Europeans, Squanto became an adviser to Massasoit. With the arrival of the Pilgrims, this last survivor of the Patuxets now resumed his former residence, but as guide and interpreter for the English. Squanto secured seed corn for the colonists and taught them how to sow and cultivate it.

Deeply in debt to its investors, always struggling to meet its payments through the Indian trade, fishing, and lumbering, the Plymouth colony was never a financial success. Most families raised their own crops and kept their own livestock, but produced little for export. Nevertheless, the Pilgrims succeeded in establishing the separate community they wanted. So strong was their communal agreement that the annual meeting of property-owning men reelected William Bradford to thirty consecutive terms as governor. By midcentury, however, the Plymouth population had dispersed into eleven separate communities, and the growth of diverse local interests had begun to disrupt this separatist retreat.

The Massachusetts Bay Colony

In England, the Puritan movement continued its struggle to reform the national church. The political climate of the late 1620s, however, convinced a number of influential Puritans that the only way to protect their congregations was to emigrate. Some went to Ireland, others to the Netherlands or the West Indies, but many decided on New England, where, according to John Winthrop—later the first governor of the colony—they could establish "a city on a hill," a model of reform for England. In 1629 a royal charter was granted to a group of wealthy Puritans who called their enterprise the Massachusetts Bay Company. The company was given exclusive rights to settle and to trade, as well as to "religiously, peaceably and civilly" govern the territory and the native people between the Merrimack and Charles rivers, from the Atlantic "to the south sea on the west part." An advance force of 200 settlers soon left for the fishing settlement of Naumkeag on Massachusetts Bay, which they renamed Salem.

The Puritan emigration to Massachusetts became known as the Great Migration, a phrase that would be repeated many times in American history.

The seal of the Massachusetts Bay Company featured an Indian (dressed more like a native of South America than southern New England) imploring Puritans to "Come over and help us." It was a cynical ploy, for English Puritans were less involved with mission efforts among the Indians than were any of the other colonists in North America.

Between 1629 and 1643 some 20,000 people relocated to New England. Boston, founded in 1630, was their central settlement; within five years it was ringed by towns as far as thirty miles inland. By 1640 settlements had spread seventy-five miles west, into the Connecticut River Valley.

Most colonists arrived in groups from long-established communities in the east of England and were frequently led by men with extensive experience in local English government. Taking advantage of a loophole in their charter, the Puritan leaders transferred company operations to America in 1629, and within a few years they had transformed the company into a civil government. The original charter had established a General Court composed of a governor and his deputy, a board of magistrates (advisers), and the members of the corporation, known as freemen. In 1632 Governor Winthrop and his advisers declared all male heads of household who were also church members to be freemen. Two years later the freemen established their right to select delegates to represent the towns in drafting the laws of the colony. These delegates and the magistrates later separated into two legislative houses. Thus the proce-

dures of a joint-stock company provided the origins for democratic suffrage and the bicameral division of legislative authority in America.

Indians and Puritans

The Algonquian Indians of southern New England found the English considerably different from the French and Dutch traders who had preceded them. The principal concern of the English was not commerce—although the fur trade remained an important part of their economy—but the acquisition of land for their growing settlements. Massasoit attempted to use the colonists to his own advantage. But he soon found that when the English attacked his enemies, their true motive was expansion.

In 1623, on Massasoit's urging, the Pilgrim military commander Miles Standish attacked a group of Massachusetts Indians north of Plymouth. When Standish brought back the sachem's head and placed it on a pike outside the settlement's gates, the meaning of the gesture was not lost on the Wampanoags. If we are allies, one Indian asked, "how cometh it to pass that when we come to Patuxet you stand upon your guard, with the mouths of your pieces [guns] presented to us?" Even the Wampanoags were soon calling their English allies *wotowquenange*, or "cutthroats."

Ravaged by disease, the Wampanoags' northern neighbors, the Massachusetts, were ill prepared for the Puritan settlement that began in 1629. The English believed they had the right to take what they deemed "unused" lands—lands not being used, that is, in the "English way"—and depopulated Massachusetts villages became prime targets. As one colonist wrote: "Their land is spacious and void, and there are few and [they] do but run over the grass, as do also the foxes and wild beasts." Conflicts between settlers over title, however, made it necessary to obtain deeds to the land, and the English used a variety of tactics to pressure the Indians into signing quitclaims, or documents in which the signers relinquish all claim to specified properties. The English allowed their livestock to graze native fields, making them useless for cultivation. They fined Indians for violations of English law, such as working on the Sabbath, and then demanded land as payment. In addition, they made deals with dishonest sachems. For giving up the land that became Charlestown, for example, the "Squaw Sachem" of the Pawtuckets, one of a number of women Algonquian leaders, received twenty-one coats, nineteen fathoms of wampum, and three bushels of corn. Disorganized and demoralized, their populations reduced by disease and warfare, many of the coastal Algonquians surrendered their autonomy and placed themselves under the protection of the English.

Indian peoples to the west, however, remained a formidable presence. They blocked Puritan expansion until they were devastated in 1633–34 by an epidemic of smallpox that spread from the St. Lawrence south to Long Island Sound just as hundreds of English migrants were crowding into coastal towns. "Without this remarkable and terrible stroke of God upon the natives," recorded a town scribe, "we would with much more difficulty have found room, and at far greater charge have obtained and purchased land." In the aftermath of the epidemic, Puritans established many new inland towns.

By the late 1630s the most powerful tribes in the vicinity of the Puritans were the Narragansets of present-day Rhode Island and their traditional enemies the Pequots, principal trading partners of the Dutch. The Pequots lived on Long Island Sound near the mouth of the Connecticut River, where they controlled the production of wampum, woven belts of sea shells used as a medium of exchange in the Indian trade. In 1637 the Narragansets, in alliance with the English, who were looking for an excuse to smash the Dutch, inaugurated the Pequot War. Narraganset warriors and English troops attacked the main Pequot village, killing most of its slumbering residents, including women and children. Unaccustomed to such tactics, the shocked Narragansets cried out to the English: "It is too furious, it slays too many."

New England Communities

Back in England, the standoff between King Charles and the Puritans in Parliament erupted in armed conflict in 1642. The civil war that followed ended in the triumph of the Parliamentarians over royalist forces. The king was executed in 1649, and England proclaimed a "Commonwealth," headed by the Puritan leader Oliver Cromwell. With Cromwell's success, Puritans no longer had the same incentive to leave the country, and in fact many Puritans returned from New England to participate in the war.

New England's economy had depended on the sale of supplies and land to arriving immigrants, but in the 1640s the importance of this "newcomer market" declined with slackening immigration. Lacking a single exportable commodity like tobacco, New Englanders were forced to diversify into farming, fishing, and lumbering. Merchants began construction of what would become, by the end of the century, the largest shipping fleet in the colonies, and became active in the carrying trade between the

Caribbean and Chesapeake colonies and Europe. Its diversified economy ultimately provided New England with considerable long-term strength.

The communities of New England were distinct from those of the Chesapeake because the vast majority of the Puritans had come in family groups with relatively few servants. The Puritan ideal was a family governed in the same way that kings ruled over society. "Surely there is in all children a stubbornness, and stoutness of mind arising from natural pride," one Puritan declared, "which must be broken and beaten down." Parents often participated in the choice of mates for their offspring, and children typically married in the order of their births, younger siblings waiting until arrangements had been made for their elders.

Unique among the seventeenth-century colonies in North America, Massachusetts built an impressive system to educate its young. In 1647 the colony required that towns with 50 families or more support a public school; those with 100 families were to establish a "grammar" school that taught Latin, knowledge of which was required for admission to Harvard College, founded in 1636. Connecticut enacted similar requirements. Literacy was higher in New England than elsewhere in the colonies, or even in much of Europe. Far fewer New England women than men could read and write, however, because girls were excluded from

The first map printed in the English colonies, this view of New England was published in Boston in 1677. With north oriented to the right, it looks west from Massachusetts Bay, the two vertical black lines indicating the approximate boundaries of the Commonwealth of Massachusetts. The territory west of Rhode Island is noted as an Indian stronghold, the homelands of the Narraganset, Pequot, and Nipmuck peoples.

Attributed to the Freake-Gibbs Painter, American, active Boston, Mass., c. 1670. *The Mason Children: David, Joanna, and Abigail*, 1670. Oil on canvas, 39 x 42½ in. The Fine Arts Museum of San Francisco, Gift of Mr. and Mrs. John D. Rockefeller 3rd, 1979.7.3.

The Mason Children, by an unknown Boston artist, c. 1670. These Puritan children—David, Joanna, and Abigail Mason— are dressed in finery, an indication of the wealth and prominence of their family. The cane in young David's hand indicates his position as the male heir, while the rose held by Abigail is a symbol of childhood innocence.

the grammar schools. By 1639 the first printing press in the English colonies was in operation in Boston, and the following year it brought out the first American English publication, *The Bay Psalm Book.*

The Politics of Gender in Massachusetts

The Puritans stressed the importance of well-ordered communities and families. Colonists often emigrated in large kin groups that made up the core of the new towns. The Massachusetts General Court granted townships to proprietors representing the congregation, who then distributed fields, pasture, and woodlands in quantities proportional to the recipient's social status, so that wealthy families received more than humble ones. Settlers clustered their dwellings at the town center, near the meetinghouse that served as both church and civic center. Some towns, particularly those along the coast such as Boston, soon became centers of shipping. These clustered settlements and strong, vital communities made seventeenth-century New England quite different from Chesapeake society.

The family farm economy operated through the combined efforts of husband and wife. Men were generally responsible for field work, women for the work of the household, which included tending the kitchen garden (crops for household use), the dairy, and the henhouse, and securing fuel and water. Women managed an array of tasks, and some housewives independently traded garden products, milk,

and eggs. One New England husband, referring to his wife's domestic management, said, "I meddle not with the geese nor turkeys, for they are hers for she hath been and is a good wife to me." Indeed, women traders helped to create and sustain many of the bonds of New England communities.

It is mistaken to regard the Puritans as "puritanical." Although adultery was a capital crime in New England, Puritans celebrated the sexual expression that took place within marriage. Courting couples were even allowed to lie in bed together, with their lower bodies wrapped in an apron, a custom known as "bundling," free to caress and pet. In the words of an old New England ballad:

> *She is modest, also chaste*
> *While only bare from neck to waist,*
> *And he of boasted freedom sings,*
> *Of all above her apron strings.*

There were certainly many loving Puritan households with contented husbands and wives. Anne Bradstreet, a Massachusetts wife and mother and the first published poet of New England, wrote about her husband and marriage:

> *If ever two are one, then surely we.*
> *If ever man were lov'd by wife, then thee;*
> *If ever wife was happy in a man,*
> *Compare with me ye women if you can.*

Nevertheless, the cultural ideal of the day was the subordination of women to men. "I am but a wife, and therefore it is sufficient for me to follow my husband," wrote Lucy Winthrop Downing, and her brother John Winthrop declared, "A true wife accounts her subjection [to be] her honor and freedom." Married women could neither make contracts nor own property, neither vote nor hold office. The extraordinarily high birth rate of Puritan women was one mark of their "subjection." The average woman, marrying in her early twenties and surviving through her forties, could expect to bear eight children. Aside from abstinence, there was no form of birth control. There was significant cultural suspicion about wives who failed to have children or widows who were economically independent.

These suspicions about women came to the surface most notably in periodic witchcraft scares. During the course of the seventeenth century, according to one historian, 342 New England women were accused by their neighbors of witchcraft. The majority of them were childless or widowed or had reputations among their neighbors for their assertiveness and independence. In the vast majority of cases these accusations were dismissed by authorities. But in Salem,

Massachusetts, in 1692, when a group of girls claimed that they had been bewitched by a number of old men and women, the whole community was thrown into a panic of accusations. Before the colonial governor finally called a halt to the persecutions in 1693, twenty people had been tried, condemned, and executed.

The Salem accusations of witchcraft probably reflected generalized social tensions that found their outlet through an attack on people perceived as outsiders. Salem was a booming port, but although some residents were prospering, others were not. Most of the victims came from the eastern, more commercial section of town, whereas the majority of their accusers lived on the economically stagnant western side. Most of the accused also came from families whose religious sympathies were with sects of Anglicans, Quakers, or Baptists, not Puritans. Finally, a majority of the victims were old women, suspect because they lived alone, without men. The Salem witchcraft trials exposed the dark side of Puritan ideas about women.

Dissent and New Communities

The Puritans emigrated in order to practice their variety of Christianity, but they had little tolerance for other religious points of view. Religious disagreements among them were not accommodated but soon provoked the founding of new colonies. Thomas Hooker, a minister in Cambridge, disagreed with Puritan leaders over the extent of their authority, and believed that suffrage should not be restricted to male church members only. In 1636 he led his followers west to the Connecticut River, where they founded the town of Hartford. Hooker helped write the Fundamental Orders that marked the beginning of the colony of Connecticut.

The second major dissenter was the clergyman Roger Williams, who came to New England in 1631 to take up duties for the congregation in Salem. Williams believed in religious toleration and the separation of church and state. (Chapter 5 discusses these issues at greater length.) He also preached that the colonists had no absolute right to Indian land but must bargain for it in good faith. Because the Puritans believed that theirs was the one true religion, because they believed in the absolute union of church and state, and because they had established their colony on what had been Indian land, they considered Williams's ideas highly dangerous, and in 1636 they banished him from the Bay colony. With a group of followers, Williams emigrated to the Narragansett country, where he purchased land from the Indians and founded the town of Providence.

The next year Boston shook with another religious controversy. Anne Hutchinson, a brilliant woman who had arrived in New England with her merchant husband in 1634, led religious discussion groups that

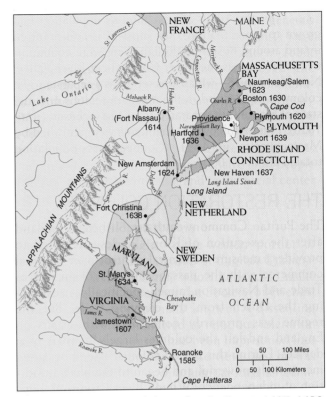

European Colonies of the Atlantic Coast, 1607–1639
Virginia on Chesapeake Bay was the first English colony in North America, but by the mid-seventeenth century Virginia was joined by settlements of Scandinavians on the Delaware River, and Dutch on the Hudson River, as well as English religious dissenters in New England. The territories indicated here reflect the vague boundaries of the early colonies.

criticized various Boston ministers for a lack of piety. The concentration of attention on good works, she argued, led people to believe that they could earn their way to heaven, a "popish" or Catholic heresy in the eyes of Calvinists. Hutchinson was called before the General Court, where the Puritan leaders made it clear that they would not tolerate a woman who publicly criticized men. Although she handled herself very skillfully, Hutchinson made the mistake of claiming that she had received a direct "revelation" from God, and so was excommunicated and banished. She and her followers moved to Roger Williams's settlement, where they established their own community in 1638.

A third group of dissenters, Samuel Gorton and his followers, were also banished from the Bay Colony and relocated, like the others, to the Narragansett haven. In 1644, Roger Williams received a charter creating the colony of Rhode Island, named for the principal island in Narragansett Bay, as a protection for these several dissenting communities. A new royal charter of 1663 guaranteed self-government and complete religious liberty and strengthened the colony's territorial claims for its approximately 2,000 English colonial inhabitants.

The Delawares presented William Penn with this wampum belt after the Shackamaxon treaty of 1682. In friendship, a Quaker in distinctive hat clasps the hand of an Indian. The diagonal stripes on either side of the figures convey information about the territorial terms of the agreement. Wampum belts like this one, made from strings of white and purple shells, were used to commemorate treaties throughout the colonial period and were the most widely accepted form of money in the northeastern colonies during the seventeenth century.

Penn wanted this colony to be a "holy experiment." In his first Frame of Government, drafted in 1682, he included guarantees of religious freedom, civil liberties, and elected representation. By attempting to deal fairly with the Algonquian Indians, Penn tried to achieve what it took the Spanish and the Pueblo Indians a great deal of bloodshed to accomplish. He refused to permit colonization until settlement rights were negotiated and lands purchased. In 1682 and 1683, he made an agreement with the sachem Tammany of the Delaware tribe at the Indian town of Shackamaxon on the Delaware River. In subsequent years Chief Tammany appeared in many popular stories and myths among the peoples of the mid-Atlantic region. By the time of the Revolution, his name had become emblematic of the American spirit of independence, and later it was adopted by a New York political club. Although Pennsylvania's relations with the Indians later soured, during Penn's lifetime his reputation for fair dealing led a number of Indian groups to take refuge in the Quaker colony.

During the first decade of Pennsylvania's settlement more than 10,000 colonists arrived from England, and agricultural communities were soon spreading from the Delaware into the fertile interior valleys. In 1704 Penn approved the creation of a separate government for the area formerly controlled by the Scandinavians and Dutch, which became the colony of Delaware. In the eighteenth century, Pennsylvania became known as America's breadbasket, and late in the century Philadelphia became the most important colonial port in North America.

CONFLICT AND WAR

Pennsylvania's ability to maintain peaceful relations with the Indians was the great exception of the late seventeenth century. Throughout all the colonial regions of the continent this proved to be a time of

OVERVIEW

CONFLICT AND WAR

King Philip's War	1675–76	The Indian peoples of southern New England and the Puritan colonies fight for the control of land
Bacon's Rebellion	1675–76	Backcountry settlers attack Indians, and colonial authorities try to suppress these attacks
Wars in the South	1670s–1720s	British colonists in the Carolinas incite Creeks, Cherokees, and other Indian tribes to attack and enslave the mission Indians of Spanish Florida
The Glorious Revolution in America	1689	Colonists in Massachusetts, New York, and Maryland rise up against the colonial governments of King James II
King William's War	1689–97	The first of a series of colonial struggles between England and France, these conflicts occur principally on the frontiers of northern New England and New York

persistent warfare between colonists and Indians and of violent conflicts within colonial communities themselves. The revolt of the Pueblo Indians in New Mexico, discussed in the opening of this chapter, was one of the most dramatic examples of such conflict, and the most effective instance of Indian resistance to colonization in the history of North America.

King Philip's War

Another Indian revolt, known as King Philip's War, which erupted in New England in 1675, turned out to be a disaster for Indian people. During the nearly forty years of relative peace that followed the Pequot War of 1637, the Algonquian and English peoples of New England lived in close if tense contact. Several Puritan ministers, including John Eliot and Thomas Mayhew, began to preach to Indian people, and several hundred Algonquian converts eventually relocated in Christian Indian communities called "praying towns." Outside the colonial boundaries, however, there remained a number of independent Indian tribes, including the Wampanoags and Narragansets of Rhode Island and the Abenakis of northern New England. The extraordinary expansion of the Puritan population, coupled with their hunger for land, created pressures for further expansion into those territories.

In 1671 the colonial authorities at Plymouth forced the Wampanoags to concede authority over their homeland territory. This humiliation convinced the Wampanoag sachem Metacomet (called King Philip by his English teachers), son of Massasoit, that his people must break their half-century alliance with Plymouth and take up armed resistance. The New England colonies, meanwhile, prepared for a war of conquest.

In the spring of 1675 Plymouth magistrates arrested three Wampanoag men and executed them for the murder of a Christian Indian. Fearing the moment of confrontation had arrived, Metacomet sent a diplomatic mission to the Narragansetts appealing for a defensive alliance. Arguing that an alliance amounted to an Indian conspiracy, the New England colonies and New York—each hoping for territorial gain—sent armed forces into Narraganset country, attacking and burning a number of villages. What became known as King Philip's War soon engulfed all of New England.

At first things went well for the Indians. They forced the abandonment of English settlements on the Connecticut River and torched several towns less than twenty miles from Boston. But by the beginning of 1676 their campaign was in collapse. A combined colonial army invaded Narraganset country, burning villages, killing women and children, and defeating a large Indian force in a battle known as the Great Swamp Fight. In western New England, Metacomet

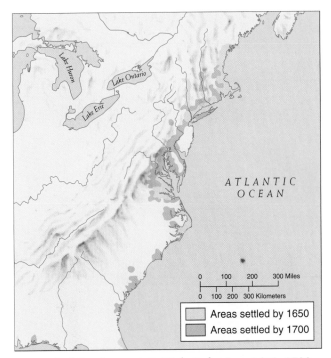

Spread of Settlement: British Colonies, 1650–1700
The spread of settlement in the English colonies in the late seventeenth century created the conditions for a number of violent conflicts, including King Philip's War, Bacon's Rebellion, the Southern Indian Wars, and King William's War.

appealed to the Iroquois for supplies and support, but instead they attacked and defeated his forces. Metacomet retreated back to his homeland, where the colonists annihilated his army in August 1676. The victors killed Metacomet and triumphantly marched his head on a pike through their towns. The colonists sold his wife and son, among hundreds of other captives, into West Indian slavery.

In their decisive attack on Metacomet's army, the Iroquois had been motivated by interests of their own. Casting themselves in the role of powerful intermediaries between other tribes and the English colonies, the Iroquois wanted to subjugate all trading rivals. In a series of negotiations conducted at Albany in 1677, the Iroquois Confederacy and the colony of New York created an alliance known as the Covenant Chain, which sought to establish both Iroquois dominance over all other tribes and New York dominance over all other colonies. During the 1680s the Iroquois pressed their claims as far west as the Illinois country, fighting the western Algonquians allied with the French trading system.

King Philip's War, which marked the end of organized Indian resistance in New England, took an enormous toll on human life and property. Approximately 4,000 Algonquians and 2,000 English colonists were dead, and dozens of colonial and native towns

Metacomet, or King Philip, in a mid-eighteenth century engraving by Paul Revere of Boston. Like his father Massasoit, Metacomet tried to cooperate with English colonists but finally had to fight to maintain his authority. For many years after the war, the leaders at Plymouth kept his severed head on display. Because his remains never received an honored burial, say the descendants of the Wampanoags, Metacomet's ghost still rises and walks about his homeland.

lay in smoking ruins. Fearing attack from Indians close at hand, colonists also attacked and destroyed most of the Christian "praying towns." Measured against the size of the population, this was one of the most destructive wars in American history.

Bacon's Rebellion

At the same time as King Philip's War, another English-Indian confrontation took place to the south in the Chesapeake. In the 1670s the Susquehannock people of the upper Potomac River came into conflict with tobacco planters expanding from Virginia. Violent raids in 1675, led by wealthy backcountry settler Nathaniel Bacon, included the indiscriminate murder of Indians. The efforts of Virginia governor

William Berkeley to suppress these unauthorized military expeditions so infuriated Bacon and his followers—many of them former indentured servants—that in the spring of 1676 they turned their fury against the colonial capital of Jamestown itself. Berkeley fled while Bacon pillaged and burned the town. When Bacon suddenly died of dysentery, however, his rebellion collapsed. Two years later, in a replay of these Virginia events, backcountry men in the Albemarle region of North Carolina overthrew the proprietary government in an episode of violence known as Culpeper's Rebellion. The rebels established a government of their own before being suppressed by English authorities.

Little immediate political change resulted from these two rebellions, but they marked an important change of direction for Virginia and North Carolina. During his tenure as "General of Virginia," Bacon had issued a manifesto demanding not only the death or removal of all Indians from the colony but also an end to the rule of aristocratic "grandees" and "parasites." The rebellion thus signaled a developing conflict of interests between the established Tidewater region, where the "Indian problem" had long since been settled, and frontier districts, where settler hunger for land created conflict with natives. Colonial authorities in Virginia and North Carolina, hoping to gain the support of backcountry men by enlarging the stock of available land, soon declared themselves in favor of armed expansion into Indian territory. But at the same time, planters' fears of disorder among former servants encouraged them to accelerate the transition to slave labor.

Wars in the South

There was also massive violence in South Carolina during the 1670s, as colonists there began the operation of a large-scale Indian slave trade. Charleston merchants encouraged Yamasees, Creeks, Cherokees, and Chickasaws to wage war on Indian tribes allied to rival colonial powers and to sell captives into slavery. Among the victims were the mission Indians of Spanish Florida, the Choctaw allies of the French, and the Tuscaroras, trading partners of the Virginians. The Florida mission Indians were hit so hard that by 1710 more than 12,000 of them had been captured and sold, thousands of others had been killed or dispersed, and the Spanish mission system, in operation for more than a century, lay in ruins.

This vicious slave trade extended well into the eighteenth century, resulting in the sale of thousands of southern Indians into captivity. Most of the men were shipped from Charleston to West Indian or northern colonies, but the Indian women remained in South Carolina. Many eventually formed relationships and had children with enslaved African men, forming a racial-ethnic group known as the mustees.

The Glorious Revolution in America

Dynastic change in England was another factor precipitating violence in North America. Upon Charles II's death in 1685, his brother and successor, James II, began a concerted effort to strengthen royal control over the colonies. During the preceding forty years colonial assemblies had grown powerful and independent, and King James was determined to reduce their status. He abolished the New York assembly, which had been particularly troublesome, and placed all power in the hands of the royal governor. Colonial assemblies continued to operate in the other colonies, but many became involved in bitter disputes with their governors.

In his most dramatic action, James abolished altogether the charter governments of the New England, New York, and New Jersey colonies, combining them into what he called the Dominion of New England. Edmund Andros, the royal governor of this dominion, imposed Anglican forms of worship in Puritan areas, violated traditions of local autonomy, and attempted to enforce the Navigation Acts (1651, 1660, 1663), which restricted colonial trade by preventing the colonies from trading directly with any nation other than England.

Within England, the same imperious style on the part of King James II alienated Parliament. In a bloodless transition in 1688, afterward known as the Glorious Revolution, some leaders in Parliament engineered replacing him with his daughter Mary and her Dutch husband, William of Orange. In 1689 the new monarchs agreed to a Bill of Rights, promising to respect traditional civil liberties, to summon and consult with Parliament annually, and to enforce and administer parliamentary legislation. These were significant concessions with profound implications for the future of English politics. England now had a "constitutional monarchy."

These changes unleashed the resentment against King James that had built up in the colonies, and a series of rebellions broke out against the authorities set in place by the king. In the spring of 1689, Governor Andros was attacked by an angry Boston mob, inflamed by rumors that he was a closet Catholic. He was able to escape their wrath but was arrested and deported by the local militia. When news of the Boston revolt arrived in New York, it inspired another uprising there. A group led by German merchant Jacob Leisler, and including many prominent Dutch residents, seized control of the city and called for the formation of a new legislature. In Maryland, rumors of a Catholic plot led to the overthrow of the propri-

etary rule of the Calvert family by an insurgent group called the Protestant Association.

The new monarchs carefully measured their response to these uprisings. When Jacob Leisler attempted to prevent the landing of the king's troops in New York, he was arrested, tried, and executed. But the monarchs consented to the dismantling of the Dominion of New England and the end of proprietary rule in Maryland. The outcome of the Glorious Revolution in America was mixed. All the affected English colonies quickly revived their assemblies and returned to their tradition of self-government. But to forestall such disorders in the future, in 1692 the crown decreed that Massachusetts, New York, and Maryland would be royal colonies, with appointed governors, thus extending the control of the monarchy over its troublesome colonists.

King William's War

The year 1689 also marked the beginning of nearly seventy-five years of armed conflict between English and French forces for control of the North American interior. The Iroquois-English Covenant Chain challenged New France to press ever harder in search of commercial opportunities in the interior. In the far North, the English countered French dominance with the establishment of the Hudson's Bay Company, a royal fur-trade monopoly that in 1670 was given exclusive rights to Rupert's Land, the watershed of the great northern Hudson Bay.

Hostilities began with English-Iroquois attacks on Montreal and violence between rival French and English traders on Hudson Bay. These skirmishes were part of a larger conflict between England and France called the War of the League of Augsburg in Europe and King William's War in the North American colonies. In 1690 the French and their Algonquian allies counterattacked, burning frontier settlements in New York, New Hampshire, and Maine and pressing the attack against the towns of the Iroquois. The same year, a Massachusetts fleet briefly captured the strategic French harbor at Port Royal, in Acadia, but a combined English colonial force failed in its attempt to conquer the French settlements along the St. Lawrence. This inconclusive war was ended by the Treaty of Ryswick of 1697, which established an equally inconclusive peace. War between England and France would resume only five years later.

The persistent violence of these years concerned English authorities, who began to fear the loss of their North American possessions either from outside attack or from internal disorder. To shore up central control, in 1701 the English Board of Trade recommended making all charter and proprietary

CHRONOLOGY

1598	Juan de Oñate leads Spanish into New Mexico
1607	English found Jamestown
1608	French found Quebec
1609	Spanish found Santa Fé
1620	Pilgrim emigration
1622	Indian uprising in Virginia
1625	Jesuit missionaries arrive in New France
1629	Puritans begin settlement of Massachusetts Bay
1637	Pequot War
1649	Charles I executed
1660	Stuart monarchy restored, Charles II becomes king

1675	King Philip's War
1676	Bacon's Rebellion
1680	Pueblo Revolt
1681–82	Robert Sieur de La Salle explores the Mississippi
1688	The Glorious Revolution
1689	King William's War
1698	Spanish reconquest of the Pueblos completed
1701	English impose royal governments on all colonies but Massachusetts, Connecticut, and Pennsylvania

governments into royal colonies. After a brief period under royal rule, William Penn regained private control of his domain, but Pennsylvania was the last remaining proprietary colony. Among the charter colonies, only Rhode Island and Connecticut retained their original governments. The result of this quarter-century of violence was the tightening of the imperial reins.

CONCLUSION

At the beginning of the seventeenth century the European presence north of Mexico was extremely limited: a Spanish base in Florida, a few Franciscan missionaries among the Pueblo Indians, and fishermen along the North Atlantic coast. By 1700, however, the human landscape of the Southwest, the South, and the Northeast had been transformed with the establishment of the Spanish colony of New Mexico, the French colonies of New France, and along the Atlantic coast

a series of English colonies from New England in the North to the Carolinas in the South. More than a quarter million Europeans and Africans now resided in colonial enclaves. Indian tribal societies had been disrupted, depopulated, and in some cases destroyed. The policies of the various European colonizers differed significantly, and outside the colonial enclaves Indians still constituted the vast majority of the continent's inhabitants, but the profound changes of the seventeenth century had ominous implications for Indian peoples.

During the long civil war in England the English colonies had been left to run their own affairs, but with the Restoration in 1660, and the establishment of the constitutional monarchy in 1689, the English state began to supervise its troublesome colonists more closely, beginning a long struggle over the limits of self-government. The violence and warfare of the last decades of the century suggested that conflict would continue to play a significant role in the future of colonial America.

REVIEW QUESTIONS

1.   Using examples drawn from this chapter, discuss the differences between colonizing "frontiers of inclusion" and "exclusion."

2.   What factors turned England's Chesapeake colony of Virginia from stark failure to brilliant success?

3. Discuss the role of religious dissent in the founding of the first New England colonies and in stimulating the creation of others.
4. Compare and contrast William Penn's policy with respect to Indian tribes with the policies of other

English settlers, in the Chesapeake and New England, and with the policies of the Spanish, the French, and the Dutch.
5. What were the principal causes of colonial violence and warfare of the late seventeenth century?

RECOMMENDED READING

James Axtell, *The European and the Indian: Essays in the Ethnohistory of Colonial America* (1981). A readable introduction to the dynamics of mutual discovery between natives and colonizers.

Carl Bridenbaugh, *Vexed and Troubled Englishmen, 1590–1642* (1968). A social history of the English people on the eve of colonization, emphasizing their religious and economic problems.

W. J. Eccles, *France in America* (1990). The most comprehensive introduction to the history of New France.

Andrew L. Knaut, *The Pueblo Revolt of 1680* (1995). The most complete and sophisticated account of the revolt.

Edmund S. Morgan, *American Slavery, American Freedom* (1975). A classic interpretation of early Virginia.

Morgan argues that early American ideas of freedom for some were based on the reality of slavery for others.

Neal Salisbury, *Manitou and Providence: Indians, Europeans, and the Making of New England* (1982). One of the best examples of the new ethnohistory of Indians; a provocative intercultural approach to the history of the Northeast.

David J. Weber, *The Spanish Frontier in North America* (1992). A powerful overview that includes the history of New Mexico and Florida.

Peter H. Wood, et al., eds., *Powhatan's Mantle: Indians in the Colonial Southeast* (1989). Essays detailing the conflict and consort between colonists and natives in the South.

ADDITIONAL BIBLIOGRAPHY

The Spanish and French in North America

James Axtell, *The Invasion Within: The Contest of Culture in Colonial North America* (1985)

Gilberto Rafael Cruz, *Let There Be Towns: Spanish Municipal Origins in the American Southwest, 1610–1810* (1988)

W. J. Eccles, *The Canadian Frontier, 1534–1760* (1983)

The Chesapeake

Kathleen M. Brown, *Good Wives, Nasty Wenches, and Anxious Patriarchs: Gender, Race, and Power in Colonial Virginia* (1996)

Wesley F. Craven, *White, Red, and Black: The Seventeenth Century Virginian* (1971)

Carville Earle, *The Evolution of a Tidewater Settlement System: All Hallow's Parish, Maryland, 1650–1783* (1975)

Jack P. Greene and J. R. Poole, eds., *Colonial British America: Essays in the New History of the Early Modern Era* (1984)

Karen Ordahl Kupperman, *Settling with the Indians: The Meeting of English and Indian Cultures in America, 1580–1640* (1980)

Gloria L. Main, *Tobacco Colony: Life in Early Maryland, 1650–1720* (1982)

Thad W. Tate and David L. Ammerman, eds., *The Chesapeake in the Seventeenth Century* (1979)

New England

David Grayson Allen, *In English Ways: The Movement of Societies and the Transferal of English Local Law and Custom* (1981)

Bernard Bailyn, *The New England Merchants in the Seventeenth Century* (1955)

Emery Battis, *Saints and Sectaries: Anne Hutchinson and the Antinomian Controversy in the Massachusetts Bay Colony* (1962)

Theodore Dwight Bozeman, *To Live Ancient Lives: The Primitivist Dimension in Puritanism* (1988)

Francis J. Bremer, ed., *Puritanism: Transatlantic Perspectives on a Seventeenth-Century Anglo-American Faith* (1993)

Carl Bridenbaugh, *Fat Mutton and Liberty of Conscience: Society in Rhode Island, 1636–1690* (1974)

David Cressy, *Coming Over: Migration and Communication between England and New England in the Seventeenth Century* (1987)

William Cronon, *Changes in the Land: Indians, Colonists, and the Ecology of New England* (1983)

Bruce Colin Daniels, *Puritans at Play: Leisure and Recreation in Colonial New England* (1995)

John Demos, *A Little Commonwealth: Family Life in Plymouth Colony* (1970)

M. Etienne and E. Leacock, eds., *Women and Colonization* (1980)

Christopher Hill, *The World Turned Upside Down: Radical Ideas during the English Revolution* (1972)

Stephen Innes, *Labor in a New Land* (1983)

Francis Jennings, *The Invasion of America: Indians, Colonialism, and the Cant of Conquest* (1975)

Amy Scrager Lang, *Prophetic Women: Anne Hutchinson and the Problem of Dissent in the Literature of New England* (1987)

Michael Walzer, *The Revolution of the Saints: A Study in the Origins of Radical Politics* (1965)

Restoration Colonies

Wesley F. Craven, *The Southern Colonies in the Seventeenth Century, 1607–1689* (1949)
Melvin B. Endy Jr., *William Penn and Early Quakerism* (1973)
Michael Kammen, *Colonial New York: A History* (1975)
Sung Bok Kim, *Landlord and Tenant in Colonial New York: Manorial Society, 1664–1775* (1978)
H. T. Merrens, *Colonial North Carolina* (1964)
Gary B. Nash, *Quakers and Politics: Pennsylvania, 1681–1726* (1968)
Oliver Rink, *Holland on the Hudson: An Economic and Social History of Dutch New York* (1986)
Robert C. Ritchie, *The Duke's Province: A Study of New York Politics and Society, 1664–1691* (1977)
M. Eugene Sirmans, *Colonial South Carolina: A Political History, 1663–1763* (1966)
Jack M. Sosin, *English America and the Restoration Monarchy of Charles II: Transatlantic Politics, Commerce, and Kinship* (1980)

Conflict and War

Thomas J. Archdeacon, *New York City, 1664–1710* (1976)
Russell Bourne, *The Red King's Rebellion: Racial Politics in New England, 1675–1678* (1990)
Paul Boyer and Stephen Nissenbaum, *Salem Possessed* (1974)
Ramón A. Gutiérrez, *When Jesus Came, the Corn Mothers Went Away: Marriage, Sexuality, and Power in New Mexico, 1500–1846* (1991)
Richard R. Johnson, *Adjustment to Empire: The New England Colonies, 1675–1715* (1981)

D. W. Jordan, *Maryland's Revolution of Government, 1689–1692* (1974)
Carol F. Karlsen, *The Devil in the Shape of a Woman: Witchcraft in Colonial New England* (1987)
Yusuhide Kawashima, *Puritan Justice and the Indian: White Man's Law in Massachusetts, 1630–1763* (1986)
Almon Wheeler Lauber, *Indian Slavery in Colonial Times within the Present Limits of the United States* (1913)
David S. Lovejoy, *The Glorious Revolution in America* (1972)
Michael J. Publisi, *Puritans Besieged: The Legacies of King Philip's War in the Massachusetts Bay Colony* (1991)
Jack M. Sosin, *English America and the Revolution of 1688* (1982)
Wilcomb E. Washburn, *The Governor and the Rebel: A History of Bacon's Rebellion in Virginia* (1957)
Stephen S. Webb, *1676: The End of American Independence* (1980)
Thomas J. Wertenbaker, *Torchbearer of the Revolution: The Story of Bacon's Rebellion and its Leader* (1940)

Biography

Mary M. Dunn, *William Penn, Politics and Conscience* (1967)
J. A. Leo Lemay, *The American Dream of Captain John Smith* (1991)
Edmund S. Morgan, *Puritan Dilemma: The Story of John Winthrop* (1958)
Ann Sanford, *Anne Bradstreet, the Worldly Puritan* (1974)
Marc Simmons, *The Last Conquistador: Juan de Oñate and the Settling of the Far Southwest* (1991)
Robert S. Tilton, *Pocahontas: The Evolution of an American Narrative* (1994)
Alvin Gardner Weeks, *Massasoit of the Wampanoags* (1919)
Selma R. Williams, *Divine Rebel: The Life of Anne Marbury Hutchinson* (1981)

CHAPTER FOUR

SLAVERY AND EMPIRE

1441–1770

AMERICAN COMMUNITIES
African Slaves Build Their Own Community in Coastal Georgia

Africans labored in the steamy heat of the coastal Georgia rice fields, the breeches of the men rolled up over their knees, the sack skirts of the women gathered and tied about their hips, leaving them, in the words of one shocked observer, "two thirds naked." Standing on the banks of canals that channeled water to the fields, African slave drivers, whips at the ready, supervised the work. Upriver, groups cut away cypress and gum trees and cleared the swampland's jungle maze of undergrowth; others constructed levees, preparing to bring more land under cultivation. An English overseer or plantation master could be seen here and there, but overwhelmingly it was a country populated by Africans.

These Georgia plantations were southern extensions of the South Carolina rice belt. Although slavery had been prohibited by Georgia's original colonial charter of 1732, the restriction was lifted when Georgia became a royal colony two decades later. By 1770, 15,000 African Americans lived on several hundred coastal plantations, and the population of the region was 80 percent African. The rice plantations were owned by a small elite, dominated by a tight circle of crown officials and their relatives and associates. Georgia's royal governor and lieutenant governor, for example, owned more than a dozen plantations with over 50,000 acres and 800 slaves. Plantations with names such as Mulberry Grove, New Settlement, and Walnut Hill were among the most recent, and most profitable, additions to the British New World empire.

Rice had become one of the most valuable commodities produced in mainland North America, surpassed in value only by tobacco and wheat. The growth of rice production in the Lower South was matched by an enormous expansion in the Atlantic slave trade. Having no experience in rice cultivation, English colonial planters pressed slave traders to supply them with Africans from rice-growing regions such as the Windward Coast of West Africa. In its workforce, its methods, and even its tools, southern rice culture was patterned on an African model.

Although in the eighteenth century the number of North American blacks who were "country-born" (native to America, and thus born into slavery) grew steadily, the majority on the rice plantations continued to be what were known as "salt-water" Africans. These men and women had endured the shock of enslavement. Ripped from their homeland communities in West Africa by slave raiders, they were brutally marched to coastal forts. There they were imprisoned, subjected to humiliating inspections of their bodies, and branded on the buttocks like animals. Packed into the holds of stinking ships, they endured a nightmarish passage across the Atlantic Ocean. When finally unloaded on a strange continent, they were sold at dockside auctions, then once again marched overland to their destinations on New World plantations. On the rice plantations of isolated coastal Georgia enslaved Africans suffered from overwork and numerous physical ailments caused by poor diet, minimal and inappropriate clothing, and inadequate housing. Mortality rates were exceptionally high, especially for infants. Colonial laws permitted masters to discipline and punish slaves indiscriminately. They were whipped, confined in irons, castrated, or sold to other landowners with little regard for their relations with family or friends.

Africans struggled to make a place for themselves in this inhospitable world. The knowledge of rice cultivation that many slaves brought with them to the rice coast gave them the bargaining power to win acceptance from their masters of the familiar work routines and rhythms of West Africa. Thus, low-country plantations operated according to the task system: once slaves finished their specific jobs, they could use their remaining time to hunt, fish, or cultivate family gardens. Masters frequently complained that "tasking" did not produce the same level of profit as the gang labor system of the sugar plantations, but African rice hands refused to work any other way.

Despite this small degree of control over the form of their servitude, slaves on the Georgia coast ran away, like slaves everywhere in the Americas. Readers of Savannah newspapers were urged to look out for fugitives: Statira, a woman of the "Gold Coast Country" with tribal markings upon her temples, or "a negro fellow named Mingo, about 40 years old, and his wife Quante, a sensible wench about 20 with her child, a boy about 3 years old, all this country born." Some fled in groups, heading for the Creek Indian settlements in northern Florida, or toward St. Augustine, where the Spanish promised them safe haven. Some struck out violently at their masters: in 1759, a group of nine Africans from a Savannah plantation killed their master and stole a boat, planning to head upriver. They were apprehended as they lay in wait to murder their hated overseers as well.

So slaves resisted. But like slaves throughout the New World, the majority of enslaved Africans and African Americans of the Georgia coast remained, and through their strategy and determination, built their own communities within the heartless world of slavery. Plantation slaves throughout the American South married, raised children, and gradually created African American kinship networks. They passed on African names and traditions and created new ones. These links between individuals and families formed the basis for reestablished communities.

African American slave communities combined elements both of African languages and of English to form dialects that allowed newly arrived people from many different African ethnic groups as well as American-born slaves to communicate with one another. Neither individuals nor families alone can make a language; that is something only a community can do. The common African heritage and a common status as slaves supplied the basis for the African American community. Communities provided both newly arrived Africans and the American-born with the opportunity to build relationships. Without African American communities there could have been no African American culture.

Traveling through the Georgia and Carolina low country during the 1740s, an English missionary heard a clamor in the woods along the road. As he peered through the trees he was startled to see a group of slaves "dancing round the fire." The African American community was refitting traditional dance, song, and story to New World circumstances, just as it was reestablishing African arts such as woodworking, iron making, and weaving. Through their culture, the slaves shared a powerful awareness of their common oppression. They told or sang dialect tales of mistreatment, as in this song of Quow, the punished slave:

Was matter Buddy Quow?
I ble Obesha bang you....
Dah Backrow Man go wrong you, Buddy Quow,
Dah Backrow Man go wrong you, Buddy Quow.

[What's the matter Brother Quow?
I believe the overseer's beat you....
The white man's wronged you, Brother Quow,
The white man's wronged you, Brother Quow.]

Just as European settlers planted colonial communities, so Africans, who constituted the largest group of people to come to North America during the colonial era, constructed distinctive communities of their own. The history of African Americans includes the story of the Atlantic slave trade, the plunder of Africa, and the profits of the empire. But it is also a story of achievement under the most difficult of circumstances and of the making of families, kin networks, and communities. They "labor together and converse almost wholly among themselves," a minister wrote of low-country slaves. "They are, as 'twere, a nation within a nation."

Georgia
Sea
Islands

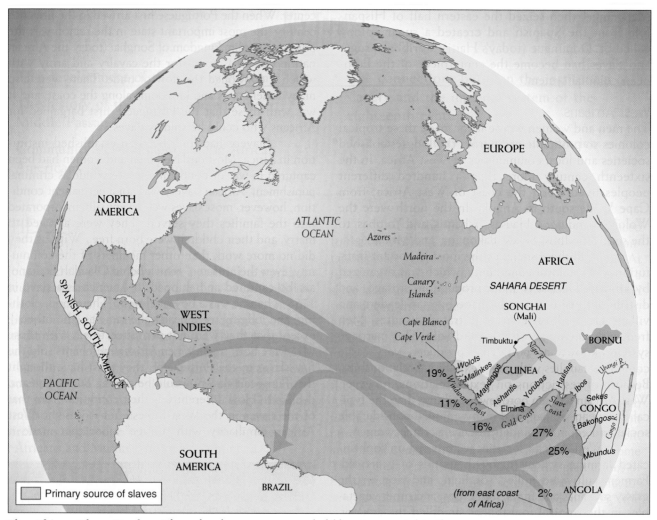

The African Slave Trade   *The enslaved men, women, and children transported to the Americas came from West Africa, the majority from the lower Niger River (called the Slave Coast) and the region of the Congo and Angola.*

possible for African and European traders to begin the trade in human merchandise.

THE AFRICAN SLAVE TRADE

The movement of Africans across the Atlantic to the Americas was the largest forced migration in world history. Moreover, Africans made up the largest group of people to come to the Americas before the nineteenth century, outnumbering European immigrants by the astounding ratio of six to one. The Atlantic slave trade, which began with the Portuguese in the fifteenth century and did not end in the United States until 1808 (it continued elsewhere in the Americas until the 1870s) is a brutal chapter in the making of America.

The Demography of the Slave Trade

Scholars today estimate that slavers transported 10 to 11 million Africans to the Americas during the four

centuries of the trade. Seventy-six percent arrived from 1701 to 1810—the peak period of colonial demand for labor, when tens of thousands of individuals were shipped from Africa each year. Of this vast multitude, about half were delivered to Dutch, French, or British sugar plantations in the Caribbean, a third to Portuguese Brazil, and 10 percent to Spanish America. A much smaller proportion—about one in twenty, or an estimated 600,000 men, women, and children—were transported from Africa to the British colonies of North America.

Among the Africans brought to the Americas, men generally outnumbered women two to one. Since most Africans were destined for field work, this ratio probably reflected the preferences of plantation owners. The majority of captured and transported Africans were young people, between the ages of fifteen and thirty, and nearly every ethnic group in West Africa was represented among them.

Slavers of All Nations

All the nations of western Europe participated in the slave trade. Dutch slavers began challenging Portuguese control at the end of the sixteenth century, and during the sugar boom of the seventeenth century Holland became the most prominent slave-trading nation. The English also entered the trade in the sixteenth century, beginning with the African voyages of John Hawkins. The Royal African Company, a slave-trading monopoly based in London, was chartered in 1672, but in 1698 England threw open the trade to independent merchants. Soon hundreds of ships from Bristol and Liverpool were competing with those from London. As a result, the number of slaves shipped to North America skyrocketed. The Dutch and Portuguese, however, continued to play important roles, alongside slave traders from France, Sweden, and several German duchies.

For the most part the European presence in Africa was confined to outposts, although the

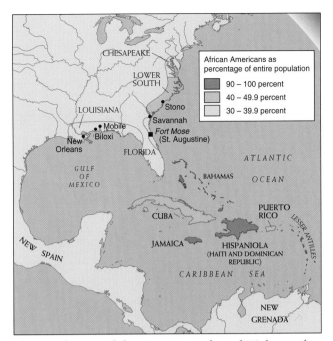

Slave Colonies of the Seventeenth and Eighteenth Centuries   *By the eighteenth century the system of slavery had created societies with large African populations throughout the Caribbean and along the southern coast of North America.*

Portrait of Olaudah Equiano, *by an unknown English artist, ca. 1780. Captured in Nigeria in 1756 when he was eleven years old, Equiano was transported to America and eventually purchased by an English sea captain. After ten years as a slave, he succeeded in buying his own freedom and dedicated himself to the antislavery cause. His book,* The Interesting Narrative of the Life of Olaudah Equiano *(1789), was published in numerous editions, translated into several languages, and became the prototype for dozens of other slave narratives in the nineteenth century.*

Portuguese established a colony in Angola. By the early eighteenth century more than two dozen trading forts dotted the 220 miles of the Gold Coast alone. As the slave trade peaked in the middle of the century, however, the forts of trading companies gave way to small coastal clusters of huts where independent traders set up operations with the cooperation of local headmen or chiefs.

This informal manner of trading offered opportunities for small operators, such as the New England slavers who entered the trade in the early eighteenth century. Often bartering rum or salt fish for human beings, these Yankees earned a reputation for crafty dealings. They came by it honestly: "Water your rum as much as possible," one New England merchant instructed his captain, "and sell as much by the short measure as you can." At first, most New England slavers sailed principally from Massachusetts, but after 1750 the center shifted to Rhode Island. Many great New England fortunes were built from profits in the slave trade.

The Shock of Enslavement

The slave trade was a collaboration between European or American and African traders. Dependent on the favor of local rulers, many colonial slave traders lived permanently in coastal forts and married African women, reinforcing their commercial ties with family relations. In many areas a mixed-ancestry group became prominent in the coastal slave trade. Continuing the

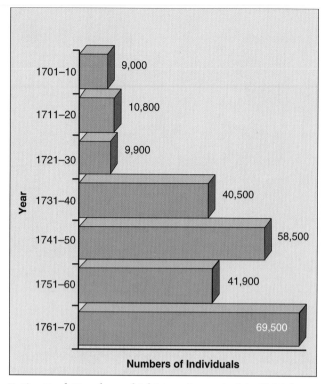

Estimated Number of Africans Imported to British North America, 1701–1775   *These official British statistics include only slaves imported legally and consequently undercount the total number who arrived on American shores. But the trend over time is clear. With the exception of the 1750s, when the British colonies were engulfed by the Seven Years War, the slave trade continued to rise in importance in the decades before the Revolution.*

Source: R. C. Simmons, The American Colonies: From Settlement to Independence (London: Longman, 1976), 186.

practice of the Portuguese, the grim business of slave raiding was left to the Africans themselves. Slaves were not at all reticent about condemning the participation of their fellow Africans. "I must own to the shame of my own countrymen," wrote Ottobah Cugoano, who was sold into slavery in the mid-eighteenth century, "that I was first kidnapped and betrayed by [those of] my own complexion."

Most Africans were enslaved through warfare. Sometimes large armies launched massive attacks, burning whole towns and taking hundreds of prisoners. More common were smaller raids in which a group of armed men attacked at nightfall, seized everyone within reach, then escaped with their captives. However, kidnapping, called *panyaring* in the jargon of the slave trade, was also common. One seaman, ashore while his slave ship awaited its cargo, amused himself by peeking at a young African woman bathing. Suddenly two raiders jumped from the bushes and dragged her off. He later saw them carry her on board and sell her to the captain, no questions asked.

As the demand for slaves increased in the eighteenth century with the expansion of the plantation system in the Americas, raids extended deeper and deeper into the African interior. The march to the coast was filled with terrors. One account describes a two-month trip in which many captives died of hunger, thirst, or exhaustion, several attempted suicide, and the whole party was forced to hide to avoid being seized by a rival band of raiders. The captives finally arrived on the coast, where they were sold to an American vessel bound for South Carolina.

Enslavement was an unparalleled shock. Venture Smith, an African born in Guinea in 1729, was eight years old when he was captured. After many years in North American slavery, he still vividly recalled the attack on his village, the torture and murder of his father, and the long march of his people to the coast. "The shocking scene is to this day fresh in my mind," he wrote, "and I have often been overcome while thinking on it." The horror was captured in the song of captives marching to the Slave Coast from the interior kingdom of Bornu, imploring the assistance of one of their gods, a song long remembered by African Americans and published by abolitionists in the nineteenth century:

> *Bornu-land was rich and good,*
> *Wells of water, fields of food;*
> *Bornu-land we see no longer,*
> *Here we thirst, and here we hunger,*
> *Here the Moor man smites in anger;*
> *Where are we going, Rubee?*
> *Where are we going? Where are we going?*
> *Hear us, save us, Rubee!*
> *Moons of marches from our eyes,*
> *Bornu-land behind us lies;*
> *Hot the desert wind is blowing,*
> *Wild the waves of sand are flowing!*
> *Hear us! Tell us, where are we going?*
> *Where are we going, Rubee?*

On the coast, European traders and African raiders assembled their captives. Prisoners waited in dark dungeons or in open pens called barracoons. To lessen the possibility of collective resistance, traders split up families and ethnic groups. Captains carefully inspected each man and woman, and those selected for transport were branded on the back or buttocks with the mark of the buyer. Olaudah Equiano remembered that "those white men with horrible looks, red faces, and long hair, looked and acted...in so savage a manner;...I had never seen among any people such instances of brutal cruelty." Equiano's narrative, written during the 1780s, after he had secured his freedom, is one of the few that

A slave coffle in an eighteenth-century print. As the demand for slaves increased, raids extended deeper and deeper into the African interior. Tied together with forked logs or bark rope, men, women, and children were marched hundreds of miles toward the coast, where their African captors traded them to Europeans.

provide an African account of enslavement. He and his fellow captives became convinced that they "had got into a world of bad spirits" and were about to be eaten by cannibals. A French trader wrote that many prisoners were "positively prepossessed with the opinion that we transport them into our country in order to kill and eat them."

The Middle Passage

In the eighteenth century English sailors christened the voyage of slave ships the Middle Passage, the middle part of a triangle from England to Africa, Africa to America, and America back to England. From coastal forts and barracoons, crews rowed small groups of slaves out to the waiting ships and packed them into shelves below deck only six feet long by two and a half feet high. "Rammed like herring in a barrel," wrote one observer, slaves were "chained to each other hand and foot, and stowed so close, that they were not allowed above a foot and a half for each in breadth." People were forced to sleep "spoon fashion," and the tossing of the ship knocked them about so violently that the skin over their elbows sometimes was worn to the bone from scraping on the planks.

Slavers debated the merits of various packing strategies. One camp argued that additional room lessened mortality and thus increased profits. But the great demand and the price for slaves in the mid-eighteenth century gave the upper hand to the "tight packers," those willing to risk life in order to carry as many men and women as possible. One ship designed to carry 450 slaves regularly crossed the Atlantic with more

than 600. Their holds filled with human cargo, the ships headed toward Cape Verde to catch the trade winds blowing toward America. A favorable voyage from Senegambia to Barbados might be accomplished in as little as three weeks, but a ship from Guinea or Angola becalmed in the doldrums or driven back by storms might take as much as three months.

The voyage was marked by a daily routine. In the morning the crew opened the hatch and brought the captives on deck, attaching their leg irons to a great chain running the length of the bulwarks. After a breakfast of beans came a ritual known as "dancing the slave": while an African thumped an upturned kettle or plucked a banjo, the crew commanded men and women to jump up and down in a bizarre session of exercise. A day spent chained on deck was concluded by a second bland meal and then the stowing away. During the night, according to one seaman, there issued from below "a howling melancholy noise, expressive of extreme anguish." Down in the hold the groans of the dying, the shrieks of women and children, and the suffocating heat and stench combined to create, in the words of Olaudah Equiano, "a scene of horror almost inconceivable."

Among the worst of the horrors was the absence of adequate sanitation. There were "necessary tubs" set below deck, but Africans, "endeavoring to get to them, tumble over their companions," one eighteenth-century ship's surgeon wrote, "and as the necessities of nature are not to be resisted, they ease themselves as they lie." Efficient captains ordered crews to scrape and swab the holds daily, but so sickening was the task that on many ships it was rarely performed and the captive Africans were forced to lie in their own urine and feces. When first taken below deck, the boy Equiano remembered, "I received such a salutation in my nostrils as I had never experienced in my life," and "became so sick and low that I was not able to eat." Atlantic sailors said you could "smell a slaver five miles down wind." Many captives sickened and died in these conditions. Many others contracted dysentery, known as the "flux." Frequent shipboard epidemics of smallpox, measles, and yellow fever added to the misery. Historians estimate that during the Middle Passage of the eighteenth century at least one in every six Africans perished.

Slaves below deck on a Spanish slaver, a sketch made when the vessel was captured by a British warship in the early nineteenth century. Slaves were "stowed so close, that they were not allowed above a foot and a half for each in breadth," wrote one observer. The close quarters and unsanitary conditions created a stench so bad that Atlantic sailors said you could "smell a slaver five miles down wind."

slavers sometimes paraded Africans off the ship to the tune of an accordion or the beat of a drum. But the toll taken by the Middle Passage was difficult to disguise. One observer described a disembarking group as "walking skeletons covered over with a piece of tanned leather."

Some cargoes were destined for a single wealthy planter or consigned to a merchant who sold the captives in return for a commission; in other cases the captain himself was responsible. Buyers painstakingly examined the Africans, who once again suffered the indignity of probing eyes and poking fingers. This caused "much dread and trembling among us," wrote Equiano, and "bitter cries." In ports like Charleston sales were generally made either by auction or by a method known as the scramble.

The unwilling voyagers offered plenty of resistance. As long as ships were still within sight of the African coast, hope remained alive and the danger of revolt was great. One historian has found references to fifty-five slave revolts on British and American ships between 1699 and 1845. Once on the open sea, however, captives' resistance took a more desperate form. The sight of the disappearing coast of Africa "left me abandoned to despair," wrote Equiano; "I now saw myself deprived of all chance of returning to my native country, or even the least glimpse of hope of gaining the shore." He witnessed several Africans jump overboard and drown, "and I believe many more would very soon have done the same if they had not been prevented by the ship's crew." Captains took the precaution of spreading netting along the sides of their ships. "Could I have got over the nettings," Equiano declared, "I would have jumped over the side."

Arrival in the New World

As the ship approached its destination, the crew made the human cargo presentable, preparing it for market. All but the most rebellious of Africans were freed from their chains and allowed to wash themselves and move about the deck. One account describes the ship's surgeon plugging captives' rectums with clumps of hemp fiber to prevent potential buyers from seeing the bloody discharge, a symptom of the flux. To impress buyers,

In the scramble, standard prices were set in advance for men, women, boys, and girls. Then the Africans were driven into a corral, and at a signal the buyers rushed among them, grabbing their pick of the lot. The noise, clamor, and eagerness of the buyers, Equiano remembered, renewed all the terrible apprehensions of the Africans. "In this manner, without scruple, are relations and friends separated, most of them never to see each other again." Bought by a Virginian, Equiano was taken to an isolated tobacco plantation where he found himself unable to communicate with any of his fellow slaves, who came from other ethnic groups.

Political and Economic Effects on Africa

Africa began the sixteenth century with genuine independence. But as surely as Europe and America grew stronger as a result of the trade and the labor of slaves, so Africa grew weaker by their loss. In the short term, slave-trading kingdoms on the coast increased their power at the expense of interior states. Thus the interior West African state of Songhai gave way to the Gold Coast state of Akwamu. In the Niger delta the slaving states of Nembe, Bonny, and Kalabari arose, and to the south the kingdom of Imbangala drew slaves from central Africa. But these coastal states found that the slave trade was a viper that could easily strike back at them. "Merchants daily seize our own subjects, sons of the land and sons of our noblemen, they grab them and cause them to be sold," King Dom Affonso of the Kongo wrote to the Portuguese monarch in the sixteenth century; "and so great, Sir, is their corruption and licentiousness that our country is being utterly depopulated."

With the loss of millions of men and women over the centuries, the West African economy stagnated. Labor was drawn away from farming and other productive activities, and imported consumer goods such as textiles and metalwares stifled local manufacturing. African traders were expert at driving a hard bargain, and over several centuries they gained an increasing price for slaves—the result of rising demand and increased competition among European slavers. But even when they appeared to get the best of the transaction, the ultimate advantage lay with the Europeans, who in exchange for mere consumer goods got human capital—wealth-producing workers.

For every man or woman taken captive, at least another died in the chronic slave raiding. Many of the new West African states became little more than machines for supplying captives to European traders, and a "gun-slave cycle" pushed neighboring kingdoms into a destructive arms race. The resulting political and cultural demoralization prepared the way for the European conquest of Africa in the nineteenth century. The leaders of West Africa during the centuries of slave trad-

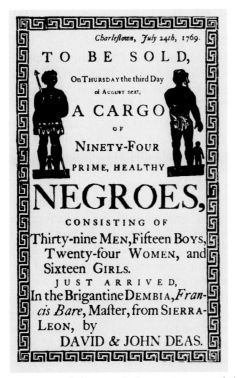

The announcement of the arrival of a consignment of slaves in Charleston, South Carolina, in 1769, where the most common method of sale was by auction. Men and women alike were subjected to intimate inspection before the bidding began. Buyers were quite interested in the ethnic origins of slaves but gave little concern to keeping family members together.

ing, writes the Nigerian poet Chinweizu, "had been too busy organizing our continent for the exploitative advantage of Europe, had been too busy with slaving raids upon one another, too busy decorating themselves with trinkets imported from Europe, too busy impoverishing and disorganizing the land, to take thought and long-range action to protect our sovereignty."

THE DEVELOPMENT OF NORTH AMERICAN SLAVE SOCIETIES

New World slavery was nearly two centuries old before it became an important system of labor in North America. There were slaves in each of the British colonies during the seventeenth century, but in 1700 they constituted only 11 percent of the colonial population. During the eighteenth century slavery greatly expanded, and by 1770 Africans and African Americans in British North America numbered 460,000, or more than 20 percent of the colonial population.

Slavery Comes to North America

The first Africans in Virginia arrived in 1619 when a Dutch slave trader exchanged "20 and odd Negroes" for badly needed provisions. But because slaves generally cost twice as much as indentured servants yet had the same appallingly short life expectancy—because of the frequent epidemics of diseases such as typhoid fever—they offered planters little economic benefit. Consequently, only a relatively small number were brought to Virginia over the next several decades. In fact, there are indications that those Africans who worked in the tobacco fields were not slaves at all, but servants.

An interesting case illustrates the ambiguous status of black Virginians. In 1654 the African John Castor told a local court that "he came unto Virginia for seven or eight years of indenture, yet Anthony Johnson his Master had kept him his servant seven years longer than he should or ought." Johnson claimed that "he had the Negro for his life." The court decided in the master's favor. But strange to say, Johnson himself was an African. He had arrived in 1621 as an indentured servant but achieved his freedom and succeeded in becoming a landowner. Property records reveal that other Africans acquired farms and servants or slaves of their own. Moreover, sexual relations among Africans, Indians, and Europeans produced a sizable group of free people of mixed ancestry known as mulattoes. It was only later that dark skin came to mean slavery, segregation, and lack of rights. Although there surely were slaves among the population in the early years, the first recorded instances of slavery date from around 1640.

In the last quarter of the seventeenth century, however, a number of developments encouraged the expansion of true slavery. As European immigrants discovered opportunities to establish themselves as free farmers in colonies such as Pennsylvania, it became increasingly difficult for southern masters to recruit them as indentured servants. Moreover, after Bacon's Rebellion and the other social conflicts of the 1670s, many colonial leaders began to worry about potential rebellions among former indentured servants in the back country. Because people were living longer, possibly the result of being better fed and more resistant to disease, more servants were surviving their indentures. But these improvements in living conditions also affected Africans, increasing their rates of survival, and planters began to see more advantage in the purchase of slaves. During these same years, the supply of slaves in North America increased when the Royal African Company inaugurated direct shipments from West Africa to the mainland.

Thus the workforce of indentured servants was gradually replaced by a workforce of slaves. By 1700 the number of African slaves had probably surpassed the number of indentured servants. There were some 19,000 Africans in Maryland and Virginia,

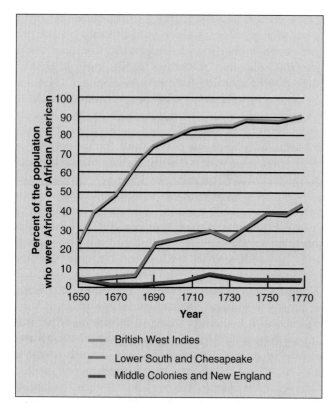

Africans as a Percentage of Total Population of the British Colonies, 1650–1770 *Although the proportion of Africans and African Americans was never as high in the South as in the Caribbean, the ethnic structure of the South diverged radically from that of the North during the eighteenth century.*

Source: Robert W. Fogel and Stanley L. Engerman, *Time on the Cross* (Boston: Little, Brown, 1974), 21.

about 22 percent of the population. In South Carolina, where indentured servants had never been an important part of the labor force, Africans constituted over 40 percent of the settler population by the end of the seventeenth century.

As the proportions of slaves in the colonial population rose, colonists wrote slavery into law, a process best observed in the case of Virginia. In 1662 colonial officials declared that children inherited the status of their slave mothers; five years later they added that baptism could no longer alter conditions of servitude. Two important avenues to freedom were thus closed. The colony then placed life-threatening violence in the hands of masters, declaring in 1669 that the death of a slave during punishment "shall not be accounted felony." Such regulations accumulated piecemeal until, in 1705, they were gathered together in the comprehensive Virginia Slave Code that became a model for other colonies.

Thus the institution of slavery was strengthened just as the Atlantic slave trade reached flood tide in the eighteenth century. During that century's first decade, more Africans were imported into North America than the total number for the preceding ninety-three years of colonial history. The English colonies were primed for an unprecedented growth of plantation slavery.

The Tobacco Colonies

During the eighteenth century the European demand for tobacco increased more than tenfold. This demand was largely supplied by increased production in the Chesapeake. Tobacco plantations spread through all sections of the sea-level coastal region known as the Tidewater, extending from the colony of Delaware south through Maryland and Virginia into the Albemarle Sound region of North Carolina. Planters eventually extended their operations above the "fall line," where waterfalls or rapids mark the end of the Tidewater and the beginning of the foothill region known as the Piedmont. Tobacco was far and away the single most important commodity produced in North America, accounting for more than a quarter of the value of all colonial exports.

The expansion of tobacco production could not have taken place without an enormous growth in the size of the slave labor force. Unlike sugar, tobacco did not require large plantations and could be produced successfully on relatively small farms. But it was a crop that demanded a great deal of hand labor and close attention, and from the beginnings of Chesapeake colonization its cultivation had been the responsibility of indentured servants and slaves. As tobacco farming grew, slaveholding became widespread. By midcentury slaves were included in a majority of upcountry households and as many as three-quarters of the households in the Tidewater. Tobacco farms varied in size, from small establishments where farmers worked side by side with one or two slaves, to large, self-sufficient plantations with dozens of slaves. By 1770 more than a quarter of a million slaves labored in the colonies of the Upper South, and because of the exploding market for tobacco, their numbers were expanding at something like double the rate of the general population.

Shipments from Africa thus accounted for part of the growth of the slave population. From 1700 to 1770 a total of perhaps 80,000 Africans were imported into the Chesapeake colonies, but natural increase in this region was much more important. Indeed, in the 1730s the slave population of the Chesapeake was the first in the Western Hemisphere to achieve self-sustained growth. In the Caribbean and Brazil, where the profits from sugar plantations were high, many masters worked their slaves literally to death, replacing them with a constant stream of new arrivals from Africa. These landowners figured that they could make greater profits through extreme exploitation of the labor force than by creating the better living and working conditions that would allow Africans to reproduce at normal rates. In contrast, in Virginia lower rates of profit may have caused tobacco planters to pay more attention to the health of their labor force, establishing work routines that were not so deadly. Food supplies were also more plentiful in North America than in the Caribbean, where nearly every morsel had to be imported, and the better-fed Chesapeake populations of Africans were more resistant to disease. Historians continue to debate these important differences. But whatever the causes, self-sustained population growth among Chesapeake slaves had begun by the 1730s, and by the 1770s the majority of them were "country-born."

The Lower South

For fifty years after the founding of the South Carolina colony in 1670, the area outside the immediate region of Charleston remained a rough and dangerous frontier. English settlers raised cattle, often using slaves with experience in the pastoral economies of West Africa. Others engaged in the deerskin trade, bartering English

An Overseer Doing His Duty, *a watercolor sketch made by Benjamin Henry Latrobe during a trip to Virginia in 1798. The majority of masters in the tobacco region owned only one or two slaves and worked with them in the fields. In his portrayal of this overseer, relaxing as he supervises his workers, Latrobe clearly expressed his disgust for slavery.*

Benjamin Henry Latrobe, An Overseer Doing His Duty. Watercolor on paper. Collection of the Maryland Historical Society, Baltimore.

goods with the numerous Indian people of the back-country. But in terms of sheer profit, the most valuable part of the early Carolina economy was the Indian slave trade. Practicing a strategy of divide and conquer, in which they encouraged Indian tribes to fight one another, Carolinians enslaved tens of thousands of Indians before the 1730s. Because Indian slaves were dangerous as long as they were near their homelands, most were shipped off to other colonies.

By 1715, as the opening of this chapter illustrates, rice production had become the most dynamic sector of the South Carolina economy, and, like cattle grazing, it depended on the expertise of West Africans. Another important crop was added in the 1740s, when Elizabeth Lucas Pinckney, a young South Carolina woman, successfully adapted West Indian indigo to the low-country climate. It is likely that here as well, the assistance of West Indian slaves skilled in indigo culture was crucial. The indigo plant, native to India, produced

TOBACCO AND RICE EXPORTS TO ENGLAND (IN THOUSANDS OF POUNDS)		
	Tobacco	Rice
1700	37,840	304
1725	21,046	5,367
1750	51,339	16,667
1775	55,968	57,692

Thomas Coram. *Residence and Slave Quarters of Mulberry Plantation*. Oil on paper, 10 × 17.6 cm. Gibbes Museum of Art. Carolina Art Association.

Residence and Slave Quarters of Mulberry Plantation, by Thomas Coram, ca. 1770. The slave quarters are on the left in this painting of a rice plantation near Charleston, South Carolina. The steep roofs of the slave cabins, an African architectural feature introduced in America by slave builders, kept living quarters cool by allowing the heat to rise and dissipate in the rafters.

a deep blue dye important in textile manufacture. Rice grew in the lowlands, but indigo could be cultivated on high ground. And because they had different seasonal growing patterns, the two crops harmonized perfectly. Rice and indigo production rose steadily over the next thirty years. By the 1770s they were among the most valuable commodities exported from the mainland colonies of North America.

Like tobacco, the expansion of rice and indigo production depended on the growth of African slavery. Before the importation of slaves to the United States ended in 1808, at least 100,000 Africans had arrived at Charleston. One of every five ancestors of today's African Americans passed through that port on his or her way to the rice and indigo fields.

By the 1740s many of the arriving Africans were being taken to Georgia, a colony created by an act of the English Parliament in 1732. Its leader, James Edward Oglethorpe, hoped to establish a buffer against Spanish invasion from Florida and to create a haven for poor British farmers who could then sell their products in the markets of South Carolina. Under Oglethorpe's influence, Parliament agreed to prohibit slavery in Georgia, but soon the colony's coastal regions were being settled by South Carolina planters with their slaves. In 1752 Oglethorpe and Georgia's trustees abandoned their experiment, and the colony was opened to slavery under royal authority. The Georgia coast had already become an extension of the Carolina low-country slave system.

By 1770 there were nearly 90,000 African Americans in the Lower South, about 80 percent of the population of coastal South Carolina and Georgia. The slave economy of the Lower South was dominated by large plantations, which had between fifty and seventy-five slaves each. The slaves' work was hard, but the task system, described at the beginning of this chapter, gave them a measure of control over their own lives. The African American communities of the Lower South, like those of the Chesapeake, achieved self-sustained growth by the middle of the eighteenth century.

Slavery in the Spanish Colonies

Slavery was basic to the Spanish colonial labor system, yet doubts about the enslavement of Africans were raised by both the Church and the crown. The papacy many times denounced slavery as a violation of Christian principles, and many priests condemned the institution. The

Catholic Church in Spanish America, however, owned slaves and profited from their labor. The slave system remained intact, and by later in the eighteenth century, when sugar production expanded in Cuba, it had become as brutal there as elsewhere in the Americas.

Still, the character of slavery varied with local conditions. One of the most benign forms operated in Florida, where Spanish colonization was undertaken primarily to create a buffer against the English. In 1699 the Spanish declared Florida a refuge for escaped slaves from the English colonies, offering free land to any fugitives who would help defend the colony and convert to Catholicism. Over the next half-century, refugee Indians and fugitive Africans established many communities in the countryside surrounding St. Augustine. North of the city, Fort Mose was manned by Negro troops commanded by their own officers. Slaves could be found in many Florida settlements, but the conditions of their servitude resembled the household slavery common in Mediterranean and African communities more than the plantation slavery of the British colonies.

In New Mexico, the Spanish depended on the forced labor of Indians. In the sixteenth century the colonial governor sent Indian workers to the mines of Mexico. And the requirement that Pueblo people labor for Spaniards was one of the causes of the Pueblo Revolt (see Chapter 3). During the eighteenth century, the Spanish were much more cautious in their treatment of the Pueblos, who were officially considered Catholics. But they captured and enslaved "infidel Indians" such as the Apaches or nomads from the Great Plains, using them as house servants and field workers.

French Louisiana

Slavery was also important in Louisiana, the colony founded by the French in the lower Mississippi Valley in the early eighteenth century. After Robert Sieur de La Salle's voyage down the Mississippi River in 1681–82, the French planned colonies to anchor their New World empire. In the early eighteenth century French Canadians established bases at Biloxi and Mobile on the Gulf of Mexico, but it was not until 1718 that they laid out the city of New Orleans on the Mississippi delta. Upriver, colonists established an alliance with the powerful Choctaw nation, and with their assistance defeated an opposing confederacy of Chickasaw and Natchez Indians during the 1720s and 1730s.

By 1750 several thousand French colonists, many from New France and the Caribbean, had established farms and plantations on the Gulf coast and in a narrow strip along the Mississippi River. Soon they were exporting rice, indigo, and tobacco, in addition to furs and skins for which they had traded with back-country Indians. Like the Spanish in St. Augustine, however, the French were more interested in defend-

ing their access to the Mississippi against rival colonial threats than in commerce and export. Consequently, African slaves amounted to no more than a third of the colonial population of 10,000. It was not until the end of the eighteenth century that the colony of Louisiana became an important North American slave society.

Slavery in the North

North of the Chesapeake, slavery was much less important. Slaves worked on some farms, but almost never in groups, and they were principally concentrated in port cities. Slaves were first shipped to Philadelphia in the 1680s, and a visitor to the city in 1750 noted that slaves were bought "by almost everyone who could afford [them]." Together with a small group of free blacks, slaves then made up about 9 percent of the city's population.

It was the Quakers, many of whom had themselves kept slaves, who voiced the first antislavery sentiment in the colonies. In *Considerations on the Keeping of Negroes* (1754), John Woolman pointed to the Bible's declaration that all peoples were of one blood. He urged his readers to imagine themselves in the place of the African people:

> Suppose that our ancestors and we had been exposed to constant servitude in the more servile and inferior employments of life; that we had been destitute of the help of reading and good company; that amongst ourselves we had had few wise and pious instructors; that the religious amongst our superiors seldom took notice of us; that while others in ease have plentifully heaped up the fruit of our labour, we had received barely enough to relieve nature, and being wholly at the command of others had generally been treated as a contemptible, ignorant part of mankind. Should we, in that case, be less abject than they now are?

It was not until the Revolution, however, that antislavery sentiment became more widespread.

In New York slavery was somewhat more important. By 1770, New York and New Jersey were home to some 27,000 African Americans, about 10 percent of these colonies' respective populations. Black people were concentrated even more highly in New York City. A British naval officer stationed in the port during the 1750s observed that "the laborious people in general are Guinea negroes." In 1770, 3,000 slaves and 100 free blacks, about 17 percent of the population, lived in the city. The most important center of slavery in the North, however, was Newport, Rhode Island. In 1760 African Americans there made up about 20 percent of the population, a concentration resulting from that port's dominance of the

Abby Aldrich Rockefeller Folk Art Center, Williamsburg, Virginia.

This eighteenth-century painting depicts a celebration in the slave quarters on a South Carolina plantation. The dance—known as "jumping the broomstick"—may have originated in Africa, and the stringed instrument was an African mbanza, which evolved into the "banjo."

Africans. Olaudah Equiano remembered his people, the Ibos, as "a nation of dancers, musicians, and poets," and Thomas Jefferson, raised on a Virginia plantation, wrote that blacks "are more generally gifted than the whites, with accurate ears for tune and time." Many Africans were accomplished players of stringed instruments and drums, and their style featured improvisation and rhythmic complexity—elements that would become prominent in African American music. In America, slaves re-created African instruments—the banjo is an example—and mastered the art of the European violin and guitar. Fearing that slaves might communicate by code, authorities frequently outlawed drums. But using bones, spoons, or sticks or simply "patting juba" (slapping their thighs), slaves produced elaborate multirhythmic patterns.

One of the most important developments of the eighteenth century was the invention of African American language. An English traveler during the 1770s complained he could not understand Virginia slaves, who spoke "a mixed dialect between the Guinea and English." But such a language made it possible for "country-born" and "salt-water" Africans to communicate. The two most important dialects were Gullah and Geeche, named after two of the African peoples most prominent in the Carolina and Georgia low country, the Golas and Gizzis of the Windward Coast. These creole languages were a transitional phenomenon, gradually giving way to distinctive forms of so-called black English, although in certain isolated areas like the sea islands of the Carolinas and Georgia they persisted into the twentieth century.

The Africanization of the South

The African American community often looked to recently arrived Africans for religious leadership. Ancestor worship, divination, and magic were strengthened by constant African infusions through the eighteenth century. Many of these beliefs and practices had much in common with European folklore, especially magic and medicinal lore. In 1729 the governor of Virginia agreed to free one of his elderly slaves, "who has performed many wonderful cures of diseases," after the man revealed the secret formulas of his medical magic. Throughout the South, many whites had as much faith in slave conjurers and herb doctors as the slaves themselves did, one example of the many ways in which white and black Southerners came to share a common culture. Acculturation was by no means a one-way street; English men and women in the South were also being Africanized.

Slaves worked in the kitchens of their masters and thus introduced an African style of cooking into colonial diets already transformed by the addition of Indian crops. African American culinary arts are responsible for such southern specialties as barbecue, fried chicken, black-eyed peas, and various greens including collard and mustard. And the liberal African use of red pepper, sesame seeds, and other sharp flavors established the southern preference for highly spiced foods. In Louisiana, a combination of African, French, and Indian elements produced a most distinctive American regional cuisine, exemplified by gumbos (soups) and jambalayas (stews).

Mutual acculturation is also evident in many aspects of material culture. Southern basket weaving used Indian techniques and African designs. Woodcarving often featured African motifs. African architectural designs featuring high, peaked roofs (to drain off the heat) and broad, shady porches gradually became part of a distinctive southern style. The West African ironworking tradition was evident throughout the South, especially in the ornamentation of the homes of Charleston and New Orleans.

Even more important were less tangible aspects of culture. Slave mothers nursed white children as well as their own. As one English observer wrote, "each child has its [black] Momma, whose gestures and accent it will necessarily copy, for children, we all know, are imitative beings." In this way, many Africanisms passed into the English language of the South: "goober" (peanut), "yam," "banjo," "okay," "tote." Some linguists have argued that the Southern "drawl," evident among both black and white speakers, derived from the incorporation of African intonations of words and syllables.

African American music and dance also deeply affected white culture. These art forms offer a good example of mutual acculturation. At eighteenth-century plantation dances, the music was usually provided by Africans playing European instruments and their own, such as the banjo. African American fiddlers were common throughout the South by the time of the Revolution, but the banjo also became the characteristic folk instrument of the white South. Toward the end of the evening, the musicians were often told to play some "Negro jigs," and slaves were asked to demonstrate the African manner of dancing. They sometimes parodied the elegant and rigid dances of their masters, while whites in turn attempted to imitate African rhythmic dance styles. In such a back-and-forth fashion the traditions of both groups were gradually transformed.

Violence and Resistance

Slavery was based on the use of force and violence. Fear underlay the daily life of both masters and slaves. Some owners were humane, but even the kindest could be cruel, and slaves had no guarantees of benevolent treatment. Even the most broad-minded plantation owners of the eighteenth century thought nothing about floggings of fifty or seventy-five lashes. "Der prayer was answered," sang the Africans of South Carolina, "wid de song of a whip." Although the typical planter punished slaves with extra work, public humiliation, or solitary confinement, the threat of the lash was omnipresent. There were also sadistic masters who stabbed, burned, maimed, mutilated, raped, or castrated their slaves.

Yet African Americans demonstrated a resisting spirit. In their day-to-day existence they often refused to cooperate: they malingered, they mistreated tools and animals, they "accidentally" destroyed the master's property.

Flight was also an option, and judging from the advertisements placed by masters in colonial newspapers, even the most trusted Africans ran away. "That this slave should run away and attempt getting his liberty, is very alarming," read the notice of one Maryland master in 1755. "He has always been too kindly used" and was "one in whom his master has put great confidence, and depended on him to overlook the rest of the slaves, and he had no kind of provocation to go off." A South Carolinian noted that his absent slave "may possibly have a ticket that I gave him, mentioning he was in quest of a runaway, [and] as I did not mention when he was to return, he may endeavour to pass by that." An analysis of hundreds of eighteenth-century advertisements for runaways reveals that 80 percent of them were men, most in their twenties, suggesting that flight was an option primarily for young, unattached men.

Runaways were sometimes called *maroons* from the Spanish *cimarrón*, meaning "wild and untamed." The African communities in Spanish Florida were often referred to as maroon colonies. Indeed, as a whole these mixed African and Creek Indian Florida peoples called themselves Seminoles, a name deriving from their pronunciation of *cimarrón*. Maroons also settled in the backcountry of the Lower South. In 1771, Georgia's governor warned that north of Savannah "a great number of fugitive Negroes had committed many robberies and insults," and he sent a detachment of

Fugitive slaves flee through the swamps in Thomas Moran's Slave Hunt (1862). Many slaves ran away from their masters, and colonial newspapers included notices urging readers to be on the lookout for them. Some fled in groups or collected together in isolated communities called "maroon colonies," located in inaccessible swamps and woods.

militia to destroy their camps. The "black Indian" violence continued, however, and reached catastrophic proportions during the Revolution. Although maroons were less common in the Upper South, a number of fugitive communities existed in the Great Dismal Swamp between Virginia and North Carolina. In the 1730s a group of escaped Africans built a community of grass houses and set up a tribal government there, but they were soon dispersed by the authorities.

The most direct form of resistance was revolt. In the Lower South, where slaves were a majority of the population, there were isolated but violent slave uprisings in 1704, 1720, and 1730. Then in 1738 a series of violent revolts throughout South Carolina and Georgia proved but a prelude to the largest slave rebellion of the colonial period. In September 1739, a group of twenty recently arrived Angolans sacked the armory in Stono, South Carolina. Arming themselves, they began marching toward Florida and freedom. Beating drums to attract other slaves to their cause, they grew to nearly a hundred. Along the way they plundered several planters' homes and killed some thirty colonists. Pausing in a field to celebrate their victory with dance and song, they were overtaken by the militia and destroyed in a pitched battle. That same year there was an uprising in Georgia, probably inspired by the Stono Rebellion, and the next year another took place in South Carolina. Attributing these revolts to the influence of newly arrived Africans, colonial officials shut off the slave trade through Charleston for the next ten years.

The second notable slave uprising of the colonial era occurred in New York City in 1712. Taking an oath of secrecy, twenty-three Africans vowed revenge for what they called the "hard usage" of their masters. They armed themselves with guns, swords, daggers, and hatchets, killed nine colonists, and burned several buildings before being surrounded by the militia. Six of the conspirators committed suicide rather than surrender. Those captured were hanged, burned at the stake, or broken on the wheel. In 1741 New York authorities uncovered what they thought was another conspiracy. Thirteen black leaders were burned alive, eighteen hanged, and eighty sold and shipped off to the West Indies. A family of colonists and a Catholic priest, accused of providing weapons, were also executed.

Wherever masters held slaves, fears of uprisings persisted. But compared with such slave colonies as Jamaica, Guiana, or Brazil, there were few slave revolts in North America. The conditions favoring revolt—large African majorities, brutal exploitation with correspondingly low survival rates, little acculturation, and geographic isolation—prevailed only in some areas of the Lower South. The very success of African Americans in British North America at establishing families, communities, and a stake in a culture of their own may have made them less likely to risk rebellion.

SLAVERY AND THE STRUCTURE OF EMPIRE

Slavery contributed enormously to the economic growth and development of Europe during the colonial era, and it was an especially important factor in Great Britain's industrial revolution in the eighteenth century. Slavery was the most dynamic force in the Atlantic economy during that century, creating the conditions for industrialization. But because colonists in the South single-mindedly committed their slave resources to the expansion and extension of the plantation system, they derived very little benefit from the economic diversification that characterized industrialization.

Slavery the Mainspring

The slave colonies accounted for 95 percent of exports from the Americas to Great Britain from 1714 to 1773. Most productive were the sugar plantations of the British West Indies (64 percent of total exports), followed by the rice, indigo, and tobacco fields of the mainland South (31 percent). Although approximately half of all Great Britain's American colonists lived in New England and the mid-Atlantic, the colonies in those regions

BRITISH COLONIAL TRADE IN THE AMERICAS, 1714–1773 (IN THOUSANDS OF BRITISH POUNDS STERLING)				
	Exports to Britain		Imports from Britain	
	£	%	£	%
British West Indies	96,808	64.0	41,653	38.8
Lower South and Chesapeake	47,192	31.2	27,561	25.7
Middle Colonies and New England	7,160	4.7	37,939	35.4
Total	151,160	99.9	107,153	99.9

Source: Eric Williams, *Capitalism and Slavery* (Chapel Hill: University of North Carolina Press, 1944), 225–26.

contributed less than 5 percent of total exports during this period. Moreover, there was the prime economic importance of the slave trade itself, which one economist of the day described as the "foundation" of the British economy, "the mainspring of the machine which sets every wheel in motion." According to another English writer, slavery was "the strength and sinews of this western world." This point is so important it bears repeating: it was the labor of African slaves that made the British empire in the Americas a success.

The profits of individual investors in the slave system varied widely, of course. Slave traders expected a return of 30 percent or more, but many ventures ended in financial disaster. Profits in sugar production during the boom of the seventeenth century easily exceeded 20 percent, but returns fell during the succeeding century. As late as 1776, however, the British economist Adam Smith wrote that "the profits of a sugar plantation in any of our West Indian colonies are generally much greater than those of any other cultivation that is known either in Europe or America." Economic historians estimate that annual profits during the eighteenth century averaged 15 percent of invested capital in the slave trade, 10 percent in plantation agriculture. Some of the first of England's great modern fortunes were made out of slavery's miseries.

The most obvious and direct economic effect of slavery was on the growth of transport: in the eighteenth century better than 10 percent of all English shipping was devoted to the African and American trades. Ships had to be outfitted and provisioned, trade goods had to be manufactured, and the commodities produced on slave plantations had to be processed. The multiplier effects of these activities are best seen in the growth of English ports such as Liverpool and Bristol. There the African and American trades provided employment for an army of ships' crews, dockmen, construction workers, traders, shopkeepers, lawyers, clerks, factory workers, and

Eighteenth-century ships being unloaded of their colonial cargoes on London's Old Custom House Quay. Most of the goods imported into England from the American colonies were produced by slave labor.

officials of all ranks down to the humblest employees of the customhouse. It was said of Bristol that "there is not a brick in the city but what is cemented with the blood of a slave."

The profits of the slave trade and slave production resulted in huge accumulations of capital, much of it invested in enterprises in these same cities. One historian estimates that in Great Britain alone during the eighteenth century the slave system generated capital valued at more than 300 million pounds. (Although converting monetary values over several centuries is always imprecise, the eighteenth-century British pound sterling was the equivalent in purchasing power of about $85 in 1990s currency; thus, £300 million would be worth about $25 billion.) This capital funded the first modern banks and insurance companies and eventually found its way into a wide range of economic activities. In the countryside surrounding Liverpool, capital acquired through slavery was invested in the cotton textile industry. Later, the demand for raw cotton to supply cotton textile factories led to the further expansion of American plantation slavery. The connections between slavery and the growth of industry were clear and dramatic.

The Politics of Mercantilism

When imperial officials argued that colonies existed solely for the benefit of the mother country, they had in mind principally the great wealth produced by slavery. To ensure that this wealth benefited their states, European imperial powers created a system of regulations that later became known as mercantilism. The essence of mercantilist policy was the political control of the economy by the state. Just as the new monarchs of western Europe had extended their control over the political affairs of their nations, so they sought to use politics to control the national and colonial economy. In the seventeenth century the French finance minister Jean-Baptiste Colbert formulated the most systematic political approach to mercantilism, and the French empire of Louis XIV became the strongest in the world. But in the eighteenth century mercantilist politics were most successfully applied in Great Britain, where the monarchy and Parliament established a uniform national monetary system, regulated workers and the poor by placing controls on wages and requiring the able-bodied to labor in workhouses, provided subsidies to encourage agriculture and manufacturing, and erected tariff barriers to protect themselves from foreign competition. England also sought to organize and control colonial trade to the maximum advantage of its own shippers, merchants, manufacturers, and bureaucrats. Mercantilists scoffed at the idea that the economy should be left to the free operation of the marketplace.

The mercantilists viewed the world economy as a "zero-sum" game in which total economic gains were equal to total losses. As an English mercantilist put it, "There is but a certain proportion of trade in the world." Profits were thought to result from successful speculation, crafty dealing, or simple plunder—all forms of stealing wealth. The institution of slavery proved the theory, for it was nothing more than a highly developed system by which masters stole the labor of slaves. The essence of the competition between nation-states, the mercantilists argued, was the struggle to acquire and hoard the wealth of the world. The nation that accumulated the largest treasure of gold and silver specie would become the most powerful.

Wars for Empire

The mercantilist era was thus a period of intense and violent competition among European nation-states. Wars usually arose out of Old World issues, spilling over into the New, but they also originated in conflicts over the colonies themselves. In the Anglo-Dutch Wars of the 1650s and 1660s, England replaced Holland as the dominant Atlantic power. Then, beginning with King William's War (1689–97), England and France (generally allied with Spain) opened a long struggle for colonial supremacy in North America that was not concluded until 1763. (For discussion of these conflicts, see Chapter 3.) The fighting took place principally at the peripheries of the empire, on the frontiers separating Spanish Florida from British Georgia and New France from New England.

In the southern region, these wars had everything to do with slavery. The first fighting of the eighteenth century took place during Queen Anne's War (known in Europe as the War of the Spanish Succession), a conflict that pitted Great Britain and its allies against France and Spain. In 1702 troops from South Carolina invaded Florida, plundering and burning St. Augustine in an attempt to destroy the refuge for fugitive slaves there. A combined French and Spanish fleet took revenge in 1706 by bombarding Charleston. But the British finally prevailed over the Spanish, and in 1713, as part of the Peace of Utrecht, Great Britain won the exclusive right to supply slaves to the Spanish colonies in the Americas, a very lucrative business.

The entrance of British slavers into Spanish ports provided an opportunity for illicit trade, and sporadic fighting between the two empires broke out a number of times over the next two decades. Robert Walpole, British prime minister from 1721 to 1748, wished to avoid the outbreak of full-scale war, but a faction in the House of Commons that wanted to bring even more slave colonies into the British orbit looked forward to smashing the Spanish in the Caribbean. In 1739, at the urging of these members of Commons, a one-eared sea captain by the name of Jenkins testified before the House to the indignities suffered by British merchant sailors at the hands of the Spanish. In a dramatic flourish he produced a dried and withered ear, which he claimed they had cut from his head. A public outrage followed, finally forcing Walpole to agree to a war of Caribbean conquest that the British called the War of Jenkins's Ear.

English troops allied with Creek Indians invaded Florida once again, laying waste the last of the old mission stations but failing to capture St. Augustine. In response, Spanish troops, including several companies of African Americans, invaded Georgia. Although the Spanish were defeated

$$\mathcal{O}\text{VERVIEW}$$

THE COLONIAL WARS		
King William's War	1689–97	France and England battle on the northern frontiers of New England and New York.
Queen Anne's War	1702–13	England fights France and Spain in the Caribbean and on the northern frontier of New France. Part of the European conflict known as the War of the Spanish Succession.
War of Jenkins's Ear	1739–43	Great Britain versus Spain in the Caribbean and Georgia. Part of the European War of the Austrian Succession.
King George's War	1744–48	Great Britain and France fight in Acadia and Nova Scotia; the second American round of the War of the Austrian Succession.
French and Indian War	1754–63	Last of the great colonial wars pitting Great Britain against France and Spain. Known in Europe as the Seven Years War.

seventy-five miles south of Savannah, the campaign produced an agreement on the boundary between British Georgia and Spanish Florida that today separates those states. Elsewhere the British were not so lucky: in the Caribbean the imperial fleet suffered disaster at the hands of the Spanish navy.

In the northern region the principal focus of the imperial struggle was control of the Indian trade. In 1704, during Queen Anne's War, the French and their Algonquian Indian allies raided New England frontier towns such as Deerfield, Massachusetts, dragging men, women, and children into captivity in Canada. In turn, the English mounted a series of expeditions against the strategic French fortress of Port Royal, which they captured in 1710. At the war's conclusion in 1713, France was forced to cede Acadia, Newfoundland, and Hudson's Bay to Great Britain in exchange for guarantees of security for the French-speaking residents of those provinces. Thirty years of peace followed, but from 1744 to 1748 England again battled France in King George's War. The French attacked the British in Nova Scotia, Indian and Canadian raids again devastated the border towns of New England and New York, and hundreds of British subjects were killed or captured.

The French, allied with the Spanish and Prussians, were equally successful in Europe. What finally turned the tide of this war was the capture in 1745 of the French fortress of Louisburg on Cape Breton Island by an expedition of Massachusetts troops in conjunction with the royal navy. Deprived of the most strategic of their American ports, and fearful of losing the wealth of their sugar islands, the French

agreed to a negotiated settlement in 1748. But despite the capture of Louisburg, the war had been fought elsewhere to a stalemate, so the treaty restored the prewar status quo, returning Louisburg to France. This disgusted merchants of New England, who wanted to expand their commercial influence in the maritime colonies, and left the North American conflict between France and Britain still simmering. Significantly, however, this was the first time that the concluding battle of a European war had been fought on North American soil, and it was a harbinger of things to come: the next war was destined to start as a conflict between French and British colonists before engulfing Europe (see Chapter 6).

British Colonial Regulation

Mercantilists used means other than war to win the wealth of the world. In the sixteenth century the Spanish monarchy became the first to create a state trading monopoly—the *Casa de Contratación*—to manage the commerce of its empire. This monopoly limited colonial trade to prescribed ports such as Seville or Veracruz, protected traders from attack and plunder, and established a system of great convoys in which merchant ships crossed the oceans under the protection of well-armed galleons. In the seventeenth century other European states followed the Spanish example. The British monarchy, for example, chartered the East India Company, the Hudson's Bay Company, and the Royal African Company as trading monopolies in their respective regions.

English manufacturers complained that the merchant-dominated trading monopolies paid too little attention to the export of their products to colonial markets. Reacting to these charges, between 1651 and 1696 Parliament passed a series of Navigation Acts (see also Chapter 3), which created the legal and institutional structure of Britain's eighteenth-century colonial system. These acts defined the colonies as both suppliers of raw materials and markets for English manufactured goods. Merchants from other nations were expressly forbidden to trade in the colonies, and all trade had to be conducted in ships built either in England or in the British colonies. The regulations specified a list of enumerated goods—colonial products that could be shipped only to England. These included the products of the southern slave colonies (sugar, molasses, rum, tobacco, rice, and indigo), those of the northern Indian trade (furs and skins), as well as the products essential for supplying the shipping industry (masts, tar, pitch, resin, and turpentine). The bulk of these products were not destined for English consumption, however; at great profit English merchants reexported them elsewhere.

England also placed limitations on colonial enterprises that might compete with those at home. A series of enactments—including the Wool Act of 1699, the Hat Act of 1732, and the Iron Act of 1750—forbade the colonial manufacture of those products. Moreover, colonial assemblies were forbidden to impose tariffs on English imports as a way to protect colonial industries. Banking was disallowed, local

coinage prohibited, and the export of coin from England forbidden. Badly in need of a circulating medium, Massachusetts illegally minted copper coin, and several colonies issued paper currency, forcing Parliament to legislate against the practice. The colonists depended mostly on "commodity money" (furs, skins, or hogsheads of tobacco) and the circulation of foreign coin, the most common being the Spanish silver peso and the German silver thaler, which Americans pronounced "dollar." Official rates of exchange between commodity money, colonial paper, foreign currency, and English pounds allowed this chaotic system to operate without too much difficulty.

Certain British interests pressed for even more stringent restrictions. But as the colonies grew more populous, and as the trade in colonial products increased, the British came to agree that it made little sense to tamper with such a prosperous system. Prime Minister Walpole pursued a policy later characterized as one of "salutory neglect": any colonial rules and regulations deemed contrary to good business practice were simply ignored and not enforced. Between 1700 and 1760 the quantity of goods exported from the colonies to the mother country rose 165 percent, while imports from Britain to North America increased by more than 400 percent. In part because of the lax enforcement, but mostly because the system operated to the profit of colonial merchants, colonists

The New England artist John Greenwood painted this amusing view of New England sea captains in Surinam in 1757. By the early eighteenth century New England merchant traders like these had become important participants in the traffic in slaves and sugar to and from the West Indies. Northern ports thus became important pivots in the expanding commercial network linking slave plantations with Atlantic markets.

complained very little about the operation of the mercantilist system before the 1760s.

The Colonial Economy

Despite seemingly harsh mercantilist regulations, then, this economic system benefited planters, merchants, and white colonists in general. Despite being restricted to English markets, southern slave owners made healthy profits on the sale of their commodities. They enjoyed a protected market, in which competing goods from outside the empire were heavily taxed. Moreover, agricultural products more than held their value against the price of manufactures, and planters found themselves with steadily increasing purchasing power.

Pennsylvania, New York, and New England, and increasingly the Chesapeake as well, produced grain and flour, meat and dairy products. None of these was included in the list of enumerated goods, and they could thus be sold freely abroad. They found their most ready market in the British West Indies and the Lower South, where food production was slighted in favor of sugar and rice. Most of this trade was carried in New England ships. Indeed, the New England shipbuilding industry was greatly stimulated by the allowance under the Navigation Acts for ships built and manned in the colonies. So many ships were built for English buyers that by midcentury nearly a third of all British tonnage was American made.

The greatest benefits for the port cities of the North came from their commercial relationship to the slave colonies. New England merchants had become important players in the slave trade by the early eighteenth century, and soon thereafter they began to make inroads as well into the export trade of the West Indian colonies. It was in the Caribbean that New England merchants most blatantly ignored mercantilist regulations. In violation of Spanish, French, and Dutch rules prohibiting foreign trade, New Englanders traded foodstuffs for sugar in foreign colonies. Then, in violation of British regulations prohibiting the importation of sugar from competing colonies, the enterprising Yankees mixed their contraband among legal shipments from the British West Indies. The Molasses Act of 1733, which Parliament enacted under pressure from British West Indian planters, placed a prohibitive duty on sugar products brought from foreign colonies to North America. Had these regulations been strictly applied, they surely would have caused conflict with the colonists, but in fact enforcement was lax. By 1750, more than sixty distilleries in Massachusetts Bay were exporting over 2 million gallons of rum, most of it produced from sugar obtained illegally. Because the restrictive rules and regulations enacted by Britain for its colonies were not enforced, the merchants and manufacturers of the port cities of the North prospered.

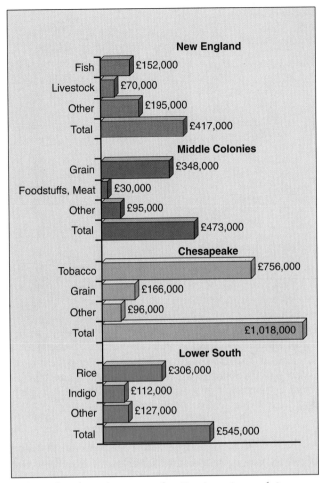

Value of Colonial Exports by Region, Annual Average, 1768–1772 *With tobacco, rice, grain, and indigo, the Chesapeake and Lower South accounted for nearly two-thirds of colonial exports in the late eighteenth century. The Middle Colonies, however, were also becoming major exporters of grain.*

Source: James F. Shepherd and Gary M. Walton, *Shipping, Maritime Trade and the Economic Development of Colonial America* (Cambridge, England: Cambridge University Press, 1972), 211–27.

As early as 1715, the exchange of New England fish, foodstuffs, and lumber for sugar and other tropical products from the West Indies accounted for more than half of the tonnage passing through the port of Boston. The volume of this trade remained steady over the next half-century, but Boston merchants greatly increased their commerce with the slave colonies of the Chesapeake and Lower South, shipping tobacco, rice, and indigo north, then reshipping it to England. A similar pattern is evident in the statistics of other northern ports. This carrying trade in the products of slave labor made it possible for New England and the Middle Colonies to earn the income necessary to purchase British imports despite the relative absence of valuable products from their own regions. Gradually, the commercial economies of the Northeast and the South were becoming integrated. From the 1730s

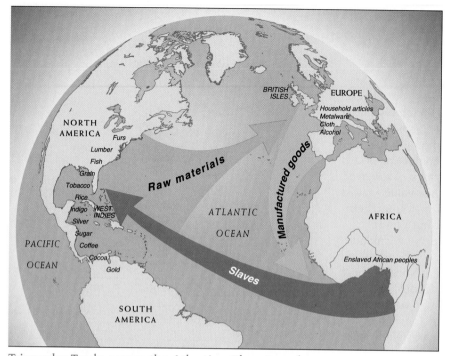

NORTH AMERICA
Furs
Lumber
Fish
Grain
Tobacco
Rice
Indigo WEST INDIES
Silver
Sugar
Coffee
Cocoa
Gold

PACIFIC OCEAN

SOUTH AMERICA

BRITISH ISLES EUROPE
Household articles
Metalware
Cloth
Alcohol

Raw materials

Manufactured goods

ATLANTIC OCEAN

AFRICA

Enslaved African peoples

Slaves

Triangular Trade across the Atlantic   *The pattern of commerce among Europe, Africa, and the Americas became known as the "Triangular Trade." Sailors called the voyage of slave ships from Africa to America the "Middle Passage" because it formed the crucial middle section of this trading triangle.*

to the 1770s, for example, while the volume of trade between Great Britain and Charleston doubled, the trade between Charleston and northern ports grew sevenfold. The same relationship was developing between the Chesapeake and the North. Merchants in Boston, Newport, New York, and Philadelphia increasingly provided southern planters not only with shipping services but with credit and insurance as well. Like London, Liverpool, and Bristol—though on a smaller scale—the port cities of the North became pivots in the expanding trade network linking slave plantations with Atlantic markets. This trade provided northern merchants with the capital that financed commercial growth and development in their cities and the surrounding countryside. Slavery thus contributed to the growth of a score of northern port cities, forming an indirect but essential part of their economies.

SLAVERY AND FREEDOM

The prosperity of the eighteenth-century plantation economy thus improved the living conditions for the residents of northern cities as well as for a large segment of the population of the South, providing them with material opportunities unknown in the preceding century. The price, however, was the oppression and exploitation of millions of Africans and African Americans. Freedom for white men based on the slavery of African Americans

is the most important contradiction in American history.

The Social Structure of the Slave Colonies

At the summit of southern colonial society stood a small elite of wealthy planters, in contrast with the mass of unfree men and women who formed the working population. Slavery had produced a society in which property was concentrated in the hands of a wealthy few. The richest 10 percent of southern colonists owned more than half the cultivated land and over 60 percent of the wealth. Although there was no colonial aristocracy—no nobility or royal appointments—the landed elite of the slave colonies came very close to constituting one.

Among the hundred wealthiest Virginians of the 1770s, for example, more than 80 percent had inherited their wealth from their fathers, and some were third- or fourth-generation colonials. Fewer than 10 percent were "self-made," and most of these men had acquired their fortunes through commerce or the law. The typical wealthy Virginia planter lived in a Tidewater county, owned several thousand acres of prime farmland and more than 100 slaves, resided in a luxurious plantation mansion, built perhaps in the fashionable Georgian style, and had an estate valued at more than 10,000 pounds. Elected to the House of Burgesses, and forming the group from which the magistrates and counselors of the colony were chosen, these "first families of Virginia"—the Carters, Harrisons, Lees, Fitzhughs, Burwells, Randolphs, and others—were a self-perpetuating governing class.

A similar elite ruled the Lower South, although wealthy landowners there spent relatively little time on their plantations. They resided instead in fashionable Charleston, where they constituted a close-knit group who controlled the colonial government. "They live in as high a style here, I believe, as any part of the world," wrote a visitor to Charleston.

A considerable distance separated this slave-owning elite from typical southern landowners. About half the adult white males were small planters and farmers. But although the gap between rich and middling colonists grew larger during the eighteenth century, the prosperity of the plantation economy created generally favorable conditions for this large landed class. Slave ownership, for example, became widespread among this group during the eighteenth century. In Virginia at midcentury, 45 percent of heads of household held one to four slaves, and even poorer farmers kept one or two.

Despite the prosperity that accompanied slavery in the eighteenth century, however, a substantial portion of colonists continued to own no land or slaves at all. Some rented land or worked as tenant farmers, some hired out as overseers or farm workers, and still others were indentured servants. Throughout the plantation region, landless white men constituted about 40 percent of the population. A New England visitor found a "much greater disparity between the rich and poor in Virginia" than at home.

White Skin Privilege

Yet all the white colonists of eighteenth-century North America shared the privileged status of their skin color. In the early seventeenth century there had been more diversity in views about race. For some, black skin was thought to be a sign of God's curse. "The blackness of the Negroes," one Englishman argued, "proceedeth of some natural infection." But not everyone shared those views. "I can't think there is any intrinsic value in one colour more than another," a second Englishman remarked, "nor that white is better than black, only we think it so because we are so." As slavery became increasingly important, however, Virginia officials took considerable care to create legal distinctions between the status of colonists and that of Africans, deliberately encouraging the growth of racism. Beginning in 1670, free Africans were prohibited from owning Christian servants. Ten years later, another law declared that any African, free or slave, who struck a Christian would receive thirty lashes on his bare back. One of the most important measures was designed to suppress intimate interracial contacts between white servants and enslaved Africans. A 1691 act "for prevention of that abominable mixture and spurious issue which hereafter may encrease in this dominion" established severe penalties for interracial sexual relationships. Such penalties were rarely applied to masters, who

frequently forced themselves on African women. But some slave women may have willingly established intimate relations with masters to better their condition or the opportunities for their children. The descendants of Sally Hemings, a slave owned by Thomas Jefferson, have long claimed that Jefferson fathered some of her children, and recent scientific tests comparing their DNA with that of descendents of Jefferson's paternal grandfather have confirmed their story. The Hemings children enjoyed a privileged position among Jefferson's slaves and were freed in his will.

Relationships between white masters or indentured servants and African slaves produced a rather large group of mulattoes. Since by law children inherited the bond or free status of their mothers, the children of African mothers became slaves, but a minority, the children of European women and African men, were free. According to a Maryland census of 1755, more than 60 percent of mulattoes were slaves. But mulattoes also made up three-quarters of a small free African American population. This group, about 4,000 in the 1770s, was denied the right to vote, to hold office, or to testify in court—all on the basis of racial

Alexander Spotswood Payne and his brother John Robert Dandridge Payne with their African American nurse, painted by an unknown Virginia artist, ca. 1790. White and black Southerners lived in intimate contact. White children were breast-fed by African nannies, and interracial sex was very much a part of plantation life. But whiteness was the universal badge of freedom, blackness a mark of bondage. Despite their close association, said Thomas Jefferson, the two peoples were divided by "deep rooted prejudices entertained by the whites" and "ten thousand recollections, by the blacks, of the injuries they have sustained."

Alexander Spotswood Payne and His Brother, John Robert Dandridge Payne, with Their Nurse, ca. 1790. Oil on canvas, 142.2 × 175.2 cm. Virginia Museum of Fine Arts, Richmond. Gift of Miss Dorothy Payne.

CHRONOLOGY

1441	African slaves first brought to Portugal		1705	Virginia Slave Code established
1518	Spain grants official license to Portuguese slavers		1706	French and Spanish navies bombard Charleston
1535	Africans constitute a majority on Hispaniola		1710	English capture Port Royal
1619	First Africans brought to Virginia		1712	Slave uprising in New York City
1655	English seize Jamaica		1713	Peace of Utrecht
1662	Virginia law makes slavery hereditary		1721–48	Robert Walpole leads British cabinet
1670	South Carolina founded		1733	Molasses Act
1672	Royal African Company organized		1739	Stono Rebellion War of Jenkins's Ear
1691	Virginia prohibits interracial sexual contact		1740–48	King George's War
1698	Britain opens the slave trade to all its merchants		1741	Africans executed in New York for conspiracy
1699	Spanish declare Florida a refuge for escaped slaves		1752	Georgia officially opened to slavery
1702	South Carolinians burn St. Augustine		1770s	Peak period of the English colonies' slave trade
			1808	Importation of slaves into the United States ends

background. Denied the status of citizenship enjoyed by even the poorest of white men, free blacks were a pariah group who raised the status of poor white colonials by contrast. Racial distinctions were a constant reminder of the freedom of white colonists and the debasement of all blacks, slave or free.

Racism set up a wall of contempt between colonists and African Americans. Jefferson wrote of "the real distinctions which nature has made" between the races. "In memory they are equal to the whites," he wrote of the slaves, but "in reason much inferior." He gave no consideration to the argument of the freed slave Olaudah Equiano that "slavery debases the mind." Jefferson was on firmer ground when he argued that the two peoples were divided by "deep rooted prejudices entertained by the whites" and "ten thousand recollections, by the blacks, of the injuries they have sustained." Perhaps he knew of these feelings from his long relationship with Sally Hemings. "I tremble for my country when I reflect that God is just," Jefferson concluded in a deservedly famous passage, and remember "that his justice cannot sleep forever."

CONCLUSION

During the eighteenth century nearly half a million Africans were kidnapped from their homes and packed into ships for up to three months before arriving in British North America. They provided the labor that made colonialism pay. Southern planters, northern merchants, and especially British traders and capitalists benefited greatly from the commerce in slave-produced crops, and that prosperity filtered down to affect many of the colonists of British North America. Slavery was "the strength and sinews" of the British empire in North America. The focus of imperial warfare was seizing the slave colonies of other powers and putting them to the service of the mother country. Mercantilism was a system designed to channel the colonial wealth produced by slaves to the nation-state, but as long as profits were high, the British were content to wink at all colonists' violations of mercantilist regulations.

Although African Americans received nothing in return, their labor helped build the greatest accumulation of capital that Europe had ever seen. But despite enormous hardship and suffering, African Americans survived by forming new communities in the colonies, rebuilding families, restructuring language, reforming culture. African American culture added important components of African knowledge and experience to colonial agri-culture, art, music, and cuisine. The African Americans of the British colonies lived better lives than the slaves worked to death on Caribbean sugar plantations, but lives of misery compared to the men they were forced to serve. As the slaves sang on the Georgia coast: "Dah Backrow Man go wrong you, Buddy Quow."

REVIEW QUESTIONS

1. Trace the development of the system of slavery and discuss the way it became entrenched in the Americas.
2. Describe the effects of the slave trade both on enslaved Africans and on the economic and political life of Africa.
3. Describe the process of acculturation involved in becoming an African American. In what ways did slaves "Africanize" the South?
4. Explain the connection between the institution of slavery and the building of a commercial empire.
5. In what ways did colonial policy encourage the growth of racism?

RECOMMENDED READING

Michael Craton, *Sinews of Empire: A Short History of British Slavery* (1974). An introduction to the British mercantilist system that emphasizes the importance of slavery. Includes a comparison of the mainland colonies with the Caribbean.

Philip D. Curtin, *The African Slave Trade: A Census* (1969). The pioneer work in the quantitative history of the slave trade. All subsequent histories of the slave trade are indebted to Curtin.

Herbert G. Gutman, *The Black Family in Slavery and Freedom, 1750–1925* (1976). A pathbreaking history of the development of the African American community in North America. The sections on the eighteenth century provide evidence of the development of multigenerational family and kin networks.

Winthrop D. Jordan, *White over Black: American Attitudes toward the Negro, 1550–1812* (1968). Remains the best and most comprehensive history of racial values and attitudes. A searching examination of British and American literature, folklore, and history.

Peter Kolchin, *American Slavery, 1619–1877* (1993). A survey that features comparisons with slavery in Brazil, the Caribbean, and serfdom in Russia. Includes a comprehensive bibliographic essay.

Walter Rodney, *How Europe Underdeveloped Africa* (1974). A highly influential book that traces the relationship between Europe and Africa from the fifteenth to the twentieth century and demonstrates how Europe's industrialization became Africa's impoverishment.

Mechal Sobel, *The World They Made Together: Black and White Values in Eighteenth-Century Virginia* (1987). Demonstrates the ways in which both Africans and Europeans shaped the formation of American values, perceptions, and identities.

Ian K. Steele, *Warpaths: Invasions of North America* (1994). A new synthesis of the colonial wars from the sixteenth to the eighteenth century that places Indians as well as empires at the center of the action.

Sterling Stuckey, *Slave Culture: Nationalist Theory and the Foundations of Black America* (1987). A study of the African origins of African American culture that concentrates on folklore. Includes important evidence on African American religion in the era before Christianization.

Hugh Thomas, *The Slave Trade: The Story of the Atlantic Slave Trade, 1440–1870* (1997). The horrifying history in brutal detail, told by a master historian.

ADDITIONAL BIBLIOGRAPHY

The African Slave Trade

Jay Coughtry, *The Notorious Triangle: Rhode Island and the African Slave Trade, 1799–1807* (1981)

Philip D. Curtin, *Economic Change in Precolonial Africa: Senegambia in the Era of the Slave Trade* (1975)

Basin Davidson, *The African Slave Trade* (1980)

Elizabeth Donnan, ed., *Documents Illustrative of the History of the Slave Trade to America* 4 vols. (1930–35)

J. E. Inikori, *Forced Migration: The Impact of the Export Slave Trade on African Societies* (1982)

Robert W. July, *A History of the African People* (1992)

Herbert S. Klein, *The Middle Passage: Comparative Studies in the Atlantic Slave Trade* (1978)

Robin Law, *The Slave Coast of West Africa, 1550–1750: The Impact of the Atlantic Slave Trade on an African Society* (1991)

Paul E. Lovejoy, ed., *Africans in Bondage: Studies in Slavery and the Slave Trade* (1986)

Daniel P. Mannix and Malcolm Crowley, *Black Cargoes: A History of the Atlantic Slave Trade* (1962)

David Northrup, ed., *The Atlantic Slave Trade* (1994)

J. A. Rawley, *The Transatlantic Slave Trade* (1981)

Edward Reynolds, *Stand the Storm: A History of the Atlantic Slave Trade* (1985)

A. C. De C. M. Saunders, *A Social History of Black Slaves and Freemen in Portugal, 1441–1555* (1982)

Jon Vogt, *Portuguese Rule on the Gold Coast, 1469–1682* (1979)

The Development of North American Slave Societies

L. R. Bailey, *Indian Slave Trade in the Southwest: A Study of Slave-Taking and the Traffic in Indian Captives* (1966)

T. H. Breen and Stephen Innes, *"Myne Owne Ground": Race and Freedom on Virginia's Eastern Shore* (1980)

Verner W. Crane, *The Southern Frontier, 1670–1732* (1929)

Richard S. Dunn, *Sugar and Slaves: The Rise of the Planter Class in the English West Indies, 1624–1713* (1972)

Laura Foner and Eugene D. Genovese, eds., *Slavery in the New World: A Reader in Comparative History* (1969)

Charles Joyner, *Down by the Riverside: A South Carolina Slave Community* (1984)

Alan Kulikoff, *Tobacco and Slaves: The Development of Southern Cultures in the Chesapeake, 1680–1800* (1986)

Daniel Littlefield, *Rice and Slaves: Ethnicity and the Slave Trade in Colonial South Carolina* (1981)

Paul E. Lovejoy, *Transformations in Slavery: A History of Slavery in Africa* (1983)

Edgar J. McManus, *Black Bondage in the North* (1973)

Gary B. Nash, *Red, White, and Black: The Peoples of Early North America* (1992)

Julia Floyd Smith, *Slavery and Rice Culture in Low Country Georgia, 1750–1860* (1985)

Brenda Stevenson, *Life in Black and White: Family and Community in the Slave South* (1996)

Peter H. Wood, *Black Majority: Negroes in Colonial South Carolina from 1670 through the Stone Rebellion* (1974)

Becoming African American

John B. Boles, *Black Southerners, 1619–1869* (1984)

Joseph E. Harris, ed., *Global Dimensions of the African Diaspora* (1982)

Annette Gordon-Reed, *Thomas Jefferson and Sally Hemings: An American Controversy,* (1997)

Gerald W. Mullin, *Flight and Rebellion: Slave Resistance in Eighteenth-Century Virginia* (1972)

Orlando Patterson, *Slavery and Social Death: A Comparative Study* (1982)

V. B. Thompson, *The Making of the African Diaspora in the Americas, 1441–1900* (1984)

The Structure of Empire

Joyce O. Appleby, *Economic Thought and Ideology in Seventeenth-Century England* (1978)

Eugene Genovese and Elizabeth Fox-Genovese, *Fruits of Merchant Capital: Slavery and Bourgeois Property in the Rise and Expansion of Capitalism* (1983)

E. J. Hobsbawn, *Industry and Empire: The Making of Modern English Society, 1750 to the Present Day* (1968)

Michael Kammen, *Empire and Interest: The American Colonies and the Politics of Mercantilism* (1970)

John J. McCusker and Russell R. Menard, *The Economy of British America, 1607–1787* (1985)

Barbara L. Solow, ed., *Slavery and the Rise of the Atlantic System* (1991)

Eric Williams, *Capitalism and Slavery* (1944)

Slavery and Freedom

David Brion Davis, *The Problem of Slavery in Western Culture* (1966)

Carl N. Degler, *Neither Black nor White: Slavery and Race Relations in Brazil and the United States* (1971)

Edmund S. Morgan, *American Slavery, American Freedom: The Ordeal of Colonial Virginia* (1975)

Joel Williamson, *New People: Miscegenation and Mulattoes in the United States* (1980)

Biography

Philip D. Curtin, ed., *Africa Remembered: Narratives of West Africans from the Era of the Slave Trade* (1967)

Paul Edwards, ed., *The Interesting Narrative of the Life of Olaudah Equiano, or Gustavus Vassa, the African, written by himself* (1987)

James B. Hedges, *The Browns of Providence Plantation* (1952)

Kenneth A. Lockridge, *The Diary and Life of William Byrd II of Virginia, 1674-1744* (1987)

Phinizy Spalding, *Oglethorpe in America* (1977)

Janet Whitman, *John Woolman, American Quaker* (1942)

CHAPTER FIVE

THE CULTURES OF COLONIAL NORTH AMERICA

1700–1780

AMERICAN COMMUNITIES
From Deerfield to Kahnawake:
Crossing Cultural Boundaries

Two hours before daylight on February 29, 1704, the Reverend John Williams and his wife Eunice of Deerfield, Massachusetts, awoke to "horrid shouting and yelling" and the crash of axes and hatchets breaking open the doors and windows of their house. Leaping out of bed they knew immediately that the town was under attack by Indians and their French allies; this frontier settlement on the northwestern fringe of New England had already been attacked six times in the perennial fighting with New France. Never before, however, had the enemy penetrated the town's stockade. Suddenly the door burst open and "with painted faces and hideous exclamations" Indians began pushing inside. "I reached up my hands for my pistol," Williams remembered, "cocked it, and put it to the breast of the first Indian that came up." It misfired, and as the couple stood trembling in their night clothes, they were bound and dragged into the central hall with their seven children. In horror they were forced to watch the invaders club and kill their resisting six-year-old son, their screaming newborn infant daughter, and the black nursemaid. The family was hustled out into the frigid dawn and, with more than a hundred other captives, marched north through snow and ice toward Canada, leaving the frightful sight of the burning town behind.

The Deerfield raid became one of the most infamous events in the long series of colonial wars. One hundred and forty residents of the town managed to hold off the invasion and survive, but fifty others died in the attack. Among the captives, twenty-one were murdered along the way, in most cases because they were too weak to travel; the murdered included Mrs. Williams, who had not yet recovered from a difficult childbirth just six weeks before. The governor of Massachusetts ordered a day of fasting and prayed that "the Designs of the barbarous Salvages against us be defeated; our exposed Plantations preserved; and the poor Christian Captives in their hands returned." Authorities raised the bounty on Indian scalps from £10 to £100 and organized bloody raids of their own on the French and Indian settlements to the north.

Most of the Deerfield captives were delivered to the French authorities in Montreal. Within two years, fifty-nine of them had been ransomed and returned home to Deerfield, the Reverend Williams and four of his surviving children among them. Williams soon published an account of his captivity, *The Redeemed Captive Returning to Zion*. In colonial America, with its many peoples and cultures, readers were fascinated by the problems and dilemmas of crossing frontiers and boundaries. What was life like for you, people wanted to know, on the other side of the frontier? How were you changed by your experience? Did you remain loyal to your community? Can you still be trusted?

Questions of this sort were vitally important to the colonists, for over the years hundreds of Europeans who had been captured by Indians had chosen to remain with their captors rather than return home. Among the Deerfield captives, thirty-one—including ten-year-old Eunice Williams, her mother's namesake—remained in Canada. Eunice and many of the other Deerfield captives lived at Kahnawake, a community of Catholic Indians near Montreal. Like Deerfield, Kahnawake was a farming town of fifty or sixty homes clustered around a central church and surrounded by a stockade to protect it from enemy raiders. The differences between the two communities, however, were more striking than the similarities.

Founded in the seventeenth century by Jesuit missionaries as a refuge for Iroquois converts, Kahnawake not only became home to a great variety of Native American Catholics but also welcomed people of mixed Indian and European ancestry. The "great mixture of the blood of whites with that of aborigines is observable in the persons of the inhabitants," wrote one visitor, struck by the appearance of people who seemed to be Indians in all respects except their blue eyes. Such mixing was also evident in the community's culture, in the exotic mélange of European and Indian clothing, in the use of both Indian and French names, and in the special ways the community bent Catholic ritual to fit traditional Iroquois practices. Community members crossed boundaries in other ways, too: many residents were smugglers who engaged in the illegal trade of furs and other Indian products across the frontier into New York. According to the frustrated authorities in Montreal, Kahnawake operated as "a sort of republic," insisting on its freedom and independence.

As the historian John Demos writes, Kahnawake was "a unique experiment in bicultural living." Its residents were skilled at offering sympathetic sanctuary to traumatized captive chil-

dren, and by the time Eunice Williams's father and siblings were ransomed she told the man who had come to fetch her that she was "unwilling to return." Soon she converted to Catholicism. Over the years the father sent several emissaries to retrieve her, but all she would say were two words of Iroquois: *jaghte oghte*, meaning "maybe not." She had apparently forgotten her English tongue, and she refused to acknowledge her English name, having taken another—A'ongonte, which in Iroquois means "she has been planted as a person." In 1713, at the age of sixteen, she married a Kahnawake Mohawk. Father and daughter would meet only once more, the following year, when he went to Kahnawake a final time to beg her to return. But she would "not so much as give me one pleasant look," Williams wrote mournfully. "She is yet obstinatly resolved to live and dye here."

And that is what happened. A'ongonte and her husband remained good Catholics, raising a family and working as traders. John Williams died in 1729, surrounded by his children and grandchildren but longing for his "unredeemed" daughter. It was not until 1739 that A'ongonte found the courage to bring her family south for a visit, for she feared being held in New England against her will. Her brother Stephen wrote in his diary that at long last "we had ye joyfull, Sorrowfull meeting of our poor Sister that we had been Sepratd from fer above 36 years." After that A'ongonte visited only rarely because of the continuing warfare. "We have a great desire of going down to see you," she wrote to her brother through an interpreter near the end of their lives in the 1770s, "but do not know when an oppertunity may offer....I pray the Lord that he may give us grace so to Live in this as to be prepared for a happey meeting in the woreld to Come." And, perhaps as a sign of reconciliation, she signed the letter, "Loving Sister until death, Eunice Williams."

KEY TOPICS

- The similarities and differences among eighteenth-century Spanish, French, and English colonies

- The impact on British colonial culture of increasing European immigration

- Cultural changes in Indian America brought about by contact with European customs and lifestyles

- Patterns of work and class in eighteenth-century America

- Tensions between Enlightenment thought and the Great Awakening's call to renewed religious devotion

NORTH AMERICAN REGIONS

American colonial history too frequently is written as if only the British colonists along the Atlantic coast really mattered. But as the experience of the Deerfield community and the Williams family suggests, this is a mistake eighteenth-century colonists could not afford to make. In the first place, Indian America was a critically important part of the eighteenth-century world. From the fringes of colonial societies into the native heart of the continent, from the eastern foothills of the Appalachians to the western flank of the Sierra Nevada in California, hundreds of Indian cultures—despite being deeply affected by the spread of colonial culture—remained firmly in control of their homelands. And in addition to the British provinces stretching along the Atlantic coast, there were Hispanic colonists who defended the northern borderlands of the Spanish Caribbean and Mexican empire in isolated communities from Florida to California, and French communities that occupied the valley of the St. Lawrence River and scattered down the Mississippi Valley from the Great Lakes to the Gulf of Mexico. There were impressive similarities among these colonial societies, representing a continuation in the New World of traditional Old World beliefs, customs, and institutions, as well as a general pattern of European adaptation to American conditions.

Indian America

As the native peoples of the Atlantic coastal plain lost their lands to colonists through battles or treaties, and moved into or beyond the Appalachian Mountains, they became active in the European fur trade and dependent on firearms, metal tools, and other manufactured goods to maintain their way of life. Yet through the American Revolution they continued to

assert a proud independence and gained considerable skill at playing colonial powers off against each other. The Iroquois Five Nations battled the French and

A portrait of the Delaware chief Tishcohan by Gustavus Hesselius, painted in 1732. In his purse of chipmunk hide is a clay pipe, a common item of the Indian trade. Tishcohan was one of the Delaware leaders forced by Pennsylvania authorities into signing a fraudulent land deal that reversed that colony's history of fair dealing with Indians over land. He moved west to the Ohio River as settlers poured into his former homeland.

their Indian allies in King William's War, but in 1701 they signed a treaty of neutrality with France that kept them out of harm's way during the next round of conflicts. The Catholic Iroquois of Kahnawake sometimes supported the French, as they did by mounting the Deerfield raid, but they also traded with the English. In the Lower South, the Creeks similarly traded with both the French and the English as a means of maintaining their autonomy.

In general, the French had significantly better relations with native peoples than the English, but inevitably as they pursued their expansionist plans they came into conflict with many Indian groups, and when opposed they could be just as cruel and violent as any other power. In the early eighteenth century the Fox Indians blocked French passage between the Great Lakes and the upper Mississippi, attempting to make themselves into middlemen in the fur trade. After several years of sporadic fighting, the French defeated the tribe in 1716. But Fox warriors rose again in 1726, and only with great violence and not until 1738 could the French force the tribe to sign a treaty. On the lower Mississippi the Natchez and Chickasaw tribes opposed the arrival of the French, engaging them in a series of bloody conflicts during the 1720s that concluded only when the French decimated the Natchez in 1731.

The preeminent concern of the Indians of the eastern half of the continent was the tremendous growth of colonial population in the British Atlantic coastal colonies, especially the movement of settlers westward. In the 1730s and 1740s Pennsylvania perpetrated a series of fraudulent seizures of western lands from the Delawares. Particularly in the light of Pennsylvania's previous history of fair dealing with Indian peoples, these acts offered yet another disturbing sign of things to come. Thus Indian alliances with the French resulted not from any great love and affection on their part toward the French but from their great fear of British expansion.

Growing Use of the Horse by Plains Indians *In the seventeenth and eighteenth centuries, Spanish settlers introduced horses into their New Mexican colony. Through trading and raiding, horses spread northward in streams both west and east of the Rocky Mountains. The horse, whose genetic ancestor had been native to the American continent in pre-Archaic times, offered the Indian peoples of the Great Plains the opportunity to create a distinctive hunting and warrior culture.*

Meanwhile, a long-term population decline continued among the Indian peoples of North America. The colonists were relatively immune from dramatic fluctuations in the death rate, but Indian America continued to take a terrific beating from epidemics of European disease. There was no systematic census of North American Indians before the nineteenth century, but historians estimate that from a high of 7 to 10 million native Americans north of Mexico in 1500 the population had probably fallen to around a million by 1800. Thus, during the eighteenth century the colonial population overtook and began to overwhelm the native population of the continent. Population loss did not affect all Indian tribes equally, however. Native peoples with a century or more of colonial contact and interaction had lost 50 percent or more of their numbers, but most Indian societies in the interior had yet to be struck by the horrible epidemics.

NEW FRANCE

NEW ENGLAND

NEW YORK
PENNSYLVANIA

NEW FRANCE

BACK COUNTRY

CHESAPEAKE

LOWER
SOUTH

NEW FRANCE

NEW SPAIN

NEW SPAIN

▢	New France
▢	New England
▢	New York
▢	Pennsylvania
▢	Chesapeake
▢	Lower South
▢	Backcountry
▢	Northern New Spain
▢	Indian America

Colonization introduced other, less-distressing changes in Indian cultures. By the early eighteenth century, Indians on the southern fringe of the Great Plains were using horses stolen from the Spanish in New Mexico. Horses enabled Indian hunters to exploit the buffalo herds much more efficiently than before, and on the base of this more productive subsistence strategy many groups built a distinctive and elaborate nomadic culture. Great numbers of Indian peoples moved onto the plains during the eighteenth century, pulled by this new way of life, pushed by colonial invasions and disruptions radiating southwest from Canada and north from the Spanish borderlands. By midcentury, the New Mexicans had become regular victims of raids by mounted hunters of the Great Plains. The invention of nomadic Plains Indian culture was another of the dramatic cultural amalgamations and innovations of the eighteenth century. The mounted Plains Indian, so frequently used as a symbol of native America, was actually a product of the colonial era.

The Spanish Borderlands

In the mid-eighteenth century what is today the Sunbelt of the United States formed the periphery of the largest and most prosperous European colony on the North American continent—the viceroyalty of New Spain, which included approximately 1 million Spanish colonists and mestizos and at least 2 million Indians. The administrative capital of Mexico City was the most sophisticated metropolis in the Western Hemisphere, the site of one of the world's great universities, with broad avenues and spectacular baroque architecture. New Spain's northern provinces of Florida, Texas, New Mexico, and California, however, were far removed from this opulence. Officials of the viceroyalty of New Spain, who oversaw these colonies, thought of them as buffer zones, protecting New Spain from the expanding colonial empires of Spain's New World rivals.

In Florida, the oldest of European colonies in North America, fierce fighting among the Spanish, the British, and the Indians had by the early eighteenth century reduced the colonial presence to little more than the forts of St. Augustine on the Atlantic and Pensacola on the Gulf of Mexico, each surrounded by small colonized territories populated with the families of Spanish troops. In their weakened condition, the Spanish had no choice but to establish cooperative relations with the Creek and Seminole Indians who dominated the region,

Region	Population
New France	70,000
New England	400,000
New York	100,000
Pennsylvania	230,000
Chesapeake	390,000
Lower South	100,000
Backcountry	100,000
Northern New Spain	20,000
Indian America	1,500,000

Regions in Eighteenth-Century North America

By the middle of the eighteenth century, European colonists had established a number of distinctive colonial regions in North America. The northern periphery of New Spain, the oldest and most prosperous European colony, stretched from Baja California to eastern Texas, then jumped to the settlements on the northern end of the Florida peninsula; cattle ranching was the dominant way of life in this thinly populated region. New France was like a great crescent, extending from the plantation communities along the Mississippi near New Orleans to the French colonial communities along the St. Lawrence; in between were isolated settlements and forts, connected only by the extensive French trading network.

as well as the hundreds of African American runaways who considered St. Augustine a refuge from the cruel slave regimes in Georgia and Carolina. Like the community of Kahnawake, eighteenth-century Florida included a growing mestizo population as well as a considerable number of free African Americans and Hispanicized Indians from the old missions.

New Mexico, nearly 2,000 miles to the west, was similarly isolated from the mainstream of New Spain. One Spanish observer characterized the province as "little populated and poverty-stricken, although endowed with natural resources." At midcentury New Mexico included some 20,000 Pueblo Indians (their numbers greatly reduced by disease since their first contact with Europeans) and perhaps 10,000 colonists. The prosperity of these colonists, who supported themselves with subsistence agriculture, was severely constrained by a restrictive colonial economic policy that forced them to exchange their wool, pottery, buffalo hides, and buckskin for imported goods at unfavorable rates. Unlike the colonial population of Florida, however, the settlements of New Mexicans were gradually expanding, following the valleys and streams that led

east and north from the original colonial outposts scattered along the upper Rio Grande.

The Spanish also founded new northern outposts during the eighteenth century. Concerned about French colonization of the Mississippi Valley, they established several military posts or *presidios* on the fringes of the colony of Louisiana and in 1716 began the construction of a string of Franciscan missions among the Indian peoples of Texas. By 1750 the settlement of San Antonio had become the center of a developing frontier province. The Spanish also established new colonial outposts west of New Mexico, in what is today southern Arizona. In the 1690s, Jesuit missionaries, led by Father Eusebio Kino, founded missions among the desert Indians of the lower Colorado and Gila River Valleys. Mission San Xavier del Bac near Tucson is acclaimed the most striking example of Spanish colonial architecture in the United States. Cattle ranching, introduced by the Jesuits, and farming as well spread along the lower Rio Grande Valley; in fact, ranching would continue to define the region's economy for the next 200 years.

Midcentury also found the Spanish considering new settlements along the California coast. Juan

The church of San Xavier del Bac, constructed in the late eighteenth century, is located a few miles south of the city of Tucson, where Jesuit Father Eusebio Kino founded a mission among the Pima Indians in 1700. Known as the White Dove of the Desert, it is acclaimed as the most striking example of Spanish colonial architecture in the United States.

Cabrillo, an associate of Hernán Cortés, had first explored the coastal waters in 1542 and was the first European to sail into the fine harbor at San Diego. In 1603 the explorer Sebastián Vizcaíno had come upon Monterey Bay. The Spanish did little to follow up on these finds, but in 1769, acting on rumors of Russian expansion along the northern Pacific coast (for a discussion of Russian America, see Chapter 9), officials in Mexico City ordered Gaspar de Portolá, governor of what is now Baja California, to establish a Spanish presence in the North. With him were Franciscan missionaries led by Junípero Serra, president of the missions in Baja. At the harbor of San Diego, Portolá and Serra founded the first mission and pueblo complex in present-day California. Portolá then proceeded overland, becoming the first European to explore the interior valleys and mountains, and in 1770 he and Serra established their headquarters at Monterey Bay on the central coast. Two years later Juan Bautista de Anza established an overland route across the blistering deserts connecting Arizona and California, and in 1776 he led a colonizing expedition that founded the pueblo of San Francisco. Over the next fifty years the number of California settlements grew to include twenty-one missions and a half-dozen presidios and pueblos, including the town of Los Angeles. Founded in 1781 by a group of mestizo settlers from Sinaloa, Mexico, by the end of the century Los Angeles, with a population of only 300, was California's largest town.

A distinguishing mark of these colonial communities was their close association with the mission system. For the Spanish, conquest demanded conversion, which, according to theory, would lead Indians toward "civilization." Like the efforts of the Jesuits at Kahnawake and elsewhere in New France, the Spanish experiment in cultural transformation was designed to make Indians over into Christians and loyal subjects by educating them and putting them to work raising cattle and crops. The most extensive mission project was in California, where under the direction of priests thousands of Indian laborers produced a flourishing local economy based on irrigation farming as well as horse, cattle, and sheep ranching. Near Los Angeles lay San Gabriel, one of the most prosperous missions, where large vineyards and orchards produced fine wines and brandies. Indian people also constructed the adobe and stone churches, built on Spanish and Moorish patterns, whose ruins symbolize California's colonial society.

But this experiment in culture change was deadly for Indian people. To keep the system functioning, the Franciscan missionaries resorted to cruel and sometimes violent means of controlling their Indian subjects: shackles, solitary confinement, and whipping posts. Indians resisted from the very beginning. In 1775 the villagers around San Diego rose up and killed several priests. The history of many missions was punctuated by revolts, but the arms and organization of Spanish soldiers were usually sufficient to suppress the uprisings. There were also smaller incidents of retaliation, as when at Mission Santa Cruz, on the central coast, a priest who thrashed Indians too often was murdered. Another form of protest was flight: whole villages sometimes fled to the inaccessible mountains.

Foreign observers noted the despondency of California's mission Indians. "I have never seen any of them laugh," one European visitor wrote. "I have never seen a single one look anyone in the face. They have the air of taking no interest in anything." The record of revolt suggests that there may have been more than a little guile in this mask of servility. But overwork, overcrowding, poor nutrition, poor sanitation, and epidemic disease took a terrible toll. The death rate, particularly high for children and women of child-bearing age, exceeded the birth rate, and California's native population fell by at least 25 percent.

As the prominence of mission settlements in California, Texas, and New Mexico suggests, the Catholic Church played a dominant role in the community life of the borderlands. In the eighteenth century, religion was no private affair. It was a deadly serious business dividing nations into warring camps, and the Spanish considered themselves the special protectors of the traditions of Rome. The object of colonization, one colonial promoter wrote in 1584, was "enlarging the glorious gospel of Christ, and leading the infinite multitudes of these simple people that are in error into the right and perfect way of salvation." Although these are the words of the English imperialist Richard Hakluyt, they could as easily have come from the Spanish padres Kino or Serra or the Jesuit missionaries at Kahnawake. There was no tradition of religious dissent. Certain of the truth of their "right and perfect way," the Spanish could see no reason for tolerating the errors of others.

The French Crescent

In France, as in Spain, Church and state were closely interwoven. During the seventeenth century the French prime ministers, Cardinal Richelieu and Cardinal Mazarin, laid out a fundamentally Catholic imperial policy, and under their guidance colonists constructed a second Catholic empire in North America. In 1674 Church and state collaborated in establishing the bishopric of Quebec.

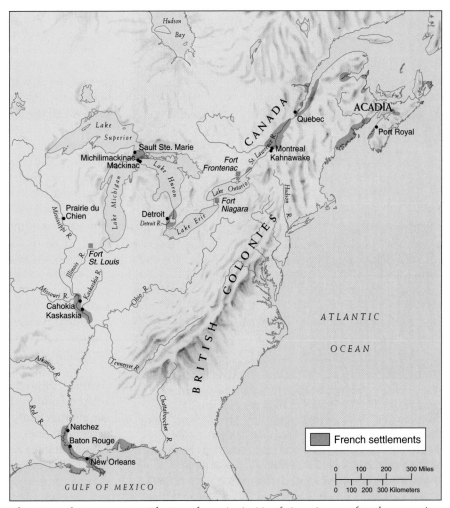

The French Crescent   *The French empire in North America was based on a series of alliances and trade relations with Indian nations linking a great crescent of colonies, settlements, and outposts that extended from the mouth of the* St. Lawrence River, *through the Great Lakes, and down the Mississippi River to the Gulf of Mexico.*

Under aggressive leadership that office founded local seminaries, oversaw the appointment and review of priests, and laid the foundation of the resolutely Catholic culture of New France. Meanwhile, Jesuit missionaries continued to carry Catholicism deep into the continent.

The number of French colonists rose at an impressive rate from fewer than 15,000 in 1700 to more than 70,000 at midcentury. During the eighteenth century the French used their trade network and alliances with the Indians to establish a great crescent of colonies, military posts, and settlements that extended from the mouth of the St. Lawrence River, southwest through the Great Lakes, then down the Mississippi River to the Gulf of Mexico. The maritime colony of Acadia, populated by fishermen and farmers, anchored the crescent on the northeast; the slave colony of Louisiana held the other end at the mouth of the Mississippi. Over this vast territory the French laid a thin colonial veneer, the beginning of what they planned as a

The persistence of French colonial long lots in the pattern of modern landholding is clear in this enhanced satellite photograph of the Mississippi River near New Orleans. Long lots, the characteristic form of property holding in New France, were designed to offer as many settlers as possible a share of good bottomland as well as a frontage on the waterways, which served as the basic transportation network.

great continental empire that would contain the Protestant British to a narrow strip of Atlantic coastline.

At the heart of the French empire in North America were the farming communities of the colony of Quebec along the banks of the St. Lawrence, including the towns of Montreal and Quebec City. There were also farming communities in the Illinois country, which shipped wheat down the Mississippi to supply the booming sugar plantations of Louisiana. By the mid-eighteenth century, those plantations—extending along the river from Natchez and Baton Rouge to New Orleans—had become the most profitable French enterprise in North America.

One of the most distinctive French stamps on the North American landscape were the "long lots" stretching back from the rivers that provided each settler family a share of good bottomland to farm as well as frontage on the waterways, the "interstate highway system" of the French Crescent. This pattern had first appeared with the seigneurial grants along the St. Lawrence, but French colonists transplanted it throughout their domain; aerial photographs reveal its persistence today. Long lots were laid out along the lower Mississippi in Louisiana and at sites on the upper Mississippi such as Kaskaskia and

Prairie du Chien, as well as at the strategic passages of the Great Lakes, the communities of Mackinac, Sault Ste. Marie, and Detroit. In 1750 Detroit was a stockaded town with a military garrison, a small administrative center, several stores, a Catholic church, and 100 households of *métis* (French for mestizo) families. French and *métis* farmers worked the land along the Detroit River, not far from communities inhabited by more than 6,000 Ottawa, Potawatomi, and Huron Indians.

Communities of this sort that combined both French and Indian elements were in the tradition of the inclusive frontier. Detroit looked like "an old French village," said one observer, except that its houses were "mostly covered with bark," in Indian style. "It is not uncommon to see a Frenchman with Indian shoes and stockings, without breeches, wearing a strip of woolen cloth to cover what decency requires him to conceal," wrote another. "Yet at the same time he wears a fine ruffled shirt and a laced waistcoat, with a fine handkerchief on his head." Detroit had much of the character of the mixed community of Kahnawake on the St. Lawrence.

Family and kinship were also cast in the Indian pattern. Households frequently consisted of several related families, but wives limited their births, having on average only two or three children. There were arranged marriages and occasional polygamy, but women had easy access to divorce and enjoyed property rights. Yet the people focused their activities on commerce and identified themselves overwhelmingly as Catholic. More frequently than not choosing a path of mutual accommodation, the French and Indians established some of the most interesting and distinct of North American communities.

New England

Just as New Spain and New France had their official church, so did the people of New England: local communities in all the New England colonies but Rhode Island were governed by Puritan congregations. Under the plan established in Massachusetts, the local church of a community was free to run its own affairs under the guidance of the General Court (the governor and the representatives selected by the towns). The Puritan colonies allotted each congregation a tract of communal land. Church members divided this land among themselves on the basis of status and seniority, laying out central villages like Deerfield and building churches (called meetinghouses) that were maintained through taxation. Adult male church members constituted the freemen of the town, and thus there was very little distinction between religious and secular authority. At the town meeting the freemen chose their minister, voted on his salary and support, and elected local men to offices ranging from town clerk to fence viewer.

The Puritan tradition, however, was a curious mix of freedom and repression. Although local communities had considerable autonomy, they were tightly bound by the restrictions of the Puritan faith and the General Court. Contrary to the beliefs of many, the Puritans did not come to America to create a society where religion could be freely practiced but to establish their own version of the "right and perfect way," which placed severe restraints on individuals. The General Court, for example, passed a statute threatening that "if any man shall exceed the bounds of moderation, we shall punish him severely." Specifics were left to the imagination. Not only did the Puritans exile dissidents such as Roger Williams and Anne Hutchinson (see Chapter 3), they banned Anglicans and Baptists and jailed, tortured, and even executed members of the Society of Friends, commonly known as the Quakers.

One of the first formal arguments for religious toleration was made by the New Englander Roger Williams, leader of dissenting Rhode Island, in his book *The Bloudy Tenent of Persecution* (1644). "Forced worship," he wrote, "stinks in God's nostrils." This argument gained increasing appeal following the religious excesses of the English civil war. In 1661, lamenting "the sad experience" of the previous generation of religious conflicts, restored King Charles II ordered a stop to religious persecution in Massachusetts. The new climate of opinion was best expressed by the English philosopher John Locke in his *Letter on Tolerance* (1688). Churches were voluntary societies, he argued, and could work only through persuasion. That a religion was sanctioned by the state was no evidence of its truth, because different nations had different official religions. Consequently, the state had no legitimate concern with religious belief. Locke's ideas were embodied in the Toleration Act, passed by Parliament in 1689. New England at first resisted it, but under pressure from English authorities, Massachusetts and Connecticut reluctantly allowed other Protestant denominations to begin worshipping openly in 1700. In both colonies, however, the Puritan, or as it was now called, Congregationalist Church (because of its self-governing congregations) continued to be officially supported through taxation. (It would not be "disestablished" in Massachusetts until 1833.) By the 1730s there were Anglican, Baptist, and Presbyterian congregations in many New England towns.

The system of town and church government was well suited to population growth. As towns grew too large for the available land, groups of residents left together, "hiving off" to form new churches and towns elsewhere. An intricate network of roads and rivers knit the region together. Seventy-five years after the Indians of southern New England suffered their final defeat in King Philip's War (see Chapter 3), Puritan farm communities had taken up most of the available land of Massachusetts, Connecticut, and Rhode Island, leaving only a few communities of Pequots, Narragansets, and Wampanoags on restricted reservations. Northern Algonquians and Catholic Iroquois allied with the French in Quebec, however, maintained a defensive barrier preventing New Englanders from expanding northward into Maine, New Hampshire, and the region later called Vermont. Deerfield represented the far northern limit of safe settlement. By midcentury, then, as the result of growing population, New England was reaching the limit of its land supply.

The Middle Colonies

The colony of New York had one of the most ethnically diverse populations on the continent, in striking contrast to the ethnically homogeneous neighboring New England colonies of Connecticut and Massachusetts. At midcentury society along the lower Hudson River, including the counties in northern New Jersey,

The House of the Seven Gables in Salem, Massachusetts, was constructed in the seventeenth century. In this style of architecture, function prevailed over form as structures grew to accommodate their residents; rooms were added where and when they were needed. In England, wood for building was scarce, but the abundance of forests in North America created the conditions for a golden age of wood construction.

was a veritable mosaic of ethnic communities: the Dutch of Flatbush, the Huguenots of New Rochelle, the Flemish of Bergen County, and the Scots of Perth Amboy were but a few. African Americans, both slave and free, made up more than 15 percent of the lower Hudson population. Congregations of Puritans, Baptists, Quakers, and Catholics worshiped without legal hindrance. New York City also was home to the oldest Jewish community in the country, established in 1654; several hundred Jewish families attended services in North America's first synagogue, built in 1730. Among these communities there was a great deal of intermingling (as there was at places such as Kahnawake), but different ethnic and religious groups would long retain their distinctions, which made New York something of a cultural "salad bowl" if not a "melting pot."

New York City grew by leaps and bounds in the eighteenth century, but the elite who had inherited the rich lands and great manors along the upper Hudson chose to rent to tenants rather than to sell, diminishing the region's attractiveness to immigrants. By contrast, Pennsylvania was what one German immigrant called "heaven for farmers." The colony's Quaker proprietors were willing to sell land to anyone who could pay the relatively modest prices. Thus as the region around New York City filled up, immigrants by the thousand made the decision to land at Philadelphia, Pennsylvania's growing port city on the Delaware River. During the eighteenth century the population of this region and an extended area that encompassed portions of New Jersey, Delaware, and Maryland grew more dramatically than any other in North America. Here, immigration played the dominant role in achieving the astonishing annual growth rate of nearly 4 percent. Boasting some of the best farmland in North America, the region was soon exporting abundant produce through Philadelphia.

The Quakers who had founded Pennsylvania quickly became a minority, but, unlike the Puritans, they were generally comfortable with religious and ethnic pluralism. Many of the founders of the Society of Friends had been imprisoned for their beliefs in pre-Restoration England, and they were determined to prevent a repetition of this injustice in their own province. William Penn himself had been prominent in the struggle for religious toleration. "Force never yet made a good Christian," he argued. Indeed, the Quakers were opposed to all signs of rank, refusing to doff their hats to superiors but greeting all comers, whatever their station, with the extended handshake of brotherhood. To a remarkable extent, these attitudes extended to relations between the sexes as well. English founder George Fox had proclaimed that "in souls there is no sex," and among American Friends, women preached equally with men.

These Quaker attitudes were well suited to the ethnically and religiously diverse population of Penn-

sylvania. Although the Society of Friends remained the affiliation of the governing elite, it never became an established church. Most German immigrants were Lutherans or Calvinists, most North Britons Presbyterians, and there were plenty of Anglicans and Baptists as well. These churches constituted one of the cornerstones of Pennsylvania community life.

The institutions of government were another pillar of community organization. Colonial officials appointed justices of the peace from among the leading local men, and these justices provided judicial authority for the countryside. Property-owning farmers chose their own local officials. Country communities were tied together by kinship bonds and by bartering and trading among neighbors. The substantial stone houses and great barns of the Pennsylvania countryside testified to the social stability and prosperity of this system. The communities of the middle colonies, however, were more loosely bound than those of New England. Rates of mobility were considerably higher, with about half the population moving on in any given decade. Because land was sold in individual lots rather than in communal parcels, farmers tended to disperse themselves at will over the open countryside. Villages gradually developed at crossroads and ferries but with relatively little forethought or planning. It was Pennsylvania, which emphasized individual settlement, that provided the basic model for American expansion.

The Backcountry

By 1750 Pennsylvania's exploding population had pushed beyond the first range of the Appalachian highlands. Settlers occupied the northern reaches of the

This two-story log house, built in Pennsylvania in the early eighteenth century, is one of the oldest surviving examples of the method and style of log construction introduced in America by the Scandinavian colonists on the lower Delaware River. Learning New World farming and woodland hunting techniques from the Indians, these settlers forged a tradition of settlement that proved enormously successful for pioneers.

Great Valley, which extended southwest from Pennsylvania into Virginia. Although they hoped to become commercial farmers, these settlers began more modestly, planting Indian corn and raising hogs, hunting in the woods for meat and furs, and building log cabins. This strategy had originated with the settlers of the New Sweden colony on the lower Delaware River. Scandinavian immigrants brought their hunting traditions and introduced log cabin construction to North America. From the Delaware Indians they incorporated the methods of New World farming and woodland hunting, just as the Indians took from them the use of firearms and metal tools and began to build log structures of their own. These were some of the most successful cross-cultural adaptations of the eighteenth century.

The movement into the Pennsylvania and Virginia backcountry that began during the 1720s was the first of the great pioneer treks that would take Americans into the continental interior. Many, perhaps most, of these pioneers held no legal title to the lands they occupied; they simply hacked out and defended their squatters' claims from Indian tribes and all other comers. Many of these backcountry settlers came from the northern borders of England and Ireland, where there was considerable clan and ethnic violence, and adapted well to the violence of the backcountry. To the Delawares and Shawnees who had been pushed into the interior, or the Cherokees who occupied the Appalachian highlands to the south, however, these pioneers presented a new and deadly threat. Their rising fears and resentments over the expanding colonial population triggered much eighteenth-century warfare.

One of the distinctive characteristics of the backcountry was the settlers' disdain for rank. "The rain don't know broadcloth from bluejeans," they said. But the myth of frontier equality was simply that—myth. Most pioneers owned little or no land, while "big men" held great tracts and dominated local communities with their bombastic style of personal leadership. Here the men were warriors, the women workers. The story was told of one pioneer whose wife began to "jaw at" him. "He pulled off his breeches and threw them down to her, telling her to 'put them on and wear them.'"

The South

The Chesapeake and the Lower South were tri-racial societies, with intermingled communities of white colonists and black slaves, along with substantial Indian communities living on the fringes of colonial settlement. Much of the population growth of the region resulted from the forced migration of enslaved Africans, who by 1750 made up 40 percent of the population. Colonial settlement had filled not only the Tidewater area of the southern Atlantic coast but much of the Piedmont as well. Specializing in rice, tobacco,

Spread of Settlement: Movement into the Backcountry, 1720–1760 *The spread of settlement from 1720 to 1760 shows the movement of population into the backcountry in the midcentury.*

and other commercial crops, these colonies were overwhelmingly rural. Farms and plantations were dispersed across the countryside, and villages or towns were few.

English authorities made the Church of England the state religion in the Chesapeake colonies. Residents paid taxes to support the Church and were required to attend services. No other churches were allowed into Virginia and Maryland, and dissenters were excluded or exiled. Before the 1750s, the Toleration Act was little enforced in the South; at the same time, the Anglican establishment was internally weak. It maintained neither a colonial bishop nor local institutions for training clergy. In Carolina and Georgia, neither Anglicanism nor any other denomination rested on a firm foundation.

Along the rice coast, the dominant institution of social life was the large plantation. Transforming the tangle of woods and swamps along the region's rivers into an ordered pattern of dams, dikes, and flooded fields required a heavy capital investment, which meant that rice cultivation could be undertaken only by men of means. By midcentury, established plantations typically were dominated by a large main house, generally located on a spot of high ground overlooking the fields. Drayton Hall near Charleston, a mansion of the period that still survives, was built of pink brick in classically symmetrical style, with hand-carved interior moldings of imported Caribbean mahogany. Nearby, but a world apart, were the slave quarters, rough wooden cabins lining two sides of a muddy pathway near the outbuildings and barns. In this contrast between "big house" and "quarters" the Lower South was the closest thing in North America to the societies of the Caribbean sugar islands.

Grand plantation houses could be found in the Chesapeake as well. However, because tobacco, unlike rice, could be grown profitably in small plots, the Chesapeake included a greater variety of farmers and a correspondingly diverse landscape. Tobacco quickly drained the soil of its nutrients, and plantings had to be shifted to fresh ground every few years. Former tobacco land could be planted with corn for several years but then required twenty years or more of rest before reuse. The landscape was thus a patchwork of fields, many in various stages of ragged second growth. The poorest farmers lived in wooden cabins little better than the shacks of the slaves. More prosperous farm families lived with two or three slaves in houses that were nevertheless considerably smaller than the substantial homes of New England.

In the Lower South, where the plantations were little worlds unto themselves, there was relatively little community life outside the plantation. But by midcentury the Chesapeake had given rise to well-developed neighborhoods based on kinship networks and economic connections. Encouraging the developing sense of community more than any other institution was the county court, which held both executive and judicial power. On court day, white people of all ranks held a great gathering that included public business, horse racing, and perhaps a barbecue. The gentleman justices of the county, appointed by the governor, included the heads of the leading planter families. These men in turn selected the grand jury, composed of substantial freeholders. One of the most significant bonding forces in this free white population was the growing sense of racial solidarity that developed in response to the increasing proportion of African slaves dispersed throughout the neighborhoods.

Traditional Culture in the New World

In each of these North American colonial societies the family and kinship, the church, and the local community were the most significant factors in everyday life. Throughout the continent, colonists tended to live much as they had in their European homelands at the time their colonies were settled. Thus the residents of New Mexico, Quebec, and New England continued to

be attached to the religious passions of the seventeenth century long after their mother countries had put those religious controversies aside in favor of imperial geopolitics. Nostalgia for Europe helped to fix a conservative colonial attitude toward culture.

These were oral cultures, depending on the transmission of information by the spoken word rather than through print, on the passage of traditions through storytelling and song, music and crafts. North American colonial folk cultures, traditional and suspicious of change, preserved an essentially medieval world view. The rhythms of life were regulated by the hours of sunlight and the seasons of the year. People rose with the sun and went to bed soon after it went down. The demands of the season determined their working routines. They farmed with simple tools and were subject to the whims of nature, for drought, flood, or pestilence might quickly sweep away their efforts. Experience told them that the natural world imposed limitations within which men and women had to learn to live. Even patterns of reproduction conformed to nature's cycle: in nearly every European colonial community of North America the number of births peaked in late winter, then fell to a low point during the summer; for African Americans, by contrast, births peaked in early summer. Historians have not yet

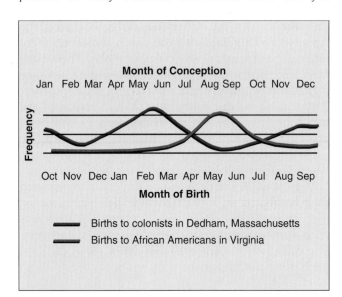

Monthly Frequency of Successful Conceptions
Human reproduction in colonial America corresponded to cycles. But European colonists and African American slaves had different patterns, with white births peaking in March, black births peaking in May and June. Historians do not yet know the cause of this variation, but it is probably tied to old English and African traditions.

Source: James A. Henretta and Gregory H. Nobles, *Evolution and Revolution: American Society, 1600–1820* (Lexington, Mass.: Heath, 1987), 37; Mechal Sobel, *The World They Made Together: Black and White Values in Eighteenth-Century Virginia* (Princeton: Princeton University Press, 1987), 67.

accounted for this intriguing pattern or provided an explanation for the differences between white and black families, but apparently there was some "inner" seasonal clock tied to old European and African patterns. Human sexual activity itself seemed to fluctuate with the rural working demands created by the seasons.

These were also communal cultures. In Quebec villagers worked side by side to repair the roads, in New Mexico they collectively maintained the irrigation canals, in New England they gathered in town meetings to decide the dates when common fields were to be plowed, sowed, and harvested. When in 1620 the Pilgrims and the other Mayflower passengers signed their compact, promising "due submission" to "the general good," they explicitly set down principles with which most North American colonists could agree. Even the artifacts of everyday life reveal this collective emphasis. Houses offered little privacy, with families often sleeping together in the same chamber, sitting together on benches rather than in chairs, and taking their supper from a common bowl or trencher. For most North American colonists of the mid-eighteenth century, the community was more important than the individual.

Throughout North America, most colonists continued the traditional European occupation of working the land. Plantation agriculture was designed to be a commercial system, in which crops were commodities for sale. Commercial farming also developed in some particularly fertile areas, notably southeastern Pennsylvania, which became known as the breadbasket of North America, as well as the country surrounding colonial cities such as New York, Boston, and Quebec. The majority of the farmers of eighteenth-century North America, however, grew crops and raised livestock for their own needs or for local barter, and communities were largely self-sufficient. Most farmers attempted to produce small surpluses as well, which they sold to pay their taxes and buy some manufactured goods. But rather than specializing in the production of one or two crops for sale, they attempted to remain as independent of the market as possible, diversifying their activities. The primary goal was ownership of land and the assurance that children and descendants would be able to settle within the community on lands nearby.

Rural households frequently practiced crafts or trades as a sideline. Farm men were also blacksmiths, coopers, weavers, or carpenters. Some farm women were independent traders in dairy products or eggs. Others became midwives and medicinal experts serving the community. In one Maine community, for example, the midwife Martha Ballard delivered 797 babies over twenty-seven years, and both male and female patients came to her for salves, pills, syrups, ointments, or advice.

In colonial cities, artisans and craftsmen worked at their trades full time. Artisans also followed tradition by organizing themselves according to the European craft system. In the colonial cities of the Atlantic coast, carpenters, iron makers, blacksmiths, shipwrights, and scores of other tradesmen had their own self-governing associations. Young men who wished to pursue a trade served several years as apprentices, working in exchange for learning the skills and secrets of the craft. After completing their apprenticeships they sought employment in a shop. Their search often required them to migrate to some other area, thus becoming "journeymen." Most craftsmen remained at the journeyman level for their whole careers. But by building a good name and carefully saving, journeymen hoped to become master craftsmen, opening shops and employing journeymen and apprentices of their own. As in farming, the ultimate goal was independence, control over one's work.

With the exception of midwifery, there were few opportunities for women outside the household. By law, husbands held managerial rights over family property, but widows received support in the form of a one-third lifetime interest, known as "dower," in a deceased husband's real estate (the rest of the estate being divided among the heirs). And in certain occupations, such as printing (which had a tradition of employing women), widows succeeded their husbands in business. As a result, some colonial women played active roles in eighteenth-century journalism. Ann Smith Franklin, Benjamin Franklin's sister-in-law, took over the operation of her husband's Rhode Island shop after his death. Widow Cornelia Smith Bradford continued to publish her deceased husband's Philadelphia paper and was an important force in publishing throughout the 1750s.

The Frontier Heritage

The colonial societies of eighteenth-century North America also shared perspectives unique to their frontier heritage. European colonists came from Old World societies in which land was scarce and monopolized by property-owning elites. They settled in a continent where, for the most part, land was abundant and cheap. This was probably the most important distinction between North America and Europe. American historians once tied the existence of this "free land" directly to the development of democracy. But although extensive lands were available in all the colonies of North America, the colonial experience encouraged assumptions that were anything but democratic.

One of the most important and widely accepted of these assumptions was that forced labor was legitimate. A woman of eighteenth-century South Carolina once offered advice on how to achieve a good

A *carpenter and spinner from* The Book of Trades, *an eighteenth-century British survey of the crafts practiced in colonial America. In colonial cities artisans organized themselves into the traditional European craft system, with apprentices, journeymen, and masters. There were few opportunities for the employment of women outside the household, but women sometimes earned income by establishing sidelines as midwives or spinners.*

living. "Get a few slaves," she declared, and "beat them well to make them work hard." In a land where free men and women could work for themselves on their own plot of ground, there was little incentive to work for wages. As a result, labor was in short supply throughout the colonies. Coercion was one of the few ways a landowner could secure an agricultural work force. In the Spanish borderlands, captured Apache children were made lifetime servants, and the Indian slave trade flourished through the eighteenth century. In Quebec one could see African American slaves from the French Caribbean working side by side with enslaved Indians captured by other tribes in the West and sold to French traders. In Philadelphia, according to Benjamin Franklin, wages for free workers were so high that most of the unskilled labor was "performed chiefly by indentured servants." All the colonists came

from European cultures that believed in social hierarchy and subordination, and involuntary servitude was easily incorporated into their world view.

At least half the immigrants to eighteenth-century British America arrived as indentured servants. This system allowed poor immigrants to arrange passage across the Atlantic in exchange for four or five years of service in America. Usually indentured servants were single men, often skilled artisans. Sometimes families without means emigrated as "redemptioners." Under this system, they arranged with the ship's owner to pay their passage on arrival in North America. If no one in the colonies stepped forth to pay, they sold themselves into service for the payment. Thus family members were sometimes separated. In addition, during the eighteenth century the British sent over, mostly to the Chesapeake, some

50,000 convicts sentenced to seven or fourteen years at hard labor. One historian, accounting for the cost of passage and upkeep, estimates that indentured servants earned their masters, on average, about fifty pounds sterling over their terms of service, the equivalent of something like four or five thousand dollars in today's values.

All classes of bound laborers remained on board ship after arrival in America, awaiting inspection by potential buyers, who poked muscles, peered into open mouths, and pinched women. Although servants were not slaves, to the men and women lined up for inspection that may have seemed a distinction without a difference. There were other similarities between indentured servitude and slavery. The ocean crossing was frequently traumatic. One immigrant described a passage across the Atlantic to Philadelphia in which several hundred people were packed like sardines in the ship's hold. "The ship is filled with pitiful signs of distress," he wrote, "smells, fumes, horrors, vomiting, various kinds of sea sickness, fever, dysentery, headaches, heat, constipation, boils, scurvy, cancer, mouth-rot, and similar afflictions. In such misery all the people on board pray and cry pitifully together." In 1750 Pennsylvania was finally compelled to pass a law to prevent the overcrowding of ships filled with indentured passengers. Especially in the Chesapeake, the life of an indentured servant could be filled with harsh and grueling labor, just like a slave's. Running away was common, although it was usually unsuccessful and resulted in extra time to serve: in Pennsylvania a runaway was liable for five times the lost service, in Maryland ten times!

Unlike slaves, however, those servants who endured had a chance of freedom. "Freedom dues" might include a suit of clothes, tools, money, and sometimes land. The social mobility of former servants was limited, however. Of the thousands of men who came to the British colonies under indenture during the seventeenth and early eighteenth centuries, only about 20 percent achieved positions of moderate comfort. The majority died before their terms were completed, returned to England, or continued in miserable poverty. But opportunities for advancement increased somewhat with the overall prosperity of the eighteenth-century British colonies. By midcentury, the chances of moderate success for former servants were probably better than fifty-fifty. The majority of redemptioners, for example, appear to have become small farmers.

The expectation of property ownership was a second important assumption that flowed from the frontier heritage and abundance of land in colonial America. This expectation led to rising popular demands in all regions that more and more land be taken from the Indian inhabitants and opened to white settlement. Some colonists justified the resulting wars of dispossession by arguing, as Puritans did, that Indians deserved to lose their lands because they had failed to use them to their utmost capacity. Others simply maintained that Indians should be dispossessed because they were "savages." But whatever their specific justifications, the majority of colonists—whether British, Spanish, or French—accepted the violence and brutality directed against the Indians as an essential aspect of colonial life. Thus did the Puritan minister Cotton Mather praise Hannah Dustin, a New England woman who escaped her captors during King William's War by killing and scalping nine sleeping Indians, including two women and six children. With this as the model for the behavior of captive women, one can understand why Eunice Williams was hesitant to return to Deerfield after she had married an Indian.

DIVERGING SOCIAL AND POLITICAL PATTERNS

Despite these important similarities among the colonial regions of North America, the eighteenth century also marked a period when the experience of the British colonies began to diverge sharply from that of the French and Spanish. Immigration, economic growth, and provincial political struggles all pushed British colonists in a radically new direction.

Population Growth

All the colonial regions of North America experienced unprecedented growth in the eighteenth century. "Our people must at least be doubled every twenty years," wrote Benjamin Franklin in a remarkable 1751 essay on population, and he was very nearly right. In 1700 there were 290,000 colonists north of Mexico; fifty years later they had grown to approximately 1.3 million, an average annual growth rate of about 3 percent. Typical preindustrial societies grow at rates of less than 1 percent per year, approximately the pace of Europe's expansion in the eighteenth century. But the colonial societies of North America experienced what English economist Thomas Malthus, writing at the end of the eighteenth century, described as "a rapidity of increase probably without parallel in history."

High fertility played an important role in this extraordinary growth. It was common for women in the British colonies to bear seven or more children, and colonial women in the French villages along the St. Lawrence or the towns of New Mexico were equally fertile. In addition, mortality rates were relatively low: in most colonial areas there were fewer than 30 deaths for every 1,000 persons, a rate 15 or 20 percent lower than in Europe. Moreover, levels of infant mortality were low. Blessed with fertile lands and the effective-

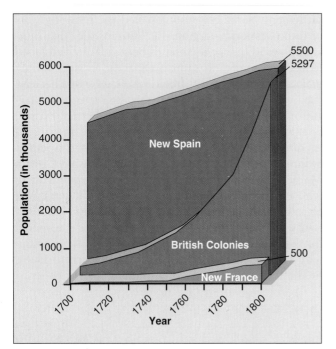

Estimated Total Population of New Spain, New France, and the British North American Colonies, 1700–1780   *Although the populations of all three North American colonial empires grew in the eighteenth century, the explosive growth of the British colonies was unmatched.*

Source: *Historical Statistics of the United States* (Washington, D.C.: Government Printing Office, 1976), 1168.

ness of Indian agricultural techniques, North America had no famines. For the colonists, North America was a remarkably healthy environment.

Yet although all North American colonial societies had high fertility rates, the British colonies grew far more rapidly than those of other nations. The reason for this contrast was the very different colonial policies on immigration. In New France and New Spain restrictive policies curbed the number of European immigrants. By contrast, English authorities allowed a massive immigration of their own subjects to North America in the seventeenth century. A total of 150,000 English men and women had relocated to the colonies by 1700, providing a substantial population base for further growth. In addition, the British were the only colonial power to encourage the immigration of foreign nationals to their colonies. (See "Immigration and Community: The Changing Face of Ethnicity in America, to 1800" on page 222.)

Social Class

Although traditional working roles were transferred to North America, attempts to transplant the European class system by creating monopolies on land were far less successful. In New France the landowning seigneurs claimed privileges similar to those

enjoyed by their aristocratic counterparts at home; the Spanish system of encomienda and the great manors created by the Dutch, and after them the English along the Hudson River, also represented attempts to bring the essence of European feudalism to North America. But in most areas, because settlers had relatively free access to land, these monopolies proved difficult or impossible to maintain. There was, of course, a system of economic rank and an unequal distribution of wealth, prestige, and power. North American society was not aristocratic, but neither was it without social hierarchy.

In New Spain the official criterion for status was racial purity. *Españoles* (Spaniards) or *gente de razón* (literally, "people of reason") occupied the top rung of the social ladder, with mestizos, mulattoes, and others on descending levels; African slaves and Indians were at the bottom. In the isolated northern borderlands, however, these distinctions tended to disappear, with *castas* (persons of mixed background) enjoying considerably more opportunity. Mestizos who acquired land might suddenly be reclassified as españoles. "The only two castes we know of here are the gente de razón and Indians," observed a missionary in California, "and all the former are considered Spaniards." Similarly, census takers in eighteenth-century Texas listed everyone but Indians as españoles, producing curious listings such as "Spaniard from Canada" or "Spaniard from France." Even so, Spanish and French colonial societies were cut in the style of the Old World, with its hereditary ranks and titles. The landlords of New France and the Spanish borderlands may have lacked the means to accumulate real wealth, but they lived lives of elegance compared to the hard toil of the people who owed them labor service or rent.

The upper class of British colonial society—the wealthiest 10 percent of all whites—was made up of large landowners, merchants, and prosperous professionals. In the eighteenth century, property valued at £2,000 marked a family as well-to-do, and £5,000 was real wealth. Leading merchants, with annual incomes in excess of £500, lived in opulence. Despite their lack of titles, the wealthy planters and merchants in the British colonies lived far more extravagantly than the seigneurs of New France or the dons of the Spanish borderlands. What separated the culture of class in the British colonies from that of New France or New Mexico, however, was not so much the material conditions of life as the prevailing attitude toward social rank. In the Catholic cultures, the upper class attempted to obscure its origins, claiming descent from European nobility. But in British North America people celebrated social mobility. The class system was remarkably open, and the entrance

An eighteenth-century Mexican painting of a mixed family, an example of a genre of portraits depicting various racial castas. Here, a Spanish father and Indian mother produce a mestizo child.

of newly successful planters, commercial farmers, and merchants into the upper ranks was not only possible but frequent—although by midcentury most upper-class families had inherited, not earned, their wealth.

To be sure, there was a large lower class in the British colonies. Slaves, bound servants, and poor laboring families made up at least 40 percent of the population. For them the standard of living did not rise above bare subsistence. Most lived from hand to mouth, often suffering through seasons of severe privation. A small proportion of poor whites could expect their condition to improve during their lifetimes, but slaves were a permanently servile population. Enslaved African Americans stood apart from the gains in the standard of living enjoyed by immigrants from Europe. Their lives had been degraded beyond measure from the conditions prevailing in their native lands.

The feature of the class system most frequently commented on by eighteenth-century observers was not the character or composition of the lower ranks but rather the size and strength of the middle class, a rank entirely absent in the colonies of France and Spain. As one Pennsylvanian wrote at midcentury, "The people of this province are generally of the middling sort." More than half the population of the British colonies, and nearly 70 percent of all white settlers, might be so classified. Most were families of landowning farmers of small to moderate means, but the group also included artisans, craftsmen, and small shopkeepers.

At the low end, the colonial middle class included families whose standard of living was barely above subsistence; at the high end were those whose holdings approached real wealth. Households solidly in the center of this broad ranking owned land or other property worth approximately £500 and earned the equivalent of about £100 per year. They enjoyed a standard of living higher than that of the great majority of people in England and Europe. The low mortality of British Americans was important testimony to generally better living conditions. Touring the British Isles at midcentury, Benjamin Franklin was shocked at the squalid conditions of farmers and workers, and he wrote of his renewed appreciation of America, where everyone "lives in a tidy, warm house, has plenty of good food and fuel, with whole cloths from head to foot, the manufacture perhaps of his own family." For the majority of British colonists in North America it was possible to achieve "roast beef and apple pie" comfort.

Economic Growth and Increasing Inequality

One of the most important differences among North American colonial regions in the eighteenth century was the economic stagnation in New France and New Spain compared with the impressive economic growth of the British colonies. Weighed down by royal bureaucracies and overbearing regulations, neither the French Crescent nor New Spain evidenced much prosperity. In British North America, however, per capita production grew at an annual rate of .5 percent. Granted, this was considerably less than the average annual growth rate of 1.5 percent that prevailed during the era of industrialization, from the early nineteenth through the mid-twentieth century. But as economic growth steadily increased the size of the economic pie, most middle- and upper-class British Americans began to enjoy improved living conditions, better than those of any people in Europe. Improving standards of living and relatively open access to land encouraged British colonists to see theirs as a society where hard work and savings could translate into prosperity, thus producing an upward spiral of economic growth.

At the same time, this growth itself produced increasing social inequality. In the commercial cities, for example, prosperity was accompanied by a concentration of assets in the hands of wealthy families. In

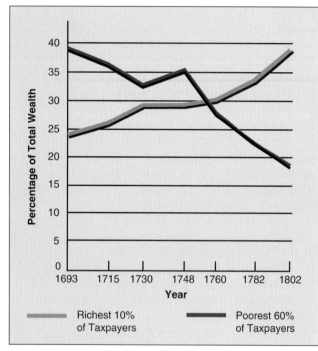

Distribution of Assessed Taxable Wealth in Eighteenth-Century Chester County *This graph charts the concentration of assets in the hands of wealthy families. From 1693 to 1802 the percentage of total wealth held by the richest 10% of taxpayers rose from 24% to 38%, while the percentage held by the poorest 60% of taxpayers fell from 39% to 18%. This pattern was typical for regions dominated by commerce.*

Source: James Lemon and Gary Nash, "The Distribution of Wealth in Eighteenth-Century America," *Journal of Social History* 2 (1968):1–24.

Boston and Philadelphia at the beginning of the century, the wealthiest 10 percent of households owned about half of the taxable property; by about midcentury this small group owned 65 percent or more. In the commercial farming region of Chester County in southeastern Pennsylvania, the holdings of the wealthiest tenth increased more modestly, from 24 to 30 percent during the first half of the century. But at the same time the share of taxable property owned by the poorest third fell from 17 to 6 percent. The general standard of living may have been rising, but the rich were getting richer and the poor poorer. The greatest concentrations of wealth occurred in the cities and in those regions dominated by commercial farming, whether slave or free, while the greatest economic equality continued to be found in areas of self-sufficient farming such as the backcountry.

Another eighteenth-century trend confounded the hope of social mobility in the countryside. As population grew, and as generations succeeded one another in older settlements, all the available land in the towns was taken up. Under the pressure of increased demand, land prices rose almost beyond the reach of families of modest means. As a family's land was divided among the heirs of the second and third generations, parcels became ever smaller and thus more intensively farmed. Eventually the soil was exhausted.

By the eighteenth century, many farm communities did not have sufficient land to provide those of the emerging generation with farms of their own. This problem was particularly acute in New England, where colonists were hemmed in by the French and Indians on the north and the great landed estates of the Hudson Valley on the west. There were notable increases in the number of landless poor in the towns of New England as well as the disturbing appearance of the "strolling poor"—homeless people who traveled from town to town looking for work or a handout. Destitute families crowded into Boston, which by midcentury was expending more than £5,000 annually on relief for the poor, who were required to wear a large red P on their clothing. In other regions, land shortages in the older settlements almost inevitably prompted people to leave in search of cheap or free land.

Young men unable to obtain land in hometowns often moved to the towns and cities of the seaboard, for New England also enjoyed a strong seafaring tradition. Fishing and shipping had first become important during the late seventeenth century, as merchants struggled to find a successful method of earning foreign exchange. The expanding slave market in the South opened new opportunities, prompting the growth of thriving coastal ports such as New Haven, Newport, Salem, and Boston. By midcentury New England had become the most urban of all North America's regions. Boston, the

WEALTH HELD BY RICHEST 10 PERCENT OF THE POPULATION: NORTHERN AND SOUTHERN BRITISH COLONIES COMPARED, 1770		
	North	South
Frontier	33	40
Rural subsistence farming	35	45
Rural commercial farming	45	65
Cities	60	65
Overall	45	55

Source: Jackson Turner Main, *The Social Structure of Revolutionary America* (Princeton: Princeton University Press, 1965), 276n.

largest city in the British colonies, was the metropolis of a region that included not only New England but also the maritime settlements of Nova Scotia and Newfoundland, where New England merchants dominated commerce and recruited seamen for their fishing and shipping fleets.

Contrasts in Colonial Politics

The administration of the Spanish and French colonies was highly centralized. French Canada was ruled by a superior council including the royal governor (in charge of military affairs), the *intendant* (responsible for civil administration), and the bishop of Quebec. New Spain was governed by the Council of the Indies, which sat in Spain, and direct executive authority over all political affairs was exercised by the viceroy in Mexico City. Although local communities enjoyed informal independence, the highly bureaucratized and centralized governments of the French Crescent and the Spanish Borderlands left little room for the development of vigorous traditions of self-government.

The situation in the British colonies was quite different. During the early eighteenth century the British government of Prime Minister Robert Walpole assumed that a decentralized administration would best accomplish the nation's economic goals. Contented colonies, Walpole argued, would present far fewer problems. "One would not strain any point where it can be of no service to our King or country," a British official advised the governor of South Carolina in 1722. "The government should be as easy and mild as possible." Each of the colonies was administered by royally appointed governors, its taxes and finances set by constituent assemblies. Those who owned property could vote for representatives to the assembly. Because many people—mostly white males—owned property, the proportion of adult white men able to vote was 50 percent or higher in all the British colonies. Proportionally, the electorate of the British colonies was the largest in the world.

That did not mean, however, that the British colonies were democratic. The basic principle of order in eighteenth-century British culture was the ideal of deference to natural hierarchies. The well-ordered family—in which children were to be strictly governed by their parents and wives by their husbands—was the common metaphor for civil order. The occupant of each rung on the social ladder was entitled to the respect of those below. Members of subordinate groups, such as women, the non-English, African American slaves, servants, and Indians—who in some colonies constituted nine of every ten adults in the population—could not vote or hold public office. Moreover, for the most part those men who did vote chose wealthy landowners, planters, or merchants to serve as their leaders. Thus, provincial assemblies were controlled by colonial elites.

The important political developments in eighteenth-century British North America, then, had nothing to do with what we commonly call democracy. To educated British colonists, the word "democracy" implied rule by the mob, the normal order of things turned upside-down. Over the century there was, however, an important trend toward stronger institutions of representative government. By midcentury most colonial assemblies had achieved considerable power over provincial affairs and enjoyed a parity of authority with governors and other imperial officials. They collected local revenues and allocated funds for government programs, asserted the right to audit the accounts of public officers, and in some cases even acquired the power to approve the appointment of provincial officials. Royal governors sometimes balked at such claims of power, but because the assemblies controlled the purse strings, most governors were unable to resist this trend.

The potential power of the assemblies was compromised somewhat by the competition among elite families for patronage and government contracts. The royal governors who were most successful at realizing their agendas were those who became adept at playing off one provincial faction against another. All this conflict had the important effect of schooling the colonial elite in the art of politics. It was not democratic politics, but schooling in the ways of patronage, coalition-building, and behind-the-scenes intrigue had important implications for the development of American institutions.

THE CULTURAL TRANSFORMATION OF BRITISH NORTH AMERICA

Despite broad similarities, therefore, the colonial regions of North America developed along divergent lines during the eighteenth century. The British colonies were marked by increasing ethnic diversity, economic growth, social tensions, and conflictual politics that proved to be training for self-government. The middle decades of the eighteenth century also witnessed significant cultural transformation as new ideas and writings associated with the Enlightenment made their way across the Atlantic on the same ships that transported European goods. In New Spain and New France, by contrast, colonial officials worked diligently to suppress these challenging new ideas. The Catholic Church effectively banned the works of hundreds of authors. In Mexico officials of the Inquisition conducted house-to-house searches in pursuit of prohibited texts that they feared had been smuggled into the country.

The Enlightenment Challenge

Drawing from the discoveries of Galileo, Copernicus, and the seventeenth-century scientists René Descartes and Sir Isaac Newton, Enlightenment thinkers in Britain and on the Continent argued that the universe was governed by natural laws that people could understand and apply to their own advantage. John Locke, for example, articulated a philosophy of reason in proposing that the state existed to provide for the happiness and security of individuals, who were endowed with inalienable rights to life, liberty, and property. Enlightenment writers emphasized rationality, harmony, and order, themes that stood in stark contrast to folk culture's traditional emphasis on the unfathomable mysteries of God and nature and the inevitability of human failure and disorder.

Enlightenment thinking undoubtedly appealed most to those whose ordered lives had improved their lot. The colonial elite had good reason to believe in progress. They sent their sons to college, where the texts of the new thinkers were promoted. Harvard, established in 1636, remained the only institution of higher education in British America until 1693, when Anglicans established the College of William and Mary at Williamsburg, soon to become the new capital of Virginia. Puritans in Connecticut, believing that Harvard was too liberal, founded Yale College in 1701. The curricula of these colleges, modeled on those of Oxford and Cambridge in England, were designed to train ministers, but gradually each institution introduced courses and professors influenced by the Enlightenment. In the 1730s Harvard endowed a chair of mathematics and natural philosophy and to fill it appointed John Winthrop, grandson of the Puritan leader and a disciple of Newton.

A mixture of traditional and Enlightenment views characterized the colonial colleges, as it did the thought of men like Cotton Mather. A conservative defender of the old order, Mather wrote a book supporting the existence of witches. On the other hand, he was also a member of the Royal Society, an early supporter of inoculation against disease, and a defender of the Copernican sun-centered model of the universe. On hearing a scientific lecture of Mather's that could have been construed as raising conflicts with a literal reading of the Bible, one old Boston minister noted in his diary, "I think it inconvenient to assert such problems."

This clergyman's views probably characterized a majority of the reading public. About half the adult men and a quarter

Peter Pelham, *Portrait of Cotton Mather,* c. 1725, oil painting, Courtesy American Antiquarian Society, Worcester, Massachusetts.

The Reverend Cotton Mather (1663–1728), pastor of Boston's Second Congregational Church and author of 450 books on theology, history, government, and science, combined both traditional and Enlightenment views. Although he defended the existence of witches, contributing to the hysteria of the Salem witchcraft trials, he also promoted Copernican science and inoculation against disease.

of the adult women of the British colonies could read, a literacy rate that was comparable to those of England and Scandinavia. In striking contrast, in the French and Spanish colonies reading was a skill confined to a tiny minority of upper-class men. In New England, where the Puritans were committed to Bible reading and had developed a system of public education, literacy rates were 85 percent among men and approximately 50 percent among women—the highest in the entire Atlantic world. But the tastes of ordinary readers ran to traditional rather than Enlightenment fare. Not surprisingly, the best-selling book of the colonial era was the Bible. In second place was that unique American literary form, the captivity narrative. The first publication of that genre was *Sovereignty and Goodness of God* (1682), Mary Rowlandson's story of her captivity among the Indians during King Philip's War, a kind of "pilgrim's progress" through the American wilderness. "It is good for me that I have been afflicted," she wrote, for "I have learned to look beyond present and smaller troubles, and to be quieted under them." Appearing in fifteen editions during the colonial period, Rowlandson's account stimulated the publication of at least 500 other such narratives, including the Reverend John Williams's *Redeemed Captive*, cited in the opening of this chapter, most with a lot less religion and a great deal more gore.

Another popular literary form was the almanac, a combination calendar, astrological guide, and sourcebook of medical advice and farming tips reflecting the concerns of traditional folk culture. The best remembered is Benjamin Franklin's *Poor Richard's Almanac* (1732–57), although it was preceded and outlived by a great many others. But what was so innovative about Franklin's almanac, and what made it so important, was the manner in which the author used this traditional literary form to promote the new Enlightenment emphasis on useful and practical knowledge. Posing as the simple bumpkin "Poor Richard," the highly sophisticated Franklin was one of the first Americans to bring Enlightenment thought to ordinary folk.

The growth of the economy in the British colonies and the development of a colonial upper class stimulated the emergence of a more cosmopolitan "Anglican" culture, particularly in the cities of the Atlantic coast. "The culture of minds by the finer arts and sciences," Franklin wrote in 1749, "was necessarily postponed to times of more wealth and leisure." And now, he added, "these times are come." A rising demand for drama, poetry, essays, novels, and history was met by urban booksellers who imported British publications. In Boston bookshops at midcentury one could buy the works of William Shakespeare and John Milton, the essays of Joseph Addison, Richard Steele, Jonathan Swift, and Samuel Johnson, and editions of the classics. In shops elsewhere around the colonies one might also find editions of novels such as *Moll Flanders* by Daniel Defoe and *Tom Jones* by Henry Fielding—but not in New England, where such works were considered indecent.

A Decline in Religious Devotion

While these new ideas flourished, religion seemed in decline. South of New England, the Anglican Church was weak, its ministers uninspiring, and many families remained "unchurched." A historian of religion has estimated that only one adult in fifteen was a member of a congregation. Although this figure may understate the impact of religion on community life, it helps keep things in perspective.

The Puritan churches of New England also suffered declining membership and falling attendance at services, and many ministers began to warn of Puritanism's "declension," pointing to the "dangerous" trend toward the "evil of toleration." By the second decade of the eighteenth century only one in five New Englanders belonged to an established congregation. When Puritanism had been a sect, membership in the church was voluntary and leaders could demand that followers testify to their religious conversion. But when Puritanism became an established church, attendance was expected of all townspeople, and conflicts inevitably arose over the requirement of a conversion experience. An agreement of 1662, known as the Half-Way Covenant, offered a practical solution: members' children who had not experienced conversion themselves could join as "half-way" members, restricted only from participation in communion. Thus the Puritans chose to manage rather than to resolve the conflicts involved in becoming an established religion. Tensions also developed between congregational autonomy and the central control that traditionally accompanied the establishment of a state church. In 1708 the churches of Connecticut agreed to the Saybrook Platform, which enacted a system of governance by councils of ministers and elders rather than by congregations. This reform also had the effect of weakening the passion and commitment of church members.

In addition, an increasing number of Congregationalists began to question the strict Calvinist theology of predestination—the belief that God had predetermined the few men and women who would be saved in the Second Coming. In the eighteenth century many Puritans turned to the much more comforting idea that God had given people the freedom to choose salvation by developing their faith and good works, a theological principle known as Arminianism (for the sixteenth-century Dutch theologian Jacobus Arminius). This belief was in harmony with the Enlightenment view that men and women were not helpless pawns but rational beings who could actively shape their own destinies. Also implicit in these new views was an image of God as a loving rather than a punishing father. Arminianism became a force at Harvard in the early eighteenth century, and soon a new generation of Arminian ministers began to assume leadership in New England's churches. These "liberal" ideas appealed to groups experiencing economic and social improvement, especially commercial farmers, merchants, and the comfortable middle class with its rising expectations. But among ordinary people, especially those in the countryside where traditional patterns lingered, there was a good deal of opposition to these "unorthodox" new ideas.

The Great Awakening

The first stirrings of a movement challenging this rationalist approach to religion occurred during the 1730s, most notably in the movement sparked by the Reverend Jonathan Edwards in the community of Northampton, in western Massachusetts. As the leaders of the community increasingly devoted their energies to the pursuit of wealth, the enthusiasm had seemed to go out of religion. The congregation adopted rules allowing church membership without evidence of a conversion experience and adopted a seating plan for the church that placed wealthy families in the prominent pews, front and center. But the same economic forces that made the "River Gods"—as the wealthy landowners of the Connecticut Valley were known—impoverished others. Young people from the community's poorer families grew disaffected as they were forced to postpone marriage because of the scarcity and expense of the land needed to set up a farm household. Increasingly they refused to attend church meeting, instead gathering together at night for "frolics" that only seemed to increase their discontent.

The Reverend Edwards made this group of young people his special concern. Believing that they needed to "have their hearts touched," he preached to them in a style that appealed to their emotions. For the first time in a generation, the meetinghouse shook with the fire and passion of Puritan religion. "Before the sermon was done," one Northampton parishioner remembered of one notable occasion, "there was a great moaning and crying through the whole house—What shall I do to be saved?—Oh I am going to Hell!—Oh what shall I do for Christ?" Religious fervor swept through the community, and church membership began to grow. There was more to this than the power of one preacher, for similar revivals were soon breaking out in other New England

communities, as well as among German pietists and Scots-Irish Presbyterians in Pennsylvania. Complaining of "spiritual coldness," people abandoned ministers whose sermons read like rational dissertations for those whose preaching was more emotional.

These local revivals became an intercolonial phenomenon thanks to the preaching of George Whitefield, an evangelical Anglican minister from England, who in 1738 made the first of several tours of the colonies. By all accounts, his preaching had a powerful effect. Even Benjamin Franklin, a religious skeptic, wrote of the "extraordinary influence of [Whitefield's] oratory" after attending an outdoor service in Philadelphia where 30,000 people crowded the streets to hear him. Whitefield began as Edwards did, chastising his listeners as "half animals and half devils," but he left them with the hope that God would be responsive to their desire for salvation. "The word was sharper than a two-edged sword," Whitefield wrote after one of his sermons. "The bitter cries and groans were enough to pierce the hardest heart. Some of the people were as pale as death; others were wringing their hands; others lying on the ground; others sinking into the arms of their friends; and most lifting their eyes to heaven and crying to God for mercy. They seemed like persons awakened by the last trumpet, and coming out of their graves to judgement." Whitefield avoided sectarian differences. "God help us to forget party names and become Christians in deed and truth," he declared.

Historians of religion consider this widespread colonial revival of religion, known as the Great Awakening, to be the American version of the second phase of the Protestant Reformation. Religious leaders condemned the laxity, decadence, and officialism of established Protestantism and reinvigorated it with calls for piety and purity. People undergoing the economic and social stresses of the age, unsure about their ability to find land, to marry, to participate in the promise of a growing economy, found relief in religious enthusiasm.

In Pennsylvania, two important leaders of the Awakening were William Tennent and his son Gilbert. An Irish-born Presbyterian, the elder Tennent was an evangelical preacher who established a school in Pennsylvania to train like-minded men for the ministry. Tennent sent many enthusiastic ministers into the field, and his lampooned "Log College" ultimately evolved into the College of New Jersey — later Princeton University—founded in 1746. In the early 1740s, disturbed by what he called the "presumptuous security" of the colonial church, Tennent toured with Whitefield and delivered the famous sermon "The Dangers of an Unconverted Ministry," in which he called upon Protestants to examine the religious

Baptism by full immersion in the Schuylkill River of Pennsylvania, an engraving by Henry Dawkins illustrating events in the history of American Baptists, was published in Philadelphia in 1770. With calls for renewed piety and purity, the Great Awakening reinvigorated American Protestantism. The Baptists preached an egalitarian message, and their congregations in the South often included both white and black Protestants.

convictions of their own ministers. Among Presbyterians, open conflict broke out between the revivalists and the old guard, and in some regions the church hierarchy divided into separate organizations.

In New England similar factions known as the New Lights and the Old Lights accused each other of heresy. The New Lights railed against Arminianism, branding it a rationalist heresy, and called for a revival of Calvinism. The Old Lights condemned emotional enthusiasm as part of the heresy of believing in a personal and direct relationship with God outside the order of the church. Itinerant preachers appeared in the countryside stirring up trouble. The followers of one traveling revivalist burned their wigs, jewelry, and fine clothes in a bonfire, then marched around the conflagration, chanting curses at their opponents, whose religious writings they also consigned to the flames. Many congregations split into feuding factions, and ministers found themselves challenged by their newly awakened parishioners. In one town members of the congregation voted to dismiss their minister, who lacked the emotional fire they wanted in a preacher. When he refused to vacate his pulpit, they pulled him down, roughed him up, and threw him out the church door. Never had there been such turmoil in New England churches.

The Great Awakening was one of the first "national" events in American history. It began some-

what later in the South, developing first in the mid-1740s among Scots-Irish Presbyterians, then achieving its full impact with the organization work of Methodists and particularly Baptists in the 1760s and early 1770s. The revival not only affected white Southerners but introduced many slaves to Christianity for the first time. Local awakenings were frequently a phenomenon shared by both whites and blacks. The Baptist churches of the South in the era of the American Revolution included members of both races and featured spontaneous preaching by slaves as well as masters. In the nineteenth century white and black Christians would go their separate ways, but the joint experience of the eighteenth-century Awakening shaped the religious cultures of both groups.

Many other "unchurched" colonists were brought back to Protestantism by the Great Awakening. But a careful examination of statistics suggests that the proportion of church members in the general population probably did not increase during the middle decades of the century. Although the number of churches more than doubled from 1740 to 1780, the colonial population grew even faster, increasing threefold. The greatest impact was on families already associated with the churches. Before the Awakening, attendance at church had been mostly an adult affair, but throughout the colonies the revival of religion had its

CHRONOLOGY

1636	Harvard College founded		1708	Saybrook Platform in Connecticut
1644	Roger Williams's *Bloudy Tenent of Persecution*		1716	Spanish begin construction of Texas missions
1662	Half-Way Covenant in New England		1730s	French decimate the Natchez and defeat the Fox Indians
1674	Bishopric of Quebec established		1732	Franklin begins publishing *Poor Richard's Almanac*
1680s	William Penn begins recruiting settlers from the European Continent		1738	George Whitefield first tours the colonies
1682	Mary Rowlandson's *Sovereignty and Goodness of God*		1740s	Great Awakening gets under way in the Northeast
1689	Toleration Act passed by Parliament		1740	Parliament passes a naturalization law for the colonies
1690s	Beginnings of Jesuit missions in Arizona		1746	College of New Jersey (Princeton) founded
1693	College of William and Mary is founded		1760s	Great Awakening achieves full impact in the South
1700s	Plains Indians begin adoption of the horse		1769	Spanish colonization of California begins
1701	Yale College founded		1775	Indian revolt at San Diego
	Iroquois sign treaty of neutrality with France		1776	San Francisco founded
1704	Deerfield raid		1781	Los Angeles founded

deepest effects on young people, who flocked to church in greater numbers than ever before. For years the number of people experiencing conversion had been steadily falling, but now full membership surged. Church membership previously had been concentrated among women, leading Cotton Mather, for one, to speculate that perhaps women were indeed more godly. But men were particularly affected by the Great Awakening, and their attendance and membership rose. "God has surprisingly seized and subdued the hardest men, and more males have been added here than the tenderer sex," wrote one Massachusetts minister.

Great Awakening Politics

The Awakening appealed most of all to groups who felt bypassed by the economic and cultural development of the British colonies during the first half of the eighteenth century. Religious factions did not divide neatly into haves and have-nots, but the New Lights tended to draw their greatest strength from small farm-ers and less prosperous craftsmen. Many members of the upper class and the comfortable "middling sort" were shocked by the excesses of the Great Awakening, viewing them as indications of anarchy, and became even more committed to rational religion.

Some historians have suggested that the Great Awakening had important political implications. In Connecticut, for example, Old Lights politicized the religious dispute by passing a series of laws in the General Assembly designed to suppress the revival. In one town, separatists refused to pay taxes that supported the established church and were jailed. New Light judges were thrown off the bench, and others were denied their elected seats in the assembly. The arrogance of these actions was met with popular outrage, and by the 1760s the Connecticut New Lights had organized themselves politically and, in what amounted to a political rebellion, succeeded in turning the Old Lights out of office. These New Light politicians would provide the leadership for the American Revolution in Connecticut.

Such direct connections between religion and politics were relatively rare. There can be little doubt, however, that for many people the Great Awakening offered the first opportunity to actively participate in public debate and public action that affected the direction of their lives. Choices about religious styles, ministers, and doctrine were thrown open for public discourse, and ordinary people began to believe that their opinions actually counted for something. Underlying the debate over these issues were insecurities about warfare, economic growth, and the development of colonial society. The Great Awakening empowered ordinary people to question their leaders, an experience that would prove critical in the political struggles to come.

CONCLUSION

By the middle of the eighteenth century a number of distinct colonial regions had emerged in North America, all with rising populations pressing for more land to be seized from the Indians. Although colonists lived in traditional and local cultures, they were fascinated with the problems presented by frontiers and boundaries within the increasingly diverse continent. Some colonies attempted to ensure homogeneity, while others embraced diversity. Within the British colonies, New England in particular seemed bound to the past, whereas the Middle Colonies and the backcountry embraced both pluralism and expansion. These developments placed them in direct competition with the expansionist plans of the French and at odds with Indian peoples committed to the defense of their homelands.

The economic development of the British colonies introduced new social and cultural tensions that led to the Great Awakening, a massive revival of religion that was the first transcolonial event in American history. Thousands of people experienced a renewal of religious passions, but rather than resuscitating old traditions, the Awakening pointed people toward a more active role in their own political futures. These transformations added to the differences among the British colonies on the one hand, and those of the Spanish and French on the other.

REVIEW QUESTIONS

1. What were the principal colonial regions of North America? Discuss their similarities and their differences. Contrast the development of their political systems.
2. Why did the Spanish and the French close their colonies to immigration? Why did the British open theirs? How do you explain the ethnic homogeneity of New England and the ethnic pluralism of New York and Pennsylvania?
3. What were the principal trends in the history of Indian America in the eighteenth century?
4. Discuss the development of class differences in the Spanish, French, and British colonies in the eighteenth century.
5. Discuss the effects of the Great Awakening on the subsequent history of the British colonies.

RECOMMENDED READING

Edward Countryman, *Americans: A Collision of Histories* (1996). An important new synthesis that includes the many peoples and cultures of North America.

John Demos, *The Unredeemed Captive: A Family Story from Early America* (1994). A moving history of the Deerfield captives, focusing on the experience of Eunice Williams, the unredeemed captive.

W. J. Eccles, *The Canadian Frontier, 1534–1760* (1983). An introduction to the history of French America by a leading scholar on colonial Canada.

David Hackett Fischer, *Albion's Seed: Four British Folkways in America* (1990). An engaging history with fascinating details on the regions of New England, Pennsylvania, Virginia, and the Backcountry.

Jack P. Greene, *Pursuits of Happiness: The Social Development of Early Modern British Colonies and the Formation of American Culture* (1986). A distillation of a tremendous amount of historical material on community life in British North America.

James A. Henretta and Gregory H. Nobles, *Evolution and Revolution: American Society, 1600–1820* (1987). A useful synthesis of the newest social history of the British colonies. Includes an excellent bibliographic essay.

Jackson Turner Main, *The Social Structure of Revolutionary America* (1965). A detailed treatment of colonial social structure, with statistics, tables, and enlightening interpretations.

Colon McEvedy, *The Penguin Atlas of North American History to 1870* (1988). An unparalleled comparative perspective on the Spanish, French, and British regions of the continent, from precolonial times to the nineteenth century.

D. W. Meinig, *The Shaping of America: Atlantic America, 1492–1800* (1986). A geographer's overview of the historical development of the North American continent in the era of European colonialism. Provides a survey of the British and French colonies.

David J. Weber, *The Spanish Frontier in North America* (1992). A magnificent treatment of the entire Spanish borderlands, from Florida to California. Includes important chapters on colonial government and social life.

Robert Wells, *The Population of the British Colonies in America before 1776* (1975). The standard source on colonial population growth.

ADDITIONAL BIBLIOGRAPHY

North American Regions

Patricia Albers and Beatrice Medicine, eds., *The Hidden Half: Studies of Plains Indian Women* (1983)

Barbara Allen and Thomas J. Schlereth, eds., *Sense of Place: American Regional Cultures* (1990)

Richard L. Bushman, *From Puritan to Yankee: Character and the Social Order in Connecticut, 1690–1765* (1967)

Edward D. Castillo, ed., *Native American Perspectives on the Hispanic Colonization of Alta California* (1992)

Cornelia Hughes Dayton, *Women before the Bar: Gender, Law, and Society in Connecticut, 1639–1789* (1995)

John C. Ewers, *The Horse in Blackfoot Indian Culture* (1955)

Joseph W. Glass, *The Pennsylvania Culture Region: A View from the Barn* (1986)

Charles E. Hambrick-Stowe, *The Practice of Piety: Puritan Devotional Disciplines in Seventeenth-Century New England* (1982)

Robert F. Heizer, *The Destruction of California Indians* (1974)

Donald A. Hutslar, *The Architecture of Migration: Log Construction in the Ohio Country, 1750–1850* (1986)

Christine Leigh Hyrman, *Commerce and Culture: The Maritime Communities of Colonial Massachusetts* (1984)

Rhys Isaac, *Worlds of Experience: Communities in Colonial Virginia* (1987)

Francis Jennings, *The Ambiguous Iroquois Empire* (1984)

Terry G. Jordan and Matti Kaups, *The American Backwoods Frontier: An Ethnic and Ecological Interpretation* (1988)

Lyle Kohler, *A Search for Power: "The Weaker Sex" in Seventeenth-Century New England, 1650–1750* (1982)

A. C. Land, et al., eds., *Law, Society, and Politics in Early Maryland* (1977)

James T. Lemmon, *The Best Poor Man's Country: A Geographical Study of Early Southeastern Pennsylvania* (1972)

Kenneth Lockridge, *Literacy in Colonial New England* (1974)

James H. Merrell, *The Indians' New World: Catawbas and Their Neighbors from European Contact through the Era of Removal* (1989)

Gary B. Nash, *The Urban Crucible* (1979)

Charles Edwards O'Neill, *Church and State in French Colonial Louisiana: Policy and Politics to 1732* (1966)

Jacqueline Peterson and Jennifer S. H. Brown, eds., *The New Peoples: Being and Becoming Métis in North America* (1985)

Daniel K. Richter, *The Ordeal of the Longhouse: The Peoples of the Iroquois League in the Era of European Colonization* (1992)

Darrett B. Rutman and Anita H. Rutman, *A Place in Time: Middlesex County, Virginia, 1650–1750* (1984)

Marylynn Salmon, *Women and the Law of Property in Early America* (1986)

Sally Schwartz, *A Mixed Multitude: The Struggle for Toleration in Colonial Pennsylvania* (1987)

William S. Simmons, *Spirit of the New England Tribes: Indian History and Folklore, 1620–1984* (1986)

Daniel Blake Smith, *Inside the Great House: Planter Family Life in Eighteenth-Century Chesapeake Society* (1980)

Helen Horbeck Tanner, ed., *Atlas of Great Lakes Indian History* (1987)

Laurel T. Ulrich, *Good Wives: Image and Reality in the Lives of Women in Northern New England, 1650–1750* (1982)

Daniel H. Usner Jr., *Indians, Settlers, and Slaves in a Frontier Exchange Economy: The Lower Mississippi Valley before 1783* (1992)

Diverging Social and Political Patterns

Bernard Bailyn, *The Peopling of British North America: An Introduction* (1986)

Bruce C. Daniels, ed., *Power and Status: Essays on Officeholding in Colonial America* (1986)

Robert J. Dinkin, *Voting in Provincial America: A Study of Elections in the Thirteen Colonies, 1680–1776* (1977)

A. Roger Ekirch, *Bound for America: The Transportation of British Convicts to the Colonies, 1718–1775* (1987)

David W. Galenson, *White Servitude in Colonial America* (1981)

Jack P. Green, *The Quest for Power: The Lower Houses of Assembly in the Southern Royal Colonies, 1689–1776* (1963)

Thomas L. Purvis, *Proprietors, Patronage, and Paper Money: Legislative Politics in New Jersey, 1703–1776* (1986)

Sharon V. Salinger, *"To Serve Well and Faithfully": Labor and Indentured Servants in Pennsylvania, 1682–1800* (1987)

The Cultural Transformation of British North America

Patricia U. Bonomi, *Under the Cope of Heaven: Religion, Society, and Politics in Colonial America* (1986)

Henry Steele Commager, *The Empire of Reason: How Europe Imagined and America Realized the Enlightenment* (1977)

Alan Heimert and Perry Miller, eds., *The Great Awakening* (1967)

Jackson Maine, *The Social Structure of Revolutionary America* (1965)

Barbara B. Oberg and Harry S. Stout, eds., *Benjamin*

Franklin, Jonathan Edwards, and the Representation of American Culture (1993)

Frank Shuffelton, ed., *The American Enlightenment* (1993)

Biography

Milton J. Coalter, *Gilbert Tennent, Son of Thunder* (1986)

Verner W. Crane, *Benjamin Franklin and a Rising People* (1952)

Harry Kelsey, *Juan Rodriguez Cabrillo* (1986)

Martin J. Morgado, *Junípero Serra's Legacy* (1987)

Kenneth Silverman, *The Life and Times of Cotton Mather* (1984)

John Edwin Smith, *Jonathan Edwards: Puritan, Preacher, Philosopher* (1992)

Harry S. Stout, *The Divine Dramatist: George Whitefield and the Rise of Modern Evangelicalism* (1991)

Laurel Ulrich, *A Midwife's Tale: The Life of Martha Ballard, Based on Her Diary, 1785–1812* (1990)

FROM EMPIRE TO INDEPENDENCE

1750–1776

Bostonians protesting the Stamp Act in 1765 by burning the stamps in a bonfire. German colored engraving, 1784. The Granger Collection.

AMERICAN COMMUNITIES
The First Continental Congress Shapes a National Political Community

Although Britain's North American colonies had enjoyed considerable prosperity during the late seventeenth and early eighteenth centuries, beginning with the Stamp Act in 1765 the British government began to put pressures on them, largely in the form of taxes and new trade restrictions, that drew increasing resistance. In convening the first Continental Congress in September 1774, the colonies made clear their displeasure with the government's actions. Fifty-six elected delegates from twelve of the colonies met at Philadelphia to draft a common response to what they called the Intolerable Acts—the closing of the port of Boston, the suspension of Massachusetts government, and several other measures of British repression—that were the latest attempt to force the colonies to accept the power of Parliament to make laws binding them "in all cases whatsoever." This was the first inter-colonial meeting since the Stamp Act Congress of 1765 (discussed later in this chapter). If the colonies now failed to act together, they would be "attacked and destroyed by piece-meal," declared Arthur Lee of Virginia. "Every part will in its turn feel the vengeance which it would not unite to repel." Abigail Adams, the politically astute wife of John Adams of Massachusetts, agreed. "You have before you," she wrote to her husband, "the greatest national concerns that ever came before any people."

The opening minutes of the first session of the Continental Congress, on September 5, did not bode well. One delegate moved that they begin with prayer, but another responded that they were "so divided in religious sentiments, some Episcopalians, some Quakers, some Anabaptists, some Presbyterians and some Congregationalists, so that we could not join in the same act of worship." Were the delegates to be stymied from the very beginning by things that separated rather than united them? John Adams's cousin, fellow Massachusetts delegate Samuel Adams, jumped to his feet. He was no bigot, he said, "and could hear a prayer from any gentleman of piety and virtue who was at the same time a friend to his country." The delegates finally agreed to ask a local clergyman, a supporter of the American cause, to officiate. The minister took for his text the Thirty-fifth Psalm: "Plead my cause, O Lord, with them that strive with me; fight against them that fight against me." John Adams was delighted. The minister "prayed with such fervor, such Ardor, such Earnestness and Pathos, and in Language so elegant and sublime," he wrote home, that "it has had an excellent Effect upon every Body here."

This incident highlighted the most important task confronting those attending the Continental Congress: they had to develop trust in one another, for what they were doing was considered treason by the British authorities. And they had to find a way to support the common cause without compromising their local identities. At first it was as if the delegates were "ambassadors from

133

a dozen belligerent powers of Europe," wrote John Adams. The delegates represented different colonies, whose traditions and histories were as distinct as those of separate countries. Moreover, these lawyers, merchants, and planters, who were leaders in their respective colonies, were strangers to one another. Their political opinions ranged from loyalty to the British crown and empire to a belief in the necessity of violent revolution. "Every man," Adams wrote, "is a great man, an orator, a critic, a statesman, and therefore every man, upon every question, must show his oratory, his criticism, and his political abilities." As a result, he continued, "business is drawn and spun out to an immeasurable length. I believe that if it was moved and seconded that we should come to a resolution that three and two make five, we should be entertained with logic and rhetorick, law, history, politicks and mathematics concerning the subject for two whole days."

During seven weeks of deliberations, however, the men of the Continental Congress succeeded in forging an agreement on both the principles and the policies they would have to follow in addressing the most serious crisis in the history of Britain's North American colonies. Equally important, the delegates found ways to work together and harmonize their interests. They immediately resolved that each colony would have one vote, thereby committing themselves to preserving provincial autonomy. They sent their most vexing problems to committees, whose members could sound each other out on the issues without speaking for the public record, and they added to their daily routine a round of dinners, parties, and late-night tippling. The greatest single accomplishment of the Continental Congress was the creation of a community of leadership for the united colonies. "It has taken us much time to get acquainted," John Adams wrote to Abigail, but he left Philadelphia thinking of his fellow representatives as "a collection of the greatest men upon this continent."

The First Continental Congress thus took the initial steps toward the creation of a national political community. The bonds of community can be local, regional, national, or international. In a town or village the feeling of association comes from daily face-to-

Philadelphia

face contact, but for larger groups these feelings must be created, or "imagined," as the historian Benedict Anderson puts it. The delegates took some of the first steps in this direction. In their final declaration they pledged to "firmly agree and associate, under the sacred ties of virtue, honor and love of our country." They urged their fellow Americans to "encourage frugality, economy, and industry, and promote agriculture, arts and the manufactures of this country," to "discountenance and discourage every species of extravagance and dissipation, especially all horse-racing, and all kinds of gaming, cock fighting, exhibitions of shows, plays, and other expensive diversions and entertainments." In other words, they called upon the common religious and cultural traditions of British Americans. They asked their countrymen to remember "the poorer sort" among them during the coming economic troubles. And in demanding that their fellow Americans "break off all dealings" and treat with contempt anyone violating the compact, the delegates were declaring who was "inside" and who was "outside" their community. Drawing boundaries is the essential first act in the construction of a new community.

Patrick Henry of Virginia, one of the delegates already committed to independence, was exuberant when the Continental Congress adjourned in late October. "The distinctions between Virginians, Pennsylvanians, New Yorkers, and New Englanders, are no more," he declared. "I am not a Virginian, but an American." Although Henry was a little premature in making this remark, he gave expression to an important truth. The Sugar Act, the Stamp Act, and the so-called Intolerable Acts that taxed and restricted colonists in various ways had also aroused a growing resistance among them. Great Britain had forced the colonists to recognize that they shared a community of interest distinct from that of the mother country. The delegates to the Continental Congress would become the core leaders of the national Revolutionary generation. Theirs was a first attempt to overcome local diversity and difference in pursuit of a common national goal. In the months and years to come the strength of local community would sometimes threaten to pull them apart, and the "imagined community" of America would be sorely tested as the colonies cautiously moved toward independence.

KEY TOPICS

- The final struggle among Great Britain, France, and native American tribes for control of eastern North America

- American nationalism in the aftermath of the French and Indian War

- Great Britain's changing policy toward its North American colonies

- The political assumptions of American republicanism

- The colonies' efforts to achieve unity in their confrontation with Great Britain

THE SEVEN YEARS WAR IN AMERICA

The first attempt at cooperation among the leaders of the British colonies had taken place twenty years earlier, in July 1754, when representatives from New England, New York, Pennsylvania, and Maryland met to consider a joint approach to the French and Indian challenge. Even as the delegates met, fighting between French Canadians and Virginians began on the Ohio River, the first shots in a great global war for empire, known in Europe as the Seven Years War, that pitted Britain (allied with Prussia) against the combined might of France, Austria, Russia, and Spain. In North America, this war—which Americans remembered as the French and Indian War—became the final and most destructive of the armed conflicts between the British and the French before the French Revolution. Ultimately it decided the imperial future of the vast region between the Appalachian Mountains and the Mississippi River, and it laid the groundwork for the conflict between the British and the colonists that led to the American Revolution.

The Albany Conference of 1754

The 1754 meeting, which included an official delegation from the Iroquois Confederacy, took place in the New York town of Albany on the Hudson River. It was convened by officials of the British Board of Trade who wanted the colonies to consider a collective response to the continuing conflict with New France and the Indians of the interior. High on the agenda was the negotiation of a settlement with the leaders of the Iroquois Confederacy, who had grown impatient with colonial land grabbing. "Brother, you are not to expect to hear of me any more," the Iroquois chief Hendrick had declared in disgust to New York officials after a swindle that resulted in the loss of a vast tract. "And brother," he added as he departed, "we desire to hear no more of you." Because the powerful Iroquois Confederacy, and its Covenant

Chain of alliances with other Indian tribes, occupied such a strategic location between New France and the British colonies, the British could ill afford Iroquois disaffection.

The Albany Conference made it clear that the British colonists were not yet ready to unite in common cause. Behind the scenes, while the negotiations took place, real estate agents bribed some minor Iroquois chiefs for their signatures on a "deed" to an enormous tract of land in Pennsylvania, turning the meeting into a vehicle for the very abuses the British were seeking to correct. Angered by these manipulations, the official Iroquois delegation walked out of the conference, refusing all offers to join a British alliance.

The Albany Conference did adopt Benjamin Franklin's Plan of Union, which proposed that Indian affairs, western settlement, and other items of mutual interest to all the colonies be placed under the authority of a grand council composed of representatives elected by the colonial assemblies and led by a royally appointed president. Franklin, who had been appointed by the British government as deputy postmaster general for all of British North America and charged with improving intercolonial communication and commerce, had become extremely sensitive to the need for cooperation among the colonies. Indeed, referring to the Iroquois Confederacy, he declared, "It would be a very strange thing if ignorant savages should be capable of forming a scheme for such a union, and yet a like union should be impracticable for ten or a dozen English colonies." But the colonial assemblies rejected the Albany Plan of Union. As one British official explained, each colony had "a distinct government, wholly independent of the rest, pursuing its own interest and subject to no general command."

Colonial Aims and Indian Interests

The absence of intercolonial cooperation proved to be one of the greatest weaknesses of the British North American empire, for the ensuing war was fought at a

The War for Empire in North America, 1754–1763   *The Seven Years War in America (also known as the French and Indian War) was fought in three principal areas: Nova Scotia and what was then Acadia, the frontier between New France and New York, and the upper Ohio River—gateway to the Great West.*

number of widespread locations. There were three principal flash points of conflict. The first was along the northern Atlantic coast. France had ceded to Britain its colony of Acadia in 1713 (which the British renamed Nova Scotia), but continued to occupy the fortress of Louisburg, from which it guarded its fishing grounds and the St. Lawrence approach to New France. New Englanders had captured this prize in 1745 during King George's War (see Chapter 4), but the French had reclaimed it upon the settlement of that conflict in 1748. They subsequently reinforced Louisburg to such an extent that it became known as the Gibraltar of the New World.

A second zone of conflict was the border region between New France and New York, from Niagara Falls to Lake Champlain, where Canadians and New Yorkers were in furious competition for the Indian trade. Unable to compete effectively against superior English goods, the French resorted to armed might, constructing fortifications on Lake George, south of Lake Champlain, and reinforcing their base at Niagara. This was the homeland of the Iroquois Confederacy, and the loyalty of these tribes would

greatly affect the strategic balance here.

It was the Ohio country—the trans-Appalachian region along the Ohio River—that became the chief focus of British and French attention. This rich land was a prime target of British backcountry settlers and frontier land speculators. The French worried that their isolated settlements at places such as Detroit, Vincennes, and Kaskaskia would be overrun by the expanding British population and that the loss of the Ohio would threaten their entire Mississippi trading empire. To reinforce their claims, in 1749 the French sent a heavily armed force down the Ohio to warn off the British, and in 1752, supported by their northern Indian allies, they expelled a large number of British traders from the region. To prevent the British from returning to the West, in 1753 they began to construct a series of forts running south from Lake Erie to the junction of the Allegheny and Monongahela rivers, a site known as the Forks of the Ohio River.

The French "have stripped us of more than nine parts in ten of North America," one British official cried, "and left us only a skirt of coast along the Atlantic shore." In preparation for a general war, the British established the port of Halifax in Nova Scotia as a counterpart to Louisburg. In northern New York, they strengthened existing forts and constructed new ones. And finally, the British king decided to directly challenge the French claim to the upper Ohio Valley: he conferred an enormous grant of land on the Ohio Company, organized by Virginia and London capitalists, and the company made plans to build a fort at the Forks of the Ohio.

The impending conflict involved more than competing colonial powers, however, for the Indian peoples of the interior had interests of their own. In addition to its native inhabitants, the Ohio country had become a refuge for Indian peoples who had fled the Northeast—Delawares, Shawnees, Hurons, and Iroquois among them. Most of the Ohio Indians opposed the British and were anxious to preserve the Appalachians as a barrier to westward expansion. They were also disturbed by the French movement into their country, although the French outposts, unlike those of the British, did not become centers of expanding agricultural settlements.

The Iroquois Confederacy maintained an official position of neutrality between the rival colonial powers. Iroquois factions allied themselves with either the British or the French, and the confederacy as a whole sought to play off one power against the other, to its own advantage. In the South, the Creeks carved out a similar role for themselves among the British, the French in Louisiana, and the Spanish in Florida; the Cherokees and the Choctaws attempted, less successfully, to do likewise. It was in the interests of these Indian tribes, in other words, to perpetuate the existing colonial stalemate. Their position would be greatly undermined by an overwhelming victory for either side.

Frontier Warfare

At the Albany Congress the delegates received news that Colonel George Washington, a young militia officer from Virginia, had been forced to surrender his troops to a French force near the headwaters of the Monongahela River. The governor of Virginia had sent Washington to expel the French from the region granted to the Ohio Company. Having forced Washington's forces back, the French Canadians now commanded the interior country from their base at Fort Duquesne, which they had built at the Forks of the Ohio and named for the governor of French Canada.

Taking up the challenge, the British government dispatched two Irish regiments under General Edward Braddock across the Atlantic in 1755 to attack and destroy Fort Duquesne. Meanwhile, colonial militias (the equivalent of today's National Guard) commanded by colonial officers were to strike at the New York frontier and the north Atlantic coast. An army of New England militiamen succeeded in capturing two important French forts on the border of Nova Scotia, but the other two prongs of the campaign were complete failures. The offensive in New York was repulsed. And in the worst defeat of a British army during the eighteenth century, Braddock's force was destroyed by a smaller force of French and Indians on the upper Ohio, and Braddock himself was killed.

Braddock's defeat was followed by the outbreak of full-scale warfare between Britain and France in 1756. The fighting of the first two years was a near catastrophe for Great Britain. Canadians captured the British forts in northern New York. Indians pounded backcountry settlements, killed thousands of settlers, and raided deep into the coastal colonies, throwing British colonists into panic. "There is no surer way to sicken the people of the English colonies," a Canadian commander mused, "and to make them desire

the return of peace." The continuing absence of colonial cooperation greatly hampered the British attempt to mount a counterattack. And when British commanders tried to exert direct control over provincial troops, they succeeded only in angering local authorities.

In this climate of defeat, the British enacted a draconian policy of retribution against the French-speaking farmers of Acadia, who had lived peacefully under British rule for over forty years. The Acadians' refusal to swear allegiance to the crown was now used as an excuse for their expulsion. In 1755 New England troops began the forcible removal of approximately 10,000 Acadians, selling their farms at bargain prices to immigrants from New England. Suffering terrible hardship and heartbreak, the Acadians were dispersed throughout the Atlantic world, although a substantial number of them ended up settling in Louisiana, then under Spanish control, where they became known as "Cajuns." The Acadian expulsion is one of the most infamous chapters in the British imperial record in North America.

The Conquest of Canada

In the darkest days of 1757, William Pitt, an enthusiastic advocate of British expansion, assumed the prime ministership of Great Britain. "I know that I can save this country," Pitt declared, "and that no one else can." Deciding that the global war could be won in North America, he subsidized the Prussians to fight in Europe and reserved Britain's own forces and resources for naval and colonial operations. Pitt committed the British to the conquest of Canada and the elimination of all French competition in North America. Such a goal could be achieved only at tremendous cost in men and money. By promising that the war would be fought "at His Majesty's expense," Pitt was able to buy colonial cooperation. A massive infusion of British currency and credit greatly stimulated the North American economy. Pitt dispatched more than 20,000 regular British troops across the Atlantic. Combining them with colonial forces, he massed more than 50,000 armed men against Canada.

The British attracted Indian support for their plans by "redressing the grievances complained of by the Indians, with respect to the lands which have been fraudulently taken from them," in the words of a British official. In 1758 officials promised the Iroquois Confederacy and the Ohio Indians that the crown would "agree upon clear and fixed boundaries between our settlements and their hunting grounds, so that each party may know their own and be a mutual protection to each other of their respective possessions."

Thus did Pitt succeed in reversing the course of the war. Regular and provincial forces captured Louisburg in July 1758, setting the stage for the penetration of the St. Lawrence Valley. A month later a

The death of General James Wolfe, at the conclusion of the battle in which the British captured Quebec in 1759, became the subject of American artist Benjamin West's most famous painting, which was exhibited to tremendous acclaim in London in 1770.

force of New Englanders captured the strategic French fort of Oswego on Lake Ontario, thereby preventing the Canadians from resupplying their western posts. Encouraged by British promises, many Indian tribes abandoned the French alliance, and the French were forced to give up Fort Duquesne. A large British force soon took control of the French fort at the Forks of the Ohio, renaming the post Fort Pitt (Pittsburgh today) in honor of the prime minister. "Blessed be God," wrote a Boston editor. "The long looked for day is arrived that has now fixed us on the banks of the Ohio." The last of the French forts on the New York frontier fell in 1759. In the South, regular and provincial British troops invaded the homeland of the Cherokees and crushed them.

British forces now converged on Quebec, the heart of French Canada. In the summer of 1759, following General James Wolfe's order to "burn and lay waste the country," British troops plundered farms and shelled the city of Quebec. Finally, in an epic battle on the Plains of Abraham before the city's walls, the

British prevailed over Quebec's defenders. More than 2,000 British, French, American, and Canadian men lost their lives in the battle, including both Wolfe and the French commander, the marquis de Montcalm. Canadian resistance continued for another year, but in 1760 British forces conquered Montreal, completing the destruction of the French Empire in America. "The great day is now come," declared the editor of the *Boston News-Letter*, "the fall of the American Carthage."

In the final two years of the war the British swept French ships from the seas, conquered important French and Spanish colonies in the Caribbean, achieved dominance in India, and even captured the Spanish Philippines. In the Treaty of Paris, signed in 1763, France lost all its possessions on the North American mainland. It ceded its claims east of the Mississippi to Great Britain, with the exception of New Orleans. This city had already been transferred, along with all other French claims to lands west of the Mississippi, to Spain—to keep these territories in the possession of a Catholic monarch. For its part, Spain ceded

Florida to Britain in exchange for the return of all its Caribbean and Pacific colonies. The imperial rivalry in eastern North America that had begun in the sixteenth century now came to an end with total victory for the British empire.

Indians and Europeans Struggle over the West

When the Ohio Indians heard of the French cession of the western country to Britain, they were shocked. "The French had no right to give away [our] country," they told a British trader. "They were never conquered by any nation." A new set of British policies soon shocked them all the more. Both the French and the British had long used gift giving as a way of gaining favor with Indians. The Spanish officials who replaced the French in Louisiana made an effort to continue the old policy. But the British military governor of the western region, General Jeffery Amherst, in one of his first official actions, banned presents to Indian chiefs and tribes, demanding that they learn to live without "charity." Not only were Indians angered by Amherst's reversal of custom, but they were also frustrated by his refusal to supply them with the ammunition they required for hunting. Many were left starving.

In this climate, hundreds of Ohio Indians became disciples of the Indian visionary Neolin (meaning "The Enlightened One," in Algonquian), known to the English as the Delaware Prophet. The core of Neolin's teaching was that Indians had been corrupted by European ways and needed to purify themselves by returning to their traditions and preparing for a holy war. "Drive them out," he declared of the settlers. A confederacy of tribes organized by a group of chiefs who had gained influence by adopting Neolin's ideas laid plans for a coordinated attack against the British in the spring of 1763. The principal figure among them was the Ottawa chief Pontiac, renowned as an orator and political leader. This combination of inspirational religious and political leadership was a pattern in the long history of Indian resistance to colonial expansion in North America. The first instance of this approach on the part of Indian tribes had taken place among the Algonquians of the Chesapeake in the early seventeenth century (see Chapter 3).

In May 1763 the Indian confederacy simultaneously attacked all the British forts in the West. Warriors overran Fort Michilimackinac, at the narrows between Lakes Michigan and Huron, by scrambling

European Claims in North America, 1750 and 1763   *As a result of the British victory in the Seven Years War, the map of colonial claims in North America was fundamentally transformed.*

most radical of his resolutions, they were all reprinted throughout the colonies. By the end of 1765 the assemblies of eight other colonies had approved similar measures denouncing the Stamp Act and proclaiming their support of "no taxation without representation."

In Massachusetts, the leaders of the opposition to the Stamp Act came from a group of upper- and middle-class men who had long opposed the conservative leaders of the colony. These men had worked for years to establish a political alliance with Boston craftsmen and workers who met at taverns, in volunteer fire companies, or at social clubs. One of these clubs, known as the Loyall Nine, included Samuel Adams (see the opening of this chapter), an associate and friend of James Otis who had made his career in local politics. Using his contacts with professionals, craftsmen, and laboring men as well, Adams helped put together an anti-British alliance that spanned Boston's social classes. "If our trade may be taxed," he reasoned with working men, "why not our lands? Why not the produce of our lands and everything we possess or make use of?" In August 1765, Adams and the Loyall Nine were instrumental in organizing a protest of Boston workingmen against the Stamp Act.

The working people of Boston had reasons of their own to be angry. While Boston's elite had prospered during the eighteenth century, the conditions for workers and the poor had worsened. Unemployment, inflation, and high taxes had greatly increased the level of poverty during the depression that followed the Seven Years War, and many were resentful. Concerted action by crowds, as when people took to the streets to demand fair prices for bread, or when posses formed to capture criminals, were commonplace in eighteenth-century communities throughout Europe and the colonies.

It was in this tradition that a large Boston crowd assembled on August 14, 1765, in the shade of a broad "liberty tree" and strung up effigies of several British officials, including Boston's stamp distributor, Andrew Oliver. The restless crowd then proceeded to vandalize Oliver's office and home. At the order of Oliver's brother-in-law, Lieutenant Governor Thomas Hutchinson, leader of the Massachusetts conservatives, the town sheriff tried to break up the crowd, but he was pelted with paving stones and bricks. Soon thereafter, Oliver resigned his commission. The unified action of Boston's social groups had its intended effect.

Twelve days later, however, a similar crowd gathered at the elegant home of Hutchinson himself. As the family fled through the back door, the crowd smashed through the front with axes. Inside they demolished furniture, chopped down the interior walls, consumed the contents of the wine cellar, and looted everything of value, leaving the house a mere shell. As these events demonstrated, it was not always possible to keep popular protests within bounds. During the fall and winter, crowds in commercial towns from Halifax in the North to Savannah in the South forced the resignation of many British tax officials.

In many colonial cities and towns, merchants, lawyers, and respectable craftsmen sought to moderate the resistance movement by seizing control of it. Groups calling themselves the Sons of Liberty encouraged moderate forms of protest. They circulated petitions, published pamphlets, and encouraged crowd actions only as a last resort; always they emphasized limited political goals. Then in October 1765 delegations from nine colonies (New Hampshire and Georgia declined the invitation to attend, and the governors of Virginia and North Carolina prevented their delegates from accepting) met at what has been called the Stamp Act Congress in New York City, where they passed a set of resolutions denying Parliament's right to tax the colonists, since taxation depended on representation. But the delegates also agreed that Parliament

Samuel Adams, a second cousin of John Adams, was a leader of the Boston radicals and an organizer of the Sons of Liberty. The artist of this portrait, John Singleton Copley, was known for setting his subjects in the midst of everyday objects; here he portrays Adams in a middle-class suit with the charter guaranteeing the liberties of Boston's freemen.

John Singleton Copley (1738–1815). *Samuel Adams*. 1772. Oil on canvas, 127 cm × 102.2 cm. Deposited by the City of Boston. Courtesy, Museum of Fine Arts, Boston.

had the authority to pass laws regulating colonial trade. These moderate efforts defused the radicals, and there were few repetitions of mob attacks, but by the end of 1765 almost all the stamp distributors had resigned or fled, making it impossible for Britain to enforce the Stamp Act.

Repeal of the Stamp Act

In the fall of 1765, British merchants, worried about the effects of the growing nonimportation movement among the colonists, began increasingly to petition Parliament to repeal the Stamp Act. About 40 percent of England's exports went to the British colonies in North America. "I rejoice that America has resisted," said William Pitt, who was no longer prime minister but spoke for the merchant interests in Parliament. "It is my opinion that this kingdom has no right to lay a tax upon the colonies." Grenville demanded that the British army be used to enforce the act. "Tell me," he demanded of Pitt, "when the Americans were emancipated." Pitt's response was memorable: "I desire to know when they were made slaves." Parliament heard the testimony of several interested parties, including Benjamin Franklin, who warned that Grenville's proposal to use troops could bring on a rebellion.

It was not, however, until Grenville was replaced by Lord Rockingham, who opposed the Stamp Act, that in March 1766 a bill for repeal passed the House of Commons. This news was greeted with celebrations throughout the American colonies, and the nonimportation associations were disbanded. Overlooked in the mood of optimism was Parliament's assertion in this Declaratory Act of its full authority to make laws binding the colonies "in all cases whatsoever." The notion of absolute parliamentary supremacy over colonial matters was basic to the British theory of empire. Even Pitt, friend of America that he was, asserted "the authority of this kingdom over the colonies to be sovereign and supreme, in every circumstance of government and legislation whatsoever." The Declaratory Act signaled that the conflict had not been resolved, merely postponed.

"SAVE YOUR MONEY AND SAVE YOUR COUNTRY"

Colonial resistance to the Stamp Act was stronger in urban than in rural communities, stronger among merchants, craftsmen, and planters than among farmers and frontiersmen. When Parliament next moved to impose its will on the colonies, as it had claimed the right to do in the Declaratory Act, it placed new duties on imported goods, and the American opposition again adopted the tactic of nonimportation. But this time resistance spread from

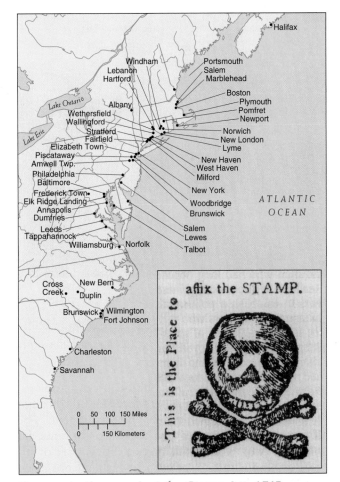

Demonstrations against the Stamp Act, 1765
From Halifax in the North to Savannah in the South, popular demonstrations against the Stamp Act forced the resignation of British tax officials. One newspaper editor cynically proposed that the stamp itself be in the form of a skull and crossbones (inset).

the cities and towns into the countryside. As the editor of the *Boston Gazette* phrased the issue, "Save your money and you save your country." It became the slogan of the movement.

The Townshend Revenue Acts

During the 1760s there was a rapid turnover of government leaders that made it difficult for Britain to form a consistent and even-handed policy toward the colonies. In 1767, after several failed governments, King George III asked William Pitt to again become prime minister. Pitt enjoyed enormous goodwill in America, and a government under his leadership stood a good chance of reclaiming colonial credibility. But, suffering from a prolonged illness, he was soon forced to retire, and his place as head of the cabinet was assumed by Charles Townshend, Chancellor of the Exchequer.

One of the first problems facing Townshend was the national debt. At home there were massive

British politicians bury the Stamp Act in this satirical engraving of 1766.

unemployment, riots over high prices, and tax protests. The large landowners forced a bill through Parliament slashing their taxes by 25 percent. The government feared continued opposition at home far more than opposition in America. So as part of his plan to close the budget gap, Townshend proposed a new measure for the colonies that placed import duties on commodities such as lead, glass, paint, paper, and tea. By means of these new Revenue Acts, enacted in 1767, Townshend hoped to redress colonial grievances against internal taxes like those imposed by the Stamp Act. The new acts provided for the collection of an external tax, that is, a duty imposed on goods at the customhouse, in colonial ports, before they entered colonial markets. In his presentation to the House of Commons, Benjamin Franklin had drawn the distinction between external taxes and internal taxes, and left the impression that colonists would be more accepting of external ones. For most colonial Americans, however, it proved to be a distinction without a difference.

The most influential response to these Revenue Acts came in a series of articles by John Dickinson, *Letters from a Farmer in Pennsylvania*, that were reprinted in nearly every colonial newspaper. In reality a wealthy Philadelphia lawyer, Dickinson posed in these articles as a humble husbandman. Parliament had the right to regulate trade through the use of duties, he conceded. It could place prohibitive tariffs, for example, on foreign products. But it had no constitutional authority to tax goods in order to raise revenues in America. As the preface to the Revenue Acts made

clear, the income they produced would be used to pay the salaries of royal officials in America. Such an arrangement, Dickinson pointed out, would render those in charge of administering colonial affairs independent of elected representatives in the colonial assemblies and thus answerable to no one within the colonies themselves.

Other Americans saw the Revenue Acts as part of a British conspiracy to suppress American liberties. Their fears were confirmed by Townshend's stringent enforcement measures. He created a new and strengthened Board of Commissioners of the Customs and established vice-admiralty courts at Boston, Philadelphia, and Charleston to prosecute violators of the duties—the first time this hated institution had appeared in the most important American port cities. And to demonstrate his power, he also suspended New York's assembly. That body had refused to vote public funds to support the British troops garrisoned in the colony. Until the citizens of New York relented, Townshend declared, they would no longer be represented.

In response to these measures, some men argued for violent resistance. But Dickinson's essays had a great effect on the public debate, not only because of their convincing argument but because of their mild and reasonable tone. "Let us behave like dutiful children," Dickinson urged, "who have received unmerited blows from a beloved parent." As yet, no sentiment for independence existed in America. The colonial response was one of resistance to what were considered unconstitutional measures by the British authorities.

Nonimportation: An Early Political Boycott

Associations of nonimportation and nonconsumption, revived in October 1767 when the Boston town meeting drew up a long list of British products to boycott, became the main weapon of the resistance movement. Over the next few months other port cities, including Providence, Newport, and New York, set up nonimportation associations of their own. Towns such as Philadelphia, however, were unable to overcome conflicts between merchants and artisans. The economy had begun to improve since the earlier boycott, and many merchants saw little advantage in curtailing imports. Craftsmen, on the other hand, supported nonimportation with enthusi-

This British cartoon, A Society of Patriotic Ladies, ridiculed the efforts of American women to support the Patriot cause by boycotting tea. The moderator of the meeting appears coarse and masculine, while an attractive scribe is swayed by the amorous attention of a gentleman. The activities under the table suggest that these women are neglecting their true duty.

asm, because it meant that consumers would buy their products rather than foreign ones. Supported by workers, artisans took to the streets in towns and cities throughout the colonies to force merchants to stop importing British goods. The associations published the names of uncooperative importers and retailers. These people then became the object of protesters, who sometimes resorted to violence. Coercion was very much a part of the movement.

Adopting the language of Protestant ethics, nonimportation associations pledged to curtail luxuries and stimulate local industry. These values held great appeal in small towns and rural districts, which previously had been relatively uninvolved in the anti-British struggle. And in 1768 and 1769, colonial newspapers paid a great deal of attention to women's support for the boycott. Groups of women, some styling themselves Daughters of Liberty, organized spinning and weaving bees to produce homespun for local consumption. The actual work performed at these bees was less important than the symbolic message. "The industry and frugality of American

ladies," wrote the editor of the *Boston Evening Post*, "are contributing to bring about the political salvation of a whole continent." Other women renounced silks and satins and pledged to stop serving tea to their husbands. Women sang:

> Throw aside your topknots of pride,
> Wear none but your own country linen.
> Of economy boast, let your pride be the most,
> To show clothes of your own make and spinning.

The poet Milcah Martha Moore urged American women to

> Stand firmly resolv'd, and bid Grenville to see,
> That rather than freedom we part with our tea,
> And well as we love the dear draught when a-dry,
> As American patriots our taste we deny.

Nonimportation appealed to the traditional values of rural communities—self-sufficiency and independence—and for the first time brought country people into the growing community of resistance.

Nonimportation was greatly strengthened in May 1769 when the Virginia House of Burgesses enacted the first provincial legislation banning the importation of goods enumerated in the Townshend Revenue Acts, and slaves and luxury commodities as well. Over the next few months all the colonies but New Hampshire enacted similar provisions. Because of these efforts, nonimportation was a great success. The value of colonial imports from Britain declined 41 percent the first year. In the largest port cities the decrease was even greater—54 percent in Philadelphia and over 80 percent in New York. The new Townshend duties, meanwhile, collected only about £20,000 in revenue. By 1770 English merchants were again protesting their hardship before Parliament.

The Massachusetts Circular Letter

Boston and Massachusetts were at the center of the agitation over the Townshend Revenue Acts. In February 1768 the Massachusetts House of Representatives approved a letter, drawn up by Samuel Adams, addressed to the speakers of the other provincial assemblies. Designed largely as a propaganda device and having little practical significance, the letter denounced the Townshend Acts, attacked the British plan to make royal officials independent of colonial assemblies, and urged the colonies to find a way to "harmonize with each other." Massachusetts governor Francis Bernard condemned the document for stirring up rebellion and dissolved the legislature. In Britain Lord Hillsborough, secretary of state for the colonies, ordered each royal governor in America to likewise dissolve his colony's assembly if it should endorse the letter. Before this demand reached America, the assemblies of New Hampshire, New Jersey, and Connecticut had commended Massachusetts. Virginia, moreover, had issued a circular letter encouraging a "hearty union" among the colonies and urging common action against the British measures that "have an immediate tendency to enslave us."

Hillsborough now ordered Massachusetts Governor Bernard to force the newly elected House of Representatives to rescind Adams's letter and delete all mention of it from its journal. The radicals could have asked for nothing better; resistance to the Townshend duties had been flagging, but there was great support for the prerogative and independence of the assembly. After protracted debate in June 1768, the representatives voted ninety-two to seventeen to defy Bernard, who immediately shut them down. The "Glorious Ninety-two" became heroes of the hour, and men in taverns throughout the colonies drank "ninety-two toasts" to the brave men of Massachusetts. The "rescinders," meanwhile, were condemned by public and press; in local elections the next year, seven of them lost their seats.

Throughout this crisis there were rumors and threats of mob rule in Boston. "I am no friend to riots, tumult, and unlawful assemblies," Samuel Adams declared, "but when the people are oppressed...they are not to be blamed." Because customs agents pressed on smugglers and honest traders alike, they enraged merchants, seamen, and dockworkers. In June 1768 a crowd assaulted customs officials who had seized John Hancock's sloop *Liberty* for nonpayment of duties. So frightened were the officials that they fled the city. Hancock, reportedly the wealthiest merchant in the colonies and a vocal opponent of the British measures, had become a principal target of the customs officers. In September, the Boston town meeting called on the people to arm themselves, and in the absence of an elected assembly it invited all the other towns to send delegates to a provincial convention. There were threats of armed resistance, but little support for it in the convention, which broke up in chaos. Nevertheless the British, fearing insurrection, occupied Boston with infantry and artillery regiments on October 1, 1768. With this action, they sacrificed a great deal of goodwill and respect and added greatly to the growing tensions.

The Politics of Revolt and the Boston Massacre

The British troops stationed in the colonies were the object of scorn and hostility over the next two years. There were regular conflicts between soldiers and radicals in New York City, often focusing on the Sons of Liberty. These men would erect "liberty poles" festooned with banners and flags proclaiming their

cause, and the British troops would promptly destroy them. When the New York assembly finally bowed to Townshend in December 1769 and voted an appropriation to support the troops, the New York City Sons of Liberty organized a demonstration and erected a large liberty pole. The soldiers chopped it down, sawed it into pieces, and left the wood on the steps of a tavern frequented by the Sons. This act led to a riot in which British troops used their bayonets against a few thousand New Yorkers armed with cutlasses and clubs. Several men were wounded.

Confrontations also took place in Boston. In September 1769, James Otis provoked a melee by picking a fight in a tavern catering to British officers. The next month an encounter between a mob and soldiers ended with the troops' firing a volley into the air. The demonstrators were "mutinous desperadoes," wrote General Thomas Gage, guilty of "sedition." Samuel Adams played up reports and rumors of soldiers harassing women, picking fights, or simply taunting residents with versions of "Yankee Doodle." Soldiers were frequently hauled into Boston's courts, and local judges adopted a completely unfriendly attitude toward these members of the occupying army. In February 1770, an eleven-year-old boy was killed when a customs officer opened fire on a rock-throwing crowd. Although no soldiers were involved, this incident heightened the tensions between citizens and troops.

A persistent source of conflict was the competition between troops and townsmen over jobs. Soldiers were permitted to work when off duty, putting them in competition with day laborers. In early March 1770, an off-duty soldier walked into a ropewalk (a long narrow building in which ropes are made) in search of a job. The proprietor told him— using an obscenity—that he could clean the outhouse. The soldier left but returned with his friends, and a small riot ensued. Fighting continued over the next few days in the streets between the wharf and the Common, where the soldiers were encamped. On the evening of March 5, a crowd gathered at the Customs House and began taunting a guard, calling him a "damned rascally scoundrel lobster", and worse. A captain and seven soldiers went to his rescue, only to be pelted with snowballs and stones. Suddenly, without orders, the frightened soldiers began to fire. In what became known as the "Boston Massacre," three of the crowd fell dead immediately, and six more were wounded, two of these dying later. The first blood shed was that of Crispus Attucks, whose mother was Indian and father African American. The soldiers escaped to their barracks, but a mob numbering in the hundreds rampaged through the streets demanding vengeance.

Fearing for the safety of his men and the security of the state, Thomas Hutchinson, now governor of Massachusetts, ordered British troops out of Boston and arrested the soldiers who had fired the shots. The soldiers were tried later that year. Defending them were John Adams and Josiah Quincy Jr., two leaders of the radicals. Adams and Quincy established a reputation for fairness and statesmanship by convincing a jury of Bostonians that the soldiers had fired in fear of their lives. The Boston Massacre became infamous throughout the colonies, in part because of the circulation of an inflammatory print produced by the Boston engraver Paul Revere, which depicted the British as firing on a crowd of unresisting civilians. But for many colonists the incident was a disturbing reminder of the extent to which relations with the mother country had deteriorated. During the next two years, many people found themselves pulling back from the brink. "There seems," one Bostonian wrote, "to be a pause in politics."

The growth of American resistance was slowed as well by the news that Parliament had repealed most of the Townshend Revenue Acts on March 5, 1770—the same day as the Boston Massacre. The nonimportation measures almost immediately collapsed. Over the next three years, the value of British imports rose by 80 percent. The parliamentary retreat on the question of duties, like the earlier repeal of the Stamp Act, was accompanied by a face-saving measure—retention of the tax on tea "as a mark of the supremacy of Parliament," in the words of Frederick Lord North, the new prime minister.

In Paul Revere's version of the Boston Massacre, issued three weeks after the incident, the British fire an organized volley into a defenseless crowd. Revere's print—which he plagiarized from another Boston engraver—may have been inaccurate, but it was enormously effective propaganda. It hung in so many Patriot homes that the judge hearing the murder trial of these British soldiers warned the jury not to be swayed by "the prints exhibited in our houses."

FROM RESISTANCE TO REBELLION

The tax revolt in America was not an isolated incident, but the largest of numerous resistance movements to taxation—in Russa, the Netherlands, Corsica, Ireland, and Great Britain itself. There was a lull in the American controversy during the early 1770s, but the situation turned violent again in 1773, when Parliament infuriated the Americans with an ill-advised tax on tea. The Tea Act propelled the colonists on a swift track from resistance to outright rebellion. The groundwork for these developments, however, was laid during the quiet years that preceded them.

Intercolonial Cooperation

The Townshend Revenue Acts, although repealed, reflected Britain's intention of using customs revenues to pay the salaries of royal officials in the colonies. In June 1772, Governor Hutchinson inaugurated another controversy by announcing that his salary and those of other royally appointed Massachusetts officials would be paid by the crown. In effect, this made the executive and judiciary branches of the colony's government independent of elected representatives. In November, the Boston town meeting appointed a Committee of Correspondence to communicate with other towns regarding this challenge. A few weeks later the meeting issued what became known as the Boston Pamphlet—a series of declarations written by Samuel Adams and other radicals concluding that British encroachments on colonial rights were signs of a plot to enslave Americans.

In March 1773 the Virginia House of Burgesses appointed a standing committee for intercolonial correspondence "to obtain the most early and authentic intelligence" of British actions affecting America, "and to keep up and maintain a correspondence and communication with our sister colonies." The Virginia committee, including Patrick Henry, Richard Henry Lee, and young Thomas Jefferson, served as a model, and within a year all the colonies except Pennsylvania, where conservatives controlled the legislature, had created committees of their own. These committees became the principal channel for sharing information, shaping public opinion, and building intercolonial cooperation before the Continental Congress of 1774.

A British tax man is tarred and feathered and forced to drink tea, while the Boston Tea Party takes place in the background, in this image of 1774.

The information most damaging to British influence came from the radicals in Boston. Governor Hutchinson put himself at the center of controversy by declaring early in 1773 that the colonists were mistaken if they thought they enjoyed all the rights of Englishmen. Furthermore, even though they had removed themselves across the Atlantic, he argued, they were still subordinate to Parliament. "I know of no line that can be drawn," he asserted, "between the supreme authority of Parliament and the total independence of the colonies." This bold declaration outraged colonists, who during the years of agitation against taxes and duties had convinced themselves of the case against parliamentary supremacy.

In June, the Boston committee circulated a set of confidential letters from Hutchinson to the ministry in Britain, obtained in London by Benjamin Franklin from friends within the British government. Because Franklin had pledged to keep the letters to himself, he became the center of a scandal in London, and was dismissed from his position as postmaster

general. But the British cause in the colonies suffered much more than Franklin's reputation. The letters revealed Hutchinson's call for "an abridgement of what are called English liberties" in the colonies. "I wish to see some further restraint of liberty," he had written, "rather than the connection with the parent state should be broken." This statement seemed to be the "smoking gun" of the conspiracy theory, and it created a torrent of anger against the British and their officials in the colonies.

The Boston Tea Party

It was in this context that the colonists received the news that Parliament had passed a Tea Act. Colonists were major consumers of tea, but because of the tax on it that remained from the Townshend duties, the colonial market for tea had collapsed, bringing the East India Company to the brink of bankruptcy. This company was the sole agent of British power in India, and Parliament could not allow it to fail. The British therefore devised a scheme in which they offered tea to Americans at prices that would tempt even the most patriotic back to the beverage. The radicals argued that this was merely a device to make palatable the payment of unconstitutional taxes—further evidence of the British conspiracy to corrupt the colonists.

In October a mass meeting in Philadelphia denounced anyone importing the tea as "an enemy of his country." A group calling itself the Committee for Tarring and Feathering plastered posters all over the city asking if the pilots of ships carrying the tea might like "ten gallons of liquid tar decanted on your pate—with the feathers of a dozen wild geese laid over that to enliven your appearance?" The Philadelphia consignees resigned in terror. Similar protests in New York City forced resignations there as well. The town meeting in Boston passed resolutions patterned on those of Philadelphia, but the tea agents there, among them two of Governor Hutchinson's sons, resisted the call to refuse the shipments.

The first of the tea ships arrived in Boston Harbor late in November. Mass meetings in Old South Church, which included many country people drawn to the scene of the crisis, resolved to keep the tea from being unloaded. Governor Hutchinson was equally firm in refusing to allow the ship to leave the harbor. On December 16, 1773, 8,000 people crowded into and around the church to hear the captain of one tea ship report to Samuel Adams that he could not move his ship. "This meeting can do nothing more to save the country," Adams declared. This was the signal for a disciplined group of fifty or sixty men, including farmers, artisans, merchants, professionals, and even apprentices, to march to the wharf disguised as Indians. There they boarded the ships and dumped into the harbor 45 tons of tea, valued at £18,000, all the while cheered on by Boston's citizens. "Boston Harbor's a tea-pot tonight," the crowd chanted.

Boston's was the first tea party, and other incidents of property destruction followed. When the New York Sons of Liberty learned that a cargo of tea had landed secretly in New York harbor, they, too, dressed themselves as Indians and dumped the tea chests over the sides. At Annapolis a ship loaded with tea was destroyed by fire, and arson also consumed a shipment stored at a warehouse in New Jersey. But it was the action in Boston at which the British railed. The government became convinced that something had to be done about the rebellious colony of Massachusetts. Strong measures were required, King George wrote to Lord North, for "we are now to dispute whether we have, or have not, any authority in that country."

The Intolerable Acts

During the spring of 1774 an angry Parliament passed a series of acts—termed by Americans the Intolerable Acts—that were calculated to punish Massachusetts and strengthen the British hand. The Boston Port Bill prohibited the loading or unloading of ships in any part of Boston harbor until the town fully compensated the East India Company and the customs service for the destroyed tea. The Massachusetts Government Act annulled the colonial charter: delegates to the upper house would no longer be elected by the assembly but henceforth be appointed by the king. Civil officers throughout the province were placed under the authority of the royal governor, and the selection of juries was given over to governor-appointed sheriffs. Town meetings, an important institution of the resistance movement, were prohibited from convening more than once a year except with the approval of the governor, who was to control their agendas. With these acts the

THE THIRTEEN REPRESSIVE BRITISH MEASURES

Legislation	Year	
Sugar Act	1764	Placed prohibitive duty on imported sugar; provided for greater regulation of American shipping to suppress smuggling
Stamp Act	1765	Required the purchase of specially embossed paper for newspapers, legal documents, licenses, insurance policies, ships' papers, and playing cards; struck at printers, lawyers, tavern owners, and other influential colonists. Repealed in 1766
Declaratory Act	1766	Asserted the authority of Parliament to make laws binding the colonies "in all cases whatsoever"
Townshend Revenue Acts	1767	Placed import duties, collectible before goods entered colonial markets, on many commodities including lead, glass, paper, and tea. Repealed in 1770
Tea Act	1773	Gave the British East India Company a monopoly on all tea imports to America, hitting at American merchants
Intolerable Acts	1774	
Boston Port Bill		Closed Boston harbor
Massachusetts Government Act		Annulled the Massachusetts colonial charter
Administration of Justice Act		Protected British officials from colonial courts by sending them home for trial if arrested
Quartering Act		Legalized the housing of British troops in private homes
Quebec Act		Created a highly centralized government for Canada

The Quebec Act of 1774 *With the Quebec Act, Britain created a centralized colonial government for Canada and extended that colony's administrative control southwest to the Ohio River, invalidating the sea-to-sea boundaries of many colonial charters.*

British terminated the long history of self-rule by communities in the colony of Massachusetts.

Additional measures affected the other colonies and encouraged them to see themselves in league with suffering Massachusetts. The Quartering Act legalized the housing of troops at public expense not only in taverns and abandoned buildings but in occupied dwellings and private homes as well. And the Administration of Justice Act sought to protect British officials from colonial courts, thereby encouraging them to pursue the work of suppression vigorously; those accused of capital crimes committed while putting down riots or collecting revenue, such as the soldiers involved in the Boston Massacre, were now to be sent to England for trial.

Finally, in the Quebec Act, the British authorized a permanent government for the territory taken from France in the late war. Originally, British officials had anticipated creating a popular assembly for Quebec, bringing it in line with the other colonies, but with the continuing American difficulties those plans were shelved. Instead Parliament established an authoritarian, antirepublican administration for

Quebec, with a royal governor and an appointed council. To curry favor with the seigneurial class, the act confirmed the feudal system of land tenure along the St. Lawrence. And the Roman Catholic Church was granted religious toleration and confirmed in its traditional right to collect tithes, thus, in effect, establishing it as the state religion.

To the American colonists the Quebec Act was a frightening preview of what imperial authorities might have in store for them, and it confirmed the prediction of the Committees of Correspondence that there was a British conspiracy to destroy American liberty. The argument was made for them in Parliament by the radical Whig Charles James Fox: "To establish a perfectly despotic government, contrary to the genius and spirit of the British constitution," he warned his colleagues, "carries with it the appearance of a love of despotism, and a settled design to enslave the people of America." Moreover, the act extended Quebec's jurisdiction to the Ohio Valley, thus violating the "sea-to-sea" provisions of many of the colonies' charters. The British appeared to be giving the West back to the very people from whom it had been won.

In May, General Thomas Gage arrived in Boston to replace Hutchinson as governor. The same day, the Boston town meeting called for a revival of nonimportation measures against Britain. In Virginia, the Burgesses declared that Boston was enduring a "hostile invasion" and made provision for a "day of fasting, humiliation, and prayer, devoutly to implore the divine interposition for averting the heavy calamity, which threatens destruction to our civil rights and the evils of civil war." For this expression of sympathy, Governor Dunmore suspended the legislature, but the members adjourned to nearby Raleigh Tavern, where they voted for a Congress of all the colonies. Despite the governor's displeasure, throughout the colony on the first of June, funeral bells tolled, flags flew at half mast, and people flocked to the churches.

The First Continental Congress

It was amid this crisis that town meetings and colonial assemblies alike chose representatives for the Continental Congress described in the opening of this chapter. The delegates who arrived in Philadelphia in September 1774 included the most important leaders of the American cause. Cousins Samuel and John Adams, the radicals from Massachusetts, were joined by Patrick Henry and George Washington from Virginia and Christopher Gadsden of South Carolina. Many of the delegates were conservatives: John Dickinson and Joseph Galloway of Philadelphia, John Jay and James Duane from New York.

With the exception of Gadsden, a hothead who proposed an attack on British forces in Boston, the delegates wished to avoid war and favored a policy of economic coercion.

In one of their first debates, the delegates passed a Declaration and Resolves, in which they asserted that all the colonists sprang from a common tradition and enjoyed rights guaranteed "by the immutable laws of nature, the principles of the English constitution, and the several charters or compacts" of their provinces. Thirteen acts of Parliament, passed since 1763, were declared in violation of these rights. Until these acts were repealed, the delegates pledged, they would impose a set of sanctions against the British. These would include not only the nonimportation and nonconsumption of British goods but a prohibition on the export of colonial commodities to Britain or its other colonies.

To enforce these sanctions, the Continental Congress urged that "a committee be chosen in every county, city, and town, by those who are qualified to vote for representatives in the legislature, whose business it shall be attentively to observe the conduct of all persons." This call for democratically elected local committees in each community had important political ramifications. The following year, these groups, known as Committees of Observation and Safety, took over the functions of local government throughout the colonies. They organized militia companies, convened extralegal courts, and combined to form colony-wide congresses or conventions. By dissolving the colonial legislatures, royal governors unwittingly aided the work of these committees. The committees also scrutinized the activities of fellow citizens, suppressed the expression of Loyalist opinion from pulpit or press, and practiced other forms of coercion. Throughout most of the colonies the committees formed a bridge between the old colonial administrations and the revolutionary governments organized over the next few years. Committees began to link localities together in the cause of a wider American community. It was at this point that people began to refer to the colonies as the American "states."

Lexington and Concord

On September 1, 1774, General Gage sent troops from Boston to seize the stores of cannon and ammunition the Massachusetts militia had stored at armories in Charlestown and Cambridge. In response, the Massachusetts House of Representatives, calling itself the Provincial Congress, created a Committee of Safety empowered to call up the militia. On October 15 the committee authorized the creation of special units, to be known as "minute-

men," who stood ready to be called at a moment's notice. The armed militia of the towns and communities surrounding Boston faced the British army, quartered in the city.

It was no rabble he was up against, Gage wrote to his superiors, but "the freeholders and farmers" of New England who believed they were defending their communities. Worrying that his forces were insufficient to suppress the rebellion, he requested reinforcements. The stalemate continued through the fall and winter. To raise their spirits, the New England militia ridiculed the British army:

> And what have you got now with all your designing,
> But a town without victuals to sit down and dine in;
> And to look on the ground like a parcel of noodles,
> And sing, how the Yankees have beaten the Doodles.
> I'm sure if you're wise you'll make peace for a dinner,
> For fighting and fasting will soon make ye thinner.

But King George was convinced that the time had come for war. "The New England governments are in a state of rebellion," he wrote privately. "Blows must decide whether they are to be subject to this country or independent." In Parliament, Pitt proposed withdrawing troops from Boston, but was overruled by a large margin. Attempting to find a balance between hard-liners and advocates of conciliation, Lord North organized majority support in the House of Commons for a plan in which Parliament would "forbear" to levy taxes for purposes of revenue once the colonies had agreed to tax themselves for the common defense. But simultaneously Parliament passed legislation severely restraining colonial commerce. "A great empire and little minds go ill together," Edmund Burke quipped in March 1775 in a brilliant speech in Parliament opposing this bill. "Let it be once understood that your government may be one thing and their privileges

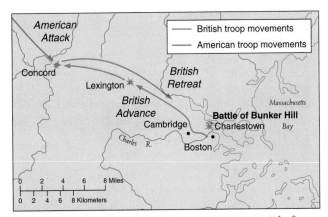

The First Engagements of the Revolution   *The first military engagements of the American Revolution took place in the spring of 1775 in the countryside surrounding Boston.*

another, that these two things may exist without any mutual relation." Then he declared in prophetic words, "The cement is gone, the cohesion is loosened, and everything hastens to decay and dissolution."

In Virginia, at almost the same moment, Patrick Henry predicted that hostilities would soon begin in New England. "Gentlemen may cry peace, peace!—but there is no peace," he thundered in prose later memorized by millions of American schoolchildren. "Is life so dear, or peace so sweet, as to be purchased at the price of chains and slavery? Forbid it, Almighty God! I know not what course others may take, but as for me give me liberty or give me death!" Three weeks later, on April 14, General Gage received instructions to strike at once against the Massachusetts militia. "It will surely be better that the conflict should be brought on upon such ground," argued his superior, "than in a riper state of rebellion."

On the evening of April 18, 1775, Gage ordered 700 men to capture the store of American ammunition at the town of Concord. Learning of the operation, the Boston committee dispatched two men, Paul Revere and William Dawes, to alert the militia of the countryside. By the time the British forces had reached Lexington, midway to their destination, it was dawn. Some seventy armed minutemen had assembled on the green in the center of town,

but they were disorganized and confused. "Lay down your arms, you damned rebels, and disperse!" cried one of the British officers. The Americans began to withdraw in the face of overwhelming opposition, but they took their arms with them. "Damn you, why don't you lay down your arms!" someone shouted from the British lines. "Damn them! We will have them!" No order to fire was given, but shots rang out, killing eight Americans and wounding ten others.

The British marched on to Concord, where they burned a small quantity of supplies and cut down a liberty pole. Meanwhile, news of the skirmish at Lexington had spread through the countryside and the militia companies of communities from miles around converged on the town. Seeing smoke, they mistakenly concluded that the troops were firing homes. "Will you let them burn the town!" one man cried, and the Americans moved to the Concord bridge. There they attacked a British company, killing three soldiers—the first British casualties of the Revolution. The British immediately turned back for Boston, but were attacked by Americans at many points along the way. Reinforcements met them at Lexington, preventing a complete disaster, but by the time they finally marched into Boston 73 were dead and 202 wounded or missing. The British troops were vastly outnumbered by the approximately 4,000 Massachusetts militiamen, who suffered 95 casualties. The engagement forecast what would be a central problem for the British: they would be forced to fight amid an armed population defending their own communities against outsiders.

DECIDING FOR INDEPENDENCE

"We send you momentous intelligence," read the letter received by the Charleston, South Carolina, Committee of Correspondence on May 8, reporting the violence in Massachusetts. Community militia companies mobilized throughout the colonies. At Boston, thousands of militiamen from Massachusetts and the surrounding provinces besieged the city, leaving the British no escape but by sea; the siege would last for nearly a year. Meanwhile, delegates from twelve colonies reconverged on Philadelphia for

Soon after the fighting at Lexington and Concord, the artist Ralph Earl and the engraver Amos Doolittle visited the location and interviewed participants. They produced a series of four engravings of the incident, the first popular prints of the battles of the Revolutionary War. This view shows the British soldiers marching back to Boston through the hail of sniper fire from colonial militiamen.

the second session of the Continental Congress. What would be the political consequences of the armed struggle now under way?

The Second Continental Congress

The members of the Second Continental Congress, which opened on May 10, 1775, represented twelve of the British colonies on the mainland of North America. From New Hampshire to South Carolina, Committees of Observation and Safety had elected colonywide conventions, and these extralegal bodies in turn had chosen delegates. Consequently, few conservatives or Loyalists were among them. Georgia, unrepresented at the first session of the Continental Congress, remained absent at the opening of the second. This newest mainland colony depended heavily on British subsidies, and its leaders were cautious, fearing both slave and Indian uprisings. But in 1775 the political balance in Georgia shifted in favor of the radicals; observing the British attempt to curry favor with Indians elsewhere, Georgia frontier settlers came to believe that the Continental Congress would be more supportive in the matter of encroachments against the Creek Indians. Leaders from the backcountry then joined Whig merchants from Savannah to form a provincial Committee of Safety, and by the end of the summer the colony had delegates in Philadelphia.

The addition of Georgia made thirteen colonies in the revolutionary camp. But what of the other British possessions? The Continental Congress made overtures to a number of them. In one of their first acts, delegates called on "the oppressed inhabitants of Canada" to join in the struggle for "common liberty." After the Seven Years War, the British had treated Quebec as a conquered province, and French Canadians had little sympathy for the British empire. On the other hand, the Americans were traditional enemies, much feared because of their aggressive expansionism. Indeed, when the Canadians failed to respond positively and immediately, the delegates reversed themselves and voted to authorize a military expedition against Quebec to eliminate any possibility of a British invasion from that quarter. They thus killed any chance of the Canadians' joining the anti-British cause and set a course toward the development of separate nations.

Many of the other British colonies, however, harbored significant sympathy for the American struggle against parliamentary authority. For example, the population of Nova Scotia (not then a part of Canada) included many New Englanders who had relocated there after the expulsion of the Acadians. When the British attempted to recruit among them for soldiers to serve in Boston, one community responded that since "[we are] almost all of us born in New England, [we are] divided betwixt natural affection to our nearest relations and good faith and friendship to our king and country." But the British had established a naval stronghold at Halifax, and the province remained secure within the empire. The presence of the British military was decisive in several other locations as well. For example, the British army was able to keep Florida, where there was minimal local government, completely outside the revolutionary struggles. The popular assemblies of Jamaica, Grenada, and Barbados all formally declared themselves in sympathy with the Continental Congress, but the powerful British navy prevented them from sending representatives. Bermuda succeeded in sending a delegation to Philadelphia to plead for support, but so preoccupied were the Americans with more pressing matters that they found themselves unable to assist. Thus it was thirteen colonies against the empire.

Among the delegates at the Continental Congress were many familiar faces and a few new ones. One of the latter was Thomas Jefferson, a plantation owner and lawyer gifted with one of the most imaginative and analytical minds of his time who had served as a junior member of Virginia's Committee of Correspondence. All the delegates carried news of the enthusiasm for war that raged in their home provinces. "A frenzy of revenge seems to have seized all ranks of people," said Jefferson. George Washington attended all the sessions in uniform. "Oh that I was a soldier," an envious John Adams wrote to his wife, Abigail. The delegates agreed that defense was the first issue on their agenda.

On May 15 this Second Continental Congress resolved to put the colonies in a state of defense, but the delegates were divided on how best to do it. They lacked the power and the funds to immediately raise and supply an army. After debate and deliberation, John Adams made the practical proposal that the delegates simply designate as a "Continental Army" the militia forces besieging Boston. On June 14 the Congress resolved to supplement the New England militiamen with six companies of expert riflemen raised in Pennsylvania, Maryland, and Virginia. The delegates agreed that in order to emphasize their national aspirations, they had to select a man from the South to command these New England forces. All eyes turned to George Washington. Although Washington had suffered defeat at the beginning of the Seven Years War, he had subsequently compiled a distinguished record and had been promoted by the British command to brigadier, the highest rank of any native-born American. On June 15, Washington was elected commander in chief of all Continental forces by a unanimous vote. He served without salary. The Continental Congress soon appointed a staff of major generals to support him. On June 22, in a highly significant move, the Congress voted to finance the army with an issue of $2 million in bills of credit, backed by the good faith of the "Confederated Colonies." Thus began the long and complicated process of financing the Revolution.

During its first session in the spring of 1775, the Continental Congress had begun to move cautiously down the path toward independence. Few would admit, even to themselves, however, that this was their goal. John Adams, who was close to advocating independence, wrote that he was "as fond of reconciliation as any man" but found the hope of peaceful resolution unreasonable. "The cancer is too deeply rooted," he thought, "and too far spread to be cured by anything short of cutting it out entire." Still, on July 5, 1775, the delegates passed the so-called Olive Branch Petition, written by John Dickinson of Pennsylvania, in which they professed their attachment to King George and begged him to prevent further hostilities so that there might be an accommodation. The next day they approved a Declaration of the Causes and Necessities of Taking Up Arms, written by Jefferson and Dickinson. Here the delegates adopted a harder tone, resolving "to die freemen rather than to live slaves." Before the Second Continental Congress adjourned at the beginning of August, the delegates appointed commissioners to negotiate with the Indian nations in an attempt to keep them out of the conflict. They also reinstated Benjamin Franklin as postmaster general to keep the mails moving and protect communication among the colonies.

Fighting in the North and South

Both North and South saw fighting in 1775 and early 1776. In May 1775, a small force of armed New Englanders under the command of Ethan Allen of Vermont surprised the British garrison at Fort Ticonderoga on Lake Champlain, demanding—"in the name of Great Jehovah and the Continental Congress"—that

The Connecticut artist John Trumbull painted The Battle of Bunker Hill in 1785, the first of a series that earned him the informal title of "the Painter of the Revolution." Trumbull was careful to research the details of his paintings but composed them in the grand style of historical romance. In the early nineteenth century he repainted this work, and three other Revolutionary scenes, for the rotunda of the Capitol in Washington, D.C.

the commander surrender. The Continental Congress, in fact, knew nothing of this campaign, and when news of its arrived, members of the New York delegation were distressed at this New England violation of their territorial sovereignty. With great effort, the Americans transported the fort's cannon overland to be used in the siege of Boston.

At Boston the British hastened to reinforce Gage's forces and by the middle of June 1775 had approximately 6,500 soldiers in the city. By that time the American forces had increased to nearly 10,000. Fearing Gage would occupy the heights south of town, the Americans countered by occupying the Charlestown peninsula to the north. On June 17, British ships in the harbor began to fire on the American positions, and Gage decided on a frontal assault to dislodge them. In bloody fighting that, although it occurred at Breed's Hill, has since been known as the Battle of Bunker Hill, the British finally succeeded in routing the Americans, killing 140 men, but not before suffering over a thousand casualties of their own, including 226 dead. The fierce reaction in England to this enormous loss ended all possibility of any last-minute reconciliation. In August 1775, King George rejected the Olive Branch Petition and issued a royal proclamation declaring the colonists to be in "open and avowed rebellion." "Divers wicked and desperate persons" were the cause of the problem, said the king, and he called on his loyal subjects in America to "bring the traitors to justice."

In June 1775, the Continental Congress had also assembled its expeditionary force against Canada. One thousand Americans moved north up the Hudson River corridor, and in November General Richard Montgomery forced the capitulation of Montreal. Meanwhile, Benedict Arnold set out from Massachusetts with another American army, and after a torturous march through the forests and mountains of Maine, he joined Montgomery outside the walls of Quebec. Unlike the assault of British General Wolfe in 1759, however, the American assault failed to take the city. Montgomery and 100 Americans were killed, and another 300 were taken prisoner. Although Arnold held his position, the American siege was broken the following spring by British reinforcements who had come down the St. Lawrence. By the summer of 1776 the Americans had been forced back from Canada.

Elsewhere there were successes. Washington installed captured British artillery on the heights above Boston, placing both the city and its harbor within cannon range. General William Howe, who had replaced Gage, had little choice but to evacuate. In March, the British sailed out of Boston harbor for the last time, heading north to Halifax with at least

1,000 American Loyalists. In the South, American militia rose against the Loyalist forces of Virginia's Governor Dunmore, who had alienated the planter class by promising freedom to any slave who would fight with the British. After a decisive defeat of his forces, Dunmore retreated to British naval vessels, from which he shelled and destroyed much of the city of Norfolk, Virginia, on January 1, 1776. In North Carolina in February, the rebel militia crushed a Loyalist force at the Battle of Moore's Creek Bridge near Wilmington, ending British plans for an invasion of that province. The British decided to attack Charleston, but at Fort Moultrie in Charleston harbor an American force turned back the assault. It would be more than two years before the British would try again to invade the South.

No Turning Back

Hopes of reconciliation died with the mounting casualties. The Second Continental Congress, which was rapidly assuming the role of a new government for all the provinces, reconvened in September 1775 and received news of the king's proclamation that the colonies were in formal rebellion. Although the delegates disclaimed any intention of denying the sovereignty of the king, they now moved to organize an American navy. They declared British vessels open to capture and authorized privateering. The Congress took further steps toward de facto independence when it authorized contacts with foreign powers through its agents in Europe. In the spring of 1776, after a period of secret negotiations, France and Spain approved the shipping of supplies to the rebellious provinces. The Continental Congress then declared colonial ports open to the trade of all nations but Britain.

The emotional ties to Britain proved difficult to break. But in 1776 help arrived in the form of a pamphlet written by Thomas Paine, a radical Englishman recently arrived in Philadelphia. In *Common Sense*, Paine proposed to offer "simple fact, plain argument, and common sense" on the crisis. For years Americans had defended their actions by wrapping themselves in the mantle of British traditions. But Paine argued that the British system rested on "the base remains of two ancient tyrannies," aristocracy and monarchy, neither of which was appropriate for America. Paine placed the blame for the oppression of the colonists on the shoulders of King George, whom he labeled the "royal Brute." Appealing to the millennial spirit of American Protestant culture, Paine wrote: "We have it in our power to begin the world over again. A situation, similar to the present, hath not happened since the days of Noah until now." *Common Sense* was the single most important piece of writing during the Revolutionary era, selling more than 100,000 copies within a few months of its publication in January 1776. It reshaped popular thinking and put independence squarely on the agenda.

In April the North Carolina convention, which operated as the revolutionary replacement for the old colonial assembly, was first to empower its delegates to vote for a declaration of independence. News that the British were recruiting a force of German mercenaries to use against the Americans provided an additional push toward what now began to seem inevitable. In May the Continental Congress voted to recommend that the individual states move as quickly as possible toward the adoption of constitutions. When John Adams wrote, in the preamble to this statement, that "the exercise of every kind of authority under the said crown should be totally suppressed," he sent a strong signal that the delegates were on the verge of approving a momentous declaration.

The Manner in which the American Colonies Declared themselves INDEPENDENT of the King of ENGLAND, *a 1783 English print. Understanding that the coming struggle would require the steady support of ordinary people, in the Declaration of Independence the upper-class men of the Continental Congress asserted the right of popular revolution and the great principle of human equality.*

The Declaration of Independence

On June 7, 1776, Richard Henry Lee of Virginia offered a motion to the Continental Congress: "That these united colonies are, and of right ought to be, free and independent states, that they are absolved from all allegiance to the British crown, and that all political connection between them and the state of Great Britain is, and ought to be, totally dissolved." After some debate, a vote was postponed until July, but a committee composed of John Adams, Thomas Jefferson, Benjamin Franklin, Roger Sherman of Connecticut, and Robert Livingston of New York was asked to prepare a draft declaration of American independence. The committee assigned the writing to Jefferson.

The intervening month allowed the delegates to sample the public discussion and debate and receive instructions from their state conventions. By the end of the month, all the states but New York had authorized a vote for independence. When the question came up for debate again on July 1, a large majority in the Continental Congress supported independence. The final vote, taken on July 2, was twelve in favor of independence, none against, with New York abstaining. The delegates then turned to the declaration itself and made a number of changes in Jefferson's draft, striking out, for example, a long passage condemning slavery. In this and a number of other ways the final version was somewhat more cautious than the draft, but it was still a stirring document.

Its central section reiterated the "long train of abuses and usurpations" on the part of King George that had led the Americans to their drastic course; there was no mention of Parliament, the principal opponent since 1764. But it was the first section that expressed the highest ideals of the delegates:

> We hold these truths to be self-evident, that all men are created equal, that they are endowed by their creator with certain inalienable rights, that among these are life, liberty, and the pursuit of happiness. That to secure these rights, governments are instituted among men, deriving their just powers from the consent of the governed. That whenever any form of government becomes destructive of these ends, it is the right of the people to alter or to abolish it, and to institute a new government, laying its foundation on such principles, and organizing its powers in such form, as to them shall seem most likely to effect their safety and happiness.

There was very little debate in the Continental Congress about these "truths" and principles. The delegates were mostly men of wealth and position,

CHRONOLOGY

1713	France cedes Acadia to Britain
1745	New Englanders capture Louisburg
1749	French send an expeditionary force down the Ohio River
1753	French begin building forts from Lake Erie to the Ohio
1754	Albany Congress
1755	British General Edward Braddock defeated by a combined force of French and Indians
	Britain expels Acadians from Nova Scotia
1756	Seven Years War begins in Europe
1757	William Pitt becomes prime minister
1758	Louisburg captured by the British for the second time
1759	British capture Quebec
1763	Treaty of Paris
	Pontiac's uprising
	Proclamation of 1763 creates "Indian Country"
	Paxton Boys massacre
1764	Sugar Act
1765	Stamp Act and Stamp Act Congress
1766	Declaratory Act
1767	Townshend Revenue Acts
1768	Treaties of Hard Labor and Fort Stanwix
1770	Boston Massacre
1772	First Committee of Correspondence organized in Boston
1773	Tea Act
	Boston Tea Party
1774	Intolerable Acts
	First Continental Congress
	Dunmore's War
1775	Fighting begins at Lexington and Concord
	Second Continental Congress
1776	Americans invade Canada
	Thomas Paine's *Common Sense*
	Declaration of Independence

but realizing that the coming struggle for independence would require the steady support of ordinary people they asserted this great principle of equality and the right of revolution without examining the implications or the potential consequences. Surely no statement would reverberate more through American history. The ideal of equality would inspire the poor as well as the wealthy, women as well as men, blacks as well as whites, indeed, people of all races and creeds.

But it was the third and final section that may have contained the most meaning for the delegates: "For the support of this declaration, with a firm reliance on the protection of divine providence, we mutually pledge to each other our lives, our fortunes, and our sacred honor." In voting for independence, the delegates proclaimed their community but they also committed treason against their king. They could be condemned as traitors, hunted as criminals, and might soon stand on the scaffold to be executed for their sentiments. Yet on July 4, 1776, these men approved the text of the Declaration without dissent.

CONCLUSION

Great Britain emerged from the Seven Years War as the dominant power in North America. Yet despite its attempts at strict regulation and determination of the course of events in its colonies, it faced consistent resistance and often complete failure. Perhaps British leaders assumed that resistance would never be unified. After all, John Adams expressed the same doubts when he likened the delegates at the Continental Congress in 1774 to "ambassadors from a dozen belligerent powers." But the British underestimated the political consensus that existed among the colonists about the importance of "republican" government. They also underestimated the ability of the colonists to inform one another, to work together, to build a sentiment of nationalism that cut across the boundaries of ethnicity, region, and economic status. Through newspapers, pamphlets, Committees of Correspondence, community organizations, and group protest, the colonists discovered the concerns they shared, and in so doing they fostered a new,

"American" identity. Without that identity it would have been difficult for them to consent to the treasonous act of declaring independence—especially when the independence they sought was from an international power that dominated much of the globe.

REVIEW QUESTIONS

1. How did overwhelming British success in the Seven Years War lead to an imperial crisis in British North America?
2. Outline the changes in British policy toward the colonies from 1750 to 1776.
3. Trace the developing sense of an American national community over this same period.
4. What were the principal events leading to the beginning of armed conflict at Lexington and Concord?
5. How were the ideals of American republicanism expressed in the Declaration of Independence?

RECOMMENDED READING

Benedict Anderson, *Imagined Communities: Reflections on the Origin and Spread of Nationalism*, revised edition (1991). An argument that the essential first act of national consciousness is the effort to create a community that encompasses more than just local individuals and groups.

Bernard Bailyn, *The Ideological Origins of the American Revolution* (1967). Whereas other accounts stress economic or social causes, this classic argument emphasizes the role of ideas in the advent of the Revolution. Includes an analysis of American views of the imperial crisis.

Eric Foner, *Tom Paine and Revolutionary America* (1976). Combines a biography of Paine with a community study of the Revolution in Philadelphia and Pennsylvania.

Lawrence H. Gipson, *British Empire before the American Revolution*, 8 vols. (1936–49). Although these volumes are heavy going, they offer what is still the best and most comprehensive treatment of the Seven Years War in America.

Robert A. Gross, *The Minute Men and Their World* (1976).

This fascinating and readable history examines the coming of the Revolution from the viewpoint of a New England community.

Francis Jennings, *Empire of Fortune: Crowns, Colonies, and Tribes in the Seven Years War in America* (1988). The French and Indian War examined from the point of view of the Iroquois Confederacy. This is opinionated but exciting history.

Pauline Maier, *American Scripture: Making the Declaration of Independence* (1997). The deep background of this foundation of American democracy.

Richard L. Merritt, *Symbols of American Community, 1735–1775* (1966). A study of colonial newspapers that provides evidence for a rising sense of national community. The French and Indian War emerges as the key period for the growth of nationalist sentiment.

Richard White, *The Middle Ground: Indians, Empires, and Republics in the Great Lakes Region, 1650–1815* (1991). This well-researched history provides a fascinating account of the West from the point of view of imperialists, settlers, and Indians.

ADDITIONAL BIBLIOGRAPHY

The Seven Years War in America

Fred Anderson, *A People's Army: Massachusetts Soldiers and Society in the Seven Years' War* (1984)

Sylvia R. Frey, *The British Soldier in America: A Social History of Military Life in the Colonial Period* (1981)

Dougles E. Leach, *Roots of Conflict: British Armed Forces and Colonial Americans, 1677–1763* (1986)

Richard Middleton, *The Bells of Victory: The Pitt-Newcastle Ministry and the Conduct of the Seven Years' War, 1757–1762* (1985)

Robert C. Newbold, *The Albany Congress and Plan of Union of 1754* (1955)

Howard H. Peckham, *Pontiac and the Indian Uprising* (1947)

William Pencak, *War, Politics, and Revolution in Provincial Massachusetts* (1981)

Alan Rogers, *Empire and Liberty* (1974)

Noel T. St. John Williams, *Red Coats along the Hudson* (1997)

Imperial Crisis in British North America

Thomas C. Barrow, *Trade and Empire: The British Customs Service in Colonial America* (1967)

John Brewer, *Party Ideology and Popular Politics at the Accession of George III* (1976)

Don Cook, *The Long Fuse: How England Lost the American Colonies, 1760–1785* (1995)

Theodore Draper, *A Struggle for Power: The American Revolution* (1996)

Marc Egnal, *A Mighty Empire: The Origins of the American Revolution* (1988)

Alice Hanson Jones, *The Wealth of a Nation to Be* (1980)

John J. McCusker, *Rum and the American Revolution* (1989)

Richard L. Merritt, *Symbols of American Community, 1735–1775* (1966)

J. G. A. Pocock, *The Machiavellian Moment: Florentine Political Thought and the Atlantic Republican Tradition* (1975)

Caroline Robbins, *The Eighteenth-Century Commonwealthman* (1959)

Arthur M. Schlesinger, *The Colonial Merchants and the American Revolution* (1917)

W. A. Speck, *Stability and Strife: England, 1714–1760* (1977)

Peter David Garner Thomas, *Revolution in America: Britain and the Colonies, 1763–1776* (1992)

John W. Tyler, *Smugglers and Patriots: Boston Merchants and the Advent of the American Revolution* (1986)

Carl Ubbelohde, *The Vice-Admiralty Courts and the American Revolution* (1960)

From Resistance to Rebellion

David Ammerman, *In the Common Cause: American Response to the Coercive Acts of 1774* (1974)

T. H. Breen, *Tobacco Culture: The Mentality of the Great Tidewater Planters on the Eve of Revolution* (1985)

Richard D. Brown, *Revolutionary Politics in Massachusetts: The Boston Committee of Correspondence and the Towns, 1772–1774* (1970)

Richard L. Bushman, *King and People in Provincial Massachusetts* (1985)

H. Trevor Colbourn, *The Lamp of Experience: Whig History and the Intellectual Origins of the American Revolution* (1965)

Bernard Donoughue, *British Politics and the American Revolution: The Path to War, 1773–1775* (1964)

Jack P. Greene, *Understanding the American Revolution: Issues and Actors* (1995)

Dirk Hoerder, *Crowd Action in Revolutionary Massachusetts* (1977)

Benjamin W. Labaree, *The Boston Tea Party* (1974)

Pauline Maier, *From Resistance to Rebellion* (1972)

Edmund S. Morgan, *The Birth of the Republic, 1763–1789* (1956)

John Shy, *Toward Lexington: The Role of the British Army in the Coming of the American Revolution* (1965)

Peter David Garner Thomas, *Tea Party to Independence: The Third Phase of the American Revolution, 1773–1776* (1991)

Morton White, *The Philosophy of the American Revolution* (1978)

Gary Wills, *Inventing America* (1978)

Biography

Bernard Bailyn, *The Ordeal of Thomas Hutchinson* (1974)

Della Gray Barthelmas, *The Signers of the Declaration of Independence* (1997)

Richard R. Beeman, *Patrick Henry: A Biography* (1974)

Jeremy Black, *Pitt the Elder* (1992)

John Brooke, *King George III* (1974)

John E. Ferling, *The Loyalist Mind: Joseph Galloway and the American Revolution* (1977)

Milton E. Flower, *John Dickinson: Conservative Revolutionary* (1983)

William M. Fowler, Jr., *The Baron of Beacon Hill: A Biography of John Hancock* (1979)

William M. Fowler, Jr., *Samuel Adams: Radical Puritan* (1997)

David A. McCants, *Patrick Henry, the Orator* (1990)

Peter Shaw, *The Character of John Adams* (1976)

Peter D. G. Thomas, *Lord North* (1974)

CHAPTER SEVEN

THE CREATION OF THE UNITED STATES

1776–1786

William Ranney, *The Battle of Cowpens*. Oil on canvas. Photo by Sam Holland. Courtesy South Carolina State House.

AMERICAN COMMUNITIES
A National Community
Evolves at Valley Forge

A drum roll ushered in a January morning in 1778, summoning the Continental Army to roll call. Along a two-mile line of log cabins, doors slowly opened and ragged men stepped out onto the frozen ground at Valley Forge. "There comes a soldier," wrote army surgeon Albigense Waldo. "His bare feet are seen through his worn-out shoes, his legs nearly naked from the tattered remains of an only pair of stockings, his breeches not sufficient to cover his nakedness, his shirt hanging in strings, his hair disheveled, his face meagre." The reek of foul straw and unwashed bodies filled the air. "No bread, no soldier!" The chant began as a barely audible murmur, then was picked up by men all along the line. "No bread, no soldier! No bread, no soldier!" At last the chanting grew so loud it could be heard at General Washington's headquarters, a mile away. The 11,000 men of the American army were surviving on little more than "firecake," a mixture of flour and water baked hard before the fire that, according to Waldo, turned "guts to pasteboard." Two thousand men were without shoes, others were without blankets and had to sit up all night about the fires to keep from freezing. Addressing the Continental Congress, Washington wrote, "Three or four days of bad weather would prove our destruction."

Valley Forge was to become a national symbol of endurance. After marching hundreds of weary miles and suffering a series of terrible defeats at the hands of a British force nearly twice their number, the soldiers of the Continental Army had retreated to this winter headquarters only to find themselves at the mercy of indifferent local suppliers. Contractors demanded exorbitant rates for food and clothing, rates the Congress had refused to pay, and as a result local farmers preferred to deal with the British, who paid in pounds sterling, not depreciated Continental currency.

The 11,000 men of the Continental Army, who had not been paid for nearly six months, were divided into sixteen brigades composed of regiments from nine states. An unsympathetic observer described them as "a vagabond army of ragamuffins," and indeed many of the men were drawn from the ranks of the poor and disadvantaged: indentured servants, landless farmers, and nearly a thousand African Americans, both slave and free. Most of the men came from thinly settled farm districts or small towns where precautions regarding sanitation had been unnecessary. Every thaw revealed ground covered with "much filth and nastiness," and officers ordered sentinels to fire on any man "easing himself elsewhere than at ye vaults." Typhoid fever and other infectious diseases spread quickly: along with dysentery, malnutrition, and exposure they claimed as many as 2,500 lives that winter. More than 700 women—wives, lovers, cooks, laundresses, and prostitutes—lived at Valley Forge that winter, and they were kept busy nursing the sick and burying the dead.

"What then is to become of this army?" Washington worried during the depth of the winter. But six months later the force he marched out of Valley Forge was considerably stronger for its experience there. Most important were the strong relationships that formed among the men, twelve of whom bunked together in each cabin, grouped by state regiments and brigade. In these units they fashioned "a band of brotherhood" and "shared with each other their hardships, dangers, and sufferings," wrote common soldier Joseph Plumb Martin, "sympathized with each other in trouble and sickness, assisted in bearing each other's burdens, [and] endeavored to conceal each other's faults." During the coming trials of battle, Washington, who referred to his staff as "family," would rely greatly on the bonds of affection his men had developed during the hard winter. As psychologists know today, it is this sense of community that contributes most to success in warfare.

To some American Patriots—as the supporters of the Revolution called themselves—the European-style Continental Army betrayed the ideals of the citizen-soldier and the autonomy of local communities, central tenets of the Revolution. Washington argued strongly, however, that the Revolution could not be won without a national army insulated from politics and able to withstand the shifting popular mood. Moreover, through the developing sense of community among these men—who came from hundreds of localities and a variety of ethnic backgrounds—the Continental soldiers became living examples of the egalitarian ideals of the Revolution. They were a popular democratic force that counterbalanced the conservatism of the new republic's elite leadership. The national spirit they built at Valley Forge would sustain them through four more years of war and provide momentum for the long process of forging a national political system out of the persistent localism of American politics. "I admire them tremendously!" wrote one European officer serving with Washington. "It is incredible that soldiers composed of men of every age, even children of fifteen, of whites and blacks, almost naked, unpaid, and rather poorly fed, can march so well and withstand fire so steadfastly." Asked to explain why his men served, another officer declared: "Nothing but virtue and that great principle, the love of our country."

Valley Forge

Key Topics

- The major alignments and divisions among Americans during the American Revolution

- Major military campaigns of the Revolution

- The Articles of Confederation and the role of the Confederation Congress during the Revolutionary War

- The states as the setting for significant political change

- The economic crisis in the aftermath of the American Revolution

THE WAR FOR INDEPENDENCE

At the beginning of the Revolution, the British had the world's best-equipped and most disciplined army as well as a navy that was unopposed in American waters. But they greatly underestimated the American capacity to fight. With a native officer corps and considerable experience in the colonial wars of the eighteenth century, the Patriot forces proved formidable. The British also misperceived the sources of the conflict. Seeing the rebellion as the work of a small group of disgruntled conspirators, initially they defined their objective as defeating this Patriot opposition. In the wake of a military victory, they believed, they could easily reassert political control. But the geography of eastern North America offered no single vital center whose conquest would end the war. The Patriots had the advantage of fighting on their own ground and among a population thinly spread over a territory stretching along 1,500 miles of coastline and extending 100 miles or more into the interior. When the British succeeded in defeating the Patriots in one area, resistance would spring up in another. The key factor in the outcome of the war for independence, then, was the popular support for the American cause.

The Patriot Forces

Most American men of fighting age had to face the call to arms. From a population of approximately 350,000 eligible men, more than 200,000 saw action, though no more than 25,000 were engaged at any one time. More than 100,000 served in the Continental Army, under George Washington's command and the authority of the Continental Congress; the others served in Patriot militia companies.

These militias—armed bodies of men drawn from local communities—proved important in the defense of their own areas, where they had homes as well as local reputations to protect. Despite legend, however, the Revolutionary War was not won by these citizen-soldiers who exchanged plows for guns, or back-country riflemen who picked off British soldiers from behind trees. In the exuberant days of 1776, many Patriots did believe that militias alone could win the war against the British. As one observer wrote, "The Rage Militaire, as the French call a passion for arms, has taken possession of the whole Continent." But, serving short terms of enlistment, often with officers of their own choosing, militiamen resisted discipline. Washington's deputy, General Nathanael Greene, declared that they lacked the fortitude "to stand the shocking scenes of war," having never been "steeled by habit or fortified by military pride." Indeed, in the face of battle militia companies demonstrated appalling rates of desertion. During the fierce fighting on Long Island, for example, three-quarters of Connecticut's 8,000 militiamen simply abandoned the field and headed home.

Initially, the Continental Congress refused to invoke a draft of men from all the colonies or to mandate army enlistments exceeding one year. As a result, and because men preferred the militia to the regular army, the states failed to meet their quotas for regiments in the Continental Army. Nevertheless, the final victory in the American Revolution was won essentially by the steady struggle of the Continental Army. And indeed, the Revolution had little in common with modern national liberation movements in which armed populations engage in guerrilla warfare. General Washington and his officers required a force that could directly engage the British, and from the beginning of the war Washington argued with a skeptical Congress that victory could be won only with a full commitment to a truly national army. This view conflicted with popular fears of a standing army: Would they not be defeating their own purpose, many Patriots wondered, by adopting the corrupt institutions of their British enemies?

The failings of the militias in the early battles of the war sobered Congress, however, and it both greatly enlarged state quotas for the army and extended the term of service to three years or the war's duration. To spur enlistment Congress offered bounties, regular wages, and promises of free land after victory. Although the states consistently failed to meet their quotas, by the spring of 1777 Washington's army had grown to nearly 9,000 men.

Discipline was essential in a conflict in which men fired at close range, charged each other with bayonets, and engaged in hand-to-hand combat. One Connecticut man wrote of the effects of cannon on his regiment: "The ball first cut off the head of Smith, a stout heavy man, and dashed it open, then took Taylor across the bowels; it then struck Sergeant Garret of our company on the hip, took off the point of the hip bone." "Oh! What a sight that was," he concluded, "to see within a distance of six rods those men with their legs and arms and guns and packs all in a heap." In New Jersey, a sergeant in the Continental Army witnessed British troops slaughtering Americans lying on the field: "The men that was wounded in the thigh or leg, they dashed out their brains with their muskets and run them through with their bayonets, made them like sieves. This was barbarity to the utmost."

According to the best estimates, a total of 25,674 American men died in the Revolution, approximately 6,000 from wounds suffered in battle, 10,000 from the effects of disease, and the rest as prisoners of war or missing in action. Regiments of the Continental Army experienced the highest casualty rates, sometimes 30 or 40 percent. Indeed, the casualty rate overall was higher than in any other American conflict up to the present day, with the exception of the Civil War. Although in most areas the war was confined to direct engagements between the armies, in the back-country and in the South, where supporters and opponents of independence waged vicious campaigns of violence against each other, there were considerable noncombatant casualties.

Both the Continentals and the militias played important political roles as well. At a time when Americans identified most strongly with their local communities or their states, the Continental Army, through experiences like the Valley Forge winter, evolved into a powerful force for nationalist sentiment. Shortages of food and pay led to many army mutinies, in the most serious of which an officer was killed and two others wounded. But, when the mutineers in this instance set out, in January 1781, for Philadelphia, where they intended to address the Continental Congress, their purpose was not to abandon the American cause but to ask Congress to uphold its commitments to the soldiers who were fighting for the nation. En route to Philadelphia, the soldiers encountered British agents who tried to persuade them to go over to the king. Angry as these Continental soldiers were at the conditions under which their Congress expected them to fight, they were enraged at this attempt at subversion, and they hanged the British agents on the spot. The men from every colony who served in the Continental Army contributed mightily to the unity of purpose—the formation of a national community—that was essential to the process of nation making.

In most communities Patriots seized control of local government during the period of committee organizing in 1774 and 1775 (see Chapter 6), and with war imminent they pressed the obligation to serve in a Patriot militia upon most eligible men. In Farmington, Connecticut, in 1776, eighteen men were imprisoned "on suspicion of their being inimical to America" when they failed to join the muster of the local militia. After individual grilling by the authorities, they petitioned for pardon. "They appeared to be penitent of their former conduct," it was reported, and understood "that there was no such thing" as remaining neutral. Probably the most important role of the Patriot militias was to force even the most apathetic of Americans to think seriously about the Revolution, and to choose sides under the scrutiny of their neighbors.

As men marched off to war, many women assumed the management of family farms and businesses; Abigail Adams, for

Jean Baptiste Antoine de Verger, a French officer serving with the Continental Army, made these watercolors of American soldiers during the Revolution. Some 200,000 men saw action, including at least 5,000 African Americans; more than half of these troops served with the Continental Army.

example, ran the family's farm at Quincy for years. Adams wrote eloquently and often to her husband, John, on issues surrounding the American struggle for independence and, later, on the structure of the new republic. Some women participated even more directly in patriotic politics. The Boston home of Mercy Otis Warren, daughter of James Otis, was a center of Patriot political activity, and this dedicated revolutionary woman published a series of satires supporting the American cause and scorning the Loyalists. When the fighting shifted to their locales, women volunteered as seamstresses, cooks, nurses, and even spies.

When the months of fighting lengthened into years, many women left their homes to join husbands and lovers, fathers and brothers, in army encampments. Some were officially employed, but most took care of their own men, and many fought with them side by side. Best known among the women who stayed by their husbands' sides even in camp were Martha Washington and Catherine Greene, wives of the two most important American generals of the war. But less socially prominent women were remembered as well. Mary Ludwig Hays (later McCauley) earned the name "Molly Pitcher" for her courage in bringing water to the Patriots during the battle of Monmouth, in June 1778. When her husband was overcome by heat, Mary took his place at the cannon. When Margaret Corbin's husband died in battle, she stepped into his position. Other women, such as Deborah Sampson of Massachusetts, disguised themselves as men and enlisted.

The Loyalists

Not all Americans were Patriots. Many sat on the fence, confused by the conflict and waiting for a clear turn in the tide of the struggle before declaring their allegiance. About a fifth of the population, perhaps as many as half a million people, remained loyal to the British crown. They called themselves Loyalists but were known to Patriots as "Tories," the popular name for the conservative party in England, which traditionally supported the authority of the king over Parliament. Loyalism was strongest in the Lower South, weakest in New England. British colonial officials were almost always Loyalists, as were most Anglican clergymen and many lawyers who had worked with colonial administrators. The British cause also attracted ethnic minorities who had been persecuted by the dominant majority, such as the Highland Scots of the Carolinas and western New York, and southern tenant farmers who had Patriot landlords. Many slaves and most Indians identified with the Loyalists, the first because the Patriot leadership in the South was drawn from the ranks of slave owners, the second because they feared aggressive expansion by independent American states. Other

John Singleton Copley's portrait of Mercy Otis Warren captured her at the age of thirty-six, in 1765. During the Revolution her home in Boston was a center of patriotic political activity.

Copley, John Singleton, U.S., 1738–1815, *Mrs. James Warren (Mercy Otis)*, ca. 1763. Oil on canvas. 51 1/4 x 41 in. (130.1 x 104.1 cm). Bequest of Winslow Warren. Courtesy, Museum of Fine Art, Boston.

Loyalists were conservatives, fearful of political or social upheaval, or were temperamentally opposed to resistance to established authority.

Patriots passed state treason acts that prohibited speaking or writing against the Revolution. They also punished Loyalists with bills of attainder, by which persons were deprived, without trial, of their civil rights and property (a process later made illegal in the United States Constitution). In some areas, notably New York, South Carolina, Massachusetts, and Pennsylvania, Loyalists faced mob violence. One favorite punishment was the "grand Tory ride," in which a crowd hauled the victim through the streets astride a sharp fence rail. Another was tarring and feathering, in which men were stripped to "buff and breeches" and their naked flesh coated liberally with heated tar and then feathers. One broadside recommended that Patriots "then hold a lighted Candle to the feathers, and try to set it all on fire." The torment rarely went that far, but it was brutally painful nonetheless.

The most infamous American supporter of the British cause was Benedict Arnold, whose name has become synonymous, in the United States, with treason. Arnold was a hero of the early battles of the Revolution. But in 1779, angry and resentful about what he

The TORY'S Day of JUDGMENT.

A Patriot mob torments Loyalists in this print published during the Revolution. One favorite punishment was the "grand Tory ride," in which a crowd hauled the victim through the streets astride a fence rail. In another men were stripped to "buff and breeches" and their naked flesh coated liberally with heated tar and feathers.

perceived to be assignments and rank below his station, he became a paid informer of General Henry Clinton, head of the British army in New York City. In 1780 Patriots uncovered Arnold's plot to betray the strategic post of West Point, which he commanded. After fleeing to the British, who paid him a handsome stipend and pension, he became a brigadier general in the British army. The *bête noire* of the Revolution, Arnold became the most hated man in America. In his hometown of Norwich, Connecticut, a crowd destroyed the gravestones of his family, and in cities and towns throughout America thousands burned his effigy. During the last two years of the war he led British raids against his home state as well as against Virginia, and after the Revolution he lived in England until his death in 1801.

The British strategy for suppressing the Revolution depended on mobilizing the Loyalists, but in most areas this proved impossible. As noted earlier, the Loyalists were not a monolithic group but were divided in their opinions, and many were covertly sympathetic to Patriot arguments. Still, as many as 50,000 Loyalists fought for the king during the Revolution. Many joined Loyalist militias or engaged in irregular warfare, especially in the Lower South. In 1780, when Washington's Continentals numbered about 9,000, there were 8,000 American Loyalists serving in the British army in America.

As many as 80,000 Loyalists fled the country during and after the Revolution, taking up residence in England, the British West Indies, or Canada. Their property was confiscated by the states and sold at public auction. Although the British government compensated many for their losses, most Loyalists were unhappy exiles. "I earnestly wish to spend the remainder of my days in America," wrote William Pepperell, formerly of Maine, from London in 1778. "I love the country, I love the people." Former governor Thomas Hutchinson of Massachusetts wrote that he "had rather die in a little country farm-house in New England than in the best nobleman's seat in old England." Despite their disagreement with the Patriots on essential political questions, they remained Americans, and they mourned the loss of their country.

The Campaign for New York and New Jersey

During the winter of 1775–76 the British developed a strategic plan for the war. From his base at Halifax, Nova Scotia, Sir William Howe was to take his army to New York City, which the British navy would make impregnable. From there Howe was to drive north along the Hudson, while another British army marched south from Canada to Albany. The two armies would converge, cutting New England off from the rest of the colonies, and then turn eastward to reduce the rebellious Yankees into submission. Washington, who had arrived at Boston to take command of the militia forces there in the summer of 1775, anticipated this strategy, and in the spring of 1776 he shifted his forces southward toward New York.

In early July, as Congress was taking its final vote on the Declaration of Independence, the British began their operation at New York City, landing 32,000 men on Staten Island, a third of them Hessian mercenaries (from the German state of Hesse). The Americans, meanwhile, set up fortified positions across the harbor in Brooklyn. Attacking in late August, the British inflicted heavy casualties on the Americans, and the militia forces under Washington's command proved unreliable under fire. The battle of Long Island ended in disaster for the Patriots, and they were forced to withdraw across the East River to Manhattan.

The British now offered Congress an opportunity to negotiate, and on September 6, Benjamin Franklin, John Adams, and Edward Rutledge sat down with General Howe and his brother, Admiral Richard Howe, on Staten Island. But the meeting broke up when the Howes demanded revocation of the Declaration of Independence. The stage was set for another round of violence. Six days later the British invaded Manhattan island, and only an American stand at Harlem Heights prevented the destruction of a large portion of the Patriot army. Enjoying naval control of the harbor, the British quickly outflanked the American positions. In a series of battles over the next few months, they forced Washington back at White Plains and overran the American posts of Fort Washington and Fort Lee, on either side of the Hudson River. By November the Americans were fleeing south across New Jersey in a frantic attempt to avoid the British under General Charles Cornwallis.

With morale desperately low, whole militia companies deserted; others, announcing the end of their terms of enlistment, left for home. American resistance seemed to be collapsing all around Washington. "Our troops will not do their duty," he wrote painfully to Congress as he crossed the Delaware River into Pennsylvania. Upon receiving his message, the delegates in Philadelphia fled to Baltimore. "I think the game is pretty near up," Washington admitted to his brother. But rather than fall back further, which would surely have meant the dissolution of his entire force, he decided to risk a counterattack. On Christmas night Washington led 2,400 troops back across the Delaware, and the next morning defeated the Hessian forces in a surprise attack on their headquarters at Trenton, New Jersey. The Americans inflicted further heavy losses on the British at Princeton, then drove them all the way back to the environs of New York City.

Although these small victories of 1776 and early 1777 had little strategic importance, they salvaged American morale. As Washington settled into winter headquarters at Morristown, he realized he had to pursue a defensive strategy, avoiding direct confrontations with the British while checking their advances and hurting them wherever possible. "We cannot conquer the British force at once," wrote General Greene, "but they cannot conquer us at all." This last sentiment was more of a hope than a conviction, but it defined the essentially defensive American strategy of the Revolution. Most important to that strategy was the survival of the Continental Army.

The Northern Campaigns of 1777

The fighting with the American forces had prevented Howe from moving north up the Hudson, and the British advance southward from Canada had been stalled by American resistance at Lake Champlain. In 1777, however, the British decided to replay their strategy. From Canada they dispatched General John Burgoyne with nearly 8,000 British and German troops. Howe was to move his force from New York, first taking the city of Philadelphia, the seat of the Continental Congress, and then moving north to meet Burgoyne.

Fort Ticonderoga fell to Burgoyne on July 6, but by August the general found himself bogged down and harassed by Patriot militias in the rough country south of Lake George. After several defeats in September at the hands of an American army commanded by General Horatio Gates, Burgoyne retreated to Saratoga. There his army was surrounded by a considerably larger force of Americans, and on October 17, lacking alternatives, he surrendered his nearly 6,000 men. It would be the biggest British defeat until Yorktown, decisive because it forced the nations of Europe to recognize that the Americans had a fighting chance to win their Revolution.

The Americans were less successful against Howe. A force of 15,000 British troops left New York in July, landing a month later at the northern end of Chesapeake Bay. At Brandywine Creek the British outflanked the Americans, inflicting heavy casualties and forcing a retreat. Ten days later the British routed the Americans a second time with a frightful bayonet charge at Paoli that left many Patriots dead. When British troops occupied Philadelphia on September 26, Congress had already fled. Washington attempted a valiant counterattack at Germantown on October 4, but initial success was followed by miscoordination that eventually doomed the operation.

After this campaign the Continentals headed for winter quarters at Valley Forge, about twenty miles from Philadelphia, the bitterness of their defeats muted somewhat by news of the surrender at Saratoga. In taking Philadelphia, the British had gained the most important city in North America, but it proved to have

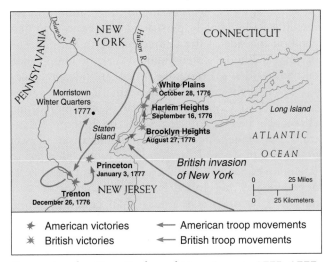

Campaign for New York and New Jersey, 1775–1777

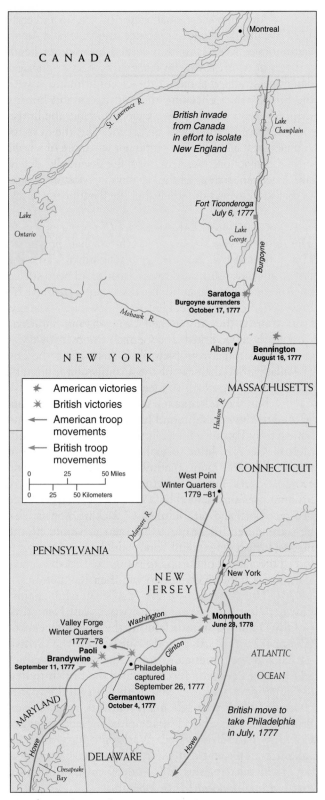

Northern Campaigns, 1777–1778

unified effort suffered little disruption. The British would have done better to move north instead, where they might have saved Burgoyne. At the end of two years of fighting, the British strategy for winning the war had to be judged a failure.

The Politics of the French and Spanish Alliance

During these first two years of fighting, the Americans were sustained by loans from France and Spain, allies in the Bourbon "family compact" of monarchies. Both saw an opportunity to win back North American territories lost to Great Britain in the Seven Years War that concluded in 1763. The Continental Congress maintained a diplomatic delegation in Paris headed by Benjamin Franklin. The urbane and cosmopolitan Franklin, who captured French hearts by dressing in homespun and wearing a "frontiersman" fur cap, maintained excellent relations with the Comte de Vergennes, the French foreign minister. Franklin negotiated with Vergennes for recognition of American independence and a Franco-American alliance against the British in addition to loans to finance the Revolution, but was unable to convince him. France, which wanted to weaken the British empire any way it could, was inclined to support the Americans, but it was reluctant to encourage a republican revolution being fought against monarchy and colonialism.

In England, meanwhile, there was rising opposition to the war among the Tories and the Whigs, their political opponents who took a less authoritarian view of things. "The measures toward America are erroneous," declared Lord Rockingham, "the adherence to them is destruction." William Pitt warned his countrymen to "beware the gathering storm" if and when France decided to support the Americans actively. When British Prime Minister Lord North received the news of Burgoyne's surrender, he dispatched agents to begin peace discussions with Franklin in Paris. The victory at Saratoga, as well as fears of British conciliation with the revolutionaries, finally persuaded Vergennes to intervene on the side of the United States. In mid-December of 1777 he informed Franklin that the king's council had decided to recognize American independence.

In February 1778 the American delegation submitted to Congress a treaty of commerce and alliance it had negotiated with the French. In the treaty, to take effect upon a declaration of war between France and Britain, the French pledged to "maintain effectually the liberty, sovereignty, and independence" of the United States. "Neither of the two parties," the document read, "shall conclude either truce or peace with Great Britain, without the formal consent of the other." The Americans had compelled France to guarantee to the United States all the "northern parts of America" conquered in the war,

little strategic value. The Continental Congress moved to the Pennsylvania backcountry. In any event, central government was virtually nonexistent, and so the ending any thought of a rebirth of New France. But they promised to recognize any French acquisitions of British islands in the West Indies. In June, France declared war, and soon began fighting with Britain.

A year later Spain also entered the war. Spanish officials in New Orleans provided substantial ammunition and provisions for American forts in the West, including herds of cattle, driven to New Orleans by *vaqueros* (cowboys) from Texas. In New Spain the viceroy levied a special tax to pay for these supplies, and borderland colonists contributed their share. Father Junípero Serra, president of the California missions, prescribed a weekly prayer for American victory, and the scene of California Indian converts praying for the freedom of European colonists on the other coast is surely one of the most ironic of the era. But American attempts to establish a formal Spanish alliance met with failure. The Spanish feared the Americans as a danger to their own empire of New Spain but regarded the Revolution as an opportunity to regain Florida from the British and extend their control of the Mississippi Valley. "Its people are active, industrious, and aggressive," one Mexican official wrote of the United States, and "it would be culpable negligence on our part not to thwart their schemes for conquest."

The Spanish zealously pursued their strategy, attacking and taking the Mississippi River towns of Natchez and Baton Rouge in 1779, and the Gulf ports of Mobile in 1780 and Pensacola in 1781; their victory at Pensacola was won with the help of several companies of African Americans. Alarmed by the quick spread of American settlements west of the Appalachians, the Spanish attempted to establish a claim of their own to the British territory north of the Ohio by sending an expedition into the Northwest in 1781, which succeeded in taking the minor British post of St. Joseph, in present-day Michigan.

The first French ambassador to the United States arrived with instructions to do everything he could to prevent the Americans from enlarging their territory at the expense of the Spanish empire in the West. Vergennes also feared the potential power of an independent United States. Several years before, he had warned the British that once the Americans gained their independence they "would immediately set about forming a great marine," and use it in the Caribbean to "conquer both your islands and ours," then sweep south, where it would "not leave a foot of that hemisphere in the possession of any European power." American leaders understood that the treaty with France and the *modus vivendi* with Spain were merely expedients for all sides, and they recognized the dangers that France and Spain posed to the United States. But far more important was the prospect the French treaty offered of victory over Britain.

The entry of France into the war forced the British to rethink their strategy. At first Lord North took a conciliatory approach, sending a peace commission to America with promises to repeal the parliamentary legislation that had provoked the crisis in the first place and pledging never again to impose revenue taxes on the colonies. Three years earlier, such pledges would surely have forestalled the movement toward independence. But the Continental Congress now declared that any person coming to terms with the peace commission was a traitor; the only possible topics of negotiation were the withdrawal of British forces and the recognition of American independence. The peace commission was reduced to attempting to bribe members of Congress and finally to threatening a war of devastation, but to no avail.

Meanwhile the British realized that with France in the war their valuable West Indies colonies were at risk, and they rushed 5,000 men from New York to the Caribbean, where they beat back a French attack. Fearing the arrival of the French fleet along the North American coast, the new British commander in America, General Henry Clinton, evacuated Philadelphia in June 1778. In hot pursuit were Washington's Continentals. At the battle of Monmouth on June 28, the British blunted the American drive and retreated to New York. The Americans, centered at West Point, took up defensive positions surrounding the lower Hudson. Confidence in an impending victory now spread through the Patriot forces. But after a failed campaign with the French against the British forces at Newport, Rhode Island, Washington settled for a defensive strategy. Although the Americans enjoyed several small successes in the Northeast over the next two years, the war there went into a stall.

The war at sea was fought mostly between the British and the French, but Continental, state, and private vessels raided British merchant ships and conducted isolated naval patrols. The foremost American naval hero of the war was John Paul Jones, who, in 1777, raided the coast of Scotland. In 1779, while commanding the French ship *Bonhomme Richard* (named in honor of Franklin's "Poor Richard"), Jones engaged in a celebrated battle with the British warship *Serapis*. When the two ships locked together, the British captain hailed Jones, asking if he were ready to surrender. Jones's reply—"I have not yet begun to fight"—became one of the most quoted lines of the Revolution. Jones won his battle, though it had little military consequence. After the war Congress decommissioned the small American navy and dismissed its officers, including Jones, who went on to serve in the imperial Russian navy.

North America after the Treaty of Paris, 1783   *The map of European and American claims to North America was radically altered by the results of the American Revolution.*

The Crisis of Demobilization

During the two years between the surrender at York-town and the signing of the Treaty of Paris, the British continued to occupy New York City, Charleston, and a series of western posts. The Continental Army remained on wartime alert, with some 10,000 men and an estimated 1,000 women encamped at Newburgh, New York, north of West Point. The soldiers had long been awaiting their pay and were concerned about the postwar bounties and land warrants promised them. The most serious problem, however, lay not among the enlisted men but in the officer corps.

Continental officers had extracted a promise from Congress of life pensions at half pay in exchange for enlistment for the duration of the war. By 1783, however, Congress had still not made specific provisions for the pensions. With peace at hand, officers began to fear that the army would be disbanded before the problem was resolved, and they would lose whatever power they had to pressure Congress. In January 1783 a group of prominent senior officers petitioned Congress, demanding that the pensions be converted to a bonus equal to five years of full pay.

"Any further experiments on their patience," they warned, "may have fatal effects." Despite this barely veiled threat of military intervention, Congress rejected their petition.

With the backing of congressional national-ists, a group of army officers associated with General Horatio Gates called an extraordinary meeting of the officer corps at Newburgh. But General Washington, on whom the officers counted for support, condemned the meeting as "disorderly" and called an official meet-ing of his own. There was enormous tension when the officers assembled on March 15; at stake was nothing less than the possibility of a military coup at the very moment of American victory. Washington strode into the room and mounted the platform. Turning his back in disdain on General Gates, he told the assembly that he wished to read a statement, and then pulled a pair of glasses from his pocket. None of his officers had seen their leader wearing glasses before. "Gentlemen, you must pardon me," said Washington when he noticed their surprise. "I have grown gray in your service and now find myself growing blind." He then went on to denounce any resort to force, but it was his offhand remark about growing gray that made the greatest impact. Who had sacrificed more than their commander in chief? After he left, the officers adopted resolutions rejecting intervention, and a week later, on Washington's urging, Congress decided to convert the pensions to bonuses after all.

Washington's role in this crisis was one of his greatest contributions to the nation. In December 1783 he resigned his commission as general of the army despite calls for him to remain. There is little doubt that he could have assumed the role of American dictator. Instead, by his actions and example, the principle of military subordination to civil authority was firmly established.

As for the common soldiers, they wanted simply to be discharged. "It is not in the power of Congress or their officers to hold them much, if any, longer," Washington wrote Alexander Hamilton in April. The next month, Congress voted the soldiers three months' pay as a bonus and instructed Washington to begin dismissing them. Some troops remained at Newburgh until the British evacuated New York in November, but by the beginning of 1784 the Continental Army had shrunk to no more than a few hundred men.

The Problem of the West

After Yorktown, the British abandoned their Indian allies in the West. When the Indians learned of the armistice, according to one British officer, they were "thunderstruck." Neither the Iroquois nor the Ohio tribes, who had fought with the British, considered themselves defeated, but the United States claimed that its victory over Great Britain was a victory over the Indians as well. A heavily armed American nation now pressed for large grants of territory according to the right of conquest. Even Patriot allies were not exempt. The Oneidas, for example, who had supported the Americans, suffered territorial demands along with the other Iroquois.

Even during the fighting the American migration to the West had continued, and

after the treaty of peace settlers streamed over the mountains and down the Ohio River. The population of Kentucky (still a part of Virginia until admitted as a state in 1792) had grown to more than 30,000 by 1785; in 1790 it numbered 74,000, and the Tennessee area held another 36,000. Thousands of Americans pressed against the Indian country north of the Ohio River, and destructive violence continued along the frontier. British troops continued to occupy posts in the Northwest and encouraged Indian attacks on vulnerable settlements. To the southwest, Spain, refusing to accept the territorial settlement of the Treaty of Paris, closed the Mississippi River to Americans. Westerners who saw that route as their primary access to markets were outraged.

The American leadership saw the West as critical to the continued development of national community sentiment. John Jay, appointed secretary for

State Claims to Western Lands   *The ratification of the Articles of Confederation in 1781 awaited settlement of the western claims of eight states. Vermont, claimed by New Hampshire and New York, was not made a state until 1791, after disputes were settled the previous year. The territory north of the Ohio River was claimed in whole or in part by Virginia, New York, Connecticut, and Massachusetts. All of them had ceded their claims by 1786, except for Connecticut, which had claimed an area just south of Lake Erie, known as the Western Reserve; Connecticut ceded this land in 1800. The territory south of the Ohio was claimed by Virginia, North Carolina, South Carolina, and Georgia; in 1802 the latter became the last state to cede its claims.*

The Northwest Territory and the Land Survey System of the United States

The greatest achievement of the Confederation government was the passing of the Land Ordinance of 1785 and the Northwest Ordinance of 1787. The first act made provision for the federal survey of newly incorporated lands. To avoid the problem of overlapping surveys that could occur under the old system of "metes and bounds" surveying, the authors of the ordinance created an ordered system of survey, dividing the land into townships composed of thirty-six sections of one square mile (640 acres) each. (The differences are clearly evident in the contrast between the patterns of landholding in Ohio, on the left side of the photo, and Pennsylvania, on the right.) The income from section 16 was reserved for the support of local schools, and sections 8, 11, 26, and 29 were held off the market for later sale. First employed in the territory north of the Ohio River, this survey system was used for all the western territory of the United States and has been adopted by many other nations.

With the Northwest Ordinance, Congress established a system of government for the territory north of the Ohio. This legislation established the important principle of eventually bringing new territory

foreign affairs by the Confederation Congress in 1784, attempted to negotiate with the British, but he was told that British troops would not evacuate the Northwest until all outstanding debts from before the war were settled. Jay also attempted to negotiate with the Spanish for guarantees of territorial sovereignty and commercial relations, but he was told that first the United States would have to relinquish free navigation of the Mississippi. Congress would approve no treaty with such terms. Under these frustrating circumstances, some Westerners considered leaving the Confederation. Kentuckians threatened to rejoin the British. The Spanish secretly employed several prominent westerners, including George Rogers Clark and General James Wilkinson, as informants and spies. The people of the West "stand as it were upon a pivot," wrote Washing-

Geographer's Base Line

First Range

Seventh Range
Sixth Range
Fifth Range
Fourth Range
Third Range
Seecond Range

Tuscarawas R.

6 miles

6 miles

Ohio R.

PENNSYLVANIA

Little Muskingum R.

0   50 Miles
0   50 Kilometers

N

Lake Erie

OHIO

PENNSYLVANIA

Ohio R.

VIRGINIA

VIRGINIA

KENTUCKY

6 miles

6	5	4	3	2	1
7	8	9	10	11	12
18	17	16	15	14	13
19	20	21	22	23	24
30	29	28	27	26	25
31	32	33	34	35	36

6 miles

Income from section 16
reserved for school support

16 One section (1 sq. mi.)

Half-section
(320 acres)

Quarter-section
(160 acres)

Half-quarter-section
(80 acres)

Quarter-quarter-sections
(40 acres)

THE SURVEY SYSTEM
A township (36 square miles)

into the states on an equal basis with the original thirteen states. The Northwest Territory was eventually divided into the five states that are the focus of this map, and each was admitted to the Union on the date that appears below its name. The Northwest Ordinance also outlawed slavery north of the Ohio River.

Before that process could begin, however, the United States had to establish sovereignty over the country. The British did not abandon the posts that they had continued to occupy after 1783 until June 1, 1796, following the agreement between the United States and Great Britain in Jay's Treaty (1794).

ton in 1784 after a trip down the Ohio. "The touch of a feather would turn them any way." In the West, local community interest continued to override the fragile development of national community sentiment.

In the context of these problems, Congress took up the problem of extending national authority over the West in 1784. Legislation was drafted, principally by Thomas Jefferson, providing for "Government

for the Western Territory." The legislation was a remarkable attempt to create a democratic colonial policy. The public domain was to be divided into states, and Congress was to guarantee the settlers in them immediate self-government and republican institutions. Once the population of a territory numbered 20,000, the residents could call a convention and establish a constitution and government of their own choosing. And once the population grew to equal that of the smallest of the original thirteen states, the territory could obtain statehood, provided it agreed to remain forever a member of the Confederation. Fortunately, Congress rejected Jefferson's proposal to provide the future states with names such as Assenisippia and Metropotamia. But it also rejected, by a vote of seven to six, his clause prohibiting slavery.

Passed the following year, the Land Ordinance of 1785 provided for the survey and sale of western lands. To avoid the chaos of overlapping surveys and land claims that had characterized Kentucky, the authors of the ordinance created an ordered system of survey, dividing the land into townships composed of thirty-six sections of one square mile (640 acres) each. This measure would have an enormous impact on the North American landscape, as anyone looking down from an airplane window on the Midwest or West can see. The Land Ordinance also reserved one section in each township for the support of schools; local officials could sell or rent this land to raise money to build schoolhouses or employ teachers. Jefferson argued that all the other land ought to be given away to actual settlers. But Congress, eager to establish a revenue base for the government, provided for the auction of public lands for not less than $1 per acre (the equivalent of $117 in 1990 currency).

In the second Treaty of Fort Stanwix in 1784 and the Treaty of Fort McIntosh in 1785, congressional commissioners forced the Iroquois and some of the Ohio Indians to cede a portion of their territory in what is now eastern Ohio. These treaties were not the result of negotiation; the commissioners dictated the terms by seizing hostages and forcing compliance. Quickly, Congress sent surveyors into the area to divide up the lands. The surveyors did not complete their work and make the lands available for settlers to purchase until the fall of 1788. In the meantime, Congress, desperate for revenue, sold a tract of more than 1.5 million acres to a new land company, the Ohio Company, for $1 million. Jefferson's vision of land for actual settlers seemed to be receding from view.

But thousands of Westerners refused to wait for the official opening of the public land north of the Ohio River. Instead they simply crossed the river and settled illegally. In 1785 Congress raised troops and evicted many of them, but once the soldiers left the squatters returned. The persistence of this problem convinced many congressmen to revise Jefferson's democratic territorial plan. It was necessary, explained Richard Henry Lee of Virginia, "for the security of property among uninformed and perhaps licentious people, as the greater part of those who go there are, that a strong toned government should exist."

In the Northwest Ordinance of 1787, Congress established a system of government for the territory north of the Ohio. Three to five states were to be carved out of the giant Northwest Territory and admitted "on an equal footing with the original states in all respects whatsoever." Slavery was prohibited. But the guarantee of initial self-government in Jefferson's plan was replaced by the rule of a court of judges and a governor appointed by Congress. Once the free white male population of the territory had grown to 5,000, these citizens would be permitted to choose an assembly, but the governor was to have the power of absolute veto on all territorial legislation. National interest would be imposed on the localistic western communities. The Northwest Territory was a huge region that included the future states of Ohio, Indiana, Illinois, Michigan, and Wisconsin. In an early instance of government in the hands of developers, Congress chose Arthur St. Clair, president of the Ohio Company, as the first governor of the Northwest Territory.

The creation of the land system of the United States was the major achievement of the Confederation government. But there were other important accomplishments. Under the Articles of Confederation, Congress led the country through the Revolution and its commissioners negotiated the terms of a comprehensive peace treaty. In organizing the departments of war, foreign affairs, the post office, and finance, the Confederation government created the beginnings of the national bureaucracy.

REVOLUTIONARY POLITICS IN THE STATES

Despite the accomplishments of the Confederation government, most Americans focused not on events in Philadelphia but on those in their own states. Although a strong national community feeling developed during the Revolutionary era, most Americans identified more strongly with their local communities and states than the American nation. People spoke of "these United States," emphasizing the plural, and were relatively unaffected by the national government. The states were the setting for the most important political struggles not only of the Confederation period but for long after.

The Broadened Base of Politics

The political mobilization that took place in 1774 and 1775 greatly broadened political participation. Mass meetings in which ordinary people expressed their opinions, voted, and gained political experience were common, not only in the cities but in small towns and rural communities as well. During these years, a greater proportion of the population began to participate in elections. South Carolina, for example, employed a system of universal white manhood suffrage for the selection of delegates to the Continental Congress, and many other states relaxed property qualifications. Compared with the colonial assemblies, the new state legislatures included more men from rural and western districts—farmers and artisans as well as lawyers, merchants, and large landowners. Many delegates to the Massachusetts provincial congress of 1774 were men from small farming communities who lacked formal education and owned little property.

This transformation was accompanied by a dramatic shift in the political debate. During the colonial period, when only the upper crust of colonial society had been truly engaged by the political process, the principal argument took place between Tory and Whig positions. Tory principles, articulated by royal officials, held that colonial governments were simply convenient instruments of the king's prerogative, serving at his pleasure. The Whig position, on the other hand, was represented by the American colonial elites, who, seeking to preserve and increase their own power, argued for stronger assemblies. They justified their position with arguments about the need for a government balanced with monarchic, aristocratic, and democratic elements, represented by the governor, the upper house, and the assembly, respectively. This debate was ended by the American Revolution. The Tory position lost all legitimacy, indelibly soiled by the taint of Loyalism and treason. There were still plenty of moderate Patriots who took a Whig position on balanced government. But farmers, artisans, and other ordinary people began to argue for a democratic government of the people themselves. For the first time in American history, democracy lost its negative connotations and became a term of approval. One of the most important consequences of the Revolution was a radical shift of the political discourse to the left.

An early post-Revolution debate focused on the appropriate governmental structure for the new states. The new thinking was indicated by the title of a New England pamphlet of 1776, *The People the Best Governors*. Power, the anonymous author argued, should be vested in a single, popularly elected assembly. There should be no property qualifications for either voting or holding office. The governor should simply execute the wishes of the people as voiced by their representatives in the assembly. Judges, too, should be popularly elected, and their decisions reviewed by the assembly. The people, the pamphlet concluded, "best know their wants and necessities, and therefore are best able to govern themselves." The ideal form of government, according to such democrats, was the community or town meeting, in which the people set their own tax rates, created a militia, controlled their own

schools and churches, and regulated the local economy. State government was necessary only for coordination among communities.

Conservative Americans took up the Whig argument on the need for a balanced government. The "unthinking many," wrote another pamphleteer, should be checked by a strong executive and an upper house. Both should be insulated from popular control by property qualifications and long terms in office, designed to draw forth the wisdom and talent of the country's wealthiest and most accomplished men. The greatest danger, according to conservatives, was the possibility of majority tyranny, which might lead to the violation of property rights and to dictatorship. "We must take mankind as they are," one conservative wrote, "and not as we could wish them to be."

The First State Constitutions

Fourteen states—the original thirteen plus Vermont—adopted constitutions between 1776 and 1780. Each of these documents was shaped by debate between radicals and conservatives, democrats and Whigs, and reflected a political balance of power. The constitutions of Pennsylvania, Maryland, and New York typified the political range of the times: Pennsylvania instituted a radical democratic government something like that proposed in *The People the Best Governors*, Maryland created a conservative set of institutions designed to keep citizens and rulers as far apart as possible, and New York adopted a system somewhere in the middle.

In Pennsylvania, a majority of the political conservatives had become Loyalists, allowing the democrats to seize power in 1776. The election of delegates to the constitutional convention was open to every man in the militia, an arrangement that further strengthened the advocates of democracy. The document this convention adopted clearly reflected a democratic agenda. It created a unicameral assembly elected annually by all free male taxpayers. So that delegates would be responsive to their constituents, sessions of the assembly were open to the public and included roll-call votes—the latter somewhat rare in colonial assemblies. There was no governor, but rather an elected executive committee. Judges were removable by the assembly.

By contrast, the Maryland constitution, adopted the same year, was written by conservative planters. It created property requirements for officeholding that left only about 10 percent of Maryland men eligible to serve in the assembly, 7 percent in the senate. A powerful governor, elected by large property owners, controlled a highly centralized government. Judges and other high executive officers served for life. These two states, Maryland and Penn-

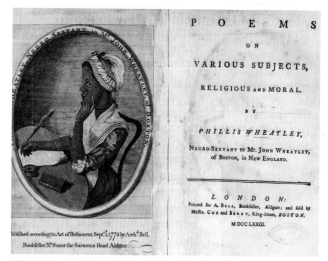

This portrait of the African American poet Phillis Wheatley was included in the collection of her work published in London in 1773, when she was only twenty. Kidnapped in Africa when a girl, then purchased off the Boston docks, she was more like a daughter than a slave to the Wheatley family, and later married and lived as a free woman of color before her untimely death in 1784.

while continuing to support the institution of slavery. Slavery was first abolished in the state constitution of Vermont in 1777, and in Massachusetts and New Hampshire in 1780 and 1784, respectively. Pennsylvania, Connecticut, and Rhode Island adopted systems of gradual emancipation during these years, freeing the children of slaves at birth. By 1786 every northern state but Delaware had provided for immediate or gradual emancipation of slaves, although as late as 1810, 30,000 African Americans remained enslaved in the North.

In the Upper South, revolutionary idealism, the Christian egalitarianism of Methodists and Baptists, and a shift from tobacco farming to the cultivation of cereal grains such as wheat and corn combined to weaken the commitment of many planters to the slave system. There was a great increase in manumissions— grants of freedom to slaves by individual masters—and a small but important movement encouraged gradual emancipation by convincing masters to free their slaves in their wills. George Washington not only freed several hundred of his slaves on his death but developed an elaborate plan for apprenticeship and tenancy for the able-bodied, lodging and pensions for the aged. Planters in the Lower South, however, heavily dependent on slave labor, resisted the growing calls for an end to slavery. Between 1776 and 1786 all the states but South Carolina and Georgia prohibited or heavily taxed the international slave trade, and this issue became an important point of contention at the Constitutional Convention in 1787 (see Chapter 8).

Perhaps the most important result of these developments was the growth of the free African American population. From a few thousand in 1750, the free African American population grew to more than 200,000 by the end of the century. The increase was most notable in the Upper South. The free black population of Virginia, for example, grew from less than 2,000 in 1780 to approximately 20,000 in 1800. Largely excluded from the institutions of white Americans, the African American community now had sufficient strength to establish schools, churches, and other institutions of its own. Initially this development was opposed. In Williamsburg, Virginia, for instance, the leader of a black congregation was seized and whipped when he attempted to gain recognition from the Baptist Association. But by the 1790s the Williamsburg African Church had more than 500 members, and the association reluctantly recognized it. In Philadelphia the Reverend Absalom Jones established St. Thomas's African Episcopal Church. The incorporation of the term "African" in the names of churches, schools, and mutual benefit societies reflected the pride that African Americans now took in their heritage. New York's African Marine Fund, to take one example, described itself as an organization for assisting "our African brethren and the descendants of our mother country."

A small group of African American writers rose to prominence during the Revolutionary era. Benjamin Banneker, born free in Maryland, where he received an education, was one of the most accomplished mathematicians and astronomers of late-eighteenth-century America. In the 1790s he published a popular almanac that both white and black Americans consulted. Jupiter Hammon, a Long Island slave, took up contemporary issues in his poems and essays, one of the most important of which was his *Address to the Negroes of the State of New York*, published in 1787. The most famous African American writer, however, was Phillis Wheatley, who came to public attention when her *Poems on Various Subjects, Religious and Moral* appeared in London in 1773, while she was still a domestic slave in Boston. Kidnapped as a young girl and converted to Christianity during the Great Awakening, Wheatley wrote poems that combined her piety with a concern for her people. "On Being Brought from Africa to America" is a good example:

> *'Twas mercy brought me from my pagan land,*
> *Taught my benighted soul to understand*
> *That there's a God, that there's a Saviour too;*
> *Once I redemption neither sought nor knew.*
> *Some view our sable race with scornful eye,*
> *"Their colour is a diabolic dye."*
> *Remember, Christians, Negros, black as Cain,*
> *May be refin'd, and join th'angelic train.*

"In every human breast God has implanted a principle, which we call love of freedom; it is impatient of oppression, and pants for deliverance," Wheatley wrote in a letter. "The same principle lives in us."

Economic Problems

During the Revolution, the shortage of goods resulting from the British blockade, the demand for supplies by the army and militias, and the flood of paper currency issued by Congress and the states combined to create the worst inflation that Americans have ever experienced. Continental dollars traded against Spanish dollars at the rate of 3 to 1 in 1777, 40 to 1 in 1779, and 146 to 1 in 1781, by which time Congress had issued more than $190 million in Continentals. Most of this paper ended up in the hands of merchants who paid only a fraction of its face value. There was a popular outcry at the incredible increase in prices, and communities and states in the North responded with laws regulating wages and prices.

The sponsors of wage and price schedules often attributed high prices to hoarding and profiteering. Although it is doubtful that such practices caused the inflation, many merchants did gouge their customers. There were demonstrations and food riots in many communities; men and women demanded fair prices, and when they did not receive them they broke into storehouses and took what they needed. People organized local committees to monitor economic activity and punish wrongdoers. Abigail Adams told of a Boston merchant who refused to sell coffee for the price demanded by the committee. "A number of females, some say a hundred, some say more," she wrote, "seized him by his neck and tossed him into the cart. Upon his finding no quarter he delivered the keys," and the women opened his warehouse and took the coffee. "A large concourse of men stood amazed, silent spectators of the whole transaction."

After the war the primary economic problem was no longer inflation but depression. Political revolution could not alter economic realities: the independent United States continued to be a supplier of raw materials and an importer of manufactured products, and Great Britain remained its most important trading partner. After the Treaty of Paris was signed in 1783, British merchants dumped their unsold goods on the American market, offering easy terms of credit. The production of exportable commodities, however, had been drastically reduced by the fighting.

With few exports to offset all the imports, the trade deficit with Great Britain for the period 1784–86 rose to approximately £5 million in British currency. The deficit acted like a magnet, drawing gold and silver coin from American accounts: according to one estimate, merchants exported £1.3 million in gold and silver coin to Britain during these two years. In turn, these merchants demanded immediate payment from their customers. Short of hard currency, the three commercial banks in the United States—the Bank of North America (Philadelphia), the Bank of New York, and the Bank of Massachusetts (Boston)—insisted on immediate repayment of old loans and refused to issue new ones. The country was left with very little coin in circulation. It all added up to a serious depression, which lasted from 1784 to 1788. At their lowest level, in 1786, prices had fallen 25 percent.

The depression struck while the country was burdened with the huge debt incurred during the Revolution. The total debt owed by the national and state governments amounted to more than $50 million in 1785. (To place this figure in perspective, consider that this debt was approximately sixty-four times greater than the value of American exports for the year 1785; by contrast, the national debt in 1990—considered a crippling burden—was only five times greater than the

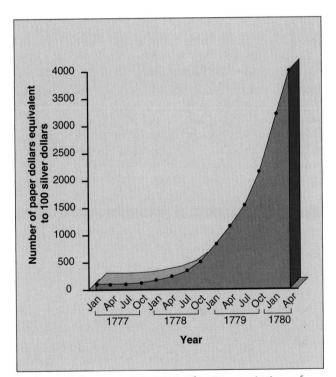

Postwar Inflation, 1777-1780: The Depreciation of Continental Currency (number of paper dollars equal to 100 silver dollars)   *The flood of Continental currency issued by Congress, combined with the shortage of goods resulting from the British blockade, combined to create the worst inflation Americans have ever experienced. Things of no value were said to be "not worth a Continental."*

Source: John McCusker, "How Much Is That in Real Money?" *Proceedings of the American Antiquarian Society*, N.S. 102 (1992): 297–359.

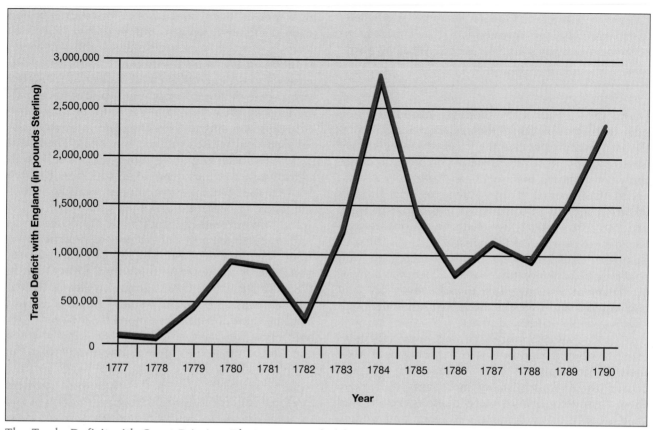

The Trade Deficit with Great Britain   *The American trade deficit with Great Britain rose dramatically with the conclusion of the Revolution.*

Source: *Historical Statistics of the United States* (Washington, D.C.:Government Printing Office, 1976), 1176.

value of exports for that year.) Not allowed to raise taxes on its own, the Confederation Congress requisitioned the states for the funds necessary for debt repayment. The states in turn taxed their residents. At a time when there was almost no money in circulation, people rightly feared being crushed by the burden of private debt and public taxes. Thus the economic problem became a political problem.

State Remedies

Where there were manufacturing interests, as in the Northeast, states erected high tariffs to curb imports and protect "infant industries." But shippers could avoid these duties simply by unloading their cargo in nearby seaboard states that lacked tariffs; domestic merchants then distributed the products overland. To be effective, commercial regulation had to be national. Local sentiment had to give way to the unity of a national community. The "means of preserving ourselves," wrote John Adams, [will] "never be secured entirely, until Congress shall be made supreme in foreign commerce, and shall have digested a plan for all the states."

The most controversial economic remedies were those designed to relieve the burden on debtors

and ordinary taxpayers. In some areas, farmers called for laws permitting payment of taxes or debts in goods and commodities, a kind of institutionalized barter. More commonly, farmers and debtors pressed their state governments for "legal tender" laws, laws that would require creditors to accept at specified rates of exchange a state's paper currency—regardless of its worth—for all debts public and private. Understandably, creditors opposed such a plan. But farmers were strong enough to enact currency laws in seven states during the depression. For the most part, these were modest programs that worked rather well, resulted in little depreciation, and did not produce the problems feared by creditors. In most instances, the notes were loaned to farmers, who put up the value of their land as collateral.

It was the radical plan of the state of Rhode Island, however, that received most of the attention. A rural political party campaigning under the slogan "To Relieve the Distressed" captured the legislature in 1786 and enacted a currency law. The supply of paper money issued in relation to the population was much greater under this program than in any other state. The law declared the currency legal tender for all debts. If creditors refused to accept it, people could satisfy their obligations by depositing the money with a county judge, who would then advertise the debt as paid. "In the state of Rogue Island," wrote a shocked merchant, "fraud and injustice" had been "enjoined by solemn law." Conservatives pointed to Rhode Island as an example of the evils that could accompany unchecked democracy. But such programs were perhaps the only alternative without effective national legislation, which required the development of national community sentiment and national political authority.

Shays' Rebellion

In 1786 a rural uprising of communities in Massachusetts shook the nation. Farmers in the western part of the state had been hit particularly hard during the depression, when country merchants pressed them to pay their debts in hard currency they did not possess. About a third of all male heads of household were sued for debt during the 1780s, and the county jails filled with debtors who could not pay. Dozens of towns petitioned the state government for relief, but the legislature, dominated by urban and merchant interests, rejected legal tender and paper currency laws. During the spring and summer of 1786, farmers throughout the rural parts of the state mustered their community militia companies and closed the courts—precisely what they had done during the Revolution. "Whenever any encroachments are made either upon the liberties or properties of the people," declared one rebel, "if redress cannot be had without, it is virtue in them to disturb government."

This uprising quickly became known as Shays' Rebellion, after Daniel Shays, a captain in the Revolution who was one of the leaders of what became known as the Committee of the People. Although the rebellion was most widespread in Massachusetts, similar disorders occurred in every other New England state except Rhode Island, where the farmers had already taken power. There were a number of incidents outside New England as well. A "tumultuary assemblage of the people" closed the court of one Maryland county, and in York, Pennsylvania, 200 armed men stopped a farm auction whose proceeds were marked for debt payment. "Following the example of the insurgents in Massachusetts," a conservative wrote, debtor associations in Virginia prevented auctions and, according to James Madison, officials throughout the state watched "prisons and courthouses and clerks' offices willfully burnt."

The crisis ended when a militia force raised in communities from eastern Massachusetts marched west and crushed the "Shaysites" in January 1787 as they attacked the Springfield armory. Fifteen rebels were subsequently sentenced to death; two were hanged before the remainder were pardoned, and several hundred farmers had to swear an oath of allegiance to the state. In fact, these men had wanted little more than temporary relief from their indebtedness, and rural discontent quickly disappeared once the depression began to lift in 1788.

The most important consequence of Shays' Rebellion was its effect on conservative nationalists unhappy with the distribution of power between the states and national government under the Articles of Confederation. The uprising "wrought prodigious changes in the minds of men respecting the powers of government," wrote the Secretary of War Henry Knox. "Everybody says they must be strengthened and that unless this shall be effected, there is no security for liberty and property." It was time, he declared, "to clip the wings of a mad democracy."

CONCLUSION

The Revolution was a tumultuous era, marked by violent conflict between Patriots and Loyalists, masters and slaves, settlers and Indian peoples. The advocates of independence emerged successful, largely because of their ability to pull together and to begin to define their national community. But fearful of the power of central authority, Americans created a relatively weak national government. People identified strongly with their local and state communities, and these governments became the site for most of the struggles over political direction that characterized the Revolution and its immediate aftermath.

By the mid-1780s, however, many nationalists were paraphrasing Washington's question of 1777: "What then is to become of this nation?" The economic crisis that followed the Revolution sorely tested the

A mocking pamphlet of 1787 pictured Daniel Shays and Job Shattuck, two leaders of Shays' Rebellion. The artist gives them uniforms, a flag, and artillery, but the rebels were actually an unorganized group of farmers armed only with clubs and simple muskets. When the rebellion was crushed, Shattuck was wounded and jailed, and Shays along with many others left Massachusetts to settle in a remote region of Vermont.

National Portrait Gallery, Smithsonian Institution/Art Resource, NY

CHRONOLOGY

1775	Lord Dunmore, royal governor of Virginia, appeals to slaves to support Britain
1776	July: Declaration of Independence August: battle of Long Island initiates retreat of Continental Army September: British land on Manhattan Island December: George Washington counterattacks at Trenton
1777	Slavery abolished in Vermont September: British General William Howe captures Philadelphia October: British General John Burgoyne surrenders at Saratoga November: Continentals settle into winter quarters at Valley Forge December: France recognizes American independence
1778	June: France enters the war June: battle of Monmouth hastens British retreat to New York July: George Rogers Clark captures Kaskaskia December: British capture Savannah
1779	Spain enters the war
1780	February: British land at Charleston July: French land at Newport September: British General Charles Cornwallis invades North Carolina
1781	February: Robert Morris appointed superintendent of finance March: Articles of Confederation ratified October: Cornwallis surrenders at Yorktown
1782	Peace talks begin
1783	March: Washington mediates issue of officer pensions September: Treaty of Paris signed November: British evacuate New York
1784	Treaty of Fort Stanwix Postwar depression begins
1785	Land Ordinance of 1785 Treaty of Fort McIntosh
1786	Jefferson's Bill for Establishing Religious Freedom Rhode Island currency law Shays' Rebellion

resources of local communities, and increasingly people found that local problems were really national problems. Conservative and moderate Patriots, who had been thrown on the defensive by the radical shift of the political debate to the left, saw this as their opportunity to successfully reenter the fray. Led by their Whiggish arguments, increasing numbers of Americans would seek to answer Washington's question by attempting to reform the national government and build a strong new national community.

REVIEW QUESTIONS

1. Assess the relative strengths of the Patriots and the Loyalists in the American Revolution.
2. What roles did Indian peoples and African Americans play in the Revolution?
3. Describe the structure of the Articles of Confederation. What were its strengths and weaknesses?
4. How did the Revolution affect politics within the states?
5. What were the issues in Shays' Rebellion? How do they help to illustrate the political conflict in the nation during the 1780s?

RECOMMENDED READING

Edward Countryman, *The American Revolution* (1985). The best short introduction to the social and political history of the Revolution. Informed by the great outpouring of studies during the twenty years preceding its publication.

Thomas Fleming, *Liberty! The American Revolution* (1997). This well-written account—derived from a public television series—includes wonderful contemporary images.

Merrill Jensen, *The New Nation: A History of the United States during the Confederation, 1781–1789* (1950). Still the standard work on the 1780s.

Charles Patrick Neimeyer, *America Goes to War: A Social History of the Continental Army* (1996). A detailed look at the men who fought and won the Revolution.

Mary Beth Norton, *Liberty's Daughters: The Revolutionary Experience of American Women, 1750–1800* (1980). A provocative and comprehensive history of women in the Revolutionary era. Treats not only legal and institutional change but also the more subtle changes in habits and expectations.

Charles Royster, *A Revolutionary People at War* (1979). A pathbreaking study of the Continental Army and popular attitudes toward it. Emphasizes the important role played by the officer corps and the enlisted men in the formation of the first nationalist constituency.

John Shy, *A People Numerous and Armed* (1976). A series of studies of the local and state militias, demonstrating that their most important contribution was political, not military.

David P. Szatmary, *Shays' Rebellion: The Making of an Agrarian Insurrection* (1980). An excellent study of the famous farmers' rebellion that stimulated conservatives to write the Constitution. Includes a great deal of general background material on the Confederation period, as well as excellent coverage of the specifics of the revolt.

Alfred F. Young, ed., *The American Revolution: Explorations in American Radicalism* (1976). Includes provocative essays on African Americans, Indians, and women.

ADDITIONAL BIBLIOGRAPHY

The War for Independence

Ira Berlin and Ronald Hoffman, eds., *Slavery and Freedom in the Age of the American Revolution* (1983)

Richard Buel Jr., *The Way of Duty: A Woman and Her Family in Revolutionary America* (1984)

Robert M. Calhoon, *The Loyalists in Revolutionary America, 1760–1781* (1973)

Charles E. Claghorn, *Women Patriots of the American Revolution* (1991)

Lawrence D. Cress, *Citizens in Arms: The Army and the Militia in American Society to the War of 1812* (1982)

Paul Finkleman, ed., *Slavery, Revolutionary America, and the New Nation* (1989)

William M. Fowler, *Rebels under Sail: The American Navy during the Revolution* (1976)

Barbara Graymont, *The Iroquois in the American Revolution* (1972)

Ronald Hoffman and Peter J. Albert, eds., *Arms and Independence: The Military Character of the American Revolution* (1984)

Ronald Hoffman and Peter J. Albert, eds., *Women in the Age of the American Revolution* (1989)

Ronald Hoffman and Thad W. Tate, eds., *An Uncivil War: The Southern Backcountry during the American Revolution* (1985)

Mark E. Kann, *A Republic of Men: The American Founders, Gendered Language, and Patriarchial Politics* (1998)

Paul C. Nagel, *The Adams Women: Abigail and Louise Adams, Their Sisters and Daughters* (1987)

Gary B. Nash, *Race and Revolution* (1990)

Mary Beth Norton, *The British Americans: The Loyalist Exiles in England, 1774–1789* (1972)

James O'Donnell, *Southern Indians in the American Revolution* (1973)

Howard W. Peckham, *The Toll of Independence: Engagements and Battle Casualties of the American Revolution* (1974)

Benjamin Quarles, *The Negro in the American Revolution*, rev. ed. (1996)

Jack M. Sosin, *The Revolutionary Frontier, 1763–1783* (1967)

James W. St. G. Walker, *The Black Loyalists* (1976)

Anthony F. C. Wallace, *The Death and Rebirth of the Seneca* (1970)

The United States in Congress Assembled

Robert A. Becker, *Revolution, Reform and the Politics of American Taxation, 1763–1783* (1980)

Richard Beeman, et al., eds., *Beyond Confederation: Origins of the Constitution and American National Identity* (1987)

E. Wayne Carp, *To Starve the Army at Pleasure: Continental Army Administration and American Political Culture, 1774–1783* (1984)

Jack Eblen, *The First and Second United States Empires* (1968)

E. J. Ferguson, *The Power of the Purse: A History of American Public Finance, 1776–1790* (1960)

Calvin C. Jillson, *Congressional Dynamics: Structure, Coordination, and Choice in the First American Congress, 1774–1789* (1994)

Jackson Turner Main, *Political Parties before the Constitution* (1973)

Jack N. Rakove, *The Beginnings of National Politics: An Interpretive History of the Continental Congress* (1979)

Gerald Sourzh, *Benjamin Franklin and American Foreign Policy* (1969)

Gordon S. Wood, *The Creation of the American Republic, 1776–1787* (1969)

Revolutionary Politics in the States

Willi Paul Adams, *The First American Constitutions: Republican Ideology and the Making of the State Constitutions* (1980)

Roger H. Brown, *Redeeming the Republic: Federalists, Taxation, and the Origins of the Constitution* (1993)

Donald S. Lutz, *Popular Consent and Popular Control: Whig Political Theory in the Early State Constitutions* (1980)

Jackson Turner Main, *The Sovereign States, 1775–1789* (1973)

Anne M. Ousterhout, *A State Divided: Opposition in Pennsylvania to the American Revolution* (1987)

Biography

Silvio A. Bedini, *The Life of Benjamin Banneker* (1972)

John Mack Faragher, *Daniel Boone: The Life and Legend of an American Pioneer* (1992)

Douglas Southall Freeman, *George Washington*, 7 vols. (1948–57)

Edith Belle Gelles, *Portia: The World of Abigail Adams* (1992)

Lowell Hayes Harrison, *George Rogers Clark and the War in the West* (1976)

Isabel Thompson Kelsay, *Joseph Brant, 1743–1807: Man of Two Worlds* (1984)

James Kirby Martin, *Benedict Arnold, Revolutionary Hero* (1997)

Willard Sterne Randall, *George Washington: A Life* (1997)

William Henry Robinson, *Phillis Wheatley and Her Writings* (1984)

Rosemarie Zagarri, *A Woman's Dilemma: Mercy Otis Warren and the American Revolution* (1995)

CHAPTER EIGHT

THE UNITED STATES OF NORTH AMERICA

1786–1800

AMERICAN COMMUNITIES
Mingo Creek Settlers Refuse to Pay the Whiskey Tax

On a hot July afternoon in 1794, the federal marshal and the federal tax collector arrived at the backcountry farm of William Miller in Mingo Creek, a community south of Pittsburgh. Like most of his neighbors, Miller had failed to pay the federal excise tax on his homemade whiskey still, and these men had come to serve him with a notice to appear in federal court in Philadelphia. "I felt myself mad with passion," said the farmer, knowing that the fine and the cost of the trip back east would "ruin" him. As the men argued, thirty or forty of Miller's neighbors suddenly appeared, armed with muskets and pitchforks. Members of the Mingo Creek Democratic Society, they had come to fight off this infringement on their liberty. There was an angry confrontation, and someone fired a gun into the air. No one was hit, and after a heated verbal exchange, the two officials rode off. But the farmers were fuming, and they decided to make a "citizen's arrest" of the officials the next day.

At Mingo Creek, poverty was the outstanding fact of life. A third of the farm families owned no land and rented or simply squatted on the acres of others. The tax collector or "exciseman" was one of the great landlords of Mingo Creek, not only controlling most of the local wealth but monopolizing political office as well. Other landlords lived outside the community, the most powerful being President George Washington himself, who owned thousands of acres in the West, much of it in the vicinity of Mingo Creek. The president had evicted so many squatters from his land that local people considered him a grasping speculator. Washington returned the compliment by describing these frontier settlers as "a parcel of barbarians" who were little better than "dogs or cats."

Farm families lived in miserable mud-floored log huts scattered along the creeks of the Monongahela Valley. But despite appearances, the farmers of Mingo Creek were bound together in networks of family and clan, work and barter, religion and politics. The militiamen acted together in what they perceived to be the interests of their community.

Like all the western territories, this was a violent place in a violent time. No-holds-barred fights at local taverns were frequent, and travelers remarked on the presence of one-eyed men, the victims of brutal gougings. Everyone knew of men or women lost in the continuing Indian wars. In 1782 militia companies from the area took their revenge by massacring ninety-six unresisting Christian Indians at Gnadenhutten, north of the Ohio River, hacking their bodies and bringing home their scalps as trophies. The new federal government had committed over 80 percent of its operating budget to defeating the Indians, but the failure of its campaigns left backcountry families resentful.

It was to help pay the costs of these campaigns that Congress had placed the tax on whiskey in 1791. The tax applied to the owners of stills, whether they produced commercially or simply for family and neighbors. Corn was not worth the cost of shipping it east, but whiskey made from corn was another matter, and many a farm family depended on the income from their stills. Farmers throughout America protested that the excise ran counter to Revolutionary principles. "Internal taxes upon consumption," declared the citizens of Mingo Creek, are "most dangerous to the civil rights of freemen, and must in the end destroy the liberties of every country in which they are introduced." Hugh Henry Brackenridge, editor of the *Pittsburgh Gazette*, argued for a tax on the "unsettled lands which all around us have been purchased by speculating men, who keep them up in large bodies and obstruct the population of the country." In other words, Congress should tax land speculators, like President Washington, instead.

Protest followed the course familiar from the Revolution. At first citizens gathered peacefully and petitioned their representatives, but when the tax collectors appeared there was vigilante action. Faces blackened or covered with handkerchiefs, farmers tarred and feathered the tax men. Although the immediate issue was taxation, larger matters were at stake. The Mingo Creek Democratic Society was part of Thomas Jefferson's political movement that supported republicanism and the French Revolution, in opposition to the conservative principles of the Washington administration. The tax protesters made this linkage explicit when they raised banners proclaiming the French slogan of "Liberty, Equality, Fraternity" and adding their own phrase, "and No Excise!" In North Carolina the rebels sang:

> *Some chaps whom freedom's spirit warms*
> *Are threatening hard to take up arms,*
> *And headstrong in rebellion rise*
> *'Fore they'll submit to that excise:*
> *Their liberty they will maintain,*
> *They fought for't, and they'll*
> *fight again.*

But it was only in western Pennsylvania that the protests turned to riot. When the Mingo Creek militia went to arrest the exciseman,

several of their number were killed in the confrontation. The exciseman and his family escaped from their house as it was consumed by a fire set by the farmers. In a community meeting afterward, the farmers resolved to attack and destroy Pittsburgh, where the wealthy and powerful local landlords resided. Terrified residents of the town saved the day by welcoming the rebels with free food and drink. "It cost me four barrels of whiskey that day," declared one man, but "I would rather spare that than a single quart of blood." Destruction was averted, but an angry farmer rode through the street waving a tomahawk and warning: "It is not the excise law only that must go down. A great deal more is to be done. I am but beginning yet."

Declaring the Whiskey Rebellion "the first ripe fruit" of the democratic sentiment sweeping the country, President George Washington organized a federal army of 13,000 men, larger than the one he had commanded during the Revolution, and ordered the occupation of western Pennsylvania. Soldiers dragged half-naked men from their beds and forced them into open pens, where they remained for days in the freezing rain. Authorities arrested twenty people and sent them in irons to Philadelphia, where a judge convicted two of treason and sentenced them to death. The protest gradually died down, and Washington pardoned the felons, sparing their lives.

Federal power had prevailed over the local community. In his Farewell Address to the nation the following year Washington warned of an excessive spirit of localism that "agitates the community with ill-founded jealousies and false alarms; kindles the animosity of one part against another; foments occasionally riot and insurrection." But resistance to the excise remained widespread, and no substantial revenue was ever collected from the tax on whiskey. More important, the whiskey rebels had raised some of the most important issues of the day: the power and authority of the new federal government; the relation of the West to the rest of the nation; the nature of political dissent; and the meaning of the Revolutionary tradition.

Mingo Creek

- The tensions and conflicts between local and national authorities in the decades after the American Revolution
- The struggle to draft the Constitution and to achieve its ratification

- Establishment of the first national government under the Constitution
- The beginning of American political parties
- The first stirrings of an authentic American national culture

FORMING A NEW GOVERNMENT

Eight years before the Whiskey Rebellion a similar rural uprising, Shays' Rebellion (see Chapter 7), had solidified beliefs that the powers of the federal government must be increased lest the budding nation wither. The action at Mingo Creek was the first test of the sovereignty of the newly formed central government, whose strength grew out of the Constitution forged in 1787 by delegates from all the colonies. In putting down the Whiskey Rebellion, federal forces exercised powers that the delegates to the Constitutional Convention agonized over but ultimately granted to the national community they wanted to build.

Nationalist Sentiment

Nationalists had long argued for a strengthened union of the states. Even before ratification of the Articles of Confederation, Alexander Hamilton, a New York lawyer and close associate of George Washington who had served during the Revolution as his aide, was advocating a "solid, coercive union" having "complete sovereignty" over the civil, military, and economic life of the states, along with permanent revenues from taxes and duties. But after emerging victorious from the Revolutionary War, most Americans turned their attention back to the states.

In general, the nationalists were drawn from the elite circles of American life. "Although there are no nobles in America, there is a class of men denominated 'gentlemen,'" the French ambassador to America wrote home in 1786. "They are creditors, and therefore interested in strengthening the government, and watching over the execution of the law. The majority of them being merchants, it is for their interest to establish the credit of the United States in Europe on a solid foundation by the exact payment of debts, and to grant to Congress powers extensive enough to compel the people to contribute for this purpose." In addition to merchants, the ambassador identified others who leaned toward national government: former officers in the Continental Army whose experience

with the Continental Congress had made them firm believers in a stronger central government, and conservatives who wanted to restrain what they considered the excessive democracy of the states.

The economic crisis that followed the Revolutionary War (see Chapter 7) provided the nationalists with their most important opportunity to organize. In March 1785 a group of men from Virginia and Maryland, including James Madison, George Mason, and George Washington, drafted an agreement to present to legislatures recommending uniform commercial regulations, duties, and currency laws. Early the next year, at Madison's urging, the Virginia legislature invited all the states to send representatives to a commercial conference to be held at Annapolis.

Only five states sent strong nationalist delegates to the Annapolis Convention in September 1786. Hamilton, who played a leading role at the meeting, drew up a report calling on Congress to endorse a new convention to be held in Philadelphia to discuss all matters necessary "to render the constitution of the federal government adequate to the exigencies of the union." By this time, although there were still serious disagreements between localists and nationalists about the powers of the national government, most Americans agreed that the Articles needed strengthening, especially in regard to commercial regulation and the generation of revenue. Early in 1787, the Confederation Congress cautiously endorsed the plan for a convention "for the sole and express purpose of revising the Articles of Confederation."

The Constitutional Convention

Fifty-five men from twelve states assembled at the Pennsylvania State House in Philadelphia where the convention opened in late May 1787. Rhode Island, where radical localists held power (see Chapter 7), refused to send a delegation. A number of prominent men were missing. Thomas Jefferson and John Adams were serving as ambassadors in Europe, and crusty Patrick Henry declared that he "smelt a rat." Henry had become a localist, and perhaps what bothered him was the predominantly cosmopolitan cast of the meeting. But most of America's best-known leaders were present: George Washington, Benjamin Franklin, Alexander Hamilton, James Madison, George Mason, and Robert Morris. Twenty-nine of them were college educated, thirty-four were lawyers, twenty-four had served in Congress, and twenty-one were veteran officers of the Revolution. At least nineteen owned slaves, and there were also land speculators and merchants. But there were no ordinary farmers or artisans present, and certainly no women, African Americans, or Indians. The Constitution was framed by white men who represented America's social and economic elite.

On their first day of work, the delegates agreed to vote by states, as was the custom in the Confederation Congress. They chose Washington to chair the meeting, and to ensure candid debate they decided to keep their sessions secret. James Madison took voluminous daily minutes, however, providing us with a record of what happened behind the convention's locked doors. Madison, a conservative young Virginian with a profound knowledge of history and political philosophy, had arrived several days before the convention opened, and with his fellow Virginians had drafted what became known as the Virginia Plan. Presented by Virginia Governor Edmund Randolph on May 29, it set the convention's agenda.

George Washington presides over a session of the Constitutional Convention, meeting in Philadelphia's State House (now known as Independence Hall), in an engraving of 1799.

The authors of the Virginia Plan proposed scrapping the Articles of Confederation in favor of a "consolidated government" having the power to tax and to enforce its laws directly rather than through the states. "A spirit of locality," Madison declared, was destroying "the aggregate interests of the community," by which he meant the great community of the nation. Madison's plan would have reduced the states to little more than administrative districts. Representation in the bicameral national legislature would be based on population: the members of the House of Representatives were to be elected by popular vote, but senators would be chosen by state legislators so that they might be insulated from democratic pressure. The Senate would lead, controlling foreign affairs and the appointment of officials. An appointed chief executive and a national judiciary would together form a Council of Revision having the power to veto both national and state legislation.

The main opposition to these proposals came from the delegates from small states, which feared being swallowed up by the large ones. After two weeks of debate, William Paterson of New Jersey introduced an alternative, a set of "purely federal" principles known since as the New Jersey Plan. He proposed increasing the powers of the central government but retaining a single-house Congress in which the states were equally represented. After much debate and a series of votes that split the convention down the middle, the delegates finally agreed to what has been called the Great Compromise: proportional representation by population in the House, representation by states in the Senate. The compromise allowed the creation of a strong national government while still providing an important role for the states.

Part of this agreement was a second, fundamental compromise that brought together the delegates from North and South. To boost their power in the new government, the southern delegates wanted to include slaves in the population to be counted for the purpose of determining state representation, but to exclude them when it came to apportioning taxes. Ultimately it was agreed that five slaves would be counted as the equal of three freemen—the "three-fifths rule." Furthermore, the representatives of South Carolina and Georgia demanded protection for the international slave trade, and after bitter debate the delegates included a provision preventing any prohibition of the importation of slaves for twenty years. Another article legitimized the return of fugitive slaves from free states. Although the word "slave" does not appear anywhere in the Constitution (the framers avoided it with such phrases as "other persons" and "persons held to labor," these provisions nonetheless amounted to national guarantees for southern slavery. Many delegates were opposed to slavery and regretted having to give in on this issue, but they agreed with Madison, who wrote that "great as the evil is, a dismemberment of the union would be worse."

There was still much to decide regarding the other branches of government. Madison's Council of Revision was scratched in favor of a strong federal judiciary with the implicit power to declare acts of Congress unconstitutional. Demands for a powerful chief executive raised fears that the office might prove to be, in the words of Edmund Randolph of Virginia, "the fetus of monarchy." But there was considerable support for a president with veto power to check the legislature. In fact, according to James McHenry, a delegate from Maryland, twenty-one delegates favored some form of monarchy, and Alexander Hamilton went on record supporting the creation of a constitutional monarch. To keep the president independent of Congress, the delegates decided he should be elected; but fearing that ordinary voters could never "be sufficiently informed" to select wisely, they insulated the process from popular choice by creating the electoral college. Voters in the states would not actually vote for president. Rather, in a manner to be determined by its legislature, each state would select a slate of "electors" equal in number to the state's total representation in the House and Senate. Following the general election, the electors in each state would meet to cast their ballots and elect the president.

In early September the delegates turned their rough draft of the Constitution over to a Committee of Style that shaped it into an elegant and concise document setting forth the general principles and basic framework of government. But Madison, known to later generations as "the Father of the Constitution," was gloomy, believing that the revisions of his original plan doomed the Union to the kind of inaction that had characterized government under the Articles of Confederation. It was left for Franklin to make the final speech to the convention. "Can a perfect production be expected?" he asked. "I consent, Sir, to this Constitution, because I expect no better, and because I am not sure that it is not the best." The delegates voted their approval on September 17, 1787, and transmitted the document to Congress, agreeing that it would become operative after ratification by nine states. Some congressmen were outraged that the convention had exceeded its charge of simply modifying the Articles of Confederation, but Congress called for a special ratifying convention in each of the states.

Ratifying the New Constitution

The supporters of the new Constitution immediately adopted the name Federalists to describe themselves. Their outraged opponents objected that the existing Confederation already provided for a "federal" government of balanced power between the states and the Union and that the Constitution would replace it with a "national" government. But in this, as in much of the subsequent process of ratification, the Federalists (or nationalists) grabbed the initiative, and their opponents had to content themselves with the label Anti-Federalists. Mercy Otis Warren, a leading critic of the Constitution, commented on the dilemma in which the Anti-Federalists found themselves. "On the one hand," she wrote, "we stand in need of a strong federal government, founded on principles that will support the prosperity and union of the colonies. On the other, we have struggled for liberty and made costly sacrifices at her shrine and there are still many among us who revere her name too much to relinquish, beyond a certain medium, the rights of man for the dignity of government."

The critics of the Constitution were by no means a unified group. Because most of them were localists, they represented a variety of social and regional interests. But most believed the Constitution granted far too much power to the center, weakening the autonomy of communities and states. As local governments "will always possess a better representation of the feelings and interests of the people at large," one critic wrote, "it is obvious that these powers can be deposited with much greater safety with the state than the general government."

All the great political thinkers of the eighteenth century had argued that a republican form of government could work only for small countries. As the French philosopher Montesquieu had observed, "In an extensive republic, the public good is sacrificed to a thousand private views." But in *The Federalist*, a series of brilliant essays in defense of the Constitution written in 1787 and 1788 by Madison, Hamilton, and John Jay, Madison stood Montesquieu's assumption on its head. Rhode Island had demonstrated that the rights of property might not be protected in even the smallest of states. Asserting that "the most common and durable source of factions has been the various and unequal distribution of property," Madison concluded that the best way to control such factions was to "extend the sphere" of government. That way, he continued, "you take in a greater variety of parties and interests; you make it less probable that a majority of the whole will have a common motive to invade the rights of other citizens; or, if such a common motive exists, it will be more difficult for all who feel it to discover their own strength and to act in unison with each other." Rather than a disability, Madison argued, great size is an advantage: interests are so diverse that no single faction is able to gain control of the state, threatening the freedoms of others.

It is doubtful whether Madison's sophisticated argument, or the arguments of the Anti-Federalists for that matter, made much of a difference in the popular voting in the states to select delegates for the state ratification conventions. The alignment of forces generally followed the lines laid down during the fights over economic issues in the years since the Revolution. For example, in Pennsylvania—the first state to convene a ratification convention, in November 1787—48 percent of the Anti-Federalist delegates to the convention were farmers. By contrast, 54 percent of the Federalists were merchants, manufacturers, large landowners, or professionals. What tipped the Pennsylvania convention in favor of the Constitution was the wide support the document enjoyed among artisans and commercial farmers, who saw their interests tied to the growth of a commercial society. As one observer pointed out, "The counties nearest [navigable waters] were in favor of it generally, those more remote, in opposition."

Similar agrarian-localist and commercial-cosmopolitan alignments characterized most of the other states. The most critical convention took place in Massachusetts in early 1788. Five states—Delaware, Pennsylvania, New Jersey, Georgia, and Connecticut—had already voted to ratify, but the states with the strongest Anti-Federalist movements had yet to convene. If the Constitution lost in Massachusetts, its fate would be in great danger. At the convention, Massachusetts opponents of ratification enjoyed a small

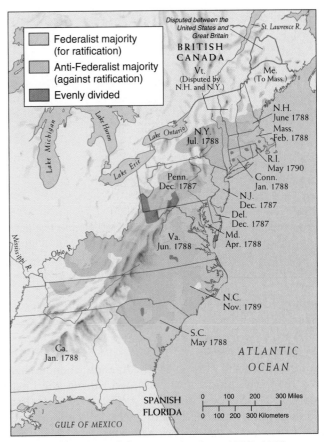

The Ratification of the Constitution, 1787–1790
The distribution of the vote for the ratification of the Constitution demonstrated its wide support in sections of the country linked to the commercial economy and its disapproval in more remote and backcountry sections. (Note that Maine remained a part of Massachusetts until admitted as a separate state in 1820.)

majority. But several important Anti-Federalist leaders, including Samuel Adams, were swayed by the enthusiastic support for the Constitution among Boston's townspeople, and on February 6 the convention voted narrowly in favor of ratification. To no one's surprise, Rhode Island rejected the Constitution in March, but Maryland and South Carolina approved it in April and May. On June 21, New Hampshire became the ninth state to ratify.

Anti-Federalist support was strong in New York, Virginia, and North Carolina. North Carolina voted to reject and did not join the union until the next year; it was followed by a still reluctant Rhode Island in 1790. In New York, the delegates were moved to vote their support by a threat from New York City to secede from the state and join the Union separately if the convention failed to ratify. The Virginia convention was almost evenly divided, but promises to amend the Constitution to protect individual rights persuaded enough delegates to produce a victory for the Consti-

A cartoon published in July 1788 when New York became the eleventh state to ratify the Constitution. After initially voting to reject, North Carolina soon reconsidered, but radical and still reluctant Rhode Island did not join the Union until 1790.

tution. The promise of a Bill of Rights, in fact, was important in the ratification vote of five of the states.

Shaping the Bill of Rights

Although the Bill of Rights—the first ten amendments to the Constitution—was adopted during the first session of the new federal Congress, it was first proposed during the debates over ratification. The Constitutional Convention had considered a Bill of Rights patterned on the declarations of rights in the state constitutions (see Chapter 7) but rejected it as superfluous, agreeing with Madison that the federal government would exercise only those powers expressly delegated to it. However, George Mason, author of Virginia's Declaration of Rights, refused to sign the Constitution because it failed to contain similar provisions. He played an important role in getting the Virginia ratifying convention to endorse a set of constitutional amendments. Campaigning for a seat in the new Congress, Madison was pressed to affirm his willingness to propose and support a set of amendments guaranteeing "essential rights."

The various state ratification conventions had proposed a grab bag of more than 200 potential amendments. Madison set about transforming these into a series that he introduced into the new Congress in June 1789. Congress passed twelve and sent them to the states in September, and ten survived the ratification process to become the Bill of Rights in 1791.

The First Amendment prohibits Congress from establishing an official religion and provides for the freedoms of speech and the press and the right of assembly and petition. The other amendments guarantee the right to bear arms, limit the government's power to quarter troops in private homes, and restrain the government from unreasonable searches or seizures; they assure the people their legal rights under the common law, includ-

ing the prohibition of double jeopardy, the right not to be compelled to testify against oneself, and due process of law before life, liberty, or property can be taken. Finally, the unenumerated rights of the people are protected, and those powers not delegated to the federal government are reserved to the states.

The first ten amendments to the Constitution have been a restraining influence on the growth of government power over American citizens. Their provisions have become an admired aspect of the American political tradition throughout the world. The Bill of Rights is the most important constitutional legacy of the Anti-Federalists.

THE NEW NATION

Ratification of the Constitution was followed by the first federal elections—for the congress and the presidency—and in the spring of 1789 the new federal government assumed power in the temporary capital of New York City. The inauguration of George Washington as the first president of the United States took place on April 30, 1789, on the balcony of Federal Hall, at the corner of Wall and Broad Streets. Reelected without opposition in 1792, Washington would serve until 1797.

The activities of the first federal government were far removed from the everyday lives of most Americans, but as the Whiskey Rebellion demonstrated, there were moments when the two intersected dramatically. Moreover, the first years under the new federal Constitution were especially important for the future, because they shaped the structure of the American state in ways that would be enormously significant for later generations.

The Washington Presidency

During its first month, the Congress debated what to call the president of the United States. Believing that no government could long endure without the awe and veneration of its citizens, Vice President John Adams, sitting as the president of the Senate, proposed "His Highness the President of the United States." But a majority in the House of Representatives saw this title as a dangerous flirtation with "monarchism." When someone proposed that the nation's coinage be stamped with a bust of the president, men of republican persuasion protested that such veneration would be too much like the customs of the British empire. The president himself finally resolved the controversy by declaring the whole topic had been raised "without any privity of knowledge of it on my part," and by custom he came to be addressed simply as "Mr. President." This issue encapsulated an important conflict of these early years—the desire of some nationalists to add to the power of executive authority, versus the faith of localists in a strong Congress.

Although he dressed in plain American broadcloth at his inauguration and claimed to be content with a plain republican title, Washington was counted among the nationalists. He was anything but a man of the people, by nature reserved and solemn, choosing to ride about town in a grand carriage drawn by six horses and escorted by uniformed liverymen. In the tradition of British royalty, he delivered his addresses personally to Congress and received from both houses an official reply. These customs were continued by John Adams, Washington's successor, but ended by Thomas Jefferson, who denounced them as "rags of royalty," and began the practice, continued throughout the nineteenth century, of sending written presidential messages to Congress. On the other hand, Washington worked hard to adhere to the letter of the Constitution, refusing, for example, to use the veto power except where he thought the Congress had acted unconstitutionally, and personally seeking the "advice and consent" of the Senate.

Congress quickly moved to establish departments to run the executive affairs of state, and Washington soon appointed Thomas Jefferson his secretary of state, Alexander Hamilton to run the Treasury, Henry Knox the War Department, and Edmund Randolph the Justice Department, as attorney general. The president consulted each of these men regularly, and during his first term met with them as a group to discuss matters of policy. By the end of Washington's presidency the secretaries had coalesced in what came to be known as the cabinet, an institution that has survived to the present despite the absence of constitutional authority or enabling legislation giving it formal recognition. Washington was a powerful and commanding personality, but he understood the importance of national unity, and in his style of leadership, his consultations, and his appointments he sought to achieve a balance of conflicting political perspectives and sectional interests. These intentions would be sorely tested during the eight years of his administration.

An Active Federal Judiciary

The most important piece of legislation to emerge from the first session of Congress was the Judiciary Act of 1789, which implemented the judicial clause of the Constitution and set up a system of federal courts.

Daniel Huntington's Republican Court *emphasized the similarities between American republican government and the royal courts of Europe. When Vice President John Adams proposed that the president be addressed as "His Highness," democrats in the Congress argued this was a dangerous flirtation with "monarchism," and Thomas Jefferson urged that the government give up such "rags of royalty."*

Congress provided that the Supreme Court consist of six justices (later increased to nine) and established three circuit and thirteen district courts. Strong nationalists argued for a powerful federal legal system that would provide a uniform code of civil and criminal justice throughout the country. But the localists in Congress fought successfully to retain the various bodies of law that had developed in the states. They wanted to preserve local community autonomy. The act gave federal courts limited original jurisdiction, restricting them mostly to appeals from state courts. But it thereby established the principle of federal judicial review of state legislation, despite the silence of the Constitution on this point.

Under the leadership of Chief Justice John Jay, the Supreme Court heard relatively few cases during its first decade. Still, it managed to raise considerable political controversy. In *Chisholm v. Georgia* (1793) it ruled in favor of two South Carolina residents who had sued the state of Georgia for the recovery of confiscated property. Thus did the Court overthrow the common law principle that a sovereignty could not be sued without its consent, and supported the Constitution's grant of federal jurisdiction over disputes "between a state and citizens of another state." Many localists feared that this nationalist ruling threatened the integrity of the states. In response, they proposed the Eleventh Amendment to the Constitution, ratified in 1798, which declared that no state could be sued by citizens from another state. The Supreme Court nevertheless established itself as the final authority on questions of law when it invalidated a Virginia statute in *Ware v. Hylton* (1796) and upheld the constitutionality of an act of Congress in *Hylton v. U.S.* (1796).

Hamilton's Controversial Fiscal Program

Fiscal and economic affairs pressed upon the new government. Lacking revenues, and faced with the massive national debt contracted during the Revolution, it took power in a condition of virtual bankruptcy. At the urging of James Madison, whose first official position in the United States government was floor leader for the Washington administration in the House of Representatives, Congress passed the Tariff of 1789, a compromise between advocates of protective tariffs (duties so high that they made foreign products prohibitively expensive, thus "protecting" American products) and those who wanted moderate tariffs that produced income. Duties on imported goods, rather than direct taxes on property or incomes, would constitute the bulk of federal revenues until the twentieth century.

After setting this system of duties in place, Congress turned to the problem of the debt. In January 1790, Hamilton submitted a "Report on the Public Credit," in which he recommended that the federal government assume the obligations accumulated by the states during the previous fifteen years and redeem the national debt—owed to both domestic and foreign leaders—by agreeing to a new issue of interest-bearing bonds. To raise the revenue required to retire the debt, Hamilton recommended an excise tax on the manufacture of distilled liquor.

By this means, Hamilton sought to inspire the confidence of domestic and foreign investors in the public credit of the new nation. Congress endorsed his plan to pay off the $11 million owed to foreign creditors but balked at funding the domestic debt of $27 million and assuming the state debts of $25 million. The funding of the domestic debt aroused debate because necessity had forced many individuals to sell off at deep discounts the notes, warrants, and securities the government had issued them during the Revolution. Yet Hamilton now advocated paying these obligations at face value, providing any speculator who held them with fabulous profits. The assumption of state debts aroused even greater debate because some states, mostly those in the South, had already arranged to liquidate their debts, whereas others had left theirs unpaid.

Congress remained deadlocked on these issues for six months, until congressmen from Pennsylvania and Virginia arranged a compromise. Final agreement, however, was stalled by a sectional dispute over the permanent location of the new national capital. Southerners supported Washington's desire to plant it on the Potomac River, but northerners argued for Philadelphia. In return for Madison's pledge to obtain enough southern votes to pass Hamilton's assumption plan—which Madison had earlier opposed as a "radically immoral" windfall for speculators—northern congressmen agreed to a location for the new federal district on the boundary of Virginia and Maryland. In July 1790, Congress passed legislation moving the temporary capital from New York to Philadelphia until the expected completion of the federal city, in 1800, in a "District of Columbia" that would be under the jurisdiction of Congress. Two weeks later it adopted Hamilton's credit program. This was the first of many sectional compromises.

Hamilton now proposed the second component of his fiscal program, the establishment of a Bank of the United States. The bank, a public corporation funded by private capital, would serve as the depository of government funds and the fiscal agent of the Treasury. Congress narrowly approved it, but Madison's opposition raised doubts in the president's mind about the constitutionality of the measure, and Washington solicited the opinion of his cabinet. Here for the first time were articulated the classic interpretations of constitutional authority. Jefferson took a "strict constructionist" position, arguing that the powers of the federal government must be limited to those specifically enumerated in the Constitution. This position came closest to the basic agreement of the men who had drafted the document. Hamilton, on the other hand, reasoned that the Constitution "implied" the power to use whatever means were "necessary and proper" to carry out its enumerated powers—a "loose constructionist" position. Persuaded by Hamilton's opinion, Washington signed the bill, and the bank went into operation in 1791.

Hamilton's "Report on Manufactures," submitted to Congress in December 1791, was the capstone to his comprehensive economic program. It contained an ambitious plan involving the use of government securities as investment capital for "infant industries," federal bounties to encourage innovation, and high protective tariffs. This system, Hamilton hoped, would promote the development of an industrial economy. Congressmen from farming areas, whose previous objections to Hamilton's preference for the "monied interests" had not prevailed, were finally able to frustrate him on this proposal. Hamilton's views, they argued, would limit them to roles exactly like those they had played within the British empire; in effect they would be exchanging British for Boston and New York masters. Of equal importance, the plan failed to inspire American capitalists, who continued to be more interested in investments in shipping or in land speculation than in industrial production.

Many of Hamilton's specific proposals for increased tariff protection became part of a revision of duties that took place in 1792. Moreover, his fiscal program as a whole dramatically restored the financial health of the United States. Foreign investment in government securities increased and along with domestic capital provided the Bank of the United States with enormous reserves. Its bank notes became the most important circulating medium of the North American commercial economy, and their wide acceptance greatly stimulated business enterprise. "Our public credit," Washington declared toward the end of his first term, "stands on that ground which three years ago it would have been considered as a species of madness to have foretold."

The Beginnings of Foreign Policy

The Federalist political coalition, forged during the ratification of the Constitution, was sorely strained by these debates over fiscal policy. By the middle of 1792, Jefferson, representing the southern agrarians, and Hamilton, speaking for northern capitalists, were locked in a full-scale feud within the Washington administration. Hamilton conducted himself more like a prime minister than a cabinet secretary, greatly offending Jefferson, who considered himself the pres-

ident's heir apparent. But the dispute went deeper than a mere conflict of personalities. Hamilton stated the difference clearly when he wrote that "one side appears to believe that there is a serious plot to overturn the State governments, and substitute a monarchy to the present republican system," whereas "the other side firmly believes that there is a serious plot to overturn the general government and elevate the separate powers of the States upon its ruins." The conflict between Hamilton and Jefferson was to grow even more bitter over the issue of American foreign policy.

The commanding event of the Atlantic world during the 1790s was the French Revolution, which had begun in 1789. Most Americans enthusiastically welcomed the fall of the French monarchy. After the people of Paris stormed the Bastille, the new French republic sent Washington the key to the prison's doors as a symbol of the relationship between the two revolutions. But with the beginning in 1793 of the Reign of Terror, whose bloody guillotine claimed the lives of hundreds of aristocrats, American conservatives began to voice their opposition. The execution of King Louis XVI, and especially the onset of war between revolutionary France and monarchical Great Britain in 1793, firmly divided American opinion.

Most at issue was whether the Franco-American alliance of 1778 required the United States to support France in its war with Britain. All of Washington's cabinet agreed on the importance of American neutrality. With France and Britain prowling for each other's vessels on the high seas, the vast colonial trade of Europe was delivered up to neutral powers, the United States prominent among them. Neutrality, in other words, meant windfall profits. Jefferson believed it highly unlikely that the French would call on the Americans to honor the 1778 treaty; the administration should simply wait and see. Hamilton argued, however, that so great was the danger that Washington should immediately declare the treaty "temporarily and provisionally suspended."

These disagreements revealed two contrasting perspectives on the course the United States should chart in international waters. Hamilton believed in the necessity of an accommodation with Great Britain, the most important trading partner of the United States and the world's greatest naval power. Jefferson and Madison, on the other hand, looked for more international independence, pinning their hopes on the future of western expansion. There was room for compromise between these two points of view, but in the debate over the French Revolution positions tended to become polarized.

The debate in the United States grew hotter with the arrival in April 1793 of French ambassador Edmond Genêt. Large crowds of supporters greeted him throughout the nation, and among them he solicited

Spain's anti-American policy in the West had several facets. Controlling both sides of the lower Mississippi, the Spanish closed the river to American shipping, making it impossible for western American farmers to market their crops through the port of New Orleans. The Spanish also sought to create a barrier to American settlement by promoting immigration to Louisiana and Florida. They succeeded in attracting several thousand of the Acadians deported by the British during the Seven Years War, who reassembled their distinctive communities in the bayou country of Louisiana (see Chapter 6). But otherwise the Spanish had little success with immigration and relied mostly on creating a barrier of pro-Spanish Indian nations in the lower Mississippi Valley. In exchange for supplies and Spanish recognition of them as "free and independent nations," the tribes of the South pledged themselves to "the preservation of the Dominion" of Spain in Louisiana and Florida. To consolidate these gains, in the early 1790s the Spanish constructed two new Mississippi River forts at sites that would later become the cities of Vicksburg and Memphis.

North of the Ohio River the situation was much the same. Thousands of Loyalists had fled the United States in the aftermath of the Revolution and settled in the country north of Lakes Ontario and Erie.

They were understandably hostile to the new republic. In 1791 the British Parliament passed the Canada Act, creating the province of Upper Canada (later renamed Ontario) and granting the Loyalists limited self-government. To protect this province British troops remained at a number of posts within American territory at places such as Detroit, where they supplied the Indian nations with arms and ammunition, hoping to create a buffer to American expansion. In early 1794 the governor general of Canada told an assembly of Indian leaders from the Ohio country that war between Britain and the United States was almost certain, and that when it broke out, "a line must then be drawn by the warriors." British soldiers began constructing Fort Miami in the Maumee Valley, west of Lake Erie, well within American territory.

Domestic and International Crises

Washington faced the gravest crisis of his presidency in 1794. In the West, the inability of the federal government to subdue the Indians, to eliminate the British from the northern fur trade, or to arrange with the Spanish for unencumbered use of the Mississippi River stirred frontiersmen to loud protests. There were rumblings of rebellion and secession from western communities. This discontent was strengthened by Hamilton's federal excise tax on whiskey, which hit backcountry farmers hardest, as the opening of this chapter illustrates. "The people of the western counties," wrote an English commentator, find "themselves grievously taxed for the support of the government without enjoying the blessings of it." London and Madrid believed that American settlers in the Northwest and Southwest might quit the Union and join themselves to Canada or Florida, and both English and Spanish secret agents worked to enhance such possibilities with liberal bribes.

In the Atlantic, Great Britain declared a blockade of France, including the seizure of vessels trading with the French West Indies. From 1793 to the beginning of 1794 the British confiscated the cargoes of more than 250 American ships, threatening hundreds of merchants with ruin. The United States was being "kicked, cuffed, and plundered all over the ocean," declared Madi-

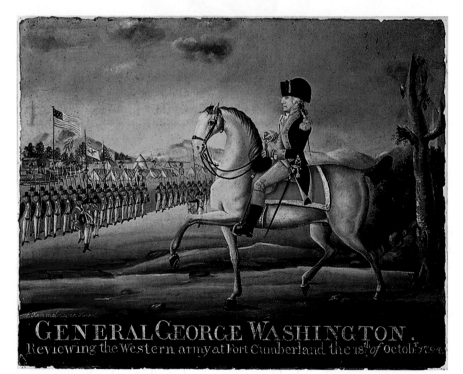

GENERAL GEORGE WASHINGTON.
Reviewing the Western army at Fort Cumberland the 18.ᵗʰ of October 1794.

In this 1794 painting, President George Washington reviews some 13,000 troops at Fort Cumberland on the Potomac before dispatching them to suppress the Whiskey Rebellion. Washington's mobilization of federal military power dramatically demonstrated the federal commitment to the preservation of the Union and the protection of the western boundary.

son, and in Congress he introduced legislation imposing retaliatory duties on British ships and merchandise.

The Whiskey Rebellion, which broke out in the summer of 1794, thus came at a time when President Washington considered the nation to be under siege. The combination of Indian attack, international intrigue, and domestic insurrection, he believed, created the greatest threat to the nation since the Revolution. In April the president had dispatched Chief Justice John Jay to London to arrange a settlement with the British. At the same time, war seemed increasingly likely, and Washington feared that any sign of federal weakness in the face of western rebellion would invite British or Spanish intervention. With Hamilton's urging he took the decisive course described in the opening of this chapter: he raised a large militia even as he pursued halfhearted negotiations with local authorities and made preparations to occupy the area around Pittsburgh, including Mingo Creek. It is clear now that the president overreacted, for although there was riot and violence in western Pennsylvania, there was no organized insurrection. Nevertheless, his mobilization of federal military power dramatically demonstrated the federal commitment to the preservation of the Union, the protection of the western boundary, and the supremacy of the national over the local community.

This action was reinforced by an impressive American victory against the Indian confederacy. Following the disastrous defeat of St. Clair by Little Turtle, Washington appointed General Anthony Wayne to lead a greatly strengthened American army to subdue the Indian confederacy and secure the Northwest. At the battle of Fallen Timbers, fought in the Maumee country of northern Ohio on August 20, 1794, Wayne crushed the Indians. Retreating, the warriors found the gates of Fort Miami closed and barred, the British inside thinking better of providing the powerful American force with a reason to attack the fort. The victory set the stage for the Treaty of Greenville in 1795, in which the representatives of twelve Indian nations ceded a huge territory encompassing most of present-day Ohio, much of Indiana, and other enclaves in the Northwest, including the town of Detroit and the tiny village of Chicago.

Jay's and Pinckney's Treaties

The strengthened American position in the West encouraged the British to settle their dispute with the United States so that they might concentrate on defeating republican France. In November 1794 Jay and the British signed an agreement providing for British withdrawal from American soil by 1796, limited American trade with the British East and West Indies, and the status of most-favored-nation for both countries (meaning that each would enjoy trade benefits

Spanish Claims to American Territory, 1783–1795
Before 1795 the Spanish claimed the American territory of the Old Southwest and barred Americans from access to the port of New Orleans, effectively closing the Mississippi River. This dispute was settled by Pinckney's Treaty in 1795.

equal to those the other accorded any other state). The treaty represented a solid gain for the young republic. With only a small army and no navy to speak of, the United States was in no position to wage war.

As it did on all matters of importance, the Senate debated the treaty in secret session. Details leaked out in a piecemeal fashion that inflamed public debate. The treaty represented a victory for Hamilton's conception of American neutrality. The Jeffersonians might well have opposed any agreement with Great Britain, but they were enraged over this accommodation that virtually unleashed Britain to attack republican France with full force. The absence in the treaty of any mention of compensation for the slaves who had fled to the British side during the Revolution further alienated Southerners. Throughout the country Democratic Societies and Jeffersonian partisans organized protests and demonstrations. Upon his return to the United States, Jay joked, he could find his way across the country by the light of his burning effigies. Despite these protests, the Senate, dominated by supporters of Hamilton, ratified the agreement in June 1795. In the House, a coalition of Southerners, Westerners, and friends of France attempted to stall the treaty by threatening to withhold the appropriations necessary for its implementation and demanding that they be allowed to examine the diplomatic correspondence regarding the whole affair. By refusing this demand, the president established the precedent of executive privilege in matters of state.

The deadlock continued until late in the year, when word arrived that the Spanish had abandoned their claims to the territory south of the Ohio River. Having declared war on revolutionary France, Spain had suffered a humiliating defeat, and fearing the loss of its American empire now found it expedient to mollify the quarrelsome Americans. In 1795 American envoy Thomas Pinckney negotiated a treaty in which Spain agreed to a boundary with the United States at the thirty-first parallel and opened the Mississippi to American shipping, with the right to dock in the port of New Orleans. This treaty fit the Jeffersonian conception of empire, and congressmen from the West and South were delighted with its terms. But administration supporters demanded their acquiescence in Jay's Treaty before the approval of Pinckney's. With this compromise, the long political controversy finally reached a conclusion.

These two important treaties finally established American sovereignty over the land west of the Appalachians and opened to American commerce a vast market extending from Atlantic ports to the Mississippi Valley. From a political standpoint, however, the battle over Jay's Treaty was costly for Washington, for it provided the Jeffersonians an opportunity to claim that in exchange for British gold the administration had sold out American neutrality as well as the republican principles embodied by the French Revolution. Washington's role in the events of 1794 and 1795 brought the president down from his pedestal and subjected him to the rough-and-tumble of political warfare. In the opposition press, he was vilified as "the source of all the misfortunes of our country" and was even accused of having been a traitor during the Revolution. Sick of politics and longing to return to private life, Washington now rejected the offer of a third term.

Washington's Farewell Address

Just two months before the presidential election of 1796, Washington published his Farewell Address to the nation, an appeal for national unity. "With slight shades of difference," Washington said to his countrymen, "you have the same religion, manners, habits, and political principles," and "union ought to be considered as a main prop of your liberty." He warned against sectional loyalty and "the baneful effects of the spirit of party." In the increasingly polarized political debate, however, this appeal fell on deaf ears.

The second part of the address was considerably more influential. "Our detached and distant situation," Washington explained, invited the nation to "defy material injury from external annoyance." He argued not for American isolation, but rather for American disinterest in the affairs of Europe. "The great rule of conduct for us in regard to foreign nations is, in extending our commercial relations to have with them as little political connection as possible." Why, he asked "entangle our peace and prosperity in the toils of European ambition, rivalship, interest, humor, or caprice?" Thomas Jefferson, in his Inaugural Address of 1801, paraphrased this first principle of American foreign policy as "peace, commerce, and honest friendship with all nations, entangling alliances with none." Jefferson's statement underscored the extent to which Washington articulated principles agreed to by all the major political figures of his day.

FEDERALISTS AND REPUBLICANS

The framers of the Constitution envisioned a one-party state in which partisan distinctions would be muted by patriotism and public virtue. "Among the numerous advantages promised by a well constructed Union," Madison had written in *The Federalist*, is "its tendency to break and control the violence of faction." Not only did he fail to anticipate the rise of political parties or factions; he saw them as potentially harmful to the new nation. It is thus ironic that when Madison broke with the Washington administration on questions of fiscal policy, he was the first to take steps toward organizing a political opposition, which would become known as the Democratic Republican Party. At the height of the agitation of the Democratic Societies in 1794, Hamilton cried that "unless soon checked," the "spirit of faction" would "involve the country in all the horrors of anarchy." Yet in acting as Washington's political lieutenant, he did more than anyone else to solidify the "Friends of Order," as his supporters were first known, into a disciplined political party known as the Federalists. Despite the framers' intentions, in the twelve years between the ratification of the Constitution and the federal election of 1800 political parties became a fundamental part of the American system of government.

The Rise of Political Parties

Evident in the debates and votes of Congress from 1789 to 1795 were a series of shifting coalitions that pitted commercial against agrarian interests, representatives from the Atlantic seaboard against those from the frontier, Anglophiles against Francophiles. The greatest potential division, that of Northerners versus Southerners, inspired the greatest fears, and congressmen worked hard to achieve sectional compromise by agreeing to avoid the troublesome issue of slavery. Antislavery petitions submitted to Congress were dismissed by nearly unanimous votes, and a law for the apprehension of fugitive slaves by federal officers anywhere in the Union was approved by a large majority in 1793.

OVERVIEW

THE FIRST AMERICAN PARTY SYSTEM

Federalist Party	Organized by figures in the Washington administration who were in favor of a strong federal government, friendship with the British, and opposition to the French Revolution; its power base was among merchants, property owners, and urban workers tied to the commercial economy. A minority party after 1800, it was regionally strong only in New England.
Democratic Republican Party	Arose as the opposition to the Federalists; its adherents were in favor of limiting federal power, sympathetic to the French Revolution, and hostile to Great Britain; it drew strength from southern planters and northern farmers. The majority party after 1800.

These shifting coalitions first began to polarize into political factions during the debate over Jay's Treaty in 1795, when agrarians, Westerners, Southerners, and supporters of France came together in opposition to the treaty. In the House, Madison acted as a leader of this coalition when it met for the first time and attempted to implement a collective strategy. By the elections of 1796, people had begun to give names to the two factions. The supporters of Hamilton claimed the mantle of Federalism. "I am what the phraseology of politicians has denominated a FEDERALIST," declared one North Carolina candidate for office, "the friend of order, of government, and of the present administration." Forced to find another term, the Jeffersonian opposition used both Democrat (from the Democratic Societies) and Republican, a name carrying the implication that the Federalists were really monarchists at heart. "There are two parties at present in the United States," wrote a New York editor sympathetic to Jefferson, "aristocrats, endeavoring to lay the foundations of monarchical government, and Republicans, the real supports of independence, friends to equal rights, and warm advocates of free elective government." Hamilton insisted on labeling his opponents the Anti-Federalists, while others scorned them as anarchists, Jacobins, or sans-culottes—all labels from the French Revolution. Historians usually call the Jeffersonian coalition the Democratic Republicans.

These two political coalitions played a fitful role in the presidential election of 1796, which pitted John Adams, Washington's vice president, against Thomas Jefferson. Partisan organization was strongest in the Middle States, where there was a real contest of political forces, weakest in New England and the South, where sectional loyalty prevailed and organized opposition infrequent. When the ballots of the presidential electors, cast in their respective state capitals, were counted in the Senate, Adams was victorious. The authors of the Constitution, not anticipating this level of partisan competition, had provided that the runner-up—Jefferson in this case—would become vice president. Thus the new administration was born divided.

The Adams Presidency

Adams was put in the difficult situation of facing a political opposition led by his own vice president. He nevertheless attempted to conduct his presidency along the lines laid down by Washington, retaining most of the former president's appointees. This arrangement presented Adams with another problem. Although Hamilton had retired the year before, the cabinet remained committed to his advice, actively seeking his opinion and following it. As a result, Adams's authority was further undercut.

On the other hand, Adams benefited from the rising tensions between the United States and France. Angered by Jay's Treaty, the French suspended diplomatic relations at the end of 1796 and inaugurated a tough new policy toward American shipping. During the next two years they seized more than 300 American vessels and confiscated cargoes valued at an estimated $20 million. Hoping to resolve the crisis, Adams sent an American delegation to France. But in dispatches sent back to the United States the American envoys reported that agents of the French foreign ministry had demanded a bribe before any negotiations could be undertaken. Pressed for copies of these dispatches by suspicious Democratic Republicans in Congress, in 1798 Adams released them after substituting the letters X, Y, and Z for the names of the French agents. The documents proved a major liability for the Democratic Republicans, sparking powerful anti-French sentiment throughout the country. To the demand for a bribe, the American delegates had actually answered "Not a sixpence," but in the inflated rhetoric of the day the response became the infinitely more memorable: "Millions for defense, but not one cent for tribute!" The XYZ Affair, as it became known, sent Adams's popularity soaring.

Adams and the Federalists prepared the country for war during the spring of 1798. Congress authorized tripling the size of the army, and Washington came out of retirement to command the force. Fears of a French invasion declined after word arrived of the British naval victory over the French in August 1798 at Aboukir Bay in Egypt, but the "quasi-war" between France and the United States continued.

The Alien and Sedition Acts

In the summer of 1798 the Federalist majority in Congress, with the acquiescence of President Adams, passed four acts severely limiting both freedom of speech and the freedom of the press and threatening the liberty of foreigners in the United States. Embodying the fear that immigrants, in the words of one Massachusetts Federalist, "contaminate the purity and simplicity of the American character" by introducing dangerous democratic and republican ideas, the Naturalization Act extended the period of residence required for citizenship from five to fourteen years. The Alien Act and the Alien Enemies Act authorized the president to order the imprisonment or deportation of suspected aliens during wartime. Finally, the Sedition Act provided heavy fines and imprisonment for anyone convicted of writing, publishing, or speaking anything of "a false, scandalous and malicious" nature against the government or any of its officers.

The Federalists intended these repressive laws as weapons to defeat the Democratic Republicans. Led by Albert Gallatin, a Swiss immigrant and congressman from Pennsylvania (replacing Madison, who had retired from politics to devote his time to his plantation), the Democratic Republicans contested all the Federalist war measures and acted as a genuine opposition party, complete with caucuses, floor leaders, and partisan discipline.

For the first time, the two parties contested the election of Speaker of the House of Representatives, which became a partisan office. The more effective the Democratic Republicans became, the more treasonous they appeared in the eyes of the Federalists. On at least one occasion acrimonious debate in the House gave way to fisticuffs. Matthew Lyon, Democratic Republican of Vermont, spit in the eye of Connecticut Federalist Roger Griswold. Griswold responded by attacking Lyon with a cane, Lyon defended himself with a pair of fire tongs, and the two had to be pulled apart. With the Revolution still fresh in memory, Americans had only a weak understanding of the concept of a loyal opposition. Disagreement with the administration was misconstrued by the Federalists as opposition to the state itself.

The Federalists thus pursued the prosecution of dissent, indicting leading Democratic Republican newspaper editors and writers, fining and imprisoning at least twenty-five of them. The most vilified was Congressman Lyon, scorned by Federalists as "Ragged Matt the Democrat." Lyon was convicted in July 1798 of publishing libelous statements about President Adams and thrown into a Vermont prison. Later that year, however, he conducted a campaign from his cell and was reelected to Congress.

From Virginia, Madison wrote that the Sedition Act "ought to produce universal alarm, because it is levelled against the right of freely examining public characters and measures, and of free commu-

In this contemporary cartoon, Congressional Pugilists, Congress Hall in Philadelphia, February 15, 1798, Roger Griswold, a Connecticut Federalist, uses his cane to attack Matthew Lyon, Vermont Democratic Republican, who retaliates with fire tongs. During the first years of the American republic there was little understanding of the concept of a "loyal opposition," and disagreement with the policy of the Federalist administration was misconstrued as disloyalty.

nication among the people thereon, which has ever been deemed the only effectual guardian of every other right." He and Jefferson anonymously authored resolutions, passed by the Virginia and Kentucky legislatures, that declared the Constitution to be nothing more than a compact between the sovereign states and advocated the power of those states to "nullify" unconstitutional laws. When threatened with overbearing central authority, the Democratic Republicans argued, the states had the right to go their own way. The Virginia and Kentucky Resolves, as they were known, had grave implications for the future of the Union, for they stamped the notion of secession with the approval of two of the founding fathers. The resolutions would later be used to justify the secession of the southern states at the beginning of the Civil War.

The Revolution of 1800

The Alien and Sedition Acts were overthrown by the Democratic Republican victory in the national elections of 1800. As the term of President Adams drew to a close, Federalists found themselves seriously divided. In 1799, by releasing seized American ships and requesting negotiations, the French convinced Adams that they were ready to settle their dispute with the United States. The president also sensed the public mood running toward peace. But the Hamiltonian wing of the party, always scornful of public sentiment, continued to beat the drums of war. When Federalists in Congress tried to block the president's attempt to negotiate, Adams threatened to resign and turn the government over to Vice President Jefferson. In the Convention of 1800, the United States abandoned its demand of compensation for seized cargoes in exchange for French abrogation of its 1778 alliance with the American colonies. "The end of war is peace," Adams declared, "and peace was offered me." Adams considered the settlement of this conflict with France to be one of the greatest accomplishments of his career, but it earned him the scorn of conservative Federalists, including Hamilton.

The Federalists also divided over a domestic controversy. Under their leadership Congress had enacted a direct tax on houses, similar to the earlier tax on whiskey. In eastern Pennsylvania in 1799 several dozen farmers, displaying symbols of the French Revolution, routed the tax collectors and freed from jail a tax resister, one John Fries, who had been involved in the Whiskey Rebellion. Adams sent federal troops to restore order, and for leading Fries's Rebellion, a court issued death sentences for three men, including Fries. The president's cabinet demanded that Adams enforce "exemplary rigor" by

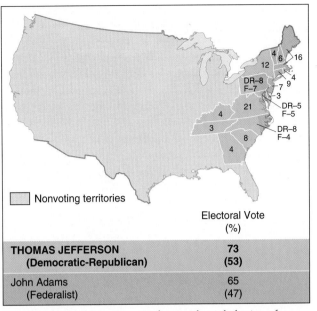

The Election of 1800   *In the presidential election of 1800, Democratic Republican victories in New York and the divided vote in Pennsylvania threw the election to Jefferson. The combination of the South and these crucial Middle States would keep the Democratic Republicans in control of the federal government for the next generation.*

	Electoral Vote	(%)
THOMAS JEFFERSON (Democratic-Republican)	**73**	**(53)**
John Adams (Federalist)	65	(47)

allowing the sentence to be carried out, but in 1800 Adams responded to popular pressure and pardoned the three. To the jeers of conservative Federalists, Adams now dumped the Hamiltonians from his cabinet. During the war scare with France, Washington had insisted that Hamilton be appointed as second in command of the enlarged army. "You crammed him down my throat!" Adams cried. Now he denounced Hamilton as "a bastard, and as much an alien as Gallatin." Hamilton responded by circulating a private letter in which he condemned Adams for his "disgusting egotism," "distempered jealousy," and "vanity without bounds." This letter fell into the hands of Aaron Burr, leader of the New York Democratic Republicans, and he published it, to the consternation of the Federalists.

The Federalists divided at precisely the time when unity was necessary to prevent the Democratic Republicans from consolidating their strengths. The defusing of the crisis with France also helped the Democratic Republicans, who could claim opposition to Federalist warmongering. They captured the state governments of Pennsylvania and New York in 1799, the first important inroads of the party in the North. These states had been taken over, cried a shocked Federalist, by "the most God-provoking Democrats on this side of Hell." From Virginia, Jefferson proclaimed his hope that "with Pennsylvania we can defy the universe!"

The presidential election of 1800 was the first to feature campaign advertising. "T. Jefferson, President of the United States of America," reads the streamer on this election banner, illustrated with an American eagle and a portrait of Jefferson; "John Adams—no more." This was mild rhetoric in a campaign characterized by wild charges. The Republicans labeled Adams a warmonger and a monarchist, while the Federalists denounced Jefferson as an atheist, Jacobin, and sexual libertine.

The presidential campaign of 1800 was the first in which Democratic Republicans and Federalists operated as two national political parties. Caucuses of congressmen nominated respective slates: Adams and Charles Cotesworth Pinckney of South Carolina for the Federalists, Jefferson and Aaron Burr of New York for the Republicans. Both tickets thus represented attempts at sectional balance. The Republicans presented themselves as the party of traditional agrarian purity, of liberty and states' rights, of "government rigorously frugal and simple," in the words of Jefferson. They were optimistic, convinced that they were riding the wave of the future. Divided and embittered, the Federalists waged a defensive struggle for strong central government and public order, and resorted frequently to negative campaigning. They denounced Jefferson as an atheist, a Jacobin, and the father of mulatto children—the first two charges were without foundation, the last apparently true, according to the results of DNA matching tests. One campaign placard put the issue succinctly: "GOD—AND A RELIGIOUS PRESIDENT" or "JEFFERSON—AND NO GOD!"

The balloting for presidential electors took place between October and December 1800. Adams took all the New England states while Jefferson captured the South and West. Jefferson called it "the Revolution of 1800." Party discipline was so effective that one of the provisions of the Constitution was shown to be badly outmoded. By this clause, the candidate receiving a majority of electoral votes became president and the runner-up became vice president. But by casting all their ballots for Jefferson and Burr, Democratic Republican electors unintentionally created a tie and forced the election into the House of Representatives. Because the new Democratic Republican-controlled Congress would not convene until March 1801, the Federalist majority was given a last chance to decide the election. They attempted to make a deal with Burr, who refused but who also would not withdraw his name from consideration. Finally, on the thirty-fifth ballot the Federalists gave up and arranged with their opponents to elect Jefferson without any of them having to cast a single vote in his favor. Congressman Lyon, "Ragged Matt the Democrat," cast the symbolic final vote in a gesture of sweet revenge. The Twelfth Amendment, creating separate ballots for president and vice-president, would be ratified in time for the next presidential election.

With the rise of partisan politics came a transformation in political participation. In 1789 state regulations limited the franchise to a small percentage of the adult population. Women, African Americans, and Indians could not vote, but neither could a third to a half of all free adult males, who were excluded by tax-paying or property-owning requirements. And even among the eligible the turnout was generally low. The traditional manner of voting was by voice: at the polling place in each community individuals announced their selections aloud to the clerk of elections, who wrote them down. Not surprisingly, this system allowed wealthy men, landlords, and employers of the community to pressure poorer voters.

These practices began to change with the increasing competition between Democratic Republicans and Federalists. Popular pressure resulted in the introduction of universal white manhood suffrage in four states by 1800 and the reduction of property requirements in others. These changes inaugurated a movement that would sweep the nation over the next quarter-century, and as a consequence, voter turnout increased in all the states. The growth of popular interest in politics was a transformation as important as the peaceful transition from Federalists to Democratic Republicans in national government.

"THE RISING GLORY OF AMERICA"

In 1771 Philip Freneau and Hugh Henry Brackenridge read an epic poem, "The Rising Glory of America," to their graduating class at Princeton. They admitted that American contributions to learning and the arts had thus far been slim, but they were boundlessly optimistic about the potential of their country. Indeed, judged against the literary and artistic work of individuals in the colonial period, artists and others of the Revolutionary generation accomplished a great deal in their effort to build a national culture.

Art and Architecture

The first American to achieve prominence in the artistic world of Europe was Benjamin West, who painted portraits in his native Pennsylvania before leaving for the Continent and England, where he became popular as a painter of historical scenes. His *Death of General Wolfe* (1770) (see p. 138) was one of the more acclaimed paintings of its day and the first to elevate an American scene to the high status of monumental historical painting. In 1774 West was joined in London by John Singleton Copley, a Boston portraitist who left America because of his loyalist sentiments. Copley's work is renowned for the truth and straightforwardness of his depictions, as in his famous portrait of Samuel Adams (1771) (see p. 144). Both West and Copley remained in England after the Revolution. Their most promising student was Gilbert Stuart, whose work in the fashionable style of the day included a portrait of Mohawk leader Joseph Brant (see p. 172). Stuart returned to the United States in 1792 to paint what became the most famous portrait of President Washington.

The preeminent painter of the Revolution was Charles Willson Peale, who studied for a time with West in London. He returned to America, however, and during the Revolution turned his talents to producing wartime propaganda. Although the almond eyes and bloated torsos of his figures suggest his technical limitations, Peale's work has a naive charm. His paintings of Washington, for example, seem more revealing of character than Stuart's placid portrait. Inspired by nationalist zeal, Peale planned a public gallery of

In this self-portrait, American artist Charles Willson Peale dramatically lifts the curtain on his Philadelphia Museum. Peale's three sons—whom he named after the artists Raphael, Rembrandt, and Titian—and two of his nieces—Anna and Sarah—also became noted painters, constituting something of a first family of American art in the early years of the new republic.

heroes in Philadelphia that eventually grew into a famous museum of curios, reflecting his interest in natural history, archaeology, and exotic cultures. Federalists joked that its chaotic arrangement of exhibits mirrored Peale's Jeffersonian politics. Part science, part circus, the collection was purchased after Peale's death by the pioneer American entertainer P. T. Barnum.

John Trumbull of Connecticut, who had predicted America's rise to his Yale classmates, served as a soldier during the Revolution, then went to London to study with West. There he painted *The Battle of Bunker's Hill* (1785), the first of a series of Revolutionary scenes (see p. 156), four of which he repainted in the Capitol rotunda in the early nineteenth century. Influenced by the grand style of eighteenth-century historical painting, Trumbull was concerned above all else with documentary detail in his scenes of the birth of America.

Nationalism was also evident in architecture. The greatest architectural project of the day was the new federal capital city, named for President Washington. In 1790, after Congress had agreed on the site, Washington retained Pierre Charles L'Enfant, a French engineer who had served as an officer during the Revolution, to lay out the city. The survey was conducted by Andrew Ellicott, assisted by the African American mathematician Benjamin Banneker. L'Enfant took full advantage of the lay of the land and the Potomac River, placing the Capitol building on a hill "which stands as a pedestal waiting for a monument." He linked public buildings such as the president's house and the Capitol with radial avenues, allowing for what he called "a reciprocity of sight." And he planned a grand mall from the Capitol to the river, along which there would be public museums, academies, and assembly halls. Development during the nineteenth century obscured L'Enfant's original design, but it was revived in 1901. Jefferson recommended "the models of antiquity" for the public buildings of the federal city, a suggestion carried out in William Thornton's original design for the Capitol.

George Town and Federal City, *or City of Washington, a colored aquatint of 1801 by T. Cartwright. When President John Adams first occupied the White House in 1800, Washington was still a small village, its streets merely muddy pathways.*

"Architecture is worth great attention," declared Jefferson, for "as we double our numbers every twenty years, we must double our houses. It is, then, among the most important arts; and it is desirable to introduce taste into an art which shows so much." In New England, architect Asher Benjamin popularized an American variant of the Georgian style, emphasizing economy of decoration and recommending the use of indigenous materials when writing handbooks such as *The Country Builder's Assistant* (1797). A great deal of the urban building undertaken in coastal cities during the shipping boom of the 1790s was characterized by this restrained classicism, which was known as the Federal style.

But the majority of Americans lived in small, bare, even squalid conditions. A nationwide tax on houses produced the first comprehensive survey of the nation's housing in 1798. There was tremendous variation in living conditions. The wealthiest 10 percent lived in dwellings estimated to be worth more than half the total value of all houses. By contrast, the value of housing owned by the wealthiest tenth of Americans today is only 30 percent of the total. Forty percent of American houses in 1798 were valued at $99 or less (the equivalent of about $1,000 today), and were little more than shacks. In the expanding cities, many residents lived along dingy back alleys and in damp basements. In the country, the typical house was a one-story structure of two or three rooms. As the population continued to grow, and Americans continued to move west, many more people would be found in log hovels like those in the community along Mingo Creek.

The Liberty of the Press

At the beginning of the Revolution in 1775 there were thirty-seven weekly or semiweekly newspapers in the thirteen colonies, only seven of which were Loyalist in sentiment. By 1789 the number of papers in the United States had grown to ninety-two, including eight dailies; three papers were being published west of the Appalachians. Relative to population, there were more newspapers in the United States than in any other country in the world—a reflection of the remarkably high literacy rate of the American people (see Chapter 5). In New England almost 90 percent of the population could read, and even on the frontier, where Brackenridge edited the *Pittsburgh Gazette*, about two-thirds of the males were literate.

During the political controversy of the 1790s, the press became the principal medium of Federalist and Democratic Republican opinion, and papers came to be identified by their politics. In 1789 John Fenno, aided by Alexander Hamilton, began publication of the *Federalist Gazette of the United States*, and in 1791 Jefferson encouraged Philip Freneau to

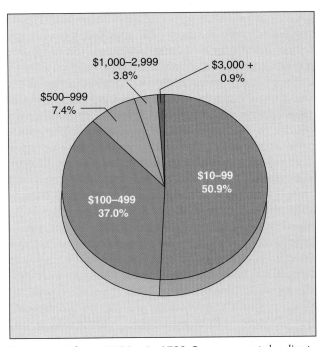

Housing Values, 1798   *In 1798 Congress enacted a direct tax on buildings, resulting in an inventory of American housing that has never been equaled. The data revealed an enormous gap between rich and poor. The majority lived in squalid cabins valued at $99 or less, while the wealthiest 10 percent of Americans lived in dwellings that, taken together, were worth just over half the total value of all the nation's houses.*

Source: Lee Soltow, "Egalitarian America and Its Inegalitarian Housing in the Federal Period," *Social Science History* 9 (1985): 199–213.

establish the competing *National Gazette*. The columns of these papers broadcast the feud between the two cabinet secretaries.

The prosecutions under the Sedition Act, however, threatened to curb the further development of the media, and in their opposition to these measures Democratic Republicans played an important role in establishing the principle of a free press. In *An Essay on Liberty of the Press* (1799), the Virginia lawyer George Hay, later appointed to the federal bench by President Jefferson, wrote that "a man may say everything which his passions suggest." Were this not true, he argued, the First Amendment would have been "the grossest absurdity that was ever conceived by the human mind." In his first Inaugural Address Jefferson echoed this early champion of the freedom of expression. "Error of opinion may be tolerated," he declared, "where reason is left free to combat it."

The Birth of American Literature

During the post-Revolutionary years there was an enormous outpouring of American publications. In the cities the number of bookstores grew in response to the demand for reading matter. Perhaps even more significant was the appearance in the countryside of numerous book peddlers who supplied farm households with Bibles, gazettes, almanacs, sermons, and political pamphlets. One such peddler was Mason Locke Weems, a man trained as a doctor and ordained an Anglican minister, who gave up these careers in the early 1790s for book selling. Parson Weems, as he was known, wrote that he found his southern backcountry customers "uninformed, their minds bitter, and their manners savage," but that they cried out for "books, books, books!"

The literature of the Revolution understandably reflected the dominating political concerns of the times. Mercy Otis Warren and Hugh Henry Brackenridge wrote propagandistic dramas, and the poet Joel Barlow composed a nationalist epic, *The Vision of Columbus* (1787). *M'Fingal* (1782), a mock epic satirizing the British, was written by John Trumbull (a cousin of the painter), a leader of the literary group known as the Connecticut Wits. It sold copies enough to be considered the best-selling fictional work of the war. But the majority of "best-sellers" during the Revolutionary era were political. The most important were Thomas Paine's *Common Sense* (1776) and his series of stirring pamphlets, published under the running title *The American Crisis* (1776–83), the first of which began with the memorable phrase, "These are the times that try men's souls."

In the cause of reform, Paine later returned to England and published *The Rights of Man* (1791), a defense of the French Revolution. Banished from Britain for this expression of radical politics, he went to France, jumped into politics, and, in one of the periodic political turns of the revolution, found himself imprisoned for a time. From his jail cell Paine wrote *The Age of Reason* (1795), a powerful attack on organized religion that became one of the most popular American books of its day, loved by Jeffersonians and loathed by Federalists. Book-selling Parson Weems, for example, made a steady profit from the sale of Paine's work, though he offered pious sermons and religious tracts to placate those objecting to Paine's politics.

Some of the most interesting American books of the postwar years examined the developing American character. The French immigrant Michel-Guillaume Jean de Crèvecoeur, in *Letters from an American Farmer* (1782), proposed that the American, a product of many cultures, was a "new man" with ideas new to the world. John Filson, the author of the *Discovery, Settlement, and Present State of Kentucke* (1784), presented the narrative of one such new man, the Kentucky pioneer Daniel Boone. In doing so he took an important step toward the creation of that most American of literary genres, the western. In a satirical novel entitled *Modern Chivalry* (1792), featuring incidents from the Whiskey Rebellion, Pittsburgh editor Brackenridge dipped his pen "in the inkstand of human nature" and produced one of the first dialect portraits of "dat son o'd a whore," the American frontiersman. Brackenridge wrote with an appreciation for his crude characters but expressed frustration that the Revolution had failed to elevate the culture of ordinary people. By shunning simple celebration, however, he was one of the first to take a critical look at the American character.

The single best-selling book of the Revolutionary era

Pages from Noah Webster's famous American Spelling Book, *the largest seller of all American books during the nineteenth century. Believing that "the King's English" reflected aristocratic standards, Webster argued for spelling reform to create "the American language."*

was Noah Webster's *American Spelling Book* (1783), the famous "Blue-Backed Speller," which soon after its publication was selling 200,000 copies annually. It became the largest-selling of all American books, a good indicator of the remarkable literacy of the American people. With it, Webster launched a life-long campaign for a distinctive American form of English, which culminated in his *American Dictionary of the English Language* (1828). In a belief that "the King's English" reflected aristocratic standards, Webster argued for a time that "the American language" must be guided by "republican principles," for example, spelling words as they sounded. "Ther iz no alternativ," he wrote. Eventually he abandoned the most radical of his suggestions, although many of his reforms stuck, dropping the "u" from the English spelling of "colour," for example, in favor of "color." The speller was the first in a graded series of textbooks that included a grammar and a reader designed to "diffuse the principles of virtue and patriotism." These texts included standard selections from not only British but also American writers. Webster compiled a list of important dates beginning with Columbus's voyage and ending with the British surrender at Yorktown—the first attempt at a distinctively American historical chronology.

Other writers produced more formal histories. Not surprisingly, Democratic Republican authors stressed the tradition of resistance to authority, whereas Federalists emphasized the importance, particularly during wartime, of central direction and unity. Fearing criticism by Federalist writers, Democratic Republican Mercy Otis Warren delayed publishing her *History of the Rise, Progress, and Termination of the American Revolution* (1805) until after Jefferson's victory in 1800.

Parson Weems found readers fascinated by the historical heroes of the Revolution, so he drew up plans for a series of "quarter of dollar books on subjects calculated to strike the popular curiosity, printed in very large numbers and properly distributed." When Washington died in December 1799, Weems was already at work on a short biography of the first president. "Washington, you know, is gone!" he wrote to his publisher. "Millions are gaping to read something about him. I am very nearly primed and cocked for 'em." His *Life of Washington* (1800, enlarged edition 1806), became the most popular history of the Revolution and introduced a series of popular and completely fabricated anecdotes, including the story of young Washington and the cherry tree. The book was a pioneering effort in mass culture, and Weems, as one historian puts it, was "the father of the Father of his Country."

Condemned by serious writers and scholars, even at the time of its publication, Weems's biography

In this 1792 cartoon from the Lady's Magazine, the allegorical figure of "Columbia" receives a petition for the "Rights of Woman." In the aftermath of the Revolution, Americans debated the issue of an expanded role for women in the new republic. Many Federalists condemned "women of masculine minds," but there was general agreement among both conservatives and democrats that the time had come for better education for American women.

was loved by ordinary Americans of all political persuasions. In the mid-nineteenth century, Abraham Lincoln recalled that he had read Weems "away back in my childhood, the earliest days of my being able to read," and had been profoundly impressed by "the struggles for the liberties of the country." In praise of Washington, Weems wrote, "all parties join with equal alacrity and earnestness." Although Washington had in fact become a partisan leader of the Federalists during his second term, Weems presented him as a unifying figure for the political culture of the new nation, and this was the way he would be remembered. Jefferson echoed these sentiments in his Inaugural Address in 1801, when as a gesture of conciliation to his opponents he

CHRONOLOGY

1786	Annapolis Convention
1787	Constitutional Convention
1787–88	*The Federalist* published
1788	Constitution ratified
	First federal elections
1789	President George Washington inaugurated in New York City
	Judiciary Act
	French Revolution begins
1790	Agreement on site on the Potomac River for the nation's capital
	Indian Intercourse Act
	Judith Sargent Murray publishes "On the Equality of the Sexes"
1791	Bill of Rights ratified
	Bank of the United States chartered
	Alexander Hamilton's "Report on Manufactures"
	Ohio Indians defeat General Arthur St. Clair's army
1793	England and France at war; America reaps trade windfall
	Citizen Genêt affair
	President Washington proclaims American neutrality in Europe

	British confiscate American vessels
	Supreme Court asserts itself as final authority in *Chisholm v. Georgia*
1794	Whiskey Rebellion
	Battle of Fallen Timbers
	Jay's Treaty with the British concluded
1795	Pinckney's Treaty negotiated with the Spanish
	Treaty of Greenville
	Thomas Paine publishes The Age of Reason
1796	President Washington's Farewell Address
	John Adams elected president
1797–98	French seize American ships
1798	XYZ Affair
	"Quasi-war" with France
	Alien and Sedition Acts
	Kentucky and Virginia Resolves
1799	Fries's Rebellion
1800	Convention of 1800
	Thomas Jefferson elected president
	Mason Locke Weems publishes *Life of Washington*

declared, "We have called by different names brethren of the same principle. We are all Republicans, we are all Federalists."

Women on the Intellectual Scene

One of the most interesting literary trends of the 1790s was the growing demand for books that appealed to women readers. Susanna Haswell Rowson's *Charlotte Temple* (1791), a tale of seduction and abandonment, ran up tremendous sales and remained in print for more than a century. Other romantic works of fiction included *The Power of Sympathy* (1789) by William Hill Brown, sometimes called the first American novel; the gothic novels of Charles Brockden Brown, such as *Arthur Mervyn* (1799); and *The Coquette* (1797) by Hannah Webster Foster. The young republic thus marked the first dramatic appearance of women writers and women readers. Although

women's literacy rates continued to be lower than men's, they rose steadily as girls joined boys in common schools. This increase was one of the most important social legacies of the democratic struggles of the Revolutionary era.

Some writers argued that the new republican order ought to provide new roles for women as well as for men. The first avowed feminist in American history was Judith Sargent Murray, who publicly stated her belief that women "should be taught to depend on their own efforts, for the procurement of an establishment in life." She was greatly influenced by the English feminist Mary Wollstonecraft, but developed her line of thinking independently, as demonstrated by her essay "On the Equality of the Sexes," written in 1779 and finally published in 1790 in a Massachusetts magazine. "I expect to see our young women forming a new era in female history," Murray predicted. Federalists listened to such opinions with horror. "Women of masculine minds," one Boston minister sneered, "have generally masculine manners."

There seemed to be general agreement among all parties, however, that the time had come for better-educated and better-informed women. Republican institutions of self-government were widely thought to depend on the wisdom and self-discipline of the American people. Civic virtue, so indispensable for the republic, must be taught at home. The share that every male citizen had in the government of the country, Benjamin Rush said in 1787, required that women have "suitable education, to concur in instructing their sons in the principles of liberty and government." By placing her learning at the service of her family, the "republican mother" was spared the criticism leveled at independent-minded women such as Murray. "A woman will have more commendation in being the mother of heroes," said a Federalist, "than in setting up, Amazon-like, for a heroine herself." Thus were women provided the opportunity to be not simply "helpmates," but people "learned and wise." But they were also expected to be content with a narrow role, not to wish for fuller participation in American democracy.

CONCLUSION

In 1800, the population of Canada numbered about 500,000. Those of European background in New Mexico and the other Spanish North American colonies numbered approximately 25,000. And the Indian people of the continent numbered anywhere from 500,000 to a million. Overwhelming all these groups was the population of the United States, which stood at 5.3 million and was growing at the astounding annual rate of 3 percent. During the last years of the eighteenth century the United States had adopted a new constitution and established a new national government. It had largely repaid the debt run up during the Revolution and made peace with adversaries abroad and Indian peoples at home. Americans had begun to learn how to channel their disagreements into political struggle. The nation had withstood a first decade of stress, but tensions continued to divide the people. As some of the rebel supporters had promised at the beginning of the Whiskey Rebellion, "their liberty they will maintain, / they fought for't, and they'll fight again." At the beginning of the new century it remained uncertain whether the new nation would find a way to control and channel the energies of an expanding people.

REVIEW QUESTIONS

1. Discuss the conflicting ideals of local and national authority in the debate over the Constitution.
2. What were the major crises faced by the Washington and Adams administrations?
3. Describe the roles of Madison and Hamilton in the formation of the first American political parties.
4. What did Jefferson mean when he talked of "the Revolution of 1800"?
5. Discuss the contributions of the Revolutionary generation to the construction of a national culture.

RECOMMENDED READING

William N. Chambers, *Political Parties in a New Nation: The American Experience, 1776–1809* (1963). An introduction to the formation of the American party system. Though several decades old, it remains essential.

Stanley Elkins and Eric McKitrick, *The Age of Federalism* (1993). A massive and informative account of the politics of the 1790s, from the ratification of the Constitution to the election of Jefferson.

Joseph J. Ellis, *After the Revolution: Profiles of Early American Culture* (1979). A series of portraits of the more important cultural innovators in the young republic.

Reginald Horsman, *The Frontier in the Formative Years, 1783–1815* (1970). A sensitive survey of developments in the West, emphasizing that the "western question" was one of the most important facing the young republic.

Jackson Turner Main, *The Antifederalists: Critics of the Constitution, 1781–1788* (1961). A detailed examination of the localist tradition in early American politics. Includes a discussion of the ratification of the Constitution from the point of view of its opponents.

Willard Sterne Randall, *George Washington: A Life* (1997). The best one-volume biography of "the Father of his Country."

Thomas P. Slaughter, *The Whiskey Rebellion: Frontier Epilogue to the American Revolution* (1986). A detailed history of the rebellion in western Pennsylvania during the 1790s. Includes a thorough examination of the politics and culture of both the backcountry and the federal government at a moment of crisis.

James M. Smith, *Freedom's Fetters: The Alien and Sedition Laws and American Civil Liberties* (1966). Remains the best overview of the Federalist threat to liberty, as well as the Democratic Republican counterattack.

Gerald Stourzh, *Alexander Hamilton and the Idea of Republican Government* (1970). A solid biography of the ultimate Federalist man and his politics.

Gordon Wood, *The Creation of the American Republic, 1776–1787* (1969). This general survey provides the best overview of the Constitutional Convention.

ADDITIONAL BIBLIOGRAPHY

Forming a New Government

Douglass Adair, *Fame and the Founding Fathers*, ed. Trevor Colbourn (1974)

John K. Alexander, *The Selling of the Constitutional Convention: A History of News Coverage* (1990)

Charles A. Beard, *An Economic Interpretation of the Constitution of the United States* (1913)

Max Farrand, ed., *Records of the Federal Convention of 1787*, 4 vols. (1911–37)

Suzette Henberger, *Creatures of the Constitution: The Federalist Constitution and the Shaping of American Politics* (1994)

John P. Kaminski and Gaspare J. Saladino, eds., *The Documentary History of the Ratification of the Constitution* (1982)

Forrest McDonald, *Novus Ordo Seclorum: The Intellectual Origins of the Constitution* (1985)

Richard B. Morris, *Witnesses at the Creation: Hamilton, Madison, Jay and the Constitution* (1985)

Peter Onuf, *Origins of the Federal Republic* (1983)

Josephine F. Pacheco, ed., *Antifederalism: The Legacy of George Mason* (1992)

Herbert J. Storing, ed., *The Complete Anti-Federalist*, 7 vols. (1981)

Garry Wills, *Explaining America: The Federalist* (1981)

The New Nation

Harry Ammon, *The Genêt Mission* (1973)

Steven R. Boyd, ed., *The Whiskey Rebellion: Past and Present Perspectives* (1985)

Collin G. Calloway, *Crown and Calumet: British-Indian Relations, 1783–1815* (1987)

Gerald A. Combs, *The Jay Treaty: Political Battleground of the Founding Fathers* (1970)

Alexander De Conde, *Entangling Alliance: Politics and Diplomacy under George Washington* (1956)

Ralph Ketcham, *Presidents above Party: The First American Presidency, 1789–1829* (1984)

Charles R. Ritcheson, *Aftermath of Revolution: British Policy toward the United States, 1783–1795* (1969)

Wiley Sword, *President Washington's Indian War: The Struggle for the Old Northwest, 1790–1795* (1985)

J. Leitch Wright, *Britain and the American Frontier, 1783–1815* (1975)

Federalists and Republicans

Joyce Appleby, *Capitalism and a New Social Order: The Republican Vision of the 1790s* (1984)

Albert H. Bowman, *The Struggle for Neutrality: Franco-American Diplomacy during the Federalist Era* (1974)

Ralph Adams Brown, *The Presidency of John Adams* (1975)

Richard Buel Jr., *Securing the Revolution: Ideology in American Politics, 1789–1815* (1972)

Nobel E. Cunningham Jr., *The Jeffersonian Republicans: The Formation of Party Organization, 1789–1801* (1957)

Alexander De Conde, *The Quasi-War: Politics and Diplomacy of the Undeclared War with France, 1797–1801* (1966)

Drew McCoy, *The Elusive Republic: Political Economy in Jeffersonian America* (1980)

Andrew W. Robertson, *The Language of Democracy: Political Rhetoric in the United States and Britain, 1790–1900* (1995)

James Roger Sharp, *American Politics in the Early Republic: The New Nation in Crisis* (1993)

Alfred F. Young, *The Democratic Republicans of New York: The Origins, 1763–1797* (1967)

"The Rising Glory of America"

R. A. Burchell, ed., *The End of Anglo-America: Historical Essays in the Study of Cultural Divergence* (1991)

Emory Elliott, *Revolutionary Writers: Literature and Authority in the New Republic* (1982)

Michael Kammen, *A Season of Youth: The American Revolution and the Historical Imagination* (1978)

Linda Kerber, *Women of the Republic: Intellect and Ideology in Revolutionary America* (1980)

Kenneth Silverman, *A Cultural History of the American Revolution* (1976)

Biography

Robert C. Alberts, *Benjamin West: A Biography* (1978)

John R. Alden, *George Washington: A Biography* (1984)

Gay Wilson Allen, *St. John de Crèvecoeur: The Life of an American Farmer* (1987)

Aleine Austin, *Matthew Lyon, "New Man" of the Democratic Revolution, 1749–1822* (1981)

Lance Banning, *The Sacred Fire of Liberty: James Madison and the Founding of the Federal Republic* (1995)

Harvey Lewis Carter, *The Life and Times of Little Turtle: First Sagamore of the Wabash* (1987)

Jacob Ernest Cooke, *Alexander Hamilton* (1982)

Helen A. Cooper, *John Trumbull: The Hand and Spirit of a Painter* (1982)

Herbert Alan Johnson, *John Jay, Colonial Lawyer* (1989)

Dumas Malone, *Jefferson and His Time*, 6 vols. (1948–81)

Jules David Prown, *John Singleton Copley* (1966)

Edgar P. Richardson et al., *Charles Willson Peale and His World* (1983)

K. Alan Synder, *Defining Noah Webster: Mind and Morals in the Early Republic* (1990)

Mason Locke Weems, *The Life of Washington*, ed. Marcus Cunliffe (1962)

Immigration contributed to the growth of the population of the colonies that became the United States of America more than any other factor. Seventeenth-century migration to these colonies was mostly from England, although small but important groups of Dutch, Swedes, and French settled areas of New York, New Jersey, and Maryland.

By 1700 the population of British colonial North America had reached 250,000. The high levels of fertility characteristic of all the colonial societies of North America—British, Spanish, and French—contributed to the growth of population. But only the British encouraged immigration. The French and the Spanish adopted highly restrictive immigration policies. Dedicated to keeping its colonies exclusively Catholic, France turned down the requests of thousands of Protestant Huguenots who desperately sought to emigrate to Canada. The Spanish, fearful of depleting their population at home, severely limited the migration of their own subjects to their colonies and absolutely forbade the immigration of foreigners, with the exception of African slaves.

Yet a veritable flood of immigrants came to British North America during the eighteenth century. Scots, Scots-Irish, Germans, and French joined the English in the trans-Atlantic crossing. Slave traders also brought tens of thousands of Africans to the southern colonies. (For a full discussion of African migration, see Chapter Four.) By 1750 European and African migrants and their descendents outnumbered the Indian population of the continent, and by 1800 had grown to more than 5.3 million, an increase of more than twenty times the population in 1700 over the course of one hundred years.

William Penn was the first British colonial official to encourage the immigration of non-British western Europeans, in the 1680s sending agents to recruit settlers in Holland, France, and the German principalities along the Rhine River. His experiment proved so successful that the leaders of other British colonies soon were employing recruiting agents of their own in Europe. Further encouraging this development, most of the British colonies enacted liberal naturalization laws in the early eighteenth century, allowing immigrants who professed Protestantism and swore allegiance to the British crown to become free "denizens" with all the freedoms and privileges of natural-born subjects. In

1740 Parliament passed a general Naturalization Act that extended these policies to all the colonies. The new legislation continued to prohibit the naturalization of Catholic and Jewish immigrants, however, and these groups remained tiny minorities in the British colonies.

Still, immigration to what would become the United States was characterized by extraordinary ethnic diversity. The two largest migrating groups were the English and the Africans, each totaling, according to good historical estimates, perhaps 400,000 to 500,000 immigrants during the colonial period. There was also substantial emigration from the northern British Isles. Squeezed by economic hardship, an estimated 250,000 Highland Scots and Protestant Irish from the Ulster region (known in America as the "Scots-Irish") emigrated to North America during the eighteenth century. The Germans were another significant group; at least 100,000 of them settled in the British colonies, where they became known as the "Dutch" (from *Deutsch*, the German-language term for German). It should be noted that from half to two-thirds of Europeans came to British North America as indentured servants, or "redemptioners," or else convicts transported to the New World to serve out their sentences laboring on plantations. The Africans were not the only people to come involuntarily to America. A majority of immigrants during the colonial period came in a state of bondage.

The first federal census, conducted in 1790, provides a snapshot of the consequences of eighteenth-century immigration. Forty-nine percent of the population of the thirteen United States was English in origin, and nearly 20 percent was African; 15 percent were Irish or Scots, 7 percent German, 3 percent Dutch, and 2 percent French.

Many of the founders of the American republic worried that the different languages and traditions of these diverse peoples would fracture the nation. In the 1750s, for example, Benjamin Franklin wrote of his fears that German immigrants would not assimilate to English ways. "Why should Pennsylvania," he asked, "founded by English, become a colony of *aliens* who will shortly be so numerous as to Germanize *us* instead of Anglifying them?" Thomas Jefferson worried that immigrants from monarchical countries, untutored in the ways of democracy, would "warp and bias" the direction of American political development. Reflecting such fears, the nation's first Naturalization Act,

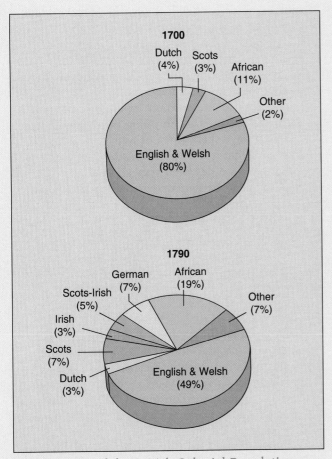

The Ancestry of the British Colonial Population
The legacy of eighteenth-century immigration to the British colonies was a population of unprecedented ethnic diversity.

Source: Thomas L. Purvis, "The European Ancestry of the United States Population," *William and Mary Quarterly* 61 (1984): 85–101.

passed in 1790, required a residency period of five years (a kind of probation period) before immigrants could apply for citizenship, and limited applications to "free white persons." In the nineteenth and early twentieth centuries this clause would be used to bar the naturalization of immigrants from Africa and Asia.

■ IN THEIR OWN WORDS

William Penn was the first colonial leader to actively seek out prospective immigrants for his colony. In 1681 he wrote a promotional account of Pennsylvania that was translated into several European languages and widely circulated.

> The place [Pennsylvania] lies 600 miles nearer the sun than England, for...[it] begins at about the latitude of Naples in Italy, or Montpellier in France. I shall say little in its praise, to excite desires in any, whatever I could truly write as to the soil, air and water. This shall satisfy me, that

by the blessing of God, and the honesty and industry of man, it may be a good fruitful land....

> What persons will be fit to go? 1st. Industrious husbandmen and day-labourers, that are hardly able (with extreme labour) to maintain their families and portion [endow] their children.

> 2dly. Laborious handicrafts, especially carpenters, masons, smiths, weavers, tailors, tanners, shoemakers, shipwrights, etc., where they may be spared or are low in the world. And as they shall want no encouragement, so their labour is worth more there than here, and their provision cheaper.

> 3dly. A plantation [colony] seems a fit place for those ingenious spirits that being low in the world, are much clogged and oppressed about a livelihood, for the means of subsisting being easy there, they may have time and opportunity to gratify their inclinations, and thereby improve science and help nurseries of people.

> 4thly. A fourth sort of men for whom a plantation would be proper, takes in those that are younger brothers of small inheritances; yet because they would live in sight of their kindred in some proportion to their quality, and can't do it without a labour that looks like farming, their condition is too straight for them; and if married, their children are often too numerous for the estate, and are frequently bred up to no trades, but are a kind of hangers-on or retainers to the elder brother's table and charity....

> Lastly, there are another sort of persons, not only fit for, but necessary in plantations, and that is men of universal spirits, that have an eye to the good of posterity, and that both understand among a plain and well-intending people. Such persons may find room in colonies for their good counsel and contrivance, who are shut out from being of much use or service to great nations under settled customs. These men deserve much esteem, and would be hearkened to...[1]

Judith Giton (ca. 1665–1711) was twenty years old when she and many other Protestant Huguenots escaped French persecution to settle in South Carolina in 1685. In the following letter to her brother, written from America, she described the harrowing experience of immigration.

> For eight months we had suffered from the contributions and the quartering of the soldiers, on account of religion, enduring many inconveniences. We therefore resolved on quitting France at night, leaving the soldiers in their beds, and abandoning the house with its furniture....We passed into Holland, in order to go to England.

Ethnic Groups in Eighteenth-Century British North America *The first federal census, taken in 1790, revealed remarkable ethnic diversity. New England was filled with people from the British Isles, but the rest of the colonies were a patchwork. Most states had at least three different ethnic groups within their borders, and although the English and Scots-Irish were heavily represented in all colonies, in some they had strong competition from Germans (eastern and southern Pennsylvania) and from African peoples (Virginia and South Carolina).*

We were detained in London for three months, waiting for a vessel ready to sail for Carolina. Once embarked, we were miserably off indeed. The scarlet fever broke out in our ship, and many died, among them our aged mother....Our vessel put in [at Bermuda] for repairs, having been badly injured in a severe storm. Our captain...was thrown into prison, and the ship was seized. It was with the greatest difficulty that we secured our passage in another ship, for our money had all been spent. After our arrival in Carolina, we suffered all sorts of evils. Our eldest brother died of a fever, eighteen months after coming here....We ourselves have been exposed, since leaving France, to all kinds of afflictions, in the forms of sickness, pestilence, famine, poverty, and the roughest labor. I have been for six months at a time in this country without tasting bread, laboring meanwhile like a slave in tilling the ground. Indeed, I have spent three or four years without knowing what it was to eat bread whenever I wanted it. God has been very good to us in enabling us to bear up under trials for every kind.[2]

Robert Parke was a Presbyterian Scot who immigrated with his family from Ireland to Pennsylvania in the early 1720s. Letters home, like this one of Parke's, were an important means of advertising the advantages of American immigration.

Chester Township, the 10th Month 1725
Dear Sister Mary Valentine:
We have not had a day's sickness in the family since we came in to the country, blessed be God for it. My father in particular has not had his health better these ten years than since he came here, his ancient age considered. You write in your letter that there was a talk went back to Ireland that we were not satisfied in coming here, which was utterly false...for there is not one of the family but what likes the country very well and would if we were in Ireland again come here directly it being the best country for working folk and tradesmen of any in the world. But for drunkards and Idlers, they cannot live well anywhere. It is likewise an Extraordinarily healthy country....

Land is of all prices even from ten pounds, to one hundred pounds a hundred, according to the goodness or else the situation thereof, and grows more dear every year by reason of vast quantities of people that come here yearly from several parts of the world, therefore, you and your family or any that I wish well I would desire to make what speed you can to come here the sooner the better....[3]

Gottlieb Mittelberger came to Pennsylvania from Germany in 1750 and served as a schoolmaster and organist in Philadelphia for three years. In this famous account, written after his return to Europe, he paints a horrid picture of the voyage to America, the conditions for indentured servants, and warns his countrymen to remain content at home.

Both in Rotterdam and in Amsterdam the people are packed densely, like herrings so to say, in the large sea vessels. One person receives a place of scarcely 2 feet width and 6 feet length in the bedstead, while many a ship carries four to six hundred souls; not to mention the innumerable implements, tools, provisions, water-barrels and other things which likewise occupy much space.

On account of contrary winds it takes the ships sometimes 2, 3, and 4 weeks to make the trip from Holland to Kaupp [Cowes] in England....When the ships have for the last time weighed their anchors near...Kaupp...., the real misery begins with the long voyage. For from there the ships, unless they have good wind, must often sail 8, 9, 10, to 12 weeks before they reach Philadelphia. But even with the best wind the voyage lasts 7 weeks.

But during the voyage there is on board these ships terrible misery, stanch, fumes, horror, vomiting, many kinds of seasickness, fever, dysentery, headache, heat, constipation, boils, scurvy, cancer, mouth-rot, and the like, all of which come from old and sharply salted food and meat, also from the very bad and foul water, so that many die miserably.

Add to this want of provisions, hunger, thirst, frost, heat, dampness, anxiety, want, afflictions and lamentations, together with other trouble, as c.v. the lice abound so frightfully, especially on sick people, that they can be scraped off the body. The misery reaches the climax when a gale rages for 2 or 3 nights and days, so that every one believes that the ship will go to the bottom with all human beings on board. In such a visitation the people cry and pray most piteously....

When the ships have landed at Philadelphia after their long voyage, no one is permitted to leave them except those who pay for their passage or can give good security; the others, who cannot pay, must remain on board the ships till they are purchased, and are released from the ships by their purchasers. The sick always fare the worst, for the healthy are naturally preferred and purchased first; and so the sick and wretched must often remain on board in front of the city for 2 or 3 weeks, and frequently die, whereas many a one, if he could pay his debt and were permitted to leave the ship immediately, might recover and remain alive....

The sale of human beings in the market on board the ship is carried on thus: Every day Englishmen, Dutchmen, and High-German people come from the city of Philadelphia and other places, in part from a great distance, say 20, 30, or 40 hours away, and go on board the newly arrived ship that has brought and offers for sale passengers from Europe, and select among the healthy persons such as they deem suitable for their business, and bargain with them how long they will serve for their passage money, which most of them are still in debt for. When they have come to an agreement, it happens that adult persons bind themselves in writing to serve 3, 4, 5 or 6 years for the amount due by them, according to their age and strength. But very young people, from 10 to 15 years, must serve till they are 21 years old.

One of Philadelphia's many wharves, featured in a hand-colored engraving of 1800. Attracted by the abundant and fertile farmland of the Pennsylvania countryside, more European immigrants passed through Philadelphia than any other North American port of the eighteenth century.

A master potter working with his indentured apprentices, from The Book of Trades, *a survey of eighteenth-century American crafts. Of all the Europeans who immigrated to British North America in the eighteenth century, half to two-thirds came as indentured servants*

Many parents must sell and trade away their children like so many head of cattle; for if their children take the debt upon themselves, the parents can leave the ship free and unrestrained; but as the parents often do not know where and to what people their children are going, it often happens that such parents and children, after leaving the ship, do not see each other again for many years, perhaps no more in all their lives....

It often happens that whole families, husband, wife, and children, are separated by being sold to different purchasers, especially when they have not paid any part of their passage money. When a husband or wife has died at sea, when the ship has made more than half of her trip, the survivor must pay or serve not only for himself or herself, but also for the deceased. When both parents have died over half-way at sea, their children, especially when they are young and have nothing to pawn or to pay, must stand for their own and their parents' passage, and serve till they are 21 years old. When one has served his or her term, he or she is entitled to a new suit of clothes at parting; and if it has been so stipulated, a man gets in addition a horse, a woman, a cow....

However hard he may be compelled to work in his fatherland, he will surely find it quite as hard, if not harder, in the new country. Besides, there is not only the long and arduous journey lasting half a year, during which he has to suffer, more than with the hardest work; he has also spent about 200 florins which no one will refund to him. If he has so much money, it will slip out of his hands; if he has it not, he must work his debt off as a slave and poor serf. Therefore let every one stay in his own country and support himself and his family honestly. Besides I say that those who suffer themselves to be persuaded and enticed away by the man-thieves, are very foolish if they believe that roasted pigeons will fly into the mouths in America or Pennsylvania without their working for them.[4]

Thomas Jefferson had doubts concerning the effect of mass immigration on American institutions. These comments come from his extended essay, *Notes on the State of Virginia*, published in 1784.

The present desire of America is to produce rapid population by as great importations of foreigners as possible. But is this founded in good policy?...Are there no inconveniences to be thrown into the scale against the advantage expected from a multiplication of numbers by the importation of foreigners? It is for the happiness of those united in society to harmonize as much as possible in matters which they must of necessity transact together. Civil government being the sole object of forming societies, its administration must be conducted by common consent. Every species of government has its specific principles. Ours perhaps are more peculiar than those of any other in the universe. It is a composition of the freest principles of the English constitution, with others derived from natural right and natural reason. To these nothing can be more opposed than the maxims of absolute monarchies. Yet, from such, we are to expect the greatest number of emigrants. They will bring with them the principles of the governments they leave, imbibed in their early youth; or, if able to throw them off, it will be in exchange for an unbounded licentiousness, passing, as is usual, from one extreme to another. It would be a miracle were they to stop precisely at the point of temperate liberty. These principles, with their language, they will transmit to their children. In proportion to their numbers, they will share with us the legislation. They will infuse into it their spirit, warp and bias its direction, and render it a heterogeneous, incoherent, distracted mass....

Suppose 20 millions of republican Americans thrown all of a sudden into France, what would be the condition of that kingdom? If it would be more turbulent, less happy, less strong, we may believe that the addition of half a million of foreigners to our present numbers would produce a similar effect here. If they come of themselves, they are entitled to all the rights of citizenship: but I doubt the expediency of inviting them by extraordinary encouragements.[5]

In contrast to Jefferson, the French immigrant J. Hector St. Jean de Crèvecoeur celebrated the American cultural blending that resulted from immigration. In his famous *Letters of an American Farmer* (1782), Crèvecoeur was the first to discuss the process by which immigrants were "melted" into a new kind of person, the American.

Whence came all these people? They are a mixture of English, Scotch, Irish, French, Dutch, Germans, and Swedes. From this promiscuous breed, that race, now called Americans, have arisen....

What then is the American, this new man? He is either an European, or the descendant of an European; hence that strange mixture of blood, which you will find in no other country. I could point out to you a man, whose grandfather was an Englishman, whose wife was Dutch, whose son married a French woman, and whose present four sons have now four wives of different nations. *He* is an American, who, leaving behind him all his ancient prejudices and manners, receives new ones from the new mode of life he has embraced, the new government he obeys, and the new rank he holds. He becomes an American by being received in the broad lap of our great Alma Mater.

Here individuals of all nations are melted into a new race of men, whose labours and posterity will one day cause great change in the world. Americans are the western pilgrims, who are carrying along with them that great mass of arts, sciences, vigour, and industry, which began long since in the east; they will finish the great circle. The Americans were once scattered all over Europe; here they are incorporated into one of the finest systems of population which has ever appeared, and which will hereafter become distinct by the power of the different climates they inhabit. The American ought, therefore, to love this country much better than that wherein either he or his forefathers were born. Here the rewards of his industry follow with equal steps the progress of his labour; his labour is founded on the basis of nature, *self-interest;* can it want a stronger allurement? Wives and children, who before in vain demanded of him a morsel of bread, now, fat and frolicsome, gladly help their father to clear those fields whence exuberant crops are to arise to feed and to clothe them all; without any part being claimed either by a despotic prince, a rich abbot, or a mighty lord. Here religion demands but little of him; a small voluntary salary to the minister, and gratitude to God; can he refuse these? The American is a new man, who acts upon new principles; he must therefore entertain new ideas, and form new opinions. From involuntary idleness, servile dependence, penury, and useless labour, he has passed to toils of a very different nature, rewarded by ample subsistence. This is an American.[6]

Questions

1. Identify the major immigrant groups of the colonial period and their proportion in the American population at the end of the eighteenth century.
2. What were the arguments made both in favor of and against immigration to British North America?
3. How would Jefferson respond to Crèvecoeur's argument about "the American, this new man"?

Sources

1. William Penn, "Account of the Province of Pennsilvania," in *Some Account of the Province of Pennsilvania in America* (London: Benjamin Clark, 1681)
2. Ruth Barnes Moynihan, Cynthia Russett, and Laurie Crumpacker, eds., *Second to None: A Documentary History of American Women* (Lincoln: University of Nebraska Press, 1993), 1, 54. Reprinted with permission of the publisher.
3. Robert Parke, "A Letter from Pennsylvania" (1725) from Charles A. Hanna, *The Scotch-Irish in America*, 2 volumes (1902), 2, 64–67
4. Gottlieb Mittelberger, *Journey to Pennsylvania in the Year 1750 and Return to Germany in the Year 1754*, translated by Carl Theo. Eben (Philadelphia: John Jos. McVey, 1898), 19–20, 22, 24–31.
5. Thomas Jefferson, *Notes on the State of Virginia* in *Thomas Jefferson: Writings* (New York, 1984), 210–212
6. J. Hector St. Jean de Crèvecoeur, *Letters from an American Farmer* (London, 1782)

CHAPTER NINE

AN AGRARIAN REPUBLIC

1790–1824

Applique quilt, late 18th–early 19th century, by Sarah Furman, with people and village at center. Henry Ford Museum and Greenfield Village.

AMERICAN COMMUNITIES
Expansion Touches Mandan Villages on the Upper Missouri

In mid-October 1804, news arrived at the Mandan villages, prominently situated on bluffs overlooking the upper Missouri, that an American expedition led by Meriwether Lewis and William Clark was coming up the river. The principal chiefs, hoping for expanded trade and support against their enemies the Sioux, welcomed these first American visitors. As the expedition's three boats and forty-three men approached the village, wrote Clark, "great numbers on both sides flocked down to the bank to view us." That evening the Mandans welcomed the Americans with an enthusiastic dance and gifts of food.

Since the fourteenth century, when they migrated from the East, the Mandans had lived along the Missouri, on the edge of the Great Plains in what is now North Dakota. They believed their homeland was "the very center of the world," and indeed it is in the heart of the North American continent. Mandan men hunted buffalo and Mandan women kept storage pits full with abundant crops of corn, beans, squash, sunflowers, and tobacco grown on the fertile soil of the river bottom. The Mandan villages were also the central marketplace of the northern Plains; at trading time in late summer they filled with Crows, Assiniboins, Cheyennes, Kiowas, and Arapahoes. Well before any of these people, or those of other tribes, had met a European, they were trading in kettles, knives, and guns acquired from the French and English to the east and leatherwork, glassware, and horses acquired form the Spanish in the Southwest.

The eighteenth century was a golden age for the Mandan, who with their closely related Hidatsa neighbors numbered about 3,000 in 1804. In each of their five villages, earth lodges surrounded a central plaza. One large ceremonial lodge was used for community gatherings, and each of the other earth lodges was home to a senior woman, her husband, her sisters (perhaps married to the same man as she, for the Mandans practiced polygamy), their daughters and their unmarried sons, along with numerous grandchildren. Matrilineal clans, the principal institution of the community, distributed food to the sick, adopted orphans, cared for the dependent elderly, and punished wrongdoers. A village council of male clan leaders selected chiefs who led by consensus and lost power when people no longer accepted their opinions.

Lewis and Clark had been sent by President Thomas Jefferson to survey the Louisiana Purchase and to find an overland route to the Pacific Ocean. They were also instructed to inform the Indians that they now owed loyalty—and trade—to the American government, thereby challenging British economic control over the lucrative North American fur trade. Meeting with the village chiefs, the Americans offered the Mandans a military and economic alliance. His people would like nothing better, responded Chief

229

Black Cat, for the Mandans had fallen on hard times over the past decade. "The smallpox destroyed the greater part of the nation" some twenty years before, the chief said. "All the nations before this malady [were] afraid of them, [but] after they were reduced the Sioux and other Indians waged war, and killed a great many." Black Cat was skeptical that the Americans would deter the Sioux, but Clark reassured him. "We were ready to protect them," Clark reported in his journal, "and kill those who would not listen to our good talk."

The Americans spent the winter with the Mandans, joining in their communal life and establishing firm and friendly relations with them. There were dances and joint hunting parties, frequent visits to the earth lodges, long talks around the fire, and, for many of the men, pleasant nights in the company of Mandan women. Lewis and Clark spent many hours acquiring important geographic information from the Mandans, who drew charts and maps showing the course of the Missouri, the ranges of the Rocky Mountains, and places where one could cross the Continental Divide. The information provided by the Mandans and other Indian peoples to the West was vital to the success of the expedition. Lewis and Clark's "voyage of discovery" depended largely on the willingness of Indian peoples to share their knowledge of the land with the Americans.

In need also of interpreters who could help them communicate with other Indian communities on their way, the Americans hired several multilingual Frenchmen who lived with the Mandans. They also acquired the services of Sacajawea, the fifteen-year-old Shoshoni wife of one of the Frenchmen, who became the only woman to join the westward journey. The presence of Sacajawea and her baby son was a signal, as Clark noted, to "all the Indians as to our friendly intentions"; everyone knew that women and children did not go on war parties.

When the party left the Mandan villages in March, Clark wrote, his men were "generally healthy, except venereal complaints which

is very common amongst the natives and the men catch it from them." After an arduous journey across the Rockies, the party reached the Pacific Ocean at the mouth of the Columbia River, where they spent the winter. Overdue and feared lost, they returned in triumph to St. Louis in September 1806. Before long the Americans had established Fort Clark at the Mandan villages, giving American traders a base for challenging British dominance of the western fur trade. The permanent American presence brought increased contact, and with it much more disease. In 1837 a terrible smallpox epidemic carried away the vast majority of the Mandans, reducing the population to fewer than 150. Four Bears, a Mandan chief who had been a child at the time of the Lewis and Clark visit, spoke these last words to the remnants of his people. "I have loved the whites," he declared. "I have lived with them ever since I was a boy." But in return for the kindness of the Mandans, the Americans had brought this plague. "I do not fear death, my friends," he said, "but to die with my face rotten, that even the wolves will shrink with horror at seeing me, and say to themselves, that is Four Bears, the friend of the whites." "They have deceived me," he pronounced with his last breath. "Them that I always considered as brothers turned out to be my worst enemies."

In sending Lewis and Clark on their "voyage of discovery" to claim the land and the loyalty of the Mandans and other western Indian communities, President Jefferson was motivated by his vision of an expanding American republic of self-sufficient farmers. During his and succeeding presidencies expansion became a key element of national policy and pride. Yet, as the experience of the Mandans showed, what Jefferson viewed as enlargement of "the empire for liberty" had a dark side—the destruction, from disease and coerced displacement, of the communities created by America's first peoples. The effects—economic, political, and social—of continental expansion dominate the history of American communities in the first half of the nineteenth century.

Mandan Villages

KEY TOPICS

- The development of America's economy in a world of warring great powers

- The role of Jefferson's presidency and his agrarian republicanism in forging a national identity

- The ending of colonial dependency by the divisive War of 1812

- Westward expansion becomes a nationalizing force

THE GROWTH OF AMERICAN COMMUNITIES FROM COAST TO COAST

At first glance, the United States of America in 1800 was little different from the scattered colonies of the pre-Revolution era. Two-thirds of the young nation's people still lived in a long thin line of settlement within fifty miles of the Atlantic coast. From New Hampshire to Georgia, most people lived on farms or in small towns, and, because they rarely traveled far from home, their horizons were limited and local.

As famed historian Henry Adams observed, at the beginning of the new century "nature was rather man's master than his servant." Travel in the young republic was slow and difficult, for the roads were poor, and a horse and carriage could go no more than three or four miles an hour. It took two days to travel from New York to Philadelphia, four days to Boston. Nevertheless, the new nation was already transforming itself, not held back by nature but plunging ahead into it. Between 1790 and 1800, according to the first and second federal censuses, the American population grew from 3.9 million to 5.3 million. Growth by migration was greatest in the trans-Appalachian West, a region that was already home to approximately 100,000 Indians. From 1800 to 1850, in an extraordinary burst of territorial expansion, Americans surged westward all the way to the Pacific. At the turn of the century few people would have predicted that within fifty years the nation would encompass the entire continent. In fact, in 1800 several European nations were still mounting significant attempts to settle parts of what is now the United States.

Russian America: Sitka

Russian settlement of what is now Alaska was an extension of its conquest of Siberia, which was driven by the fur trade. In 1741, commissioned by Tsar Peter the Great, the Danish-born naval officer Vitus Bering sailed east from Kamchatka across the sea that now bears his name, explored the Aleutian Islands, and made landfall on the southern coast of Alaska. Although Bering died in a shipwreck on his return voyage, his associates brought back a cargo of sea otter furs, news of the discovery of Alaska, and a navigational report on the Arctic waters of the northern Pacific. In the aftermath of these voyages, Russian and Siberian fur trappers, known as *promyshleniki*, became regular visitors to the Aleutian Islands and the Alaskan coast. By the late 1750s they were shipping a steady supply of furs from Russian America.

The Russians sometimes took furs by force, holding whole villages hostage and brutalizing the native Inuit and Aleut peoples. Within a decade, native resistance had broadened beyond sporadic and local efforts. In 1762, for example, the Aleuts destroyed a fleet of Russian ships from Kamchatka, beginning a series of attacks known as the Aleut Revolt. Finally crushing the Aleuts in 1766, the Russians promised to protect them from abuse, but by the end of the century, the precontact population of 25,000 Aleuts had been greatly reduced. At the same time, sexual relations and intermarriage between fur trappers and Aleut women created a large group of Russian creoles who assumed an increasingly prominent position in the Alaskan fur trade as navigators, explorers, clerks, and traders.

In 1784, the merchant trader Gregory Shelikhov set up a post on Kodiak Island, and over the next several years he established the first permanent Russian settlements in the Gulf of Alaska. In 1799, after his death, Shelikhov's company received a state charter as a quasi-governmental monopoly with rights to the lucrative trade in sea otter pelts. The Russian-American Company set up American headquarters first at Kodiak. When overhunting caused a scarcity of furs, the Russians moved their headquarters south to Sitka, in what is now the southeastern panhandle of Alaska. This was the homeland of the Tlingits, a warrior society, who destroyed the Russians' first fortress in the Tlingit Revolt of 1802. The Russians reestablished

From an engraving by Freidrich H. von Kittlitz, 1827.

This view shows Sitka, the center of Russian activities in Alaska, in 1827. Russian architectural styles and building techniques are apparent in the Church of St. Michael the Archangel in the right background, contrasting with the Asian and Indian origins of most of Sitka's inhabitants.

Sitka by force in 1804, and over the next generation established Russian settlements along the Pacific coast as far south as Fort Ross, which was just north of San Francisco Bay and well within what Spain considered Spanish territory.

Northern New Spain: Los Angeles

Spain had long been concerned about threats to its New World empire from other nations. Fearing incursions by the Russians and British, the Spanish sent naval squadrons north from Mexico to establish their claim to the Pacific coast. By the 1770s, Spain had explored and made claim to the mouth of the Columbia River, Nootka Sound (on Vancouver Island), and the coast of southeastern Alaska. But Spanish attempts to seal off the rich seaborne fur trade from other nations failed. The Russians were a strong presence in Alaska, and the British, already the major power in the land-based fur trade, built a trading post for sea otter furs at Nootka Sound in 1789 in spite of Spanish protests. Americans, who soon dominated the sea otter trade, made their first voyage to the Pacific Northwest in 1787.

In another effort to protect their rich colony of Mexico the Spanish pushed north into Alta (Upper) California, establishing a chain of twenty-one missions that stretched north from San Diego (1769) to Sonoma (1823). The largest of these missions was Los Angeles, which in 1800 had a largely mestizo population of 300. The town, which was the social center for the vast countryside

surrounding it, functioned chiefly as a center of government authority (see Chapter 5). Despite Spain's desire to seal its territory from commerce with other nations, a brisk but illegal trade in otter skins, hides, and tallow developed between the United States and California after the first American ship, the *Lelia Bird*, arrived in 1803.

A French Legacy: New Orleans and St. Louis

For a half-century after its founding by Jean Baptiste le Moyne, Sieur de Bienville, in 1718, New Orleans was controlled by the French. Originally little more than a small port at the mouth of the Mississippi River, its location gave it access to the vast and vaguely defined continental interior that the French called Louisiana. New Orleans came under Spanish rule in 1763 as a result of the Seven Years War, but it continued to be a polyglot, French-dominated society. By 1800 it had a population of about 8,000, half white and half black. Two-thirds of the black population were slaves; the remainder were "free persons of color," who under French law enjoyed legal rights equal to those of white people. The white population was a mixture of French people of European and West Indian origin. Among them were French-speaking exiles from Acadia, who became known in New Orleans as Cajuns (see Chapters 6 and 8). But there were also Spanish, Germans, English, Irish, Americans, and native-born creoles, causing one observer to call the community "a veritable tower of Babel."

All these people were there because New Orleans was becoming a thriving international port. In 1801 it shipped more than $3 million worth of tobacco, sugar, rice, cotton, fruits, and vegetables to Europe. Every year, a greater proportion of the New Orleans trade was supplied by Americans living some distance up the Mississippi River. In 1801 alone, an observer in Natchez counted nearly 600 flatboats on their way to New Orleans from American settlements upriver. Pinckney's 1795 treaty with Spain guaranteed Americans free navigation of the Mississippi River and the right to deposit goods at the port of New Orleans. Nevertheless, Americans were uncomfortably aware that the city's crucial location at the mouth of the Mississippi meant that whatever foreign nation possessed New Orleans had the power to

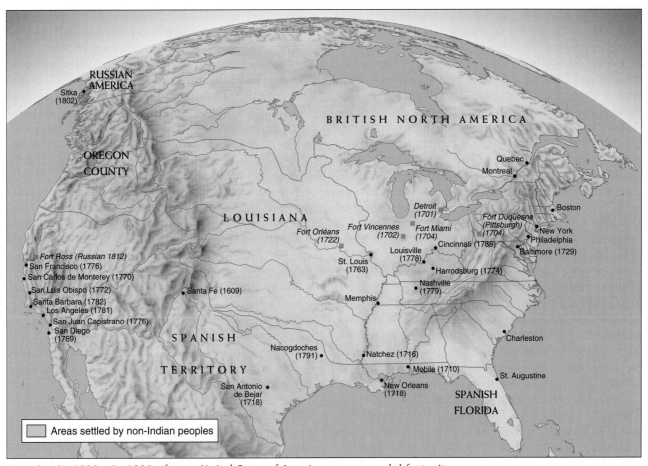

RUSSIAN AMERICA
Sitka (1802)

BRITISH NORTH AMERICA

OREGON COUNTY

LOUISIANA

Quebec
Montreal

Detroit (1701)
Fort Orléans (1722)
Fort Vincennes (1702)
Fort Miami (1704)
Fort Duquesne (Pittsburgh) (1704)
Boston
New York
Philadelphia
Cincinnati (1788)
Baltimore (1729)
Louisville (1778)
St. Louis (1763)
Harrodsburg (1774)
Nashville (1779)
Memphis

Fort Ross (Russian 1812)
San Francisco (1776)
San Carlos de Monterey (1770)
San Luis Obispo (1772)
Santa Barbara (1782)
Los Angeles (1781)
San Juan Capistrano (1776)
San Diego (1769)

Santa Fé (1609)

SPANISH

TERRITORY

Nacogdoches (1791)

Natchez (1716)

Charleston

Mobile (1710)
St. Augustine

San Antonio de Bejar (1718)

New Orleans (1718)

SPANISH FLORIDA

Areas settled by non-Indian peoples

America in 1800   *In 1800, the new United States of America was surrounded by territories held by the European powers: British Canada, French Louisiana (secretly ceded that year to France by Spain), Spanish Florida, Spanish Mexico, and Russian Alaska expanding southward along the Pacific coast. Few people could have imagined that by 1850 the United States would span the continent. But the American settlers who had crossed the Appalachians to the Ohio River Valley were already convinced that opportunity lay in the West.*

choke off the flourishing trade in the vast Mississippi Valley river system.

More than 600 miles north was the small trading town of St. Louis, founded by the New Orleans trader Pierre Laclède in 1763. By 1800 the town had fewer than a thousand residents, three-quarters of whom were involved in the Indian trade of the Missouri River. Spanish officials tried to supervise that trade from their offices in the town, but real control rested in the hands of the Laclèdes and other French traders. Americans visiting this shabby little place laughed at Pierre Laclède's prediction that St. Louis would become "one of the finest cities in America," but he was right.

Trans-Appalachia: Cincinnati

Within the United States itself, the region of greatest growth was the area west of the Appalachian Mountains. By 1800, 500,000 people (the vast majority from

Virginia and North Carolina) had found rich and fertile land along the splendid rivers of the interior—the Tennessee, the Cumberland, and the Ohio, all draining into the Mississippi River, which marked the western boundary of the United States. Soon there was enough population for statehood. Kentucky (1792) and Tennessee (1796) were the first trans-Appalachian states admitted to the Union.

Migration was a principal feature of American life. Probably 5 to 10 percent of all American households moved each year. In the rural areas of the Atlantic seaboard, a third of the households counted in the 1790 census had moved by 1800; in cities the proportion was closer to half. In the West, meanwhile, rates of migration rose to as high as two-thirds of the community every ten years. Most moves were between neighboring communities or towns, but many families underwent the painful process of long-distance relocation. Migration was generally a family affair, with groups of kin moving together to a new area. One observer wrote of a caravan moving across the mountains, "They had prepared baskets made of fine hickory withe or splints, and fastening two of them together with ropes they put a child in each basket and put it across a pack saddle." Once pioneers had managed to struggle by road over the Appalachians, they gladly took to the rivers, especially the Ohio River, to move farther west.

Cincinnati, strategically situated 450 miles downstream from Pittsburgh, was a particularly dramatic example of the rapid community growth and development that characterized the trans-Appalachian region. Founded in 1788, Cincinnati began life as a military fort defending settlers in the fertile Miami River valley of Ohio from resistance by Shawnee and Miami Indians. Conflict between these Indian peoples and the new settlers was so fierce that the district was grimly referred to as "the slaughterhouse." Trans-Appalachian settlement was not individual but communal: fear of attack led the white settlers to group together for protection. The basic form of settlement in early Kentucky was the "station," or fort; north of the Ohio River, compact settlements on the New England model were favored.

After the battle of Fallen Timbers broke Indian resistance in 1794, Cincinnati became the point of departure for immigrants arriving by the Ohio River on their way to settle the interior of the Old Northwest: Ohio, Indiana, and Illinois. In the boom years of settlement, the number of people passing through was so great that the entire town seemed to consist of hotels and eating places. In 1800, Cincinnati had a population of about 750 people. By 1810, it had tripled in size, confirming its boast to be "the Queen City of the West."

Cincinnati merchants were soon shipping farm goods from the fertile Miami Valley down the Ohio–Mississippi River system to New Orleans, 1,500 miles away. River hazards like snags and sandbars made the downriver trip by barge or keelboat hazardous, and the return trip upriver was slow, more than three months from New Orleans to Cincinnati. Frequently rivermen simply abandoned their flatboats in New Orleans and traveled home overland, on foot or horseback, by the long and dangerous Natchez Trace, an old Indian trail that linked Natchez with Nashville, Tennessee. Nevertheless, river traffic increased yearly, and the control of New Orleans became a key concern of western farmers and merchants. If New Orleans refused to accept American goods, Cincinnati merchants and many thousands of trans-Appalachian farmers would be ruined.

Atlantic Ports: From Charleston to Boston

Although only 3 percent of the nation's population lived in cities, the Atlantic ports continued, as in the colonial era, to dominate the nation economically and politically. Seaports benefited from the advantage of waterborne trade and communication over much slower land travel. Merchants in the seaboard cities found it easier to cross the Atlantic than to venture into their own backcountry in search of trade. In 1800 the nation's most important urban centers were all Atlantic seaports: Charleston (which had a population of 20,000), Baltimore (26,000), Philadelphia (70,000), New York (60,000), and Boston (25,000). Each had a distinctive regional identity.

Charleston, South Carolina, was the South's premier port. In colonial days, Charleston had grown rich on its links with the British West Indies and on trade with England in rice, long-staple cotton, and indigo. The social center for the great low-country plantation owners, Charleston was a multicultural city of white people, African Americans (2,000 of them free), Indian people, and the mixed race offspring of the three groups. One was as likely to hear French, Spanish, or Gullah and Geeche (African-based dialects of low-country slaves) as English. This graceful, elegant city was a center for the slave trade until 1808.

Baltimore was the major port for the tobacco of the Chesapeake Bay region and thus was connected with the slave-owning aristocracy of the Upper South. But proximity to the wheat-growing regions of the Pennsylvania backcountry increasingly inclined the city's merchants to look westward and to consider ways to tap the trade of the burgeoning Ohio country.

Philadelphia, William Penn's "City of Brotherly Love," was distinguished by the commercial and banking skills of Quaker merchants. These merchants had built international trade networks for shipping the farm produce of Pennsylvania's German farmers. Philadelphia served as the nation's capital in the 1790s and was acknowledged as its cultural and intellectual leader as well.

New York, still faintly Dutch in architecture and social customs, was soon to outgrow all the other cities. New York merchants were exceptionally aggressive in their pursuit of trade. Unlike their counterparts in Philadelphia and Boston, New Yorkers accepted the British auction system, which cut out the middleman and offered goods in large lots at wholesale prices at open auctions. Increasingly, British imports entered America through the port of New York. New York's shipping, banking, insurance, and supporting industries boomed, and as early as 1800 a quarter of all American shipping was owned by New York merchants.

Boston, the cockpit of the American Revolution, was also the capital of Massachusetts. The handsome State House, built on Beacon Hill, reflected the origins of Boston's merchant wealth: a carved wooden codfish occupied a place of honor in the new building. By the late eighteenth century, however, Boston's commercial wealth had diversified into shipbuilding and shipping, banking and insurance.

Though small in population, these Atlantic cities led the nation socially, politically, and above all economically. In 1800, the merchants in these seaports still primarily looked across the Atlantic to Europe. In the coming half-century, however, it was the cities that developed the strongest ties with the trans-Appalachian West that were to thrive.

A NATIONAL ECONOMY

In 1800, the United States was a producer of raw materials. The new nation faced the same challenge that developing nations confront today. At the mercy of fluctuating world commodity prices they cannot control, such countries have great difficulty protecting themselves from economic dominance by stronger, more established nations. In 1800, America was in just such a situation.

The Economy of the Young Republic

In 1800 the United States was predominantly rural and agricultural. According to the census of 1800, 94 in 100 Americans lived in communities of fewer than 2,500 people, and 4 in 5 families farmed the land, either for themselves or for others. Farming families followed centuries-old traditions of working with hand tools and draft animals, producing most of their own food and fiber, and most Americans dressed in cloth that had been spun, woven, and tailored by women in their own families. Seaboard farmers of the Middle States and those near urban centers engaged in commercial farming, but for most, crops were grown for home use rather than for sale. Production of a "surplus" to sell was a small sideline. Commodities such as whiskey and hogs (both easy to transport) provided small and irregular cash incomes or items for barter. As late as 1820, only 20 percent of the produce of American farms was consumed outside the local community.

In contrast to this pattern, the plantation agriculture of the South was wholly commercial and international. Slave owners, however, faced a growing dilemma: their heavy capital investment in African American slave labor was not matched by a growth in the demand for tobacco and rice, the traditional export crops. The tobacco trade, which accounted for about a third of the value of all colonial exports, remained at or below pre-Revolutionary levels, and the demand for rice had actually declined.

The demand for a third crop, cotton, was growing rapidly in response to the boom in the industrial production of textiles in England and Europe, but extracting the seeds from the fibers of the variety of cotton that grew best in the southern interior required an enormous investment of labor. The cotton gin, which mechanized this process, was invented in 1793, but not until the nineteenth century did cotton assume a commanding place in the foreign trade of the United States.

In 1790, increasing foreign demand for American goods and services hardly seemed likely. Trade with Britain, still the biggest customer for American raw materials, was considerably less than it had been before the Revolution. As an independent nation, the United States no longer benefited from British mercantilist trade privileges. Britain and France both excluded Americans from their lucrative West Indian trade and taxed American ships with discriminatory duties. It was difficult to be independent in a world dominated by great powers.

Shipping and the Economic Boom

Despite these restrictions on American commerce, the strong shipping trade begun during the colonial era and centered in the Atlantic ports became a major asset in the 1790s, when events in Europe provided America with extraordinary opportunities.

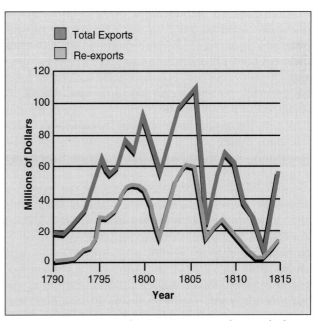

American Export Trade, 1790–1815   *This graph shows how completely the American shipping boom was tied to European events. Exports, half of which were reexports, surged when Britain and France were at war and America could take advantage of its status as neutral. Exports slumped in the brief period of European peace in 1803–1805 and plunged following the Embargo Act of 1807 and the outbreak of the War of 1812.*

Source: Douglass C. North, *The Economic Growth of the United States, 1790–1860* (New York: Norton, 1966), p. 26.

This picture shows the launching of the ship Fame *from Becket's Shipyard in Essex, Massachusetts, in 1802. Shipbuilding was a major New England industry, and a launching was a community event.*

The French Revolution, which began in 1789, soon initiated nearly twenty-five years of warfare between Britain and France. As the European powers converted their ships from international trade to military purposes, American vessels were ready to replace them. All along the Atlantic seaboard, urban centers thrived as American ships carried European goods that could no longer be transported on British ships without danger of French attack (and vice versa). Because America was neutral, its merchants had the legal right to import European goods and promptly reexport them to other European countries. In spite of British and French efforts to prevent the practice (see Chapter 8), reexports amounted to half of the profits in the booming shipping trade.

The vigorous international shipping trade had dramatic effects within the United States. The coastal cities all grew substantially from 1790 to 1820. In 1790, only twelve cities in the United States held more than 5,000 people and only 3 percent of the population was urban; by 1820 city dwellers made up 7 percent of the population and thirty-five cities had a population exceeding 5,000. This rapid urbanization was a sign of vigorous economic growth (rather than a sign that poverty was pushing rural workers off the farms, as occurs in some third world countries today), for it reflected expanding opportunities in the cities. In fact, the rapid growth of cities stimulated farmers to produce the food to feed the new urban dwellers.

The long series of European wars also allowed enterprising Americans to seize such lucrative international opportunities as the China trade. In 1784 the *Empress of China* set sail from New York for Canton with forty tons of ginseng. When it returned in 1785 with a cargo of teas, silks, and chinaware, the sponsors of the voyage, Philadelphia financier Robert Morris and his partners, made a 30 percent profit. Other merchants were quick to follow Morris's example, and to improve on it. In 1787 Robert Gray left Boston in the *Columbia,* sailing south around Cape Horn, then north to Nootka Sound in the Pacific Northwest, where he bought sea otter skins cheaply from the coastal Indians. Then, in 1789, Gray sailed west across the Pacific to China, where he sold the furs at fabulous profits before rounding the Cape of Good Hope and returning to Boston laden with tea. In his second voyage in 1792, Gray discovered the mouth of a major Northwest river, which he named for his ship. (When Lewis and Clark ventured west in 1804, part of their task was to chart the exact path of Gray's "Columbia's River.") Soon New England so dominated the seaborne trade in furs to China that the Pacific Northwest Indians called all Americans "Bostons."

The active American participation in international trade fostered a strong and diversified shipbuilding industry. All the major Atlantic ports boasted expanding shipbuilding enterprises. The average size of full-rigged ships built in one shipyard in Portsmouth, New Hampshire, increased from 361 tons in 1825 to 2,145 tons in 1855. Demands for speed increased as well, resulting in what many people have regarded as the flower of American shipbuilding, the clipper ship. The narrow-hulled, many-sailed clipper ships of the 1840s and 1850s set records for ships of their size. In 1854, *Flying Cloud,* built in the Boston shipyards of Donald McKay, sailed from New York to San Francisco—a 16,000-mile trip that usually took 150 to 200 days—in a mere 89 days. The clipper ships' average of 300 miles a day made them competitive with steamships through the 1850s.

In every seaport, this booming trade stimulated the development of financial services, such as insurance companies, banks, and brokers, geared more to international than to local concerns. By 1820, the United States was well on its way to building a strong and diversified national economy. At the same time, the wealth, confidence, and power of the merchants in the seacoast cities greatly increased.

THE JEFFERSON PRESIDENCY

Thomas Jefferson began his presidency with a symbolic action worthy of a twentieth-century media-wise politician. At noon on March 4, 1801, he walked from his

modest boardinghouse through the swampy streets of the new federal city of Washington to the unfinished Capitol. George Washington and John Adams had ridden in elaborate carriages to their inaugurals. Jefferson, although accepting a military honor guard, demonstrated by his actions that he rejected the elaborate, quasi-monarchical style of the two Federalist presidents, and their (to his mind) autocratic style of government as well.

For all its lack of pretension, Jefferson's inauguration as the third president of the United States was a momentous occasion in American history, for it marked the peaceful transition from one political party, the Federalists, to their hated rivals, the Democratic Republicans. Beginning in an atmosphere of exceptional political bitterness, Jefferson's presidency was to demonstrate that a strongly led party system could shape national policy without leading either to dictatorship or to revolt. It was a great achievement.

Republican Agrarianism

Jefferson brought to the presidency a clearly defined political philosophy. Behind all the events of his administration (1801–09) and those of his successors in what became known as the Virginia Dynasty (James Madison, 1809–17; James Monroe, 1817–25) was a clear set of beliefs that embodied Jefferson's interpretation of the meaning of republicanism for Americans.

Jefferson's years as ambassador to France in the 1780s were particularly important in shaping his political thinking. Recoiling from the extremes of wealth and poverty he saw there, he came to believe that it was impossible for Europe to achieve a just society that could guarantee to most of its members the "life, liberty and…pursuit of happiness" of which he had written in the Declaration of Independence.

Tall, ungainly, and diffident in manner, Thomas Jefferson was nonetheless a man of genius. Jefferson designed and supervised every aspect of the building and furnishing of Monticello, his classical home atop a hill near Charlottesville, Virginia. The process took almost forty years (from 1770 to 1809), for Jefferson constantly changed and refined his design, subjecting both himself and his family to years of uncomfortable living in the partially completed structure. The result, however, was one of the most civilized—and most autobiographical— houses ever built.

military conquests. Four years later, Great Britain went to war against him. Following one year of peace, Britain and France were again at war by 1803, beginning a twelve-year duel that ended only with Napoleon's defeat at the battle of Waterloo in 1815. As had his predecessors, Napoleon looked at North America as a potential battleground on which to fight the British. In 1800, in a secret treaty, France reacquired the Louisiana Territory, the vast western drainage of the Mississippi and Missouri Rivers, from Spain, which had held the region since 1763. From Louisiana, if he chose, Napoleon could launch an attack to regain Canada from the British.

When President Jefferson learned of the secret agreement in 1801, he was alarmed. He feared that French control would threaten the growing American trade on the Mississippi River and force the young nation to take military action. In fact, in 1802 the Spanish commander at New Orleans (the French had not yet taken formal control) closed the port to American shippers, thus disrupting commerce as far away as Cincinnati. As Jefferson feared, Federalists in Congress clamored for military action to reopen the port, and he himself was determined to end this threat to American commerce.

Initially, Jefferson offered to buy New Orleans and the surrounding area for $2 million (or up to $10 million, if necessary). As it happened, Napoleon was eager to sell. A French army of 30,000 men had just withdrawn from the Caribbean island of Santo Domingo (now Haiti), defeated by yellow fever and an army of former slaves led by François Toussaint L'Ouverture. In the wake of the defeat, and in need of money for European military campaigns, Napoleon offered the entire Louisiana Territory, including the crucial port of New Orleans, to the Americans for $15 million. Exceeding his instructions, special American envoy James Monroe seized the opportunity and bought the entire Louisiana Territory from Napoleon in Paris in April 1803.

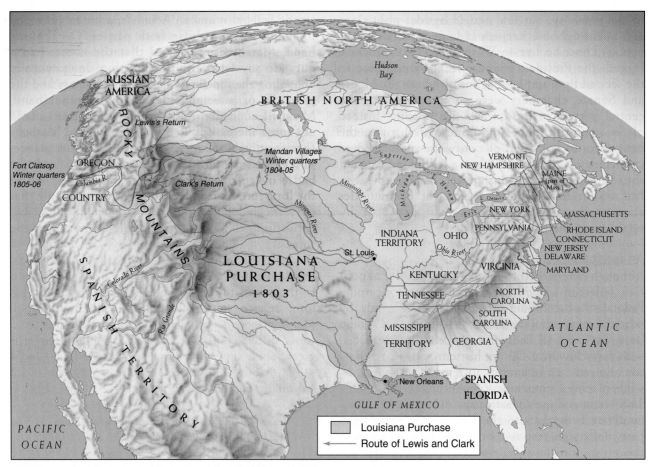

Louisiana Purchase   *The Louisiana Purchase of 1803, the largest peaceful acquisition of territory in United States history, more than doubled the size of the nation. The Lewis and Clark expedition (1804–1806) was the first to survey and document the natural and human richness of the area. The American sense of expansiveness and continental destiny owes more to the extraordinary opportunity provided by the Louisiana Purchase than to anything else.*

Overnight, the size of the United States more than doubled. It was the largest peaceful acquisition of territory in United States history.

At home, Jefferson suffered brief qualms. The Constitution did not authorize the president to purchase territory, and Jefferson had always rigidly insisted on a limited interpretation of executive rights. But he had also long held a sense of destiny about the West and had planned the Lewis and Clark expedition before the Louisiana Purchase was a reality. In any case, the prize was too rich to pass up. Jefferson now argued that Louisiana was vital to the nation's republican future. "By enlarging the empire of liberty," Jefferson wrote, "we…provide new sources of renovation, should its principles, at any time, degenerate, in those portions of our country which gave them birth." In other words, expansion was essential to liberty.

Congress and the general public joined Jefferson in welcoming the purchase. Of course, the support was not unanimous. Some Federalists disputed Jefferson's claim that expansion would foster liberty and predicted that it would doom the republican form of government. As Federalist Fisher Ames dramatically warned, "By adding an unmeasured world beyond [the Mississippi]…we rush like a comet into infinity."

Incorporating Louisiana

The immediate issue following the Louisiana Purchase was how to treat the French and Spanish inhabitants of the Louisiana Territory. Many people thought that the only way to deal with a population so "foreign" was to wipe out its customs and laws and impose American ones as quickly as possible. But this did not happen. The incorporation of Louisiana into the American federal system was a remarkable story of adaptation between two different communities—American and French.

In 1803, when the region that is now the state of Louisiana became American property, it had a racially and ethnically diverse population of 43,000 people, of whom only 6,000 were American. French and French-speaking people were numerically and culturally dominant, especially in the city of New Orleans. There the French community effectively challenged the initial American plan of rapidly supplanting French culture and institutions with American ones. At a public ball held in New Orleans in January 1804, for example, American and French military officers almost came to blows over whether an English country dance or a French waltz would be played first.

Officials in Washington dismissed the reported conflict as mere frivolity, but the U.S. representative in New Orleans and governor of Lower Louisiana Territory, William Claiborne, did not. Over the next four years Claiborne came to accept the value of French institutions to the region. As a result, with Claiborne's full support, Louisiana adopted a legal code in 1808 that was based on French civil law rather than English common law. This was not a small concession. French law differed from English law in many fundamental respects, such as family property (communal versus male ownership), inheritance (forced heirship versus free disposal), and even contracts, which were much more strictly regulated in the French system. Remnants of the French legal system remain part of Louisiana state law to this day. In 1812, with the required 60,000 free inhabitants, Louisiana was admitted to the Union. New Orleans remained for years a distinctively French city, illustrating the flexibility possible under a federal system.

Texas and the Struggle for Mexican Independence

Spain objected, in vain, to Napoleon's 1803 sale of Louisiana to America. For years Spain had attempted to seal off its rich colony of Mexico from commerce with other nations. Now, American Louisiana shared one vague and disputed boundary with Mexico's northern province of Texas (a parcel of land already coveted by some Americans) and, on the east, a similarly uncertain boundary with Spanish Florida.

Soon Napoleon brought turmoil to all of Mexico. In 1808, he installed his brother Joseph Bonaparte as king of Spain, forcing Spain's king, Charles IV, to renounce his throne. For the next six years, as warfare convulsed Spain, the country's long-prized New World empire slipped away. Mexico, divided between royalists loyal to Spain and populists seeking social and economic justice for mestizos and Indians, edged bloodily toward independence. Two populist revolts—one in 1810 led by Father Miguel Hidalgo and the other in 1813 led by Father José María Morelos—were suppressed by the royalists, who executed both revolutionary leaders. In 1812 a small force, led by Mexican republican Bernardo Gutiérrez but composed mostly of American adventurers, invaded Texas, capturing San Antonio, assassinating the provincial governor Manuel Salcedo, and declaring Texas independent. A year later, however, the Mexican republicans were defeated by a royalist army that then killed suspected collaborators and pillaged the province so thoroughly that the local economy was devastated and the Mexican population declined to fewer than 2,000. Mexico's difficult path toward independence seemed, at least to some Americans, to offer yet another opportunity for expansion.

RENEWED IMPERIAL RIVALRY IN NORTH AMERICA

Fresh from the triumph of the Louisiana Purchase, Jefferson scored a major victory over the Federalist Charles Cotesworth Pinckney in the presidential election of 1804, garnering 162 electoral votes to Pinckney's 14. Jefferson's shrewd wooing of moderate Federalists had been so successful that the remaining Federalists dwindled to a highly principled but sectional group unable to attract voters outside of its home base in New England. Jefferson's Louisiana success was not repeated, however, and few other consequences of the ongoing struggle between Britain and France were so easy to solve. Their rivalry caused problems for America both on the high seas and on the nation's western borders.

Problems with Neutral Rights

In his first Inaugural Address in 1801, Jefferson had announced a foreign policy of "peace, commerce, and honest friendship with all nations, entangling alliances with none." This was a difficult policy to pursue after 1803, when the Napoleonic Wars resumed. By 1805 Napoleon had conquered most of Europe, but Britain, the victor at the great naval battle of Trafalgar, controlled the seas. The United States, trying to profit from trade with both countries, was caught in the middle. The British did not look kindly as their former colonists tried to evade their blockade of the French by claiming neutrality. Beginning in 1805, the British targeted the American reexport trade between the French West Indies and France by seizing American ships bringing French West Indian goods to Europe. Angry Americans viewed these seizures as violations of their neutral rights as shippers.

An even more contentious issue arose from the substantial desertion rate of British sailors. Many deserters promptly signed up on American ships, where they drew better pay and sometimes obtained false naturalization papers as well. The numbers involved were large: as many as a quarter of the 100,000 seamen on American ships were British. Soon the British were stopping American merchant vessels and removing any man they believed to be British, regardless of his papers. The British refusal to recognize genuine naturalization papers (on the principle "once a British subject, always a British subject") was particularly insulting to the new American sense of nationhood.

At least 6,000 innocent American citizens suffered forced impressment into the British navy from 1803 to 1812. In 1807 impressment turned bloody when the British ship *Leopard* stopped the American ship *Chesapeake* in American territorial waters and demanded to search for deserters. When the American captain refused, the *Leopard* opened fire, killing three men, wounding eighteen, and removing four deserters (three with American naturalization papers) from the damaged ship. An indignant public protested British interference and the death of innocent sailors. Had Congress been in session and the country militarily strong, public pressure might very well have forced a declaration of war against Britain then.

The Embargo Act

Fully aware that commerce was essential to the new nation, Jefferson was determined to insist on America's right as a neutral nation to ship goods to Europe. But Britain possessed the world's largest and strongest navy, one the small American navy could not effectively challenge. Jefferson first tried diplomatic protests, then negotiations, and finally threats, all to no avail. In 1806 Congress passed the Non-Importation Act, hoping that a boycott of British goods, which had worked so well during the Revolutionary War, would be effective once again. Presumably, denied their customary American markets British manufacturers would force a change in their government's policy. They did not. The boycott was suspended late in 1806 while the Jefferson administration tried to negotiate with the British; when that effort failed, the boycott was resumed.

Finally, in desperation, Jefferson imposed the Embargo Act in December 1807. This act forbade American ships from sailing to any foreign port, thereby cutting off all exports as well as imports. The act was directed at French as well as British disregard for the neutral rights of American vessels. Its intent was to force both countries to recognize those rights by depriving them of American-shipped raw materials. Jefferson hoped especially for a speedy change of British policy, because Britain's large navy caused much more harm to American shipping than did the smaller French navy.

But the results were a disaster for American trade. The commerce of the new nation, which Jefferson himself had done so much to promote, came to a standstill. Exports fell from $108 million in 1807 to $22 million in 1808, and the nation was driven into a deep depression. There was widespread evasion of the embargo. A remarkable number of ships in the coastal trade found themselves "blown off course" to the West Indies or Canada. Other ships simply left port illegally. Smuggling flourished. Pointing out that the American navy's weakness was due largely to the deep cuts Jefferson had inflicted on it, the Federalists sprang to life with a campaign of outspoken opposition to Jefferson's policy and found a ready audience in New England, the area hardest hit by the embargo.

Madison and the Failure of "Peaceable Coercion"

In this troubled atmosphere, Thomas Jefferson despondently ended his second term, acknowledging the failure of what he called "peaceable coercion." He was followed in office by his friend and colleague, James Madison of Virginia. Although Madison defeated the Federalist candidate—again Charles Cotesworth Pinkney—by 122 electoral votes to 47, Pinckney's share of the votes was three times what it had been in 1804, a reflection of the resentment New Englanders felt to the disproportionate hardships they suffered from the Embargo Act.

Ironically, the Embargo Act had almost no effect on its intended victims. The French used the embargo as a pretext for seizing American ships, claiming they must be British ships in disguise. The British, in the absence of American competition, developed new markets for their goods in South America. And at home, as John Randolph sarcastically remarked, the embargo was attempting "to cure corns by cutting off the toes."

In March 1809 Congress admitted failure, and the Embargo Act was repealed. But the struggle to remain neutral in the confrontation between the European giants continued. The next two years saw passage of several acts—among them the Non-Intercourse Act of 1809 and Macon's Bill Number 2 in 1810—that unsuccessfully attempted to prohibit trade with Britain and France unless they ceased their hostile treatment of U.S. shipping. Frustration with the ineffectiveness of government policy mounted.

A Contradictory Indian Policy

The United States faced other conflicts than those with Britain and France over neutral shipping rights. In the West, the powerful Indian nations of the Ohio Valley were determined to resist the wave of expansion that had carried thousands of white settlers onto their lands. North of the Ohio River lived the Northwest Confederation of the Shawnees, Delawares, Miamis, Potawatomis, and several smaller tribes. To the south of the Ohio were the so-called "Five Civilized Tribes," the Cherokees, Chickasaws, Choctaws, Creeks, and (in Florida) the Seminoles.

According to the Indian Intercourse Act of 1790, the United States could not simply seize Indian land; it could only acquire it when the Indians ceded it by treaty. But this policy conflicted with the harsh reality of westward expansion. Commonly, settlers

This double portrait of two Sac Indians by John Wesley Jarvis, painted in 1833, symbolized the hopes of official American Indian policy. The traditional Indian ways represented by Whirling Thunder's attire would be superseded by the "civilized" attitude represented by his father Black Hawk's European dress.

John Wesley Jarvis, *Black Hawk and His Son, Whirling Thunder*, 1833. Oil on canvas. 23 × 30 in. (60.3 × 76 cm). Gilcrease Museum, Tulsa, Oklahoma.

pushed ahead of treaty boundaries. When Indian peoples resisted the invasion of their lands, the pioneers fought back and called for military protection. Defeat of an Indian people led to further land cessions. The result for the Indians was a relentless cycle of invasion, resistance, and defeat.

Thomas Jefferson was deeply concerned with the fate of the western Indian peoples. Unlike most of the pioneers, who saw them simply as dangerous obstacles to be removed, Jefferson believed in coexistence and acculturation. His Indian policy was designed to solve the fundamental dilemma of expansion—the conflicting needs of white and Indian peoples. The Indians would cede the lands the pioneers craved, and in return white people would teach them how to farm and live like whites on their new, compressed reservations. Convinced that Indians had to give up hunting in favor of the yeoman-farmer lifestyle he so favored for all Americans, Jefferson directed the governors of the Northwest Territories to "promote energetically" his vision for civilizing the Indians.

Although he himself was notoriously indifferent to organized religion, Jefferson strongly supported efforts to Christianize Indian peoples and educate them in white ways. A number of denominations, among them the Moravians, Quakers, and Baptists, sent missionaries to the western Indians. Others formed special missionary societies, such as the Society for Propagating the Gospel among Indians (1797) and the American Board of Commissioners for Foreign

History and the Land

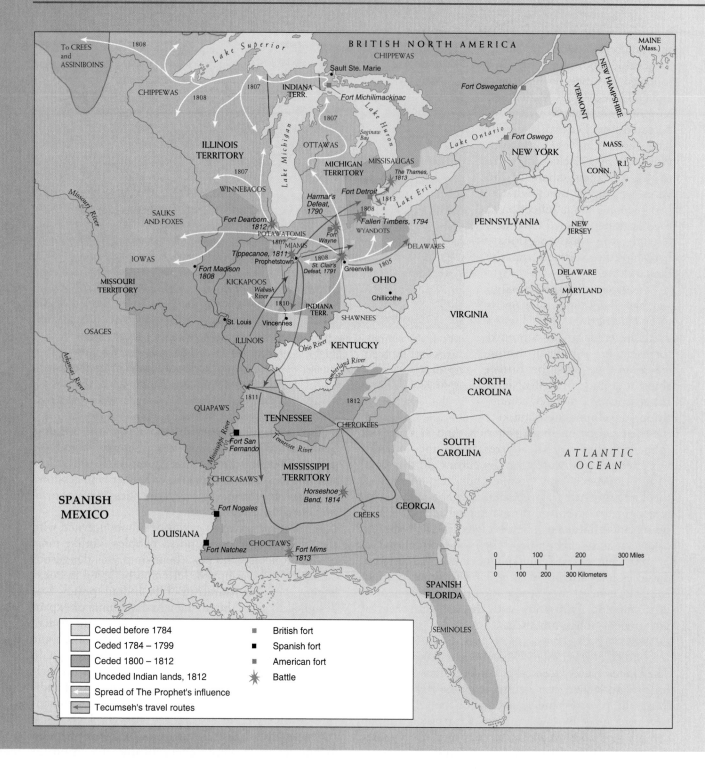

Map legend

- Ceded before 1784
- Ceded 1784 – 1799
- Ceded 1800 – 1812
- Unceded Indian lands, 1812
- ← Spread of The Prophet's influence
- ← Tecumseh's travel routes
- British fort
- Spanish fort
- American fort
- Battle

Missions (1810). The latter was a joint effort of the Congregationalist, Presbyterian, and Dutch Reformed churches. Jefferson's Indian civilization plan was never adequately funded by Congress or supported by territorial governors and settlers. Although missionaries promoted literacy and a knowledge of white ways, they were generally disdainful of Indian culture and created deep divisions within Indian tribes between those who converted to Christianity and those who actively resisted conversion and were unwilling to give up traditional ways, especially hunting. Thus missionary efforts unwittingly weakened tribes already disoriented by the loss of their lands and life ways.

After the Louisiana Purchase, Jefferson offered traditionalist Indian groups new lands west of the Mississippi River, claiming that they would be able to live there undisturbed by white settlers for centuries. But he failed to consider the pace of westward expan-

Tecumseh

Tenskwatawa, The Prophet

Indian Resistance, 1790–1816

American westward expansion put relentless pressure on the Indian nations in the Trans-Appalachian South and West. The Trans-Appalachian region was marked by constant warfare from the time of the earliest settlements in Kentucky in the 1780s to the War of 1812. Tecumseh's Alliance in the Northwest (1809–11) and the Creek Rebellion in the Southwest (1813–14) were the culminating struggles in Indian resistance to the American invasion of the Trans-Appalachian region. Tecumseh, a Shawnee military leader, and his brother Tenskwatawa, a religious leader called The Prophet, led a pan-Indian revitalization and resistance movement that posed a serious threat to American westward expansion. As the map shows, Tenskwatawa's message had wide appeal in the Northwest. Tecumseh traveled widely, attempting to build a military alliance on his brother's spiritual message. He achieved considerable success in the Northwest, but less in the Southwest, where many Indian peoples put their faith in accommodation. Tecumseh's death at the Battle of the Thames (1813) and British abandonment of their Shawnee allies at the end of the War of 1812 brought an end to organized Indian resistance in the Old Northwest. In the South, Andrew Jackson crushed Creek resisters in the Battle of Horseshoe Bend in 1814, and then demanded the cession of 23 million acres of land from both hostile and friendly Creek peoples.

sion. Less than twenty years later, Missouri, the first trans-Mississippi state, was admitted to the Union. The Indians living in Missouri, some of whom had been removed from the Old Northwest in accord with Jefferson's plan, were forced to move again to lands farther west. Western Indians like the Mandans, who had seemed so remote when Lewis and Clark wintered with them in 1804–05, were now threatened by further westward expansion.

In fact, Jefferson's Indian policy, because it did nothing to slow down the ever-accelerating westward expansion, offered little hope to Indian peoples. The alternatives they faced were stark: acculturation, removal, or extinction. Deprived of hunting lands, decimated by disease, increasingly dependent on the white economy for trade goods and annuity payments in exchange for land cessions, many Indian peoples despaired. Like the Mandans after Lewis and Clark's visit, they came to dread the effects of white contact. Nearly every tribe found itself bitterly split between accommodationists and traditionalists. Some, like groups of Cherokees and associated tribes in the South, advocated adapting their traditional agricultural lifestyles and pursuing a pattern of peaceful accommodation. In the Northwest Territory, however, many Indians chose the path of armed resistance.

Indian Resistance

The Shawnees, a seminomadic hunting and farming tribe (the men hunted, the women farmed) of the Ohio Valley, had resisted white settlement in Kentucky and Ohio since the 1750s. The decisive defeat of the Indian Confederacy led by Little Turtle, a Miami Indian, at Fallen Timbers (1794) and the continuing pressure of American settlement, however, left the Shawnees divided. One group, led by Black Hoof, accepted acculturation. Soon Quaker and Moravian missionaries were converting Black Hoof's band and teaching them farming. The rest of the tribe tried to maintain traditional ways. Most broke into small bands and tried to eke out a living by hunting, but their numbers were reduced by disease and the survivors further demoralized by the alcohol offered them illegally by private traders. One group of traditional Shawnees, however, led by the warrior Tecumseh, sought refuge farther west.

But there was no escape from white encroachment. Between 1801 and 1809, William Henry Harrison, governor of Indiana Territory, concluded fifteen treaties with the Delawares, Potawatomis, Miamis, and other tribes. These treaties opened eastern Michigan, southern Indiana, and most of Illinois to white settlement and forced the Indians into ever-smaller reservations. Many of these treaties were obtained by coercion, bribery, and outright trickery, and most Indians did not accept them.

In 1805 Tecumseh's brother, Tenskwatawa, known as The Prophet, began preaching a message of Indian revitalization: a rejection of all contact with the Americans, including use of American alcohol, clothing, and trade goods, and a return to traditional practices of hunting and farming. He preached an end to quarreling, violence, and sexual promiscuity and to the accumulation of private property. Wealth was valuable only if it was given away, he said. If the Northwest Indians returned to traditional ways, Tenskwatawa promised, "the land will be overturned so that all the white people will be covered and you alone shall inhabit the land."

This was a powerful message, but it was not new. Just six years earlier, Handsome Lake had led the Seneca people of upstate New York in a similar revitalization movement. Tecumseh, however, succeeded in molding his brother's religious following into a powerful pan-Indian military resistance movement. With each new treaty that Harrison concluded, Tecumseh gained new followers among the Northwest Confederation tribes. Significantly, he also had the support of the British, who, after 1807, began sending food and guns to him from Canada.

The pan-Indian strategy was at first primarily defensive, aimed at preventing further westward expansion. But the Treaty of Fort Wayne in 1809, in which the United States gained 3 million acres of Delaware and Potawatomi land in Indiana, led to active resistance. Confronting Harrison directly, Tecumseh argued that the land belonged to the larger community of all the Indian peoples; no one tribe could give away the common property of all. He then warned that any surveyors or settlers who ventured into the 3 million acres would risk their lives.

Tecumseh took his message of common land ownership and military resistance to all the Indian peoples of the Northwest Confederacy. He was not uniformly successful, even among the Shawnees. Black Hoof, for example, refused to join. Tecumseh also recruited, with mixed success, among the tribes south of the Ohio River. In councils with Choctaws, Chickasaws, Creeks, and Cherokees, he promoted active resistance:

> The white race is a wicked race. Since the days when the white race first came in contact with the red men, there has been a continual series of aggressions. The hunting grounds are fast disappearing, and they are driving the red man farther and farther to the west. Such has been the fate of the Shawnees, and surely will be the fate of all tribes if the power of the whites is not forever crushed. The mere presence of the white man is a source of evil to the red men. His whiskey destroys the bravery of our warriors, and his lust corrupts the virtue of our women. The only hope for the red man is a war of extermination against the paleface.

In November 1811, while Tecumseh was still recruiting among the southern tribes, Harrison marched to the pan-Indian village of Tippecanoe with 1,000 soldiers. The 600 to 700 Indian warriors at the town, urged on by Tenskwatawa, attacked Harrison's forces before dawn on November 7, hoping to surprise them. The attack failed, and in the battle that followed the Americans inflicted about 150 Indian casualties, while sustaining about as many themselves. Although Harrison claimed victory, the truth was far different. Dispersed from Tippecanoe, Tecumseh's angry followers fell on American settlements in Indiana and southern Michigan, killing many pioneers and forcing the rest to flee to fortified towns. Tecumseh himself entered into a formal alliance with the British. For western settlers, the Indian threat was greater than ever.

THE WAR OF 1812

Many westerners blamed the British for Tecumseh's attacks on pioneer settlements in the Northwest. British support of western Indians and the long-standing difficulties over neutral shipping rights were the two grievances cited by President Madison when he asked Congress for a declaration of war against Britain on June 1, 1812; Congress obliged him on June 18. But the war had other, more general causes as well.

The War Hawks

A rising young generation of political leaders, first elected to Congress in 1810, strongly resented the continuing influence of Britain, the former mother country, on American affairs. These War Hawks, who included such future leaders as Henry Clay of Kentucky and John C. Calhoun of South Carolina, were young Democratic Republicans from the West and South. They found all aspects of British interference, such as impressment and support for western Indians, intolerable. Eager to assert independence from England once and for all, these young men saw themselves finishing the job begun by the aging revolutionary generation.

The War Hawks were vehemently expansionist, and their dreams of expansion entailed control of peoples of other races—resistant Indians and rebellious African Americans—at the edges of the national boundaries. Southerners wanted to occupy Florida to prevent runaway slaves from seeking refuge with the Seminole Indians. Westerners wanted to invade Canada, hoping thereby to end threats from British-backed Indians in the Northwest such as Tecumseh. As resentments against England and frustrations over border issues merged, the pressure for war—always a strong force for national unity—mounted.

Unaware that the British, seriously hurt by the American trade embargo, were about to adopt a more conciliatory policy, President James Madison yielded to the War Hawks' clamor for action in June 1812, and his declaration of war passed the U.S. Senate by the close vote of 19 to 13, the House by 79 to 49. All the Federalists voted against the war. (The division along party lines continued in the 1812 presidential election, in which Madison garnered 128 electoral votes to 89 for his Federalist opponent, DeWitt Clinton.) The vote was sectional, with New England and the Middle States in opposition and the West and South strongly prowar. Thus the United States entered the War of 1812 more deeply divided along sectional lines than during any other foreign war in American history.

Nor was that the end of the difficulties. As a result of Jefferson's economizing, the American army and navy were small and weak. In contrast, the British,

The War of 1812   *On land, the War of 1812 was fought to define the nation's boundaries. In the North, American armies attacked British forts in the Great Lakes region with little success, and the invasion of Canada was a failure. In the South, the battle of New Orleans made a national hero of Andrew Jackson, but it occurred after the peace treaty had been signed. On the sea, with the exception of Oliver Perry's victory in the Great Lakes, Britain's dominance was so complete and its blockade so effective that British troops were able to invade the Chesapeake and burn the capital of the United States.*

after almost ten years' entanglement in the Napoleonic Wars, were in fighting trim. As a result, although the War of 1812 brought Americans a few moments of glory, it was on the whole an ignominious struggle that gained them little.

The Campaign against Canada

The American goal of expansion fared badly. Americans envisaged a quick victory over sparsely populated British Canada that would destroy British support for Tecumseh and his Northwest Indian allies, but instead the British-Indian alliance defeated them. In July 1812, a foray into western Canada by General William Hull of Michigan Territory was repulsed by a joint British and Indian force, which went on, in August, to capture Detroit, Fort Dearborn (site of Chicago), and Hull's army of 2,000 men. The American burning of York (now Toronto) in April 1813 achieved little, but in September, at the battle of Put-in-Bay, Captain Oliver H. Perry defeated a British naval squadron on Lake Erie, sending out the famous message, "We have met the enemy and they are ours." Without control of Lake Erie, the British could no longer assure their hold on Detroit. In October, William Henry Harrison retook Detroit and followed its retreating British and Indian defenders. Assisted by naval forces commanded by Perry, Harrison defeated them in the battle of the Thames. Among those slain in the battle was Tecumseh. Later attempts by the United States to invade Canada in the Niagara area failed, but so too did British attempts to invade the United States in the same area.

One reason for the failure of the Canadian invasion, aside from failure to appreciate the strength of the British-Indian forces, was that the New England states actively opposed the war. Massachusetts, Rhode Island, and Connecticut refused to provide militia or supplies, and other New England governors turned a blind eye to the flourishing illegal trade across the U.S.–Canadian border. Another reason was the reaction of Canadians themselves, the majority of whom were former Americans. Ironically, the most decisive effect of the abortive American attacks was the formation of a Canadian sense of national identity and a determination never to be invaded or absorbed by the United States.

War in the South

In the South, warfare similar to that waged against Tecumseh's pan-Indian resistance movement in the Northwest dramatically affected the southern Indian peoples. The first of the southern Indian peoples to battle the Americans were the Creeks, a trading nation with a long history of contacts with the Spanish and the French. When white settlers began to occupy Indian lands in

northwestern Georgia and central Alabama early in the century, the Creeks, like the Shawnees in the Northwest, were divided in their response. Although many Creek bands argued for accommodation, a group known as the Red Sticks were determined to fight. During the War of 1812 the Red Sticks, allied with the British and Spanish, fought not only the Americans but other Indian groups.

In August 1813 the Red Sticks attacked Fort Mims on the Alabama River, killing more than 500 Americans and mixed-race Creeks who had gathered there for safety. Led by Andrew Jackson, troops from the Tennessee and Kentucky militias combined with the Creeks' traditional foes—the Cherokees, Choctaws, and Chickasaws—and some opposing bands of Creeks to exact revenge. Jackson's troops matched the Creeks in ferocity, shooting the Red Sticks "like dogs," one soldier reported. At the battle of Horseshoe Bend in March 1814, the Creeks were trapped between American cannon fire and their Indian enemies: more than 800 were killed, more than in any other battle in the history of Indian-white warfare. Jackson then marched on the remaining Red Stick villages, burning and killing as he went. Cornered, one remaining Red Stick leader, Red Eagle, personally confronted Jackson:

> General Jackson, I am not afraid of you. I fear no man, for I am a Creek warrior. I have nothing to request in behalf of myself....But I come to beg you to send for the women and children of the war party, who are now starving in the woods....If I could fight you any longer I would most heartily do so. Send for the women and children. They never did you any harm. But kill me, if the white people want it done.

At the end of the Creek War in 1814 Jackson demanded huge land concessions from the Creeks (including from some Creek bands that had fought on his side): 23 million acres, or more than half the Creek domain. The Treaty of Fort Jackson (1814) confirming these land concessions earned Jackson his Indian name, Sharp Knife.

The war failed to achieve another of its initial goals, that of capturing Florida from Spain. Mobile was captured in 1813, but although Jackson captured Pensacola in 1814, he was unable to hold it. In early 1815 (after the peace treaty had been signed but before news of it arrived in America), Andrew Jackson achieved his best-known victory, an improbable win over veteran British troops in the battle of New Orleans.

The Naval War

At sea the British navy quickly established a strong blockade, harassing coastal shipping along the Atlantic seaboard and attacking coastal settlements at will. In the most humiliating attack, the British burned Washington in the summer of 1814, forcing the president and Congress to flee. Dolley Madison, the president's wife, achieved a permanent footnote in history by saving a portrait of George Washington from the White House as she fled. The indignity of the burning of Washington was somewhat assuaged in September, when Americans beat back a British attack on Baltimore and Fort McHenry. Watching the "rockets' red glare" in the battle, onlooker Francis Scott Key was moved to write the words to the "Star-Spangled Banner." There were a few American naval successes. The American frigate *Constitution* destroyed two British men-of-war, the *Guerrière* and the *Java*, in classic naval battles but failed to lift the British blockade.

The Hartford Convention

America's occasional successes failed to diminish the angry opposition of the New England Federalists to the War of 1812. In late 1814, Federalist representatives from the five New England states met in Hartford, Connecticut, to air their grievances. At first the air was full of talk of secession from the Union, but soon cooler heads prevailed.

The Hartford Convention's final document contained a long list of grievances, but it did not mention secession. It did, however, insist that a state had the right "to interpose its authority" to protect its citizens against unconstitutional federal laws. This nullification doctrine was not new; Madison and Jefferson had proposed it in the Virginia and Kentucky Resolves opposing the Alien and Sedition Acts in 1798 (see Chapter 8). In any event, the nullification threat from Hartford was ignored, for peace with Britain was announced as delegates from the convention made their way to Washington to deliver their message to Congress. There the convention's grievances were treated not as serious business but as an anticlimactic joke.

The Treaty of Ghent

In 1814, as the long Napoleonic Wars in Europe were drawing to a close, the British decided to end their minor war with the Americans. The peace treaty, after months of hard negotiation, was signed at Ghent, Belgium, on Christmas Eve in 1814. Like the war itself, the treaty was inconclusive. The major issues of impressment and neutral rights were not mentioned, but the British did agree to evacuate their western posts, and late in the negotiations they abandoned their insistence on a buffer state for neutral Indian peoples in the Northwest.

For all its international inconsequence, the war did have an important effect on national morale. As one historian has said, Americans had fought "for their chance to grow up." Andrew Jackson's victory at New Orleans allowed Americans to believe that they had defeated the British. It would be more accurate to say that by not losing the war the Americans had ended their own feelings of colonial dependency. Equally important, they convinced the British government to stop thinking of America as its colony. As it turned out, the War of 1812 was the last war the United States and Britain were to fight against each other.

At the same time, the war was a dangerous risk to new and fragile ideas of national unity. It was one of America's most divisive wars, and what made the opposition so serious was its sectional nature. Had the conflict continued, it might have led to the secession of New England.

The only clear losers of the war were the Indian nations in the Northwest and their southern allies. With the death of Tecumseh in 1813 and the defeat of the southern Creeks in 1814, the last hope of a united Indian resistance to white expansion perished forever. Britain's abandonment of its Indian allies in the Treaty of Ghent sealed their fate. By 1815, American settlers were on their way west again.

The burning of Washington by the British was the worst indignity the young American nation suffered in the War of 1812. This contemporary woodcut shows Washington aflame on August 2, 1814.

Spread of Settlement: Westward Surge, 1800–1820
Within a period of twenty years, a quarter of the nation's population had moved west of the Appalachian Mountains. The westward surge was a dynamic source of American optimism.

DEFINING THE BOUNDARIES

With the War of 1812 behind them, Americans turned, more seriously than ever before, to the tasks of expansion and national development. The so-called Era of Good Feelings (1817–23) found politicians largely in agreement on a national agenda, and a string of diplomatic achievements forged by John Quincy Adams gave the nation sharper definition. But the limits to expansion also became clear: the Panic of 1819 showed the dangers in economic growth, and the Missouri Crisis laid bare the sectional split that attended westward expansion.

Another Westward Surge

The end of the War of 1812 was followed by a westward surge to the Mississippi River that populated the Old Northwest (Ohio, Indiana, Illinois, Michigan, and Wisconsin) and the Old Southwest (western Georgia, Alabama, Mississippi, Louisiana). The extent of the population redistribution was dramatic: in 1790, 95 percent of the nation's population had lived in states bordering the Atlantic Ocean; by 1820 fully 25 percent of the population lived west of the Appalachians.

What accounted for the westward surge? There were both push and pull factors. Between 1800 and 1820, the nation's population almost doubled, increasing from 5.3 million to 9.6 million. Although many easterners were attracted to the rapidly growing seacoast cities, 2.5 million, most of them farmers, chose to go westward. Overpopulated farmland in all of the seaboard states pushed farmers off the land, while new land pulled them westward. Defeat and removal of Indians in the War of 1812 was another important pull factor. In the Southwest, the Creeks ceded a huge tract of land amounting to three-fifths of Alabama and one-fifth of Georgia in the Treaty of Fort Jackson (1814); in the Northwest, the threat to settlers posed by Tecumseh's alliance had been removed.

The most important pull factor, however, was the attractive price of western land. The Land Ordinance of 1785 priced western lands too high for all but speculators and the wealthy (see Chapter 7), but since that time realities had slowly forced Congress to

Settlement of the heavily forested Old Northwest and Old Southwest required much heavy labor to clear the land. One common laborsaving method settlers learned from Indians was to "girdle" the trees (cutting the bark all around), thereby killing them. Dead trees could be more easily chopped and burned.

enact land laws more favorable to the small farmer. The most sustained challenge came from "squatters," who repeatedly took up land before it was officially open for sale and then claimed a "preemption" right of purchase at a lower price that reflected the value of improvements made to the land. Congress sought to suppress this illegal settlement and ordered the expulsion of squatters on several occasions, but to no avail. When federal lands were officially opened for sale in Illinois in 1814, for example, there were already 13,000 settlers, forcing Congress to reverse itself and grant them all preemption rights. Finally, in the Land Act of 1820, Congress set the price of land at $1.25 an acre, the minimum purchase at eighty acres (in contrast to the 640-acre minimum in 1785), and a down payment of $100 in cash. This was the most liberal land law yet passed in American history, but the cash requirement still favored speculators, who had more cash than most small farmers.

There were four major migration routes. In upstate New York, the Mohawk and Genesee Turnpike led New England migrants to Lake Erie, where they traveled by boat to northern Ohio. In the Middle States region, the turnpike from Philadelphia to Pittsburgh led to the Ohio River, as did the National Road that began in Baltimore and led to Wheeling. In the South, the Wilderness Road through the Cumberland Gap led to Kentucky, and passes in the mountains of North and South Carolina led to Tennessee. The Federal Road skirted the southern edge of the Appalachians and allowed farmers from South Carolina and eastern Georgia to move directly into Alabama and Mississippi. In this way, geography facilitated lateral westward movement (Northerners tended to migrate to the Old Northwest, Southerners to the Old Southwest). Except in southern Ohio and parts of Kentucky and Tennessee, there was very little contact between regional cultures. New Englanders carried their values and lifestyles

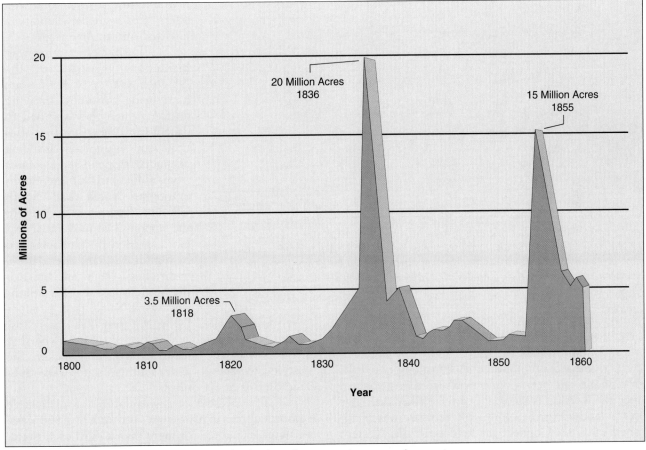

Western Land Sales   *Surges in western land sales reflect surges in westward expansion. Western land sales following the War of 1812 reached an unprecedented 3.5 million acres, but that was small in comparison with what was to come in the 1830s and 1850s. Not all land sales reflected actual settlement, however, and speculation in western lands was rampant. Collapse of the postwar speculative boom contributed to the Panic of 1819, and the abrupt end to the boom of the 1830s led to the Panic of 1837.*

Source: Robert Riegel and Robert Athearn, *America Moves West* (New York: Holt, Rinehart, 1964).

Major Migration Routes, 1800–1820 *The barrier of the Appalachian Mountains permitted only a few routes to the west. Settlers from the northern states took the Genesee Turnpike, Middle States migrants favored the Philadelphia-Pittsburgh Turnpike and the National Road, and Southerners used the Wilderness and Federal Roads. Because most westward movement was lateral, regional mixing among western settlers was rare. New Englanders carried their attitudes West, and Southerners did the same.*

Source: Donald Meinig, *The Shaping of America*, Vol. 2, *Continental America* (New Haven: Yale University Press, 1994).

directly west and settled largely with their own communities; Southerners did the same.

One section of northern Ohio along Lake Erie, for example, had been Connecticut's western land claim since the days of its colonial charter. Rather than give up the land when the Northwest Territory was established in 1787, Connecticut held onto the Western Reserve (as it was known) and encouraged its citizens to move there. Group settlement was common. General Moses Cleaveland of the Revolutionary War led one of the first groups of Yankees, fifty-two in all. In 1795 they settled the community that bears his name (though not his spelling of it). Many other groups followed, naming towns such as Norwalk after those they had left in

Connecticut. These New Englanders brought to the Western Reserve their religion (Congregational), their love of learning (tiny Norwalk soon boasted a three-story academy), and their adamant opposition to slavery.

Western migration in the South was very different. Just as on other frontiers, pioneers hacked wagon roads through the wilderness, encountered resistance from Indian peoples, and cleared the land for settlements and farms. But on this frontier, the hands on the ax handle were likely to be black, the people clearing the land doing it not for themselves but to create plantations for slave owners. More than half of the migrants to the Old Southwest after 1812 were involuntary—enslaved African Americans.

Even before the war, plantation owners in the Natchez district of Mississippi had made fortunes growing cotton, which they shipped to Britain from New Orleans. After the war, as cotton growing expanded, hopeful slave owners from older parts of the South (Virginia, North and South Carolina, Georgia), flooded into the region. The movement was like a gold rush, characterized by high hopes, land speculation, and riches—for a few. Most of the settlers in the Old Southwest were small farm families living in forest clearings. Most did not own slaves, but they hoped to, for ownership of slaves was the means to wealth. Quickly, the lifestyle and values of older southern states were replicated on this new frontier.

This western transplantation of distinctive regional cultures explains why, although by 1820 western states accounted for more than a third of all states (eight out of twenty-three), the West did not form a third, unified political region. Although there were common western issues—in particular, the demand for better roads and other transportation routes—in general, communities in the Old Northwest shared New England political attitudes, whereas those in the Old Southwest shared southern attitudes.

Camp Meeting. Color lithograph by Kennedy and Lucas, after painting by A. Rider, ca. 1835, negative number 26275. Collection of the New York Historical Society, New York City

The rural and community nature of the Second Great Awakening is captured in this illustration. The preacher exhorts the large audience, which responds with emotion. Many of the most enthusiastic converts were women, who gained a new feeling of moral and social consequence through their religious experience.

The Second Great Awakening on the Frontier

The religious movement known as the Second Great Awakening began quietly in the 1790s in New England, but by 1800 it had spread through the Protestant churches of the entire country. It was most dramatic on the frontier, where church organization was naturally weak. The great institution of western Protestantism became the camp meeting, an outdoor gathering that included many sects and might go on for days. The greatest of the early camp meetings took place at Cane Ridge, Kentucky, in 1801, when an estimated 20,000 people came together for a week of preaching and singing. This was a remarkable assembly considering that the largest town in the West at the time had fewer than 2,000 inhabitants. Preachers shouted from the stand, and in the flickering firelight of evening hundreds of people, overcome with religious enthusiasm, fell to speaking in tongues or jerking uncontrollably. "Many things transpired there," one observer wrote, "that had the same effects as miracles on infidels and unbelievers."

Organized religion became one of the most important institutions within the continuing westward migration. Camp meetings frequently provided the first occasion for the new settlers of an area to come together, and religious meetinghouses were often the first public buildings erected in a community. In the absence of resident ministers, preaching was provided by Methodist circuit riders or perhaps a Baptist farmer who heard "the call" and had himself licensed as a lay preacher. On the frontier as well as in the East, women were often in the majority among church members. They thus played an important role in an institution that was fundamental to the planting of new American communities.

The Election of 1816 and the Era of Good Feelings

In 1816 James Monroe, the last of the Virginia Dynasty, was easily elected president over his Federalist opponent, Rufus King (183 to 34 electoral votes). This was the last election in which Federalists ran a candidate. Monroe had no opponent in 1820 and was reelected nearly unanimously (231 to 1). The triumph of the Democratic Republicans over the Federalists seemed complete. But although the Democratic Republicans kept their name, they had accepted so many Federalist political principles that it was not easy to tell which party had actually triumphed.

Tall, dignified, dressed in the old-fashioned style of knee breeches and white-topped boots that Washington had worn, Monroe looked like a traditional figure. But his politics reflected changing times. Soon after his inauguration, the president made a goodwill tour of the country, the first president since Washington to do so. Reflecting the new geography of the nation, he went the farthest west any president had yet traveled to visit the frontier post of Detroit. When he visited Boston, as recently as 1815 the heart of a secession-minded Federalist region, he received an enthusiastic welcome, prompting the Federalist *Columbian Centinel* to proclaim an "Era of Good Feelings." The phrase has been applied to Monroe's presidency (1817–25) ever since.

Monroe sought a government of national unity, and he chose men from North and South, Democratic Republicans and Federalists, for his cabinet. He selected John Quincy Adams, a former Federalist, as his secretary of state, virtually assuring that Adams, like his father, would become president. To balance Adams, Monroe picked John C. Calhoun of South Carolina, a prominent War Hawk, as secretary of war. And Monroe supported the American System, a program of national economic development that became identified with Westerner Henry Clay, Speaker of the House of Representatives.

In supporting the American System, Monroe was following President Madison, who had proposed the program in his message to Congress of December 1815. Madison and Monroe broke with Jefferson's agrarianism to embrace much of the Federalist program for economic development, including the chartering of a national bank, a tax on imported goods to protect American manufacturers, and a national system of roads and canals. All three of these had first been proposed by Alexander Hamilton in the 1790s (see Chapter 8). At the time they had met with bitter Democratic Republican opposition. The support that Madison and Monroe gave to Hamilton's ideas following the War of 1812 was a crucial sign of the dynamism of the American commercial economy. Many Democratic Republicans now acknowledged that the federal government had a role to play in fostering the economic and commercial conditions in which both yeoman farmer and merchant could succeed. This active support for capitalist development explained why so many former Federalists were willing to join Monroe's party of national unity.

In 1816 Congress chartered the Second Bank of the United States for twenty years. Located in Philadelphia, the bank had a capital of $35 million, of which the government contributed $7 million. The bank was to provide large-scale financing that the smaller state banks could not handle and to create a strong national currency. Because they feared concentrated economic power, Democratic Republicans had allowed the charter of the original Bank of the United States, founded in 1791, to expire in 1811. The Democratic Republican about-face in 1816 was a sign that the strength of commercial interests had grown to rival that of farmers, whose distrust for central banks persisted.

The Tariff of 1816 was the first substantial protective tariff in American history. In 1815, British manufacturers, who had been excluded for eight years (from the Embargo Act of 1807 to the end of the War of 1812), flooded the United States market with their products. American manufacturers complained that the British were dumping goods below cost to prevent the growth of American industries. Congress responded with a tariff on imported woolens and cottons, on iron, leather, hats, paper, and sugar. The measure had southern as well as northern support, although in later years differences over the passage of higher tariffs would become one of the most persistent sources of sectional conflict.

The third item in the American System, funding for roads and canals—internal improvements, as they came to be known—was more controversial. Monroe and Madison both supported genuinely national (that is, interstate) projects such as the National Road from Cumberland, Maryland to Vandalia, Illinois. Congressmen, however, aware of the urgent need to improve transportation in general and scenting the political advantages that could accrue to them from directing funds to their districts, proposed spending federal money on local projects. Both Madison and Monroe vetoed such local proposals, believing them to be unconstitutional. Thus it was that some of the most famous projects of the day, such as the Erie Canal, which lay wholly within New York state, and the early railroads, were financed by state or private money.

The support of Madison and Monroe for measures initially identified with their political oppo-

sition was an indicator of their realism. The three aspects of the American System—bank, tariff, roads—were all parts of the basic infrastructure that the American economy needed in order to develop. Briefly, during the Era of Good Feelings, politicians agreed about the need for all three. Later, each would be a source of heated partisan argument.

The Diplomacy of John Quincy Adams

The diplomatic achievements of the Era of Good Feelings were due almost entirely to the efforts of one man, John Quincy Adams, Monroe's secretary of state. Adams set himself the task of tidying up the borders of the United States. Two accords with Britain—the Rush-Bagot Treaty of 1817 and the Convention of 1818—fixed the border between the United States and Canada at the 49th parallel and resolved conflicting U.S. and British claims to Oregon with an agreement to occupy it jointly for ten (eventually twenty) years. The American claim to Oregon (present-day British Columbia, Washington, Oregon, northern Idaho, and parts of Montana) was based on China trader Robert Gray's discovery of the Columbia River in 1792 and on the Lewis and Clark expedition of 1804–06. The British Hudson's Bay Company, however, had land-based fur-trading operations in the region, and established a major base at Fort Vancouver on the Columbia River in 1825.

Adams's major diplomatic accomplishment was the Adams-Onís or Transcontinental Treaty of 1819, in which he skillfully wrested concessions from the faltering Spanish empire. In 1818 General Andrew Jackson led an American force on a mission purportedly to end raids on the Florida border by Seminole Indians against American settlements. Exceeding his orders, Jackson invaded Florida itself, and Spain, preoccupied with revolts throughout its Latin American empire, was unable to repulse him. Jackson's success made it clear that the United States could easily snatch Florida from Spain by force. Adams convinced Spain not only to cede Florida but also to drop all previous claims it had to the Louisiana Territory and Oregon. In return, the United States relinquished claims on Texas and assumed responsibility for the $5 million in claims U.S. citizens had against Spain. Although many Westerners believed Adams should have been able to obtain Texas as well as Florida, the Transcontinental Treaty was hailed at the time as a success. It proved an important spur to American expansionism and highlighted Americans' growing confidence in foreign affairs.

That growing confidence was also apparent in Adams's culminating diplomatic success. In 1821, Mexico achieved its independence from Spain; by 1822, Argentina, Chile, and Colombia were independent as well. Adams picked his way through these remarkable changes in Latin America to the policy that bears his president's name, the Monroe Doctrine. The

United States was the first country outside Latin America to recognize the independence of Spain's former colonies. Many Americans enthusiastically supported the Latin American revolts and were proud to think that they were modeled on the American Revolution, as the Latin American liberator, Simón Bolívar, claimed.

But then the European powers (France, Austria, Russia, and Prussia) began talk of a plan to help Spain recover the lost colonies. What was the United States to do? The British, suspicious of the European powers, proposed a British-American declaration against European intervention in the hemisphere. Others might have been flattered by an approach from the British empire, but Adams would have none of it. Showing the national pride that was so characteristic of the era, Adams insisted on an independent American policy. He therefore drafted for the president the hemispheric policy that the United States has followed ever since. On December 2, 1823, the president presented the Monroe Doctrine to Congress and the world. He

called for the end of colonization of the Western Hemisphere by European nations (this was aimed as much at Russia and its Pacific coast settlements as at other European powers). Intervention by European powers in the affairs of the independent New World nations would be considered by the United States a danger to its own peace and safety. Finally, Monroe pledged that the United States would not interfere in the affairs of European countries or in the affairs of their remaining New World colonies.

All of this was a very large bark from a very small dog. In 1823, the United States lacked the military and economic force to back up its grand statement. In fact, what kept the European powers out of Latin America was British opposition to European intervention, enforced by the Royal Navy. But the Monroe Doctrine was to take on quite another aspect at the end of the century, when the United States did have the power to enforce it. The Monroe Doctrine was more immediately useful in Adams's last diplomatic achievement, the Convention of 1824, in which Russia gave up its claim to the Oregon

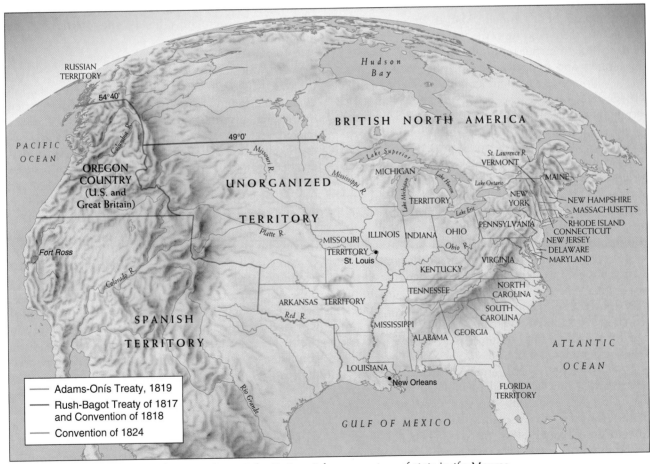

John Quincy Adams's Border Treaties   *John Quincy Adams, secretary of state in the Monroe administration (1817–25), solidified the nation's boundaries in several treaties with Britain and Spain. The Rush-Bagot Treaty of 1817 and the Conventions of 1818 and 1824 settled the northern boundary with Canada and the terms of a joint occupancy of Oregon. The Adams-Onís Treaty of 1819 added Florida to the United States and settled the disputed border between the American Louisiana Territory and Spanish possessions in the West.*

Territory and accepted 54° 40′ as the southern border of Russian America. Thus Adams contained another possible threat to American continental expansion.

This string of diplomatic achievements—the treaties with Russia, Britain, and Spain and the Monroe Doctrine—represented a great personal triumph for the stubborn, principled John Quincy Adams. A committed nationalist and expansionist, he showed that reason and diplomacy were in some circumstances more effective than force. Adams's diplomatic achievements were a fitting end to the period dominated by the Virginia Dynasty, the trio of enlightened revolutionaries who did so much to shape the new nation.

The Panic of 1819

Across this impressive record of political and economic nation building fell the shadow of the Panic of 1819. A delayed reaction to the end of the War of 1812 and the Napoleonic Wars, the panic forced Americans to come to terms with their economic place in a peaceful world. As British merchant ships resumed trade on routes they had abandoned during the wars, the American shipping boom ended. And as European farm production recovered from the wars, the international demand for American foodstuffs declined and American farmers and shippers suffered.

Domestic economic conditions made matters worse. The western land boom that began in 1815 turned into a speculative frenzy. Land sales, which had totaled 1 million acres in 1815, mushroomed to 3.5 million in 1818. Some lands in Mississippi and Alabama, made valuable by the international demand for cotton, were selling for $100 an acre. Many settlers bought on credit, aided by loans from small and irresponsible "wildcat" state banks. A number of speculators, carried away by the excitement of it all, also bought large tracts of land on credit and promoted them heavily. This was not the first—or the last—speculative boom in western lands. But it ended like all the rest—with a sharp contraction of credit, begun on this occasion by the Second Bank of the United States, which in 1819 forced state banks to foreclose on many bad loans. Many small farmers were ruined, and six years of depression followed.

In response to farmer protests, Congress passed a relief act in 1821 that extended the payment period for western lands, and some state legislatures passed "stay laws" that prevented banks from executing foreclosures. Nonetheless, many small banks failed, taking down their creditors with them. Many western farmers blamed the faraway Bank of the United States for their troubles. In the 1830s Andrew Jackson would build a political movement on their resentment.

Urban workers suffered both from the decline in international trade and from manufacturing failures caused by competition from British imports. As urban workers lobbied for local relief (there was no federal welfare), they found themselves deeply involved in urban politics, where they could express their resentment against the merchants and owners who had laid them off. Thus developed another component of Andrew Jackson's new political coalition.

Another confrontation arose over the tariff. Southern planters, hurt by a decline in the price of cotton, began to actively protest the protective tariff, which kept the price of imported goods high even when cotton prices were low. Manufacturers, hurt by British competition, lobbied for even higher rates, which they achieved in 1824 over southern protests. Southerners then began to express doubts about the fairness of a political system in which they were always outvoted.

The Panic of 1819 was a symbol of this transitional time. It showed how far the country had moved since 1800 from Jefferson's republic of yeoman farmers toward a nation dominated by commerce. And the anger and resentment expressed by the groups harmed by the depression—farmers, urban workers, and southern planters—were portents of the politics of the upcoming Jackson era.

The Missouri Compromise

In the Missouri Crisis of 1819–21, the nation confronted the momentous issue that had been buried in the general enthusiasm for expansion: As America moved west, would the largely southern system of slavery expand as well? Until 1819, this question was decided regionally. As residents of the northern states moved west, the territory into which they expanded (the Old Northwest) was free of slavery. As southerners moved into Alabama, Mississippi, and Louisiana (the Old Southwest), they brought their slaves with them. This regional difference had been mandated by Congress in the Northwest Ordinance of 1787, which explicitly banned slavery in the northern section of trans-Appalachia but made no mention of it elsewhere. Because so much of the expansion into the Old Northwest and Southwest was lateral (Northerners stayed in the north, Southerners in the south), there was little conflict over sectional differences. In 1819, however, the sections collided—in Missouri.

In 1819, Missouri applied for admission to the Union as a slave state. To the slave-owning Kentuckians and Tennesseans who were the territory's major settlers, this extension of slavery seemed natural and inevitable. But Illinois, also an adjacent state, prohibited slavery. The northern states, all of which had abolished slavery by 1819, looked askance at the extension of slavery northward.

In addition to the moral issue of slavery, the Missouri question raised the political issue of sectional balance. Northern politicians did not want to admit another slave state. To do so would tip the balance of power in the Senate, where the 1819 count of slave and free states was eleven apiece. For their part, Southerners believed they needed an advantage in the Senate; because of faster population growth in the North, they were already outnumbered (105 to 81) in the House of Representatives. But above all, Southerners did not believe Congress had the power to limit the expansion of slavery. They were alarmed that Northerners were considering national legislation on the matter. Slavery, in southern eyes, was a question of property and therefore a matter for state rather than federal legislation. Thus, from the very beginning the expansion of slavery raised constitutional issues.

The urgency of these considerations among politicians in 1819 illustrates how delicate matters of sectional balance had already become. Indeed, the

aging politician of Monticello, Thomas Jefferson, immediately grasped the seriousness of the question of the expansion of slavery. As he prophetically wrote to a friend, "This momentous question like a fire bell in the night, awakened and filled me with terror. I considered it at once the [death] knell of the Union."

In 1819 Representative James Tallmadge Jr. of New York began more than a year of congressional controversy when he demanded that Missouri agree to the gradual end of slavery as the price of entering the Union. At first, the general public paid little attention, but religious reformers (Quakers prominent among them) organized a number of antislavery rallies in northern cities that made politicians take notice. Former Federalists in the North who had seen their party destroyed by the achievements of Jefferson and his successors in the Virginia Dynasty eagerly seized on the Missouri issue. This was the first time that the growing northern reform impulse

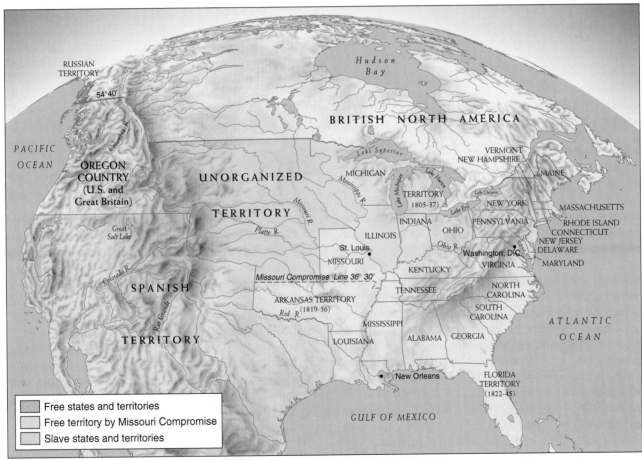

The Missouri Compromise   *Before the Missouri Compromise of 1820, the Ohio River was the dividing line between the free states of the Old Northwest and the slaveholding states of the Old Southwest. The compromise stipulated that Missouri would enter the Union as a slave state (balanced by Maine, a free state), but slavery would be prohibited in the Louisiana Territory north of 36° 30′ (Missouri's southern boundary). This awkward compromise lasted until 1846 when the Mexican-American War reopened the issue of the expansion of slavery.*

CHRONOLOGY

1790s	Second Great Awakening begins			Louisiana admitted to the Union
1800	Thomas Jefferson elected president		**1814**	Hartford Convention
1802	Russian-American Company headquarters established at Sitka, Alaska			Treaty of Ghent
			1815	Battle of New Orleans
1803	Louisiana Purchase		**1816**	James Monroe elected president
	Marbury v. Madison			Congress charters Second Bank of the United States
	Ohio admitted to the Union			Indiana admitted to the Union
1804	Lewis and Clark expedition begins		**1817**	Mississippi admitted to the Union
	Thomas Jefferson reelected president		**1818**	Illinois admitted to the Union
	Russians reestablish Sitka following the Tlingit Revolt			Andrew Jackson invades Florida
1807	*Chesapeake-Leopard* incident		**1819**	Panic of 1819
	Embargo Act			Adams-Onís Treaty
1808	James Madison elected president			Alabama admitted to the Union
1809	Tecumseh forms military alliance among Northwest Confederacy peoples		**1819–20**	Missouri Crisis and Compromise
			1820	James Monroe reelected president
1811	Battle of Tippecanoe			Maine admitted to the Union
1812	War of 1812 begins		**1821**	Missouri admitted to the Union as a slave state
	James Madison reelected president		**1823**	Monroe Doctrine

had intersected with sectional politics. It was also the first time that southern threats of secession were made openly in Congress.

The Senate debate over the admission of Missouri, held in the early months of 1820, was the nation's first extended debate over slavery. Observers noted the high proportion of free African Americans among the listeners in the Senate gallery. They, like Thomas Jefferson, realized that the fate of the Union and the fate of the black race in America were inseparable. But the full realization that the future of slavery was central to the future of the nation would not become apparent to the general public until the 1850s.

In 1820, Congress achieved compromise over the sectional differences. Henry Clay forged the first of the many agreements that were to earn him the title of "the Great Pacificator" (peacemaker). A glance at the map shows the state of Missouri as an awkward intrusion into an otherwise slave-free area, a visual break in the smooth westward continuation of sectionalism. This visual impression is reflected in the Missouri Compromise itself, which was difficult to arrange and had an awkward air about it. The compromise maintained the balance between free and slave states: Maine (which had been part of Massachusetts) was admitted as a free state in 1820 and Missouri as a slave state in the following year. A policy was also enacted with respect to slavery in the rest of the Louisiana Purchase: slavery was prohibited north of 36° 30′ north latitude—the southern boundary of Missouri—and permitted south of that line. This meant that the vast majority of the Louisiana Territory would be free. In reality, then, the Missouri Compromise could be only a temporary solution, because it left open the question of how the balance between slave and free states would be maintained. The seriousness of the sectional struggle over the Missouri question also directed popular attention to the changing nature of national politics.

CONCLUSION

In complex ways a developing economy, geographical expansion, and even a minor war helped shape American unity. Locally, small, settled, face-to-face communities in both the North and the South began to send their more mobile, expectant members to new occupations in urban centers or west to form new settlements, displacing Indian communities in the process.

The westward movement was the novel element in the American national drama. Europeans believed that large size and a population in motion bred instability and political disintegration. Thomas Jefferson thought otherwise, and the Louisiana Purchase was the gamble that confirmed his guess. The westward population movement dramatically changed the political landscape and Americans' view of themselves. Few of those changes, though, were fully apparent in 1820.

Expansion would not create the settled communities of yeoman farmers Jefferson had hoped for. Rather, it would breed a nation of restless and acquisitive people and a new kind of national democratic politics that reflected their search for broader definitions of community.

REVIEW QUESTIONS

1. What economic and political problems did the United States face as a new nation in a world dominated by war between Britain and France? How successful were the efforts by the Jefferson, Madison, and Monroe administrations to solve these problems?
2. The anti-European cast of Jefferson's republican agrarianism made it appealing to many Americans who wished to believe in their nation's uniqueness, but how realistic was it?
3. Some Federalists opposed the Louisiana Purchase, warning of the dangers of westward expansion. What are arguments for and against expansion?
4. What contradictions in American Indian policy did the confrontations between Tecumseh's alliance and soldiers and settlers in the Old Northwest reveal? Can you suggest solutions to them?
5. What did the War of 1812 accomplish?
6. What were the issues that made it impossible for the Era of Good Feelings to last?

RECOMMENDED READING

Frank Bergon, ed., *The Journals of Lewis and Clark* (1989). A handy abridgment of the fascinating history of the expedition. (For more intensive study, Gary Moulton's six-volume unabridged edition of the expedition journals is unsurpassed.)

John Boles, *The Great Revival, 1787–1805* (1972). The standard work on the Second Great Awakening.

George Drago, *Jefferson's Louisiana: Politics and the Clash of Legal Traditions* (1975). Provides an illuminating example of the cultural flexibility of the federal system.

R. David Edmunds, *Tecumseh and the Quest for Indian Leadership* (1984). A sympathetic portrait.

Joseph J. Ellis, *American Sphinx: The Character of Thomas Jefferson* (1998). An engaging exploration of Jefferson's many contradictions.

John Mack Faragher, *Sugar Creek* (1987). The fullest examination of the lives of pioneers in the Old Northwest.

Donald Hickey, *The War of 1812: A Forgotten Conflict* (1989). Takes a fresh look at the events and historiography of the war.

Drew McCoy, *The Elusive Republic: Political Economy in Jeffersonian America* (1980). The most useful discussion of the ties between expansion and republican agrarianism.

Glover Moore, *The Missouri Controversy, 1819–1821* (1953). The standard account.

Curtis P. Nettels, *The Emergence of a National Economy, 1775–1815* (1962). A useful overview.

Merrill Peterson, *Thomas Jefferson and the New Nation* (1970). A good one-volume political biography of Jefferson. (The major biography, by Dumas Malone, is a multivolume work.)

James Ronda, *Lewis and Clark among the Indians* (1984). An innovative look at the famous explorers through the eyes of the Indian peoples they encountered.

ADDITIONAL BIBLIOGRAPHY

American Communities from Coast to Coast

James Gibson, *Imperial Russia in Frontier America* (1976)

Marcel Giraud, *A History of French Louisiana, 1698–1715* (1974)

Carey McWilliams, *North from Mexico: The Spanish-Speaking People of the United States* (1948)

Douglas Monroy, *Thrown among Strangers: The Making of Mexican Culture in Frontier California* (1990)

Barbara Sweetland Smith and Redmond Barnett, eds., *Russian America* (1990)

David Weber, *The Spanish Frontier in North America* (1993)

The National Economy

Robert G. Albion, *The Rise of New York Port, 1815–1860* (1939)

W. Eliot Brownlee, *Dynamics of Ascent: A History of the American Economy* (1979)

Stuart Bruchey, *The Roots of American Economic Growth, 1607–1861* (1965)

Samuel Eliot Morison, *Maritime History of Massachusetts: 1783–1860* (1921)

Douglass C. North, *The Economic Growth of the United States, 1790–1860* (1966)

The Jefferson Presidency

Thomas P. Abernathy, *The Burr Conspiracy* (1954)

Henry Adams, *The United States in 1800* (1955)

Noble E. Cunningham, *The Jeffersonian Republicans and Power: Party Operations, 1801–1809* (1963)

Richard E. Ellis, *The Jeffersonian Crisis: Courts and Politics in the Young Republic* (1971)

David Hackett Fischer, *The Revolution of American Conservatism: The Federalist Party in the Era of Jeffersonian Democracy* (1965)

Charles G. Haines, *The Role of the Supreme Court in American Government and Politics, 1789–1835* (1944)

Linda K. Kerber, *Federalists in Dissent: Imagery and Ideology in Jeffersonian America* (1970)

Burton Spivak, *Jefferson's English Crisis: Commerce, Embargo, and the Republican Revolution* (1979)

Robert W. Tucker and David Hendrickson, *Empire of Liberty: The Statecraft of Thomas Jefferson* (1990)

G. Edward White, *The Marshall Court and Cultural Change, 1815–1835*, abridged ed. (1991)

Robert H. Wiebe, *The Opening of American Society: From the Adoption of the Constitution to the Eve of Disunion* (1984)

James S. Young, *The Washington Community: 1800–1828* (1966)

Renewed Imperial Rivalry

Robert F. Berkhofer Jr., *Salvation and Savage: An Analysis of Protestant Missions and American Indian Response, 1787–1862* (1965)

Henry Warner Bowden, *American Indians and Christian Missions: Studies in Cultural Conflict* (1981)

Gregory Evans Dowd, *A Spirited Resistance: The North American Indian Struggle for Unity, 1745–1815*

Reginald Horsman, *Expansion and American Indian Policy, 1783–1812* (1967)

Dorothy Jones, *License for Empire: Colonialism by Treaty in Early America* (1982)

Drew R. McCoy, *The Last of the Fathers: James Madison and the Republican Legacy* (1989)

Francis Paul Prucha, *The Great Father: The United States Government and the American Indians*, 2 vols. (1984)

Bernard Sheehan, *Seeds of Extinction: Jeffersonian Philanthropy and the American Indian* (1973)

The War of 1812

Reginald Horsman, *The Causes of the War of 1812* (1962)

Steven Watts, *The Republic Reborn: War and the Making of Liberal America, 1790–1820* (1987)

Defining the Boundaries

John Boles, *Religion in Antebellum Kentucky* (1976)

Andrew Cayton, *The Frontier Republic: Ideology and Politics in the Ohio Country, 1789–1812* (1986)

———, *Frontier Indiana* (1996)

Paul Conklin, *Cane Ridge: America's Pentecost* (1990)

George Dangerfield, *The Era of Good Feelings* (1952)

Anita Shafer Goodstein, *Nashville, 1780–1860: From Frontier to City* (1989)

Harlan Hatcher, *The Western Reserve: The Story of New Connecticut in Ohio* (1991)

Walter LaFeber, ed., *John Quincy Adams and the American Continental Empire* (1965)

Ernest R. May, *The Making of the Monroe Doctrine* (1975)

Malcolm J. Rohrbough, *The Land Office Business* (1968)

———, *The Trans-Appalachian Frontier: Peoples, Societies, and Institutions, 1775–1850* (1978)

William Ganson Rose, *Cleveland: The Making of a City* (1990)

Richard Slotkin, *Regeneration through Violence: The Mythology of the American Frontier* (1973)

Richard C. Wade, *The Urban Frontier: The Rise of Western Cities, 1790–1850* (1973)

Kenneth J. Winkle, *The Politics of Community: Migration and Politics in Antebellum Ohio* (1988)

Biography

Harry Ammon, *James Monroe: The Quest for National Identity* (1971)

Leonard Baker, *John Marshall: A Life in Law* (1974)

Irving Brant, *James Madison* (1950–61)

Dumas Malone, *Jefferson the President: First Term, 1801–1805* (1970)

———, *Jefferson the President: Second Term, 1805–1809* (1974)

CHAPTER TEN

THE GROWTH OF DEMOCRACY

1824–1840

George Caleb Bingham, *Stump Speaking*, from the Art Collection of NationsBank.

AMERICAN COMMUNITIES
Martin Van Buren Forges a New Kind of Political Community

When Martin Van Buren left Albany for Washington in the fall of 1821 to take up his new position as junior senator from New York, he wrote complacently: "I left the service of the state [of New York] for that of the federal government with my friends in full and almost unquestioned possession of the state government in all its branches, at peace with each other and overflowing with kindly feelings towards myself." Thus did Van Buren sum up more than ten years of intense activity in New York State politics in which he and his allies, nicknamed the Bucktails (for the Indian-inspired insignia, the tail of a buck, that members wore on their hats), created one of the first modern democratic political parties. How could it be, Washington politicians asked, that this short, invariably pleasant but rather nondescript man had triumphed over the renowned DeWitt Clinton?

Tall, handsome, arrogant DeWitt Clinton, governor of New York from 1817 to 1823 (and again from 1825 until his death in 1828), had been swept into office on a tide of enthusiasm for his plan to build a canal the length of the state. Clinton soon gained legislative approval for the project—the Erie Canal—the most ambitious and most successful canal project in an era of canal building. An aristocrat in wealth, connections, and attitude, Clinton represented old style politics. During his first terms as governor he ran the New York Democratic Republican Party as though it were his personal property, dispensing patronage to relatives and friends (many of whom were Federalists) on the basis of their loyalty to him rather than their political principles.

Martin Van Buren was a new kind of politician. Born in the small, Dutch-dominated town of Kinderhook, New York, Van Buren was the son of a tavern keeper, not a member of the wealthy elite. He grew up with an enduring resentment of the aristocratic landowning families such as the Van Schaacks and the Van Rensselaers (and, by extension, the Clintons) who disdained him when he was young. Masking his anger with charming manners, Van Buren took advantage of the growing strength of the Democratic Republican Party in New York State to wrest control of it from Clinton and forge it into a new kind of political organization. Clinton's use of patronage to reward friends at the expense of young party loyalists infuriated Van Buren and other rising politicians. Two years after Clinton became governor, Van Buren wrote bitterly to a friend: "A man to be a sound politician and in any degree useful to his country must be guided by higher and steadier considerations than those of personal sympathy and private regard. . . . In the name of all that is holy, where is the evidence of that towering mind and those superior talents which it has been the business of puffers and toad eaters to attribute to [Clinton]?"

By 1819, Van Buren had gathered together enough other disgruntled Democratic Republicans to form the Bucktail faction and openly challenge Clinton. Two years later, at the state constitutional convention of 1821 (where they made up three fourths of the delegates), the Bucktails sealed their victory. Meeting in Albany to revise the out-of-date constitution of 1777, the convention voted to streamline the organization of state government and sharply curtail the patronage powers of the governor. To cement these changes, delegates enacted nearly total manhood suffrage: all adult male citizens who paid state or local taxes; served in the militia, or worked on state roads—more than four-fifths of the adult male population—were now eligible to vote directly for state legislators, governor, and members of Congress.

This dramatic democratization of politics reflected the state's changing population. Already the bustling port of New York was the nation's largest city, and the state's commercial opportunities were attracting shrewd Yankee traders from New England "whose laws, customs and usages," conservative senator Rufus King complained, "differ from those of New York." The old ruling families, failing to recognize the new commercial and social values of the newcomers, were losing their grip on politics. Rising politicians like Van Buren and other Bucktails, in contrast, found opportunity in these changing conditions. Attuned to popular feeling, they responded to the state's growing and increasingly diverse population by creating a new kind of political community. A political party, they maintained, should be a democratic organization expressing the will of all its members, not an organization dominated by an elite group like Clinton's and bound together only by family ties and political favors. All party members, including leaders, would have to abide by majority rule. Party loyalty, rather than personal opinion or friendship, would be the bond that kept the party together and, rather than aristocratic background, the principal requirement for party leadership. "The first man we see step to the rear," wrote Bucktail Silas Wright Jr., still smarting from the factionalism and favoritism of the Clinton years, "we cut down."

By the time he departed for Washington in the fall of 1821, Van Buren left in Albany a closely knit group of friends and allies who practiced these new political principles. Party decisions, reached by discussion in legislative caucus and publicized by the party newspaper, the *Albany Argus*, were binding on all members and enforced by patronage decisions. The group, dubbed the Albany Regency, ran New York State politics for twenty years. For all those years Martin Van Buren was in Washington, where he was a major architect of the new democratic politics of mass participation that has been called the Second American Party System. This new movement created, for the first time in American history, national communities of political partisans. Van Buren understood how to create these new communities. Organization and discipline were essential not for their own sake but because they allowed the political leader to reach out to public opinion. "Those who have wrought great changes in the world," Van Buren wrote, " never succeeded by gaining over chiefs; but always by exciting the multitude. The first is the resource of intrigue and produces only secondary results, the second is the resort of genius and transforms the face of the universe." The sources and expression of the new politics were linked to wider economic and cultural factors that encouraged national cohesion.

KEY TOPICS

- The role of Andrew Jackson's presidency in affirming and solidifying the new democratic politics

- The part played by the transportation revolution in unifying the nation

- Establishment of the basic two-party pattern of American political democracy

- The creation of a distinctive American cultural identity by writers and artists

THE NEW DEMOCRATIC POLITICS

The early years of the nineteenth century were a time of extraordinary growth and change for the new republic. The changes pulled the nation in two contradictory directions, toward both sectionalism and nationalism.

The two major sections of the country, the North and the South, had always had different social systems, and from the time of the first Continental Congress they had also always disagreed as to the nature of the political compromises they needed to make. Economic development in the early nineteenth century increased the difference between the sections as the South committed itself to cotton growing and the slave system and the North moved rapidly to a commercial, industrializing economy. Although both North and South were still economically interconnected, the two sections were on very different paths. Had the United States of America still consisted only of the thirteen original states, North-South compromises might well have broken down by the 1820s and split the nation into two parts.

Westward expansion, however, provided a nationalizing force. Because of developments in transportation, in 1840 the larger United States was more closely knit than the original thirteen states had been in 1787. And the nine new states west of the Appalachians that entered the Union between 1800 and 1840—making up one-third of the membership of the U.S. Senate—contributed their own regional perspective to national politics. Although settlement patterns tended to align people in what is now called the Old Northwest (Ohio, Indiana, Illinois, Wisconsin, and Michigan) with New England and those in the Old Southwest (Mississippi and Alabama) and the slave states of the Louisiana Purchase (Louisiana, Arkansas, and Missouri) with the South, Westerners as a whole shared common concerns and attitudes that national politicians from the two older areas could not ignore if they wished to build strong political allegiances in the new region. The political effect of westward expansion in the period 1820–40 was to modify although not to eliminate the basic sectional differences between North and South. But the most dramatic effect of westward expansion was the encouragement it gave to democratic politics.

The Expansion and Limits of Suffrage

Before 1800 most of the original thirteen states limited the vote to property owners or taxpayers, or less than half the white male population. In DeWitt Clinton's New York and other states the wealthy held the levers of political power. In national politics as well, in spite of occasional revolts from below such as the Whiskey Rebellion of 1794 (see Chapter 8), political control remained in the hands of the traditional elite until the end, in 1825, of the Virginia Dynasty of presidents.

Westward expansion changed the nature of American politics. Mobility itself promoted change by undermining the traditional authority structures in the older states. "Old America seems to be breaking up and moving westward," an observer commented in 1817. Rapid westward expansion bolstered the national pride that Americans felt in their successful republican revolution and fostered a spirit of self-reliance. As Andrew Jackson, recruiting troops for the War of 1812, boasted, "We are the free born sons of America; the citizens of the only republic now existing in the world; and the only people on earth who possess rights, liberties, and property which they dare call their own."

The new western states extended the right to vote to all white males over the age of twenty-one. Kentucky entered the Union with universal manhood suffrage in 1792, Tennessee (1796), and Ohio (1803) with low taxpayer qualifications that approached universal suffrage. Soon older states such as New Jersey (1807) and Maryland (1810) dropped their property qualification for voting. By 1820, most of the older states had followed suit. Some states liberalized voting in the hopes of dissuading disgruntled nonvoters from moving west or because it seemed unfair to recruit men to fight in the War of 1812 but not allow them to vote. In most states, however, the driving force behind reform was competition for votes between parties or factions of parties (such as the Bucktails and the Clintonians in New York).

In Connecticut, the Democratic Republicans, appealing to young, democratically minded but propertyless young men, first challenged the state's controlling Federalists in 1802 and finally in 1817 achieved suffrage for all men who paid taxes or served in the militia (that is, nearly everyone). In South Carolina, the rivalry was geographical, pitting the more numerous up-country residents who supported Jefferson's Democratic Republicans against the wealthy Federalist slave-owning political elite of the low country who controlled the state legislature. A compromise agreement of 1808 allocated votes to the lower house by population (favoring the up-country), and to the upper house by wealth (favoring the low country). This redistribution of power led directly to a demand for universal white manhood suffrage, which became law (with a two-year residency requirement) in South Carolina in 1810. There were laggards— Rhode Island, Virginia, and Louisiana did not liberalize their voting qualifications until later— but by 1840, more than 90 percent of adult white males in the nation could vote. And they could vote for more officials: governors and (most important) presidential electors were now elected by direct vote, rather than chosen by small groups of state legislators.

Universal white manhood suffrage, of course, was far from true universal suffrage: The right to vote remained barred to most of the nation's 500,000 free African Americans and to women of any race. Only in five New England states (Maine, New Hampshire, Vermont, Massachusetts, and Rhode Island) could free African American men vote before 1865. In most of the other northern states the right of free African American men to vote was limited, first by custom and later by law. In 1821 in New York, for example, the same Bucktail-dominated legislature that voted to

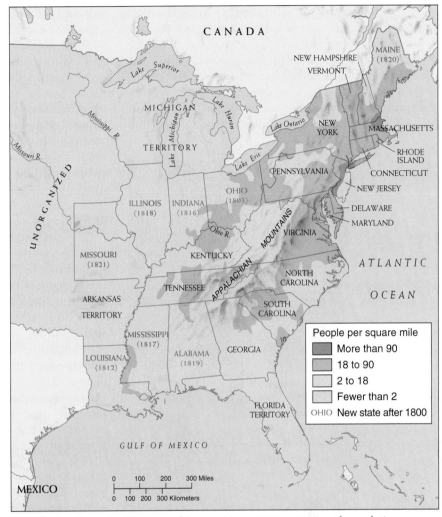

Population Trends: Westward Expansion, 1830 *Westward population movement, a trickle in 1800, had become a flood by 1830. Between 1800 and 1830 the U.S. white and African American population more than doubled (from 5.3 million to 12.9 million), but the trans-Appalachian population grew tenfold (from 370,000 to 3.7 million). By 1830 more than a third of the nation's inhabitants lived west of the original thirteen states.*

extend the franchise to most white men also restricted it among African American men to those with property valued at $250 or more, a very high amount at the time. As a result, only 68 of the nearly 13,000 African Americans in New York City qualified to vote in 1825.

Free African Americans were denied the vote in all southern states—and surprisingly, in the new western states as well. The Ohio constitution of 1802 denied African Americans the rights to vote, to hold public office, and to testify against white men in court cases. Later restrictions barred black men from serving in the state militia and on juries. The constitutions of other western states—Illinois, Indiana, Michigan, Iowa, Wisconsin, and, later, Oregon—attempted to solve the "problem" of free African Americans by simply denying them entry into the state at all.

The denial of suffrage to white women stemmed from the patriarchal belief that men headed households and represented the interests of all household members. Even wealthy single women who lived alone were considered subordinate to male relatives and denied the right to vote. (New Jersey was an exception to this rule until it amended its constitution in 1807 to withdraw the franchise from propertied

The Growth of Universal White Manhood Suffrage
Kentucky was the first western state to enact white male suffrage without tax or property qualifications. Other western states followed, and by 1820 most of the older states had dropped their suffrage restrictions as well. By 1840, more than 90 percent of the nation's white males could vote. But although voting was democratized for white men, restrictions on free African American male voters grew tighter, and women were excluded completely.

women.) Although unable to vote, women of the upper classes had long played important informal roles in national politics. Presidents' wives like Abigail Adams and Dolley Madison were famous for their ability to provide the social settings in which their husbands could quietly conduct political business. Another unrecognized group of skilled politicians were the women who ran the Washington boardinghouses where most congressmen lived during the legislative term. These women, longtime Washington residents, often served as valuable sources of information and official contacts for their boarders. At the state and local level of politics as well, women—often the wives of politicians—engaged in political activities.

Although the extension of suffrage to all classes of white men seemed to indicate that women had no role in public affairs, in fact women's informal involvement in politics grew along with the increasing pace of political activity. At the same time, however, as "manhood" rather than property became the qualification for voting, men began to ignore women's customary political activity and to regard their participation as inappropriate, an attitude that politically active women increasingly resented.

Thus, in this period famous for democratization and "the rise of the common man" the exclusion of important groups—African American men, and women of all races—marked the limits of liberalization. It is also true that nowhere else in the world was the right to vote so widespread as it was in the United States. The extension of suffrage to the common man marked a major step beyond the republicanism advocated by the Revolutionary generation. Thomas Jefferson had envisaged a republic of property-owning yeoman farmers. Now, however, propertyless farm workers and members of the laboring poor in the nation's cities could vote as well. European observers were curious about the democratization of voting: Could "mob rule" possibly succeed? And how would it affect traditional politics? The election of 1824 provided the first outline of the answer.

The Election of 1824

The 1824 election marked a dramatic end to the political truce that James Monroe had established in 1817. In that "Era of Good Feelings," one big political party, the expanded Democratic Republicans, had absorbed the remaining Federalists. This brief moment of unanimity did not survive the Panic of 1819 and the Missouri Crisis (see Chapter 9). Thus five candidates, all of them members of the Democratic Republican Party, ran for president in the elections of 1824. The candidate chosen by the usual method of congressional caucus was William H. Crawford of Georgia. The traditional stepping stone to the presidency, however, had been the office of secretary of state, giving a strong claim to John Quincy Adams of Massachusetts, who held that position in President Monroe's administration. Adams was nominated by his state legislature, as were two other candidates, Henry Clay of Kentucky and Andrew Jackson of Tennessee. The fifth candidate, John C. Calhoun of South Carolina, Monroe's secretary of war, withdrew before the election to run for vice president. Each candidate was clearly identified with a region: Adams with New England, Crawford and Calhoun with the South, Clay and Jackson with the West. Jackson, a latecomer to the race, was at first not taken seriously because his record as a legislator was lackluster and his political views unknown. His reputation as a military hero, however, enabled him to run as a national candidate despite his regional identification. He won 43 percent of the popular vote and more electoral votes—99—than any other candidate. The runner-up, John Quincy Adams, won 31 percent of the popular vote and 84 electoral votes. But neither had an electoral majority, leaving it up to the House of Representatives, as in the election of 1800, to pick the winner.

After some political dealing, Henry Clay threw his support to Adams and the House elected Adams president. This was customary and proper: the Constitution gave the House the power to decide, and Clay had every right to advise his followers how to vote. But when Adams named Clay his secretary of state, the traditional stepping-stone to the highest office, Jackson's supporters promptly accused them of a "corrupt bargain." Popular opinion, the new element in politics, supported Jackson. John Quincy Adams served four miserable years as president, knowing that Jackson would challenge him, and win, in 1828.

The legislative accomplishments of Adams's presidency were scanty. Adams's ambitious proposals for national development were rebuffed by a hostile Congress, although he did succeed in obtaining funding for an extension of the National Road west from Wheeling—significantly, an issue on which he could count on western votes. Congress stalled Adams's request to send American delegates to a conference in Panama called by the Latin American liberator Simón Bolívar, in part because Southerners feared attendance might lead to recognition of the revolutionary black republic of Haiti. Thus Adams's desire to lead the nation from a position above politics was frustrated by a political opposition that he thought illegitimate but that was in reality an early portent of the emerging two-party system.

Organizing Popular Politics

As the election of 1824 showed, hand-in-hand with the spread of universal manhood suffrage went a change in popular attitudes that spelled the end of personal, elitist politics. The triumph of Van Buren and the Buck-

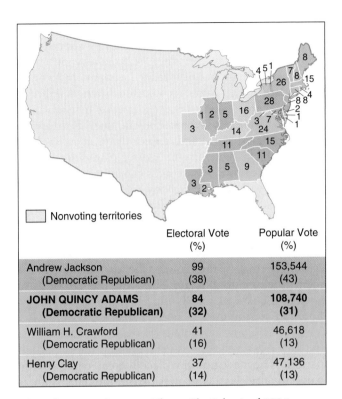

	Electoral Vote (%)	Popular Vote (%)
Andrew Jackson (Democratic Republican)	99 (38)	153,544 (43)
JOHN QUINCY ADAMS (Democratic Republican)	**84 (32)**	**108,740 (31)**
William H. Crawford (Democratic Republican)	41 (16)	46,618 (13)
Henry Clay (Democratic Republican)	37 (14)	47,136 (13)

Nonvoting territories

The Election of 1824   *The presidential vote of 1824 was clearly sectional. John Quincy Adams carried his native New England and little else, Henry Clay carried only his own state of Kentucky and two adjoining states, and Crawford's appeal was limited to Virginia and Georgia. Only Andrew Jackson moved beyond the regional support of the Old Southwest to wider appeal and the greatest number of electoral votes. Because no candidate had a majority, however, the election was thrown into the House of Representatives, which chose Adams.*

tails in New York in 1821 was one example of this sort of change, but politicians in other states shared Van Buren's vision of tightly organized, broad-based political groups. John C. Calhoun of South Carolina was first elected to his state legislature in 1808, the year that the iron political grip of the low-country planters was weakened. Calhoun, himself from the up-country, depended throughout his political career on the up-country voters who achieved universal white manhood suffrage in 1810. In Virginia a group known as the Richmond Junto had control of state politics by 1816, and in Tennessee the Nashville Junto, masterminded by John Overton, held sway by 1822. In New Hampshire, Isaac Hill's Concord Regency was firmly in control by 1825. Each of these organizations, to a greater or lesser extent, aspired to the same discipline and control as the Albany Regency aspired to, and each had wider aspirations. The Nashville Junto led the way by nominating Andrew Jackson for president in 1824.

The crucial element in the success of the new party system, as Van Buren realized, was its mass appeal.

Just as the religion of the day emphasized emotion over reason, so too the new political parties appealed to popular enthusiasms. The techniques of mass campaigns—huge political rallies, parades, and candidates with wide "name recognition" such as military heroes—were quickly adopted by the new political parties. So were less savory techniques such as the distribution of lavish food and (especially) drink at polling places, which frequently turned elections into rowdy, brawling occasions. These mass campaigns were something new. In 1834, the French visitor Michel Chevalier witnessed a mile-long nighttime parade in support of Andrew Jackson. Stunned by the orderly stream of banners lit by torchlight, the portraits of George Washington, Thomas Jefferson, and Jackson, and the enthusiastic cheering of the crowd, Chevalier wrote, "These scenes belong to history. They are the episodes of wondrous epic which will bequeath a lasting memory to posterity, that of the coming of democracy."

As Chevalier noted, the spirit that motivated the new mass politics was democratic pride in participation. The new politics placed great emphasis on party loyalty. Just as professional politicians such as Van Buren were expected to be loyal, so the average voter was encouraged to make a permanent commit-

Politics, abetted by the publication of inexpensive party newspapers, was a great topic of conversation among men in early nineteenth-century America, as Richard Caton Woodville's 1845 painting Politics in an Oyster House *suggests.*

ment to a political party. The party provided some of the same satisfactions that popular sports offer today: excitement, entertainment, and a sense of belonging. In effect, political parties functioned as giant national men's clubs. They made politics an immediate and engrossing topic of conversation and argument for men of all walks of life. In this sense, the political party was the political manifestation of a wider social impulse toward community. But the glue that held political parties together went beyond the appeal of a particular leader or loyalty to one's friends. Political parties were based on genuine differences of political opinion. The task of politicians, as Van Buren recognized, was to emphasize those differences in ways that forged support not just for one election but for permanent, national communities of political interest.

The Election of 1828

The election of 1828 was the first to demonstrate the power and effectiveness of the new party system. With the help of Martin Van Buren, his campaign manager, Andrew Jackson rode the wave of the new democratic politics to the presidency. Jackson's party, the Democratic Republicans (they soon dropped "Republicans" and became simply the Democrats), spoke the language of democracy, and they opposed the special privilege personified for them by President John Quincy Adams and his National Republican (as distinguished from "Democratic Republican") Party. Neither Jackson nor Adams campaigned on his own—that was considered undignified. But the supporters of both candidates campaigned vigorously, freely, and negatively. Jackson's supporters portrayed the campaign as a contest between "the democracy of the country, on the one hand, and a lordly purse-proud aristocracy on the other." In their turn, Adams's supporters depicted Jackson as an illiterate backwoodsman, a murderer (he had killed several men in duels), and an adulterer (apparently unwittingly, he had married Rachel Robards before her divorce was final).

Jackson's running mate for vice president was John C. Calhoun of South Carolina. Although this choice assured Jackson of valuable southern support, it also illustrated the transitional nature of politics, for Calhoun was currently serving as vice president to John Quincy Adams, Jackson's opponent. That Calhoun was able easily to lend his support to a rival faction was a holdover from the old elite and personal politics that would soon be impossible in the new democratic political system.

Jackson won 56 percent of the popular vote (well over 80 percent in much of the South and West) and a decisive electoral majority of 178 votes to Adams's 83. The vote was interpreted as a victory for the common man. But the most important thing about

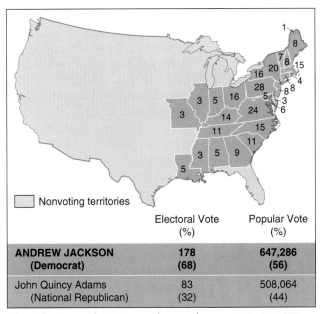

	Electoral Vote (%)	Popular Vote (%)
ANDREW JACKSON (Democrat)	**178 (68)**	**647,286 (56)**
John Quincy Adams (National Republican)	83 (32)	508,064 (44)

Nonvoting territories

The Election of 1828   *Andrew Jackson's victory in 1828 was the first success of the new national party system. The coalition of state parties that elected him was national, not regional. Although his support was strongest in the South and West, his ability to carry Pennsylvania and parts of New York demonstrated his national appeal.*

Jackson's victory was the coalition that achieved it. The new democratically based political organizations—the Richmond and Nashville Juntos, the Albany and Concord Regencies, with help from Calhoun's organization in South Carolina—worked together to elect him. Popular appeal, which Jackson the military hero certainly possessed, was not enough to ensure victory. To be truly national, a party had to create and maintain a coalition of North, South, and West. The Democrats were the first to do this.

THE JACKSON PRESIDENCY

Andrew Jackson's election ushered in a new era in American politics, an era that historians have called "the Age of the Common Man." Jackson himself, however, was no "common man": he was a military hero, a rich slave owner, and an imperious and decidedly undemocratic personality. "Old Hickory," as Jackson was affectionately called, was tough and unbending, just like hickory itself, one of the hardest of woods. Yet he had a mass appeal to ordinary people unmatched—and indeed unsought—by earlier presidents. The secret to Jackson's extraordinary appeal lies in the changing nature of American society. Jackson was the first to respond to the ways in which westward expansion and the extension of the suffrage were changing politics at the national as well as the local and state levels.

A Popular Figure

Jackson was born in 1767 and raised in North Carolina. During the American Revolution he was captured and beaten by the British, an insult he never forgot. As a young man without wealth or family support, he moved west to the frontier "station" of Nashville, Tennessee, in 1788. There he made his career as a lawyer and his considerable wealth as a slave-owning planter. He had a touchy sense of pride and honor that led him into many duels. As he showed in his campaigns against the "Five Civilized Tribes" in the Old Southwest during the War of 1812, he was ruthless toward Indians. He first became a national hero with his underdog win against the British in the battle of New Orleans. In the popular mind, his fierce belligerence came to symbolize pioneer independence. The fact that he had little political experience, which would have made his nomination impossible under the traditional system of politics, was not a hindrance in the new age of popular politics.

On March 4, 1829, Andrew Jackson was inaugurated as president of the United States. Jackson himself was still in mourning for his beloved wife Rachel, whose recent death he attributed to the slanders of the campaign. But everyone else was celebrating. The small community of Washington was crowded with strangers, many of them Westerners and common people who had come especially for Jackson's inauguration. Their celebrating dismayed the city's more respectable citizens. Jackson's brief Inaugural Address was almost drowned out by the cheering of the crowd, and after the ceremony the new president was mobbed by well-wishers. The same unrestrained enthusiasm was evident at a White House reception, where the crowd was large and disorderly. People stood on chairs and sofas to catch glimpses of Jackson and shoved and pushed to reach the food and drink, which was finally carried out to the lawn. In the rush to follow, some people exited through windows rather than the doors. All in all, a disapproving observer noted, this behavior indicated the end of proper government and the beginning of "the reign of King Mob." Indeed, Jackson's administration was different from all those before it.

The Spoils System and the New Politics

Jackson began his term rewarding party loyalists by giving them positions in the national government. Although Jackson himself spoke loftily of democratizing the holding of public office, New York Bucktail William Marcy put the matter more bluntly: there was "nothing wrong in the rule, that to the victor belong the spoils of the enemy." Hence the expression "spoils system" to describe the practice of awarding government appointments to loyalists of the winning party. This attitude toward public office was one of the strongest points of difference between the new politics and the old.

Until 1829, presidential inaugurations had been small, polite, and ceremonial occasions. Andrew Jackson's popularity, however, brought a horde of well-wishers to Washington for his inaugural. Conservative critics, dismayed by the disorderly crowd at Jackson's frontier-style open house at the White House, feared "the reign of King Mob" had begun.

What Jackson did was to transfer a common state practice to the national level and to set a precedent that was followed in national politics until passage of the Pendleton Act of 1883, which began the reform of the civil service system. Jackson opened up all federal positions to party loyalists, and his opponents quickly found examples of corruption and inefficiency among the new officeholders. It is doubtful, though, if any alternative to the spoils system—such as the elite, independent civil service that the British were developing at the time—would have been consistent with the democratic spirit of American politics in the 1820s.

In fact, although the spoils system upset Jackson's opponents more than most of his other controversial actions, the number of officeholders he replaced was rather small—only about 10 percent (of a total of 10,093 offices). As was true in so many other cases, it was not so much the appointments themselves as the manner in which Jackson made them—brooking no argument, not even from supporters—that opponents found so aggravating.

The Nation's Leader vs. Sectional Spokesmen

Despite his western origins, Jackson was a genuinely national figure. He was more interested in asserting strong national leadership than promoting sectional compromise. He believed that the president, who symbolized the popular will of the people, ought to dominate the government. As he put it in his first annual message, "the first principle of our system [is that] the majority is to govern." This was new. Voters were much more accustomed to thinking of politics in

sectional terms. Jackson faced a Congress full of strong and immensely popular sectional figures. Three stood out: Southerner John C. Calhoun, Northerner Daniel Webster, and Westerner Henry Clay.

Intense, dogmatic, and uncompromising, John C. Calhoun of South Carolina had begun his political career as an ardent nationalist and expansionist in his early days as a War Hawk before the War of 1812. Since the debate over the Missouri Compromise in 1820, however, Calhoun had wholeheartedly identified with southern interests, first and foremost among which was the expansion and preservation of slavery. As the South's minority position in Congress became clear over the years, Calhoun's defense of southern economic interests and slavery became more and more rigid. Not for nothing did he earn his nickname "the Cast-Iron Man."

Senator Daniel Webster of Massachusetts was the outstanding orator of the age. Large, dark, and stern, Webster delivered his speeches in a deep, booming voice that, listeners said, "shook the world." He was capable of pathos as well, bringing tears to the eyes of those who heard him say, while defending Dartmouth College before the Supreme Court (in the case of the same name), "It is a small college, sir, but there are those who love it." Webster, a lawyer for business interests, became the main spokesman for the new northern commercial interests, supporting a high protective tariff, a national bank, and a strong federal government. Webster's fondness for comfortable living, and especially brandy, made him less effective as he grew older, but then, as a contemporary of his remarked, "No man could be as great as Daniel Webster looked."

In contrast with the other two, Henry Clay of Kentucky, spokesman of the West, was charming, witty, and always eager to forge political compromises. Clay held the powerful position of Speaker of the House of Representatives from 1811 to 1825 and later served several terms in the Senate. A spellbinding storyteller and well known for his ability to make a deal, Clay worked to incorporate western desires for cheap and good transportation into national politics. It was he who promoted the political agenda known as the American System: a national bank, a protective tariff, and the use of substantial federal funds for internal improvements such as roads, canals, and railroads (see Chapter 9). Clay might well have forged a political alliance between the North and the West if not for the policies of President Jackson, his fellow Westerner and greatest rival. Jackson's preeminence thwarted Clay's own ambition to be president.

The prominence and popularity of these three politicians show that sectional interests remained strong even under a president as determined as Jackson to override them and disrupt "politics as usual" by imposing his own personal style.

A Strong Executive

The mob scene that accompanied Jackson's inauguration was more than a reflection of the popular enthusiasm for Old Hickory. It also signaled a higher level of controversy in national politics. Jackson's personal style quickly stripped national politics of the polite and gentlemanly aura of cooperation it had acquired during the Era of Good Feelings and that Adams had vainly tried to maintain. Jackson had played rough all his life, and he relished controversy. His administration (1829–37) had plenty of it.

Andrew Jackson dominated his administration. Except for Martin Van Buren, whom he appointed secretary of state, he mostly ignored the heads of government departments who made up his official cabinet. Instead he consulted with an informal group, dubbed the "Kitchen Cabinet," made up of Van Buren and old western friends. The Kitchen Cabinet did not include John C. Calhoun, the vice president, or either of the other two great sectional representatives, Henry Clay and Daniel Webster. Jackson never forgave Clay for his role in the "corrupt bargain" of 1825, and he saw Daniel Webster as a representative of his favorite political target, the privileged elite.

Jackson used social distance to separate himself from other politicians. When Jackson's secretary of war, John Henry Eaton, married a beautiful woman of flamboyant reputation, he transgressed the social code of the time. It was rumored that Peggy Eaton had been John's mistress and that there were other men in her past. She was, in nineteenth-century thinking, a fallen woman and unfit for polite society. The respectable ladies of Washington shunned her. But Jackson, aroused by memories of the slanders against his own wife, defended Peggy Eaton and urged his cabinet members to force their wives to call on her. When, to a woman, they refused, Jackson called the husbands henpecked. This episode chilled the social life of cabinet members and their families and drove a wedge between Jackson and Calhoun, whose wife was a leader in the anti-Eaton group. Although Jackson claimed to be motivated only by chivalry, he wanted to keep his distance from Calhoun, and this episode helped him do it. Ironically, it may never have occurred had Jack-

son not been a widower. His wife Rachel would surely have sided with Mrs. Calhoun in upholding the moral code of the time.

Jackson freely used the tools of his office to strengthen the executive branch of government at the expense of the legislature and judiciary. By using the veto more frequently than all previous presidents combined (twelve vetoes compared with nine by the first six presidents), Jackson forced Congress to constantly consider his opinions. Even more important, Jackson's "negative activism" restricted federal activity, thereby allowing more power to remain in state hands.

In one of his most famous and unexpected actions, the veto of the Maysville Road Bill of 1830, Jackson refused to allow federal funding of a southern spur of the National Road in Kentucky, claiming such funding should be left to the state. Like Presidents James Madison and James Monroe before him, Jackson believed that federal funding for extensive and expensive transportation measures was unconstitutional because it infringed on the "reserved powers" the Constitution left to the states. The veto was unexpected because it disappointed Jackson's strongest supporters, Westerners who wanted better transportation. But by addressing his veto message to a popular audience, not just to Congress, and by dramatically portraying federal funding as a threat to the popular political principle of states' rights (and by making it clear that he was not opposed to federal funding of all internal improvements), Jackson actually gained political support. He also had the satisfaction of defeating a measure central to the American System proposed by his western rival, Henry Clay.

INTERNAL IMPROVEMENTS: BUILDING AN INFRASTRUCTURE

Despite the ongoing constitutional debate over who should fund internal improvements, no one argued that they should not be funded at all. On the contrary, ordinary people and politicians of all persuasions agreed that both federal and state governments had an important role in encouraging economic growth and in fostering the development of a national market. And that role included subsidizing the costs of the basic infrastructure—the canals and railroads—that would tie the national market together.

The Transportation Revolution

Between 1800 and 1840 the United States experienced truly revolutionary improvements in transportation. More than any other development, these improvements encouraged Americans to look beyond their local communities to broader ones and to foster the enterprising commercial spirit for which they became so widely known.

Improved transportation had dramatic effects both on individual mobility and on the economy. By 1840 it was easier for people to move from one locale to another, but even more remarkably people now had easy access in their own cities and towns to commercial goods made in distant centers. Thus even for people who remained in one place, horizons were much broader in 1840 than they had been forty years before. The difference lay in better roads, in improvements in water transport, and in the invention and speedy development of railroads.

In 1800, travel by road was difficult for much of the year. Mud in the spring, dust in the summer, and snow in the winter all made travel by horseback or carriage uncomfortable, slow, and sometimes dangerous. Over the years, localities and states tried to improve local roads or contracted with private turnpike companies to build, maintain, and collect tolls on important stretches of road. In general, however, local roads remained poor.

The federal government demonstrated its commitment to the improvement of interregional transportation by funding the National Road in 1808, at the time the greatest single federal transportation expense (its eventual cost was $7 million). Built of gravel on a stone foundation, it crossed the Appalachian Mountains at Cumberland, Maryland, thereby opening up the West. Built in stages—to Wheeling, Virginia (now West Virginia), by 1818, to Columbus, Ohio, by 1833, to Vandalia, Illinois, almost at the Mississippi River, by 1850—the National Road tied the East and the West together, providing strong evidence of the nation's commitment to both expansion and cohesion and helping to foster a national community.

Although the federal commitment was great, the states actually spent more than the federal government on internal improvements—canals and railroads as well as roads. In the 1820s, state spending for internal improvements totaled $26 million. Half of this amount was incurred by two states, New York and Pennsylvania, but even smaller states such as South Carolina spent $2 million, largely on canals. In the next decade, state spending for canals, railroads, and turnpikes soared to $108 million. States and towns, especially in newly populated areas of the West, competed against each

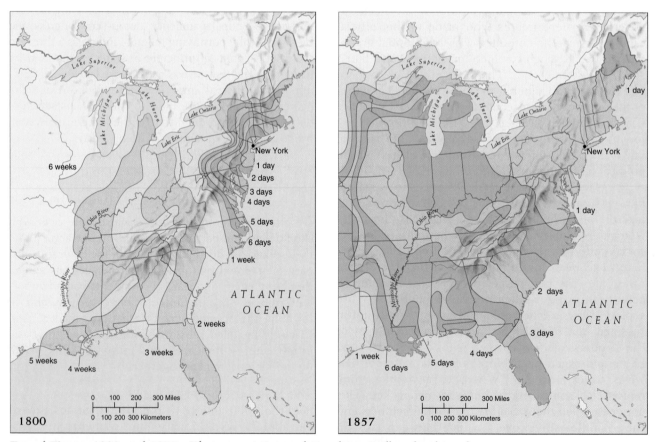

Travel Times, 1800 and 1857   *The transportation revolution dramatically reduced travel times and vastly expanded everyone's horizons. Improved roads, canals, and steamboats and the introduction of railroads made it easier for Americans to move than ever before, and made even those who did not move less isolated. Better transportation linked the developing West to the eastern seaboard and fostered a national identity and pride.*

This 1829 painting of Fairview Inn on the National Road just three miles west of Baltimore illustrates the importance of good transportation. The busy traffic attests to commercial activity and to confidence in westward expansion—the canvas-covered wagons were able to travel as far west as Ohio on the National Road at the time.

Thomas Coke Ruckle, Fairview Inn or Three Mile House on Old Frederick Road, c. 1829?, watercolor on paper. Collection of the Maryland Historical Society, Baltimore, Maryland.

other in giving land, subsidies, and other forms of encouragement to road, canal, and railroad companies to provide transportation to their particular localities. Some of these commitments were overly generous and led to financial difficulty: by 1842, nine states (Arkansas, Florida, Illinois, Indiana, Louisiana, Maryland, Michigan, Mississippi, and Pennsylvania) had defaulted on some of their transportation loans, and Ohio and New York were forced to suspend dividends to investors.

Canals and Steamboats

However much they helped the movement of people, the National Road and other roads were unsatisfactory in a commercial sense. Shipment of bulky goods like grain was too slow and expensive by road. Waterborne transportation was much cheaper and still the major commercial link among the Atlantic seaboard states and in the Mississippi-Ohio River system. But before the 1820s most water routes were north-south or coastal (Boston to Charleston, for example); east-west links were urgently needed. Canals turned out to be the answer.

The Erie Canal—the most famous canal of the era—was the brainchild of New York governor DeWitt Clinton, who envisioned a link between New York City and the Great Lakes through the Hudson River and a 364-mile-long canal stretching from Albany to Buffalo. When Clinton proposed the canal in 1817 it was derisively called

"Clinton's Ditch"; the longest then existing American canal was only 27 miles long and had taken nine years to build. Nevertheless, Clinton convinced the New York legislature to approve a bond issue for the canal, and investors (New York and British merchants) subscribed to the tune of $7 million, an immense sum for the day.

Building the canal—40 feet wide, 4 feet deep, 364 miles long, with 83 locks and more than 300 bridges along the way—was a vast engineering and construction challenge. What came to be called Yankee ingenuity showed at every step of the way, from the creation of stump pullers to remove trees from the route, to substitutes for cement (previously imported from England), and to the widespread use of Dupont blasting powder, the forerunner of dynamite (which was not invented for another forty years).

Manpower was another concern. In the early stages nearby farmers worked for $8 a month, but when malaria hit the workforce in the summer of 1819, many went home. They were replaced by 3,000 Irish contract laborers, who were much more expensive—50 cents a day plus room and board—but more reliable (if they survived). Local people regarded the Irish workers as different and frightening, but the importation of foreign contract labor for this job was a portent of the future. Much of the heavy construction work on later canals and railroads was performed by immigrant labor.

DeWitt Clinton had promised, to general disbelief, that the Erie Canal would be completed in less than ten years, and he made good on his promise. The canal was the wonder of the age. On October 26, 1825, Clinton declared it open in Buffalo and sent the first boat, the *Seneca Chief*, on its way to New York at the incredible speed of four miles an hour. (Ironically, the Seneca Indians, for whom the boat was named, had been "removed" from the path of the canal and confined to a small reservation.) The boat reached New York City on November 4, where it was greeted with elaborate ceremonies, including one in which vials of water from the great rivers of the world—the Nile, Ganges, Mississippi, Rhine, and Danube—were emptied into New York harbor to symbolize the opening of commerce between the heart of America and the world.

This grand gesture was appropriate. The Erie Canal provided easy passage to and from the interior, both for people and for goods. It drew settlers like a magnet from the East and, increasingly, from overseas: by 1830, 50,000 people a year were moving west on the canal to the rich farmland of Indiana, Illinois, and territory farther west. Earlier settlers now had a national, indeed an international, market for their produce. Moreover, farm families began purchasing household goods and cloth, formerly made at home. Indeed, one of the most dramatic illustrations of the canal's impact is a rapid decline in the production of homespun cloth. In 1825, the year the Erie Canal opened, New York homesteads produced 16.5 million yards of textiles. By 1835 this figure had shrunk by almost half—8.8 million yards—and by 1855 it had dropped to less than 1 million.

Towns along the canal—Utica, Rochester, Buffalo—became instant cities, each an important commercial center in its own right. Perhaps the greatest beneficiary was the city of New York, which quickly established a commercial and financial supremacy no American city could match. The Erie Canal decisively turned New York's merchants away from Europe and toward America's own heartland, building both interstate commerce and a feeling of community. As the famous song put it,

> *You'll always know your neighbor,*
> *You'll always know your pal,*
> *If you've ever navigated*
> *On the Erie Canal.*

The phenomenal success of the Erie Canal prompted other states to construct similar waterways to tap the rich interior market. Between 1820 and 1840, $200 million was invested in canal building, three-quarters of it provided by state governments. The Blackstone Canal linked Worcester, Massachusetts, with Providence, Rhode Island; the Pennsylvania Main Line Canal ran all the way from Philadelphia to Pittsburgh; and many other canals were built in Maine, Maryland, Ohio, Indiana, and Illinois. None of these waterways achieved the success of the Erie, which collected $8.5 million in tolls in its first nine years. And the port cities they were meant to benefit—Philadelphia and Baltimore, for example—never threatened New York's commercial supremacy. Nevertheless, the spurt of canal building ended the geographical isolation of much of the country. For example, Ohio's

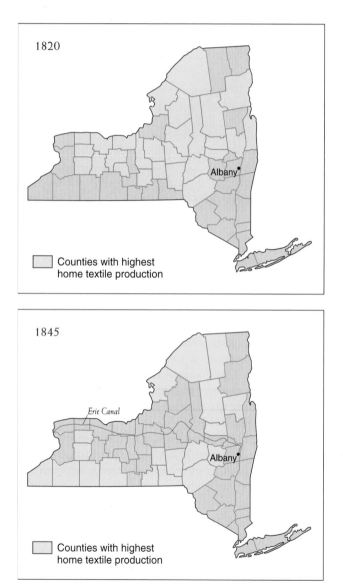

The Impact of the Erie Canal on Household Textile Manufacture In 1820 *the household manufacture of woolen cloth for home use was widespread in New York State, but in 1845, twenty years after the Erie Canal opened, many fewer counties were producing significant quantities of fabric. Because they could now buy cheap manufactured textiles, New York women living near the canal were freed from the time-consuming task of making cloth for their families.*

Source: Arthur Harrison Cole, *The American Wool Manufacture* (Cambridge, Mass.: Harvard University Press, 1926), p. 280.

canal system opened up the American interior by linking the Ohio River to Lake Erie in the north and to the Pennsylvania canals to the east.

An even more important improvement in water transportation, especially in the American interior, was the steamboat. Robert Fulton first demonstrated the commercial feasibility of steamboats in 1807, and they were soon operating in the East. Redesigned with more efficient engines and shallower, broader hulls, steamboats transformed commerce on the country's great inland river system: the Ohio, the Mississippi, the Missouri, and their tributaries. Steamboats were extremely dangerous, however; boiler explosions, fires, and sinkings were common. Public outrage at these conditions led to one of the first uses of federal regulatory power in the public interest. The first Steamboat Act, passed in 1838 and strengthened in 1852, set standards for the construction, equipment, and operation of steamboat boilers, required measures to prevent fire and collisions, and established an inspection system to make sure the new regulations were carried out. Although steamboats were privately owned and operated, the public that they served insisted on the need for safety standards to promote the wider community welfare.

Dangerous as they were, steamboats greatly stimulated trade in the nation's interior. There had long been downstream trade on flatboats along the Mississippi River system, but it was limited by the return trip overland on the arduous and dangerous Natchez Trace. For a time, steamboats actually increased the downriver flatboat trade, because boatmen could now make more round trips in the same amount of time, traveling home by steamboat in speed and comfort.

The increased river- and canal-borne trade, like the New England shipping boom of a generation earlier, stimulated urban growth and all kinds of commerce. Cities such as Cincinnati, already notable for its rapid growth, experienced a new economic surge. A frontier outpost in 1790, Cincinnati was by the 1830s a center of steamboat manufacture and machine tool production as well as a central shipping point for food for the southern market. Even in sleepy agricultural villages like Mark Twain's hometown of Hannibal, Missouri, the steamboat was a powerful symbol of energy and international

Mary Keys, a local artist, painted this watercolor in 1832 illustrating one of the Erie Canal's engineering triumphs, the famous "combined" locks—two sets of five locks rising side by side for 60 feet—at Lockport. One observer boasted, "Here the great Erie Canal has defied nature."

Mary Keys, American (active 1832) Lockport on the Erie Canal, 1832. Watercolor on paper 15¼ x 20½ inches. Munson–Williams–Proctor Institute Museum of Art, Utica, NY 55.45.

commerce. As Twain recounts in "Old Times on the Mississippi," the steamboat brought the town to life:

A negro drayman, famous for his quick eye and prodigious voice, lifts up the cry, "S-t-e-a-m-boat a comin'!"...The town drunkard stirs, the clerks wake up, a furious clatter of drays follows, every house and store pours out a human contribution, and all in a twinkling the dead town is alive and moving. Drays, carts, men, boys, all go hurrying from many quarters to a common center, the wharf....Then such a scramble as there is to get aboard, and to get ashore, and to take in freight and to discharge freight, all at one and the same time; and such a yelling and cursing as the mates facilitate it all with! Ten minutes later the steamer is under way again....After ten more minutes the town is dead again, and the town drunkard asleep by the skids once more.

Railroads

Remarkable as all these transportation changes were, the most remarkable was still to come. Railroads, new in 1830 (when the Baltimore and Ohio Railroad opened with 13 miles of track), grew to an astounding 31,000 miles by 1860. By that date, New England and the Old Northwest had laid a dense network of rails, and several

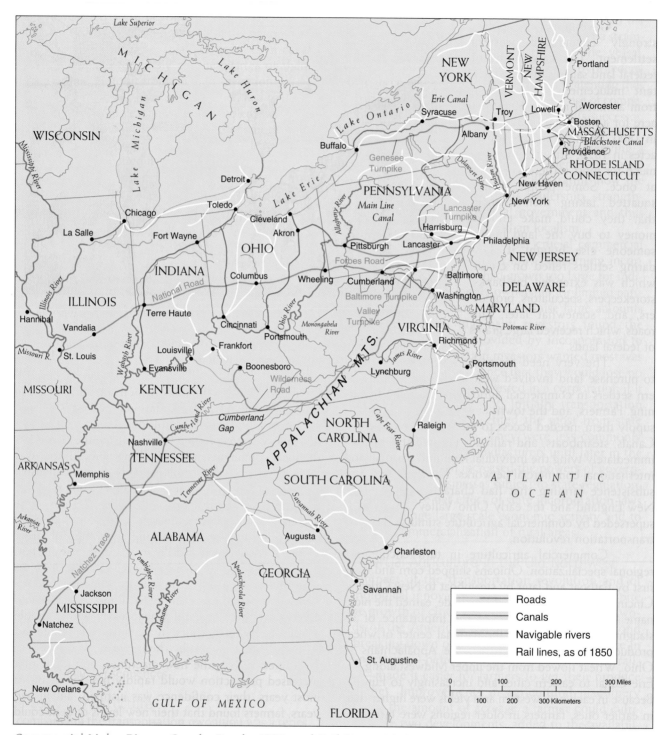

Commercial Links: Rivers, Canals, Roads, 1830, and Rail Lines, 1850   By 1830, the United States was tied together by a network of roads, canals, and rivers. This "transportation revolution" fostered a great burst of commercial activity and economic growth. Transportation improvements accelerated the commercialization of agriculture by getting farmers' products to wider, nonlocal markets. Access to wider markets likewise encouraged new textile and other manufacturers to increase their scale of production. By 1850, another revolutionary mode of transportation, the railroad, had emerged as a vital link to the transportation infrastructure.

growth. In turn, the transportation revolution fostered an optimistic, risk-taking mentality in the United States that stimulated invention and innovation. More than anything, the transportation revolution allowed people to move with unaccustomed ease. Already a restless people compared with Europeans, Americans took advantage of new transport to move even more often—and farther away—than they had before.

There were other, less directly economic effects. Every east-west road, canal, and railroad helped to reorient Americans away from the Atlantic and toward the heartland. This new focus was decisive in the creation of national pride and identity. Transportation improvements such as the Erie Canal and the National Road linked Americans in larger communities of interest beyond the local community in which they lived. Other results were less positive. The technological triumphs of canal building and rail laying fostered a brash spirit of conquest over nature that was to become part of the American myth of the frontier. Furthermore, although every new transportation or communication link broke down local and regional isolation and helped to build a spirit of pride in the nation, it also refocused attention on questions of national politics. The new transportation system caused a subtle political shift, for it strengthened the influence of the North by improving the North's ties with the West more than those of the South. In this way, the new modes of communication and transportation served to heat up the politics of the era.

JACKSON AND HIS OPPONENTS: THE RISE OF THE WHIGS

As transportation improvements, increased commercialization, and the new politics drew the people of the United States out of localism into larger networks, fundamental questions about national unity arose. What was the correct balance between local interests—the rights of the states—and the powers of the central government? The men who wrote the federal Constitution in Philadelphia in 1787 had not been able to reach agreement on this question. Because the Constitution deliberately left the federal structure ambiguous, all subsequent sectional disagreements automatically became constitutional issues that carried a threat to national unity. The great issues of Jackson's presidency expressed this continuing tension between nationalism and sectionalism. Jackson's responses to them created such controversy that a permanent opposition—another political party, known as the Whigs—was born.

The Nullification Crisis

The political issue that came to symbolize the divergent sectional interests of North and South, pitting the rights of individual states against the claims of a federal major-

ity, was the protective tariff. The first substantial protective tariff was enacted in 1816 after northern manufacturing interests clamored for protection from the ruthless British competition that followed the War of 1812 (see Chapter 9). As a group, wealthy southern planters were opposed to tariffs, both because tariffs raised the cost of the luxury goods they imported from Europe and because they believed in the principle of free trade, fearing that American tariffs would cause other countries to retaliate with tariffs against southern cotton. Most southern congressmen, assured that the 1816 tariff was a temporary postwar recovery measure, voted for it. But it was not temporary. As the North industrialized and new industries demanded protection, tariff bills in 1824 and 1828 raised rates still higher and protected more items. Southerners protested, but they were outvoted in Congress by northern and western representatives, who agreed both on the need to protect industry and on the tariff as a way to raise federal revenue.

The 1828 tariff, nicknamed "the Tariff of Abominations," was a special target of southern anger, because Jackson's supporters in Congress had passed it in order to increase northern support for him in the presidential campaign of that year. It imposed especially high tariffs on imported textiles and iron that ranged from a third to half their total value. Southerners in Congress lacked the votes to block the tariff and faced the bleak prospect that their economic interests would always be ignored by the majority. Southern opponents of the tariff insisted that it was not a truly national measure but a sectional one that helped only some groups while harming others. Thus it was unconstitutional because it violated the rights of some of the states.

South Carolina, Calhoun's home state, reacted the most forcefully to the tariff of 1828. Of the older southern states, South Carolina had been the hardest hit by the opening of the new cotton lands in the Southwest, which had drained both population and commerce from the state. One index of South Carolina's changed status was the declining position of Charleston. In 1800 it was still as important a seaport as New York and Boston, but by the 1820s it had been eclipsed by all the major northern ports as well as by Mobile and New Orleans, then the major ports for exporting cotton. To these economic woes were added the first real fears about national attitudes toward slavery. South Carolinians, who had always had close personal ties with slave owners in the Caribbean islands, were shaken by the news that the British Parliament, bowing to popular pressure at home, was planning to emancipate all the slaves in the British West Indies. If Congress had the power to impose tariffs that were harmful to some states, South Carolinians asked, what would prevent it from enacting legislation like Britain's, depriving Southerners of their slaves and, thus, of their livelihood?

The result of these fears was a renewed interest in the doctrine of nullification, a topic that became the subject of widespread discussion in South Carolina in 1828. The doctrine upheld the right of a state to declare a federal law null and void and to refuse to enforce it within the state. This was not a new argument. Thomas Jefferson and James Madison had used it in the Kentucky and Virginia Resolves of 1798, which they wrote in opposing the Alien and Sedition Acts (see Chapter 8). The Hartford Convention of 1814–15, at which Federalists protested grievances related to the War of 1812, had adopted the same position (see Chapter 9). At issue in each case was the power of the state against that of the federal government. Now the same constitutional issue emerged again, this time, linked to the most intractable sectional issue, the South's determination to protect the institution of slavery.

South Carolina had an important supporter of nullification in the person of John C. Calhoun, who wrote a widely circulated defense of the doctrine, the *Exposition and Protest,* in 1828. Because Calhoun was soon to serve as Andrew Jackson's vice president, he wrote the *Exposition* anonymously. He hoped to use his influence with Jackson to gain support for nullification, but he was disappointed.

Where Calhoun saw nullification as a safeguard of the rights of the minority, Jackson saw it as a threat to national unity. As the president said at a famous exchange of toasts at the annual Jefferson Day dinner in 1830, "Our Federal Union, it must be preserved." In response to Jackson, Calhoun offered his own toast: "The Union—next to our liberty most dear. May we always remember that it can only be preserved by distributing equally the benefits and burdens of the Union." The president and the vice president were thus in open disagreement on a matter of crucial national importance. The outcome was inevitable: Calhoun lost all influence with Jackson, and two years later he took the unusual step of resigning the vice presidency. Martin Van Buren was elected to the office for Jackson's second term. Calhoun, his presidential aspirations in ruins, became a senator from South Carolina, and in that capacity participated in the last act of the nullification drama.

In 1832 the nullification controversy became a full-blown crisis. In passing the tariff of 1832, Congress (in spite of Jackson's urging) retained high taxes on woolens, iron, and hemp, although it reduced duties on other items. South Carolina responded with a special convention and an Ordinance of Nullification, in which it rejected the tariff and refused to collect the taxes it required. The state further issued a call for a volunteer militia and threatened to secede from the Union if Jackson used force against it. Jackson responded vehemently, denouncing the nullifiers—"Disunion by armed force is treason"—and obtaining from Congress a Force Bill

authorizing the federal government to collect the tariff in South Carolina at gunpoint if necessary. Intimidated, the other southern states refused to follow South Carolina's lead. More quietly, Jackson also asked Congress to revise the tariff. Henry Clay, the Great Pacificator, swung into action and soon, with Calhoun's support, had crafted the Tariff Act of 1833. This measure appeared to meet southern demands by pledging a return to the tariff rate of 1816 (an average of 20 percent) by 1842 through a series of very small annual decreases for nine years, followed by a large cut in the final year. (In fact, in 1842 Congress quickly voted a return to higher tariff rates.) In 1833 the South Carolina legislature, unwilling to act without the support of other southern states, quickly accepted this face-saving compromise and repealed its nullification of the tariff of 1832. In a final burst of bravado, the legislature nullified the Force Bill, but Jackson defused the crisis by ignoring this second nullification.

The nullification crisis was the most serious threat to national unity that the United States had ever experienced. South Carolinians, by threatening to secede, had forced concessions on a matter they believed of vital economic importance. They—and a number of other Southerners—believed that the resolution of the crisis illustrated the success of their uncompromising tactics. Most of the rest of the nation simply breathed a sigh of relief, echoing Daniel Webster's sentiment, spoken in the heat of the debate over nullification, "Liberty and Union, now and forever, one and inseparable!" Most Americans firmly believed that although every effort should be made to address sectional concerns, national unity and majority rule came first. But another event of the Jackson years, Indian removal, clearly showed how unfair majority rule could be when the minority was not strong enough to force a compromise.

Indian Removal

The official policy of the United States government from the time of Jefferson's administration was to promote the assimilation of Indian peoples by encouraging them to adopt white ways. To Indian groups who resisted "civilization" or who needed more time to adapt, Jefferson offered the alternative of removal from settled areas in the East to the new Indian Territory west of the Mississippi River. Following this logic, at the end of the War of 1812 the federal government signed removal treaties with a number of Indian nations of the Old Northwest, thereby opening up large tracts of land for white settlement (see Chapter 9). In the Southwest, however, the "Five Civilized Tribes"—the Cherokees, Chickasaws, Choctaws, Creeks, and Seminoles—remained. By the 1830s, under constant pressure from settlers, each of the five tribes had ceded most of its lands, but sizable self-governing groups lived in

Georgia, Alabama, Mississippi, and Florida. All of these (except the Seminoles) had moved far in the direction of coexistence with whites, and they resisted suggestions that they should voluntarily remove themselves.

The Cherokees took the most extensive steps to adopt white ways. Their tribal lands in northwestern Georgia boasted prosperous farms, businesses, grain and lumber mills, and even plantations with black slaves. Intermarriage with whites and African Americans had produced an influential group of mixed bloods within the Cherokee nation, some of whom were eager to accept white ways. Schooled by Congregationalist, Presbyterian, and Moravian missionaries, the Cherokees were almost totally literate in English. They took special pride in the alphabet for their own language that was developed by the Cherokee scholar Sequoyah, and in 1828 they began publishing a tribal newspaper, the *Cherokee Phoenix*, in both Cherokee and English. A year earlier the tribe abolished its traditional form of government and established a constitutional republic.

Despite the evidence of the Cherokees' successful adaptation to the dominant white culture, in the 1820s the legislatures of Georgia, Alabama, and Mississippi, responding to pressures from land-hungry whites, voted to invalidate federal treaties granting special self-governing status to Indian lands. Because the federal government, not the states, bore responsibility for Indian policy, these state actions constituted a sectional challenge to federal authority. In this instance, however, unlike the Nullification Crisis, the resisting states had presidential support. Living up to his reputation as a ruthless Indian fighter, Jackson determined on a federal policy of wholesale removal of the southern Indian tribes.

In 1830, at President Jackson's urging, the U.S. Congress passed the hotly debated Indian Removal Act, which appropriated funds for relocation, by force if necessary. When Jackson increased the pressure by sending federal officials to negotiate removal treaties with the southern tribes, most reluctantly signed and prepared to move. The Cherokees, however, fought their removal by using the white man's weapon—the law. At first they seemed to have won: in *Cherokee Nation v. Georgia* (1831) and *Worcester v. Georgia* (1832) Chief

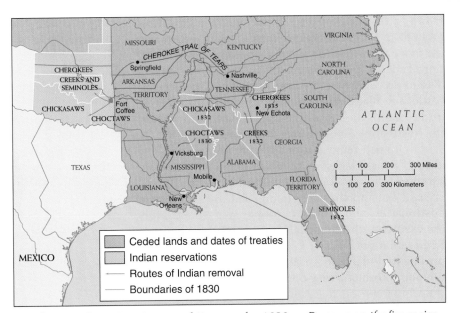

Southern Indian Cessions and Removals, 1830s   *Pressure on the five major southern Indian peoples—the Cherokees, Chickasaws, Choctaws, Creeks, and Seminoles—that began during the War of 1812 culminated with their removal in the 1830s. Some groups from every tribe ceded their southern homelands peacefully and moved to the newly established Indian Territory west of Arkansas and Missouri. Some, like the Seminoles, resisted by force. Others, like the Cherokees, resisted in the courts but finally lost when President Andrew Jackson refused to enforce a Supreme Court decision in their favor. The Cherokees, the last to move, were forcibly removed by the U.S. Army along "the Trail of Tears" in 1838.*

Justice John Marshall ruled that the Cherokees, though not a state or a foreign nation, were a "domestic dependent nation" that could not be forced by the state of Georgia to give up its land against its will. However, when President Jackson heard the Supreme Court's decision, he is reputed to have said, "John Marshall has made his decision. Now let him enforce it." Ignoring the decision, Jackson continued his support for removal.

Faced by the Cherokees' de facto defeat, what could the other Indian tribes do? Some Seminoles of Florida chose to fight. Aided by runaway slaves and by their unsurpassed knowledge of their homeland, the Florida Everglades, some Seminole bands fought a guerrilla war that lasted into the 1840s before the U.S. military gave up and allowed them to remain. The majority of Seminoles and members of other tribes were much less fortunate: most of the Choctaws moved west in 1830; the last of the Creeks were forcibly moved by the military in 1836, and the Chickasaws a year later. And in 1838, in the last and most infamous removal, resisting Cherokees were driven west to Oklahoma along what came to be known as "the Trail of Tears." A 7,000-man army escorting them watched thousands (perhaps a quarter of the 16,000 Cherokees) die along the way. Another futile effort to resist removal, the Black Hawk "war," occurred in the Old Northwest. In 1832, Sac and Fox Indians, led by Black

Hawk, attempted to move back to their old tribal grounds in Illinois following removal, but settlers saw the move as an invasion and demanded military protection. Federal troops chased the Black Hawk band to Wisconsin, where more than 300 Indians died in a final battle, and Black Hawk himself was taken prisoner. As in the South, the last of the remaining Indians east of the Mississippi were removed by the end of the 1830s.

Indian removal was a deeply divisive national issue. President Jackson's sweeping policy undoubtedly expressed the opinion of most Southerners and Westerners. But northern opinion, led by Protestant missionaries and reform groups, was so strongly opposed that the Removal Act passed the House of Representatives by only 3 votes (out of 200). Jackson's presidential claim to speak for popular opinion was running into increasing opposition.

The Bank War

The last major event of Jackson's presidency, his refusal to renew the charter of the Second Bank of the United States, had lasting political consequences. Jackson's opponents, already angry about his earlier actions, were so infuriated by the bank episode that they formed the permanent opposition party known as the Whigs. It was from the heat of the Bank War that the now characteristic American two-party system emerged.

The first Bank of the United States had been chartered by Congress in 1791, at Alexander Hamilton's urging. Federalists supported it, Jeffersonians opposed it and allowed its charter to expire in 1811. But after the War of 1812 almost all Democratic Republicans came to appreciate the stability provided by a central bank. Thus in 1816 Congress granted a twenty-year charter to the Second Bank of the United States. Like its predecessor, the Bank played a powerful role in the expanding American economy, encouraging the growth of strong and stable financial interests and curbing less stable and irresponsible ones.

Also, like its predecessor, the Bank was not a government agency but a private institution, the majority of whose directors were appointed by the government. Its stockholders were some of the nation's richest men (New York's John Jacob Astor and Philadelphia's Stephen Girard among them). The bank was directed by the erudite and aristocratic Nicholas Biddle of Philadelphia. Biddle, a friend of Thomas Jefferson and an avid amateur scientist, was the editor of the journals of Lewis and Clark.

The Bank, which with thirty branches was the nation's largest, performed a variety of functions: it held the government's money (about $10 million), sold government bonds, and made commercial loans. But its most important function was the control it exercised over state banks. At the time, America

This figurehead of Andrew Jackson, carved in 1834 for the navy frigate Constitution, *captures the unmoveable resolve that made Jackson so popular early in his presidency and so reviled during the Bank War.*

Museum of the City of New York (M52.11)

lacked a national currency. The money in circulation was a mixture of paper money (U.S. notes and the notes of state banks) and gold and silver coins (specie, or hard currency), many of them of foreign origin. Because state banks tended to issue more paper money than they could back with hard currency, the Bank always demanded repayment of its loans to them in coin. This policy forced state banks to maintain adequate reserves, curbed inflationary pressures (overprinting of banknotes), and restricted speculative activities such as risky loans. In times of recession, the bank eased the pressure on state banks, demanding only partial payment in coin. Thus the Bank acted as a currency stabilizer by helping to control the money supply. It brought a semblance of order to what we today would consider a chaotic money system—coins of various weights and a multitude of state banknotes, many of which were discounted (not accepted at full face value) in other states.

The concept of a strong national bank was supported by the majority of the nation's merchants and businessmen and was a key element in Henry Clay's American System. Nevertheless, the Bank had many opponents. The objections arose from both sectional and political resentments. A number of state bank directors felt overshadowed by the central bank's size and power. Western land speculators, and many western farmers, chafed at the bank's tight control over the currency reserves of state banks, claiming it was harmful to western development. Both western farmers and urban workers had bitter memories of the Panic of 1819, which the Bank had caused (at least in part) by sharply contracting credit. To some people, the economic power of the Bank was frightening; they feared that monied elites would use it to their own advantage. Although the rapid growth of the national economy made some sort of control necessary, many ordinary people were uneasy not only about the Bank but about banks of all kinds. They believed that a system based on paper currency would be manipulated by bankers in unpredictable and dangerous ways. Among those who held that opinion was Andrew Jackson, who had hated and feared banks ever since the 1790s, when he had lost a great deal of money in a speculative venture.

Early in his administration, Jackson hastened to tell Nicholas Biddle, "I do not dislike your Bank any more than all banks." By 1832, Jackson's opinion had changed and he and Biddle were locked in a personal conflict that harmed not only the national economy but the reputations of both men. Biddle, urged on by Henry Clay and Daniel Webster, precipitated the conflict by making early application for rechartering the Bank. Congress approved the application in July 1832. Clay and Webster, though well aware of Jackson's antibank feelings, believed the president would not risk a veto in an election year. They were wrong. Jackson immediately decided on a stinging veto, announcing to Van Buren, "The bank…is trying to kill me, but I will kill it!"

And kill it he did that same July, with one of the strongest veto messages in American history. Denouncing the Bank as unconstitutional, harmful to states' rights, and "dangerous to the liberties of the people," Jackson presented himself as the spokesman for the majority of ordinary people and the enemy of special privilege. Asserting that the Bank's "exclusive privileges" were benefiting only the rich, Jackson claimed to speak for the "humble members of society— the farmers, mechanics and laborers"—and to oppose injustice and inequality. Nor did Jackson's veto message speak only of the sharp division between social classes. It also aroused sectional and national feelings by its allusions to the many British and eastern bank stockholders who were profiting from the debts of poor Southerners and Westerners. In short, the veto spoke directly to many of the fears and resentments that Americans felt at this time of exceptionally rapid economic and social change. Jackson's message was a campaign document, written to appeal to voters. Most of the financial community was appalled, believing both the veto and the accompanying message to be reckless demagoguery.

Jackson's Reelection in 1832

Nevertheless, Jackson's veto message was a great popular success, and it set the terms for the presidential election of 1832. Henry Clay, the nominee of the anti-Jackson forces, lost the battle for popular opinion. Democrats successfully painted Clay as the defender of the Bank and of privilege. His defeat was decisive: he drew only 49 electoral votes, to Jackson's 219. A handful of votes went to the first third party in American history, the short-lived Anti-Masonic Party. This party played on the resentments of the newly enfranchised "common man" against the traditional political elite, many of whom (including both Jackson and Clay) were members of the Masonic order, a fraternal society with secret rituals and special customs. The Anti-Masonic Party did make one lasting contribution to the political process. It was the first to hold a national nominating convention, an innovation quickly adopted by the other political parties.

Although the election was a triumph for Jackson, the Bank War continued. It was to have serious effects on the economy and on political principle. The Bank charter did not expire until 1836, but Jackson, declaring that "the hydra of corruption is only scotched, not dead," decided to kill the Bank by transferring its $10 million in government deposits to favored state banks ("pet banks," critics called them). Cabinet members objected, but Jackson ignored them. Two secretaries of the treasury refused to carry out Jackson's orders and were abruptly removed. Jackson then found a more pliant man, Roger Taney, for the job. (Jackson later rewarded him with the post of chief justice of the Supreme Court.) Henry Clay led an unprecedented vote of censure in the Senate, but in the House loyal Democrats prevented a censure vote. To all of these protests, Jackson responded that the election had given him a popular mandate to act against the Bank. The president was the direct representative of the people, he claimed, and could act upon the popular will, regardless of the opinion of Congress or even the cabinet. Short of impeachment, there was nothing Congress could do to prevent Jackson from acting on his expansive—and novel—interpretation of presidential powers.

Whigs, Van Buren, and the Election of 1836

But there was someone outside Congress with power to respond: the Bank's director, Nicholas Biddle. "This worthy President thinks that because he has scalped Indians…he is to have his way with the Bank," Biddle commented. "He is mistaken." As the government withdrew its deposits, Biddle abruptly called in the Bank's commercial loans, thereby causing a sharp panic and recession in the winter of 1833–34. Merchants, businessmen, and southern planters were all furious— at Jackson. His opponents, only a loose coalition up to this time, coalesced into a formal opposition party that called itself the Whigs. Evoking the memory of the Patriots who had resisted King George III in the American Revolution, the new party called on everyone to resist tyrannical "King Andrew." Just as Jackson's own calls for popular democracy had appealed to voters in all regions, so his opponents overcame their sectional differences to unite in opposition to his economic policies and arbitrary methods.

The Whigs first tested their strength against Vice President Martin Van Buren, Jackson's designated successor, in the presidential election of 1836. Still not completely free of the methods and attitudes of traditional politics, the Whigs ran four sectional candidates: William Henry Harrison of Ohio, Hugh Lawson White of Tennessee, W. P. Mangum of North Carolina, and Daniel Webster of Massachusetts. The Whigs hoped the combined votes for these regional candidates would deny Van Buren a majority and force the election into the House of Representatives, where they hoped to win. The strategy failed, but not by much: although Van Buren captured 170 electoral votes to the Whigs' 124, the popular vote was much closer, 50.9 percent to 49.1 percent. A shift of only 2,000 votes in Pennsylvania would have thrown the election into the House of Representatives, vindicating the Whig strategy. The Whig defeat drove home the weakness of the traditional sectional politics, but the closeness of the popular vote showed that the basis for a united national opposition did exist. In 1840, the Whigs would prove that they had learned this lesson.

The Panic of 1837

Meanwhile, the consequences of the Bank War continued. The recession of 1833–34 was followed by a wild speculative boom, caused as much by foreign investors as by the expiration of the Bank. Many new state banks were chartered that were eager to give loans, the price of cotton rose rapidly, and speculation in western lands was feverish (in Alabama and Mississippi, the mid-1830s were known as "the Flush Times"). A government surplus of $37 million distributed to the states in 1836 made the inflationary pressures worse. Jackson became alarmed at the widespread use of paper money (which he blamed for the inflation), and in July 1836 he issued the Specie Circular, announcing that the government would accept payment for public lands only in hard currency. At the same time, foreign investors, especially British banks, affected by a world recession, called in their American loans. The sharp contraction of credit led to the Panic of 1837 and a six-year recession, the worst the American economy had yet known. Ironically, Andrew Jackson, whose bad experience with speculation had led him to destroy the Bank of the United States, set in motion the events that caused the boom and bust he so feared. And he left his successor, Martin Van Buren, an impossible political legacy.

In 1837, 800 banks suspended business, refusing to pay out any of their $150 million in deposits. The collapse of the banking system led to business closures and outright failures. Nationwide, the unemployment rate is estimated to have reached more than 10 percent. In the winter of 1837–38 in New York City alone, one-third of all manual laborers were unemployed and an estimated 10,000 were living in abject poverty. New York laborers took to the streets. Four or five thousand protesters carrying signs reading "Bread, Meat, Rent, Fuel!" gathered at City Hall on February 10, 1838, then marched to the warehouse of a leading merchant, Eli Hart. Breaking down the door, they took possession of the thousands of barrels of flour Hart had stored there rather than sell at what the mob considered a fair price. Policemen and state militia who tried to prevent the break-in were beaten by the angry mob.

Nor were the working class and the poor the only victims. Among the many hurt by the panic was Philip Hone, former mayor of New York and once a man of considerable wealth. Hone lost two-thirds of his own fortune and was unable to help his three grown sons when they lost their jobs. "Business of all kinds [is] completely at a stand," Hone noted in 1840, wondering "how the poor man manages to get a dinner for his family." The Panic of 1837 lasted six long years, causing widespread misery. Not until 1843 did the economy show signs of recovery.

In neither 1837 nor 1819 did the federal government take any action to aid victims of economic recession. No banks were bailed out, no bank depositors were saved by federal insurance, no laid-off workers got unemployment payments. Nor did the government undertake any public works projects or pump money into the economy. All of these steps, today seen as essential to prevent economic collapse and to alleviate human suffering, were unheard of in 1819 and 1837. Soup kitchens and charities were mobilized in major cities, but only by private, volunteer groups, not by local or state governments. Panics and depressions were believed to be natural stages in the business cycle, and government intervention was considered unwarranted—although it was perfectly acceptable for government to intervene to promote growth. As a result, workers, farmers, and members of the new business middle class suddenly realized that participation in America's booming economy was very dangerous. The rewards could be great, but so could the penalties.

Martin Van Buren (quickly nicknamed "Van Ruin") spent a dismal four years in the White House presiding over bank failures, bankruptcies, and massive unemployment. Van Buren, who lacked Jackson's compelling personality, could find no remedies to the

This contemporary cartoon bitterly depicts the terrible effects of the Panic of 1837 on ordinary
people—bank failures, unemployment, drunkenness, and destitution—which the artist links
to the insistence of the rich on payment in specie (as Jackson had required in the Species
Circular of 1836). Over the scene waves the American flag, accompanied by the ironic
message, "61st Anniversary of our Independence."

depression. His misfortune gave the opposition party,
the newly formed Whigs, their opportunity.

THE SECOND AMERICAN PARTY SYSTEM

The First American Party System, the confrontation
between the Federalists and the Jeffersonian Democratic Republicans that began in the 1790s, had been
widely viewed as an unfortunate factional squabble that
threatened the common good of the republic (see
Chapter 8). By the 1830s, with the expansion of
suffrage, politics and the reality of continuing political
disagreements had come to be taken as a fact of life.
The political struggles of the Jackson era, coupled with
the dramatic social changes caused by expansion and
economic growth, created the basic pattern of American politics: two major parties, each with at least some
appeal among voters of all social classes and in all
sections of the country. That pattern, which we call "the
Second American Party System," remains to this day.

Whigs and Democrats

There were genuine differences between the Whigs
and the Democrats, but they were not sectional differences. Instead, the two parties reflected just-emerging
class and cultural differences. The Democrats, as they
themselves were quick to point out, had inherited
Thomas Jefferson's belief in the democratic rights of
the small, independent yeoman farmer. Because most of
the country was rural, it is not surprising that the
Democrats had nationwide appeal, especially in the
South and West, the most rural regions. As a result of
Jackson's presidency, Democrats came to be identified
with independence and a distaste for interference,
whether from the government or from economic
monopolies such as the Bank of the United States.
They favored expansion, Indian removal, and the freedom to do as they chose on the frontier. In the politics of the time, these were conservative values. They
reflected the opposition of most Democratic voters to
the rapid social and economic changes that accompanied the transportation revolution.

OVERVIEW

THE SECOND AMERICAN PARTY SYSTEM

Democrats	First organized to elect Andrew Jackson to the presidency in 1828. The Democratic Party spoke for Jeffersonian democracy, expansion, and the freedom of the "common man" from interference from government or from financial monopolies like the Bank of the United States. It found its power base in the rural South and West and among some northern urban workers. The Democratic Party was the majority party from 1828 to 1860.
Whigs	Organized in opposition to Andrew Jackson in the early 1830s. Heir to Federalism, the Whig Party favored a strong role for the national government in the economy (for example, it promoted Henry Clay's American System) and supported active social reform. Its power base lay in the North and Northwest among voters who benefited from increased commercialization and among some southern planters and urban merchants. The Whigs won the elections of 1840 and 1848.

The Whigs were themselves often the initiators and beneficiaries of economic change and were more receptive to it. Heirs of the Federalist belief in the importance of a strong federal role in the national economy (see Chapter 8), they supported the elements of Henry Clay's American System: a strong central government, the Bank of the United States, a protective tariff, and internal improvements. In fact, when it came to improvements, the Whigs wanted to improve people as well as roads. Religion was an important element in political affiliation, and many Whigs were members of evangelical reforming denominations. Reformers believed that everyone, rich and poor, was capable of the self-discipline that would lead to a good life. Thus Whigs favored government intervention in both economic and social affairs, calling for education and social reforms such as temperance that aimed to improve the ordinary citizen. Many rich men were Whigs, but so were many poorer men who had a democratic faith in the perfectibility of all Americans. The Whigs' greatest strength was in New England and the northern part of the West (the Old Northwest), the areas most affected by commercial agriculture and factory work.

Yet neither party was monolithic. As has continued to be true of American political parties, both the Democrats and the Whigs were a coalition of interests affected by local and regional factors. The job of the party leader, as the Democrats' Martin Van Buren had been among the first to realize, was to forge the divergent local party interests into a winning national majority. Although Jackson's appeal was strongest in the rural South and West, the Democrats also appealed to some workers in northern cities. Reflecting the emerging issues of class and ethnicity, these Democrats, many

of them immigrants, voted against the wealthier, native-born Americans, who were mostly Whigs. Urban workers cared little about rural issues, and they were less committed to the slave system than many Southerners, but they shared with Democrats from other regions a dislike of big business. On the other hand, a number of southern planters, who had close ties to merchant and banking interests, and residents of the South's commercial cities were attracted to the Whig policy of a strong federal role in economic development, though they were less active than many northern Whigs in advocating sweeping social reform.

The Campaign of 1840

In 1840, the Whigs set out to beat the Democrats at their own game. Passing over the ever-hopeful Henry Clay, the Whigs nominated a man as much like Andrew Jackson as possible, the aging Indian fighter William Henry Harrison, former governor of the Indiana Territory from 1801 to 1812. In an effort to duplicate Jackson's winning appeal to the South as well as the West, the Whigs balanced the ticket by nominating a Southerner, John Tyler, for vice president. The campaign slogan was "Tippecanoe and Tyler too" (Tippecanoe was the site of Harrison's famous victory over Tecumseh's Indian confederation in 1811). As if this were not enough, Whigs made Harrison out to be a humble man who would be happy to live in a log cabin, although he actually lived in a large and comfortable house. Thus began another long-lived political legend. The Whigs reached out to ordinary people with torchlight parades, barbecues, songs, coonskin caps, bottomless jugs of (hard) cider, and claims that Martin Van Buren, Harrison's hapless opponent, was a man of privilege and aristocratic tastes. Nothing could be further from the truth: Van Buren was the son of a tavern keeper. But Van Buren, a short man who lacked a commanding presence, had always dressed meticulously, and now even his taste in coats and ties was used against him.

The Whig campaign tactics, added to the popular anger at Van Buren because of the continuing depression, gave Harrison a sweeping electoral victory, 234 votes to 60. Even more remarkable, the campaign achieved the greatest voter turnout up to that time (and rarely equaled since), 80 percent.

The Whig Victory Turns to Loss: The Tyler Presidency

Although the Whig victory of 1840 was a milestone in American politics, the triumph of Whig principles was short-lived. William Henry Harrison, who was sixty-eight, died of pneumonia a month after his inauguration. For the first time in American history the vice president stepped up to the presidency. Not for the last time, important differences between the dead president and his successor reshaped the direction of American politics.

John Tyler of Virginia was a former Democrat who had left the party because he disagreed with Jackson's autocratic style. The Whigs had sought him primar-

ily for his sectional appeal and had not inquired too closely into his political opinions, which turned out to be anti-Whig as well as anti-Jackson. President Tyler vetoed a series of bills embodying all the elements of Henry Clay's American System: tariffs, internal improvements, a new Bank of the United States. In exasperation, congressional Whigs read Tyler out of the party, and his entire cabinet of Whigs resigned. To replace them, Tyler appointed former Democrats like himself. Thus the Whig triumph of 1840, one of the clearest victories in American electoral politics, was negated by the stalemate between Tyler and the Whig majority in Congress. The Whigs were to win only one more election, that of 1848.

Although the circumstances that robbed the Whigs of their victory were accidental, the Tyler debacle laid bare the great division that the two-party system was intended to hide: the sectional difference between the North and the South. The Whigs were a short-lived national party because they could not bridge that gap. And by the 1850s not even the Democrats could remain united.

AMERICAN ARTS AND LETTERS

Jackson's presidency was a defining moment in the development of an American identity. His combination of western belligerency and combative individualism was the strongest statement of American distinctiveness since Thomas Jefferson's agrarianism. Did Jackson speak for all of America? The Whigs did not think so. And the definitions of American identity that were beginning to emerge in popular culture and in intellectual circles were more complex than the message coming from the White House. Throughout the nation, however, there was a widespread interest in information and literature of all kinds. The Age of the Common Man would prove to be the period when American writers and painters found the national themes that allowed them to produce the first distinctively American literature and art.

The Spread of the Written Word

The transportation revolution improved communication. The number of newspapers, magazines, and books grew rapidly, helping broaden people's horizons beyond their own community. A print revolution began in 1826 when a reform organization, the American Tract Society, installed the country's first steam-powered press. Three years later the new presses had turned out 300,000 Bibles and 6 million religious tracts, or pamphlets. The greatest growth, however, was in newspapers that reached a mass audience. The number of newspapers soared from 376 newspapers in 1810 to 1,200 in 1835. This rise paralleled the growth of interest in politics, for most newspapers were published by political parties and were

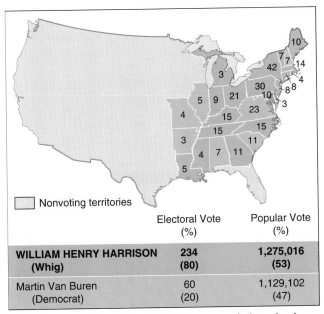

	Electoral Vote (%)	Popular Vote (%)
WILLIAM HENRY HARRISON (Whig)	**234 (80)**	**1,275,016 (53)**
Martin Van Buren (Democrat)	60 (20)	1,129,102 (47)

The Election of 1840   *The Whigs triumphed in the election of 1840 by beating the Democrats at their own game. Whigs could expect to do well in the commercializing areas of New England and the Old Northwest, but their adopted strategy of popular campaigning worked well in the largely rural South and West as well, contributing to Harrison's victory. The Whigs' choice of John Tyler as vice-presidential candidate, another strategy designed to appeal to southern voters, backfired when Harrison died and Tyler, who did not share Whig principles, became America's first vice president to succeed to the presidency.*

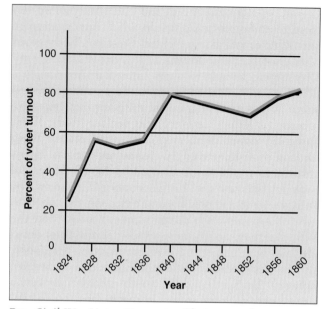

Pre–Civil War Voter Turnout   *The turnout of voters in presidential elections more than doubled from 1824 to 1828, the year Andrew Jackson was first elected. Turnout surged to 80 percent in 1840, the year the Whigs triumphed. The extension of suffrage to all white men and heated competition between two political parties with nationwide membership turned presidential election campaigns into events with great popular appeal.*

openly partisan. Packed with articles that today would be considered libelous and scandalous, newspapers were entertaining and popular reading. For western readers, the popular Crockett almanacs offered a mix of humorous stories and tall tales attributed to Davy Crockett (the boisterous Tennessee "roarer" who died defending the Alamo in 1836) along with meteorological and climate information. Throughout the country, religious literature was still the most widely read, but a small middle-class audience existed for literary magazines and, among women especially, for sentimental magazines and novels.

Accompanying all these changes in print communication was an invention that outsped them all: the telegraph, so innovative that its inventor spent years fruitlesssly seeking private funds to back its application. Finally, with financing from the federal government, Samuel F. B. Morse sent his first message from Washington to Baltimore in 1844. Soon messages in Morse code would be transmitted instantaneously across the continent. The impact of this revolutionary invention, the first to separate the message from the speed at which a human messenger could travel, was immediate. The timeliness of information available to the individual, from important national news to the next train's arrival time, vastly increased. Distant events gained new and exciting immediacy. Everyone's horizon and sense of community was widened.

Creating an American Culture

For all the improvements in communication, the United States was a provincial culture, still looking to Britain for values, standards, and literary offerings, and still mocked by the British. In a famous essay in the *Edinburgh Review* in 1820, Sidney Smith bitingly inquired, "In the four quarters of the globe, who reads an American book? or goes to an American play? or looks at an American picture or statue? What does the world yet owe to American physicians or surgeons? What new substances have their chemists discovered?" The answer was nothing—yet.

In the early years of the nineteenth century, eastern seaboard cities actively built the cultural foundation that would nurture American art and literature. Philadelphia's American Philosophical Society, founded by Benjamin Franklin in 1743, boasted a distinguished roster of scientists, including Thomas Jefferson—concurrently its president and president of the United States—and Nicholas Biddle, Jackson's opponent in the Bank War. Culturally, Boston ran a close second to Philadelphia, founding the Massachusetts General Hospital (1811) and the Boston Athenaeum (1807), a gentlemen's library and reading room containing "the works of learning and science in all languages; particularly such rare and expensive publications as are not generally to be obtained in this country." The *North American Review*, published in Boston, emerged as the country's most

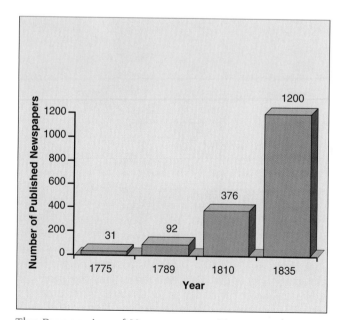

The Burgeoning of Newspapers   *Newspapers have a long history in the United States. Even before the American Revolution the colonies boasted 37 newspapers (see Chapter 6), and within little more than a decade that number had nearly tripled. Toward the end of the century, however, the number of newspapers expanded rapidly, by 1835 numbering more than 30 times that of 1775.*

LIBRARY OF THE ATHENÆUM.

*The Boston Athenaeum was one of Boston's leading cultural institutions. The library, shown
in this engraving, was probably the finest in the country in the early nineteenth century.*

important and long-lasting intellectual magazine. Devoted to keeping its readers in touch with European intellectual developments, the *Review* had a circulation of 3,000 in 1826, about the same as similar British journals. Southern cities were much less successful in supporting culture. Charleston had a Literary and Philosophical Society (founded in 1814), but the widely dispersed residences of the southern elite made urban cultural institutions difficult to sustain. Thus, unwittingly, the South ceded cultural leadership to the North.

The cultural picture was much spottier in the West. A few cities, such as Lexington, Kentucky, and Cincinnati, Ohio, had civic cultural institutions, and some transplanted New Englanders maintained connections with New England culture. A group of pioneers in Ames, Ohio, for example, founded a "coonskin library" composed of books purchased from Boston and paid for in coonskins. But most pioneers were at best uninterested and at worst actively hostile to traditional literary culture. This was neither from lack of literacy nor from failure to read. Newspaper and religious journals both had large readerships in the West: The Methodist *Christian Advo-*

cate, for example, reached 25,000 people yearly (compared with the *North American Review*'s 3,000). The frontier emphasis on the practical was hard to distinguish from anti-intellectualism. As writer Hugh Henry Brackenridge lamented from Pittsburgh, it was not "the want of learning I consider as a defect, but the contempt of it."

Thus in the early part of the nineteenth century, the gap between the intellectual and cultural horizons of a wealthy Bostonian and a frontier farmer in Michigan widened. Part of the unfinished task of building a national society was the creation of a national culture that could fill this gap. For writers and artists, the challenge was to find distinctively American themes.

Of the eastern cities, New York produced the first widely recognized American writers. In 1819, Washington Irving published *The Sketch Book*, thus immortalizing Rip Van Winkle and the Headless Horseman. Within a few years James Fenimore Cooper's Leatherstocking novels (of which *The Last of the Mohicans*, published in 1826, is the best known) achieved wide success in both America and Europe. Cooper's novels featured a heroic frontiersman, Natty Bumppo (modeled on Daniel Boone) who observes favorably the nobility of the Indians even as he participates in their defeat by the forces of civilization. Cooper's novels established the long American experience of westward expansion, of which the conquest of the Indians was a vital part, as a serious and distinctive American literary theme.

It was New England, however, that claimed to be the forge of American cultural independence from Europe. As Ralph Waldo Emerson proclaimed in "The American Scholar," a lecture he delivered in 1837 to the Harvard faculty, "Our day of dependence, our long apprenticeship to the learning of other lands, draws to a close." He went on to encourage American writers to find inspiration in the ordinary details of daily life. The stuff of literature, he declared, were to be found in "the familiar, the low…the milk in the pan; the ballad in the street; the news of the boat." Immensely popular, Emerson was the star of the lyceum circuit, a lecture network that sent speakers on cultural subjects to all parts of the country. He gave more than 1,500 lectures in twenty states between 1833 and 1860. "The American Scholar," his most famous lecture, carried a message of cultural self-sufficiency that Americans were eager to hear.

Artists and Builders

Artists were as successful as novelists in finding American themes. Thomas Cole, who came to America from England in 1818, found great inspiration in the American landscape, painting scenes of New York State's Catskill and Adirondack Mountains that reflect the influence of the British romantic school of landscape painting. With these works, Cole founded the Hudson River school of American painting. The frankly nationalistic style and subject matter of this school are reflected in the comment of New Yorker Philip Hone: "Every American is bound to prove his love of country by admiring Cole."

The western painters—realists such as Karl Bodmer and George Catlin as well as the romantics who followed them, like Albert Bierstadt and Thomas Moran—drew on the dramatic western landscape and its peoples. Their art was an important contribution to the American sense of the land and to the nation's identity. Catlin, driven by a need to document Indian life before it disappeared, spent eight years among the tribes of the upper Missouri River. Then he assembled his collection—more than 500 paintings in all—and toured the country from 1837 to 1851 in an unsuccessful attempt to arouse public indignation about the plight of the western Indian nations. Another unusual western painter, John James Audubon, could at first find no publisher in this country for his striking and sometimes grotesque etchings of American birds. George Caleb Bingham, an accomplished genre painter, produced somewhat tidied-up scenes of real-life American workers, such as flatboatmen on the Missouri River. All these painters found much to

Asher Durand, a member of the Hudson River School of landscape painting, produced this work, Kindred Spirits, in 1849 as a tribute to Thomas Cole, the school's leader. Cole is one of the figures depicted standing in a romantic wilderness.

record and to celebrate in American life. Ironically, the inspiration for the most prevalent theme, the American wilderness, was profoundly endangered by the rapid western settlement of which the nation was so proud.

The haste and transiency of American life are nowhere so obvious as in the architectural record of this era, which is sparse. The monumental neoclassical style (complete with columns) that Jefferson had recommended for official buildings in Washington continued to be favored for public buildings elsewhere and by private concerns trying to project an imposing image, such as banks. A few southern planters built impressive mansions, and there were odd experiments such as the prison built in Philadelphia in the 1820s that was designed to look like a medieval castle. The effect of this building on the imagination, one admiring commentator remarked, was "peculiarly impressive, solemn and instructive."

But in general Americans were in too much of a hurry to build for the future, and in balloon-frame construction they found the perfect technique for the present. Balloon-frame structures—which consist of a basic frame of wooden studs fastened with crosspieces top and bottom—could be put up quickly, cheaply, and without the help of a skilled carpenter. Covering the frame with wooden siding was equally simple, and the

CHRONOLOGY

1817	Erie Canal construction begins
1818	National Road completed to Wheeling
1819	*Dartmouth College v. Woodward*
1821	Martin Van Buren's Bucktails defeat DeWitt Clinton in New York
1824	*Gibbons v. Ogden* John Quincy Adams elected president by the House of Representatives
1825	Erie Canal opens
1826	First American use of the steam-powered printing press
1828	Congress passes "Tariff of Abominations" Andrew Jackson elected president John C. Calhoun publishes *Exposition and Protest* anonymously
1830	Jackson vetoes Maysville Road Bill Congress passes Indian Removal Act Baltimore and Ohio Railroad opens
1832	Nullification Crisis begins Jackson vetoes renewal of Bank of the United States charter Jackson reelected president
1833	National Road completed to Columbus, Ohio
1834	Cyrus McCormick patents the McCormick reaper Whig party organized
1836	Jackson issues Specie Circular Martin Van Buren elected president
1837	*Charles River Bridge v. Warren Bridge* John Deere invents steel plow Ralph Waldo Emerson first presents "The American Scholar" Panic of 1837
1838	Cherokee removal along the "Trail of Tears"
1840	Whig William Henry Harrison elected president
1841	John Tyler assumes presidency at the death of President Harrison
1844	Samuel F. B. Morse operates first telegraph

resultant dwelling was as strong, although not as well insulated, as a house of solid timber or logs. Balloon-frame construction was first used in Chicago in the 1830s, where it created the city almost instantly. The four-room balloon-frame house, affordable to many who could not have paid for a traditionally built dwelling, became standard in that decade. This was indeed housing for the common man and his family.

CONCLUSION

Andrew Jackson's presidency witnessed the building of a strong national party system based on nearly universal white manhood suffrage. At the same time that the nation expanded politically (nine new western states were admitted between 1800 and 1840), construction of new roads, canals, and railroads and other improvements in transportation and communication created the infrastructure that united the nation physically. Sectionalism and localism seemed to have been replaced by a more national consciousness that was clearly expressed in the two national political parties, the Whigs and the Democrats. The Second American Party System created new democratic political communities united by common political opinions. Culturally, American writers and artists began to establish a distinctive American identity in the arts. But as the key battles of the Jackson presidency—the Nullification Crisis, Indian removal, the Bank War—attested, the forces of sectionalism resisted the strong nationalizing tendencies of the era. As the next two chapters will show, economic and social forces continued to force the South and the North apart.

REVIEW QUESTIONS

1. What reasons might a person of the 1820s and 1830s give for opposing universal white manhood suffrage? Suffrage for free African American men? For women of all races?
2. Opponents believed that Andrew Jackson was unsuited in both political experience and temperament to be president of the United States, yet his presidency is considered one of the most influential in American history. Explain the changes in political organization and attitude that made his election possible.
3. Both the Nullification Crisis and Indian Removal raised the constitutional issue of the rights of a minority in a nation governed by majority rule. What rights, in your opinion, does a minority have, and what kinds of laws are necessary to defend those rights?
4. Why was the issue of government support for internal improvements so controversial? Who benefited from the transportation revolution? Who lost ground?
5. What were the key differences between Whigs and Democrats? What did each party stand for? Who were their supporters? What were the links between each party's programs and party supporters?
6. What distinctive American themes did the writers, artists, and builders of the 1820s and 1830s express in their works? Are they still considered American themes today?

RECOMMENDED READING

Donald B. Cole, *Martin Van Buren and the American Political System* (1984). An excellent study of Van Buren's key role in the transformation of politics.

Donald B. Cole, *The Presidency of Andrew Jackson* (1993). In this recent work, Jackson is seen as just as influential, but less commanding and more ambiguous in his political attitudes than in earlier studies.

Daniel Feller, *The Jacksonian Promise* (1995). A recent overview of the period 1815–1840 that stresses the optimism and enterprising spirit of the era rather than the anxiety some other historians have discerned.

Ronald P. Formisano, *The Transformation of Political Culture: Massachusetts Parties, 1790s–1840s* (1983). One of many detailed studies that have contributed to our understanding of the development of the second party system.

William W. Freehling, *Prelude to Civil War* (1966). An examination of the Nullification Crisis that stresses the centrality of slavery to the dispute.

Paul W. Gates, *The Farmer's Age: Agriculture, 1815–1860* (1966). The standard source on the growth of commercial agriculture.

Jean V. Matthews, *Toward a New Society: American Thought and Culture, 1800–1830* (1991). A valuable survey of American attitudes toward religion, politics, science, nature, and culture in the early nineteenth century.

Robert Remini, *Andrew Jackson and the Source of American Freedom* (1981). An account of Jackson's White House years by his major biographer.

Carol Sheriff, *The Artificial River: The Erie Canal and the Paradox of Progress, 1817–1862* (1996). Shows how the building of the canal changed personal lives and fostered religious beliefs in human perfectability.

Alan Taylor, *William Cooper's Town: Power and Persuasion on the Frontier of the Early American Republic* (1995). The Pulitzer Prize-winning study of the founding and development of Cooperstown, New York, by the father of novelist James Fenimore Cooper. An engrossing study of the effects of the democratization of politics.

George Rogers Taylor, *The Transportation Revolution, 1815–1860* (1951). The indispensable book on all aspects of the American economy during this period.

Harry L. Watson, *Liberty and Power: The Politics of Jacksonian America* (1990). An excellent recent overview of Jacksonian politics.

ADDITIONAL BIBLIOGRAPHY

The New Democratic Politics and the Jackson Presidency

William L. Anderson, *Cherokee Removal: Before and After* (1991)
Ralph S. Cotterill, *The Southern Indians* (1954)

John Ehle, *Trail of Tears* (1988)
Richard E. Ellis, *The Union at Risk* (1987)
Paul Goodman, *Towards a Christian Republic: Antimasonry and the Great Tradition in New England, 1826–1836* (1988)

Michael D. Green, *The Politics of Indian Removal* (1982)

Lucy Maddox, *Removals: Nineteenth-Century American Literature and the Politics of Indian Affairs* (1991)

Michael Rogin, *Fathers and Children: Andrew Jackson and the Destruction of American Indians* (1975)

Ronald N. Satz, *American Indian Policy in the Jacksonian Era* (1975)

Arthur M. Schlesinger Jr., *The Age of Jackson* (1945)

John Ward, *Andrew Jackson: Symbol for an Age* (1955)

Chilton Williamson, *American Suffrage: From Property to Democracy, 1760–1860* (1960)

Internal Improvements

Allan G. Bogue, *From Prairie to Corn Belt: Farming on the Illinois and Iowa Frontier* (1968)

Clarence Danhof, *Changes in Agriculture: The Northern United States, 1820–1870* (1969)

E. M. Dodd, *American Business Corporations until 1860* (1954)

Albert Fishlow, *American Railroads and the Transformation of the Ante-Bellum Economy* (1965)

Robert W. Fogel, *Railroads and American Economic Growth: Essays in Econometric History* (1964)

Carter Goodrich, *Government Promotion of American Canals and Railroads, 1800–1890* (1960)

John Denis Haeger, *The Investment Frontier: New York Businessmen and the Economic Development of the Old Northwest* (1981)

Oscar Handlin and Mary Handlin, *Commonwealth: A Study of the Role of Government in the American Economy: Massachusetts, 1774–1861* (1947)

Louis Hartz, *Economic Policy and Democratic Thought: Pennsylvania, 1776–1860* (1948)

Erik F. Hiates, James Mak, and Gary M. Walton, *Western River Transportation: The Era of Early Internal Development, 1800–1860* (1975)

Morton J. Horwitz, *The Transformation of American Law, 1780–1860* (1977)

Philip Jordan, *The National Road* (1948)

Karl Raitz, ed., *The National Road* (1995)

Harry N. Scheiber, *The Ohio Canal Era: A Case Study of Government and the Economy, 1820–1861* (1969)

Ronald E. Shaw, *Canals for a Nation: The Canal Era in the United States, 1790–1860* (1990)

Ronald Shaw, *Erie Water West: History of the Erie Canal* (1966)

Peter Temin, *Iron and Steel in Nineteenth-Century America* (1964)

———, *The Jacksonian Economy* (1965)

Peter Way, *Common Labour: Workers and the Digging of North American Canals, 1780-1860* (1993)

The Rise of the Whigs and the Second American Party System

John Ashworth, *Agrarians and Aristocrats: Party Ideology in the United States, 1837–1846* (1983)

R. G. Gunderson, *The Log Cabin Campaign* (1957)

Bray Hammond, *Banks and Politics in America* (1957)

Daniel W. Howe, *The Political Culture of the American Whigs* (1980)

Lawrence F. Kohl, *The Politics of Individualism: Parties and the American Character in the Jacksonian Era* (1989)

Richard P. McCormick, *The Second American Party System: Party Formation in the Jacksonian Era* (1966)

James Roger Sharp, *The Jacksonians versus the Banks: Politics in the United States after the Panic of 1837* (1970)

Joel H. Sibley, *The Partisan Imperative: The Dynamics of American Politics before the Civil War* (1985)

Harry L. Watson, *Jacksonian Politics and Community Conflict: The Emergence of the Second American Party System in Cumberland County, North Carolina* (1981)

American Arts and Letters

John L. Brooke, *Knowledge Is Power: The Diffusion of Information in Early America, 1700–1865* (1989)

Cathy N. Davidson, *Revolution and the Word: The Rise of the Novel in America* (1986)

William J. Gilmore, *Reading Becomes a Necessity of Life: Material and Cultural Life in Rural New England, 1780–1835* (1989)

Neil Harris, *The Artist in American Society: The Formative Years, 1790–1860* (1966)

Nathan O. Hatch, *The Democratization of American Christianity* (1989)

Barbara Novak, *Nature and Culture: American Landscape Painting 1825–1875* (1982)

Albert Von Frank, *The Sacred Game: Provincialism and Frontier Consciousness in American Literature, 1630–1860* (1985)

Gwendolyn Wright, *Building the Dream: A Social History of Housing in America* (1981)

Biography

Irving H. Bartlett, *Daniel Webster* (1978)

Richard Current, *Daniel Webster and the Rise of National Conservatism* (1955)

———, *John C. Calhoun* (1963)

Robert V. Remini, *Henry Clay: Statesman for the Union* (1991)

Leonard L. Richards, *The Life and Times of Congressman John Quincy Adams* (1986)

C. M. Wiltse, *John C. Calhoun: Nullifier, 1829–1839* (1949)

THE SOUTH AND SLAVERY

1790s–1850s

Taylor. *An American Slave Market*, 1852. Oil on canvas. Chicago Historical Society.

AMERICAN COMMUNITIES
Natchez-under-the-Hill

The wharfmaster had just opened the public auction of confiscated cargoes in the center of Natchez when a great cry was heard. An angry crowd of flatboatmen, Bowie knives in hand, was storming up the bluffs from the Mississippi shouting, as the local newspaper reported, "threats of violence and death upon all who attempted to sell and buy their property." It was November 1837, and the town council had just enacted a restrictive tax of $10 per flatboat, a measure designed to rid the wharf district known as Natchez-under-the-Hill of the most impoverished and disreputable of the riverboatmen. The council had made its first confiscation of cargo after nine captains refused to pay this tax. As the boatmen approached, merchants and onlookers shrank back in fear. But the local authorities had called out the militia, and a company of farmers and planters now came marching into the square with their rifles primed and lowered. "The cold and sullen bayonets of the Guards were too hard meat for the Arkansas toothpicks," reported the local press, and "there was no fight." The boatmen sullenly turned back down the bluffs. It was the first confrontation in the "Flatboat Wars" that erupted as Mississippi ports tried to bring their troublesome riverfronts under regulation.

The first European to take notice of this "land abundant in subsistence" was a member of Hernando de Soto's expedition in the sixteenth century. The area was "thickly peopled" by the Natchez Indians, he wrote. It was not until the French established the port of Fort Rosalie in the 1720s, however, that Europeans settled in the area. The French destroyed the highly organized society of the Natchez Indians in the 1730s and the port became a major Mississippi River trading center. From Fort Rosalie, the French conducted an extensive frontier trade that brought peoples of different races together, leading to intermarriage and the growth of a mixed-race population. French traders bought deerskins, for which there was a large export market, from Choctaw, Chickasaw, and Creek hunters. During the same period, some Africans who had been imported by the French to work as slaves on plantations found roles in the French-Indian trade as boatmen, hunters, soldiers, and interpreters.

When the Spanish took control of the territory in 1763 they laid out the new town of Natchez high on the bluffs, safe from Mississippi flooding. Fort Rosalie, rechristened Natchez-under-the-Hill, continued to flourish as the produce grown by American farmers in Kentucky and Tennessee moved downriver on flatboats. Thus Americans became the newest additions to the ethnic diversity of this well-established trading center. When Americans took possession of Mississippi in 1798, the district surrounding the port became the most important center of settlement in the Old Southwest. Once again this abundant land of rich, black soil became thickly peopled, but this time with cotton planters and their African American slaves.

CHAPTER OUTLINE

Under-the-Hill gained renown as the last stop for boatmen before New Orleans. Minstrel performers sang of their exploits:

Den dance de boatmen dance,
O dance de boatmen dance,
O dance all night till broad daylight,
An go home wid de gals in de morning.

According to one traveler, "They feel the same inclination to dissipation as sailors who have long been out of port." There were often as many as 150 boats drawn up at the wharves. The crowds along the riverfront, noted John James Audubon, who visited in the 1820s, "formed a medley which it is beyond my power to describe." Mingling among American rivermen of all descriptions were trappers and hunters in fur caps, Spanish shopkeepers in bright smocks, French gentlemen from New Orleans in velvet coats, Indians wrapped in their trade blankets, African Americans both free and slave—a pageant of nations and races. Clapboard shacks and flatboats dragged on shore and converted into storefronts served as grog shops, card rooms, dance halls, and hotels. Whorehouses with women of every age and color abounded.

On the bluffs, meanwhile, the town of Natchez had become the winter home to the southwestern planter elite. They built their mansions with commanding views of the river. A visitor attending a ball at one of these homes was dazzled by the display: "Myriads of wax candles burning in wall sconces, sparkling chandeliers, entrancing music, the scent of jasmine, rose and sweet olive, the sparkle of wine mellowed by age, the flow of wit and brilliant repartee, all were there." Sustaining this American aristocracy was the labor of thousands of enslaved men and women, who lived in the squalid quarters behind the great house and worked the endless fields of cotton. It was they who made possible the greatest accumulations of wealth in early-nineteenth-century America.

The Natchez planters, their wealth and confidence growing with cotton's growing dominance of the local economy, found Under-the-Hill an increasing irritant. "A gentleman may game with a gambler by the hour," one resident remembered, "and yet despise him and refuse to recognize him afterward." The Under-the-Hill elite, however—gamblers, saloon keepers, and pimps—disturbed this social boundary when they began staying at hotels and even

building town houses in Natchez town. And in the wake of the slave revolt led by Nat Turner in Virginia in 1831 in which fifty-five white people were killed, the planters began to feel increasingly threatened by the racial mingling of the riverfront.

In the late 1830s the Natchez elite was jolted by rumors that their slaves were conspiring to murder them during Fourth of July celebrations while Under-the-Hill desperadoes looted their mansions. The rumors reinforced the growing conviction among planters that they could no longer tolerate the polyglot community of the riverfront. The measures that ultimately provoked the flatboatmen's threats in November 1837 soon followed.

In response to these threats, the planters issued an extralegal order giving all the gamblers, pimps, and whores of Under-the-Hill twenty-four hours to evacuate the district. As the Mississippi militia sharpened their bayonets, panic swept the wharves, and that night dozens of flatboats loaded with a motley human cargo headed for the more tolerant community of New Orleans. Other river ports issued similar orders of expulsion. "The towns on the river," one resident remembered, "became purified from a moral pestilence which the law could not cure." Three years later a great tornado hit Under-the-Hill, leveling the shacks that had served so long as a rendezvous for the rivermen, and gradually the Mississippi reclaimed the bottom.

These two communities—Natchez, home to the rich slave-owning elite, and Natchez-under-the-Hill, the bustling polyglot trading community—epitomize the paradox of the American South in the early nineteenth century. Enslaved African Americans grew the region's most lucrative crop, cotton. On the resulting profits, aristocratic Southerners built a sumptuous and distinctive lifestyle for themselves. The boatmen and traders of Natchez-under-the-Hill who brought the cotton and other products to market were vital to the planters' prosperity. But the polyglot racial and social mixing of Natchez-under-the-Hill threatened the system of control, built on a rigid distinction between free white people and enslaved black people, by which the planters maintained slavery. Because the slave owners could not control the boatmen, they expelled them. This defensive reaction—to seal off the world of slavery from the wider commercial world—exposed the vulnerability of the slave system at the very moment of its greatest commercial success.

Natchez

KEY TOPICS

- The domination of southern life by the slave system
- The economic implications of "King Cotton"
- The creation of African American communities under slavery
- The social structure of the white South and its increasing defensiveness

KING COTTON AND SOUTHERN EXPANSION

Slavery had long dominated southern life. African American slaves grew the great export crops of the colonial period—tobacco, rice, and indigo—on which slave owners' fortunes were made, and their presence shaped southern society and culture (see Chapter 4). Briefly, in the early days of American independence, the slave system waned, only to be revived by the immense profitability of cotton in a newly industrializing world. Cotton became the dominant crop in a rapidly expanding South that included not only the original states of Maryland, Delaware, Virginia, North and South Carolina, and Georgia, but Kentucky, Tennessee, Missouri, Alabama, Mississippi, Louisiana (the Old Southwest), Arkansas, Florida, and Texas as well. The overwhelming economic success of cotton and of the slave system on which it depended created a distinctive regional culture quite different from that developing in the North.

The Cotton Gin and Expansion into the Old Southwest

Short-staple cotton had long been recognized as a crop ideally suited to southern soils and growing conditions. But it had one major drawback: the seeds were so difficult to remove from the lint that it took an entire day to hand-clean a single pound of cotton. The invention in 1793 that made cotton growing profitable was the result of collaboration between a young Northerner named Eli Whitney, recently graduated from Yale College, and Catherine Greene, a South Carolina plantation owner and widow of Revolu-

tionary War General Nathanael Greene, who hired Whitney to tutor her children. Whitney built a prototype cotton engine, dubbed "gin" for short, a simple device consisting of a hand-cranked cylinder with teeth that tore the lint away from the seeds. At Greene's suggestion, the teeth were made of wire. With the cotton gin it was possible to clean more than fifty pounds of cotton a day. Soon large and small planters in the inland regions of Georgia and South Carolina had begun to grow cotton. By 1811, this area was producing 60 million pounds of cotton a year, and exporting most of it to England.

Other areas of the South quickly followed South Carolina and Georgia into cotton production. New land was wanted because cotton growing rapidly depleted the soil. The profits to be made from cotton growing drew a rush of southern farmers into the so-called black belt—an area stretching through western

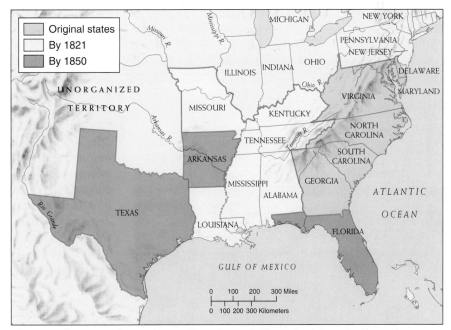

The South Expands, 1790–1850 *This map shows the dramatic effect cotton production had on southern expansion. From the original six states of 1790, westward expansion, fueled by the search for new cotton lands, added another six states by 1821, and three more by 1850.*

Georgia, Alabama, and Mississippi that was blessed with exceptionally fertile soil. Following the War of 1812, southerners were seized by "Alabama fever." In one of the swiftest migrations in American history, white southerners and their slaves flooded into western Georgia and the areas that would become Alabama and Mississippi (the Old Southwest). On this frontier, African American pioneers (albeit involuntary ones) cleared the forests, drained the swamps, broke the ground, built houses and barns, and planted the first crops.

This migration caused the population of Mississippi to double (from 31,306 to 74,448) and that of Alabama to grow sixteenfold (from 9,046 to 144,317) between 1810 and 1820. This and subsequent western land booms dramatically changed the population of the original southern states as well. Nearly half of all white South Carolinians born after 1800 eventually left the state, usually to move west. By 1850 there were more than 50,000 South Carolina natives living in Georgia, almost as many in Alabama, and 26,000 in Mississippi.

Southerners had historically taken the lead in westward expansion. Backcountry residents of Virginia and North Carolina were the first to venture over the Appalachians, and Virginians and Carolinians were the major settlers of the first two trans-Appalachian states, Kentucky (1792) and Tennessee (1796). John C. Calhoun of South Carolina and Henry Clay of Kentucky had been two of the most prominent expansionist War Hawks in Congress before the War of 1812. Like the simultaneous expansion into the Old Northwest, settlement of the Old Southwest took place at the expense of the region's Indian population (see Chapter 9). Beginning with the defeat of the Creeks at Horseshoe Bend in 1814 and ending with the Cherokee forced migration along "the Trail of Tears" in 1838, the "Five Civilized Tribes"—

the Cherokees, Chickasaws, Choctaws, Creeks, and Seminoles—were forced to give up their lands and move to Indian Territory (see Chapter 10).

On the southern frontier, as on the northern frontier, the killing, confinement, and removal of Indian peoples was the result of white expansion and settlement motivated by the hunger for land and profit. In the South, however, there was an additional motivation, rooted in slavery, for Indian removal: there was simply no room in the southern social order for anything other than white and black, master and slave. Literate, slave-owning "redskins" confused this simple picture: they were too "civilized" to be like slaves, but the wrong color to be masters. Thus southern Indian removal, like southern expansion, was dictated by the needs of the slave system.

Following "the Alabama Fever" of 1816–20, several later surges of southern expansion (1832–38, and again in the mid–1850s) carried cotton planting over the Mississippi River into Louisiana and deep into Texas. Each surge ignited feverish speculative frenzies, remembered in terms like "the Flush Times" for the heated rush of the 1830s. In the minds of the mobile, enterprising Southerners who sought their fortunes in the West, cotton profits and expansion went hand in hand. But the expansion of cotton meant the expansion of slavery.

The Question of Slavery

Cotton growing was well suited to the southern plantation system of agriculture. That system was characterized by large plantings of a single crop tended by gangs of workers who performed the same operation (planting, hoeing, or picking) under the supervision of an overseer. The southern labor system shifted from white indentured servitude to African slavery during the colonial period because servants would not perform plantation work for others when they could farm their own land (see Chapter 4). White Southerners believed that only African slaves could be forced to work day after day, year after year, at the rapid and brutal pace required in the cotton fields of large plantations in the steamy southern summer. As the production of cotton climbed higher every year in response to a seemingly inexhaustible international demand, so too did the demand for slaves and the conviction of Southerners that slavery was an economic necessity.

At the very moment that the South was committing its future to cotton, however, and assuring the persistence of slavery there, opinion about slavery was changing. Britain outlawed the international slave trade in 1807 and the United States took the same step in 1808. In the preceding quarter century, all the northern states had abolished slavery or passed laws for gradual emancipation (see Chapter 7). Between 1776 and 1786 all the states except South Carolina and Georgia either banned or

Steamboats at New Orleans await loads of cotton, the nation's major export. Just as the giant bales crowd the wharf, so too the culture created by "King Cotton" dominated southern life.

The immense size of the internal slave trade made sights like this commonplace on southern roads. Groups of slaves, chained together in gangs called coffles, were marched from their homes in the Upper South to cities in the Lower South, where they were auctioned to new owners.

heavily taxed the international slave trade, and it was only at the insistence of these two states that the Constitutional Convention prohibited Congress from passing a federal law to outlaw the slave trade for twenty years. All the southern states banned the importation of foreign slaves after the successful slave revolt in Haiti in 1791; Southerners feared that Caribbean revolutionaries might incite their own slaves to rebellion.

Attitudes changed again following the invention of the cotton gin in 1793 and the realization of the riches to be made from cotton. Slave smuggling became so rampant that South Carolina officially reopened the trade in 1804. For the next four years, Charleston boomed as one of the world's largest slaving ports: at least 40,000 Africans were imported. It was clear, however, that national opinion found the international slave trade abhorrent, and on January 1, 1808, the earliest date permitted by the Constitution, a bill to abolish the importation of slaves became law. Although a small number of slaves continued to be smuggled from Africa, the growth of the slave labor force after 1808 depended primarily on natural increase. And the ban on foreign importations vastly increased the importance of the internal slave trade.

The Internal Slave Trade

The cotton boom caused a huge increase in the domestic slave trade. Plantation owners in the Upper South (Delaware, Kentucky, Maryland, Virginia, and Tennessee) sold their slaves to meet the demand for labor in the new and expanding cotton-growing regions of the Old Southwest. In every decade after 1820 at least 150,000 slaves were uprooted either by slave trading or planter migration to the new areas, and in the expansions of the 1830s and the 1850s, the number reached a quarter of a million. Cumulatively, between 1820 and 1860 nearly 50 percent of the slave population of the

Upper South took part against their will in southern expansion.

Purchased by slave traders from owners in the Upper South, slaves were gathered together in notorious "slave pens" like the ones in Richmond and Charleston and then moved south by train or boat. In the interior, they were carried as cargo on steamboats on the Mississippi River, hence the phrase "sold down the river." Often slaves moved on foot, chained together in groups of fifty or more known as "coffles." Coffles were a common sight on southern roads, and one difficult to reconcile with the notion of slavery as a benevolent institution. Arriving at a central market in the Lower South like Natchez, New Orleans, or Mobile, the slaves, after being carefully inspected by potential buyers, were sold at auction to the highest bidder.

Although popular stereotype portrayed slave traders as unscrupulous outsiders who persuaded kind and reluctant masters to sell their slaves, the historical truth is much harsher. Traders, far from being shunned by slave-owning society, were often respected community members. One Charleston trader, Alexander McDonald, served as both an alderman and a bank president and was described as "a man of large means and responsible for all his engagements" who had "the confidence of the public." Similarly, the sheer scale of the slave trade makes it impossible to believe that slave owners only reluctantly parted with their slaves at times of economic distress. Instead, it is clear that many owners sold slaves and separated slave families not out of necessity but to increase their profits. The sheer size and profitability of the internal slave trade made a mockery of Southern claims for the benevolence of the slave system.

The Economics of Slavery

The rapid growth of cotton production was an international phenomenon, prompted by events occurring far from the American South. The insatiable demand for cotton was a result of the technological and social changes that we know today as the industrial revolution. Beginning early in the eighteenth century, a series of inventions resulted in the mechanized spinning and weaving of cloth in the world's first factories in the north of England. The ability of these factories to produce unprecedented amounts of cotton cloth revolutionized the world economy. The invention of the cotton gin came at just the right time. British textile manufacturers were eager to buy all the cotton that the South could produce.

Was the southern plantation system profitable? Clearly, in the years before 1860, southern farmers believed so. The figures for cotton production support this conclusion: from 720,000 bales in 1830, to 2.85 million bales in 1850, to nearly 5 million in 1860. By the time of the Civil War, cotton accounted for almost 60 percent of American exports, representing a total value of nearly $200 million a year.

Cotton's central place in the national economy and its international importance led Senator James Henry Hammond of South Carolina to make a famous boast in 1858:

> Without firing a gun, without drawing a sword, should they make war on us, we could bring the whole world to our feet....What would happen if no cotton was furnished for three years?...England would topple headlong and carry the whole civilized world with her save the south. No, you dare not to make war on cotton. No power on the earth dares to make war upon it. Cotton is King.

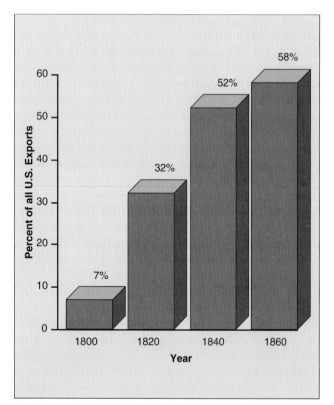

Cotton Exports as a Percentage of All U.S. Exports, 1800–1860 *One consequence of the growth of cotton production was its importance in international trade. The growing share of the export market, and the great value (nearly $200 million in 1860) led southern slave owners to believe that "Cotton Is King." The importance of cotton to the national economy entitled the South to a commanding voice in national policy, many Southerners believed.*

Indeed, the export of cotton from the South was the dynamic force in the developing American economy in the period 1790–1840. Just as the international slave trade had been the dynamic force in the Atlantic economy of the eighteenth century (see Chapter 4), southern slavery financed northern industrial development in the nineteenth century.

The connection between southern slavery and northern industry was very direct. Most mercantile services associated with the cotton trade (insurance, for example) were in northern hands and, significantly, so was shipping. This economic structure was not new. In colonial times, New England ships dominated the African slave trade. Some New England families—like the Browns of Providence who made fortunes in the slave trade—invested some of their profits in the new technology of textile manufacturing in the 1790s. Other merchants—such as the Boston Associates who financed the cotton textile mills at Lowell—made their money from cotton shipping and brokerage. Thus as cotton boomed, it provided capital for the new factories of the North.

Cotton Culture

Northerners, who were caught up in rapid industrialization and urbanization, failed to recognize their economic connection to the South and increasingly regarded it as a backward region. Senator from New York William H. Seward, on his first visit to Virginia, found ample justification for his antislavery convictions:

> It was necessary that I should travel in Virginia to have any idea of a slave state....An exhausted soil, old and decaying towns, wretchedly-neglected roads, and in every respect, an absence of enterprise and improvement, distinguish the region through which we have come, in contrast to that in which we live. Such has been the effect of slavery.

Concentration on plantation agriculture did divert energy and resources from the South's cities. At a time when the North was experiencing the greatest spurt of urban growth in the nation's history, southern cities did not keep pace. Charleston, for example, one of America's five largest cities in 1800, had a population of only 41,000 in 1860, compared with Boston's 177,840 and Baltimore's 212,418. The one exception was New Orleans, the great port at the mouth of the extensive Mississippi River transportation system. In 1860 New Orleans was the nation's fifth largest city, with a population of 169,000. The nine other leading cities were all northern or western. Most of the South remained rural: less than 3 percent of Mississippi's population lived in cities of more than 2,500 residents, and only 10 percent of Virginia's did.

The South also lagged behind the North in industrialization and in canals and railroads. In 1860, only 15 percent of the nation's factories were located in the South. Noteworthy exceptions were the iron industry near Richmond, which in 1860 boasted four rolling mills, fourteen foundries, and various machine shops employing 1,600 mechanics, and William Gregg's cotton textile mills in Graniteville, just east of Augusta, Georgia. Similarly, the South was initially left behind by the transportation revolution. In 1850, only 26 percent of the nation's railroads were in the South, increasing to still only 35 percent in 1860.

The failure of the South to industrialize at the northern rate was not a matter of ignorance but of choice. Southern capital was tied up in land and slaves, and Southerners, buoyed by the world's insatiable demand for cotton, saw no reason to invest in economically risky railroads, canals, and factories. Nor were they eager to introduce the disruptive factor of free wage labor into the tightly controlled slave system. Cotton was safer. Cotton was King.

Thus the cotton boom created a distinctive regional culture. Although cotton was far from being the only crop (the South actually devoted more acreage to corn than to cotton in 1860), its vast profitability affected all aspects of society. In the first half of the nineteenth century, King Cotton reigned supreme over an expanding domain as Southerners increasingly tied their fortunes to the slave system of cotton production. As a British tourist to Mobile wryly noted in the 1850s, the South was a place where "people live in cotton houses and ride in cotton carriages. They buy cotton, sell cotton, think cotton, eat cotton, drink cotton, and dream cotton. They marry cotton wives, and unto them are born cotton children." The South was truly in thrall to King Cotton.

TO BE A SLAVE

The slave population, estimated at 700,000 by 1790, grew to more than 4 million. After 1808 (when official American participation in the international slave trade ceased) the growth occurred because of natural increase—that is, births within the slave population. In spite of the burden of slavery, a distinctive African American community, which had first emerged in the eighteenth century (see Chapter 4), flourished in the years before the Civil War.

The Maturing of the American Slave System

Dependence on King Cotton meant dependence on slave labor. In 1850, 55 percent of all slaves were engaged in cotton growing. Another 20 percent labored to produce other crops: tobacco (10 percent), rice, sugar, and hemp. About 15 percent of all slaves were domestic servants, and the remaining 10 percent worked in mining, lumbering, industry, and construction.

Agriculture, Industry, and Slavery, 1850   *The distribution of the slave population in the South was determined by agricultural and industrial patterns. In 1850, 55 percent of all slaves worked in cotton, 10 percent in tobacco, and another 10 percent in rice, sugar, and hemp. Ten percent worked in mining, lumbering, industry, and construction, and 15 percent worked as domestic servants. Slaves were not generally used to grow corn, the staple crop of the yeoman farmer.*

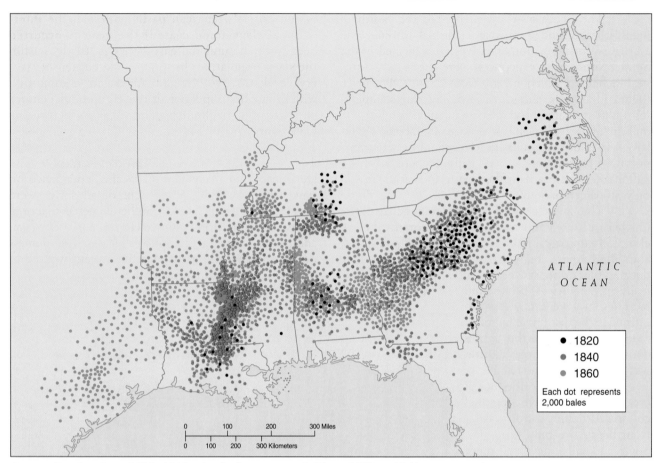

Cotton Production, 1820–1860 In the forty-year period from 1820 to 1860, cotton production grew dramatically both in quantity and in extent. The westward expansion that cotton production encouraged in the 1830s and 1850s is reflected in the symbols for 1840 and 1860, and the growing concentration of cotton production in the black belt (so-called for its rich soils) of the Lower South is clearly evident.

Source: Sam Bowers Hilliard, *Atlas of Antebellum Southern Agriculture* (Baton Rouge: Louisiana State University Press, 1984), pp. 67–71.

Slavery had become distinctively southern: by 1820, as a result of laws passed after the Revolution, all of the northern states had abolished slaveholding. Slaves were increasingly clustered in the Lower South, as Upper South slave owners sold slaves downriver or migrated westward with their entire households. An estimated 1 million slaves migrated involuntarily to the Lower South between 1820 and 1860. Moreover, as expansion to the Southwest accelerated, so did the demand for slaves in the newly settled regions, thus fueling the internal slave trade.

Slaves were not distributed equally among southern slave owners. More than half of all slave owners owned five slaves or fewer, but 75 percent of all slaves lived in groups of ten or more. This disproportionate distribution could have a major impact on a slave's life, for it was a very different matter to be the single slave of a small farmer as opposed to a member of a 100-person black community on a large plantation.

Finally, of all the New World slave societies, the one that existed in the American South was the only one that grew by natural increase rather than the constant importation of captured Africans. This fact alone made the African American community of the South different from the slave societies of Cuba, the Caribbean islands, and Brazil. The first thing to understand, then, are the circumstances of survival.

The Challenge to Survive

The primary challenge facing African Americans was survival. The very young were at risk: mortality rates for slave children under five were twice those for their white counterparts. The reason was clear: pregnant black women were inadequately nourished, worked too hard, or were too frequently pregnant, giving birth to six to eight children at year-and-one-half intervals. When the British actress Fanny Kemble came to live on her husband's Georgia plantation in 1837, what

Slave Population, 1820–1860 *The growth of cotton production caused a redistribution of the enslaved African American population in the South. Although slaves were still used to grow tobacco in Virginia and rice in coastal South Carolina, after 1830 an increasing number were sold "down the river" to work new cotton plantations in the Lower South. Thus although U.S. participation in the international slave trade was outlawed in 1808, the domestic trade in slaves flourished.*

Source: Sam Bowers Hilliard, *Atlas of Antebellum Southern Agriculture* (Baton Rouge: Louisiana State University Press, 1984), pp. 29–34.

shocked her more deeply than any other aspect of the slave system was the treatment of pregnant black women. Sensing her sympathy, pregnant slave women came to Kemble to plead for relief from field work, only to be brusquely ordered back to the fields by the overseer and Kemble's husband.

Health remained a lifelong issue for slaves. Malaria and infectious diseases such as yellow fever and cholera were endemic in the South. White people as well as black died, as the life expectancy figures for 1850 show: 40–43 years for white people and 30–33 years for African Americans. Slaves were more at risk because of the circumstances of slave life: poor housing, poor diet, and constant, usually heavy work. Sickness was chronic: 20 percent or more of the slave labor force on most plantations were sick at any one time. Many owners believed sick slaves were only "malingering." Because of the poor medical knowledge

of the time, they failed to realize that adequate diet, warm housing, and basic sanitation might have prevented the pneumonia and dysentery that killed or weakened many slaves, and that exacted an especially high toll on very young children.

From Cradle to Grave

Slavery was a lifelong labor system, and the constant and inescapable issue between master and slave was how much work the slave would—or could be forced to—do. Southern white slave owners claimed that by housing, feeding, and clothing their slaves from infancy to death they were acting more humanely than northern industrialists who employed people only during their working years. But in spite of occasional instances of manumission—the freeing of a slave—the child born of a slave was destined to remain a slave.

Children lived with their parents (or with their mother if the father was a slave on another farm or plantation) in housing provided by the owner. Slaves owned by small farmers usually had only a bed or mattress to sleep on in the attic or a back room. Larger slave owners housed slaves in one-room cabins with dirt floors and few furnishings (a table, stools, a cooking pot and a few dishes, a bed or corn-shuck mattresses). Fanny Kemble described, with some horror, the one-room slave cabins she found on her husband's plantation:

> These cabins consist of one room, about twelve feet by fifteen, with a couple of closets smaller and closer than the state-rooms of a ship, divided off from the main room and each other by rough wooden partitions, in which the inhabitants sleep. They have almost all of them a rude bedstead, with the gray moss of the forests for mattress, and filthy, pestilential-looking blankets for covering. Two families (sometimes eight and ten in number) reside in one of these huts, which are mere wooden frames pinned, as it were, to the earth by a brick chimney outside.

Masters supplied food to their slaves. One common ration for a week was three pounds of meat, a quart of corn meal, and some molasses for each person. Often slaves were encouraged to supplement their diet by keeping their own gardens, and by hunting—though not, of course, with guns. Slaves were also provided with clothes, usually of rough homespun cloth: two shirts, two pairs of pants, and a pair of shoes a year for men, and enough cloth for women to make an equal number of smocks for themselves and their children yearly. This clothing was barely adequate, and in severe winters slaves suffered badly.

From birth to about age seven, slave children played with one another and with white children, observing and learning how to survive. They saw the penalties: black adults, perhaps their own parents, whipped for disobedience; black women, perhaps their own sisters, violated by white men. And they might see one or both parents sold away as punishment or for financial gain. They would also see signs of white benevolence: special treats for children at holidays, appeals to loyalty from the master or mistress, perhaps friendship with a white child. One former slave recalled:

> Yessum, when they used to have company in the big house, Miss Ross would bring them to the door to show them us children. And, my blessed, the yard would be black with us children, all string up there next the doorstep looking up in they eyes. Old Missus would say, "Ain't I got a pretty crop of little niggers coming on?"

The children would learn slave ways of getting along: apparent acquiescence in white demands; pilfering; malingering, sabotage, and other methods of slowing the relentless work pace. Fanny Kemble, an accomplished actress, was quick to note the pretense in the "outrageous flattery" she received from her husband's slaves. But many white Southerners genuinely believed that their slaves were both less intelligent and more loyal than they really were. An escaped slave, Jermain Loguen, recalled with some distaste the charade of "servile bows and counterfeit smiles…and other false expressions of gladness" with which he placated his master and mistress. Frederick Douglass, whose fearless leadership of the abolitionist movement made him the most famous African American of his time, wryly noted, "As the master studies to keep the slave ignorant, the slave is cunning enough to make the master think he succeeds."

Most slaves spent their lives as field hands, working in gangs with other slaves under a white overseer, who was usually quick to use his whip to keep up the work pace. But there were other occupations. In the "big house" there were jobs for women as cooks, maids, seamstresses, laundresses, weavers, and nurses. Black men became coachmen, valets, and gardeners, or skilled craftsmen—carpenters, mechanics, and blacksmiths. Some children began learning these occupations at age seven or eight, often in an informal apprentice system. Other children, both boys and girls, were expected to take full care of younger children while the parents were working. Of course black children had no schooling of any kind: in most of the southern states, it was against the law to teach a slave to read, although indulgent owners often rewarded their "pet" slaves by teaching them in spite of the law. At age twelve, slaves were considered full grown and put to work in the fields or in their designated occupation. As Mary Raines, a former slave in South Carolina, recalled, "I was a strong gal, went to de field when I's twelve years old, hoe my acre of cotton, 'long wid de grown ones, and pick my 150 pounds of cotton."

House Servants

At first glance, working in the big house might seem to have been preferable to working in the fields. Physically it was much less demanding, and house slaves were often better fed and clothed. They also had much more access to information, for white people, accustomed to servants and generally confident of their loyalty, often forgot their presence and spoke among themselves about matters of interest to the slaves: local gossip, changes in laws or attitudes, policies toward disobedient or rebellious slaves. As Benjamin Russel, a former slave in South Carolina, recalled:

How did we get the news? Many plantations were strict about this, but the greater the precaution the alerter became the slave, the wider they opened their ears and the more eager they became for outside information. The sources were: girls that waited on the tables, the ladies' maids and the drivers; they would pick up everything they heard and pass it on to the other slaves.

For many white people, one of the worst surprises of the Civil War was the eagerness of their house slaves to flee. Considered by their masters the best treated and the most loyal, these slaves were commonly the first to leave or to organize mass desertions. Even the Confederacy's first family, President Jefferson Davis and his wife Varina, were chagrined by the desertion of their house servants in 1864.

From the point of view of the slave, the most unpleasant thing about being a house servant (or the single slave of a small owner) was the constant presence of white people. There was no escape from white supervision. Many slaves who were personal maids and children's nurses were required to live in the big house and rarely saw their own families. Cooks and other house servants were exposed to the tempers and whims of all members of the white family, including the children, who prepared themselves for lives of mastery by practicing giving orders to slaves many times their own age. And house servants, more than any others, were forced to act grateful and ingratiating. The demeaning images of Uncle Tom and the ever-smiling mammy derive from the roles slaves learned as the price of survival. At the same time, genuine intimacy was possible, especially between black nurses and white children. But these were bonds that the white children were ultimately forced to reject as the price of joining the master class.

Artisans and Skilled Workers

A small number of slaves were skilled workers: weavers, seamstresses, carpenters, blacksmiths, mechanics. More slave men than women achieved skilled status (partly because many jobs considered appropriate for women, like cooking, were not thought of as skilled). Solomon Northup, a northern free African American kidnapped into slavery, explained in his 1853 narrative, *Twelve Years a Slave*, that he had been forced to do a variety of work. He had had three owners and had been hired out repeatedly as a carpenter and as a driver of other slaves in a sugar mill; he had also been hired out to clear land for a new Louisiana plantation and to cut sugar cane. Black people worked as lumberjacks (of the 16,000 lumber workers, almost all were slaves), as miners, as deckhands and stokers on Mississippi riverboats, as stevedores loading cotton on the docks of Charleston, Savannah, and New Orleans, and in the handful of southern factories.

Because slaves were their masters' property, the wages of the slave belonged to the owner, not the slave.

The extent to which slaves made up the laboring class was most apparent in cities. A British visitor to Natchez in 1835 noted slave "mechanics, draymen, hostelers, labourers, hucksters and washwomen and the heterogeneous multitude of every other occupation." In the North, all these jobs were performed by white workers. In part because the South failed to attract as much immigrant labor as the North, southern cities offered both enslaved and free black people opportunities in skilled occupations such as blacksmithing and carpentering that free African Americans in the North were denied.

Field Work

A full 75 percent of all slaves were field workers. Field hands, both men and women, worked from "can see to can't see" (sunup to sundown) summer and winter, and frequently longer at harvest, when eighteen-hour days were common. On most plantations, the bell sounded an hour before sunup, and slaves were expected to be on their way to the fields as soon as it was light. The usual pattern of working in groups of twenty to twenty-five harked back to African communal systems of agricultural work. Many work gangs had black drivers in addition to white overseers. Work continued till noon, and after an hour or so for lunch and rest the slaves worked nearly until dark. In the evening the women prepared dinner at the cabins and everyone snatched a few hours of socializing before bedtime. Work days were shorter in the winter, perhaps only ten hours.

Work was tedious in the hot and humid southern fields, and the overseer's whip was never far away. Cotton growing was hard work: plowing and planting, chopping weeds with a heavy hoe, and picking the ripe cotton from the stiff and scratchy bolls at the rate of 150 pounds a day. In the rice fields, slaves worked knee-deep in water. On sugar plantations, harvesting the cane and getting it ready for boiling was exceptionally heavy work. A strong, hardworking slave—a "prime field hand"—was valuable property, worth at least $1,000 to the master. Slaves justifiably took pride in their strength, as observed by a white Northerner traveling in Mississippi in 1854 who came across a work gang happy to be going home early because of rain:

> First came, led by an old driver carrying a whip, forty of the largest and strongest women I ever saw together...they carried themselves loftily, each having a hoe over the shoulder, and walking with a free, powerful stride. Behind them came the ...[plowhands and their mules], thirty strong, mostly men, but a few of them women....A lean and vigilant white overseer, on a brisk pony, brought up the rear.

That, of course, is only one side of the story. Compare Solomon Northup's memory of cotton picking:

> It was rarely that a day passed by without one or more whippings. The delinquent [who had not picked enough cotton] was taken out, stripped, made to lie upon the ground, face downwards, when he received a punishment proportioned to his offence. It is the literal, unvarnished truth, that the crack of the lash, and the shrieking of the slaves, can be heard from dark till bed time, on [this] plantation, any day almost during the entire period of the cotton-picking season.

Slaves aged fast in this regime. Poor diet and heavy labor undermined health. When they were too old to work, they took on other tasks within the black community, such as caring for young children. Honored by the slave community, the elderly were tolerated by white owners, who continued to feed and clothe them until their deaths. Few actions show the hypocrisy of southern paternalism more clearly than the speed with which white owners evicted their elderly slaves in the 1860s when the end of the slave system was in sight.

THE AFRICAN AMERICAN COMMUNITY

Surely no group in American history has faced a harder job of community building than the black people of the antebellum South. Living in intimate, daily contact with their oppressors, African Americans nevertheless created an enduring culture of their own, a culture that had far-reaching and lasting influence on all of southern society (see Chapter 4). Within their own communities, African American values and attitudes, and especially their own forms of Christianity, played a vital part in shaping a culture of endurance and resistance.

Few African Americans were unfortunate enough to live their lives alone among white people. Over half of all slaves lived on plantations with twenty or more other slaves, and others, on smaller farms, had links with slaves on nearby properties. Urban slaves were able to make and sustain so many secret contacts with other African Americans in cities or towns that slave owners wondered whether slave discipline could be maintained in urban settings. There can be no question that the bonds among African Americans were what sustained them during the years of slavery.

In law, slaves were property, to be bought, sold, rented, worked, and otherwise used (but not abused or killed) as the owner saw fit. But slaves were also human beings, with feelings, needs, and hopes.

Even though most white Southerners believed black people to be members of an inferior, childish race, all but the most brutal masters acknowledged the humanity of their slaves. Furthermore, as a practical matter, white owners had long since learned that unhappy or rebellious slaves were poor workers. White masters learned to live with the two key institutions of African American community life: the family and the African American church.

Slave Families

No southern state recognized slave marriages in law. Most owners, though, not only recognized but encouraged them, sometimes even performing a kind of wedding ceremony for the couple. James Henry Hammond conducted a special ceremony for his slaves, to whom he gave $5.00 for a first marriage and $3.50 for a second marriage. Masters sometimes tried to arrange marriages, but slaves usually found their own mates, sometimes on their own plantation, sometimes elsewhere. Masters encouraged marriage among their slaves, believing it made the men less rebellious, and for economic reasons they were eager for women to have children. Thomas Jefferson, always a clear thinker, put the matter bluntly: "I consider a [slave] woman who [gives birth to] a child every two years as more profitable than the best man on the farm.... What she produces is an addition to the capital." Whatever marriages meant to the masters, to slaves they were a haven of love and intimacy in a cruel world and the basis of the African American community. Husbands and wives had a chance, in their own cabins, to live their own lives among loved ones. The relationship between slave husband and wife was different from that of the white husband and wife. The patriarchal system dictated that the white marriage be unequal, for the man had to be dominant and the woman dependent and submissive. Slave marriages were more equal, for husband and wife were both powerless within the slave system. Both knew that neither could protect the other from abuse at the hands of white people.

Husband and wife cooperated in loving and sheltering their children and teaching them survival skills. Above all, family meant continuity. Parents made great efforts to teach their children the family history. As Alex Haley's *Roots* illustrated, many African American families today maintain strong oral traditions dating back to their African origins. Parents did their best to surround children with a supportive and protective kinship network.

The strength of these ties is shown by the many husbands, wives, children, and parents who searched for each other after the Civil War when slavery came to an end. Observing African Americans' postwar migrations, a Freedmen's Bureau agent commented that "every mother's son among them seemed to be in search of his mother; every mother in search of her children." As the ads in black newspapers indicate, some family searches went on into the 1870s and 1880s, and many ended in failure.

Given the vast size of the internal slave trade, fear of separation was constant—and real. Far from being a rare event prompted only by financial necessity, separations of slave families were common. One in every five slave marriages was broken, and one in every three children sold away from their families. These figures clearly show that slave owners' support for slave marriages was secondary to their desire for profits. The scale of the trade was a strong indication of the economic reality that underlay their protestations of paternalism.

In the face of constant separation, slave communities attempted to act like larger families. Following practices developed early in slavery, children were taught to respect and learn from all the elders, to call all adults of a certain age "aunt" or "uncle," and to call children of their own age "brother" or "sister" (see Chapter 4). Thus, in the absence of their own family, separated children could quickly find a place and a source of comfort in the slave community to which they had been sold.

This emphasis on family and on kinship networks had an even more fundamental purpose. The kinship of the entire community, where old people were respected and young ones cared for, represented a conscious rejection of white paternalism. The slaves' ability, in the most difficult of situations, to structure a community that expressed their values, not those of their masters, was extraordinary. Equally remarkable was the way in which African Americans reshaped Christianity to serve their needs.

African American Religion

Slaves brought religions from Africa but were not allowed to practice them, for white people feared religion would create a bond among slaves that might lead to rebellion. African religions managed to survive in the slave community in forms that white people considered "superstition" or "folk belief," such as the medicinal use of roots by conjurers. Religious ceremonies survived, too, in late-night gatherings deep in the woods where the sound of drumming, singing, and dancing could not reach white ears (see Chapter 4). In the nineteenth century, these African traditions allowed African Americans to reshape white Christianity into their own distinctive faith.

Most masters of the eighteenth century made little effort to Christianize their slaves, afraid they might take the promises of universal brotherhood and

Five generations of one family on a South Carolina plantation are gathered together for this 1862 picture, providing living evidence of the importance of kinship in the building of African American communities.

equality too literally. The Great Awakening, which swept the South after the 1760s, introduced many slaves to Christianity, often in mixed congregations with white people (see Chapter 5). The transformation was completed by the Second Great Awakening, which took root among black and white Southerners in the 1790s. The number of African American converts, preachers, and lay teachers grew rapidly, and a distinctive form of Christianity took shape.

Free African Americans founded their own independent churches and denominations. The first African American Baptist and Methodist churches were founded in Philadelphia in 1794 by the Reverend Absalom Jones and the Reverend Richard Allen. In 1816, the Reverend Allen joined with African American ministers from other cities to form the African Methodist Episcopal (AME) denomination. By the 1830s, free African American ministers like Andrew Marshall of Savannah and many more enslaved black preachers and lay ministers preached, sometimes secretly, to slaves. Their message was one of faith and love, of deliverance, of the coming of the promised land.

African Americans found in Christianity a powerful vehicle to express their longings for freedom and justice. But why did their white masters allow it? Some white people, themselves converted by the revivals, doubtless believed that they should not deny

African cultural patterns persisted in the preference for night funerals and for solemn pageantry and song, depicted in British artist John Antrobus's Plantation Burial, ca. 1860. Like other African American customs, the community care of the dead contained an implied rebuke to the masters' care of the living slaves.

their slaves the same religious experience. But the evangelical religion of the early nineteenth century was also a powerful form of social control. Southern slave owners, seeking to counteract the appeal of African American religion, expected their Christianity to make their slaves obedient and peaceful. Forbidding their slaves to hold their own religious gatherings, owners insisted that their slaves attend white church services. Slaves were quick to realize the owners' purpose. As a former Texas slave recalled: "We went to church on the place and you ought to heard that preachin'. Obey your massa and missy, don't steal chickens and eggs and meat, but nary a word 'bout havin' a soul to save." On many plantations, slaves attended religious services with their masters every Sunday, sitting quietly in the back of the church or in the balcony as the minister preached messages justifying slavery and urging obedience. But at night, away from white eyes, they held their own prayer meetings. Another former Texas slave recalled:

> [We] used to have a prayin' ground down in the hollow and sometimes we come out of the field, between eleven and twelve at night, scorchin' and burnin' up with nothin' to eat, and we wants to ask the good Lawd to have mercy. We put grease in a snuff pan or bottle and make a lamp. We takes a pine torch, too, and goes down to the hollow to pray. Some gits so joyous they starts to holler loud and we has to stop up they mouth [so the whites won't hear].

In churches and in spontaneous religious expressions, the black community made Christianity its own. Fusing Christian texts with African elements of group activity such as the circle dance, the call-and-response pattern, and, above all, group singing, black people created a unique community religion full of emotion, enthusiasm, and protest. Nowhere is this spirit more compelling than in the famous spirituals: "Go Down Moses," with its mournful refrain "Let my people go"; the rousing "Didn't My Lord Deliver Daniel...and why not every man"; the haunting "Steal Away." Some of these spirituals became as well known to white people as to black people, but only African Americans seem to have appreciated the full meaning of their subversive messages.

Nevertheless, this was not a religion of rebellion, for that was unrealistic for most slaves. Black Christianity was an enabling religion: it helped slaves to survive, not as passive victims of white tyranny but as active opponents of an oppressive system that they daily protested in small but meaningful ways. In their faith, African Americans expressed a spiritual freedom that white people could not destroy.

Freedom and Resistance

Whatever their dreams, most slaves knew they would never escape. Freedom was too far away. Almost all successful escapes in the nineteenth century (approximately 1,000 a year) were from the Upper South (Delaware, Maryland, Virginia, Kentucky, Missouri). A slave in the Lower South or the Southwest simply had too far to go to reach freedom. In addition, white Southerners were determined to prevent escapes. Slave patrols were a common sight on southern roads. Any black person without a pass from his or her master was captured (usually roughly) and returned home to certain punishment. But despite almost certain recapture, slaves continued to flee and to help others do so. Escaped slave Harriet Tubman of Maryland, who made nineteen rescue missions freeing 300 slaves in all, had extraordinary determination and skill. As a female runaway, she was unusual, too: most escapees were young men, for women often had small children they were unable to take and unwilling to leave behind.

Much more common was the practice of "running away nearby." Slaves who knew they could not reach freedom still frequently demonstrated their desire for liberty or their discontent over mistreatment by taking unauthorized leave from their plantation. Hidden in nearby forests or swamps, provided with food smuggled by other slaves from the plantation, the runaway might return home after a week or so, often to rather mild punishment. Although in reality most slaves could have little hope of gaining freedom, even failed attempts at rebellion shook the foundations of the slave system and thus temporary flight by any slave was a warning sign of discontent that a wise master did not ignore.

Slave Revolts

The ultimate resistance, however, was the slave revolt. Southern history was dotted with stories of former slave conspiracies and rumors of current plots (see Chapter 4). Every white Southerner knew about the last-minute failure of Gabriel Prosser's insurrection in Richmond in 1800 and the chance discovery of Denmark Vesey's plot in Charleston in 1822. But when in 1831, Nat Turner actually started a rebellion in which a number of white people were killed, southern fears were greatly magnified.

Gabriel Prosser, a literate blacksmith, had gathered more than a thousand slaves for an assault on Richmond. Although the attempt was aborted at the last minute and Prosser and thirty-five others were caught and hanged, white people were especially frightened to learn that Prosser had organized under a banner proclaiming "Death or Liberty" and had hoped for help from the independent black people of Haiti. The notion of an international force of revolutionary slaves demanding their freedom was a fundamental challenge to slave owners' assumptions about their own liberty and power.

Denmark Vesey's conspiracy raised fears among white people concerning African American religion and free black people. Vesey was a well-traveled former seaman who lived in Charleston and worked as a carpenter. Free, well read, and eloquent, he was a lay preacher at Charleston's African Methodist Episcopal Church, where he drew on quotations from the Bible and from the congressional debates during the Missouri Crisis (1819–20) to make a forceful argument against slavery. His co-conspirator, Gullah Jack, was a "conjure-man" who drew on the

African religious traditions that flourished among the slaves in the South Carolina low country. Vesey and Gullah Jack drew up a plan to evade the lax city patrol and steal weapons from the Charleston arsenal and horses from livery stables. Then, while mounted and armed slaves beat back white counterattacks in the streets of Charleston, house slaves would capture their owners and murder any who tried to escape. Vesey's aim was to seize Charleston and ultimately to sail to the free black Caribbean nation of Haiti.

Vesey and Gullah Jack recruited at least eighty country and city slaves into the conspiracy, including several trusted house slaves of South Carolina governor Thomas Bennett. Two weeks before the date fixed for the insurrection, the plot was betrayed by a house servant who reported the two slaves who had tried to recruit him into the conspiracy. The accused slaves laughed at the charge and coolly managed to convince the authorities that there was no plot. But two days before the revolt, another house servant confessed, and this time the authorities believed him. In the frantic roundup that followed, thirty-five black people were hanged (Vesey among them) and thirty-seven others sold down the river. But some rebels were not caught because their fellow conspirators died without betraying them. Charlestonians had to live with the knowledge that some of their city's most trusted black servants had conspired to kill their masters—and might still plan to do so.

In the wake of the Vesey conspiracy, Charlestonians turned their fear and anger outward. Planter Robert J. Turnbull wrote bitterly, "By the Missouri question, our slaves thought, there was a charter of liberties granted them by Congress....[The Vesey conspiracy] will long be remembered, as

Harriet Tubman escaped in 1849 from slavery in Maryland, and returned nineteen times to free almost 300 other slaves. Here Tubman (at left), the most famous "conductor" on the Underground Railroad, is shown with some of those she led to freedom.

This drawing shows the moment, almost two months after the failure of his famous and bloody slave revolt, when Nat Turner was accidentally discovered in the woods near his home plantation. Turner's cool murder of his owner and methodical organization of his revolt deeply frightened many white Southerners.

amongst the choicest fruits of that question in Congress." White people attempted to seal off the city from dangerous outside influences. The AME Church (where radical ideas such as the Missouri question had been discussed) was destroyed, and in December 1822 the South Carolina legislature passed a bill requiring that all black seamen be seized and jailed while their ships were in Charleston harbor. Initially most alarmed about free black people from Haiti, Charlestonians soon came to believe that northern free black seamen were spreading antislavery ideas among their slaves.

The most famous slave revolt—Nat Turner's revolt in Southampton County, Virginia—was a partial success. A literate man, Nat Turner was, like Denmark Vesey, a lay preacher, but unlike Vesey he was also a slave. It was Turner's intelligence and strong religious commitment that made him a leader in the slave community and, interestingly, these very same qualities led his master, Joseph Travis, to treat him with kindness even though Turner had once run away for a month after being mistreated by an overseer. Turner began plotting his revolt after a religious vision in which he saw "white spirits and black spirits engaged in battle"; "the sun was darkened—the thunder rolled in the Heavens, and blood flowed in streams." Turner and five other slaves struck on the night of August 20, 1831, first killing Travis, who, Turner said, "was to me a kind master, and placed the greatest confidence in me; in fact, I had no cause to complain of his treatment of me."

Moving from plantation to plantation and killing a total of fifty-five white people, the rebels numbered sixty by the next morning, when they fled from a group of armed white men. More than forty blacks were executed after the revolt, including Turner, who was captured accidentally after he had hidden for two months in the woods. Thomas R. Gray, a white lawyer to whom Turner dictated a lengthy confession before his death, was impressed by Turner's composure. "I looked on him," Gray said, "and my blood curdled in my veins." If intelligent, well-treated slaves such as Turner could plot revolts, how could white Southerners ever feel safe?

Gabriel's Rebellion, the Denmark Vesey plot, and Nat Turner's Revolt were the most prominent examples of organized slave resistance, but they were far from the only ones. Conspiracies and actual or rumored slave resistance began in colonial times (see Chapter 4) and never ceased. These plots exposed the truth white Southerners preferred to ignore: Only force kept Africans and African Americans enslaved, and because no system of control could ever be total, white Southerners could never be completely safe from the possibility of revolt. Nat Turner brought white Southerners' fears to the surface. After 1831, the possibility of slave insurrection was never far from their minds.

Free African Americans

Another source of white disquiet was the growing number of free African Americans. By 1860 nearly 250,000 free black people lived in the South. For most, freedom dated from before 1800, when antislavery feeling among slave owners in the Upper South was widespread and cotton cultivation had yet to boom. In Virginia, for example, the number of manumitted (freed) slaves jumped tenfold in twenty years (see Chapter 7). But a new mood became apparent in 1806 when Virginia tightened its lenient manumission law: now the freed person was required to leave the state within a year or be sold back into slavery. After 1830 manumission was virtually impossible throughout the South.

Most free black people lived in the countryside of the Upper South, where they worked as tenant farmers or farm laborers. Urban African Americans were much more visible. Life was especially difficult for female-headed families because only the most menial work—street peddling and laundry work, for example—was available to free black women. The situation for African American males was somewhat better. Although they were discriminated against in employment and in social life, there were opportunities for skilled black craftsmen in trades such as blacksmithing and carpentering.

Cities such as Charleston, Savannah, and Natchez were home to flourishing free African American communities that formed their own churches and fraternal orders. In Natchez, a free black barber, William Johnson, owned several barber shops, a small farm, and an estate valued at $25,000 in 1851 that included fifteen slaves. Johnson had a white attorney and friends among the city's leading politicians, and he lived in a white neighborhood. Half a dozen other free African Americans in Natchez were similarly prosperous, and they, too, were slave owners. This tiny elite kept a careful social distance from most of Natchez's approximately 1,000 free black people (one-quarter of all free African Americans in Mississippi in 1840), who were miserably poor. This free black elite treated white people with great tact and deference.

Free African Americans had reason to be careful, for their position was increasingly precarious. Throughout the South in the 1830s, state legislatures tightened black codes—laws concerning free black people. Free African Americans could not carry firearms, could not purchase slaves (unless they were members of their own family), and were liable to the criminal penalties meted out to slaves (that is, whippings and summary judgments without a jury trial). They could not testify against whites, hold office, vote, or serve in the militia. In other words, except for the right to own property, free blacks had no civil rights. Following the cleanup of the alarming race mixing in Natchez-under-the-Hill, the Natchez elite focused on free African Americans. In 1841, whites mounted a campaign to deport from the state any free black person who adopted "the practices of the rogue, the incendiary, and the abolitionist." Many poor free African Americans were deported from Natchez that summer and in the following years. William Johnson, whose own security was not threatened, aided some poor black people by quietly helping them obtain attestations of good character from white planters. For

all of his (comparative) wealth, as a black man he could do nothing openly to help his own people.

As this episode shows, white people increasingly feared the influence free black people might have on slaves, for free African Americans were a living challenge to the slave system. Their very existence disproved the basic southern equations of white equals free, and black equals slave. No one believed more fervently in those equations than the South's largest population group, white people who did not own slaves.

YEOMEN AND POOR WHITE PEOPLE

The pervasive influence of the slave system in the South is reflected in the startling contrast of two facts: two-thirds of all Southerners did not own slaves, yet slave owners dominated the social and political life of the region. Who were the two-thirds of white Southerners who did not own slaves, and how did they live? Throughout the south, slave owners occupied the most productive land: tobacco-producing areas in Virginia and Tennessee, coastal areas of South Carolina and Georgia where rice and cotton grew, sugar lands in Louisiana, and large sections of the cotton-producing black belt, which stretched westward from South Carolina to Texas. Small farmers, usually without slaves, occupied the rest of the land. This land ranged from adequate to poor, from depleted, once-rich regions in Virginia to the Carolina hill country and the pine barrens of Mississippi.

Yeomen

The word "yeoman," originally a British term for a farmer who works his own land, is often applied to independent farmers of the South, most of whom lived on family-sized farms. Although yeoman farmers sometimes owned a few slaves, in general they and their families worked their land by themselves. Typical of the yeoman-farmer community was northwestern Georgia, once home to the Creeks and Cherokees, but now populated by communities of small farmers who grew enough vegetables to feed their families, including corn, which they either ate themselves or fed to hogs. In addition, these farmers raised enough cotton every year (usually no more than one or two bales) to bring in a little cash. At least 60 percent owned their own farms, but some were wealthier than others. Isaac Cobb of Carroll County owned 700 acres of land on which he grazed cattle, sheep, and hogs. On 200 of these acres, twelve slaves helped him produce 2,000 bushels of grain and twelve bales of cotton. In contrast, Richard White, of the same county, used only family labor to farm 50 acres devoted to food and grains and the grazing of a few cattle, sheep, and hogs. These two men, and thou-

One of the ways Charleston attempted to control its African American population was to require all slaves to wear badges showing their occupation. After 1848, free black people also had to wear badges, which were decorated, ironically, with a liberty cap.

sands like them, were the yeomen Thomas Jefferson celebrated—economically independent yet intimately tied to a larger but still very local group.

The local community was paramount. Farm men and women depended on their relatives and neighbors for assistance in large farm tasks such as planting, harvesting, and construction. Events requiring lots of hands like logrollings, corn shuckings, and quilting bees were community events. Farmers repaid this help, and obtained needed goods, through complex systems of barter with other members of the community. In their organization, southern farm communities were no different from northern ones, with one major exception—slavery. In the South, one of the key items in the community barter system was the labor of slaves, who were frequently loaned out to neighbors by small slave owners such as Isaac Cobb to fulfill an obligation to another farmer.

Where yeomen and large slave owners lived side by side, as in the Georgia black belt where cotton was the major crop, slavery again provided a link between richer and poorer. Large plantation owners often bought food for their slaves from small local farmers, ground the latter's corn in the plantation mill, ginned their cotton, and transported and marketed it as well. But although planters and much smaller yeomen were part of a larger community network, in the black belt the large slave owners were clearly dominant. Only in their own up-country communities did yeomen feel truly independent.

Poor White People

Not all small farmers were on an equal footing. One-third of the farmers in the Georgia up-country were tenant farmers. Some were farmers' sons, striking out on their own while waiting to inherit their fathers' land. But others were poor whites with little hope of improving their condition. From 30 to 50 percent of all southern white people were landless, a proportion similar to that in the North. But the existence of slavery affected the opportunities for southern poor white people. Slaves made up the permanent, stable work force in agriculture and in many skilled trades. Many poor white people led highly transient lives in search of work, such as farm labor at harvest time, which was only temporary. Others were tenant farmers working under share-tenancy arrangements that kept them in debt to the landowner. Although they farmed poorer land with less equipment than landowning farmers, most tenant farmers grew enough food to sustain their families. Like the yeomen, but with more difficulty, tenant farmers aspired to independence.

Relationships between poor whites and black slaves were complex. White men and women often worked side by side with black slaves in the fields and were socially and sexually intimate with enslaved and free African Americans. White people engaged in clandestine trade to supply slaves with items like liquor that slave owners prohibited, helped slaves to escape, and even (in an 1835 Mississippi case) were executed for their participation in planning a slave revolt. At the same time, the majority of poor white people insisted, sometimes violently, on their racial superiority over blacks. For their part, many African American slaves, better dressed, better nourished, and healthier, dismissed them as "poor white trash." But the fact was that the difficult lives of poor whites, whom one contemporary described as "a third class of white people," served to blur the crucial racial distinction between independent whites and supposedly inferior, dependent black people on which the system of slavery rested. Like the boatmen whom the Natchez slave owners viewed with such alarm, poor white people posed a potential threat to the slave system.

The goal of yeoman farm families was economic independence. Their mixed farming and grazing enterprises, supported by kinship and community ties, afforded them a self-sufficiency epitomized by Carl G. von Iwonski's painting of this rough but comfortable log cabin in New Braunfels, Texas.

Yeoman Values

In 1828 and 1832, southern yeomen and poor white men voted overwhelmingly for Andrew Jackson. They were drawn variously to his outspoken policy of ruthless expansionism, his appeals to the common man, and his rags-to-riches ascent from poor boy to rich slave owner. It was a career many hoped to emulate. The dominance of the large planters was due at least in part to the ambition of many yeomen, especially those with two or three slaves, to expand their holdings and become rich. These farmers, enthusiastic members of the lively democratic politics of the South, supported the leaders they hoped to join.

But for a larger group of yeomen, independence and not wealth was most important. Many southern yeomen lived apart from large slaveholders, in the up-country regions where plantation agriculture was unsuitable. The very high value southern yeomen placed on freedom grew directly from their own experience as self-sufficient property-owning farmers in small, family-based communities. This was a way of life that southern "plain folk" were determined to preserve. It made them resistant to the economic opportunities and challenges that capitalism and industrialization posed for northern farmers, which southern yeomen perceived as encroachments on their freedom.

The irony was that the freedom yeomen so prized rested on slavery. White people could count on slaves to perform the hardest and worst labor, and the degradation of slave life was a daily reminder of the freedom they enjoyed in comparison. Slavery meant that all white people, rich and poor, were equal in the sense that they were all free. This assumption of white skin privilege had formed in the eighteenth century as slavery became the answer to the South's labor problem (see Chapter 4). The democratization of politics in the early nineteenth century and the enactment of nearly universal white manhood suffrage perpetuated the belief in white skin privilege, even though the gap between rich and poor white people was widening.

Southern yeomen did not blindly follow the rich slave owners who were their political leaders. Rather, they supported a freedom they believed they would not have under any other system. But southern unanimity on this point, which looked so strong, was actually very fragile. Anything that appeared to threaten slavery threatened the entire southern social structure, trapping Southerners in ever more rigid and defensive positions.

PLANTERS

Remarkably few slave owners fit the popular stereotype of the rich and leisured plantation owner with hundreds of acres of land and hundreds of slaves. Only

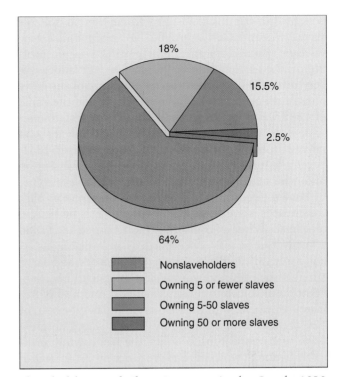

Slaveholding and Class Structure in the South, 1830
The great mass of the southern white population were yeoman farmers. In 1830, slave owners made up only 36 percent of the southern white population; owners of more than fifty slaves constituted a tiny 2.5 percent. Yet they and the others who were middling planters dominated politics, retaining the support of yeomen who prized their freedom as white men above class-based politics.

Source: U.S. Bureau of the Census.

36 percent of southern white people owned slaves in 1830, and only 2.5 percent owned fifty slaves or more. Just as yeomen and poor whites were diverse, so, too, were southern slave owners.

Small Slave Owners

The largest group of slave owners were small yeomen taking the step from subsistence agriculture to commercial production. To do this in the South's agricultural economy, they had to own slaves. But upward mobility was difficult. Owning one or two slaves increased farm production only slightly, and it was hard to accumulate the capital to buy more. One common pattern was for a slave owner to leave one or two slaves to farm while he worked another job (this arrangement usually meant that his wife had unacknowledged responsibility for their supervision). In other cases, small farmers worked side by side with their slaves in the fields. In still other cases, owners hired out their slaves to larger slave owners.

In every case, the owner was economically vulnerable: a poor crop or a downturn in cotton prices could wipe out his gains and force him to sell his slaves. When times improved, he might buy a new slave or two and try again, but getting a secure footing on the bottom rung of the slave owner ladder was very difficult. The roller-coaster economy of the early nineteenth century did not help matters, and the Panic of 1837 was a serious setback to many small farmers.

John Flintoff was an aspiring slave owner who moved from North Carolina to Mississippi in 1841, hoping to make his fortune. Working as an overseer on his uncle's land, Flintoff began his career as a slave owner by buying three slave children (one was seven years old), the cheapest slaves available. Over the years he bought nine in all. While an overseer, Flintoff married and began a family. But he was unsuccessful as an overseer. As he confessed in his diary, "managing negroes and large farms is soul destroying." In 1853 his uncle fired him. Flintoff was forced to sell his slaves and return to North Carolina, where, with the help of his in-laws, he bought 124 acres of land. Assisted by several slaves he grew corn, wheat, and tobacco—not the wonderfully profitable cotton of which he had dreamed. By 1860, Flintoff was modestly successful; wealthy enough to send his son to college and to free his wife from routine farm chores. As he boasted, his wife "has lived a Lady."

For a smaller group of slave owners, the economic struggle was not so hard. Middle-class professional men—lawyers, doctors, and merchants—frequently managed to become large slave owners because they already had capital (the pay from their professions) to invest in land and slaves. Sometimes they received payment for their services not in money but in slaves. These owners were the most likely to own skilled slaves—carpenters, blacksmiths, other artisans—and to rent them out for profit. By steady accumulation, the most successful members of this middle class were able to buy their way into the slave-owning elite and to confirm that position by marrying their sons or daughters into the aristocracy.

Here the career of Andrew Jackson of Tennessee is instructive. Jackson, an orphan, had no family money. He began a profitable career as a prosecutor in Nashville in the 1790s, frequently taking small plots of land as payment for his services. In 1796, the year he was elected Tennessee's delegate to the U.S. House of Representatives, he owned 10 slaves. In 1798 Jackson owned 15 slaves. He widened his economic activities, buying land, partnership in a store, a plantation for himself (the Hermitage), and a racetrack. Then came some bad years—the mercantile business failed, and debts on land came due—and Jackson was soon preoccupied with military matters. But he continued to accumulate slaves: 44 by 1820, 95 by 1828 (the year he was elected president), 150 a few years later, and almost 200 by the time of his death in 1845.

The Old Planter Elite

The slave-owning elite, those 2.5 percent who owned fifty slaves or more, enjoyed the prestige, the political leadership, and the lifestyle to which many white Southerners aspired. Almost all great slave owners inherited their wealth. They were rarely self-made men, although most tried to add to the land and slaves they had inherited. Men of wealth and property had led southern politics since colonial times, but increasingly after 1820 it was men from the middle classes who were most often elected to political office. As the nation moved toward universal manhood suffrage, planters tried to learn how to appeal to the popular vote, but most never acquired "the common touch." It was the smaller slave owners who formed a clear majority in every southern state legislature before 1860.

The eastern seaboard had first given rise to a class of rich planters in the colonial period, as attested by the plantations of William Byrd and Robert "King" Carter of Virginia and the cultured life of the planter elite, centered in Charleston, that had established itself in the South Carolina low country and Sea Islands.

One such planter was Thomas Chaplin, descended from an indentured servant who arrived in 1672 from the British sugar-producing island of Barbados. In 1839 he married Mary McDowell, granddaughter of a rich Charleston merchant, and in 1840 they moved into the old family house on the 376-acre Tombee Plantation on St. Helena Island near Beaufort, South Carolina. Master of sixty to seventy slaves, Chaplin grew sea-island cotton (a long-staple variety), potatoes, and corn and raised beef and mutton. Although St. Helena land was rich and fertile, the climate bred mosquito-borne malaria, epidemic from mid-May until November. Most planters and their families lived in Charleston or the healthier up-country during the "sickly season," and few poorer white people lived on St. Helena at all. As a consequence, by 1845 black people outnumbered white people eight to one on the island (2,000 African Americans to 250 whites). St. Helena and the other Sea Islands of South Carolina were unique in the relative autonomy of their black population and the persistence of African customs and language.

Soon after he took possession of Tombee Plantation, Chaplin was forced to sell off more than half his slaves to settle family debts and lawsuits. Land rich but labor poor, Chaplin fretted in 1850: "So many mouths to feed & so few to work that it is impossible for me to get along." Although completely dependent on his black labor force, Chaplin was indifferent to them as individuals. Unlike many planters, Chaplin refused to attend slave weddings, dismissing them as "tomfoolery," and only grudgingly did he permit his slaves to choose husbands and wives from other plantations. He complained unceasingly about the high rate of infant mortality among slaves, going so far as to accuse mothers of killing their own babies. He failed to realize that overwork and poor nutrition (counteracted only in part by the constant pilfering from his storehouses and barns) were to blame. Unlike most planters, Chaplin never hired an overseer for the work in his fields, but after 1852 he increasingly left the details of management to a black slave driver.

The Natchez "Nabobs"

As Southerners and slave owning spread westward, membership in the elite broadened to include the new wealth of Alabama, Mississippi, Louisiana, and Texas. The rich planters of the Natchez community were popularly called "nabobs" (from a Hindi word for Europeans who had amassed fabulous wealth in India). Frederick Stanton, owner of Stanton Hall in Natchez, was a physician who had immigrated from Northern Ireland. The source of his wealth was not medicine but the cotton commission (brokerage) business. At the time of his death he owned 444 slaves and 15,109 acres of land on six Louisiana and Mississippi plantations that produced more than 3,000 bales of cotton a year. Another great Natchez family, the Surgets, of French origin, traced their wealth further back, to a Spanish land grant of 2,500 acres to Pierre Surget. In the 1850s his grandsons Frank and James Surget controlled some 93,000 acres in Mississippi, Arkansas, and Louisiana (half of it plantation land and half bought on speculation, for resale). Each brother sold 4,000 bales of cotton a year, and between them they owned upwards of 1,000 slaves. Each also owned palatial mansions in Natchez—Cherry Hill and Clifton.

The extraordinary concentration of wealth in Natchez—in 1850 it was the richest county in the nation—fostered a self-consciously elite lifestyle that derived not from long tradition but from suddenly acquired riches. Fastidious Northerners such as Thomas Taylor, a Pennsylvania Quaker who visited Natchez in 1847, noted: "Many of the chivalric gentry whom I have been permitted to see dashing about here on highbred horses, seem to find their greatest enjoyment in recounting their bear hunts, 'great fights,' and occasional exploits with revolvers and Bowie knives—swearing 'terribly' and sucking mint juleps & cherry cobblers with straws."

Plantation Life

The urban life of the Natchez planters was unusual. Many wealthy planters, especially those on new lands in the Old Southwest, lived in isolation on their plantations with their families and slaves. Through family networks, common boarding school experience, political activity, and frequent visiting, the small planter elite consciously worked to create and maintain a distinctive lifestyle that was modeled on that of the English aristocracy, as Southerners understood it. This

William H. Brown, *Hauling the Whole Week's Picking* (detail), 1842. Watercolor. The Historic New Orleans Collection.

This scene is part of a larger mural, created by artist William Henry Brown in 1842, which depicts everyday life at Nitta Yuma, a Mississippi cotton plantation. The elegant white woman, here seen elaborately dressed to go riding, depended for her leisure status on the work of African American slaves, such as this one feeding her horse.

entailed a large estate, a spacious, elegant mansion, and lavish hospitality. For men, the gentlemanly lifestyle meant immersion in masculine activities such as hunting, soldiering, or politics and a touchy concern with "honor" that could lead to duels and other acts of bravado. Women of the slave-owning elite, in contrast, were expected to be gentle, charming, and always welcoming of relatives, friends, and other guests.

But this gracious image was at odds with the economic reality. Large numbers of black slaves had to be forced to work to produce the wealth of the large plantations. Each plantation, like the yeoman farm but on a larger scale, aimed to be self-sufficient, producing not only the cash crop but most of the food and clothing for both slaves and family. There were stables full of horses for plowing, transportation, and show. There were livestock and vegetable gardens to be tended, and carpentering, blacksmithing, weaving, and sewing to be done. A large plantation was an enterprise that required many hands, many skills, and a lot of management. Large plantation owners might have overseers or black drivers to supervise field work, but frequently they themselves had direct financial control of daily operations. Even if they were absentee landlords (like, for example, Thomas Chaplin in South Carolina and the richest of the Natchez elite), planters usually required careful accounts from their overseers and often exercised the right to overrule their decisions.

A paternalistic ideology infused the life of large plantations that permitted the planter elite to rationalize their use of slaves and the submissiveness

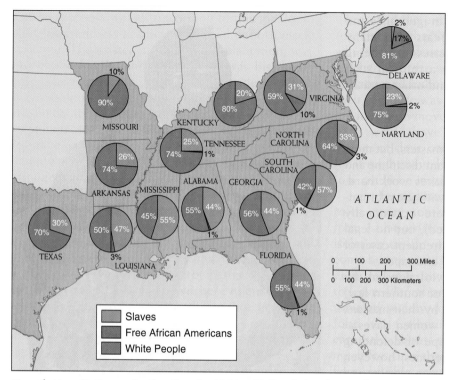

Population Patterns in the South, 1850   *In South Carolina and Mississippi the enslaved African American population outnumbered the white population; in four other Lower South states the percentage was above 40 percent. These ratios frightened many white Southerners. White people also feared the free black population, though only three states in the Upper South and Louisiana had free black populations of over 3 percent. Six states had free black populations that were so small (less than 1 percent) as to be statistically insignificant.*

12 million people who lived in the South in 1860, 4 million were slaves. Indeed, in the richest agricultural regions, such as the Sea Islands of South Carolina and Georgia and parts of the black belt, black people outnumbered whites. These sheer numbers of African Americans reinforced white people's perpetual fears of black retaliation for the violence exercised by the slave master. Every rumor of slave revolts, real or imagined, kept those fears alive. The basic question was this: What might slaves do if they were not controlled? Thomas Jefferson summed up this dilemma: "We have the wolf by the ears; and we can neither hold him nor safely let him go. Justice is in one scale, and self-preservation in the other."

Developing Proslavery Arguments

In the flush of freedom following the American Revolution, a number of slave owners in the Upper South freed their slaves, and Thomas Jefferson, ever the optimist, claimed that "a total emancipation with the consent of the masters" could not be too far in the future. Nevertheless, southern legislatures were unwilling to write steps toward emancipation into law, preferring to depend on the charity of individual slave

owners. Once the cotton boom began in the 1790s, this charity was rarely exercised and Jefferson's vision of peaceful emancipation faded. On the contrary, Southerners increasingly sought to justify slavery.

Southern apologists had several conventional lines of defense. They found justifications for slavery in the Bible and in the histories of Greece and Rome, both slave-owning societies. The strongest defense was a legal one: the Constitution allowed slavery. Though never specifically mentioned in the final document, slavery had been a major issue between North and South at the Constitutional Convention in 1787. In the end, the delegates agreed that seats in the House of Representatives would be apportioned by counting all of the white population and three-fifths of the black people (Article I, Section 2, Paragraph 3); they included a clause requiring the return of runaway slaves who had crossed state lines (Article IV, Section 2, Paragraph 3); and they agreed that Congress could not abolish the international slave trade for twenty years (Article I, Section 9, Paragraph 1). There was absolutely no question: the Constitution did recognize slavery.

The Missouri Crisis of 1819–20 alarmed most Southerners, who were shocked by the evidence of widespread antislavery feeling in the North. South Carolinians viewed Denmark Vesey's conspiracy, occurring only two years after the Missouri debate, as an example of the harm that irresponsible northern antislavery talk could cause. After Nat Turner's revolt in 1831, Governor John Floyd of Virginia blamed the uprising on "Yankee peddlers and traders" who supposedly told slaves that "all men were born free and equal." Thus northern antislavery opinion and the fear of slave uprisings were firmly linked in southern minds.

After Nat Turner

In 1831 the South began to close ranks in defense of slavery. Several factors contributed to this regional solidarity. Nat Turner's revolt was important, linked as it was in the minds of many Southerners with antislavery agitation from the North. Militant abolitionist William

Lloyd Garrison began publishing the *Liberator*, the newspaper that was to become the leading antislavery organ, in 1831. The British gave notice that they would soon abolish slavery on the sugar plantations of the West Indies, an action that seemed to many Southerners much too close to home. Emancipation for West Indian slaves came in 1833. Finally, 1831 was the year before the Nullification Crisis (see Chapter 10) was resolved. Although the other southern states did not support the hotheaded South Carolinians who called for secession, they did sympathize with the argument that the federal government had no right to interfere with a state's special interest (namely, slavery). Following the crisis, other southern states joined with South Carolina in the belief that the only effective way to prevent other federal encroachment was militant and vehement defense of slavery.

In the 1830s, southern states began to barricade themselves against "outside" antislavery propaganda. In 1835, a crowd broke into a Charleston post office, made off with bundles of antislavery literature, and set an enormous bonfire, to fervent state and regional acclaim. By 1835, every southern legislature had tightened its laws concerning control of slaves. For example, they tried to blunt the effect of abolitionist literature by passing laws forbidding slaves to learn how to read. In only three border states—Kentucky, Tennessee, and Maryland—did slave literacy remain legal. By 1860, it is estimated, only 5 percent of all slaves could read. Slaves were forbidden to gather for dances, religious services, or any kind of organized social activity without a white person present. They were forbidden to have whiskey because it might encourage them toward revolt. The penalty for plotting insurrection was death. Other laws made manumission illegal and placed even more restrictions on the lives of free black people (as in Natchez). In many areas slave patrols were augmented and became more vigilant in restricting African American movement and communication between plantations.

In 1836, Southerners introduced a "gag rule" in Washington to prevent congressional consideration of abolitionist petitions. Attempts were made to stifle all open debate about slavery within the South; dissenters were pressured to remain silent or to leave. A few, such as James G. Birney and Sarah and Angelina

Grimké of South Carolina, left for the North to act on their antislavery convictions, but most chose silence. Among those under the greatest pressure to conform were Christian ministers, many of whom professed to believe that preaching obedience to slaves was a vital part of making slavery a humane system.

In addition to fueling fears of slave rebellions, the growing abolitionist sentiment of the 1830s raised the worry that southern opportunities for expansion would be cut off. Southern politicians painted melodramatic pictures of a beleaguered white South hemmed in on all sides by "fanatic" antislavery states, while at home Southerners were forced to contemplate what might happen when they had "to let loose among them, freed from the wholesome restraints of patriarchal authority…an idle, worthless, profligate set of free negroes" whom they feared would "prowl the…streets at night and [haunt] the woods during the day armed with whatever weapons they could lay their hands on."

Finally, southern apologists moved beyond defensiveness to develop proslavery arguments. One of the first to do this was James Henry Hammond, elected a South Carolina congressman in 1834. In 1836 Hammond delivered a major address to Congress in which he denied that slavery was evil. Rather, he claimed, it had produced "the highest toned, the purest, best organization of society that has ever existed on the face of the earth." One wonders what Hammond's slaves, especially Sally and Louisa Johnson, would have thought of this argument.

This 1841 proslavery cartoon contrasts healthy, well-cared-for African American slaves with unemployed British factory workers living in desperate poverty. The comparison between contented southern slaves and miserable northern "wage slaves" was frequently made by proslavery advocates.

CHAPTER TWELVE

INDUSTRY AND THE NORTH

1790s–1840s

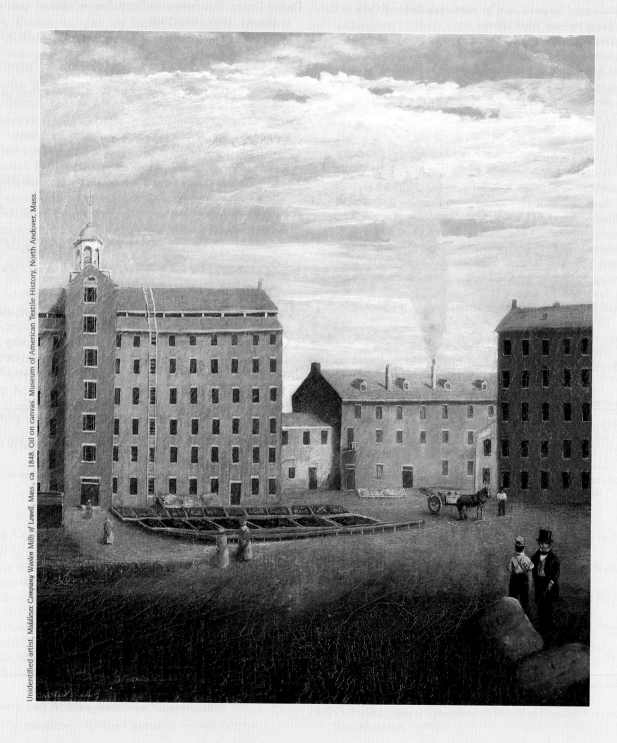

Unidentified artist. *Middlesex Company Woolen Mills of Lowell, Mass.* ca. 1848. Oil on canvas. Museum of American Textile History, North Andover, Mass.

AMERICAN COMMUNITIES
Women Factory Workers Form a Community in Lowell, Massachusetts

In the 1820s and 1830s, young farm women from all over New England flocked to Lowell to work a twelve-hour day in one of the first cotton textile factories in America. Living six to eight to a room in nearby boardinghouses, the women of Lowell earned an average of $3 a week. Some also attended inexpensive nighttime lectures or classes. Lowell, considered a model factory town, drew worldwide attention. As one admirer of its educated workers said, Lowell was less a factory than a "philanthropic manufacturing college."

The Boston investors who financed Lowell were businessmen, not philanthropists, but they wanted to keep Lowell free of the dirt, poverty, and social disorder that made English factory towns notorious. Built in 1823, Lowell boasted six neat factory buildings grouped around a central clock tower, the area pleasantly landscaped with flowers, shrubs, and trees. Housing was similarly well ordered: a Georgian mansion for the company agent; trim houses for the overseers; row houses for the mechanics and their families; and boardinghouses, each supervised by a responsible matron, for the workforce that made Lowell famous—young New England farm women.

The choice of young women as factory workers seemed shockingly unconventional. In the 1820s and 1830s, young unmarried women simply did not live alone; they lived and worked with their parents until they married. In these years of growth and westward expansion, however, America was chronically short of labor, and the Lowell manufacturers were shrewd enough to realize that young farm women were an untapped labor force. For farmers' sons, the lure of acquiring their own farms in the West was much stronger than factory wages, but for their sisters, escaping from rural isolation and earning a little money was an appealing way to spend a few years before marriage. To attract respectable young women, Lowell offered supervision both on the job and at home, with strict rules of conduct, compulsory religious services, cultural opportunities such as concerts and lectures, and cash wages.

When they first arrived in Lowell, the young women were often bewildered by the large numbers of townspeople and embarrassed by their own rural clothing and ways of speech. The air of the mill was hot, humid, and full of cotton lint, and the noise of the machinery—"The buzzing and hissing and whizzing of pulleys and rollers and spindles and flyers"—was constant. Very quickly, however, other women workers—often their own sisters or neighbors who had preceded them to the mill—helped them adjust. It was company policy for senior women to train the newcomers. The work itself was simple, consisting largely of knotting broken threads on spinning machines and power looms. Most women enjoyed the work. They were not bothered by the long hours; farm people were accustomed to long days. One woman wrote home: "The work is not disagreeable. It tried my patience sadly at first, but in general I like it very much. It is easy to do, and does not require very violent exertion, as much of our farm work does."

The most novel aspect of textile mills was a rigid work schedule. Power-driven machinery operated at a sustained, uniform pace throughout every mill; human workers had to learn to do the same. Each mill published elaborate schedules and imposed fines and penalties on latecomers. It was this kind of precise work schedule that represented the single largest change from preindustrial work habits; it was the hardest for workers to adjust to. Moreover, each mill positioned one or two overseers on every floor to make sure the pace was maintained. Men held these positions, and they earned more than the women who made up most of the workforce; this arrangement was unquestioned.

Why did young women come to Lowell? Some worked out of need and some to add to their family's income, but most regarded Lowell as opportunity. It was escape from rural isolation and from parental supervision, a chance to buy the latest fashions and learn "city ways," to attend lectures and concerts, to save for a dowry or to pay for an education. As writer Lucy Larcom, one of the most famous workers, said, the young farm women who came to Lowell sought "an opening into freer life." Working side by side and living in company boardinghouses with six to twelve other women, some of whom might be relatives or friends from home, the Lowell women built a close, supportive community for themselves.

The owners of Lowell made large profits. They also drew praise for their carefully managed community with its intelligent and independent workforce. But their success was short-lived. In the 1830s, because of competition and poor economic conditions, the owners imposed wage cuts and work speedups that their model workforce did not take lightly. Although the Lowell women had been brought together under a system of paternalistic control, the close bonds they forged in the boardinghouses gave them the courage and solidarity to "turn out" in spontaneous protests, which were, however, unsuccessful in reversing the wage cuts. By 1850 the "philanthropic manufacturing college" was no more. The original Lowell workforce of New England farm girls had been replaced by poor Irish immigrants of both sexes, who tended more machines for much less pay than their predecessors. Now Lowell was simply another mill town.

The history of Lowell epitomizes the process by which the North (both New England and the Middle Atlantic states) began to change from a society composed largely of self-sufficient farm families (Jefferson's "yeoman farmers") to one of urban wage-workers in an industrial economy. Industrialization did not occur overnight. Large factories were not common until the 1880s, but by that decade most workers had already experienced a fundamental change in their working patterns. Once under way, the market revolution changed the very basis of community: how people worked, how they thought, how they lived. In the early years of the nineteenth century, northern communities led this transformation, fostering attitudes far different from those prevalent in the South.

Lowell

KEY TOPICS

- Preindustrial ways of working and living
- The nature of the market revolution
- The effects of industrialization on workers in early factories
- Ways the market revolution changed the lives of ordinary people
- The emergence of the middle class

PREINDUSTRIAL WAYS OF WORKING

The Lowell mill was a dramatic example of the changes factories imposed on people's accustomed ways of working and interacting with each other. To fully understand the novelty of these changes in long-established patterns of work, it is important to understand traditional ways of working on farms—where 97 percent of all Americans lived in 1800—and in cities.

Rural Life: The Springer Family

The young family of Thomas and Elizabeth Springer began farming near the city of Wilmington in Mill Creek, Delaware, in the 1790s. Although no single family can represent all of the nation's farmers, a close look at the Springers can help to identify traditional patterns and the seeds of commercial change. The Springers, who had two infant daughters, owned 129 acres of farmland, 104 of which Thomas Springer had bought from his father for less than the market price. At twenty-nine, Springer, to whom family wealth had given a substantial advantage, owned four African American slaves: Ace, a young man; Sara and Amelia, young girls; and Will, aged sixty. Ace was in the process of buying his freedom, something he could not have done further south.

Although Delaware remained a slave state until the Civil War, as the case of Ace suggests, it developed differently from states further south. By 1861, only 2 percent of the state's population was still enslaved. In part this decline reflected the strong antislavery feeling that many residents of Delaware shared with people in the neighboring free state of Pennsylvania. But it was primarily because farmers like Thomas Springer found their soil was not suitable for growing cotton, the crop that fastened slavery on the states of the deep south (see Chapter 11).

The Springers had access to a commercial market for their crops. From their herd of thirty or forty sheep and at least fifteen milking cows, the Springers provided Wilmington butchers with some livestock, and they sold wool, milk, and butter in local

markets. They also raised oats, hay, and Indian corn to feed the livestock, as well as wheat and vegetables for both family use and commercial sale. They may have sold some of the wheat to Wilmington merchants for transshipment to Philadelphia and then Europe, but in general the Springers, like most preindustrial farm families, planted and produced a diverse range of crops for their own use. Only after their own needs were met did they sell their surplus on the commercial market.

It was Elizabeth Springer who, with the help of the female slaves and perhaps female relatives, was in charge of spinning the wool and collecting the dairy cows' milk that was intended for sale, and she was also responsible for preparing all the farm meals and preserving the vegetables and fruits grown for the family. Both the Springers, who had family living nearby, and all the neighboring farmers who made up the larger community shared their labor with each other in a barter system. They helped each other construct houses and barns, pick apples, thresh wheat, cut firewood, and prune trees. Neighbor women assisted one another in childbirth. Thus the Springers, like their neighbors, produced goods for their own use, for a community network, and for a larger, cash market, in that order. This kind of community network of barter and mutual obligation characterized traditional farming families throughout the nation. But because of the thriving market in nearby Wilmington, the Springers already, in a small way, had begun the transition from traditional to commercial agriculture.

The Family Labor System

In the traditional, preindustrial economy, people like the Springers did most of their work at or near their homes. One kind of traditional work was the labor of caring for the home itself and for its members, including spinning, weaving, and sewing clothes for everyone. These jobs, which fell to the women of the family, were time-consuming, multistage activities that occupied much of the year. Mothers introduced their daughters to the easiest tasks, such as carding wool, at a young age, and taught them the more difficult skills of spinning and weaving as they grew older. This infor-

In the 1840s Edward Hicks painted his childhood home, rendering an idealized image of rural harmony that owes more to faith in republican agrarianism than to the artist's accurate memory. The prosperous preindustrial farm depicted was similar to the Springers' farm described in the text in its mixed yield—sheep, cattle, dairy products, and field crops—and in its employment of an African American farm worker, shown plowing.

goods and services originating in the home were part of the complicated reciprocal arrangements among community residents who knew each other well. The "just price" for an item was set by agreement among neighbors, not by some impersonal market. Another characteristic of traditional rural work was its relatively slow, unscheduled, task-oriented pace. There was no fixed production schedule or specified period of time for task completion. People did their jobs as they needed to be done, along with the daily household routine. "Home" and "work" were not separate locations or activities, but intermixed.

Urban Artisans and Workers

In urban areas, skilled craftsmen had controlled preindustrial production since the early colonial period. Trades were perpetuated through a formal system of apprenticeship in which a boy went to work in the shop of a master, usually at the age of twelve or fourteen. Over the next three to seven years the young apprentice learned all aspects of the craft, gaining increasing responsibility and status as the day approached when he could strike out on his own. During that time, the master not only taught the apprentice his trade but housed, fed, and clothed him. Usually the apprentice lived with the master craftsman and was treated more like a member of the family than an employee. Thus the family-learning model used on farms was formalized in the urban apprenticeship system. At the end of the contract period the apprentice became a journeyman craftsman. Journeymen worked for wages in the shop of a master craftsman until they had enough capital to set up shop for themselves. Generally, they could not afford to marry until they achieved master status.

Like farmers, urban artisans usually kept long hours—sunup to sundown was common—but the pace of work varied enormously with the time of year and the number of orders. And work was frequently interrupted by family activities and neighborliness. Most cities were densely settled, and one bumped into one's neighbors all the time. Sales, business contracts, meals, and other occasions were often accompanied by a friendly drink of rum or other spirits. There was no clear separation between work and leisure.

mal family apprenticeship system was echoed in the barn and field tasks sons learned from their fathers. In this way one generation passed along essential skills to the next generation.

On the rocky farms of New England, where farm surpluses were rare and a home-produced item was cheaper and easier to obtain than an item from Britain or even Boston, many farmers worked off the farm at some other job. Sometimes an entire family developed a skill such as shoemaking that they could practice over the long New England winters. Much of what families crafted was for local and immediate use, not for a distant market. Among New England farmers, the need to find several jobs bred ingenuity and flexibility. As Noah Webster observed in 1785, "Every man is in some measure an artist—he makes a variety of utensils, rough indeed, but such as will answer his purpose—he is a husbandman [farmer] in summer and mechanic in winter."

Two other notable characteristics of rural home production were slated soon to disappear. First, things had no fixed prices, and money rarely exchanged hands. People usually paid for a home-crafted item or a neighbor's help with a particular task in foodstuffs or a piece of clothing or by helping the neighbor with a job he needed to have done. Thus

Although women as well as men did task-oriented skilled work, the formal apprenticeship system was exclusively for men. Because it was assumed that women would marry, most people thought that all girls needed to learn were domestic skills. Women who needed or wanted work, however, found a small niche of respectable occupations as domestic servants, laundresses, or seamstresses, often in the homes of the wealthy, or as cooks in small restaurants or street food vendors. Some owned and managed boardinghouses. Prostitution, another common female occupation (especially in seaport cities) was not respectable.

Patriarchy in Family, Work, and Society

Like the farm family, an entire urban household was commonly organized around one kind of work. Usually the family lived at the shop or store, and all family members worked with the craftsman at his trade. A printer's wife, for example, would be capable of keeping most of the shop's functions going in the printer's absence and of supervising the work of apprentices and

Every small community had artisans such as blacksmiths and wheelwrights who did such essential work as shoeing horses and mending wagons for local farmers. Artist John Neagle's heroic image of the blacksmith Pat Lyon presents him as the very model of honest industry.

her children. Some artisans, like blacksmiths, needed shops separate from their homes but probably relied on their children to fetch and carry and to help with some of the work. Others, like bakers, who generally had to get up in the middle of the night to perform their work, relied on their wives to sell their products during the day.

In both rural and urban settings, working families were organized along strictly patriarchal lines. The man had unquestioned authority to direct the lives and work of family members and apprentices and to decide on occupations for his sons and marriages for his daughters. His wife had many crucial responsibilities—feeding, clothing, child rearing, taking care of apprentices, and all the other domestic affairs of the household—but in all these duties she was subject to the direction of her husband. Men were heads of families and bosses of artisanal shops; although entire families were engaged in the enterprise, the husband and father was the trained craftsman, and assistance by the family was informal and generally unrecognized.

The patriarchal organization of the family was reflected in society as a whole. Legally, men had all the power: neither women nor children had property or legal rights. For example, a married woman's property belonged to her husband, a woman could not testify on her own behalf in court, and in the rare cases of divorce the husband kept the children, for they were considered his property. When a man died, his son or sons inherited his property. It was customary to allow widows the use of one-third of the property, but unfilial sons could deprive their mothers of support if they chose. Some widows successfully continued a family business, and some single daughters received inheritances from rich fathers, but these were exceptions. The basic principle was that the man, as head of the household, represented the common interests of everyone for whom he was responsible—women, children, servants, apprentices. He thus controlled everything of value, and he alone could vote for political office.

The Social Order

In this preindustrial society everyone, from the smallest yeoman farmer to the largest urban merchant, had a fixed place in the social order. The social status of artisans was below that of wealthy merchants but decidedly above that of common laborers. Yeoman farmers, less grand than large landowners, ranked above tenant farmers and farm laborers. Although men of all social ranks mingled in their daily work, they did not mingle as equals, for great importance was placed on rank and status, which were distinguished by dress and manner. Although by the 1790s many artisans who owned property were voters and vocal participants in urban politics, few directly challenged the traditional

WEALTH IN BOSTON, 1687–1848

Percent of the Population	Percent of Wealth Held			
	1687	1771	1833	1848
Top 1 percent	10%	16%	33%	37%
Top 10 percent	42	65	75	82
Lowest 80 percent	39	29	14	4

This table tracing the distribution of wealth in Boston reflects the gains made by merchants during the international shipping boom of 1790–1807 and the way in which intermarriage between wealthy families consolidated these gains.

authority of the rich and powerful to run civic affairs. The rapid spread of universal white manhood suffrage after 1800 democratized politics (see Chapter 10). At the same time, economic changes undermined the preindustrial social order.

Beginning to upset this social order were a few wealthy artisans in seacoast cities like New York. Cabinetmaker Duncan Phyfe, who gave his name to a distinctive style of furniture, is one example. Phyfe, immigrating from Scotland, opened his first shop in 1792. By 1815 he had an elegant salesroom, three workshops employing up to 100 journeymen, and a fortune of $500,000, much of it from real estate investments. Another successful New York artisan, Stephen Allen, began as an apprentice sailmaker. Allen made his fortune when he arranged to bypass the traditional middlemen and buy his materials directly from wholesalers. His sailmaking operation made a profit of $100,000 between 1802 and 1825, and when he retired he was elected mayor of New York, customarily a position reserved for gentlemen. These New York artisans, and others like them in other cities, owed much of their success to the ever-expanding effects of the economic upheaval known as the market revolution.

THE MARKET REVOLUTION

The market revolution, the most fundamental change American communities ever experienced, was the outcome of three interrelated developments: rapid improvements in transportation (see Chapter 10), commercialization, and industrialization. Improved transportation allowed both people and goods to move with new ease and speed. Commercialization involved the replacement of household self-sufficiency and barter with the production of goods for a cash market. And industrialization involved the use of power-driven machinery to produce goods once made by hand. Taken together, these three developments rapidly joined most ordinary Americans into a commercial market that supplied them with abundant quantities of inexpensive manufactured goods.

The Accumulation of Capital

In the northern states, the business community was composed largely of merchants in the seaboard cities: Boston, Providence, New York, Philadelphia, and Baltimore. Many had made substantial profits in the international shipping boom of the period 1790–1807 (as discussed in Chapter 9). During those years, the proportion of American trade carried in American ships jumped from 59 percent to 92 percent, and earnings to American merchants rose from $5.9 million to $42.1 million.

Such extraordinary opportunities attracted enterprising people. Established merchants like Philadelphia's Robert Morris opened up new markets such as the China trade, but there was room for newcomers as well. John Jacob Astor, who had arrived penniless from Germany in 1784, made his first fortune in the Pacific Northwest fur trade with China and eventually dominated the fur trade in the United States through his American Fur Company. Astor made a second fortune in New York real estate, and when he retired in 1834 with $25 million he was reputed to be the wealthiest man in America. Many similar stories of success, though not so fabulous as Astor's, demonstrated that risk-takers might reap rich rewards in international trade.

But the early years of the nineteenth century posed difficulties for international trade. Following the 1807 Embargo Act only the most daring American merchants were willing to risk restrictions and the chance of capture to reap exceptional profits. More cautious men perceived opportunity in the potentially huge domestic American market, deprived of cheap British goods by war in Europe (and later, the War of 1812) and underserved by the traditional family-centered, slow-paced, and localized system of skilled craftsmanship. Mobilizing the capital available within the business community, merchants began to control, transform, and increase American home-based production.

Some of the nation's wealthiest men turned to local investments. In Providence, Rhode Island, Moses Brown and his son-in-law William Almy began to invest some of the profits the Brown family had reaped from a worldwide trade in iron, candles, rum, and African slaves in the new manufacture of cotton textiles. Philadelphia merchant and banker Stephen

Girard, who had made his fortune in the West Indies trade, invested in the Lehigh Valley coalfields and in the canals and railroads that linked the coalfields to Philadelphia. Cincinnati merchants banded together to finance the building of the first steamboats to operate on the Ohio River. And even in rural towns, local merchants and shopkeepers invested in the work of local craftsmen.

Much of the capital for the new investments came from banks, both those in seaport cities that had been established for the international trade and those, like the Lynn, Massachusetts, Mechanics Bank, founded in 1814 by a group of Lynn's Quaker merchants, that served local clients. An astonishing amount of capital, however, was raised through family connections. In the late eighteenth century, members of the business communities in the seaboard cities had begun to consolidate their position and property by intermarriage. In Boston, such a strong community developed that when Francis Cabot Lowell needed $300,000 in 1813 to build the world's first automated cotton mill in Waltham, Massachusetts (the prototype of the Lowell mills), he had only to turn to his family network.

Although much of the original capital for American manufacturing, such as Almy and Brown's collaboration with Samuel Slater, came from the shipping boom of 1790–1807, southern cotton provided the capital for continuing development. Because Northerners built the nation's ships, controlled the shipping trade, and provided the nation's banking, insurance, and financial services, the astounding growth in southern cotton exports enriched northern merchants almost as much as southern planters. In 1825, for example, of the 204,000 bales of cotton shipped from New Orleans, about one-third (69,000) were transshipped through the northern ports of New York, Philadelphia, and Boston. Southerners complained that their combined financial and shipping costs diverted forty cents of every dollar paid for their cotton to northerners. Profits from cotton shipping provided some of the funds the Boston Associates made available to Francis Cabot Lowell. In another example, New York merchant Anson Phelps invested the profits he made from cotton shipping in iron mines in Pennsylvania and metalworks in Connecticut. Although imperfectly understood at the time, the truth is that the development of northern industry was paid for by southern cotton produced by enslaved African American labor.

The Putting-Out System

Initially, the American business community invested not in machinery and factories but in the "putting-out system" of home manufacture, thereby expanding and transforming it. In this significant departure from preindustrial work, people still produced goods at home but under the direction of a merchant, who "put out" the raw materials to them, paid them a certain sum per finished piece, and sold the completed item to a distant market.

A crucial aspect of the new putting-out system was the division of labor. In the preindustrial system, an individual worker or his household made an entire item—a shoe, for example. Now an unskilled worker often made only a part of the finished product in large quantities for low per-piece wages.

The change in the shoe industry in Lynn, Massachusetts, shows how the putting-out system transformed American manufacturing. Long a major center of the shoe industry, Lynn, in 1800, produced 400,000 pairs of shoes—enough for every fifth person in the country. The town's 200 master artisans and their families, including journeymen and apprentices, worked together in hundreds of small home workshops called "ten-footers" (from their size, about ten feet square). The artisans and journeymen cut the leather, the artisans' wives and daughters did the binding of the upper parts of the shoe, the men stitched the shoe together, and children and apprentices helped where needed. In the early days, the artisan commonly bartered his shoes for needed products. For example, in 1773, a Lynn shopkeeper wrote to Providence merchant Nicholas Brown (Moses Brown's brother) offering to trade 100 pairs of shoes for 100 pounds of tea! Sometimes an artisan sold his shoes to a larger retailer in Boston or Salem, and sometimes a sea captain arranged to lend an artisan money for the raw materials and then sold the finished shoes at every port his ship visited. Although production of shoes in Lynn increased yearly from 1780 to 1810 as markets widened, shoes continued to be manufactured in traditional artisanal ways.

The investment of merchant capital in the shoe business changed everything. In Lynn, a small group of Quaker shopkeepers and merchants, connected by family, religious, and business ties, took the lead in reorganizing the trade. Financed by the bank they founded in 1814, Lynn capitalists like Micajah Pratt built large, two-story central workshops to replace the scattered ten-footers. Pratt employed a few skilled craftsmen to cut leather for shoes, but he put out the rest of the shoemaking to less-skilled workers who were no longer connected by family ties. Individual farm women and children sewed the uppers, which, when completed, were soled by farm men and boys. Putting-out workers were paid on a piecework basis; the men and boys earned more than the women and children but much less than a master craftsman or a journeyman. This arrangement allowed the capitalist to employ much more labor for the same investment than with the traditional artisan workshop. Shoe production increased enormously: the largest central shop in 1832 turned out ten times more shoes

Woman at Spinning Wheel, ca. 1850–70. Carved and painted wood and iron. Photographed by Ken Burris. Shelburne Museum, Shelburne, Vermont.

This carved and painted figure, designed as a whirligig and trade sign, shows a woman at a spinning wheel. Until cotton textile mills industrialized this work, spinning was one of the most time-consuming tasks that women and young girls did at home.

than the largest shopkeeper had sold in 1789. Gradually the putting-out system and central workshops replaced artisan's shops. Some artisans became wealthy owners of workshops, but most became wage earners, and the apprenticeship system eventually disappeared.

The putting-out system moved the control of production from the individual artisan households to the merchant capitalists, who could now control labor costs, production goals, and shoe styles to fit certain markets. For example, the Lynn trade quickly monopolized the market for cheap boots for southern slaves and western farmers, leaving workshops in other cities to produce shoes for wealthier customers. This specialization of the national market—indeed, even thinking in terms of a national market—was new. Additionally, and most important from the capitalist's point of view, the owner of the business controlled the workers and could cut back or expand the labor force as economic and marketplace conditions warranted. The unaccustomed severity of economic slumps like the Panics of 1819 and 1837 made this flexibility especially desirable.

While the central workshop system prevailed in Lynn and in urban centers like New York City, the

putting-out system also fostered a more dispersed form of home production. By 1810 there were an estimated 2,500 so-called outwork weavers in New England, operating handlooms in their own homes. Other crafts that rapidly became organized according to the putting-out system were flax and wool spinning, straw braiding, glove making, and the knitting of stockings. For example, the palm-leaf hat industry that supplied farm laborers and slaves in the South and West relied completely on women and children, who braided the straw for the hats at home part-time. Absorbed into families' overall domestic routines, the outwork activity seemed small, but the size of the industry itself was surprising: in 1837, 33,000 Massachusetts women braided palm-leaf hats, whereas only 20,000 worked in the state's cotton textile mills. They were producing for a large national market, made possible by the dramatic improvements in transportation that occurred between 1820 and 1840.

Although the putting-out system meant a loss of independence for artisans such as those in Lynn, New England farm families liked it. From their point of view, the work could easily be combined with domestic work, and the pay was a new source of income that they could use to purchase mass-produced goods—among them shoes, boots, hats, buttons, stockings, suspenders, horsewhips, machine-made textiles, and men's work clothes—rather than spend the time required to make these things themselves. It was in this way that farm families moved away from the local barter system and into a larger market economy. The longer-term consequences of industrial capitalism—the destruction of the artisan tradition and the undermining of the patriarchal family—took some years to emerge. For example, apprentices were still taken on in the Lynn shoemaking trade until 1840.

British Technology and American Industrialization

Important as were the transportation revolution and the commercialization made possible by the putting-out system, the third component of the market revolution, industrialization, brought the greatest changes to personal lives. Begun in Britain in the eighteenth century, industrialization was the result of a series of technological changes in the textile trade. Mechanization moved the production of cotton and woolen yarn out of the home to the "manufactory" ("factory" for short), where power-driven machines did the work. In marked contrast to the putting-out system, in which capitalists had dispersed work into many individual households, industrialization required workers to concentrate in factories and pace themselves to the rhythms of power-driven machinery.

Many British people, especially the elite, looked on factories with horror. In England, the first factory workers were orphaned children, women, and poor Irish immigrants. These people flooded into ill-prepared rural factory towns. Horrified at the dirt and squalor of these towns, and by the relentless pace of the machinery, British poet William Blake condemned the entire concept of industrialization, writing ominously of "dark, satanic mills." If this was progress, he wanted no part of it.

Some Americans, most notably Thomas Jefferson, shared these sentiments, basing their dream of American development on the independent yeoman farmer rather than on industrialization. But conditions in New England favored rapid industrialization. New England had swift rivers that could power factory machinery, and it had wealthy merchants looking for new ways to invest their capital. Some of these merchants, whose fortunes derived from shipping southern cotton to textile factories in England, quickly realized that the manufacturing could be done in New England—if Americans could learn the secrets of British industrial technology.

Slater's Mill

The simplest and quickest way for America to industrialize was to copy the British, but the British, well aware of the value of their machinery, enacted laws forbidding its export and even the emigration of skilled workers. Over the years, however, Americans managed to lure a number of British artisans to the United States.

In 1789 Samuel Slater, who had just finished an apprenticeship in the most up-to-date cotton spinning factory in England, disguised himself as a farm laborer and slipped out of England without even telling his mother good-bye. In Providence, Rhode Island, he met Moses Brown and William Almy, who had been trying without success to duplicate British industrial technology. Having carefully committed the designs to memory before leaving England, Slater promptly built copies of the latest British machinery for Brown and Almy. Slater's mill, as it became known, began operation in 1790. It was the most advanced cotton mill in America. Although Slater was a skilled mechanic and improved on the original British machines, it is nonetheless true that American industrialization owed its start to technology that the British had not wished to share.

Following British practice, Slater drew his workforce primarily from among young children (ages seven to twelve) and women, whom he paid much less than the handful of skilled male workers he hired to keep the machines working. The yarn spun at Slater's mill was then put out to local home weavers, who turned it into cloth on handlooms. As a result, home weaving flourished in areas near the mill, giving families a new opportunity to make money at a task with which they were already familiar. In 1790, home weavers had no way of knowing that their profitable occupation would soon be challenged by power looms in factories.

Many others followed Slater's lead, and the rivers of New England were soon dotted with mills wherever waterpower could be tapped. Embargo and war sheltered American factories from British competition from 1807 to 1815, but when the War of 1812 ended, the British cut prices ruthlessly in an effort to drive the newcomers out of business. In 1816 Congress passed the first tariff, aimed largely against British cotton textiles, in response to the clamor by New England manufacturers for protection for their young industry. Interestingly, the issue of tariff protection, usually regarded as a sectional issue between North and South (see "The Nullification Crisis" in Chapter 10) initially aroused controversy in New England, where many seaport merchants opposed it because they saw it as a threat to the international free trade from which they had so richly profited.

This early nineteenth-century watercolor shows Slater's mill, the first cotton textile mill in the United States, which depended on the waterpower of Pawtucket Falls for its energy. New England was rich in swiftly flowing streams that could provide power to spinning machines and power looms.

The Lowell Mills

Another way to deal with British competition was to beat the British at their own game. With the intention of designing better machinery, a young Bostonian, Francis Cabot Lowell, made an apparently casual tour of British textile mills in 1810. Lowell, the founder of the Lowell mills described in the opening of this chapter, made a good impression on his English hosts, who were pleased by his interest and his intelligent questions. They did not know that each night, in his hotel room, Lowell made sketches from memory of the machines he had inspected during the day.

Lowell was more than an industrial spy, however. When he returned to the United States, he went to work with a Boston mechanic, Paul Moody, to improve on the British models. Lowell and Moody not only made the machinery for spinning cotton more efficient, but they also invented a power loom. This was a great advance, for now all aspects of textile manufacture, from the initial cleaning and carding (combing) to the production of finished lengths of cloth, could be gathered together in the same factory. Such a mill required a much larger capital investment than a small spinning mill such as Slater's, but Lowell's family network gave him access to the needed funds. In 1814 he opened the world's first integrated cotton mill in Waltham, near Boston. It was a great success: in 1815, the Boston Associates (Lowell's partners) made profits of 25 percent, and their efficiency allowed them to survive the intense British competition. Many smaller New England mills did not survive, even with the tariff protection voted in 1816. The lesson was clear: size mattered.

Lowell, Massachusetts, 1832   *This town plan of Lowell, Massachusetts, in 1832 illustrates the comprehensive relationship the owners envisaged between the factories and the workforce. The mills are located on the Merrimack River, while nearby are the boardinghouses for the single young female workers, row houses for the male mechanics and their families, and houses for the overseers. Somewhat farther away is the mansion of the company agent.*

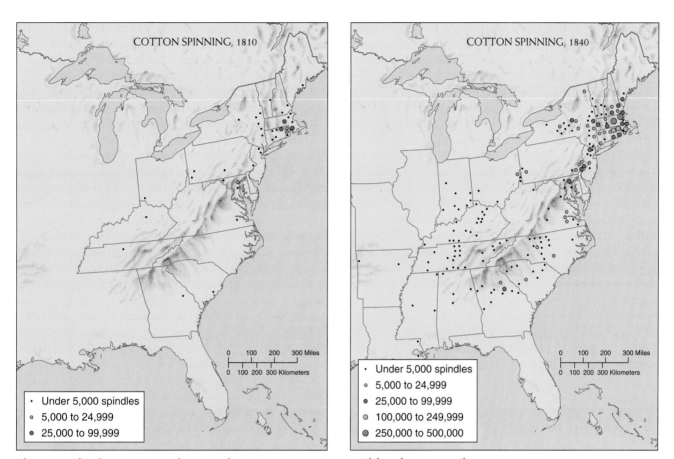

The Growth of Cotton Textile Manufacturing, 1810–1840   *Although cotton textile manufacturing spread to other parts of the country after 1810, New England never lost its early lead. By 1839, the extent of industrialization in New England far outstripped that of other regions. Although much of New England was still rural, more and more residents were drawn into the market economy. Nationally, the proportion of wage laborers rose from 12 percent in 1800 to 40 percent in 1860. The majority of them were New Englanders who had made the transition from artisan to worker.*

Source: *Atlas of the Historical Geography of the United States,* © Carnegie Institute of Washington, Plate 186.

The Boston Associates took the lesson to heart, and when they moved their enterprise to a new location in 1823, they thought big. They built an entire town at the junction of the Concord and Merrimack Rivers where the village of East Chelmsford stood, renaming it Lowell in memory of Francis, who had died, still a young man, in 1817. As the opening of this chapter describes, the new industrial community boasted six mills and company housing for all the workers. In 1826 the town had 2,500 inhabitants; ten years later the population was 17,000.

Family Mills

Lowell was unique. No other textile mill was ever such a showplace. None was as large, integrated so many tasks, or relied on such a homogeneous workforce. Its location in a new town was also unusual. Much more common in the early days of industrialization were small rural spinning mills, on the model of Slater's first

mill, built on swiftly running streams near existing farm communities. Although the economic benefits to local residents were considerable, the presence of the mills and mill workers brought rural communities troubling new issues of authority and diversity.

Because the owners of smaller mills often hired entire families, their operations came to be called family mills. The employment pattern at these mills followed that established by Slater at his first mill in 1790. Children aged eight to twelve, whose customary job was doffing (changing) bobbins on the spinning machines, made up 50 percent of the workforce. Women and men each made up about 25 percent of the workforce, but men had the most skilled and best-paid jobs.

The engagement of an entire family in a particular line of work was hardly new; both farm and artisan families were accustomed to working at a family enterprise. And unless a family member was very highly skilled, more than one worker per family was a necessity. To take one example, in the Rockdale mills, located on Chester Creek in Delaware, wages in the 1840s ranged from $1 a week for unskilled children to $12 a week for skilled workers. Unskilled adult laborers earned between $2.50 and $3.50 a week, or between $110 and $150 a year, allowing for sickness and temporary layoffs. Wages of $300 a year were necessary to keep a family safely above the poverty line. Single workers, who had to pay $70 to $100 a year for room and board, were at a disadvantage compared with a family, who could rent a house for $25 a year and survive on an estimated $200 a year for food.

Relations between these small rural mill communities and the surrounding farming communities were often difficult, as the history of the towns of Dudley and Oxford, Massachusetts, shows. Samuel Slater, now a millionaire, built three small mill communities near these towns in the early years of the century. Each consisted of a small factory, a store, and cottages and a boardinghouse for workers. Slater

In 1816 Connecticut gunsmith Simeon North did what Eli Whitney had only hoped to do. North produced the first gun with interchangeable parts. North's invention, taken up and improved by the national armories at Springfield and Harpers Ferry, formed the basis of the American system of manufactures.

or one of his sons ran the mills personally; they were not absentee owners. Most of Slater's workers came from outside the Dudley-Oxford area. They were a mixed group—single young farm women of the kind Lowell attracted, the poor and destitute, and workers from other factories looking for better conditions. They rarely stayed long: almost 50 percent of the workforce left every year.

Slater's mills provided a substantial amount of work for local people, putting out to them both the initial cleaning of the raw cotton and the much more lucrative weaving of the spun yarn. But in spite of this economic link, relations between Slater and his workers on one side and the farmers and shopkeepers of the Dudley and Oxford communities on the other were stormy. They disagreed over the building of mill dams (essential for the mill power supply, they sometimes flooded local fields), over taxes, over the upkeep of local roads, and over schools. Slater, hoping to save money and exercise more control over his mill workers' time, wanted to set up his own school for factory children. The debates were so constant, and so heated, that in 1831 Slater petitioned the Massachusetts General Court to create a separate town, Webster, that would encompass his three mill communities. For their part, the residents of Dudley and Oxford became increasingly hostile to Slater's authoritarian control, which they regarded as undemocratic. Their dislike carried over to the workers as well. Disdaining the mill workers for their poverty and transiency, people in the rural communities began referring to them as "operatives," making them somehow different in their work roles from themselves. Industrial work thus led to new social distinctions. Even though the people of Dudley and Oxford benefited from the mills, they did not fully accept the social organization on which their new prosperity rested, nor did they feel a sense of community with those who did the work that led to their increased well-being.

"The American System of Manufactures"

Not all American industrial technology was copied from British inventions, for there were many homegrown inventors. Indeed, calling Americans "mechanic[s] by nature," one Frenchman observed that "in Massachusetts and Connecticut there is not a labourer who had not invented a machine or tool." By the 1840s, to take but one example, small towns like St. Johnsbury, Vermont, boasted many small industries based on local inventions such as those by Erastus Fairbanks in scales and plows, Lemuel Hubbard in pumps, and Nicanor Kendall in guns. But perhaps most important was the pioneering American role in the development of standardized parts.

The concept of interchangeable parts, realized first in gun manufacturing, was so unusual that the British soon dubbed it "the American system of manufactures." In this system, a product such as a gun was broken down into its component parts and an exact mold was made for each. All pieces made from the same mold (after being hand filed by inexpensive unskilled laborers) matched a uniform standard. As a result, repairing a gun that malfunctioned required only installing a replacement for the defective part rather than laboriously making a new part or perhaps an entirely new gun.

Eli Whitney, the co-inventor of the cotton gin, was the first to take up the challenge of interchangeable parts, and in 1798 he contracted with the government to make 10,000 rifles in twenty-eight months, an incredibly short period had he been planning to produce each rifle by hand in the traditional way. Whitney's ideas far outran his performance. It took him ten years to fulfill his contract, and even then he had not managed to perfect the production of all the rifle parts. Two other New Englanders, Simeon North and John Hall, created milling machines that could grind parts to the required specifications and brought the concept to fruition, North in 1816 and Hall in 1824. Subsidized by the government to make rifles for the national armory at Harpers Ferry, Virginia, Hall wrote triumphantly to the secretary of war, "I have succeeded in an object which has hitherto baffled…all the endeavors of those who have heretofore attempted it— I have succeeded in establishing methods of fabricating arms exactly alike." When the system of interchangeable machine-made parts was adopted by the other national armory, at Springfield, Massachusetts, the Springfield rifle got its name.

America's early lead in interchangeable parts was a substantial source of national pride. As American gunmaker Samuel Colt boasted, "There is nothing that cannot be made by machine." Standardized production quickly revolutionized the manufacture of items as simple as nails and as complicated as clocks. By 1810 a machine had been developed that could produce 100 nails a minute, cutting the cost of nail making by two-thirds. Finely made wooden and brass clocks, previously made (expensively) by hand, were replaced by mass-produced versions turned out in the Connecticut factories of Eli Terry, Seth Thomas, and Chauncey Jerome and sold nationwide by Yankee peddlers. Now ordinary people could keep precise time rather than estimate time by the sun, and factories could require workers to come to work on time. The need of railroads for precise timekeeping gave further support to the new system of manufacture.

Like the factory system itself, the American system spread slowly. For example, Isaac Singer's sewing machine, first patented in 1851, was not made with fully interchangeable parts until 1873, when the company was already selling 230,000 machines a year. The sewing machine revolutionized the manufacture of clothing, which up to this time had been made by women for their families at home and by hand.

American businesses mass-produced high-quality goods for ordinary people earlier than manufacturers in Britain or any other European country were able to do. The availability of these goods was a practical demonstration of American beliefs in democracy and equality. As historian David Potter has perceptively remarked: "European radical thought is prone to demand that the man of property be stripped of his carriage and his fine clothes. But American radical thought is likely to insist, instead, that the ordinary man is entitled to mass-produced copies, indistinguishable from the originals."

Other Factories

Although cotton textile mills were the first and best known of the early factories, some factories produced other items, among them metal and iron. Like the textile mills, many of these factories were rural because they depended on natural water sources for power or because they needed to be near their raw materials, such as iron ore. And like the early textile mills, these first heavy industries initially coexisted with the traditional artisanal system.

The rapid development of the steamship industry in Cincinnati illustrates both the role of merchant capital and the coexistence of old and new production methods. The first steamboat appeared on the Ohio River in 1811, and Cincinnati's merchants, who had heretofore invested their profits in land and real estate speculation, were quick to see its advantages. Cincinnati's first steamboat, financed by local merchant capital, was commissioned in 1816. It proved so successful that by 1819 one-quarter of all western steamboats were being built in Cincinnati. By 1826, Cincinnati's steamship industry had grown to include four iron foundries employing 54 men, five steam engine and finishing factories employing 126 people, and three boatyards with 200 workers. At the same time, much of the detail work on the steamboat was performed by traditional artisans such as cabinetmakers, upholsterers, tinsmiths, and blacksmiths, who did record-breaking amounts of work in their small, independent shops. In this way, new factory methods and industrial techniques were often coupled with old craft techniques.

The new concepts of specialization and standardization and the increased production they brought about were basic to the system of industrial capitalism. In turn, the system led to vast increases in wealth and in living standards for many—eventually most—of the inhabitants of industrial nations. But for many workers

Steamboats transformed commerce on western rivers and helped to make the fortune of Cincinnati, which became a center of steamboat manufacture. This Currier and Ives print of 1855 shows the Mayflower, one of the most elegant and handsome steamboats on the Mississippi River.

in early-nineteenth-century America, the transition from the old method of production to the new one did not come without a price.

FROM ARTISAN TO WORKER

The changes wrought by the market revolution had major and lasting effects on ordinary Americans. The proportion of wage laborers in the nation's labor force rose from 12 percent in 1800 to 40 percent by 1860. Most of these workers were employed in the North, and almost half were women, performing outwork in their homes. The young farm woman who worked at Lowell for a year or two, then returned home; the master craftsman in Lynn who expanded his shop with the aid of merchant capital; the home weaver who prospered on outwork from Slater's mill—all were participating, often unknowingly, in fundamental personal and social changes.

Personal Relationships

The putting-out system, with its division of each craft into separate tasks, effectively destroyed artisan production and the apprenticeship system. For example, in New York by the mid-1820s, tailors and shoemakers were teaching apprentices only a few simple operations, in effect using them as helpers. Printers undercut the system by hiring partly trained apprentices as journeymen. In almost every trade, apprentices no longer lived with the master's family, and their parents received cash payment for the child's work. Thus in effect the apprenticeship system was replaced by child labor.

Artisans who helped to destroy the older system did so unwillingly, in response to harsh new competition caused by improvements in transportation. For example, in the 1850s Philadelphia's 7,000 shoemakers, shut out of the cheap shoe market by the success of the shoe manufacturers of Lynn, turned to the specialty markets of ladies' shoes and expensive men's shoes and boots. But even in this luxury market, the pressure of cheaper competition forced them to accept the central shop and the putting-out system rather than the individual artisanal shop. To compete, they had to change and adopt the same new labor organization as their rivals.

Although the breakdown of the family work system undoubtedly harmed independent urban artisans, it may have had a liberating effect on the women and children of farm families. About a third of the Lowell women workers did not return to their farm homes, instead remaining in town and marrying urban men or continuing to work. And of the women who did return home, fewer than half married farmers. There is no doubt that working at Lowell provided these women with new options. Women and children who earned wages by doing outwork at home may have found their voices strengthened by this evidence of their power and worth. Patriarchal control over family members was no longer absolute.

The breakdown of the patriarchal relationship between the master craftsman and his workers became an issue in the growing political battle between the North and the South over slavery. Southern defenders of slavery compared their cradle-to-grave responsibility to their slaves with northern employers' "heartless" treatment of their "wage slaves." Certainly the new northern employer assumed less responsibility for individual workers than had the traditional artisan. Although the earliest textile manufacturers, like those at Lowell, provided housing for their workers, workers soon became responsible for their own food and housing. Moreover, northern employers felt no obligation to help or care for old or disabled workers. Southerners were right: this was a heartless system. But Northerners were also right: industrialization was certainly freer than the slave system, freer even than the hierarchical craft system, although it sometimes offered only the freedom to starve.

Mechanization and Women's Work

Industrialization posed a major threat to the status and independence of skilled male workers. In trade after trade, mechanization meant that most tasks could be performed by unskilled labor. For example, the textile mills at Lowell and elsewhere hired a mere handful of skilled mechanics; most of the rest of the workers were unskilled and lower paid. In fact, the work in the textile mills was so simple that children came to form a large part of the workforce. By 1850 in New York City, many formerly skilled trades, including shoemaking, weaving, silversmithing, pottery making, and cabinetmaking, were filled with unskilled, low-paid workers who did one specialized operation or tended machinery. Many former artisans were reduced to performing wage labor for others. Because women were so frequently hired in the putting-out system, male workers began to oppose female participation in the workforce, fearing that it would lower their own wages.

Mechanization changed the nature of women's work in other ways as well. The industrialization of textiles—first in spinning, then in weaving—relieved women of a time-consuming home occupation. To supplement family income, women now had the choice of following textile work into the factory or finding other kinds of home work. At first, these were attractive options, but negative aspects soon developed, especially in the nation's cities.

The 1820s saw the birth of the garment industry. In New York City, employers began hiring women to sew ready-made clothing, at first rough, unfitted clothing for sailors and southern slaves, but later overalls and shirts for Westerners and finer items such as men's shirts. Most women performed this work at low piecework rates in their homes. Although by 1860 Brooks Brothers, the famous men's clothing firm, had 70 "inside" workers in a model central workshop, the firm relied primarily on putting out sewing to 3,000 women who worked at home.

Soon the low pay and seasonal nature of the industry became notorious. Two basic problems were overcrowding of the market and low wages. Women were pushed into the garment trade because they were barred from many occupations considered inappropriate for them, and the oversupply of workers led to wage cutting. To make matters worse, most people

believed that "respectable" women did not do factory work (Lowell in its "model" years was the exception that proved the rule), and this disparagement fostered low pay and poor working conditions.

Manufacturers in the garment trade made their profits not from efficient production but by obtaining intensive labor for very low wages. The lower the piece rate, the more each woman, sewing at home, had to produce to earn enough to live. The invention of the sewing machine only made matters worse. Manufacturers dropped their piecework rates still lower, and some women found themselves working fifteen to eighteen hours a day, producing more than they ever had, but earning the same pay.

Time, Work, and Leisure

Preindustrial work had a flexibility that factory work did not, and it took factory workers a while to get accustomed to the constant pace of work. Long hours did not bother them, for they were accustomed to

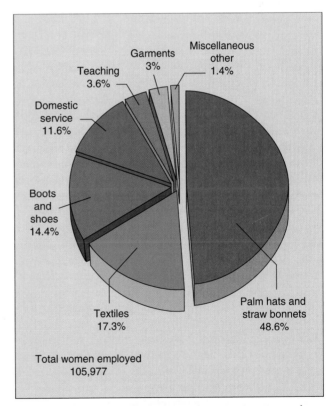

Occupations of Women Wage Earners in Massachusetts, 1837   *This chart shows how important outwork was for women workers. Textile work in factories occupied less than 20 percent of women, while outwork in palm-leaf hats, straw bonnets, and boots and shoes accounted for over half of the total workforce. Teaching was a new occupation for women in 1837. The small percentage of 3.6 would grow in the future.*

Source: Based on Thomas Dublin, *Transforming Women's Work* (Ithaca, N.Y.: Cornell University Press, 1991), table 1.1, p. 20.

twelve-hour workdays and six-day weeks on the farm and in the shop. But in the early days of Slater's mill in Rhode Island, workers sometimes took a few hours off to go berry picking or to attend to other business. And when Slater insisted on a twelve-hour day that required candles for night work, one upset father demanded that his children be sent home at sunset, the traditional end of the workday.

Factory workers gradually adjusted to having their lives regulated by the sound of the factory bell, but they did not necessarily become the docile "hands" the owners wanted. Absenteeism was common, accounting for about 15 percent of working hours, and there was much pilfering. Workers were beginning to think of themselves as a separate community whose interests differed from those of owners, and the tyranny of time over their work was certainly one reason for this.

Another adjustment required by the constant pace was that time now had to be divided into two separate activities—work and leisure. In preindustrial times work and leisure were blended for farmers and artisans.

This timetable from the Lowell Mills illustrates the elaborate time schedules that the cotton textile mills expected their employees to meet. For workers, it was difficult to adjust to the regimentation imposed by clock time, in contrast to approximate times common to preindustrial work.

The place of work—often the home—and the pace made it possible to stop and have a chat or a friendly drink with a visitor. Now, however, the separation of home and workplace and the pace of production not only squeezed the fun out of the long workday but left a smaller proportion of time for leisure activities.

For many workingmen, the favored spot for after-hours and Sunday leisure became the local tavern. Community-wide celebrations and casual sociability, still common in rural areas, began to be replaced in cities by spectator sports—horse racing, boxing, and (beginning in the 1850s) baseball—and by popular entertainments such as plays, operas, minstrel shows, concerts, and circuses. Some of these diversions, such as plays and horse racing, appealed to all social classes, but others, like parades, rowdy dance halls, and tavern games like quoits and ninepins were favored working-class amusements. The effect of these changes was to make working-class amusements more distinct, and visible, than they had been before.

The Cash Economy

Another effect of the market revolution was the transformation of a largely barter system into a cash economy. For example, a farm woman might pay in butter and eggs for a pair of shoes handmade for her by the local shoemaker. A few years later that same woman, now part of the vast New England outwork industry, might buy new footwear with the cash she had earned from braiding straw for hats, making gloves, or sewing shirts at home. Moreover, the shoes would have been commercially manufactured, perhaps in Lynn. In this way, in hundreds of thousands of small transactions, community economic ties were replaced by distant, sometimes national ones.

The rise of the cash economy also changed the relationships among workers and their employers. In some cases the pay envelope was the only direct contact between factory worker and (often absentee) owner. For workers, this change was both unsettling and liberating. On the minus side, workers were no longer part of a settled, orderly, and familiar community. On the plus side, they were now free to labor wherever they could, at whatever wages their skills or their bargaining power could command. That workers took their freedom seriously is evidenced by the very high rate of turnover in the New England textile mills. By the 1830s, at both the small family mills and the model mills at Lowell, almost half the workforce left every year.

But if moving on was a sign of increased freedom of opportunity for some workers, for others it was an unwanted consequence of the market revolution. In New England, for example, many quite prosperous artisans and farmers faced disruptive competition from factory goods and western commercial agriculture. They could remain where they were only if they were willing to become factory workers or commercial farmers. Often the more conservative choice was to move west and try to reestablish one's traditional lifestyle on the frontier.

Free Labor

At the heart of the industrializing economy was the notion of free labor. Originally, "free" referred to individual economic choice—that is, to the right of workers to move to another job rather than be held to a position by customary obligation or the formal contract of apprenticeship or journeyman labor. But "free labor" soon came to encompass as well the range of attitudes—hard work, self-discipline, and a striving for economic independence—that were necessary for success in a competitive, industrializing economy. These were profoundly individualistic attitudes, and owners cited them in opposing labor unions and the use of strikes to achieve wage goals. As the *Cincinnati Gazette* put it in 1857: "We are not speaking of leaving work—that all men have the right to do; but of combining to interrupt and arrest the machinery. The first is a plain, individual right. The last is a conspiracy against the interest, and even the safety of the public." Owners opposed government action, such as proposals for legislation mandating a ten-hour day, on the same grounds: it denied workers wishing to work a twelve-hour day the opportunity to do so!

For their part, many workers were inclined to define freedom more collectively, arguing that their just grievances as free American citizens were not being heard. As a group of New Hampshire female workers rhetorically asked, "Why [is] there...so much want, dependence and misery among us, if forsooth, we are freemen and freewomen?" Or, as the Lowell strikers of 1836 sang as they paraded through the streets:

> Oh! Isn't it a pity, such a pretty girl as I,
> Should be sent to the factory to pine away and die?
> Oh! I cannot be a slave,
> I will not be a slave,
> For I'm so fond of liberty
> That I cannot be a slave.

Early Strikes

Rural women workers led some of the first strikes in American labor history. Because young women formed the majority of the workforce in early textile mills like Lowell, their participation in spontaneous protests is not surprising. What was surprising was that women, whose public role and activities were limited at the time, were the ones who led these protests. In 1824, in one of the first of these actions, women workers at a

Pawtucket, Rhode Island, textile mill led their coworkers, female and male, out on strike to protest wage cuts and longer hours.

More famous were the strikes that the women at the model mill at Lowell led. The first serious trouble came in 1834, when 800 women participated in a spontaneous turnout to protest a wage cut of 25 percent. The owners were shocked and outraged by the strike, considering it both unfeminine and ungrateful. The workers, however, were bound together by a sense of sisterhood and were protesting not just the attack on their economic independence but the blow to their position as "daughters of freemen still." Nevertheless the wage cuts were enforced, as were more cuts in 1836, again in the face of a turnout. Many women simply packed their clothes in disgust and returned home to the family farm.

Like these strikes, most turnouts by factory workers in the 1830s—male or female—were unsuccessful. Owners, claiming that increasing competition made wage cuts inevitable, were always able to find new workers—Irish immigrants, for example—who would work at lower wages. The preindustrial notion of a community of interest between owner and workers had broken down.

Collective labor action by the women workers of Lowell underlined that point. In 1845 they formed the first chapter of the New England Female Labor Reform Association. The chapter soon had over 400 members, and other chapters sprang up in mill towns such as Fall River, Dover, Nashua, and Manchester. The Lowell chapter, led by Sarah Bagley, submitted a petition to the Massachusetts legislature demanding a law limiting the workday to ten hours, which the Lowell owners were unwilling to consider. The ten-hour day, a major labor goal throughout the nation, had first been demanded by skilled male workers in Boston in 1825. When the Massachusetts legislature ignored the Lowell petition on the grounds that many of the signers were nonvoters (because they were women), Bagley broke with customary notions of female propriety and challenged the legislature in a formal address: "For the last half century, it has been deemed a violation of woman's sphere to appear before the public as a speaker: but when our rights are trampled upon and we appeal in vain to our legislator, what are we to do?...Shall not our voice be heard...shall it be [said] to the daughters of New England that they have not political rights?"

The answer seemed at first to be yes. The Massachusetts legislature continued adamantly to ignore the ten-hour-day proposal even when presented with another petition in 1846 that had 10,000 signatures, 4,000 from Lowell women. But in 1847, legislators in New Hampshire, responding to a petition from women workers in Nashua who had refused to work after "lighting up" (after dark), made theirs the first state to enact a ten-hour-day law. Maine followed in 1848 and Pennsylvania in 1849. For the first time, thanks to women's pioneering role in factory protests, a group of workers had obtained state legislation improving their working conditions.

A NEW SOCIAL ORDER

The market revolution reached into every aspect of life, down to the most personal family decisions. It also fundamentally changed the social order, creating a new middle class with distinctive habits and beliefs.

Wealth and Class

There had always been social classes in America. Since the early colonial period planters in the South and merchants in the North had comprised a wealthy elite. Somewhere below the elite but above the mass of people were the "middling sort": a small professional group that included lawyers, ministers, schoolteachers, doctors, public officials, some prosperous farmers, prosperous urban shopkeepers and innkeepers, and a few wealthy artisans such as Boston silversmith Paul Revere. "Mechanics and farmers"—artisans and yeoman farmers—made up another large group, and the laboring poor, consisting of ordinary laborers, servants, and marginal farmers were below them. At the very bottom were the paupers—those dependent on public charity—and the enslaved. This was the "natural" social order that fixed most people in the social rank to which they were born. Although many a male servant in early America aspired to become a small farmer or artisan, he did not usually aspire to become a member of the wealthy elite, nor did serving maids often marry rich men.

The market revolution ended the old social order, creating the dynamic and unstable one we recognize today: upper, middle, and working classes, whose members all share the hope of climbing as far up the

WEALTH IN NEW YORK CITY, 1828–1845

Percent of the Population	Percent of Wealth Held	
	1828	1845
Top 1 percent	40%	50%
Top 4 percent	63	80

The impact of the market revolution on New York City, the nation's largest seaport, is shown by the dramatic increase in wealth of the already wealthy elite in a period of less than 20 years.

social ladder as they can. This social mobility was new, and it fascinated French observer Alexis de Tocqueville: "The first thing that strikes one in the United States is the innumerable crowd of those striving to escape from their original social condition." In the early nineteenth century the upper class remained about the same in size and composition. In the seacoast cities, as the example of Francis Cabot Lowell showed, the elite was a small, intermarried group, so distinctive in its superior cultural style that in Boston its members were nicknamed "Brahmins" (after the highest caste in India). The expanding opportunities of the market revolution enriched this already rich class: by the 1840s, the top 1 percent of the population owned about 40 percent of the nation's wealth. At the other extreme, fully one-third of the population possessed little more than the clothes they wore and some loose change.

The major transformation came in the lives of the "middling sort." As discussed earlier, the market revolution downgraded many independent artisans but elevated others, like Duncan Phyfe and Stephen Allen of New York, who became wealthy businessmen and manufacturers. Other formerly independent artisans or farmers (or more frequently, their children) joined the rapidly growing ranks of managers and white-collar workers such as accountants, bank tellers, clerks, bookkeepers, and insurance agents. Occupational opportunities shifted dramatically in just one generation. In Utica, New York, for example, 16 percent of the city's young men held white-collar jobs in 1855, compared with only 6 percent of their fathers. At the same time, 15 percent fewer younger men filled artisanal occupations than older men.

These new, white-collar workers owed not only their jobs but their lifestyles to the new structure and organization of industry. The new economic order demanded certain habits and attitudes of workers: sobriety, responsibility, steadiness, and hard work. Employers, for their part, were expected to maintain both physical and psychological distance from their workers and to rein in employees' traditional spontaneity and boisterous sociability. Historian Paul Johnson has sketched this change in lifestyle in his study of the city of Rochester: "In 1825 a northern businessman dominated his wife and children, worked irregular hours, consumed enormous amounts of alcohol, and seldom voted or went to church. Ten years later the same man went to church twice a week, treated his family with gentleness and love, drank nothing but water, worked steady hours and forced his employees to do the same." Rochester, a town transformed by the opening of the Erie Canal in 1825, grew from 300 in 1815 to 10,000 in 1830. In this pressure-cooker environment, new middle-class attitudes like that of Johnson's businessman were formed.

The Tea Party *painted by Henry Sargent in 1821 depicts an elegant gathering of what were known as the Boston Brahmins—a small and wealthy group of New England elite. Intermarriage tended to concentrate wealth in this group and to separate them from the "middling sort."*

Religion and Personal Life

Religion, which had undergone dramatic changes since the 1790s, played a key role in the emergence of the new attitudes. The Second Great Awakening (see Chapter 9) had supplanted the orderly and intellectual Puritan religion of early New England. The new evangelistic religious spirit, which stressed the achievement of salvation through personal faith, was more democratic and more enthusiastic than the earlier faith. The old concern with sin survived in dramatic sermons that vividly portrayed hellfire and damnation, but the way to salvation was broader. The concept of original sin, the cornerstone of Puritan belief, was replaced by the optimistic belief that a willingness to be saved was enough to ensure salva-tion. Conversion and repentance were now community experiences, often taking place in huge revival meetings in which an entire congregation focused on the sinners about to be saved. But although continued support from the community was important, the converted bore a heavy personal responsibility to demonstrate their faith in their own daily lives through morally respectable behavior. In this way the new religious feeling fostered individualism and self-discipline.

The Second Great Awakening had its greatest initial success on the western frontier in the 1790s, but by the 1820s evangelical religion was reaching a new audience: the people whose lives were being changed by the market revolution and who needed help in adjusting to the demands made by the new economic conditions. In 1825 in Utica, New York, and other towns along the recently opened Erie Canal, evangelist Charles G. Finney began a series of dramatic revival meetings. His spellbinding message reached both rich and poor, converting members of all classes to the new evangelistic religion. In 1830, made famous by these gatherings, Finney was invited by businessmen to preach in Rochester. Finney preached every day for six months—three times on Sundays—and his wife, Lydia, made home visits to the unconverted and mobilized the women of Rochester for the cause. Under the Finneys' guidance and example, prayer meetings were held in schools and businesses, and impromptu religious services were held in people's homes. As one person recalled, "You could not go upon the streets and hear any conversation, except upon religion."

Evangelism rapidly became the religion of the new middle class. Men soon found that evangelism's stress on self-discipline and individual achievement helped them adjust to new business conditions. Moreover, it gave them a basis for demanding the same behavior from their workers. Businessmen now argued that traditional paternalism had no role in the new business world. Because achievement depended on individual character, each worker was responsible for making his own way.

Master artisans, themselves successful businessmen, often took the lead in reforming the habits of younger workers. Stephen Allen, the New York sailmaker who became mayor, attributed his success to long workdays, avoidance of debt, and "employing the utmost economy in all my concerns." Another New York artisan, master baker Thomas Mercein, took advantage of the opening of the Apprentices' Library, founded by the General Society of Mechanics and Tradesmen in 1820, to preach a similar message. "Cherish, I beseech you, a deep-rooted abhorrence of the alluring but fatal paths of vice and dissipation," Mercein told the apprentices. "Industry, ardour, sobriety, and perseverance in your different pursuits will lead to a successful competition in the world."

The New Middle-Class Family

The market revolution and the new evangelism also affected women's family roles. To begin with, the "softer," more emotional aspects of the new religious approach often especially appealed to women, and it was they who made certain that their families joined them in conversion. And as men increasingly concentrated their energies on their careers and occupations, women assumed major new responsibilities for rearing the children and inculcating in them the new attitudes necessary for success in the business world.

As the work roles of middle-class men and women diverged, so did social attitudes about appropriate male and female characteristics and behavior. Men were expected to be steady, industrious, responsible, and painstakingly attentive to their business. They had little choice: in the competitive, uncertain, and rapidly changing business conditions of the early nineteenth century, these qualities were essential for men who hoped to hold their existing positions or to get ahead. In contrast, women were expected to be nurturing, gentle, kind, moral, and selflessly devoted to their families. They were expected to operate within the "woman's sphere"—the home. Neither this division of responsibilities nor the distinction between men's and women's desirable characteristics and behavior was completely new; they were implicit in much earlier thinking about appropriate gender roles. But now clearly defined gender roles became a matter of social importance.

The unsettling demands of the market revolution forced a dramatic change in family life. When the master craftsman became a small manufacturer, or the small subsistence farmer began to manage a large-scale commercial operation, production moved away from both the family home and its members. Husbands and

fathers became managers of paid workers—or workers themselves—and although they were still considered the heads of their households, they spent most of the day away from their homes and families. The husband was no longer the undisputed head of a family unit that combined work and personal life. Their wives, on the other hand, remained at home, where they were still responsible for cooking, cleaning, and other domestic tasks but no longer contributed directly to what had previously been the family enterprise. Instead, women took on a new responsibility, that of providing a quiet, well-ordered, and relaxing refuge from the pressures of the industrial world. As Utica author John Mather Austin advised in his manual, *A Voice to the Married*, the husband should regard his home as "an elysium to which he can flee and find rest from the stormy strife of a selfish world."

The invention of photography made possible family portraits that earlier were too expensive for all but the wealthiest. This portrait of the Edward Miner Gallaudet family, photographed by Mathew Brady in the 1860s, exhibits the gender differences expected in the middle-class family: strong, self-reliant men and softer, more clinging women.

Women's magazines like Sarah Josepha Hale's *Ladies' Magazine* gave homemakers some help in creating this refuge for their husbands and families, describing "patterns of virtue, of piety, of intelligence and usefulness in private life." By 1850 this magazine, which Hale merged in 1837 with *Godey's Lady's Book*—a magazine that concentrated on fashion—offered 70,000 readers a popular mixture of advice, recipes, and patterns for everything from simple embroidery to ballgowns to "model cottages," as the new suburban ideal middle-class homes were called.

A sure sign that traditional methods were inadequate for new needs was the appearance of housekeeping guides such as Catharine Beecher's book *Treatise on Domestic Economy*. First published in 1841, this book became the standard guide for a generation of middle-class American women. In it, Beecher combined innovative ideas for household design—she introduced important principles of organization for the kitchen in particular—with medical information, child-rearing advice, recipes, and much discussion of the mother's moral role in the family. Beecher's attempt to help women modernize their traditional housekeeping tasks within the context of their newly defined family role clearly filled a need: her book and the Bible were the only books that many pioneer women carried west.

The maintenance or achievement of a middle-class lifestyle required the joint efforts of husband and wife. More cooperation between them was called for than in the preindustrial, patriarchal family. The nature of the new, companionate marriage that evolved in response to the market revolution was reflected most clearly in decisions concerning children.

Family Limitation

Middle-class couples chose to have fewer children than their predecessors. Children who were being raised to succeed in the middle class placed considerable demands on family resources: they required more care, training, and education than children who could be put to work at traditional tasks at an early age. The dramatic fall in the birth rate during the nineteenth century (from an average of seven children per woman in 1800 to four in 1900) is evidence of conscious decisions about family limitation, first by members of the new middle class and later by working-class families. Few couples used mechanical methods of contraception such as the condom, partly because these were difficult to obtain and partly because most people associated their use with prostitution and the prevention of venereal disease rather than with family planning. Instead, people used birth control methods that relied on mutual consent: coitus interruptus (withdrawal before climax), the rhythm method (intercourse only during the woman's infertile period), and, most often, abstinence or infrequent intercourse. Medical manuals suggested that couples consider ending their sex life after they had reached the desired number of children.

When mutual efforts at birth control failed, married women often sought a surgical abortion, a new technique that was much more reliable than the folk remedies women had always shared among themselves. Surgical abortions were widely advertised after 1830, and widely used, especially by middle-class married women seeking to limit family size. Some historians estimate that one out of every four pregnancies was aborted in the years 1840–60 (about the same rate as in 1990). The rising rate of abortion by married women (in other words, its use as birth control) prompted the first legal bans; by 1860, twenty states had outlawed the practice. Even in the absence of accurate statistics, it is clear that dangerous illegal abortions continued, especially among unmarried women who believed they lacked alternatives.

Accompanying the interest in family limitation was a redefinition of sexuality. Doctors generally recommended that sexual urges be controlled, but they believed that men would have much more difficulty exercising such control than women, partly because, they also believed, women were uninterested in sex. (Women who were visibly interested ran the risk of being considered immoral or "fallen," and thereupon shunned by the middle class.) Medical manuals of the period suggested that it was the task of middle-class women to help their husbands and sons restrain their sexuality by appealing to their higher, moral natures. Although it is always difficult to measure the extent to which the suggestions in advice books were applied in actual practice, it seems that many middle-class women accepted this new and limited definition of their sexuality because of their desire to limit the number of pregnancies.

Many women of the late eighteenth century wanted to be free of the medical risks and physical debility that too-frequent childbearing brought, but they had little chance of achieving that goal until men became equally interested in family limitation. The rapid change in attitudes toward family size that occurred in the early nineteenth century has been repeated around the world as other societies undergo the dramatic experience of industrialization. It is a striking example of the ways economic changes affect our most private and personal decisions.

Motherhood

New responsibilities toward children led to another major redefinition of women's roles. Child rearing had been shared in the preindustrial household, boys learning farming or craft skills from their fathers while girls learned domestic skills from their mothers. The children of the new middle class, however, needed a new kind of upbringing, one that involved a long period of nurturing in the beliefs and personal habits necessary for success. Mothers assumed primary responsibility for this training, in part because fathers were too busy but also because people believed that women's superior qualities of gentleness, morality, and loving watchfulness were essential to the task.

Fathers retained a strong role in major decisions concerning children, but mothers commonly turned to other women for advice on daily matters. Through their churches, women formed maternal associations for help in raising their children to be religious and responsible. In Utica, New York, for example, these extremely popular organizations enabled women to form strong networks sustained by mutual advice and by publications such as *Mother's Magazine*, issued by the Presbyterian Church, and *Mother's Monthly Journal*, put out by the Baptists.

Middle-class status required another sharp break with tradition. As late as 1855, artisanal families expected all children over fifteen to work. Middle-class families, on the other hand, sacrificed to keep their sons in school or in training for their chosen professions, and they often housed and fed their sons until the young men had "established" themselves financially and could marry.

Collection of the New York Historical Society

This watercolor, The Happy Home, *illustrates the importance of domesticity for middle class families and the powerful new role for women as they used their moral influence in childrearing.*

Mothers continued to be concerned about their children's character and morality, as women's activities in the great religious revivals of the 1830s showed. They also took the lead in an important informal activity: making sure their children had friends and contacts that would be useful when they were old enough to consider careers and marriage. Matters such as these, rarely considered by earlier generations living in small communities, now became important in the new middle-class communities of America's towns and cities.

Contrary to the growing myth of the self-made man, middle-class success was not a matter of individual achievement. Instead it was usually based on a family strategy in which women's efforts were essential. The reorganization of the family described in this section was successful: from its shelter and support emerged generations of ambitious, responsible, and individualistic middle-class men. But although boys were trained for success, this was not an acceptable goal for their sisters. Women were trained to be the nurturing, silent "support system" that undergirded male success. And women were also expected to ease the tensions of the transition to new middle-class behavior by acting as models and monitors of traditional values.

Sentimentalism

The individualistic competitiveness engendered by the market revolution caused members of the new middle class to place extraordinary emphasis on sincerity and feeling. So-called sentimentalism sprang from nostalgia for the imagined trust and security of the familiar, face-to-face life of the preindustrial village. Sermons, advice manuals, and articles now thundered warnings to young men of the dangers and deceits of urban life, and especially of fraudulent "confidence men and painted ladies" who were not what they seemed. Middle-class women were expected to counteract the impersonality and hypocrisy of the business world by the example of their own morality and sincere feeling.

For guidance in this new role women turned to a new literary form, the sentimental novel. In contrast to older forms like sermons and learned essays, the novel was popular, accessible, and emotionally engrossing. Although denounced by ministers and scholars as frivolous, immoral, and subversive of authority, the novel found a ready audience among American women. Publishers of novels found a lucrative market, one that increased from $2.5 million in 1820 to $12.5 million in 1850. By 1850, *Harper's Magazine* estimated, four-fifths of the reading public were women, and they were reading novels written by women.

To be a "lady novelist" was a new and rather uncomfortably public occupation for women. Several authors, such as Susan Warner, were driven to novel writing when their fathers lost their fortunes in the Panic of 1837. Novel writing could be very profitable: Warner's 1850 novel *The Wide Wide World* went through fourteen editions in two years, and works by other authors such as Lydia Maria Child, Catherine Sedgwick, and E.D.E.N. Southworth sold in the thousands of copies. Sentimental novels concentrated on private life. Religious feeling, antipathy toward the dog-eat-dog world of the commercial economy, and the need to be prepared for unforeseen troubles were common themes. Although the heroines usually married happily at the end of the story, few novels concentrated on romantic love. Most of these domestic novels, as they were known, presented readers with a vision of responsibility and community based on moral and caring family life.

Although sentimentalism originally sprang from genuine fear of the dangers individualism posed to community trust, it rapidly hardened into a rigid code of etiquette for all occasions. Moments of genuine and deep feeling, such as death, were smothered in elaborate rules concerning condolences, expressions of grief, and appropriate clothing. A widow, for example, was expected to wear "deep mourning" for a year—dresses of dull black fabrics and black bonnets covered with long, thick black veils—and in the following year "half mourning"—shiny black silk dresses, perhaps with trim of gray, violet, or white, and hats without veils. Thus sentimentalism rapidly became concerned not with feelings but social codes. Transformed into a set of rules about genteel manners to cover all occasions, sentimentalism itself became a mark of middle-class status. And it became one of the tasks of the middle-class woman to make sure her family conformed to the social code and associated only with other respectable families. In this way, women forged and enforced the distinctive social behavior of the new middle class.

Transcendentalism and Self-Reliance

As the new middle class conformed to the rules of sentimental behavior, it also sought a more general intellectual reassurance. Middle-class men, in particular, needed to feel comfortable about their public assertions of individualism and self-interest. One source of reassurance was the philosophy of transcendentalism and its well-known spokesman, Ralph Waldo Emerson. Originally a Unitarian minister, Emerson quit the pulpit in 1832 and became what one might call a secular minister. Famous as a writer and lecturer, he popularized transcendentalism, a romantic philosophical theory claiming that there was an ideal, intuitive reality transcending ordinary life. The best place to achieve that individual intuition of the Universal Being, Emerson suggested, was not in church or in society but alone in the natural world. As

he wrote in "Nature" (1836), "Standing on the bare ground—my head bathed by the blithe air, and uplifted into infinite space—all mean egotism vanishes. I become a transparent Eyeball; I am nothing; I see all; the currents of the Universal Being circulate through me; I am part and parcel of God." The same assertion of individualism rang through Emerson's stirring polemic "Self-Reliance" (1841). Announcing that "Whoso would be a man, must be a nonconformist," Emerson urged that "Nothing is at last sacred but the integrity of your own mind." Inspirational but down-to-earth, Emerson was just the philosopher to inspire young businessmen of the 1830s and 1840s to achieve success in a responsible manner.

Emerson's younger friend, Henry David Thoreau, pushed the implications of individualism further than the more conventional Emerson. Determined to live the transcendental ideal of association with nature, Thoreau lived in solitude in a primitive cabin for two years at Walden Pond, near Concord, Massachusetts, confronting "the essential facts of life." His experience was the basis for *Walden* (1854), a penetrating criticism of the spiritual cost of the market revolution. Denouncing the materialism that led "the mass of men [to] lead lives of quiet desperation," Thoreau recommended a simple life of subsistence living that left time for spiritual thought. Margaret Fuller, perhaps the most intellectually gifted of the transcendental

Emerson's romantic glorification of nature included the notion of himself as a "transparent eyeball," as he wrote in "Nature" in 1836. A contemporary produced this cartoon.

CHRONOLOGY

1790	Samuel Slater's first mill opens in Rhode Island
1793	Cotton gin invented
1798	Eli Whitney contracts with the federal government for 10,000 rifles, which he undertakes to produce with interchangeable parts
1807	Embargo Act excludes British manufactures
1810	Francis Cabot Lowell tours British textile factories First steamboat on the Ohio River
1812	Micajah Pratt begins his own shoe business in Lynn, Massachusetts
1813	Francis Cabot Lowell raises $300,000 to build his first cotton textile factory at Waltham, Massachusetts
1815	War of 1812 ends; British competition in manufactures resumes
1816	First protective tariff
1820s	Large-scale outwork networks develop in New England
1823	Lowell mills open
1824	John Hall successfully achieves interchangeable parts at Harpers Ferry armory Women lead strike at Pawtucket textile mill
1825	Erie Canal opens
1830	Charles G. Finney's Rochester revivals
1834	First strike at Lowell mills
1836	Ralph Waldo Emerson lecture "Nature" published
1841	Catharine Beecher's *Treatise on Domestic Economy* published
1845	New England Female Labor Reform Association formed
1847	New Hampshire passes first ten-hour-day law

circle, was patronized by Emerson because she was a woman. She expressed her sense of women's wasted potential in her pathbreaking work *Woman in the Nineteenth Century* (1845). Intellectually and emotionally, however, Fuller achieved liberation only when she moved to Europe and participated in the liberal Italian revolution of 1848. The romantic destiny she sought was tragically fulfilled when she, her Italian husband, and their child died in a shipwreck off the New York coast as they returned to America in 1850.

Although Thoreau and Fuller were too radical for many readers, Emerson's version of the romantic philosophy of transcendentalism, seemingly so at odds with the competitive and impersonal spirit of the market revolution, was in fact an essential component of it. Individualism, or, as Emerson called it, self-reliance, was at the heart of the personal transformation required by the market revolution. Sentimentalism, transcendentalism, and evangelical religion all helped the new middle class to forge values and beliefs that were appropriate to their social roles.

CONCLUSION

The market revolution involved three transformations: improvements in transportation, commercialization, and industrialization. Each began at different times. The transportation revolution (discussed in Chapter 10), usually dated from 1825 (the year of the opening of the Erie Canal), accelerated with the building of railroads in the 1830s and 1840s. Commercialization began earlier, around 1805, as a consequence of the reorganization of manufacturing through the putting-out system by northern entrepreneurs. After 1805, the cash purchase of items manufactured elsewhere slowly eroded local barter arrangements. American industrialization began with Samuel Slater's small cotton spinning mill in Rhode Island in 1790, but the most famous early example was the mill town of Lowell, whose factories opened in 1823. These three transformations, taken together, constituted the market revolution that, by changing the ways people worked, changed how they thought.

For most people the changes were gradual. Until midcentury, the lives of rural people were still determined largely by community events, although the spread of democratic politics and the availability of newspapers and other printed material increased their connection to a larger world. Wage earners made up only 40 percent of the working population in 1860, and factory workers made up an even smaller percentage.

The new middle class was most dramatically affected by the market revolution. All aspects of life, including intimate matters of family organization, gender roles, and the number and raising of children, changed. New values—evangelical religion, sentimentalism, and transcendentalism—helped the members of the new middle class in their adjustment. As the next chapter describes, the nation's cities were the first arena where old and new values collided.

REVIEW QUESTIONS

1. What changes in preindustrial life and work were caused by the market revolution?
2. This chapter argues that when people begin doing new kinds of work, their beliefs and attitudes change. Give three examples of such changes described in the chapter. Can you think of other examples?
3. Discuss the opinion offered by historian David Potter that mass production has been an important democratizing force in American politics. Do you agree? Why or why not?
4. Consider the portrait of the nineteenth-century middle-class family offered in this chapter and imagine yourself as a member of such a family. What new aspects of family relations would you welcome? Which would be difficult? Why?

RECOMMENDED READING

Christopher Clark, *The Roots of Rural Capitalism: Western Massachusetts, 1780–1860* (1990). The most thorough examination to date of how the commercial spirit changed rural life.

Alan Dawley, *Class and Community: The Industrial Revolution in Lynn* (1976). A pathbreaking study of the shift from artisanal to wage labor.

Thomas Dublin, *Women at Work: The Transformation of Work and Community in Lowell, Massachusetts, 1826–1860* (1979). A careful look at the female workers of Lowell and their changing conditions.

Thomas Dublin, *Transforming Women's Work: New England Lives in the Industrial Revolution* (1994). A thoughtful study of the effects of women's outwork.

Karen Halttunen, *Confidence Men and Painted Women: A Study of Middle-Class Culture in America* (1982). Explores the development and importance of sentimentalism to the new middle class.

David Houndshell, *From the American System to Mass Production, 1800–1932* (1984). Shows how not only Eli Whitney but an entire network of New England "mechanics" contributed to the invention of interchangeable parts.

Paul Johnson, *A Shopkeeper's Millennium: Society and Revivals in Rochester, New York, 1815–1837* (1978). A study of the changing relationship between masters and workers in Rochester.

Bruce Laurie, *Artisans into Workers: Labor in Nineteenth-Century America* (1989). Using many specific examples, traces the changes in labor described in this chapter.

Jonathan Prude, *The Coming of Industrial Order: Town and Factory Life in Rural Massachusetts, 1810–1860* (1983). A major source of information on family mills.

Steven J. Ross, *Workers on the Edge: Work, Leisure and Politics in Industrializing Cincinnati, 1788–1890* (1985). Studies the growth of wage labor in a major western city.

Mary Ryan, *The Making of the Middle Class* (1981). A study of Utica, New York, that was the first to clearly discern the role of women in the family strategies of the new middle class.

Charles Sellers, *The Market Revolution: Jacksonian America 1815–1846* (1991). A synthesis of the political, religious, and economic change of the period.

Christine Stansell, *City of Women: Sex and Class in New York, 1789–1860* (1983). Exceptionally useful in exploring the range of women's work and the social dynamics of rapidly growing New York City.

ADDITIONAL BIBLIOGRAPHY

The Market Revolution

Thomas C. Cochran, *Frontiers of Change: Early Industrialism in America* (1981)

Robert F. Dalzell Jr., *Enterprising Elite: The Boston Associates and the World They Made* (1987)

L. C. Hunter, *A History of Industrial Power in the United States, 1780–1930*, vol. 1: *Waterpower in the Century of the Steam Engine* (1979)

David J. Jeremy, *Transatlantic Industrial Revolution: The Diffusion of Textile Technology between Britain and America* (1981)

Benjamin W. Labaree, *Patriots and Partisans, The Merchants of Newburyport, 1764–1815* (1962)

Walter Licht, *Industrializing America: The Nineteenth Century* (1995)

Diane Linstrom, *Economic Development in the Philadelphia Region, 1810–1850* (1978)

Merritt R. Smith, *Harpers Ferry Armory and the New Technology* (1977)

Barbara Tucker, *Samuel Slater and the Origins of the American Textile Industry, 1790–1860* (1984)

Caroline F. Ware, *Early New England Cotton Manufacturing* (1931)

From Artisan to Worker

Mary H. Blewett, *Men, Women, and Work: Class, Gender, and Protest in the New England Shoe Industry, 1780–1910* (1988)

John L. Brooke, *The Heart of the Commonwealth: Society and Political Culture in Worcester County, Massachusetts, 1713–1861* (1989)

Robert Doherty, *Society and Power: Five New England Towns, 1800–1860* (1977)

Paul G. Faler, *Mechanics and Manufacturers in the Early Industrial Revolution: Lynn, Massachusetts* (1981)

Michael H. Glickstein, *Concepts of Free Labor in Antebellum America* (1991)

Susan E. Hirsch, *Roots of the American Working Class: The Industrialization of Crafts in Newark, 1800–1860* (1978)

Joan M. Jensen, *Loosening the Bonds: Mid-Atlantic Farm Women, 1750–1850* (1986)

Jack Larkin, *The Reshaping of Everyday Life, 1790–1840* (1988)

Bruce Laurie, *Working People of Philadelphia, 1800–1850* (1980)

Scott C. Martin, *Killing Time: Leisure and Culture in Southwestern Pennsylvania, 1800–1850* (1995)

Howard Rock, *Artisans of the New Republic: Tradesmen of New York City in the Age of Jefferson* (1979)

W. J. Rorabaugh, *The Craft Apprentice: From Franklin to the Machine Age in America* (1986)

Charles G. Steffan, *The Mechanics of Baltimore: Workers and Politics in the Age of Revolution, 1763–1812* (1984)

A New Social Order

Jeanne Boydston, *Home and Work* (1990)

Nancy E. Cott, *The Bonds of Womanhood: "Woman's Sphere" in New England, 1780–1835* (1977)

Betty G. Farrell, *Elite Families: Class and Power in Nineteenth Century Boston* (1993)

Clyde Griffen and Sally Griffen, *Natives and Newcomers: The Ordering of Opportunity in Mid-Nineteenth-Century Poughkeepsie* (1978)

James C. Mohr, *Abortion in America: The Origins and Evolution of National Policy, 1800–1900* (1978)

Edward Pessen, *Riches, Class, and Power before the Civil War* (1973)

James Reed, *From Private Vice to Public Virtue: The Birth Control Movement and American Society since 1830* (1978)

Anthony F. C. Wallace, *Rockdale: The Growth of an American Village in the Early Industrial Revolution* (1977)

Middle-Class Culture

Barbara A. Bardes and Suzanne Gossett, *Declarations of Independence: Women and Political Power in Nineteenth-Century American Fiction* (1990)

Nina Baym, *Woman's Fiction: A Guide to Novels by and about Women in America* (1978)

———, *Feminism and American Literary History* (1992)

Paul F. Boller, *American Transcendentalism, 1830–1860* (1974)

John F. Kasson, *Rudeness and Civility: Manners in Nineteenth-Century America* (1990)

Mary Kelley, *Private Women, Public Stage: Literary Domesticity in Nineteenth-Century America* (1984)

F. O. Matthiessen, *American Renaissance* (1941)

Walter Benn Michaels and Donald E. Pease, eds., *The American Renaissance Reconsidered* (1985)

Leonard Neufeldt, *The Economist: Henry Thoreau and Enterprise* (1989)

Russell Nye, *Society and Culture in America, 1830–1860* (1974)

Lewis Perry, *Intellectual Life in America* (1984)

Ann Rose, *Transcendentalism as a Social Movement* (1981)

Shirley Samuels, ed., *The Culture of Sentiment: Race, Gender, and Sentimentality in Nineteenth-Century America* (1992)

Jane Tompkins, *Sensational Designs: The Cultural World of American Fiction, 1790–1860* (1986)

Joyce W. Warren, *The (Other) American Traditions: Nineteenth-Century Women Writers* (1993)

Biography

Paul Blanchard, *Margaret Fuller: From Transcendentalism to Revolution* (1978)

Walter Harding, *Thoreau: Man of Concord* (1960)

Joel Porte, *Representative Man: Ralph Waldo Emerson in His Time* (1979)

R. D. Richardson Jr., *Henry Thoreau: A Life of the Mind* (1986)

CHAPTER THIRTEEN

COMING TO TERMS
WITH THE NEW AGE

1820s–1850s

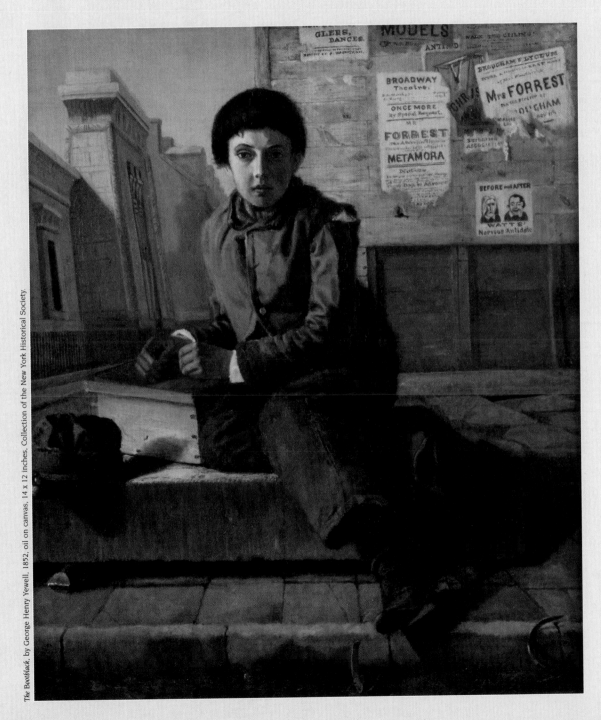

The Bootblack, by George Henry Yewell, 1852, oil on canvas, 14 x 12 inches. Collection of the New York Historical Society.

AMERICAN COMMUNITIES
Seneca Falls: Women Reformers Respond to the Market Revolution

In the summer of 1848, a small advertisement appeared in an upstate New York newspaper announcing a "convention to discuss the social, civil, and religious condition and rights of woman," to be held at Seneca Falls on the 19th and 20th of July.

Charlotte Woodward, a nineteen-year-old glove maker who did outwork in her rural home, saw the advertisement and persuaded six friends to join her in the 40-mile journey to the convention. "At first we travelled quite alone," she recalled. "But before we had gone many miles we came on other wagon-loads of women, bound in the same direction. As we reached different crossroads we saw wagons coming from every part of the country, and long before we reached Seneca Falls we were a procession."

To the surprise of the convention organizers, almost 300 people—men as well as women—attended the two-day meeting. The focus of their discussions was the Declaration of Sentiments, a petition for women's rights modeled on the Declaration of Independence. "We hold these truths to be self-evident," it announced: "That all men and women are created equal." As the Declaration of Independence detailed the oppressions King George III had imposed on the colonists, the Declaration of Sentiments detailed, in a series of resolutions, the oppressions men had imposed on women. Men had deprived women of legal rights, of the right to own their own property, of custody of their children in cases of divorce, of the right to higher education (at that time only Oberlin College and Mount Holyoke Female Seminary admitted women), of full participation in religious worship and activity, and of the right to vote. After discussion, the attendees approved all the resolutions, and all but the last of them, which a minority found too radical, unanimously. "Why Lizzie, thee will make us ridiculous!" Quaker Lucretia Mott had exclaimed when Elizabeth Cady Stanton proposed the voting rights measure. Indeed the newspapers reporting on the convention thought the demand for the vote was ridiculously unfeminine. But the group that assembled in Seneca Falls was undeterred. Buoyed by the success of this first women's rights convention, they promptly planned another one three weeks later in New York's largest upstate city, Rochester, to reach new supporters and to develop strategies to implement their resolutions.

The fight for women's rights was only one of many reform movements that emerged in the United States in the wake of the economic and social disruptions of the market revolution. The Seneca Falls region was itself deeply affected by that revolution. A farming frontier in 1800, it had been drawn into national commerce in 1828 when it was reached by an offshoot of the Erie Canal. It was drawn even further into the modern age when the railroad arrived in 1841. A village of 200 in 1824, Seneca Falls had grown to a town of over 4,000 by 1842. It was now a center for flour milling (in 1845, the nine mills in the town produced a total of 2,000 barrels of flour a day) and manufacturing, and a hub of the outwork network of which Charlotte Woodward was a part. Swamped by newcomers (among them a growing number of poor Irish Catholics), the inhabitants of Seneca Falls struggled to maintain a sense of community. They formed volunteer organizations of all kinds—religious, civic, social, educational, recreational. And they became active participants in reform movements seeking to counteract the effects of industrialization, rapid growth, and the influx of newcomers.

Many reformers belonged to liberal religious groups with wide social perspectives. Perhaps a third of those attending the women's rights convention, for example, were members of the Wesleyan Methodist Society of Seneca Falls, which had broken with the national Methodist organization because it would not take a strong stand against slavery. Another quarter were Progressive Quakers of the nearby town of Waterloo, who had broken with their national organization for the same reason. Both groups were outspoken in their belief in the moral equality of all humankind and in their commitment to social activism. The Wesleyans, for example, resolved in 1847 that "we cannot identify our Christian and moral character with societies where women and colored persons are excluded." Seneca Falls had been the site of a "Temperance Reformation" in the early 1840s, and many attendees at the Women's Rights convention were also active in the temperance movement, a more limited but extremely popular reform cause dedicated to promoting abstinence from alcohol.

The idea for the Women's Rights convention emerged during a meeting in early July, 1848, between Lucretia Mott—a Philadelphia Quaker and the nation's best-known woman reformer—and Elizabeth Cady Stanton of Seneca Falls, wife of a well-known antislavery orator and niece of a leading reform philanthropist. Reflecting her many concerns, Mott had just finished a tour of the new penitentiary at Auburn and a nearby Indian reservation and was visiting her sister in Waterloo. Stanton called for tea to renew her acquaintance with Mott, and it was in this context of friendship and shared concern for reform that the two began planning the convention that was held two weeks later.

Stanton and her family had moved from Boston, where, she remembered, they had "near neighbors, a new home with all the modern conveniences, and well-trained servants." Living in a house on the outskirts of Seneca Falls, her three children suffering from malaria, she had none of those things. "I now fully understood," she mused,

> the practical difficulties most women had to contend with....The general discontent I felt with woman's portion as wife, mother, housekeeper, physician and spiritual guide, the chaotic conditions into which everything fell without her constant supervision, and the wearied anxious look of the majority of women impressed me with a strong feeling that some active measures should be taken to remedy the wrongs of society in general, and of women in particular.

As she and Mott spoke of the changes that would be necessary to allow women to care for their families but have energy left over to reform "the wrongs of society," the idea of a women's rights convention was born. The women's rights movement that took shape from this convention proved exceptionally long-lasting. Stanton, soon to form a working partnership with former temperance worker Susan B. Anthony, devoted the rest of her life to women's rights.

But what of Charlotte Woodward, a local farm girl, unaware of the national reform community? Why was she there? In this age of hopefulness and change she wanted a better life for herself. She was motivated, she said, by "all the hours that I sat and sewed gloves for a miserable pittance, which, after it was earned, could never be mine." By law and custom her father, as head of the household, was entitled to her wages. "I wanted to work," she explained, "but I wanted to choose my task and I wanted to collect my wages." The reforming women of Seneca Falls, grouped together on behalf of social improvement, had found in the first women's rights convention a way to speak for the needs of working women such as Charlotte Woodward

All over the North, in communities like Seneca Falls as well as in cities like New York, Americans gathered together in reform organizations to try to solve the problems that the market revolution posed for work, family life, personal and social values, and urban growth. Through these organizations local women and men became participants in wider communities of concern.

Seneca Falls

KEY TOPICS

- The new social problems that accompanied urbanization and immigration

- The responses of reformers

- The origins and political effects of the abolitionist movement

- The involvement of women in reform efforts

URBAN AMERICA

Although the market revolution affected all aspects of American life, nowhere was its impact so noticeable as in the cities. It was within the urban environment, with its stimulating, frightening confusion of rapid physical growth, occupational and ethnic change, and economic competition, that new American political and social forms began to emerge.

The Preindustrial City

The preindustrial cities of eighteenth-century America were small and compact. They were "walking cities," in which people mostly got around on foot. Philadelphia, for example, which had been laid out by William Penn himself in 1682, was an orderly grid of streets bordered by neat row houses in a dense, small-scale housing pattern that fostered neighborliness.

In these cities, rich and poor lived side by side. Merchants lived next door to their businesses, and in the busy streets and public places they daily rubbed elbows with their employees and with artisans and laborers. The wealthy enjoyed unquestioned authority. Merchants sat on the city council, which had broad powers to regulate the public markets, to set prices for basic foodstuffs, to grant licenses to artisans and traders, and to encourage community harmony. The same wealthy men organized charity and relief for the poor in hard times, often walking door to door in their neighborhood to solicit donations. Wealthy men were active in neighborhood volunteer fire departments and in the volunteer watch societies that prevented crime and kept neighborhood order. When larger disturbances such as bread riots broke out, the mayor and other city officials were expected to appear and disperse the mob by force of their own authority.

The Growth of Cities

The market revolution dramatically increased the size of America's cities, with the great seaports leading the way. The proportion of America's population living in cities increased from only 7 percent in 1820 to almost 20 percent in 1860, a rate of growth greater than at any other time in the country's history.

The nation's five largest cities in 1850 were the same as in 1800, with one exception. New York, Philadelphia, Baltimore, and Boston still topped the list, but New Orleans had edged out Charleston (see Chapter 9). The rate of urban growth was extraordinary. All four Atlantic seaports grew at least 25 percent each decade between 1800 and 1860, and often much more. New York, which grew from 60,000 in 1800 to 202,600 in 1830 and to more than 1 million in 1860, emerged as the nation's most populous city, its largest port, and its financial center. Between 1820 and 1830, the decade in which the Erie Canal added commerce with the American interior to the city's long-standing role in international trade, New York's population grew 64 percent.

Philadelphia, which had been the nation's largest city in 1800, was half the size of New York in 1850. Nevertheless, its growth was substantial—from 70,000 in 1800 to 389,000 in 1850 and to 565,529 in 1860. Philadelphia became as much an industrial as a commercial city. Old artisanal industries such as handloom weaving, tailoring, and shoe manufacture coexisted with new industries such as the huge Baldwin locomotive works, foundries, and chemical companies.

Baltimore, with 212,418 residents in 1860 was about half the size of Philadelphia. The city's merchants, hoping to counter the threat posed by the Erie Canal to their trade links with the trans-Appalachian West, financed the nation's first important railroad, the Baltimore and Ohio, which began operation in 1830. Although Baltimore remained the east coast center of the tobacco trade with Europe, by 1850 its major partner in foreign trade was Brazil, to which it shipped flour and from which it imported coffee.

Boston, in colonial times, had dominated the triangular trade linking Britain and the West Indies. By 1860, with a population of 177,840, the city had emerged as the center of a new triangular trade: the ships of Boston merchants carried New England cotton cloth, shoes, and other manufactured goods to the South, delivered southern cotton to British and European ports, and returned to Boston with European manufactured goods. Boston still dominated the China trade as well.

New Orleans, fed by the expansion of cotton throughout the South and commercial agriculture in the Mississippi Valley, had a population of 168,675 in 1860. In the 1850s, New Orleans handled about half the nation's cotton exports and by 1860, its exports—$5 million in 1815—had risen to $107 million.

The market revolution oriented the attention of each of these major seaports away from the oceans and toward trade with the nation's interior. Prosperous merchants in these cities now depended on American exports rather than European imports for their profits.

Another result of the market revolution was the appearance of "instant" cities at critical points on the new transportation network. Utica, New York, once a frontier trading post, was transformed by the opening of the Erie Canal into a commercial and manufacturing center. By 1850 the city's population had reached 22,000. Chicago, on the shores of Lake Michigan, was transformed by the coming of the railroad into a major junction for water and rail transport. The city, which emerged as a fur trading center around Fort Dearborn, an army post built in 1803, had become, by the 1850s, a hub of trade boasting grain storage facilities, slaughterhouses, and warehouses of all kinds. Farm implement manufacturers such as Cyrus McCormick built manufacturing plants there to serve the needs of Midwest farmers. By 1860 Chicago had a population of 100,000, making it the nation's eighth largest city (after Cincinnati and St. Louis).

Patterns of Immigration

One of the key aspects of urban growth was a surge in immigration to the United States that began in the 1820s and accelerated dramatically after 1830 (see "Immigration and Community: The Changing Face of Ethnicity in the United States, 1800–1860," on page 380). From an annual figure of about 20,000 in 1831, immigration ballooned to a record 430,000 in 1854 before declining in the years prior to the Civil War. The proportion of immigrants in the population jumped from 1.6 percent in the 1820s to 11.2 percent in 1860. In the nation's cities the proportion was vastly larger: by 1860, nearly half of New York's population (48 percent) was foreign-born.

Most of the immigrants to the United States during this period came from Ireland and Germany. Political unrest and poor economic conditions in Germany and the catastrophic Potato Famine of 1845–1850 in Ireland was responsible for an enormous surge in immigration from those countries between 1845 and 1854. The starving, desperate "Famine Irish" who crowded into eastern seaports were America's first large refugee group. Between them, the Germans and the Irish represented the largest influx of non-English immigrants the country had known (many Americans found the Irish dialect as strange as a foreign language). They were also the poorest: most of the Irish arrived destitute. In addition most of the Irish and half of the Germans were Catholics, an unwelcome novelty to many Protestant Americans.

Many German immigrants made their way to agricultural communities in Ohio, Indiana, Missouri, and Texas, but many others, and most Irish immigrants, settled in America's major cities. Few immigrants found life in the United States pleasant or easy. In addition to the psychological difficulties of leaving a home and familiar ways behind, most immigrants endured harsh living and working conditions. One common immigrant response was to construct ethnic neighborhoods and communities for mutual support. For their inhabitants, these Irish and German neighborhoods were a positive response that eased the difficulties of adaptation to American circumstances. But native-born Americans, unprepared for the "foreignness" and poverty of many new immigrants, reacted with hostility to immigrant clustering, and indeed, to the immigrants themselves. Because the immigrant influx widened the social gap between rich and poor and dramatically altered living patterns, immigration contributed to the social problems that America's urban centers faced—and were unable to solve—in the early nineteenth century.

Class Structure in the Cities

Although per capita income in America is estimated to have doubled between 1800 and 1850, the gap between rich and poor increased and became glaringly apparent in the nation's cities. The benefits of the market revolution were unequally distributed: by the 1840s the top 1 percent of the population owned about 40 percent of the nation's wealth, while, at the other extreme, one-third of the population owned virtually nothing. In the cities, then, there was a very small group of wealthy people worth more than $5,000 (about 3 percent of the population), a very large group of poor people worth $100 or less (nearly 70 percent), and a middle class with incomes in between (25–30 percent).

Differences in income affected every aspect of urban life. Very poor families, including almost all new immigrants, performed unskilled labor in jobs whose future was uncertain at best, lived in cheap rented housing, moved frequently, and depended on more than one income to survive. Artisans and skilled workers with incomes of $500 or more could live adequately, though often in cramped quarters that also served as their shops. A middle-class family with an income of more than $1,000 a year could live comfortably in a house of four to six rooms complete with carpeting, wallpaper, and good furniture. The very rich

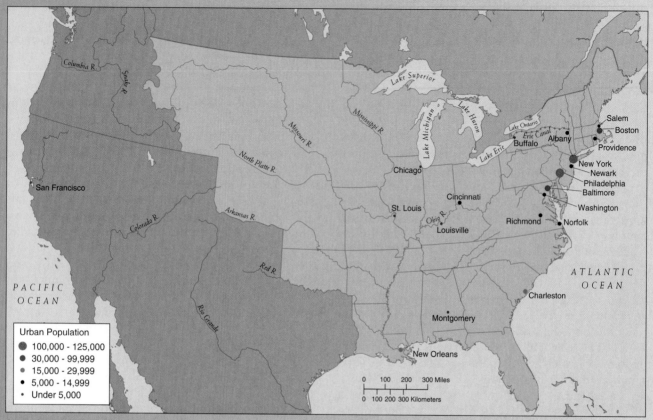

American Cities, 1820

Source: *Statistical Abstract of the United States*

The Growth of Cities, 1820–1860

The cities of North America grew more rapidly between 1820 and 1860 than at any other time in the nation's history. Eastern seaport cities remained the largest, but New York grew to twice the size of the second largest city, Philadelphia. New York's growth, due in large part to the increase in trade following the opening of the Erie Canal, illustrates

built mansions and large town houses and staffed them with many servants. In the summer they left the cities for country estates or homes at seaside resorts such as Newport, Rhode Island, which attracted wealthy families from all over the country.

Sanitation and Living Patterns

Early-nineteenth-century cities lacked municipal water supplies, sewers, and garbage collection. People drank water from wells, used outdoor privies that often contaminated the water supply, and threw garbage and slop out the door to be foraged by roaming herds of pigs. Clearly, this was a recipe for disease, and every American city suffered epidemics of sanitation-related diseases such as yellow fever, cholera, and typhus. Philadelphia's yellow fever epidemic of 1793 caused 4,000 deaths and stopped all business with the outside world for more than a month.

Yet the cities were slow to take action. In response to the yellow fever epidemic Philadelphia completed a city water system in 1801, but users had to pay a fee, and only the richest subscribed in the early days. Neither New York nor Boston had a public water system until the 1840s. Garbage collection remained a private service, and cities charged property owners for the costs of sewers, water mains, and street paving. Poorer areas of the cities could not afford the costs.

Provision of municipal services forced residential segregation. Richer people clustered in neighborhoods that had the new amenities. One of New York's first wealthy areas, Gramercy Park, was developed in 1831 by a speculator who transformed what had been Gramercy Farm into "an ornamental private square or park, with carriageways and footwalks." Only purchasers of the surrounding lots had keys to the park; everyone else was

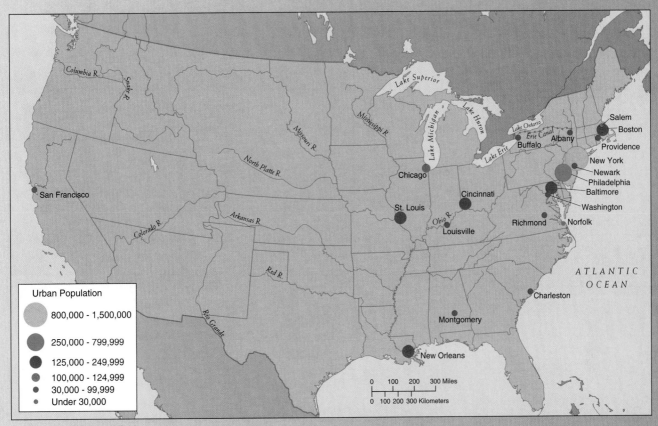

American Cities, 1860

Source: *Statistical Abstract of the United States*

Urban Population

- 800,000 – 1,500,000
- 250,000 – 799,999
- 125,000 – 249,999
- 100,000 – 124,999
- 30,000 – 99,999
- Under 30,000

the importance of trade between port cities and the nation's interior. Inland river cities like Cincinnati and St. Louis and the great Mississippi seaport of New Orleans grew rapidly. San Francisco, Louisville, and Buffalo—still villages in 1820—grew also, but Chicago, which rapidly emerged as a hub for both water and rail transport, surpassed them all.

excluded. By the 1850s the middle class began to escape cities completely by moving to the new "streetcar suburbs," named for the new mode of urban transportation that connected these nearby areas to the city itself.

As the middle class left the city, the poor clustered in bad neighborhoods that became known as slums. The worst New York slum in the nineteenth century was Five Points, a stone's throw from city hall. There immigrants, free black people, and criminals were crammed into rundown buildings known in the slang of the time as "rookeries." Notorious gangs of thieves and pickpockets with names such as the Plug Uglies and the Shirt Tails dominated the district. Starvation and murder were commonplace.

Five Points was grim even in comparison with the notorious slums of London. As knowledgeable an Englishman as the author Charles Dickens exclaimed on a visit to the district in 1842, "All that is loathsome, drooping and decayed is here...Where dogs would howl to lie, women, and men and boys slink off to sleep, forcing the dislodged rats to move away in quest of better lodgings." With the influx of European immigrants after 1830, middle-class Americans increasingly saw slums as the home of strange and foreign people, who deserved less than American-born citizens. In this way, residential patterns came to embody larger issues of class and citizenship.

Ethnic Neighborhoods

To poverty-stricken Irish immigrants, these same slums represented not only family ties and familiar ways but community support as they learned how to survive in new surroundings. Isolated partly by their own beliefs (for Catholics fully reciprocated the hatred and fear

The Five Points neighborhood in lower Manhattan illustrates the segregated housing patterns that emerged as New York City experienced rapid growth. Immigrants, free African Americans, the poor and criminals were crowded together in New York's most notorious slum, while wealthier people moved to more prosperous neighborhoods.

Protestants showed them), Irish immigrants created their own communities in Boston and New York, their major destinations. They raised the money to erect Catholic churches with Irish priests. They established parochial schools with Irish nuns as teachers and sent their children to them in preference to the openly anti-Catholic public schools. They formed mutual aid societies based on kinship or town of origin in Ireland. Men and women formed religious and social clubs, lodges, and brotherhoods and their female auxiliaries. Irishmen manned fire and militia companies as well. This dense network of associations served the same purpose that social welfare organizations do today: providing help in time of need and offering companionship in a hostile environment.

Germans who settled in urban areas also built their own ethnic enclaves—"Little Germanies"—in which they sought to duplicate the rich cultural life of German cities. In general, German immigrants were skilled workers and not as poor as the Irish. Like the Irish, however, the Germans formed church societies, mutual benefit societies, and fire and militia companies to provide mutual support. Partly because their communities were more prosperous than those of the Irish, the Germans also formed a network of leisure organizations: singing societies, debating and political clubs, concert

halls like New York's Beethoven Hall, theaters, *turnvereins* (gymnastics associations), and beer gardens. They published German-language newspapers as well.

Ethnic clustering, then, allowed new immigrants to hold onto aspects of their culture that they valued and to transplant them to American soil. Many native-born Americans, however, viewed ethnic neighborhoods with deep suspicion. The Boston *American* expressed the sentiments of many in 1837 when it remarked:

> our foreign population are too much in the habit of retaining their own national usages, of *associating too* exclusively *with each other*, and living in groups together. *It would be the part of wisdom, to ABANDON AT ONCE ALL USAGES AND ASSOCIATIONS WHICH MARK THEM AS FOREIGNERS, and to become in feeling and custom, as well as in privileges and rights, citizens of the United States.*

Urban Popular Culture

The size, diversity, and changing working conditions in American cities bred a new urban popular culture with New York, the largest city, leading the way. In the period 1820–60, urban workers experienced the replacement of artisanal labor by wagework, two serious depressions (1837–43 and 1857), and vastly increased competition from immigrant labor. In response to these pressures, working-class amusements became rougher and rowdier. Taverns that served as neighborhood centers of drink and sociability were also frequent centers of brawls and riots. Community groups such as fire engine companies that had once included men of all social classes now attracted rough young laborers who formed their own youth gangs and defended "their" turf against other gangs. Some trades, such as that of butcher, became notorious for starting fights in taverns and grog shops.

Theaters, which had been frequented by men of all social classes, provided another setting for violence. Few women, except for the prostitutes who met their customers in the third tier of the balcony, attended. In the 1820s, a long-standing tradition of small-scale rioting by poorer patrons against unpopular actors began to change into more serious violence. The Astor Place Riot of 1849 began as a theater riot against a British actor but escalated into a pitched battle between the mob and the militia that left twenty-two dead.

By the 1830s, middle-class and upper-class men withdrew to more respectable theaters to which they could bring their wives and daughters. Workers found new amusements in theaters such as the Lafayette Circus that featured dancing girls and horseback riders as well as theatrical acts. Another popular urban working-class amusement was the blackface minstrel show. White actors (often Irish) blacked their faces and entertained audiences with songs (including the famous "Dixie," written by an Irishman as a blackface song), dances, theatrical skits, and antiblack political jokes. Cruel stereotypes such as Zip Coon, an irresponsible free black man, and Jim Crow, a slow-witted slave, entertained white audiences. Historians have speculated that the popularity of blackface expressed not only white racism but also nostalgia for the freer behavior of preindustrial life that was now impossible for white workers but that

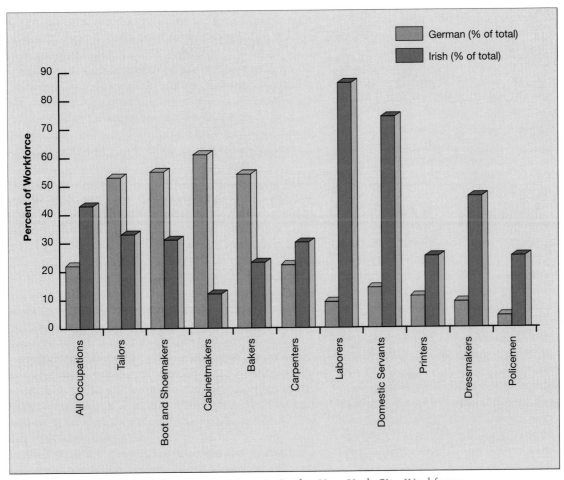

Participation of Irish and German Immigrants in the New York City Workforce for Selected Occupations, 1855

Source: Robert Ernst, *Immigrant Life in New York City* 1825-1863 (Syracuse: Syracuse University Press, 1994).

they imagined African American slaves continued to enjoy in carefree dependency.

The new working-class culture flourished especially on the Bowery, a New York City street filled with artisanal workshops, small factories, shops with cheap goods, dance halls, theaters, ice cream parlors, and oyster bars. Here working-class youth, the "Bowery b'hoys" (slang pronunciation of "boy") and "gals," found Saturday night amusements and provided it for themselves with outrageous clothing and behavior. The deliberately provocative way they dressed was in effect a way of thumbing their noses at the more respectable classes. The costumes worn by the characters in one long-running series of melodramas staged by the Bowery Theater imitated this style. Mose, the hero of the series, dressed more like a pirate captain

This 1848 playbill promotes A Glance at New York, *which featured two well-known working-class figures, Mose, the Bowery B'hoy, and his gal, Lise. His exaggerated clothing and hairstyle and her flashy colors were deliberate parodies aimed at New York's respectable middle class for the benefit of the rowdy working-class culture that grew up in the Bowery district of the city in the 1830s.*

than a worker, and his gal Lise wore a bright-colored, body-hugging dress that challenged the discreet, sober fashions worn by middle-class women.

Another challenge to middle-class respectability came from the immensely popular "penny papers" (so called from their price), the *New York Morning Post* and the *New York Sun*, which began appearing in 1833. These papers, with lurid headlines such as "Double Suicide," and "Secret Tryst," and "Bloody Murder," fed the same popular appetite for scandal, as did other popular reading such as the *Police Gazette* magazine, pamphlets about murder trials, swindlers, and pirates, and temperance dime novels such as *Franklin Evans; or, The Inebriate* written in 1842 by the struggling young newspaperman, Walter (later Walt) Whitman. Urban journalist, Democratic Party activist, and poet, Whitman distilled his passionate love for the variety and commonness of the American people in *Leaves of Grass*, a book of free-verse poems published in 1855. Regarded at the time as scandalous because of its frank language, Whitman's poetry nevertheless captured the driving energy and democratic spirit of the new urban popular culture. In a rather more sinister way, so did the writings of Edgar Allan Poe, who found the inspiration for his gothic horror stories such as "The Murders in the Rue Morgue" (1841) and "The Mystery of Marie Roget" (1842) not in Europe (as his titles might suggest) but in contemporary American crimes.

This fascination with urban violence led one observer to comment cynically in 1859 that "No narrative of human depravity or crime can shock or horrify an American reader." But Alexis de Tocqueville, the famous French observer who visited the United States in 1831–32 wrote with foreboding, "I look upon the size of certain American cities, and especially on the nature of their population, as a real danger." Here was an expression of a new fear in American urban life—concern about civic order.

Civic Order

Tocqueville's fears for civic order echoed that of the urban middle class, who now found menacing even traditions of lower-class amusement that dated back to colonial times. New York City's tradition of New Year's Eve "frolics," in which laborers, apprentices, and other members of the lower classes paraded through the streets playing drums, trumpets, whistles, and other noisemakers, was an example. By the 1820s the revelry had been taken over by gangs of young workers from the lower classes who called themselves the Callithumpian Band. On New Year's Eve 1828, the band, 4,000 strong and equipped with drums, tin kettles, rattles, horns, and whistles, marched through the city. On their way they overturned carts and broke windows in the commercial district, in some wealthy homes, near Battery Park, and in an African American church. They then marched to the City Hotel, where middle-class couples were just leaving a ball, and obstructed traffic. The indignant couples watched helplessly as several hundred watchmen called to disperse the mob cautiously declined to do so. In the following year, the traditional New Year's Eve parade was banned by the city government.

The prosperous classes were frightened by the urban poor and by working-class rowdyism. They resented having to avoid many parts of the city that were unsafe for them, and they disliked even more the disturbances in "their" parts of the city, as this irritable notation in the diary of merchant Philip Hone indicates: "Riot, disorder, and violence increase in our city, every night is marked by some outrage committed by gangs of young ruffians who prowl the streets insulting females, breaking into the houses of unoffending publicans [tavern keepers], making night hideous by yells of disgusting inebriety, and—unchecked by the city authorities—committing every sort of enormity with apparent impunity."

In colonial days, civic disturbances had been handled informally: members of the city watch asked onlookers for such assistance as was necessary to keep the peace. New York City's first response in the 1820s and 1830s to increasing civic disorder was to hire more city watchmen and to augment them with constables and marshals. When riots occurred, the militia were called, and deaths were increasingly common as they forcibly restrained mobs. Finally, in 1845, the city created a permanent police force with a mandate to keep the poor in order. There had been substantial opposition to the idea of this first professional police force in the United States on the grounds that it infringed personal liberty, but as middle-class fear of what became known as "the dangerous classes" grew, police protection came to seem necessary. Here was an indication that the harmonious preindustrial urban community no longer existed.

But even with police forces in place, the pressures of rapid urbanization, immigration, and the market revolution proved to be more than America's cities could contain. The violence was more than just rowdyism and socially disapproved behavior. Beginning in the 1830s, a series of urban riots broke out against the two poorest urban groups: Catholics and free black people. As if their miserable living conditions were not enough, Irish immigrants were met with virulent anti-Catholicism. In 1834 rioters burned an Ursuline convent in Charlestown, Massachusetts; in 1844 a Philadelphia mob attacked priests and nuns and vandalized Catholic churches; in 1854 a mob destroyed an Irish neighborhood in Lawrence, Massachusetts. Often the Irish replied in kind—for

example, in the 1806 riot in New York when they counterattacked a mob that disrupted their Christmas Eve mass in a Catholic church on Augustus Street. But the most common targets of urban violence were free African Americans.

Urban Life of Free African Americans

By 1860, there were nearly half a million free African Americans in the United States, constituting about 11 percent of the country's total black population. More than half of all free African Americans lived in the North, mostly in cities, where they competed with immigrants and native-born poor white people for jobs as day laborers and domestic servants. Their relative social position is reflected in statistics on per capita annual income in Boston in the 1850s—$91 for black people and $131 for Irish immigrants compared to $872 for the population at large. Philadelphia and New York had the largest black communities: 22,000 African Americans in Philadelphia and 12,500 in New York (another 4,313 lived just across the East River in Brooklyn). There were much smaller but still significant black communities in the New England cities of Boston, Providence, and New Haven and in Ohio cities like Cincinnati.

Free African Americans in northern cities faced residential segregation (except for the domestic servants who lived in with white families), pervasive job discrimination, segregated public schools, and severe limitations on their civil rights. In addition to these legal restrictions there were matters of custom: African Americans of all economic classes endured daily affronts, such as exclusion from public concerts, lectures, and libraries and segregation or exclusion from public transportation. For example, in Massachusetts—which had the reputation of being more hospitable to black people than any other northern state—the famed African American abolitionist Frederick Douglass was denied admission to a zoo on Boston Common, a public lecture and revival meeting, a restaurant, and a public omnibus, all within the space of a few days.

In common with Irish and German immigrants, African Americans created defenses against the larger hostile society by building their own community structures. They formed associations for aiding the poorest members of the community, for self-improvement, and for socializing. Tired of being insulted by the white press, African American communities supported their own newspapers. The major community organization was the black Baptist or African Methodist Episcopal (AME) church, which served, as one historian put it, as "a place of worship, a social and cultural center, a political meeting place, a hiding place for fugitives, a training ground for potential community leaders, and one of the few places where blacks could express their true feelings."

Free African Americans suffered many forms of discrimination, but as this 1850 daguerreotype of an unknown woman shows, they sought to achieve the same levels of education and economic comfort as other Americans.

Employment prospects for black men deteriorated from 1820 to 1850. Those who had held jobs as skilled artisans were forced from their positions, and their sons denied apprenticeships, by white mechanics and craftsmen who were themselves suffering from the effects of the market revolution. Limited to day labor, African Americans found themselves in direct competition with the new immigrants, especially the Irish, for jobs. On the waterfront, black men lost their jobs as carters and longshoremen to the Irish. One of the few occupations to remain open to them was that of seaman. More than 20 percent of all American sailors in 1850 were black, and over the years their ranks included an increasing number of runaway slaves. The pay was poor and the conditions miserable, but many black men found more equality aboard ship than they did ashore. Mothers, wives, and daughters were left ashore to work as domestic servants (in competition with Irishwomen), washerwomen, and seamstresses.

Free African Americans remained committed to their enslaved brethren in the South. In New York, for example, black communities rioted four times—in 1801, 1819, 1826, and 1832—against slave catchers taking escaped slaves back to slavery. But even more frequently, free African Americans were themselves

targets of urban violence. An 1829 riot in Cincinnati sent a thousand black people fleeing to Canada in fear for their lives; a three-day riot in Providence in 1831 destroyed an African American district; and an 1834 New York riot destroyed a church, a school, and a dozen homes. Philadelphia, "the City of Brotherly Love," had the worst record. Home to the largest free African American community in the North, Philadelphia was repeatedly rocked by antiblack riots in the period between 1820 and 1859. A riot in 1834 destroyed two churches and thirty-one homes and left one African American dead and many injured. In 1842, a predominantly Irish mob attacked black marchers celebrating Jamaican Emancipation Day. The marchers counterattacked, wounding three Irish boys and provoking widespread arson, which firemen refused to put out for fear of the mob. The disturbance ended only when the mayor called out seven companies of the militia. Other cities had similar stories. Urban riots of all kinds had cost 125 lives by 1840, by 1860 more than 1,000.

THE LABOR MOVEMENT AND URBAN POLITICS

Universal white manhood suffrage and the development of mass politics (see Chapter 10), coupled with the rapid growth of cities, changed urban politics. The traditional leadership role of the wealthy elite waned, and members of the wealthiest class gradually withdrew from direct participation in urban politics. In New York City, elite political leaders had disappeared by 1845. In their place were professional politicians whose job it was to make party politics work. In New York and in other large cities, this change in politics was spurred by working-class activism.

The Tradition of Artisanal Politics

The nation's urban centers had long been strongholds of craft associations for artisans and skilled workers. These organizations, and their parades and celebrations, were recognized parts of the urban community. Groups of master craftsmen marching in community parades with signs such as "By Hammer and Hand All Arts Do Stand" were visible symbols of the strength and solidarity of workers' organizations.

Also traditional were riots and demonstrations by workers (usually journeymen or apprentices, not the master artisans themselves) over matters as political and far-reaching as the American Revolution or as practical and immediate as the price of bread. In fact, protests by urban workers had been an integral part of the older social order controlled by the wealthy elite. In the eighteenth century, when only men of property could vote, such demonstrations usually indicated widespread discontent or economic difficulty among workers. They served as a warning signal that the political elite rarely ignored.

By the 1830s the status of artisans and independent craftsmen in the nation's cities had changed. As discussed in Chapter 12, the artisanal system was crumbling, undercut by competition between cities (the result of the transportation revolution) and by the growth of the putting-out system. Furthermore, the rapid influx of immigrants changed the character of the labor force. New York provides a particularly dramatic example. The city's rapid growth as a manufacturing center was based on the labor of Irish and German immigrant workers, who made up 65 percent of the workforce by 1855. Germans clustered primarily in the skilled trades, while the Irish performed most of the low-paid labor. Indeed, 86 percent of day laborers were Irishmen, while Irishwomen made up 74 percent of the domestic servants.

This seal of the General Society of Mechanics and Tradesmen illustrates in its motto— "By Hammer and Hand All Arts Do Stand"—the personal and community pride artisans took in their work.

There was no safety net for workers who lost their jobs—no unemployment insurance or welfare— and no public regulation of wages and conditions of work. The first protests against these harsh conditions came from the women workers at the new cotton textile factories in Lowell and elsewhere. The members of urban workers' associations, increasingly angry over their declining status in the economic and social order, also became—tentatively at first, but then with growing conviction—active defenders of working-class interests.

What was new was the open antagonism between workers and employers. The community of interest between masters and workers in preindustrial times broke down. Workers realized they had to depend on other workers, not employers, for support. In turn, employers and members of the middle class began to take urban disorders much more seriously than their grandfathers might have done.

The Union Movement

Urban worker protest against changing conditions quickly took the form of party politics. The Workingmen's Party was founded in Philadelphia in 1827, and chapters quickly formed in New York and Boston as well. Using the language of class warfare—"two distinct classes...those that live by their own labor and they

that live upon the labor of others"—the "Workies" campaigned for the ten-hour day and the preservation of the small artisanal shop. They also called for the end of government-chartered monopolies—banks were high on the list—and for a public school system and cheap land in the West. Although the Workies themselves did not survive as a party, Jacksonian Democrats were quick to pick up on some of their themes. The Democrats attracted many workers' votes in 1832, the year Andrew Jackson campaigned against the "monster" Bank of the United States.

Both major parties competed for the votes of urban workers. In New York City in 1835 a radical antimonopoly branch of the Democratic Party known officially as the Equal Rights Party attracted some worker support. For their part, the Whigs wooed workers by assuring them that Henry Clay's American System, and tariff protection in particular, would be good for the economy and for workers' jobs. Nevertheless, neither major political party really spoke to the primary need of workers—for well-paid, stable jobs that assured them independence and respect. Unsatisfied with the response of political parties, workers turned to labor organization to achieve their goals.

Between 1833 and 1837 a wave of strikes in New York City cut the remaining ties between master craftsmen and the journeymen who worked for them. In 1833, journeymen carpenters struck for higher wages. Workers in fifteen other trades came to their support, and within a month the strike was won. The lesson was obvious: if skilled workers banded together across craft lines, they could improve their conditions. The same year, representatives from nine different craft groups formed the General Trades Union of New York. By 1834 similar groups had sprung up in over a dozen cities—Boston, Louisville, and Cincinnati among them. In New York alone, the GTU helped organize almost forty strikes between 1833 and 1837, and it encouraged the formation of more than fifty unions. In 1834 also, representatives of several local GTUs met in Baltimore and organized the National Trades Union. In its founding statement the NTU criticized the "unjustifiable distribution of the wealth of society in the hands of a few individuals," which had created for working people "a humiliating, servile dependency, incompatible with…natural equality."

Naturally, employers disagreed with the NTU's criticism of the economic system. Convinced that unions were dangerous, New York employers took striking journeymen tailors to court in 1836. Judge Ogden Edwards pronounced the strikers guilty of conspiracy and declared unions un-American. He assured the strikers that "the road of advancement is open to all" and that they would do better to strive to be masters themselves rather than "conspire" with their fellow workers. The GTU responded with a mass rally at which Judge Edwards was burned in effigy. A year later, stunned by the effects of the Panic of 1837, the GTU collapsed. The founding of these general unions, a visible sign of a class-based community of interest among workers, is generally considered to mark the beginning of the American labor movement. However, these early unions included only white men in skilled trades who made up only a small percentage of all workers. The majority of workers—men in unskilled occupations, all free African Americans, and all women—were excluded.

Big-City Machines

Although workers were unable to create strong unions or stable political parties that spoke for their economic interests, they were able to shape urban politics. As America's cities experienced unprecedented growth, the electorate mushroomed. In New York, for example,

By 1855, half the voters in New York City were foreign-born. This 1858 engraving of an Irish bar in the Five Points area appeared in the influential Harper's Weekly. It expressed the dislike of temperance reformers for immigrants and their drinking habits and the dismay of political reformers that immigrant saloons and taverns were such effective organizing centers for urban political machines.

the number of voters grew from 20,000 in 1825 to 88,900 in 1855. Furthermore, by 1855 half of the voters were foreign-born. At the time, America was the only country in the world where propertyless white men had the vote. The job of serving this largely working-class electorate and making the new mass political party work at the urban level fell to a new kind of career politician—the boss—and a new kind of political organization—the machine.

Just as the old system of elite leadership had mirrored the social unity of eighteenth-century cities, so the new system of machine politics reflected the class structure of the rapidly growing nineteenth-century cities. Feelings of community, which had arisen naturally out of the personal contact that characterized neighborhoods in earlier, smaller cities, now were cultivated politically. The existence of distinct ethnic neighborhoods fostered political organization. Because immigrants clustered in neighborhoods, their impact on politics could be concentrated and manipulated. Legally, three years' residence in the United States was required before one could apply for citizenship, but there was clear evidence of swifter naturalization in large cities with effective political organizations. In New York, for example, the Irish-dominated districts quickly became Democratic Party strongholds. Germans, who were less active politically than the Irish, nevertheless voted heavily for the new Republican Party in the 1850s. Between them, these two new blocs of immigrant voters destroyed the Whig Party that had controlled New York politics before the immigrants arrived.

In New York City, the Tammany Society, begun in the 1780s as a fraternal organization of artisans, slowly evolved into the key organization of the new mass politics. (Named after the Delaware chief mentioned in Chapter 3, the society met in a hall called the Wigwam and elected "sachems" as their officers.) Tammany, which was affiliated with the national Democratic Party, reached voters by using many of the techniques of mass appeal made popular earlier by craft organizations—parades, rallies, current songs, and party newspapers.

Along with these new techniques of mass appeal went new methods of organization: a tight system of political control beginning at the neighborhood level with ward committees and topped by a chairman of a citywide general committee. At the citywide level, ward leaders—bosses—bartered the loyalty and votes of their followers for positions on the city payroll for party members and community services for their neighborhood. This was machine politics. Through it workers, although they lacked the political or organizational strength to challenge the harmful effects of the market revolution, could use their

numbers to ameliorate some of its effects at the local level. Machine politics served to mediate increasing class divisions and ethnic diversity as well. The machines themselves offered personal ties and loyalties—community feeling—to recent arrivals in the big cities (increasingly, immigrants from Europe) and help in hard times to workers who cast their votes correctly.

In America's big cities the result was apparent by midcentury: the political "machine" controlled by the "boss"—the politician who represented the interests of his group and delivered their votes in exchange for patronage and favors.

Critics said that big-city machines were corrupt, and indeed they often were. Antagonism between reformers, who were usually members of the upper and middle classes, and machine politicians, who spoke for the working class, was evident by the 1850s. This antagonism was to become chronic in American urban politics. One result of the market revolution was the political expression, in a democratic society, of the conflict of interests between owners and workers.

SOCIAL REFORM MOVEMENTS

The passion for reform that had become such an important part of the new middle-class thinking was focused on the problems of the nation's cities. As the opening of this chapter describes, the earliest response to the dislocations caused by the market revolution was community-based and voluntary. Middle-class people tried to deal with social changes in their communities by joining organizations devoted to reforms such as temperance, education, prisons and asylums, women's rights, abolitionism, and, above all, the spread of evangelical religion. The reform message was vastly amplified by inventions such as the steam printing press, which made it possible to publish reform literature in great volume. Soon there were national networks of reform groups.

Alexis de Tocqueville commented on the vast extent of American voluntary associations and their many purposes. "In no country in the world," he noted, "has the principle of association been more successfully used, or more unsparingly applied to a multitude of different objects, than in America." The widespread reform movements of the era depended on the energy and hope of communities of like-minded people.

Evangelism, Reform, and Social Control
Evangelical religion was fundamental to social reform. Men and women who had been converted to the enthusiastic new faith assumed personal responsibility for making changes in their own lives. Personal reform quickly led to social reform; recall, for example, the northern businessman described in Chapter 12 who

gave up drinking alcohol and insisted that his employees do the same. Religious converts were encouraged in their social activism by such leading revivalists as Charles G. Finney, who preached a doctrine of "perfectionism," claiming it was possible for all Christians to personally understand and live by God's will and thereby become "as perfect as God." Furthermore, Finney predicted, "the complete reformation of the whole world" could be achieved if only enough converts put their efforts into moral reform. This new religious feeling was intensely hopeful: members of evangelistic religions really did expect to convert the world and create the perfect moral and religious community on earth.

Much of America was swept by the fervor of moralistic reform, and it was the new middle class, who applied new notions of morality to the movement, that set the agenda for reform. Reform efforts arose from the recognition that the traditional methods of small-scale local relief were no longer adequate. In colonial times, families (sometimes at the request of local government) had housed and cared for the ill or incapacitated. Small local almshouses and prisons had housed the poor and the criminal. Reformers now realized that large cities had to make large-scale provisions for social misfits and that institutional rather than private efforts were needed. This thinking was especially true of the institutional reform movements that began in the 1830s, such as the push for insane asylums. At this time, of course, the federal government provided no such relief.

A second characteristic of the reform movements was a belief in the basic goodness of human nature. All reformers believed that the condition of the unfortunate—the poor, the insane, the criminal—would improve in a wholesome environment. Thus insane asylums were built in rural areas, away from the noise and stress of the cities, and orphanages had strict rules that were meant to encourage discipline and self-reliance. Prison reform carried this sentiment to the extreme. On the theory that bad social influences were largely responsible for crime, some "model" prisons completely isolated prisoners from one another, making them eat, sleep, work, and do required Bible reading in their own cells. The failure of these prisons to achieve dramatic changes for the better in their inmates (a number of isolated prisoners went mad, and some committed suicide) or to reduce crime was one of the first indications that reform was not a simple task.

A third characteristic of the reform movements was their moralistic dogmatism. Reformers were certain they knew what was right and were determined to see their improvements enacted. It was a short step from developing individual self-discipline to imposing discipline on others. The reforms that

were proposed thus took the form of social controls. Lazy, sinful, intemperate, or unfit members of society were to be reformed for their own good, whether they wanted to be or not. This attitude was bound to cause controversy; by no means did all Americans share the reformers' beliefs, nor did those for whom it was intended always take kindly to being the targets of the reformers' concern.

Indeed, some aspects of the social reform movements were harmful. The evangelical Protestantism of the reformers promoted hostility to Catholic immigrants from Ireland and Germany beginning in the 1830s. The temperance movement, in particular, targeted immigrants for their free drinking habits. Seeking uniformity of behavior rather than tolerance, the reformers thus helped to promote the virulent nativism that infected American politics between 1840 and 1860 (see Chapter 15 and "Immigration and Community: The Changing Face of Ethnicity in America, 1800–1865" on page 380).

Regional and national reform organizations quickly grew from local projects to deal with social problems such as drinking, prostitution, mental illness, and crime. In 1828, for example, Congregationalist minister Lyman Beecher joined other ministers in forming a General Union for Promoting the Observance of the Christian Sabbath; the aim was to prevent business on Sundays. To achieve its goals, the General Union adopted the same methods used by political parties: lobbying, petition drives, fund-raising, and special publications. These and other efforts, Beecher said, were all for the purpose of establishing "the moral government of God."

In effect, the sabbath reformers engaged in political action but remained aloof from direct electoral politics, stressing their religious mission. In any case, their goal was controversial. Workingmen (who usually worked six days a week) were angered when the General Union forced the Sunday closure of their favorite taverns and were quick to vote against the Whigs, the party most sympathetic to reform thinking. Other reforms likewise muddied the distinction between political and social activity. It is not surprising that women, who were barred from electoral politics but not from moral and social activism, were major supporters of reform.

Education and Women Teachers

Women became deeply involved in reform movements through their churches. It was they who did most of the fund-raising for the home missionary societies that were beginning to send the evangelical message worldwide—at first by ministers alone, later by married couples. Nearly every church had a maternal association, where mothers gathered to discuss ways to raise

Catharine Beecher, a member of one of America's leading families of religious reformers, advocated teaching as a suitable employment for young single women because it called for the nurturing skills and moral values she claimed all women possessed.

their children as true Christians. These associations reflected a new and more positive definition of childhood. The Puritans had believed that children were born sinful and that their wills had to be broken before they could become godly. Early schools reflected these beliefs: teaching was by rote, and punishment was harsh and physical. Educational reformers, however, tended to believe that children were born innocent and needed gentle nurturing and encouragement if they were to flourish. At home, mothers began to play the central role in child rearing. Outside the home, women helped spread the new public education pioneered by Horace Mann, secretary of the Massachusetts State Board of Education.

Although literacy had long been valued, especially in New England, schooling since colonial times had been a private enterprise and a personal expense. Town grammar schools, required in Massachusetts since 1647, had been supported primarily by parents' payments, with some help from local property taxes. In 1827, Massachusetts pioneered compulsory education by legislating that public schools be supported by public taxes. Soon schooling for white children between the ages of five and nineteen was common, although, especially in rural schools, the term might be only a month or so long. Uniformity in curriculum

and teacher training, and the grading of classes by ability—measures pioneered by Horace Mann in the 1830s—quickly caught on in other states. In the North and West (the South lagged far behind), more and more children went to school, and more and more teachers, usually young single women, were hired to teach them.

The spread of public education created the first real career opportunity for women. Horace Mann insisted that to learn well, children needed schools with a pleasant and friendly atmosphere. One important way to achieve that atmosphere, Mann recommended, was to group children by ages rather than combining everyone in the traditional ungraded classroom and to pay special attention to the needs of the youngest pupils. Who could better create the friendly atmosphere of the new classroom than women? The great champion of teacher training for women was Catharine Beecher, daughter of Lyman, who clearly saw her efforts as part of the larger work of establishing "the moral government of God." Arguing that women's moral and nurturing nature ideally suited them to be teachers, Beecher campaigned tirelessly on their behalf. Since "the mind is to be guided chiefly by means of the affections," she argued, "is not woman best fitted to accomplish these important objects?"

By 1850 women were dominant in primary school teaching, which had come to be regarded as an acceptable occupation for educated young women during the few years between their own schooling and marriage. For some women, teaching was a great adventure; they enthusiastically volunteered to be "schoolmarms" on the distant western frontiers of Wisconsin and Iowa. Still others thought globally. The young women who attended Mary Lyon's Mount Holyoke Female Seminary in Massachusetts, founded in 1837, hoped to be missionary teachers in distant lands. For others, a few years of teaching was quite enough. Low pay (half of what male schoolteachers earned) and community supervision (women teachers had to board with families in the community) were probably sufficient to make almost any marriage proposal look appealing.

Temperance

Reformers believed not only that children could be molded but that adults could change. The largest reform organization of the period, the American Society for the Promotion of Temperance founded in 1826, boasted more than 200,000 members by the mid-1830s. Dominated by evangelicals, local chapters used revival methods—lurid temperance tracts detailing the evils of alcohol, large prayer and song meetings, and heavy group pressure—to encourage young men to stand up, confess their bad habits, and

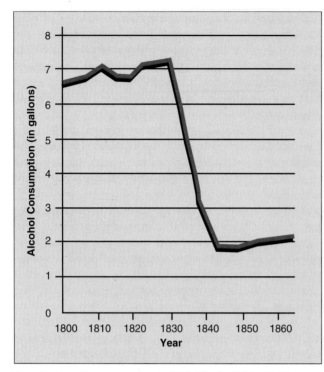

Per Capita Consumption of Alcohol, 1800–1860
The underlying cause for the dramatic fall in alcohol consumption during the 1830s was the changing nature of work brought about by the market revolution. Contributing factors were the shock of the Panic of 1837 and the untiring efforts of temperance reformers.

Source: W. J. Rorabaugh, *The Alcoholic Republic: An American Tradition* (New York: Oxford University Press, 1979).

"take the pledge" (not to drink). Here again, women played an important role.

Excessive drinking was a national problem, and it appears to have been mostly a masculine one, for respectable women did not drink in public. (Many did, however, drink alcohol-based patent medicines. Lydia Pinkham's Vegetable Compound, marketed for "female complaints," was 19 percent alcohol.) Men drank hard liquor—whiskey, rum, and hard cider—in abundance. Traditionally, drinking had been a basic part of men's working lives. It concluded occasions as formal as the signing of a contract and accompanied such informal activities as card games. Drink was a staple offering at political speeches, rallies, and elections. In the old artisanal workshops, drinking had been a customary pastime. Much of the drinking was well within the bounds of sociability, but the widespread use (more than seven gallons of hard liquor per capita in 1830— more than twice as much as today's rate) must have encouraged drunkenness.

There were many reasons to support temperance. Heavy-drinking men hurt their families economically by spending their wages on drink. Women had no recourse: the laws of the time gave men complete financial control of the household, and divorce was difficult as well as socially unacceptable. Excessive drinking also led to violence and crime, both within the family and in the larger society.

But there were other reasons as well. The new middle class, preoccupied with respectability and morality, found the old easygoing drinking ways unacceptable. As work patterns changed, employers banned alcohol at work and increasingly considered drinking men not only unreliable but immoral. Temperance became a social and political issue. Whigs, who embraced the new morality, favored it; Democrats, who in northern cities consisted increasingly of immigrant workers, were opposed. Both German and Irish immigrants valued the social drinking that occurred in beer gardens and saloons and were hostile to temperance reform.

The Panic of 1837 affected the temperance movement. Whereas most temperance crusaders in the 1820s had been members of the middle class, the long depression of 1837–43 prompted artisans and skilled workers to give up or at least cut down substantially on drinking. Forming associations known as Washington Temperance Societies, these workers spread the word that temperance was the workingman's best chance to survive economically and to maintain his independence. Their wives, gathered together in Martha Washington Societies, were frequently even more committed to temperance than their husbands. While the men's temperance groups were often deeply involved in working-class politics, the women's groups stressed the harm that alcoholism could do to homes and families and provided financial help to distressed women and children.

Campaigns against alcohol were frequent and successful. By the mid-1840s alcohol consumption had been more than halved, to less than two gallons per capita, about the level of today. Concern over drinking would remain constant throughout the nineteenth century and into the twentieth.

Moral Reform, Asylums, and Prisons

Alcohol was not the only "social evil" that reform groups attacked. Another was prostitution, which was common in the nation's port cities. The customary approach of evangelical reformers was to "rescue" prostitutes, offering them the salvation of religion, prayer, and temporary shelter. The success rate was not very high. As an alternative to prostitution, reformers usually offered domestic work, a low-paying and restrictive occupation that many women scorned. Nevertheless, campaigns against prostitution, generally organized by women, continued throughout the nineteenth century.

One of the earliest and most effective antiprostitution groups was the Female Moral Reform Society. Founded by evangelical women in New York in 1834 (the first president was Lydia Finney), it boasted 555 affiliates throughout the country by 1840. It was surprising that so many respectable women were willing to acknowledge the existence of something so disreputable as prostitution. Even more surprising was the speed with which the societies realized that prostitution was not so much a moral as an economic issue. The societies rapidly moved to organize charity and work for poor women and orphans. They also took direct action against the patrons of prostitutes by printing their names in local papers, and they successfully lobbied the New York state legislature for criminal penalties against the male clients as well as the women themselves.

Another dramatic example of reform was the asylum movement, spearheaded by a woman evangelist, Dorothea Dix. In 1843, Dix horrified the Massachusetts state legislature with the results of her several years of study into the conditions to which insane women were subjected. She described in graphic detail how the women were incarcerated with ordinary criminals, locked up in "cages, closets, stalls, pens! Chained, naked, beaten with rods, and lashed into obedience!" Dix's efforts led to the establishment of a state asylum for the insane in Massachusetts and to similar institutions in other states. Between 1843 and 1854 Dix traveled more than 30,000 miles to publicize the movement for humane treatment of the insane. By 1860 twenty-eight states had public institutions for the insane.

Other reformers were active in related causes, such as prison reform and the establishment of orphanages, homes of refuge, and hospitals. Model penitentiaries were built in Auburn and Ossining (known as "Sing Sing"), New York, and in Philadelphia and Pittsburgh. Characterized by strict order and discipline, these prisons were supposed to reform rather than simply incarcerate their inmates, but their regimes of silence and isolation caused despair more often than rehabilitation.

Utopianism and Mormonism

Amid all the political activism and reform fervor of the 1830s, a few people chose escape into utopian communities and new religions. The upstate New York area along the Erie Canal was the seedbed for this movement, just as it was for evangelical revivals and reform movements like the Seneca Falls convention. The area was so notable for its reform enthusiasms that it has been termed "the Burned-Over District," a reference to the waves of reform that swept through like forest fires.

Apocalyptic religions tend to spring up in places experiencing rapid social change. The Erie Canal region, which experienced the full impact of the

Temperance tracts, produced in the hundreds of thousands, painted lurid pictures of the perils of alcohol. Both melodramatic stories of ruin and cartoons like this 1826 tract, "The Drunkard's Progress," spread the temperance message in popular, easily understood forms.

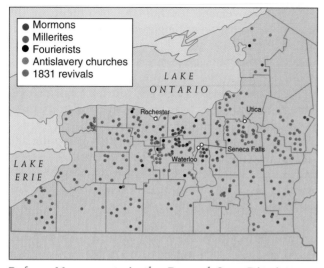

Reform Movements in the Burned-Over District
The so-called Burned-Over District, the region of New York State most changed by the opening of the Erie Canal, was a seedbed of religious and reform movements. The Mormon Church originated there and Utopian groups and sects like the Millerites and the Fourierists thrived. Charles G. Finney held some of his most successful evangelical revivals in the district. Antislavery feeling was common in the region, and the women's rights movement began at Seneca Falls.

Source: Whitney Cross, *The Burned-Over District* (1950; reprint, New York: Hippocrene Books, 1981).

market revolution in the early nineteenth century, was such a place. A second catalyst is hard times, and the prolonged depression that began with the Panic of 1837 led some people to embrace a belief in imminent catastrophe. The Millerites (named for their founder, William Miller) believed that the Second Coming of Christ would occur on October 22, 1843. In anticipation, members of the church sold their belongings and bought white robes for their ascension to heaven. When the Day of Judgment did not take place as expected, most of Miller's followers drifted away. But a small group persisted. Revising their expectations, they formed the core of the Seventh-Day Adventist faith, which is still active today.

The Shakers, founded by "Mother" Ann Lee in 1774, were the oldest utopian group. An offshoot of the Quakers, the Shakers espoused a radical social philosophy that called for the abolishment of the traditional family in favor of a family of brothers and sisters joined in equal fellowship. Despite its insistence on celibacy, the Shaker movement grew between 1820 and 1830, eventually reaching twenty settlements in eight states with a total membership of 6,000. The Shaker's simple and highly structured lifestyle, their isolation from the changing world, and their belief in equality drew new followers, especially among women. In contrast, another utopian commu-

nity, the Oneida Community, became notorious for its sexual freedom. Founded by John Humphrey Noyes in 1848, the Oneida community, like the Shaker community, viewed itself as one family. But rather than celibacy, members practiced "complex marriage," a system of highly regulated group sexual activity. Only "spiritually advanced" males (Noyes himself and a few others) could father children, who were raised communally. These practices gave the sect a notorious reputation as a den of "free love" and "socialism," preventing Noyes from increasing its membership beyond 200.

Still other forthrightly socialist communities flourished briefly. New Harmony, Indiana, founded by the famous Scottish industrialist Robert Owen in 1825, was to be a manufacturing community without poverty and unemployment. The community survived only three years. Faring little better were the "phalanxes," huge communal buildings structured on the socialist theories of the French thinker Charles Fourier. Based on his belief that there was a rational way to divide work, Fourier suggested, for example, that children would make the best garbage collectors because they didn't mind dirt! And Louisa May Alcott (who later wrote *Little Women* and many other novels and stories) lived with her family at Fruitlands in Massachusetts, which had begun as a rural community of transcendentalists. The rapid failure of these socialist communities was due largely to inadequate planning and organization. Another reason may have been, as Alcott suggested in her satirical reminiscence, *Transcendental Wild Oats*, that the women were left to do all the work while the men philosophized. Nevertheless, it is striking that at a time when so many voluntary associations successfully organized the activities of their members so few cooperative communities succeeded.

The most successful of the nineteenth-century communitarian movements was also a product of the Burned-Over District. In 1830, a young man named Joseph Smith founded the Church of Jesus Christ of Latter-Day Saints based on the teachings of the *Book of Mormon*, which he claimed to have received from an angel in a vision.

Initially, Mormonism, as the new religion became known, seemed little different from the many other new religious groups and utopian communities of the time. But under the benevolent but absolute authority of its patriarch, Joseph Smith, it rapidly gained distinction for its extraordinary communitarianism. Close cooperation and hard work made the Mormon community successful, attracting both new followers and the animosity of neighbors, who resented Mormon exclusiveness and economic success. The Mormons were harassed in New York and driven west to Ohio and then Missouri. Finally they seemed to find an ideal home in Nauvoo, Illinois, where in 1839 they built a model community, achieving almost complete self-government and isolation from non-Mormon neighbors. But in 1844, dissension within the community over Joseph Smith's new doctrine of polygamy (marriage between one man and more than one woman, simultaneously) gave outsiders a chance to intervene. Smith and his brother were arrested peacefully but were killed by a mob from which their jailers failed to protect them.

The beleaguered Mormon community decided to move beyond reach of harm. Led by Brigham Young, the Mormons migrated in 1846 to the Great Salt Lake in present-day Utah. After several lean years (once, a grasshopper plague was stopped by the providential arrival of sea gulls, who ate the insects), the Mormon method of communal settlement proved successful. Their hopes of isolation were dashed, however, by the California Gold Rush of 1849.

ANTISLAVERY AND ABOLITIONISM

The antislavery feeling that was to play such an important role in the politics of the 1840s and 1850s also had its roots in the religious reform movements that began in the 1820s and 1830s. Three groups—free African Americans, Quakers, and militant white reformers—worked to bring an end to slavery, but each in different ways. Their efforts eventually turned a minor reform movement into the dominant political issue of the day.

Antislavery activity was not new. For free African Americans the freedom of other black people had always been a major goal, but in order to achieve legal change they needed white allies. In 1787 antislavery advocates had secured in the Constitution a clause specifying a date after which American participation in the international slave trade could be made illegal, and Congress outlawed it in 1808. By 1800 slavery had been abolished or gradual emancipation enacted in most northern states. In 1820 the Missouri Compromise prohibited slavery in most of the Louisiana Purchase lands. None of these measures, however, addressed the continuing reality of slavery in the South.

The American Colonization Society

The first attempt to "solve" the problem of slavery was a plan for gradual emancipation of slaves (with compensation to their owners) and their resettlement in Africa. This plan was the work of the American Colonization Society, formed in 1817 by northern religious reformers (Quakers prominent among them) and a number of southern slave owners, most from the Upper South and the border states (Kentuckian Henry Clay was a supporter). Northerners were especially eager to send the North's 250,000 free black people back to Africa, describing them, in the words of the society's 1829 report, as "notoriously ignorant, degraded and miserable, mentally diseased, [and] broken-spirited," a characterization that completely ignored the legal and social discrimination they faced. Some northern members of the society also supported laws disenfranchising and restricting the rights of free African Americans. The American Colonization Society was remarkably ineffective; by 1830, it had managed to send only 1,400 black people to a colony in Liberia, West Africa. Critics pointed out that more slaves were born in a week than the society sent back to Africa in a year.

African Americans' Fight against Slavery

Most free African Americans rejected colonization, insisting instead on a commitment to the immediate end of slavery and the

Shaker Hannah Cohoon's 1845 painting of the Tree of Life—*her effort to reproduce a vision she had seen while in a religious trance—communicates the intense spirituality of Shaker life.*

The Mormon Migration, 1830—1847 *The Mormon church and community, founded by Joseph Smith of Palmyra, New York, in 1830, aroused intense opposition. Two early settlements, one in Kirtland, Ohio, and another near Independence, Missouri, were driven out in 1838. The Mormons regrouped and prospered in Nauvoo, Illinois, until the mob murder of Joseph Smith in 1844. Their escape to the west began in 1846, first to Winter Quarters, Nebraska, and finally to the desolate Great Salt Lake region of Utah, where the Mormons hoped to be free of outside interference.*

equal treatment of black people in America. "We are natives of this country," an African American minister in New York pointed out. Then he added bitterly, "We only ask that we be treated as well as foreigners." By 1830 there were at least fifty black abolitionist societies in the North. These organizations held yearly national conventions, where famous African American abolitionists like Frederick Douglass, Harriet Tubman, and Sojourner Truth spoke. The first African American newspaper, founded in 1827 by John Russwurm and Samuel Cornish, announced its antislavery position in its title, *Freedom's Journal.*

In 1829 David Walker, a free African American in Boston, wrote a widely distributed pamphlet, *Appeal to the Colored Citizens of the World,* that encouraged slave rebellion. "We must and shall be free...in spite of you," Walker warned whites. "And woe, woe will be it to you if we have to obtain our freedom by fighting." White Southerners blamed pamphlets such

as these and the militant articles of African American journalists for stirring up trouble among southern slaves, and in particular for Nat Turner's revolt in 1831. The vehemence of white southern reaction testifies to the courage of that handful of determined free African Americans who persisted in speaking for their enslaved brothers and sisters long before most white Northerners even noticed.

Abolitionists

The third and best-known group of antislavery reformers was headed by William Lloyd Garrison. In 1831 Garrison broke with the gradualist persuaders of the American Colonization Society and began publishing his own paper, the *Liberator.* In the first issue Garrison declared, "I am in earnest—I will not equivocate—I will not excuse—I will not retreat a single inch—AND I WILL BE HEARD." Garrison, the embodiment of moral indignation, was totally incapable of compromise. His approach was to mount a sweeping crusade condemning slavery as sinful and demanding its immediate abolishment. Garrison's crusade, like evangelical religion, was personal and moral. In reality, Garrison did not expect that all slaves would be freed immediately, but he did want and expect everyone to acknowledge the immorality of slavery. On the other hand, Garrison took the truly radical step of demanding full social equality for African Americans, referring to them individually as "a man and a brother" and "a woman and a sister." Garrison's determination electrified the antislavery movement, but his inability to compromise limited his effectiveness as a leader.

Garrison's moral vehemence radicalized northern antislavery religious groups. Theodore Weld, an evangelical minister, joined Garrison in 1833 in forming the American Anti-Slavery Society. The following year, Weld encouraged a group of students at Lane Theological Seminary in Cincinnati to form an antislavery society. When the seminary's president, Lyman Beecher, sought to suppress it, the students moved en masse to Oberlin College in northern Ohio, where they were joined by revivalist Charles Finney, who became president of the college. Oberlin soon became known as the most liberal college in the country, not only for its antislavery stance but for its acceptance of African American students and of women students as well.

Moral horror over slavery engaged many Northerners deeply in the abolitionist movement. They flocked to hear firsthand accounts of slavery by Frederick Douglass and Sojourner Truth, and by the white sisters from South Carolina, Angelina and Sarah Grimké. Northerners eagerly read slave narratives and books such as Theodore Weld's 1839 *American Slavery As It Is* (based in part on the recollections of Angelina Grimké, whom Weld had married) that provided graphic details of abuse. Lyman Beecher's daughter, Harriet Beecher Stowe, was to draw on the

The different dates on these two widely used antislavery images are important. The title page of Thomas Branagan's 1807 book includes a then already commonly used image of a male slave. The engraving of a chained female slave was made by Patrick Reason, a black artist, in 1835. The accompanying message, "Am I Not a Woman and a Sister?" spoke particularly to white female abolitionists in the North, who were just becoming active in antislavery movements in the 1830s.

The Philadelphia Anti-Slavery Society was one of the largest and best-known local chapters of the American Anti-Slavery Society, founded in 1833. The national society depended on local chapters to collect signatures for petitions, organize local meetings, and raise the money to print and distribute more than a million pieces of antislavery literature. The Philadelphia chapter, founded in 1832, included a number of Quakers, among whom Lucretia Mott (second from right in the front row) was prominent.

Grimké-Weld book for her immensely popular anti-slavery novel, *Uncle Tom's Cabin*, published in 1852.

The style of abolitionist writings and speeches was similar to the oratorical style of the religious revivalists. Northern abolitionists believed that a full description of the evils of slavery would force southern slave owners to confront their wrongdoing and lead to a true act of repentance—freeing their slaves. They were confrontational, denunciatory, and personal in their message, much like the evangelical preachers. Southerners, however, regarded abolitionist attacks as libelous and abusive.

Abolitionists adopted another tactic of revivalists and temperance workers when, to enhance their powers of persuasion, they began to publish great numbers of antislavery tracts. In 1835 alone they mailed more than a million pieces of antislavery literature to southern states. This tactic also drew a backlash: southern legislatures banned abolitionist literature, encouraged the harassment and abuse of anyone distributing it, and looked the other way when (as in South Carolina) proslavery mobs seized and burned it. The Georgia legislature even offered a $5,000 reward to anyone who would kidnap William Lloyd Garrison and bring him to the South to stand trial for inciting rebellion. Most seriously, most southern states reacted by toughening laws concerning emancipation, freedom of movement, and all aspects of slave behavior. Hoping to prevent the spread of the abolitionist message, most southern states reinforced laws making it a crime to teach a slave how to read. Ironically, then, the immediate impact of abolitionism in the South was to stifle dissent and make the lives of slaves harder (see Chapter 11).

Even in the North, controversy over abolitionism was common. Some places were prone to anti-abolitionist violence. The Ohio Valley, settled largely by Southerners, was one such place, as were northern cities experiencing the strains of rapid growth, such as Philadelphia. Immigrant Irish, who found themselves pitted against free black people for jobs, were often violently antiabolitionist. A tactic that abolitionists borrowed from revivalists—holding large and emotional meetings—opened the door to mob action. Crowds of people often disrupted such meetings, especially those addressed by Theodore Weld, whose oratorical style earned him the title of "the Most Mobbed Man in the United States." William Lloyd Garrison was stoned, dragged through the streets, and on one occasion almost hanged by a Boston mob. In the three-day New York riot of 1834, abolitionist Arthur Tappan's home and store were sacked at the same time that black churches and homes were damaged and free blacks attacked. In 1837, antislavery editor Elijah P. Lovejoy of Alton, Illinois, was killed and his press destroyed. In 1838, a mob threatened a meeting of the Philadelphia Female Anti-Slavery Society one night and, the next night, burned down the hall in which they had met.

Abolitionism and Politics

Abolitionism began as a social movement but soon intersected with sectional interests and became a national political issue. In the 1830s, massive abolitionist petition drives gathered a total of nearly 700,000 petitions requesting the abolition of slavery and the slave trade in the District of Columbia but were rebuffed by Congress. At southern insistence and with President Andrew Jackson's approval, Congress passed a "gag rule" in 1836 that prohibited discussion of antislavery petitions.

Many Northerners viewed the gag rule and censorship of the mails, which Southerners saw as necessary defenses against abolitionist frenzy, as alarming threats to free speech. First among them was Massachusetts representative John Quincy Adams, the only former president ever to serve in Congress after leaving the executive branch. Adams so publicly and persistently denounced the gag rule as a violation of the constitutional right to petition that it was repealed in 1844. Less well-known Northerners like the thousands of women who canvassed their neighborhoods with petitions made personal commitments to abolitionism that they did not intend to abandon.

John Quincy Adams was also a key figure in the abolitionists' one undoubted victory, the fight to free the fifty-three slaves on the Spanish ship *Amistad* and return them to Africa. Although the Africans successfully mutinied against the *Amistad's* crew in 1839, when the ship was found in American waters a legal battle over their "ownership" ensued, during which the Africans themselves were held in jail. Prominent abolitionists, most notably Lewis Tappan, financed the legal fight which went all the way to the Supreme Court, where Adams won the case for the *Amistad* defendants against the American government, which supported the Spanish claim.

Although abolitionist groups raised the nation's emotional temperature, they failed to achieve the moral unity they had hoped for, and they began to splinter. One perhaps inevitable but nonetheless distressing split was between white and black abolitionists. Frederick Douglass and William Lloyd Garrison parted ways when Douglass, refusing to be limited to a simple recital of his life as a slave, began to make specific suggestions for improvements in the lives of free African Americans. When Douglass chose the path of political action, Garrison denounced him as "ungrateful." Douglass and other free African Americans worked under persistent discrimination, even from antislavery whites; some of the latter refused to hire black people or to meet with them as equals. For example, some Philadelphia Quaker meetings, though devoted to the antislavery cause, maintained segregated seating for black people in their churches. While many white reformers eagerly pressed for civil equality for African Americans, they did not accept the idea of social equality. On the other hand, black and white "stations" worked closely in the risky enterprise of passing fugitive slaves north over the famous Underground Railroad, as the various routes by which slaves made their way to freedom were called. Contrary to abolitionist legend, however, it was free African Americans, rather than white people, who played the major part in helping the fugitives.

Among white abolitionists, William Lloyd Garrison remained controversial, especially after 1837, when he espoused a radical program that included women's rights, pacifism, and the abolition of the prisons and asylums that other reformers were working to establish. In 1840 the abolitionist movement formally split. The majority moved toward party politics (which Garrison abhorred), founding the Liberty Party and choosing James G. Birney (whom Theodore Weld had converted to abolitionism) as their presidential candidate. Thus the abolitionist movement, which began as an effort at moral reform, took its first major step into politics, and this step in turn led to the formation of the Republican Party in the 1850s and to the Civil War.

For one particular group of antislavery reformers, the abolitionist movement opened up new possibilities for action. Through their participation in antislavery activity, some women came to a vivid realization of the social constraints on their activism.

THE WOMEN'S RIGHTS MOVEMENT

American women, without the vote or a role in party politics, found a field of activity in social reform movements. There was scarcely a reform movement in which women were not actively involved. Often men

Women's gatherings, like the first women's rights convention in Seneca Falls in 1848 and this meeting of strikers in Lynn in 1860, were indicators of widespread female activism.

speaking to mixed gatherings. The meetings got larger and larger, and soon the sisters realized that they had become the first female public speakers in America. In 1837 Angelina Grimké became the first woman to address a meeting of the Massachusetts state legislature (Sarah Bagley, the Lowell worker, was the second).

The sisters challenged social norms on two grounds. The antislavery movement was widely disapproved, and many famous male orators were criticized by the press and mobbed at meetings. The Grimké sisters were criticized for speaking because they were women. A letter from a group of ministers cited the Bible in reprimanding the sisters for stepping out of "woman's proper sphere" of silence and subordination. Sarah Grimké answered the ministers in her 1838 *Letters on the Equality of the Sexes and the Condition of Women*, claiming that "men and women were CREATED EQUAL.…Whatever is right for a man to do, is right for woman." She followed with this ringing assertion: "I seek no favors for my sex. I surrender not our claim to equality. All I ask of our brethren is, that they will take their feet from off our necks and permit us to stand upright on that ground which God designed us to occupy."

Not all female assertiveness was as dramatic as Sarah Grimké's, but women in the antislavery movement found it a constant struggle to be heard. Some solved the problem of male dominance by forming their own groups, like the Philadelphia Female Anti-Slavery Society. In the antislavery movement and other reform groups as well, men accorded women a secondary role, even when—as was frequently the case—women constituted a majority of the members.

were the official leaders of such movements, and some women—especially those in the temperance, moral reform, and abolitionist movements—formed all-female chapters to define and implement their own policies and programs.

The majority of women did not participate in these activities, for they were fully occupied with housekeeping and child rearing (families with five children were the average). A few women—mostly members of the new middle class, who could afford servants—had the time and energy to look beyond their immediate tasks. Touched by the religious revival, these women enthusiastically joined reform movements. Led thereby to challenge social restrictions, some, like the Grimké sisters, found that their commitment carried them beyond the limits of what was considered acceptable activity for women.

The Grimké Sisters

Sarah and Angelina Grimké, members of a prominent South Carolina slaveholding family, rejected slavery out of religious conviction and moved north to join a Quaker community near Philadelphia. In the 1830s, these two sisters found themselves drawn into the growing antislavery agitation in the North. Because they knew about slavery firsthand, they were in great demand as speakers. At first they spoke to "parlor meetings" of women only, as was considered proper. But interested men kept sneaking into the talks, and soon the sisters found themselves

Women's Rights

The Seneca Falls Convention of 1848, the first women's rights convention in American history, was an outgrowth of almost twenty years of female activity in social reform. Every year after 1848 women gathered to hold women's rights conventions and to work for political, legal, and social equality. Over the years, in response to persistent lobbying, states passed property laws more favorable to women and altered divorce laws to allow women to retain custody of

CHRONOLOGY

1817	American Colonization Society founded
1820s	Shaker colonies grow
1825	New Harmony founded, fails three years later
1826	American Society for the Promotion of Temperance founded
1827	Workingmen's Party founded in Philadelphia
	Freedom's Journal begins publication
	Public school movement begins in Massachusetts
1829	David Walker, *Appeal to the Colored Citizens of the World*, published
1830	Joseph Smith founds Church of Jesus Christ of Latter-Day Saints (Mormon Church)
	Charles G. Finney's revivals in Rochester
1831	William Lloyd Garrison begins publishing antislavery newspaper, the *Liberator*
1832	Immigration begins to increase
1833	American Anti-Slavery Society founded by Garrison and Theodore Weld
1834	First Female Moral Reform Society founded in New York
	National Trades Union formed
1836	Congress passes "gag rule" to prevent discussion of antislavery petitions
1837	Antislavery editor Elijah P. Lovejoy killed
	Angelina Grimké addresses Massachusetts legislature
	Sarah Grimké, *Letters on the Equality of the Sexes and the Condition of Women*
	Panic begins seven-year recession
1839	Theodore Weld publishes *American Slavery As It Is*
1840s	New York and Boston complete public water systems
1840	Liberty Party founded
1843	Millerites await the end of the world
	Dorothea Dix spearheads asylum reform movement
1844	Mormon leader Joseph Smith killed by mob
1845	New York creates city police force
	Beginning of Irish Potato Famine and heavy Irish immigration
1846	Mormons begin migration to the Great Salt Lake
1848	Women's Rights Convention at Seneca Falls
	John Noyes founds Oneida Community

children. Teaching positions in higher education opened up to women, as did jobs in some other occupations, and women gained the vote in some states, beginning with Wyoming Territory in 1869. In 1920, seventy-two years after universal woman suffrage was first proposed at Seneca Falls, women's right to vote was at last guaranteed in the Nineteenth Amendment to the Constitution.

Historians have only recently realized how much the reform movements of this "Age of the Common Man" were due to the efforts of the "common woman." Women played a vital role in all the social movements of the day. In doing so they implicitly challenged the popular notion of separate spheres for men and women—the public world for him, home and family for her. The separate spheres argument, although it heaped praise on women for their allegedly superior moral qualities, was meant to exclude them from political life. The reforms discussed in this chapter show clearly that women reformers believed they had a right and a duty to propose solutions for the moral and social problems of the day. Empowered by their own religious beliefs and activism, the Seneca Falls reformers spoke for all American women when they demanded an end to the unfair restrictions they suffered as women.

CONCLUSION

Beginning in the 1820s, the market revolution changed the size and social order of America's preindustrial cities and towns. Immigration, dramatically rapid population growth, and changes in working life and class structure created a host of new urban problems ranging from sanitation to civic order. These changes occurred so rapidly that they seemed overwhelming. Older, face-to-face methods of social control no longer worked. To fill the gap, new kinds of associations—the political party, the religious crusade, the reform cause, the union movement—sprang up. These associations were new manifestations of the deep human desire for social connection, for continuity, and—especially in the growing cities—for social order. A striking aspect of these associations was the uncompromising nature of the attitudes and beliefs on which they were based. Most groups were formed of like-minded people who wanted to impose their will on others. Such intolerance boded ill for the future. If political parties, religious bodies, and reform groups were to splinter along sectional lines (as happened in the 1850s), political compromise would be very difficult. In the meantime, however, Americans came to terms with the market revolution by engaging in a passion for improvement. As a perceptive foreign observer, Francis Grund, noted, "Americans love their country not as it is but as it will be."

REVIEW QUESTIONS

1. What impact did the new immigration of the 1840s and 1850s have on American cities?
2. Why did urbanization produce so many problems?
3. What motivated the social reformers of the period? Were they benevolent helpers or dictatorial social controllers? Study several reform causes and discuss similarities and differences among them.
4. Abolitionism differed little from other reforms in its tactics, but the effects of antislavery activism were politically explosive. Why was this so?

RECOMMENDED READING

Arthur Bestor, *Backwoods Utopias* (1950). The standard work on utopian communities.

Paul Boyer, *Urban Masses and Moral Order in America, 1820–1920* (1978). Interprets reform as an effort to reestablish the moral order of the preindustrial community.

Amy Bridges, *A City in the Republic: Antebellum New York and the Origins of Machine Politics* (1984). An innovative look at the transition from elite political control to machine politics.

Paul A. Gilje, *The Road to Mobocracy: Popular Disorder in New York City, 1763–1834* (1987). Provides an interesting and entertaining description of the many varieties of civic disorder of the day.

Oscar Handlin, *Boston's Immigrants: A Study in Acculturation* (rev. ed., 1959). A pathbreaking exploration of conflict and adaptation among Boston's Irish community.

Daniel Walker Howe, "The Evangelical Movement and Political Culture in the North during the Second Party System," *Journal of American History*, 78:1 (March 1991). An award-winning article that explores the connections among religion, politics, and reform.

Leon Litwack, *North of Slavery: The Negro in the Free States, 1790–1860* (1961). The standard source on free black people in the North.

Eric Lott, *Love and Theft: Blackface Minstrelsy and the American Working Class* (1993). Explores the complicated relationships between working-class amusements and racial attitudes.

Steven Mintz, *Moralists and Modernizers: America's Pre-Civil War Reformers* (1995). A brief but inclusive study of reforms and reformers.

David Roediger, *The Wages of Whiteness* (1991). Explores the links between artisanal republicanism, labor organization, and white racism.

David Rothman, *The Discovery of the Asylum: Social Order and Disorder in the New Republic* (1971). Explores institutional reforms.

Kathryn Sklar, *Catharine Beecher: A Study in American Domesticity* (1973). An absorbing "life and times" that explores the possibilities and limits of women's roles in the early nineteenth century.

Sean Wilentz, *Chants Democratic: New York City and the Rise of the American Working Class, 1788–1850* (1983). An important book, rooted in social history, that reveals how workers acted upon their understanding of republicanism in confronting the changes wrought by the market revolution.

ADDITIONAL BIBLIOGRAPHY

Immigration

Kathleen Neils Conzen, *Immigrant Milwaukee, 1836–1860* (1976)

Hasia Diner, *Erin's Daughters in America* (1983)

Jay P. Dolan, *The Immigrant Church: New York's Irish and German Catholics, 1815–1865* (1975)

Oscar Handlin, *The Uprooted* (1951; 2nd ed. 1973)

Noel Ignatiev, *How the Irish Became White* (1995)

Kerby A. Miller, *Emigrants and Exiles: Ireland and the Irish Exodus to North America* (1985)

Stanley Nadel, *Little Germany: Ethnicity, Religion, and Class in New York City, 1845–1880* (1990)

LaVern J. Rippley, *The German-Americans* (1976)

Dennis P. Ryan, *Beyond the Ballot Box: A Social History of the Boston Irish, 1845–1917* (1989)

Urban and Labor

Oliver E. Allen, *The Tiger: The Rise and Fall of Tammany Hall* (1995)

W. Jeffrey Bolster, *Black Jacks: African American Seamen in the Age of Sail* (1997)

Michael Feldberg, *The Philadelphia Riots of 1844: A Study of Ethnic Conflict* (1975)

Herbert G. Gutman, *Work, Culture, and Society in Industrializing America: Essays in American Working-Class History* (1976)

James Oliver Horton, *Free People of Color: Inside the African American Community* (1993)

James Oliver Horton and Lois E. Horton, *Black Bostonians: Family Life and Community Struggle in the Antebellum North* (1979)

David Montgomery, *Citizen Worker: The Experience of Workers in the United States with Democracy and the Free Market during the Nineteenth Century* (1993)

Gary B. Nash, *Forging Freedom: Philadelphia's Black Community, 1720–1840* (1988)

Edward Pessen, *Most Uncommon Jacksonians: The Radical Leaders of the Early Labor Movement* (1967)

Mary Ryan, *Civic Wars: Democracy and Public Life* (1997)

Amy Gilman Srebnick, *The Mysterious Death of Mary Roberts, Sex and Culture in the Nineteenth Century* (1995)

Sam Bass Warner, *The Private City: Philadelphia in Three Periods of Its Growth* (1968)

Religion, Reform, and Utopianism

Lawrence Cremin, *American Education: The National Experience, 1783–1861* (1981)

Whitney R. Cross, *The Burned-Over District: The Social and Intellectual History of Enthusiastic Religion in Western New York, 1800–1850* (1950)

Jed Dannenbaum, *Drink and Disorder: Temperance Reform in Cincinnati from the Washingtonian Revival to the WCTU* (1984)

Barbara Epstein, *The Politics of Domesticity: Women, Evangelism, and Temperance in Nineteenth Century America* (1981)

Michael Fellman, *The Unbounded Frame: Freedom and Community in Nineteenth-Century American Utopianism* (1973)

Lori D. Ginzberg, *Women and the Work of Benevolence: Morality, Politics, and Class in the Nineteenth-Century United States* (1990)

Klaus J. Hansen, *Mormonism and the American Experience* (1981)

Carl F. Kaestle, *Pillars of the Republic: Common Schools and American Society, 1780–1860* (1983)

Louis J. Kern, *An Ordered Love: Sex Roles and Sexuality in Victorian Utopias–The Shakers, the Mormons, and the Oneida Community* (1981)

W. J. Rorabaugh, *The Alcoholic Republic: An American Tradition* (1979)

Ann C. Rose, *Transcendentalism as a Social Movement, 1830–1850* (1981)

Timothy L. Smith, *Revivalism and Social Reform: American Protestantism on the Eve of the Civil War* (1980)

Abolitionism

R.J.M. Blackett, *Building an Antislavery Wall: Black Americans in the Abolitionist Movement, 1830–1860* (1983)

David Brion Davis, *The Problem of Slavery in the Age of Revolution, 1770–1823* (1975)

Louis Gerteis, *Morality and Utility in American Antislavery Reform* (1987)

Howard Jones, *Mutiny on the Amistad* (1987).

Jean Fagan Yellin, *Women and Sisters: The Antislavery Feminists in American Culture* (1989)

Women's Rights

Carl N. Degler, *At Odds: Women and the Family in America from the Revolution to the Present* (1980)

Ellen C. Dubois, *Feminism and Suffrage: The Emergence of an Independent Women's Movement in America, 1848–1869* (1978)

Keith Melder, *Beginnings of Sisterhood: The American Women's Rights Movement, 1800–1850* (1977)

Sandra S. Weber, *Special History Study, Women's Rights National Historical Park, Seneca Falls, New York* (1985)

Biography

Robert H. Abzug, *Passionate Liberator, Theodore Dwight Weld and the Dilemma of Reform* (1980)

Frederick Douglass, *The Narrative of the Life of Frederick Douglass, An American Slave* (1845)

Elisabeth Griffith, *In Her Own Right: The Life of Elizabeth Cady Stanton* (1984)

Nathan I. Huggins, *Slave and Citizen: The Life of Frederick Douglass* (1980)

Gerda Lerner, *The Grimké Sisters from South Carolina: Pioneers for Women's Rights and Abolition* (1967)

John L. Thomas, *The Liberator: William Lloyd Garrison* (1963)

The Changing Face of Ethnicity in America
1800 – 1860

Between 1790 and 1820, the rate of immigration to the United States was low, held in check by the Napoleonic Wars in Europe. It began to pick up in the 1820s, increased sharply in the 1830s, and reached a record 430,000 in 1854. As immigration increased, the ethnic composition of the immigrant stream changed. Most of the new immigrants were Irish, driven from home by the Potato Famine of 1845, and German, driven by economic and political unrest in the German Principalities.

Until the 1880s, the task of receiving immigrants fell completely on cities and states, not the federal government. New York City, by far the largest port of entry, did not even establish an official reception center until 1855, when Castle Garden, at the bottom of Manhattan Island (near present-day Battery Park), was so designated.

The influx of mostly poor, mostly Catholic foreigners provoked nativist hostility among many Protestant, native-born Americans, including many leaders of the major reform movements. It would be a mistake, however, to think that immigration was unwelcome to everyone. Industries needed willing workers, and western states were eager for settlers. In 1852 Wisconsin appointed a commissioner of emigration with responsibility for attracting Europeans to the state. Soon Iowa and Minnesota joined Wisconsin in advertising widely in Europe for settlers.

Immigrant labor fueled the nation's expanding economy and helped turn wilderness into farmland. Many of the changes in industry and transportation that accompanied the market revolution would have been impossible without immigrants. Irish contract workers, for example, were essential to the completion of the Erie Canal in 1825. And Irish women and men kept the mills at Lowell operating when the mill operators, facing increasing competition, sought cheaper labor to replace their original labor force of farm women.

Irish immigration to the United States dated from colonial times. Many of Ireland's young people, with no hope of owning land at home, had long looked to America for better opportunities. But in 1845 Ireland's green fields of potato plants turned black with blight, and for five years a catastrophic famine ravaged the land. The Irish had two choices: starve or leave. One million people died, and another 1.5 million emigrated, most to the United States. The Famine Irish were America's first major refugee group. Starving, suffering from disease

(thousands died of typhus during the voyage), and destitute, hundreds of thousands disembarked in the east-coast ports of New York, Philadelphia, Boston, and Baltimore. Lacking the money to go inland, they remained in the cities. Crowded together in miserable housing, desperate for work at any wages, foreign in their religion and pastimes (drinking and fighting, their critics said), tenaciously nationalistic and bitterly anti-British, they created ethnic enclaves of a kind new to American cities.

The largest number of Irish immigrants settled in New York. Fewer settled in Boston, but that city, smaller and more homogeneous than New York, was overwhelmed by the influx. By 1850, a quarter of Boston's population was Irish. The home of Puritanism and the center of American intellectualism, Boston was not welcoming. All over the city in places of business and in homes normally eager for domestic servants the signs went up: "No Irish Need Apply." The Irish were able to get only the worst and poorest-paying jobs and could afford housing only in an area of East Boston that was described by a health committee in 1849 as "a perfect hive of human beings, without comforts and mostly without common necessaries; in many cases, huddled together like brutes, without regard to sex or age or sense of decency."

Despite poverty and local hostility, the Irish created within their neighborhoods an impressive network of Catholic churches and schools, mutual aid societies, and religious and social clubs. And almost from the moment of their arrival, the Irish sent huge sums of money back to Ireland so that relatives could join them in America. For however bad the conditions in the adopted country, they were better than those in Ireland. As one newcomer wrote, "There is a great many ill conveniences here, but no empty bellies."

Irish immigrants changed American urban politics. In Boston, they quickly took over the local Democratic Party, opposing that city's traditional, Whig-dominated power structure. Irish political strength lay at the neighborhood level. Many politicians were saloonkeepers, for the saloon was the secular center of Irish society—much to the horror of temperance reformers. One Irish saloonkeeper, Patrick Joseph Kennedy, founded one of America's most famous political dynasties. Barely a century after Patrick's birth into a poor immigrant family in Boston, his grandson John Fitzgerald Kennedy was elected the first Irish Catholic president of the United States.

Immigration to the United States, 1820–1860

The typical German immigrant was a small farmer or artisan dislodged by the same market forces that were at work in America: the industrialization of manufacturing and the commercialization of farming. The first two major ports of embarkation for the Germans were Bremen (in northern Germany) and Le Havre (in northern France), which were also the main ports for the importation of American tobacco and cotton. The tobacco boats bore the Bremen passengers to Baltimore, and the cotton ships took them to New Orleans, a major entry point for European immigrants until the Civil War. From these ports, many Germans made their way up the Mississippi and Ohio valleys, where they settled in Milwaukee, Pittsburgh, Cincinnati, and St. Louis and on farms in Ohio, Indiana, Missouri, and Texas. In Texas the nucleus of a German community began with a Mexican land grant in the 1830s. Few Germans settled in the South.

German agricultural communities took a distinctive form that fostered cultural continuity. Immigrants formed predominantly German towns by clustering, or taking up adjoining land. A small cluster could support German churches, German-language schools, and German customs and thereby attract other Germans, some directly from Europe and some from other parts of the United States. Non-German neighbors often sold out and moved on, but the Germans stayed and passed on

their land to succeeding generations. They used soil conservation practices that were unusual for the time. German cluster communities still endure in Texas, the Midwest, and the Pacific Northwest, and more American farm families are today of German origin than of any other background.

Large German populations settled in "little Germanies" in New Orleans, St. Louis, Cincinnati, and Milwaukee, and in the eastern cities of New York, Philadelphia, and Baltimore. There they developed a flourishing community culture, with German language schools, theater groups, and a German-language press. In the summer, entire families frequented beer gardens, where there was always music, in the semi-rural outskirts of the cities. At first the Germans were greeted with hostility (temperance societies were especially unhappy about the beer gardens), but by 1860, German culture, with its emphasis on music, intellectual interests, and love of nature, had become widely influential. Among its contributions to American life were not only beer (then a new drink to most Americans) but gymnasiums and candle-lit Christmas trees. Germans also had an important impact on American public education, which was then in its formative years. The first kindergarten in America was founded by Margarethe Schurz in Watertown, Wisconsin, where she and her husband, Carl Schurz, settled in 1856. German ideas were also influential in the development of music programs, gymnastics, vocational training, and high schools.

Other areas attracting immigrants in the early nineteenth century were Gold Rush California, which drew, among others, numbers of Chinese, and Utah Territory, where the Mormon Church recruited many former English factory workers to its new Zion. In Texas and Mexico, a high proportion of residents were listed as foreign-born in 1860 who were in fact native-born Mexicans who had become foreigners only by virtue of the conquest of their homeland by the United States in the Mexican-American war.

The Chinese who came to California in the 1850s following the Gold Rush worked in the mines, most as independent prospectors. Other miners disliked their industriousness and their clannishness. One reporter noted groups of twenty or thirty "Chinamen, stools, tables,

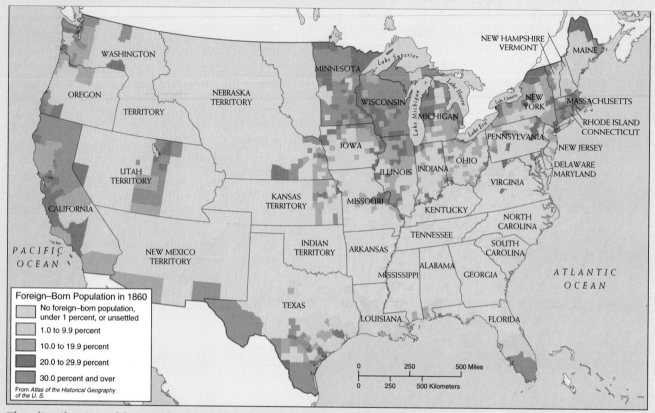

The distribution of foreign-born residents of the United States in 1860.

Foreign–Born Population in 1860
- No foreign–born population, under 1 percent, or unsettled
- 1.0 to 9.9 percent
- 10.0 to 19.9 percent
- 20.0 to 29.9 percent
- 30.0 percent and over

From Atlas of the Historical Geography of the U. S.

cooking utensils, bunks, etc., all huddled up together in indiscriminate confusion, and enwreathed with dense smoke, inhabiting close cabins, so small that one would not be of sufficient size to allow a couple of Americans to breathe in it." In 1852 the California legislature enacted a Foreign Miner's Tax aimed at the Chinese. By the time the tax was repealed in 1870, it had cost Chinese miners five million dollars. By the mid-1860s, Chinese workers made up 90 percent of the laborers building the Central Pacific Railroad, replacing more expensive white laborers and sowing the seeds of the long-lasting hostility of American workers toward Chinese. In the meantime, however, San Francisco's Chinatown, the oldest Chinese ethnic enclave in America, became a well established, thriving community. In the years to come, as hostility against the Chinese broke into violence, Chinatowns in San Francisco and elsewhere served a vital function as safe refuges for the Chinese who remained in the United States.

■ IN THEIR OWN WORDS

The unprecedented immigration of the 1840s and 1850s evoked the first organized nativist (antiforeign) movement in American history. As immigration swelled the country's previously small Catholic population, Protestant ministers became alarmed. One of them was Reverend Lyman Beecher, who equated Catholicism with the antidemocratic powers of Europe and suggested that Catholic immigrants followed their bidding. Despite his disclaimer, Beecher viewed immigration as a religious as well as a political threat.

Catholic Europe is throwing swarm on swarm [of immigrants] upon our shores. There is evidently a supervision abroad—and one here—by which they come, and set down together, in city or country, as a Catholic body, and are led or followed quickly by a Catholic priesthood, who maintain over them in the land of strangers and unknown tongues an ascendency as absolute as they are able to exert in Germany itself.

In the beginning this eruption of revolutionary Europe was not anticipated, and we opened our doors wide to the influx and naturalization of foreigners. But it is becoming a terrific inundation; it has increased upon our native population from five to thirty-seven percent, and is every year advancing. It seeks, of course, to settle down upon the unoccupied territory of the West, and may at no distant day equal, and even outnumber the native population.

But what if this emigration, self-moved and slow in the beginning, is now rolling its broad tide at the bidding of the powers of Europe hostile to free institutions, and associated in holy alliance to arrest and put them down? Is this a vain fear? Are not the continental powers alarmed at the march of liberal opinions, and associated to put them down?...A tenth part of the suffrage of the nation,...condensed and wielded by the Catholic powers of Europe, might decide our elections, perplex our policy, inflame and divide the nation, break the bond of our union, and throw down our free institutions....

I have no fear of the Catholics, considered simply as a religious denomination, and unallied to the church and state establishments of the European governments hostile to republican institutions.

Let the Catholics mingle with us as Americans, and come with their children under the full action of our common schools and republican institutions, and the various powers of assimilation, and we are prepared cheerfully to abide the consequences. If in these circumstances the Protestant religion cannot stand before the Catholic, let it go down, and we will sound no alarm, and ask no aid, and make no complaint. It is no ecclesiastical quarrel to which we would call the attention of the American nation.[1]

Compelled by the Potato Famine to migrate to America, many Irish felt an enduring longing for their homeland, as the following song of lament reflects.

> Farewell to thee, Erin mavourneen,
> Thy valleys I'll tread nevermore;
> This heart that now bleeds for thy sorrows,
> Will waste on a far distant shore.
> The green sods lie cold on my parents,
> A cross marks the place of their rest,—
> The wind that moans sadly above them,
> Will waft their poor child to the West.[2]

Few personal memoirs from Irish immigrants of this period survive, but the combined effects of the Famine Exodus and the hostile American reception were felt in later generations, as William Alfred's memoir of his great-grandmother, Anna Maria Gavin, attests.

Of Ireland she rarely spoke, save to recall that she was often hungry there and that for her main meal she often ate cress out of the brooks on oaten bread with a bit of lard. Although she always used to say she had no desire to return to Ireland to live, she lived out of a trunk to her dying day, and taught her children to do the same. I myself, till well on in my twenties, felt that Ireland, which I had never seen, was my true country. When, over eighty, she died, it did not seem strange six months afterward to receive a clipping from an Irish newspaper, which read: "Died in Exile: Anna Maria Gavin Egan."

Of her first years here, she never tired of speaking. She and her mother landed at Castle Garden and walked up Broadway to City Hall, with bundles of clothes and pots and featherbeds in their arms. The singing of the then exposed telegraph wires frightened them, as did the bustle of the people in the streets. They lost their fear when they met an Irish policeman who directed them to a rooming house on Baxter Street.

Her training as a "manty-maker" (mantua-maker, in other words, dressmaker) gave her an advantage over other girls of her age. She got a job fast. On her way from work the first year, she nightly passed a house in whose tall, lit first-floor windows sat the most beautiful women she had ever seen, dressed to the nines, their hair as trimly curled, their faces painted fresh as new French china dolls. After weeks of gawking, she built up the courage to hazard a smile. "Come up here...," one of the women called to her, "and we'll wipe that smile off your face."[3]

On the other edge of the continent in California, another new immigrant group, the Chinese, were making their presence felt. By 1852 there were nearly 25,000 Chinese in California, attracted by the Gold Rush. They did not always, at first, encounter hostility, as the following report in a California paper of 1852 suggests.

Quite a large number of the Celestials [Chinese] have arrived among us of late, enticed thither by the golden romance that has filled the world. Scarcely a ship arrives that does not bring an increase to this worthy integer of our population. [Soon] the China boys will vote at the same polls, study at the same schools and bow at the same altar as our own countrymen.[4]

German Beer Halls, like this one pictured on New York's Bowery, offered music and contact with nature as well as beer from the owners' own breweries. Much to the dismay of American temperance reformers, German immigrants viewed beer halls and gardens as gathering places for the entire family.

Samuel Waugh's The Bay and Harbor of New York, *painted in 1855, shows the newly opened Castle Garden, the city's first official reception center for immigrants, receiving a boat-load of newcomers from Ireland and perhaps from Germany. Note the anti-Irish caricatures, including the trunk on the right labeled "Pat Murfy for Ameriky." A Chinese junk rides at anchor in the harbor, a reminder that not all immigration in this period was from Europe.*

Another newspaper report described the emerging Chinatown of San Francisco.

The majority of the houses were of Chinese importation and were stores, stocked with hams, tea, dried fish, dried ducks, and other Chinese eatables, besides copper pots and kettles, fans, shawls, chessmen, and all sorts of curiosities. Suspended over the doors were brilliantly-colored boards covered with Chinese writings, and with several yards of red ribbon streaming from them; while the streets thronged with Celestials, chattering vociferously as they rushed about from store to store.[5]

The large German immigrant population was more geographically dispersed than either the Irish or the Chinese. Their experience is also better documented with firsthand accounts, because many more German immigrants than Irish sent letters home to family members and wrote reminiscences. Many German immigrants brought farming skills with them to America and put them to use, often in company with kin and friends, in rural ethnic clusters. Wilhelmina Stille, her brother Wilhelm Stille, and her fiance Wilhelm Krumme settled together along the Ohio River near Wheeling, Virginia (now West Virginia). The following letter, written in October 1838, is from Wilhelmina Stille to her mother.

We got married on August 10th. We've bought 80 acres of land and our brother has too, they are next to one another but his is so much better it cost 400 talers and ours 300 talers, we paid 200 talers of it since we didn't have any more. So we're asking you, dear mother and brothers in the name of the Lord, send me the rest of my money, please don't fail me because we have nowhere else to turn. I also want to tell you that my brother Wilhelm left his boss last fall and went down the river on a boat that was loaded with all kinds of goods, flour, potatoes, string beans, cabbage, onions, apples and two others had a quarter of it each. The city is called Neuoliens [New Orleans] which is 15 hundred miles away it's in South America there they can't grow such things. When he got back he started to work on his land, he's built himself a house and has already cleared 3 acres of farmland. We live 3 hours away from Wilingen [Wheeling] right on the road and are very happy for I have a happy marriage and live in peace.[6]

Another German immigrant, Carl Blümer, settled in Santa Fé before the Mexican-American War. As the following letter of October 31, 1852, suggests, he and his brother August were caught up in some of the dramatic events of America's westward expansion.

My dearest, my eternally beloved mother: Your reproach, my dear mother, is justified; years have passed without my writing to you; I don't

384

want to try to excuse myself, only to the extent that I knew for certain that August [his brother] had sent you all my news until he left for California. Mother! Mother! Brother August is no more! August came here, to Santa Fé, in the spring of 1849; but he only stayed with me for a few months, and went from here to California, thinking and hoping to make a fortune more quickly there. He arrived safely in California; went to the gold mines and wrote his *last* letter to me from the gold mines in Mariposa, in California, in the winter of 1849. Then I didn't hear anything from him for a long time, until I finally received a letter the following year from his brother-in-law, who informed me that he had died in August 1850 in the gold mines on the Yuba River in California. He fell ill with abdominal ailments, and he passed away, calm and composed, after about a month. A German, who worked with him, wrote that he was buried decently. Peace be to his ashes in a foreign land, in an unknown place! His spirit will hover about us in love!...

I myself, my dear mother, have almost always been well, in this country, since 1836; the climate here is one of the nicest, at least the healthiest, on earth. I've been married for about 4 years; my wife is a Mexican, the youngest daughter of a good but poor family; she is named Felisiana Quintana y Alarid. She is pretty about 26 years old. She presented me with a daughter as a first-born child, whom we baptized Carlota, (Charlotte). My second is a boy; named Carlos (Karl or Charles) and is about 15 months old. My business here has almost always been as a merchant; about a year ago I gave up my trading company and am mostly employed in the service of the government. Since the United States of North America took possession of this country, as a result of the war, since the year 1846, I have always had one or other government post; *Treasurer* I have had since 1846 and I still have; my yearly salary is 500 dollars, about 700 Prussian talers. Felisiana sends you, dear mother, her filial love and devotion, and all of you a dear and sisterly kiss.

Farewell!/Forever/ Your true son
and your true brother and uncle, Carl Blümer[7]

Carl Schurz, who emigrated from Germany in 1852 when the nativist political movement was at its height, gained great prominence in the United States, becoming a general in the Union Army, a senator from Missouri, and secretary of the interior in the administration of Rutherford B. Hayes. In this letter to a German friend, he reflects with pride on some of his accomplishments in his adopted country.

Here in America I lived for several years quietly and unobtrusively in an ideally happy family circle until at last in the year '56, when the movement against slavery developed magnificently, I found myself drawn into public life. I knew that I should accomplish something. America is the country for ambitious capability, and the foreigner who studies its conditions thoroughly, and with full appreciation, can procure for himself an even greater field of activity than the native. My success surprised even myself; I found my boldest expectations outdone. I flung myself with all my heart into the Antislavery Movement and thus showed the Americans something new....It is said that I made Lincoln President. That is certainly not true; but the fact that people say it indicates that I did contribute something toward raising the wind which bore Lincoln into the presidential chair and thus shook the slave system to its very foundations.[8]

Study Questions

1. Why did immigrant groups of the 1830s through the 1850s generate more controversy than earlier groups?
2. Many immigrants regarded ethnic neighborhoods as essential to their economic and cultural survival, but many native-born Americans regarded them as hindrances to complete adoption of "American" customs and attitudes. What is your opinion?
3. In what ways did Irish, German, and Chinese immigrants participate in the social, political, economic, and cultural life of the United States?
4. Do you see any validity in the arguments of nativists like Lyman Beecher?

Sources

1. Lyman Beecher, *Plea for the West* (1835)
2. "The Emigrant's Farewell," *Boston Pilot*, August 16, 1862
3. William Alfred, "An Irish Integrity," in Thomas C. Wheeler, ed., *The Immigrant Experience: The Anguish of Becoming American* (1972)
4. *Daily Alta California* (San Francisco), May 12, 1852, quoted in Ronald Takaki, *A Different Mirror: A History of Multicultural America* (1993)
5. Thomas Chinn, H.M. Lai, and Philip Choy, *A History of the Chinese in California* (1969)
6. Walter D. Kamphoefner, Wolfgang Helbich, and Ulrike Summer, eds., *News from the Land of Freedom: German Immigrants Write Home* (1991)
7. *Ibid.*
8. Letter from Carl Schurz to Theodor Petrasch, Bonn, September 24, 1863, quoted in A.E. Zucker, ed. *The Forty-Eighters, Political Refugees of the German Revolution of 1848* (1950)

CHAPTER FOURTEEN

THE TERRITORIAL EXPANSION OF THE UNITED STATES

1830s–1850s

Samuel Chamberlain, *General Wool Crossing the Military Plaza*, San Antonio, c. 1856. San Jacinto Museum of History Association.

AMERICAN COMMUNITIES
Texans and Tejanos
"Remember the Alamo!"

For thirteen days in February and March 1836, a force of 187 Texans held the mission fortress known as the Alamo against a siege by 5,000 Mexican troops under General Antonio López de Santa Anna, president of Mexico. Santa Anna had come north to subdue rebellious Texas, the northernmost part of the Mexican province of Coahuila y Texas, and to place it under central authority. On March 6 he ordered a final assault, and in brutal fighting that claimed over 1,500 Mexican lives, his army took the mission. All the defenders were killed, including Commander William Travis and the well-known frontiersmen Jim Bowie and Davy Crockett. It was a crushing defeat for the Texans, but the cry "Remember the Alamo!" rallied their remaining forces, which, less than two months later, routed the Mexican army and forced Santa Anna to grant Texas independence from Mexico. Today the Alamo, in San Antonio, is one of the most cherished historic shrines in the United States.

But memory is selective: some things tend to be forgotten. Within a generation of the uprising few remembered that many *Tejanos*, Spanish-speaking people born in Texas, had joined with American settlers fighting for Texas independence. The Americans were concentrated in the central and eastern portions of the huge Texas territory, where during the 1820s the Mexican government had authorized several colonies managed by *empresarios* (land agents) like Stephen F. Austin. These settler communities consisted mostly of farmers from the Mississippi Valley, who introduced slavery and cotton growing to the rich lands of coastal and upland Texas.

The Tejano community, descended from eighteenth-century Spanish and Mexican settlers, included wealthy *rancheros* who raised cattle on the shortgrass prairies of south Texas, as well as the cowboys known as *vaqueros* and the *peónes*, or poor tenant farmers. Although there was relatively little contact between the Americans and Tejanos, their leaders interacted in San Antonio, the center of regional government. The Tejano elite welcomed the American immigrants and were enthusiastic about their plans for the economic development of Texas. Many Americans married into elite Tejano families, who hoped that by thus assimilating and sharing power with the Americans they could not only maintain but strengthen their community.

The Mexican state, however, was politically and socially unstable during these first years after its successful revolt against Spain in 1821. Liberals favored a loose federal union, conservatives a strong central state. As a northern frontier province, Texas did not have the benefits of statehood; as a result most Tejanos found themselves taking the liberal side in the struggle, opting for more local control over government activities. When, in 1828, the conservative centralists came to power in Mexico City and decided the Americans had too much influence in Texas, many Tejanos rose up with the Americans in opposition. In 1832 the Tejano elite of San Antonio and many prominent rancheros went on record in favor of provincial autonomy and a strong role for the Americans.

One of the leaders of the San Antonio community was the wealthy ranchero Juan Nepomuceno Seguín. As Santa Anna's army approached from the south, Seguín recruited a company of Tejano volunteers and joined the American force inside the walls of the Alamo. During the siege, Commander Travis sent Seguín and some of his men for reinforcements. Stopped by Mexican troops on his way across the lines, Seguín called out, "¡Somos paisanos!" (We are countrymen), confusing the guards just long enough for Seguín and his men to make their escape despite the hail of gunfire that quickly ensued. Seguín returned from his unsuccessful mission to find the burned bodies of the Alamo defenders, including seven San Antonio Tejanos. "Texas será libre!" Seguín called out as he directed the burial of the Alamo defenders—"Texas shall be free!" In April, Seguín led a regiment of Tejanos in the decisive battle of San Jacinto that won independence for Texas.

At first Tejanos were pleased with independence and played an important political role in the new Republic of Texas. The liberal Lorenzo de Zavala was chosen vice president, and Seguín became the mayor of San Antonio. But soon things began to change, illustrating a recurring pattern in the American occupation of new lands—a striking shift in the relations between different cultures in frontier areas. Most commonly, in the initial stage newcomers blended with native peoples, creating a "frontier of inclusion." The first hunters, trappers, and traders on every American frontier—west of the Appalachians, in the Southwest, and in the Far West—married into the local community and tried to learn native ways. Outnumbered Americans adapted to local societies as a matter of simple survival.

A second, unstable stage occurred when the number of Americans increased and they began occupying more and more land or, as in California, "rushing" in great numbers to mine gold, overrunning native communities. The usual result was warfare and the rapid growth of hostility and racial prejudice—all of which was largely absent in earlier days. A third stage—that of stable settlement—occurred when the native community had been completely "removed" or isolated. In this "frontier of exclusion," racial mixing was rare. Generally, when Europeans pushed American Indians onto reservations they cut themselves off from sources of human history that could have helped them more fully understand the country into which they had moved. And in Texas, American settlers—initially invited in by Mexicans and Tejanos—developed an anti-Mexican passion, regarding all Spanish-speakers as Mexican enemies rather than Tejano allies.

Unscrupulous Americans exploited these prejudices to acquire Tejano property. If the rancheros were "sufficiently scared," one wrote, they would "make an advantageous sale of their lands," and if "two or three hundred of our troops should be stationed here, I have no doubt but a man could make some good speculations." Tejanos were attacked and forced from their homes; some of their villages were burned to the ground. "On the pretext that they were Mexicans," Seguín wrote, Americans treated Tejanos "worse than brutes…My countrymen ran to me for protection against the assaults or exactions of these adventurers." But even in his capacity as mayor Seguín could do little, and in 1842 he and his family, like hundreds of other Tejano families, fled south to Mexico in fear for their lives.

Thus the Tejanos became symbols of a romanticized past rather than full participants in the building of western communities. Spanish-speaking communities in Texas, and later in New Mexico and California, like the communities of Indians throughout the West, became conquered peoples. "White folks and Mexicans were never made to live together," a Texas woman told a traveler a few years after the revolution. "The Mexicans had no business here," she said, and the Americans might "just have to get together and drive them all out of the country." The descendants of the first European settlers of the American Southwest had become foreigners in the land their people had lived in for two centuries.

San Antonio

388

KEY TOPICS

- Continental expansion and the concept of Manifest Destiny

- The contrasting examples of frontier development in Oregon, Texas, and California

- How the political effects of expansion heightened sectional tensions

EXPLORING THE WEST

There seemed to be no stopping the expansion of the American people. By 1840 they had occupied all of the land east of the Mississippi River and had organized all of it (except for Florida and Wisconsin) into states. Of the ten states admitted to the Union between 1800 and 1840, all but one were west of the Appalachian Mountains. Less than sixty years after the United States gained its independence, the majority of its population lived west of the original thirteen states.

The speed and success of this expansion were a source of deep national pride that whetted appetites for more. Many Americans looked eagerly westward to the vast unsettled reaches of the Louisiana Purchase: to Texas, Santa Fé, and trade with Mexico, and even to the Far West, where New England sea captains had been trading for furs since the 1790s. By 1848 the United States had gained all of these coveted western lands. This chapter examines the way the United States became a continental nation, forming many frontier communities in the process. Exploring the vast continent of North America and gaining an understanding of its geography took several centuries and the efforts of many people.

The Fur Trade

The fur trade, which flourished from the 1670s to the 1840s, was an important spur to exploration on the North American continent. In the 1670s the British Hudson's Bay Company and its French Canadian rival, Montreal's North West Company, began exploring beyond the Great Lakes in the Canadian West in search of beaver pelts. Traders and trappers for both companies depended on the goodwill and cooperation of the native peoples of the region, in particular the Assiniboins, Crees, Gros Ventres, and Blackfeet, all of whom moved freely across what later became the U.S.-Canadian border. From the marriages of European men with native women arose a distinctive mixed-race group, the *métis* (see Chapter 5). In 1821 the Hudson's Bay Company absorbed its Montreal rival and ran the fur trade from trading posts in the far Canadian North

such as Norway House, Cumberland House, and Fort George. British, French Canadian, and métis employees of the Hudson's Bay Company also trapped and explored throughout the Canadian West and in the Oregon Country, then jointly occupied by the British and Americans (see Chapter 9).

Not until the 1820s were American companies able to challenge British dominance of the trans-Mississippi fur trade. In 1824, William Henry Ashley of the Rocky Mountain Fur Company instituted the "rendezvous" system. This was a yearly trade fair, held deep in the Rocky Mountains (Green River and Jackson Hole were favored locations), to which trappers brought their catch of furs. There they traded them for goods transported by the fur companies from St. Louis: traps, guns, ammunition, tobacco, beads and fabrics (for later trade with Indian peoples), and alcohol. These yearly fur rendezvous were modeled on traditional Indian trade gatherings such as the one at the Mandan villages on the upper Missouri and the huge gathering that took place every year at Celilo Falls on the Columbia River during the annual salmon run. Like its Indian model, the fur rendezvous was a boisterous, polyglot, many-day affair at which trappers of many nationalities—Americans and Indian peoples, French Canadians and métis, as well as Mexicans from Santa Fé and Taos—gathered to trade, drink, and gamble.

For the "mountain men" employed by the American fur companies, the rendezvous was their only contact with American society. The rest of the year they spent deep in the mountains trapping beaver and living in some sort of relationship with local Indian peoples. Some lived in a constant state of danger, always alert to the possibility of attack by parties of local people. But most trappers sought accommodation and friendship: nearly half of them contracted long-lasting marriages with Indian women, who not only helped in the trapping and curing of furs but also acted as vital diplomatic links between the white and Indian worlds. Contemporaries often viewed the mountain men—tough, bearded, leather-clad, fluent in Indian tongues—as half-savage, but we should perhaps see them as an example of successful adaptation to frontier life. Indeed, one

The artist Alfred Jacob Miller, a careful observer of the western fur trade, shows us a mountain man and his Indian wife in his 1837 Bourgeois Walker and His Wife. Both Walker and his wife worked together to trap and prepare beaver pelts for market.

legendary trapper became a Crow chief: the African American Jim Beckwourth, who married a Crow woman and was accepted into her tribe.

For all its adventure, the American fur trade was short-lived. By the 1840s, the population of beaver in western streams was virtually destroyed, and the day of the mountain man was over. But with daring journeys like that of Jedediah Smith, the first American to enter California over the Sierra Nevada mountains, the mountain men had helped forge a clear picture of western geography. Soon permanent settlers would follow the trails they had blazed.

Government-Sponsored Exploration

The federal government played a major role in the exploration and development of the West. Thomas Jefferson decisively influenced American westward expansion with the Louisiana Purchase of 1803. When he dispatched the Lewis and Clark expedition the next year it may have been largely to satisfy his own intense scientific and geographic curiosity about the West, but he also instructed Meriwether Lewis and William Clark to draw the western Indians into the American trading network, away from the British.

The exploratory and scientific aspects of the Lewis and Clark expedition set a precedent for many government-financed quasi-military expeditions. In 1806 and 1807, Lieutenant Zebulon Pike led an expedition to the Rocky Mountains in Colorado. Major

Stephen Long's exploration and mapping of the Great Plains in the years 1819–20 was part of a show of force meant to frighten British fur trappers out of the West. Then, in 1843 and 1844, another military explorer, John C. Frémont, mapped the overland trails to Oregon and California. In the 1850s, the Pacific Railroad surveys explored possible transcontinental railroad routes. The tradition of government-sponsored western exploration continued after the Civil War in the famous geological surveys, the best known of which is the 1869 Grand Canyon exploration by Major John Wesley Powell.

Beginning with Long's expedition, the results of these surveys were published by the government, complete with maps, illustrations, and, after the Civil War, photographs. These publications fed a strong popular appetite for pictures of the breathtaking scenery of the Far West and information about its inhabitants. Artists like Karl Bodmer, who accompanied a private expedition by the scientifically inclined German prince Maximilian in the years 1833–34, produced stunning portraits of American Indians. Over the next three decades Thomas Moran, Albert Bierstadt, and other landscape artists traveled west with government expeditions and came home to paint grand (and sometimes fanciful) pictures of Yosemite Valley and Yellowstone (later designated among the first national parks). All these images of the American West made a powerful contribution to the emerging American self-image. American pride in the land—the biggest of this, the longest of that, the most spectacular of something else—was founded on the images brought home by government surveyors and explorers.

In the wake of the pathfinders came hundreds of government geologists and botanists as well as the surveyors who mapped and plotted the West for settlement according to the Land Ordinance of 1785. The basic pattern of land survey and sale established by these measures (see Chapter 7) was followed all the way to the Pacific Ocean. The federal government sold the western public lands at low prices and, to veterans of the War of 1812, gave away land in the Old Northwest. And following policies established in the Old Northwest (see Chapter 9), the federal government also shouldered the expense of Indian removal, paying

Exploration of the Continent, 1804–1830   *Lewis and Clark's "voyage of discovery" of 1804–06 was the first of many government-sponsored western military expeditions. Crossing the Great Plains in 1806, Lieutenant Zebulon Pike was captured by the Spanish in their territory and taken to Mexico but returned in 1807 via Texas. Major Stephen Long, who crossed the Plains in 1819–20, found them "arid and forbidding." Meanwhile fur trappers, among them the much-traveled Jedediah Smith, became well acquainted with the West as they hunted beaver for their pelts.*

the soldiers or the officials who fought or talked Indian peoples into giving up their lands and making long-term commitments to compensate the Indian people themselves. The government also supported the forts and soldiers whose task was to maintain peace between settlers and Indian peoples in newly opened areas.

Expansion and Indian Policy

While American artists were painting the way of life of western Indian peoples, eastern Indian tribes were being removed from their homelands to Indian Territory (present-day Oklahoma, Kansas, and Nebraska), west of Arkansas, Missouri, and Iowa on the eastern edge of the

Great Plains, a region widely regarded as unfarmable and popularly known as the Great American Desert. The justification for this western removal, as Thomas Jefferson had explained early in the century, was the creation of a space where Indian people could live undisturbed by white people while they slowly adjusted to "civilized" ways. But the government officials who negotiated the removals failed to predict the tremendous speed at which white people would settle the West.

As a result, encroachment on Indian Territory was not long in coming. The territory was crossed by the Santa Fé Trail, established in 1821; in the 1840s the northern part was crossed by the heavily traveled

Overland Trails to California, Oregon, and the Mormon community in Utah. In 1854, the government abolished the northern half of Indian Territory, establishing the Kansas and Nebraska Territories in its place and opening them to immediate white settlement. The tribes of the area—the Potawatomis, Wyandots, Kickapoos, Sauks, Foxes, Delawares, Shawnees, Kaskaskias, Peorias, Piankashaws, Weas, Miamis, Omahas, Otos, and Missouris—signed treaties accepting either vastly reduced reservations or allotments. Those who accepted allotments—sections of private land—often sold them, under pressure, to white people. Thus many of the Indian people who had hoped for independence and escape from white pressures in Indian Territory lost both their autonomy and their tribal identity.

The people in the southern part of Indian Territory, in what is now Oklahoma, fared somewhat better. Those members of the southern tribes—the Cherokees, Chickasaws, Choctaws, Creeks, and Seminoles—who had survived the trauma of forcible removal from the Southeast in the 1830s quickly created impressive new communities. The five tribes divided up the territory and established self-governing nations with their own schools and churches. The societies they created were not so different from the American societies from which they had been expelled. The five tribes even carried slavery west with them: an elite economic group established plantations and shipped their cotton to New Orleans like other Southerners. Until after the Civil War, these southern tribes were able to withstand outside pressures and remain the self-governing communities that treaties had assured them they would be.

The removal of the eastern tribes did not solve "the Indian Problem," the term many Americans used to describe their relationship with the first occupants of the land. West of Indian Territory were the nomadic and warlike Indians of the Great Plains: the Sioux, Cheyennes, Arapahoes, Comanches, and Kiowas. Beyond them were the seminomadic tribes of the Rocky Mountains—the Blackfeet, Crows, Utes, Shoshonis, Nez Percé, and Salish peoples—and, in the Southwest, the farming cultures of the Pueblos, Hopis, Acomas, Zunis, Pimas, and Papagos and the migratory Apaches and Navajos. Even farther west were hundreds of small tribes in California and the Pacific Northwest. Clearly, all of these people could not be "removed," for where could they go? The first western pioneers ignored the issue. Beginning in the 1840s, they simply passed through the far western tribal lands on their way to establish new frontiers of settlement in California and Oregon. Later, after the Civil War, the government would undertake a series of Indian wars that ultimately left the remaining Indian peoples penned up on small reservations.

THE POLITICS OF EXPANSION

America's rapid expansion had many consequences, but perhaps the most significant was that it reinforced Americans' sense of themselves as pioneering people. In the 1890s Frederick Jackson Turner, America's most famous historian, observed that the repeated experience of settling new frontiers across the continent had shaped Americans into a uniquely adventurous, optimistic, and democratic people. Other historians have disagreed with Turner, but there is no question that his view of the frontier long ago won the battle for popular opinion. Ever since the time of Daniel Boone, venturing into the wilderness has held a special place in the American imagination, seen almost as an American right.

Manifest Destiny, an Expansionist Ideology

How did Americans justify their restless expansionism? After all, the United States was already a very large country with much undeveloped land. To push beyond existing boundaries was to risk war with Great Britain, which claimed the Pacific Northwest, and with Mexico, which held what is now Texas, New Mexico, Arizona, Utah, Nevada, California, and part of Colorado. If the United States prevailed it would be reducing 75,000 Spanish-speaking people and 150,000 Indian people to subject status. Undertaking such a conquest required a rationale.

In 1845 newspaperman John O'Sullivan provided it. It was, he wrote, "our manifest destiny to overspread the continent allotted by Providence for the free development of our yearly multiplying millions." Sullivan argued that Americans had a God-given right to bring the benefits of American democracy to other, more backward peoples—meaning Mexicans and Indians—by force, if necessary. The notion of manifest destiny summed up the powerful combination of pride in what America had achieved and missionary zeal and racist attitudes toward other peoples that lay behind the thinking of many expansionists. Americans were proud of their rapid development: the surge in population, the remarkable canals and railroads, the grand scale of American enterprise. Why shouldn't it be even bigger? Almost swaggering, Americans dared other countries—Great Britain in particular—to stop them.

Behind the bravado was concern about the economic future of the United States. After the devastating Panic of 1837 (see Chapter 10), many politicians became convinced that the nation's prosperity depended on vastly expanded trade with Asia. Senator Thomas Hart Benton of Missouri had been advocating trade with India by way of the Missouri and Columbia Rivers since the 1820s (not the easiest of routes, as Lewis and Clark had shown). Soon Benton and others were pointing out

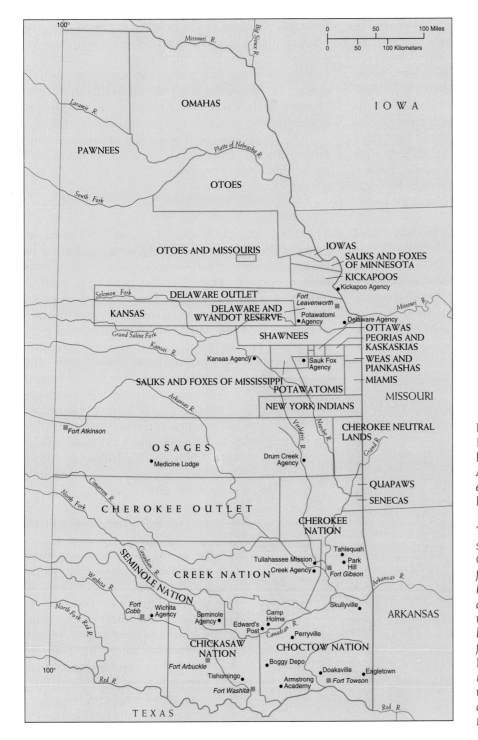

Indian Territory before the Kansas-Nebraska Act of 1854
Indian Territory lay west of Arkansas, Missouri, and Iowa and east of Spanish Territory. Most of the Indian peoples who lived there in the 1830s and the 1840s had been "removed" from east of the Mississippi River. The southern part (now Oklahoma) was inhabited by peoples from the Old Southwest: the Cherokees, Chickasaws, Choctaws, Creeks, and Seminoles. North of that (in what is now Kansas and Nebraska) lived peoples who had been removed from the Old Northwest. All these Indian peoples had trouble adjusting not only to a new climate and a new way of life but to the close proximity of some Indian tribes who were their traditional enemies.

how greatly Pacific trade would increase if the United States held the magnificent harbors of the west coast, among them Puget Sound in the Oregon Country held jointly with Britain and the bays of San Francisco and San Diego, both in Mexican-held California.

In one sense, manifest destiny was evangelical religion on a larger scale. The same revivalist fervor that Charles G. Finney had sparked in Rochester in 1830 had a continental echo: missionaries were among the first to travel to the Far West to Christianize Indian people. Just as many of Finney's eastern converts mounted reform movements aimed at changing the lives of workers, so did the western missionaries attempt to "civilize" the Indian peoples. They believed that the only way to do so was to destroy their cultures and to surround them with good American examples.

Expansionism was also tied to national politics. O'Sullivan, whose "manifest destiny" became the expansionist watchword, was not a neutral observer: he was the editor of the *Democratic Review*, a party newspaper. Most Democrats were wholehearted supporters of expansion, whereas many Whigs (especially in the North) opposed it. Whigs welcomed most of the changes wrought by industrialization but advocated strong government policies that would guide growth and development within the country's existing boundaries; they feared (correctly) that expansion would raise the contentious issue of the extension of slavery to new territories.

On the other hand, many Democrats feared the industrialization that the Whigs welcomed. Where the Whigs saw economic progress, Democrats saw economic depression (the Panic of 1837 was the worst the nation had experienced), uncontrolled urban growth, and growing social unrest. For many Democrats, the answer to the nation's social ills was to continue to follow Thomas Jefferson's vision of establishing agriculture in the new territories in order to counterbalance industrialization (see Chapter 9). Another factor in the political struggle over expansion in the 1840s was that many Democrats were Southerners, for whom the continual expansion of cotton-growing lands was a matter of social faith as well as economic necessity.

These were politicians' reasons. The average farmer moved west for many other reasons: land hunger, national pride, plain and simple curiosity, and a sense of adventure.

The Overland Trails

The 2,000-mile trip on the Overland Trails from the banks of the Missouri River to Oregon and California usually took seven months, sometimes more. Travel was slow, dangerous, tedious, and exhausting. Forced to lighten their loads as animals died and winter weather threatened, pioneers often arrived at their destination with little food and few belongings. Uprooted from family and familiar surroundings, pioneers faced the prospect of being, in the poignant and much-used biblical phrase, "strangers in a strange land." Yet despite the risks, settlers streamed west: 5,000 to Oregon by 1845 and about 3,000 to California by 1848 (before the discovery of gold). Some arrived by ship, but this was more expensive than the overland journey, which itself was not cheap: a wagon, a team of oxen, food, clothing, and essential tools cost between $500 and $1,000.

Pioneers had many motives for making the trip. Glowing reports from Oregon's Willamette Valley, for example, seemed to promise economic opportunity and healthy surroundings, an alluring combination to farmers in the malaria-prone Midwest who had been hard hit by the Panic of 1837. But rational motives do not tell the whole story. Many men were motivated by a sense of adventure, by a desire to experience the unknown, or, as they put it, to "see the elephant." Women were more likely to think of the trip as *A Pioneer's Search for an Ideal Home*, the title that Phoebe Judson chose for

The Overland Trails, 1840 *All the great trails west started at the Missouri River. The Oregon, California, and Mormon Trails followed the Platte River into Wyoming, crossed South Pass, and divided in western Wyoming. The much harsher Santa Fé Trail stretched 900 miles southwest across the Great Plains. All of the trails crossed Indian Territory and, to greater or lesser extent, Mexican possessions as well.*

her account of her family's 1852 trip to Oregon.

Few pioneers traveled alone, partly because they feared Indian attack (which was rare) but largely because they needed help fording rivers or crossing mountains with heavy wagons. Most Oregon pioneers traveled with their families but usually also joined a larger group, forming a "train." In the earliest years, when the route was still uncertain, trains hired a "pilot," generally a former fur trapper. Often the men of the wagon train drew up semimilitary constitutions, electing a leader. Democratic as this process appeared, not everyone was willing to obey the leader, and many trains experienced dissension and breakups along the trail. But in essence all pioneers—men, women, and children—were part of a new, westward-moving community in which they had to accept both the advantages and disadvantages of community membership.

J. Goldsborough Bruff, one of thousands who rushed to California for gold in 1849, sketched many events in his Overland Trail journey. Here he depicts several wagons being ferried over the Platte River. The need for individuals to cooperate is obvious. Less obvious in this sketch is the danger: most river crossing points lacked ferries, and both people and livestock often drowned trying to ford them.

Wagon trains started westward as soon as the prairies were green (thus ensuring feed for the livestock). The daily routine was soon established. Men took care of the moving equipment and the animals, while the women cooked and kept track of the children. Slowly, at a rate of about fifteen miles a day, the wagon trains moved west along the Platte River, crossing the Continental Divide at South Pass in present-day Wyoming. West of the Rockies the climate was much drier. The long, dusty stretch along the Snake River in present-day southern Idaho finally gave way to Oregon's steep and difficult Blue Mountains and to the dangerous rafting down the Columbia River, in which many drowned and all were drenched by the cold winter rains of the Pacific Northwest. California-bound migrants faced even worse hazards: the complete lack of water in the Humbolt Sink region of northern Nevada and the looming Sierra Nevadas, which had to be crossed before the winter snows came. (Members of the ill-fated Donner party, snowbound on the Nevada side of that range in 1846–47, resorted to cannibalism before they were rescued.)

In addition to the ever-present tedium and exhaustion, wagon trains were beset by such trail hazards as illness and accident. Danger from Indian attack, which all pioneers feared, was actually very small. Before the 1849 California Gold Rush, conflicts between wagon trains and Indians claimed the lives of only thirty-four white people (twenty-

four in one wagon train) and twenty-five Indians. In subsequent years, as thousands of gold rushers flocked west, the deaths increased, but, significantly, more Indians than white people died. It appears that unprovoked white attacks on Indians were more common than the reverse.

In contrast, cholera killed at least a thousand people a year in 1849 and the early 1850s when it stalked sections of the trail along the Platte River. Spread by contaminated water, cholera caused vomiting and diarrhea, which in turn led to extreme dehydration and death, often in one night. In the afflicted regions, trailside graves were a frequent and grim sight. Drownings were not uncommon, nor were accidental ax wounds or shootings, and children sometimes fell out of wagons and were run over. The members of the wagon train community did what they could to arrange decent burials, and they provided support for survivors: men helped widows drive their wagons onward, women nursed and tended babies whose mothers were dead, and at least one parentless family, the seven Sager children, were brought to Oregon in safety.

By 1860 almost 300,000 people had traveled the Overland Trails to Oregon or California. Ruts from the wagon wheels can be seen in a number of places along the route even today. In 1869 the completion of the transcontinental railroad marked the end of the wagon train era (although many people made shorter trips to other western locations by wagon). In retrospect, the pioneers remembered their journey as more dangerous and less tedious than it actually was. The stories that came down to their grandchildren told of a heroic adventure. These "pioneers' tales" were not the truth as it had

Missouri, was a forbidding 900 miles of arid plains, deserts, and mountains. On the Santa Fé trail, unlike the Oregon Trail, there was serious danger of Indian attack, for neither the Comanches nor the Apaches of the southern high plains tolerated trespassers. In 1825, at the urging of Senator Benton and others, Congress voted federal protection for the Santa Fé Trail, even though much of it lay in Mexican territory. The number of people venturing west in the trading caravans increased yearly because the profits were so great (the first American trader to reach Santa Fé, William Becknell, realized a thousand percent profit). By the 1840s a few hundred American trappers and traders (called *extranjeros*, or foreigners) lived permanently in New Mexico. In Santa Fé, some American merchants married daughters of important local families, suggesting the start of the inclusive stage of frontier contact.

Settlements and trading posts soon grew up along the long Santa Fé Trail. One of the most famous was Bent's Fort, on the Arkansas River in what is now eastern Colorado, which did a brisk trade in beaver skins and buffalo robes. Like most trading posts, it had a multiethnic population. In the 1840s the occupants included housekeeper Josefa Tafoya of Taos, whose husband was a carpenter from Pennsylvania; an African American cook; a French tailor from New Orleans; Mexican muleteers; and a number of Indian women, including the two Cheyenne women who were the (successive) wives of William Bent, cofounder of the fort. The three small communities of Pueblo, Hardscrabble, and Greenhorn, spinoffs of Bent's Fort, were populated by men of all nationalities and their Mexican and Indian wives. All three communities lived by trapping, hunting, and a little farming. This racially and economically mixed existence was characteristic of all early trading frontiers, but another western frontier, the American agricultural settlement in Texas, was different from the start.

Mexican Texas

In 1821, when Mexico gained its independence from Spain, there were 2,240 *Tejano* (Spanish-speaking) residents of Texas. Established in 1716 as a buffer against possible French attack on New Spain, the main Texas settlements of Nacogdoches, Goliad, and San Antonio remained small, far-flung frontier outposts (see Chapter 5). As was customary throughout New Spain, communities were organized around three centers: missions and *presidios* (forts), which formed the nucleus of towns, and the large cattle-raising *ranchos* on which rural living depended. As elsewhere in New Spain, society was divided into two classes: the *ricos* (rich), who claimed Spanish descent, and the mixed-blood *pobres* (poor). Tejano town life was traditionally hierarchical, dominated by the ricos who were connected by blood or marriage with the great ranching families. The most colorful figures on the ranchos were mestizo (mixed-blood) vaqueros, renowned for their horsemanship; Americanization of their name made "buckaroos" of the American cowboys to whom they later taught their skills. Most Tejanos were neither ricos nor vaqueros but small farmers or common laborers who led hardscrabble frontier lives. But all Tejanos, rich and poor, faced the constant threat of raids by Comanche Indians.

The Comanches exemplified the revolutionary changes brought about in the lives of Plains Indians by the reintroduction of horses into the American continent (see Chapter 5). "A Comanche on his feet is out of his element...but the moment he lays his hands upon his horse," said artist George Catlin, "I doubt very much whether any people in the world can surpass [him]." Legendary warriors, the Comanches raided the small Texas settlements at will and even struck deep into Mexico itself. Once they raided so far

Alfred Jacob Miller painted the busy life of Fort Laramie, a multiracial trading fort, in 1837. Bent's Fort, another multiracial trading center, would have looked much like this.

south that they saw brightly plumed birds (parrots) and "tiny men with tails" (monkeys); apparently they had reached the tropical Yucatán. The nomadic Comanches followed the immense buffalo herds on which they depended for food and clothing. Their relentless raids on the Texas settlements rose from a determination to hold onto this rich buffalo territory, for the buffalo provided all that they wanted. They had no interest in being converted by mission priests or incorporated into mixed-race trading communities.

Americans in Texas

In 1821, seeking to increase the strength of its buffer zone between the heart of Mexico and the

Painted by George Catlin about 1834, this scene, Comanche Village, shows how the everyday life of the Comanches was tied to buffalo. The women in the foreground are scraping buffalo hide, and buffalo meat can be seen drying on racks. The men and boys may be planning their next buffalo hunt.

marauding Comanches, the Mexican government granted Moses Austin of Missouri an area of 18,000 square miles within the territory of Texas. Moses died shortly thereafter, and the grant was taken up by his son Stephen F. Austin, who became the first American *empresario* (land agent). From the beginning the American settlement of Texas differed markedly from that of other frontiers. Elsewhere, Americans frequently settled on land to which Indian peoples still held title, or, as in the case of Oregon, they occupied lands to which other countries also made claim. In contrast, the Texas settlement was fully legal: Austin and other empresarios owned their lands as a result of formal contracts with the Mexican government. In exchange, Austin agreed that he and his colonists would become Mexican citizens and would adopt the Catholic religion. It is difficult to say which of these two provisions was the more remarkable, for most nineteenth-century Americans defined their Americanness in terms of citizenship and the Protestant religion.

Additionally, in startling contrast with the usual frontier free-for-all, Austin's community was populated with handpicked settlers, Austin insisting that "no frontiersman who has no other occupation than that of hunter will be received—no drunkard, no gambler, no profane swearer, no idler." Neither Austin nor later empresarios had any trouble finding Americans to apply, for the simple reason that Mexican land grants were magnificent: a square league (4,605 acres) per family. Soon Americans (including African American slaves, to whose presence the Mexican government turned a blind eye) outnumbered Tejanos by nearly two to one: in 1830 there were an estimated 7,000 Americans and 4,000 Tejanos living in Texas.

The Austin settlement of 1821 was followed by others, twenty-six in all, concentrating in the fertile river bottoms of east Texas (along the Sabine River) and south central Texas (the Brazos and the Colorado). These large settlements were highly organized farming enterprises whose principal crop was cotton, grown by African American slave labor, which was sold in the international market. By the early 1830s, Americans in Texas were exporting an estimated $500,000 worth of goods yearly to New Orleans, two-thirds of it cotton.

Austin's colonists and those who settled later were predominantly Southerners who viewed Texas as a natural extension of settlement in Mississippi and Louisiana. These settlers created enclaves (self-contained communities) that had little contact with Tejanos or Indian peoples. In fact, although they lived in Mexican territory, most Americans never bothered to learn Spanish. Nor, in spite of Austin's promises, did they become Mexican citizens or adopt the Catholic religion. Yet because of the nature of agreements made by the empresarios, the Americans could not set up local American-style governments like the one created by settlers in Oregon. Like the immigrants who flooded into east coast cities (see Chapter 13) the Americans in Texas were immigrants to another country—but one they did not intend to adapt to.

The one exception to American exclusiveness occurred in San Antonio, the provincial government center. There, just as in Santa Fé, a handful of wealthy Americans married into the Tejano elite with ease. One such marriage in San Antonio linked wealthy Louisianan James Bowie, the legendary fighter for whom the Bowie knife is named, and Ursula Veramendi, daughter of the vice governor of Texas. With the marriage, Bowie became a wealthy, honored, and well-connected Mexican citizen. Only after the death of his wife and children in a cholera epidemic in 1833 did Bowie support the cause of Anglo-Texan independence, going on to fight—and die—at the Alamo.

The great ranchos excited the admiration of many Americans, who later made cattle raising a major western industry. In these early days in Texas, Americans watched and learned as Tejanos rounded up range cattle, branded them, and drove more than 20,000 each year to Nacogdoches for the U.S. market. Praise for Tejano horsemanship was unstinting: they are "not surpassed perhaps by any other people in the Globe," enthused one American immigrant. Tejano customs, especially multiday celebrations that mixed religious ceremonies, feasting, horse racing, and elaborate *fandangos* (dances), offered striking evidence of the richly textured community life created by Tejanos of all social classes.

For a brief period Texas was big enough to hold three communities: Comanche, Tejano, and American. The nomadic Comanches rode the high plains of northern and western Texas, raiding settlements primarily for horses. The Tejanos maintained their ranchos and missions mostly in the South, while American farmers occupied the eastern and south central sections. Each group would fight to hold its land: the Comanches, their rich hunting grounds, the Mexicans, their towns and ranchos; and the newcomers, the Americans, their rich land grants.

The Texas Revolt

The balance between the three communities in Texas was broken in 1828, when centrists gained control of the government in Mexico City and, in a dramatic shift of policy, decided to exercise firm control over the northern province. As the Mexican government restricted American immigration, outlawed slavery, levied customs duties and taxes, and planned other measures, Americans seethed and talked of rebellion. Bolstering their cause were as many as 20,000 additional Americans, many of them openly expansionist, who flooded into Texas after 1830. These most recent settlers did not intend to become Mexican citizens. Instead, they planned to take over Texas. What ensued was reminiscent of the American Revolution, at least in the eyes of some Americans. But for all the invocations of the Revolution, the real issue in Texas was conquest.

Whereas many of the older American settlers in Texas found much that was admirable, or at least understandable, in Spanish Mexican culture, many of the post-1830 immigrants were vehemently anti-Mexican. Many had grievances: failure to obtain a land grant, restrictions on trade because of Mexican customs regulations, difficulties in understanding Hispanic law, which differed markedly from the Anglo-American legal tradition. Above all, in the eyes of many Americans, there was the matter of race. Statements of racial superiority were commonplace, and even Stephen Austin wrote in 1836 that he saw the Texas conflict as one of barbarism on the part of "a mongrel Spanish-Indian and negro race, against civilization and the Anglo-American race." Most recent American migrants to Texas had come from the South, and racist statements of this sort made political compromise with the Mexican government, a step favored by many of the older American settlers, impossible.

Between 1830 and 1836, in spite of the mediation efforts of Austin (who was imprisoned for eighteen months by the Mexican government for his pains), the mood on both the Mexican and the American-Texan sides became more belligerent. In the fall of 1835 war finally broke out, and a volunteer American Texan and Tejano army seized Goliad and San Antonio, in the heart of Mexican Texas, from the small Mexican army that was sent to quell them. Believing they had won, the Americans were caught off guard by a major counterattack led by the Mexican general and president Antonio López de Santa Anna. As described in the opening of this chapter, on March 6, 1836, Santa Anna and his forces overwhelmed the 187 men who refused to surrender—or to escape from—the Alamo in San Antonio. At Santa Anna's orders, the women at the Alamo—one American woman and several Tejanas—and an African American slave named Joe were spared so that Texans could hear their eyewitness accounts. From those accounts the legend of the Alamo was born.

From San Antonio, Santa Anna divided his army and led part of it in pursuit of the remaining army of American and Tejano volunteers commanded by General Sam Houston. On April 21, 1836, at the San Jacinto River in eastern Texas, Santa Anna thought he had Houston trapped at last. Confident of victory against the exhausted Texans, Santa Anna's army rested in the afternoon, failing even to post sentries. Although Houston advised against it, Houston's men voted to attack immediately rather than wait till the next morning. Shouting "Remember the Alamo!" for the first time, the Texans completely surprised their opponents and won an overwhelming victory. On May 14, 1836, Santa Anna signed a treaty fixing the southern boundary of the newly independent Republic of Texas at the Rio Grande. The Mexican Congress, however, repudiated the treaty and refused to recognize Texan independence. It also rejected the offer by President Andrew Jackson to solve the matter through purchase.

The Republic of Texas

Despite the military triumph of the Americans who had proclaimed the Republic of Texas, the land between the Rio Grande and the Nueces River remained disputed territory. In the eyes of the Mexicans, the American insistence on the Rio Grande boundary was little more than a blatant effort to stake a claim to New Mexico, an older and completely separate Spanish settlement. An effort by the Republic of Texas in 1841 to capture Santa Fé was easily repulsed.

The Republic of Texas was unexpectedly rebuffed in another quarter as well. The U.S. Congress refused to grant it statehood when, in 1837, Texas applied for admission to the Union. Petitions opposing the admission of a fourteenth slave state (there were then thirteen free states) poured into Congress.

Texas: From Mexican Province to U.S. State   *In the space of twenty years, Texas changed shape three times. Initially part of the Mexican province of Coahuila y Tejas, it became the Republic of Texas in 1836, following the Texas Revolt, and was annexed to the United States in that form in 1845. Finally, in the Compromise of 1850 following the Mexican-American War, it took its present shape.*

Congressman John Quincy Adams of Massachusetts, known as the conscience of New England, led the opposition to the admission of Texas. Adams was (and is still) the only former president to subsequently serve in Congress, and his unprecedented position gave immense authority to his opinions. Congress debated and ultimately dropped the Texas application. Although President Jackson was sympathetic to the Texan cause, he knew that he did not have the power to quell the controversy that the admission of Texas would arouse. But he did manage to extend diplomatic recognition to the Republic of Texas, on March 3, 1837, less than twenty-four hours before he left office. Breaking the good news to Texas agents at the White House, Jackson offered toasts to the Republic of Texas and to its president, his old friend Sam Houston.

Sam Houston must often have wondered whether the presidency of the Republic of Texas was an honor worth having. The unresolved conflict with Mexico put heavy stress on American-Tejano relations. Immediately after the revolt, many Tejano residents fled to Mexico, and American squatters moved in to claim their lands. In some regions, vigilantes forced Tejanos to leave. San Antonio, however, the most important city of Mexican Texas, saw an accommodation between the old elite and the new American authorities. Although they slowly lost political power, members of the Tejano elite were not immediately dispossessed of their property. As before, ambitious Anglos married into the Tejano elite. The intermarriages made it easier for the Tejano elite to adjust to the changes in law and commerce that the Americans quickly enacted. But following a temporary recapture of San Antonio by Mexican forces in 1842, positions hardened. Many more of the Tejano elite fled to Mexico, and Americans discussed banishing or imprisoning all Tejanos until the border issue was settled. This was, of course, impossible. Culturally, San Antonio remained a Mexican city long after the Americans had declared independence. The Americans in the Republic of Texas were struggling to reconcile American ideals of democracy with the reality of subordinating those with a prior claim, the Tejanos, to the status of a conquered people.

Ethnocentric attitudes quickly triumphed. Tejanos and other Mexicans were soon being blamed by Americans for their own subordination. Senator Edward Hannegan of Indiana was one of the most outspoken: "Mexico and the United States are peopled by two distinct and utterly unhomogeneous races," he announced in 1847. "In no reasonable period could we amalgamate." In the same year, the *Democratic Review*, completely ignoring the Spanish discovery and conquest of the Americas, offered the following rationalization: "Had Mexico been settled by a vigorous race of Europeans...that would have turned its advantages to account, developed its wealth, increased its commerce and multiplied its settlements, she would not now be in danger of losing her lands by emigration from the North."

American control over the other Texas residents, the Indians, was also slow in coming. Although the coastal Indian peoples were soon killed or removed, the Comanches still rode the high plains of northern and western Texas. West of the Rio Grande, equally fierce Apache bands were in control. Both groups soon learned to distrust American promises to stay out of their territory, and they did not hesitate to raid and to kill trespassers. Not until after the Civil War and major campaigns by the U.S. Army were these fierce Indian tribes conquered.

Texas Annexation and the Election of 1844

Martin Van Buren, who succeeded Andrew Jackson as president in 1837, was too cautious to raise the Texas issue during his term of office. But Texans themselves continued to press for annexation to the United States while at the same time seeking recognition and support from Great Britain. The idea of an independent and expansionist republic on its southern border that might gain the support of America's traditional enemy alarmed many Americans. Annexation thus became an urgent matter of national politics. This issue also added to the troubles of a governing Whig Party that was already deeply divided by the policies of John Tyler, who had become president by default when William Harrison died in office (see Chapter 10). Tyler raised the issue of annexation in 1844, hoping thereby to ensure his reelection, but the strategy backfired. Presenting the annexation treaty to Congress, Secretary of State John Calhoun awakened sectional fears by connecting Texas with the urgent need of southern slave owners to extend slavery.

In a storm of antislavery protest, Whigs rejected the treaty proposed by their own president and ejected Tyler himself from the party. In his place they chose Henry Clay, the party's longtime standard-bearer, as their presidential candidate. Clay took a noncommittal stance on Texas, favoring annexation, but only if Mexico approved. Since Mexico's emphatic disapproval was well known, Clay's position was widely interpreted as a politician's effort not to alienate voters on either side of the fence.

In contrast, in the Democratic Party wholehearted and outspoken expansionists seized control. Sweeping aside their own senior politician, Van Buren, who like Clay tried to remain uncommitted, the Democrats nominated their first "dark horse" candidate, James K. Polk of Tennessee. Southerners and Westerners among the Democrats—including such notables as Robert Walker of Mississippi, Stephen Douglas of Illinois, and Lewis Cass of Michigan—beat the drum of manifest destiny, promising that expansion meant a glorious extension of democracy. They enthusiastically endorsed Polk's platform, which called for "the re-occupation of Oregon and the re-annexation of Texas at the earliest practicable period."

Polk won the 1844 election by the narrow margin of 40,000 popular votes (although he gained 170 electoral votes to Clay's 105). An ominous portent for the Whigs was the showing of James G. Birney of the Liberty Party, who polled 62,000 votes, largely from northern antislavery Whigs. Birney's third-party campaign was the first political sign of the growing strength of antislavery opinion. Nevertheless, the 1844 election was widely interpreted as a mandate for expansion. Thereupon John Tyler, in one of his last actions as president, pushed through Congress a joint resolution (which did not require the two-thirds approval by

the Senate necessary for treaties) for the annexation of Texas. Three months later the Texas congress approved annexation, and thus nine years after its founding the Republic of Texas disappeared. Florida had just been approved for statehood as well, and when Texas entered the Union in December 1845 it was the twenty-eighth state and the fifteenth slave state.

THE MEXICAN–AMERICAN WAR

James K. Polk lived up to his campaign promises. In 1846 he peacefully added Oregon south of the forty-ninth parallel to the United States; in 1848, following the Mexican-American War, he acquired Mexico's northern provinces of California and New Mexico as well. Thus, with the annexation of Texas, the United States, in the short space of three years, had added 1.5 million square

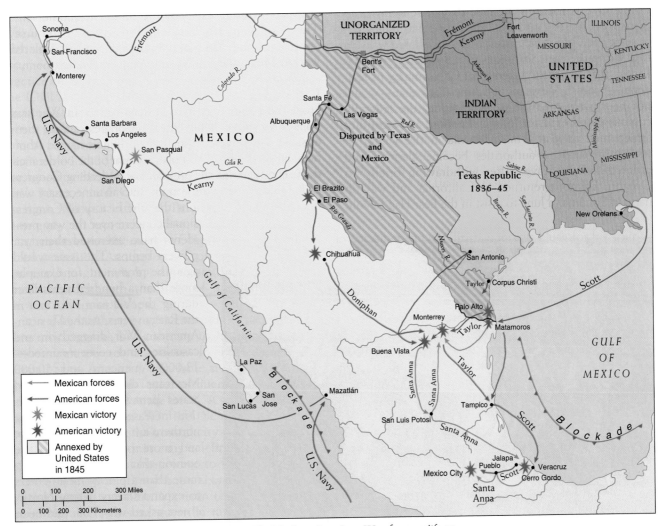

The Mexican-American War, 1846–1848   The Mexican-American War began with an advance by U.S. forces into the disputed area between the Nueces River and the Rio Grande in Texas. The war's major battles were fought by General Zachary Taylor in northern Mexico and General Winfield Scott in Vera Cruz and Mexico City. Meanwhile Colonel Stephen Kearny secured New Mexico and, with the help of the U.S. Navy and John C. Frémont's troops, California.

warned, "The United States will conquer Mexico, but it will be as the man swallows arsenic, which brings him down in turn. Mexico will poison us." The second group was composed of Southerners who realized that Mexicans could not be kept as conquered people but would have to be offered territorial government as Louisiana had in 1804. Senator John C. Calhoun of South Carolina, leading the opposition, warned against admitting "colored and mixed-breed" Mexicans "on an equality with people of the United States." "We make a great mistake, sir," he argued on the floor of the Senate, "when we suppose that all people are capable of self-government." Bowing to these political protests, Polk reluctantly accepted the treaty. A later addition, the $10 million Gadsden Purchase of parts of present-day New Mexico and Arizona, added another 30,000 square miles to the United States in 1853. This purchase, made to facilitate a southern transcontinental railroad route through arid borderland, was a far cry from the rich heartland of Mexico that Polk had hoped to annex.

The Press and Popular War Enthusiasm

The Mexican-American War was the first war in which regular, on-the-scene reporting by representatives of the press caught the mass of ordinary citizens up in the

The unprecedented immediacy of the news reporting of the Mexican-American War, transmitted for the first time by telegraph, is captured here by Richard Caton Woodville in War News from Mexico *(1848). By including an African American man and child, the artist is also voicing a political concern about the effect of the war on slavery.*

war's daily events. Thanks to the recently invented telegraph, newspapers could get the latest news from their reporters, who were among the world's first war correspondents. The "penny press," with more than a decade's experience of reporting urban crime and scandals, was quick to realize that the public's appetite for sensational war news was apparently insatiable. For the first time in American history, accounts by journalists, and not the opinions of politicians, became the major shapers of popular attitudes toward a war. From beginning to end, news of the war stirred unprecedented popular excitement.

The reports from the battlefield united Americans in a new way: they became part of a temporary but highly emotional community linked by newsprint and buttressed by public gatherings. In the spring of 1846, news of Zachary Taylor's victory at Palo Alto prompted the largest meeting ever held in the cotton textile town of Lowell, Massachusetts. In May 1847, New York City celebrated the twin victories at Veracruz and Buena Vista with fireworks, illuminations, and a "grand procession" estimated at 400,000 people. Generals Taylor and Scott became overnight heroes, and in time both became presidential candidates. Exciting, sobering, and terrible, war news had a deep hold on the popular imagination. It was a lesson newspaper publishers never forgot.

CALIFORNIA AND THE GOLD RUSH

In the early 1840s California was inhabited by many seminomadic Indian tribes whose people numbered approximately 50,000. There were also some 7,000 Californios, descendants of the Spanish Mexican pioneers who had begun to settle in 1769. The American presence in California at first consisted of a few traders and settlers who often intermarried with Californios. Even American annexation at the end of the Mexican-American War changed little for the handful of Americans on this remote frontier. But then came the Gold Rush of 1849, which changed California permanently.

Russian-Californio Trade

The first outsiders to penetrate the isolation of Spanish California were not Americans but Russians. Because the distance between California and Mexico City was so great, the Spanish had found it difficult to maintain the elaborate system of twenty-one missions first established in the eighteenth century (see Chapter 5). Nevertheless, Spanish officials in Mexico insisted on isolation, forbidding the colonists to trade with other nations. Evading Spanish regulations, Californios conducted a small illegal trade in cattle hides with American merchant ships (for the shoes made in the workshops of Massachusetts), and

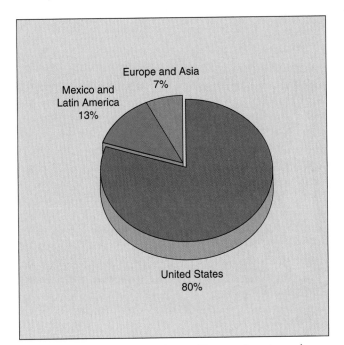

Where the Forty-Niners Came From   *Americans drawn to the California Gold Rush of 1849 encountered a more diverse population than most had previously known. Nearly as novel to them as the 20 percent from foreign countries was the regional variety from within the United States itself.*

a much larger trade with the Russian American Fur Company in Sitka, Alaska. A mutually beneficial barter of California food for iron tools and woven cloth from Russia was established in 1806. This arrangement became even brisker after the Russians settled Fort Ross (near present-day Mendocino) in 1812, and led in time to regular trade with Mission San Rafael and Mission Sonoma. That the Russians in Alaska, so far from their own capital, were better supplied with manufactured goods than the Californios is an index of the latter's isolation.

When Mexico became independent in 1821, the California trade was thrown open to ships of all nations. Nevertheless, Californios continued their special relationship with the Russians, exempting them from the taxes and inspections that they required of Americans. However, agricultural productivity declined after 1832, when the Mexican government ordered the secularization of the California missions, and the Russians regretfully turned to the rich farms of the Hudson's Bay Company in the Pacific Northwest for their food supply. In 1841, they sold Fort Ross, and the Russian-Californio connection came to an end.

Early American Settlement

It was Johann Augustus Sutter, a Swiss who had settled in California in 1839, becoming a Mexican citizen, who served as a focal point for American settlement in

the 1840s. Sutter held a magnificent land grant in the Sacramento Valley. At the center of his holdings was Sutter's Fort, a walled compound that was part living quarters and part supply shop for his vast cattle ranch, which was run largely on forced Indian labor. In the 1840s, Sutter offered valuable support to the handful of American overlanders who chose California over Oregon, the destination preferred by most pioneers. Most of these Americans, keenly aware that they were interlopers in Mexican territory, settled near Sutter in California's Central Valley, away from the Californios clustered along the coast.

The 1840s immigrants made no effort to intermarry with the Californios or to conform to Spanish ways. They were bent on taking over the territory. In June 1846 these Americans banded together at Sonoma in the Bear Flag Revolt (so called

California in the Gold Rush   *This map shows the major gold camps along the Mother Lode in the western foothills of the Sierra Nevada mountains. Gold seekers reached the camps by crossing the Sierra Nevadas near Placerville on the Overland Trail or by sea via San Francisco. The main area of Spanish-Mexican settlement, the coastal region between Monterey and Los Angeles, was remote from the gold fields.*

Source: Warren A. Beck and Ynez D. Haase, *Historical Atlas of California* (Norman: University of Oklahoma Press, 1974), map 50.

Frank Marryat, *The Bar of A Gambling Saloon*, published 1855. Lithograph. Collection of the New York Historical Society, New York City.

This drawing of the bar of a gambling saloon in San Francisco in 1855 shows the effects of the Gold Rush on California. Men from all parts of the world are gathered at this elegant bar in the large cosmopolitan city of San Francisco, which had been only a small trading post before gold was discovered in 1849.

because their flag bore a bear emblem), declaring independence from Mexico. The American takeover of California was not confirmed until the Treaty of Guadalupe Hidalgo in 1848. In the meantime, California was regarded by most Americans merely as a remote, sparsely populated frontier, albeit one with splendid potential. Polk and other expansionists coveted the magnificent harbors in San Diego and San Francisco as the basis for Pacific trade with Asia, but in 1848 this prospect was still only a dream.

Gold!

In January 1848 carpenter James Marshall noticed small flakes of gold in the millrace at Sutter's Mill (present-day Coloma). Soon he and all the rest of John Sutter's employees were panning for gold in California's streams. The news, which they had hoped to keep secret, spread, and before long it seemed that all the men in California were at the mines. When explorer John Frémont returned to San Francisco in June 1848, he found it almost deserted because of the "gold fever."

In the autumn of 1848, the east coast heard the first rumors about the discovery of gold in California. The reports were confirmed in mid-November when an army courier arrived in Washington carrying a tea caddy full of gold dust and nuggets. The spirit of excitement and adventure so recently aroused by the Mexican-American War was now directed toward California, the new El Dorado. Thousands left farms and jobs and headed west, by land and by sea, to make their fortune. Later known as "forty-niners" for the year the gold rush began in earnest, these people came from all parts of the

United States—and indeed, from all over the world. They transformed what had been a quiet ranching paradise into a teeming and tumultuous community in search of wealth in California's rivers and streams.

Eighty percent of the forty-niners were Americans. They came from every state. The Gold Rush was an eye-opening expansion of their horizons for the many who had known only their hometown folks before. The second largest group of migrants were from nearby Mexico and the west coast of Latin America (13 percent). The remainder came from Europe and Asia.

The presence of Chinese miners surprised many Americans. Several hundred Chinese arrived in California in 1849 and 1850, and in 1852 more than 20,000 landed in San Francisco hoping to share in the wealth of Gum Sam (Golden Mountain). Most came, like the Americans, as temporary sojourners, intending to return home as soon as they made some money. Again, like most of the American miners, the majority of Chinese were men who left their wives at home. Dressed in their distinctive blue cotton shirts, baggy pants, and broad-brimmed hats, and with long queues hanging down their backs, hardworking Chinese miners soon became a familiar sight in the gold fields, as did the presence of "Chinatowns." The distinctive appearance of the Chinese, added to the threat of economic competition that they posed, quickly aroused American hostility. A special tax was imposed on foreign miners in 1852, and in the 1870s, Chinese immigration was sharply curtailed.

In 1849, as the gold rush began in earnest, San Francisco, the major entry port and supply point, sprang to life. From a settlement of 1,000 in 1848 it grew to a city of 35,000 in 1850. This surge suggested that the real money to be made in California was not in panning for gold but from feeding, clothing, housing, provisioning, and entertaining the miners. Among the first to learn that lesson was the German Jewish immigrant Levi Strauss, who sold so many tough work pants to miners that his name became synonymous with his product. And Jerusha Marshall, who opened a twenty-room boardinghouse in the city, candidly wrote to her eastern relatives: "Never was there a better field for making money than now presents itself in this place....We are satisfied to dig our gold in San Francisco." From these "instant" beginnings San Francisco stabilized to become a major American city. Meanwhile, the white population of California had jumped from an estimated pre-Gold Rush figure of 11,000 to more than 100,000 by 1852. California was admitted as a state in 1850.

Mining Camps

Most mining camps, like San Francisco, boomed almost instantly to life, but unlike San Francisco, they were empty again within a few years. In spite of the aura of glamour that surrounds the names of the famous camps—Poker Flat, Angels Camp, Whiskey Bar, Placerville, Mariposa—they were generally dirty and dreary places. Most miners lived in tents or hovels, unwilling to take time from mining to build themselves decent quarters. They cooked monotonous meals of beans, bread, and bacon or, if they had money, bought meals at expensive restaurants and boardinghouses (where the table might be no more than a plank over two flour barrels). Many migrants traveled to the mines with relatives or fellow townspeople. But often they split up in California—each man with his own idea of where he could find gold the easiest—and ended up on their own. They led a cheerless, uncomfortable, and unhealthy existence, especially during the long, rainy winter months, with few distractions apart from the saloon, the gambling hall, and the prostitute's crib.

Most miners were young, unmarried, and unsuccessful. Only a small percentage ever struck it rich in California. Gold deposits that were accessible with pick and shovel were soon exhausted, and the deeper deposits required capital and machinery. Some of the workings at the Comstock Lode in Virginia City, Nevada, a later mining center, were half a mile deep. But many men were ashamed to come home until they had "made their pile." Increasingly, as they stayed on in California, they had to give up the status of independent miners and become wage earners for large mining concerns.

As in San Francisco, a more reliable way to earn money in the camps was to supply the miners. Every mining community had its saloonkeepers, gamblers, prostitutes, merchants, and restauranteurs. Like the miners themselves, these people were tran-

sients, always ready to pick up and move at the word of a new gold strike. The majority of women in the early mining camps were prostitutes. Some grew rich or married respectably, but most died young of drugs, venereal disease, or violence. Most of the other women were hardworking wives of miners, and in this predominantly male society they made good money doing domestic work: keeping boardinghouses, cooking, doing laundry. Even the wives of professional men who in the East might have been restrained by propriety succumbed to the monetary opportunities and kept boardinghouses.

Partly because few people put any effort into building communities—they were too busy seeking gold—violence was endemic in mining areas, and much of it was racial. Discrimination, especially against Chinese, Mexicans, and African Americans, was common. Frequently miners' claims were "jumped": thieves would rob them of the gold they had accumulated, kill them, or chase them away, and then file their own claim for the victims' strike. Or unscrupulous miners might use the law to their advantage to secure the claims of others without violence—for example by taking advantage of the prohibitively high mining tax on foreigners.

In the end, most mining camps were at best temporary communities. The gold "played out" and people moved on, leaving ghost towns behind. By the

Chinese first came to California in 1849 attracted by the Gold Rush. Frequently, however, they were forced off their claims by intolerant whites. Rather than enjoy an equal chance in the gold fields they were often forced to work as servants or in other menial occupations.

mid-1850s, the immediate effects of the Gold Rush had passed. California had a booming population, a thriving agriculture, and a corporate mining industry. The Gold Rush also left California with a population that was larger, more affluent, and (in urban San Francisco) more culturally sophisticated than that in other newly settled territories. It was also significantly more multicultural than the rest of the nation, for many of the Chinese and Mexicans, as well as immigrants from many European countries, remained in California after the Gold Rush subsided. But the Gold Rush left some permanent scars, and not just on the foothills landscape: the virtual extermination of the California Indian peoples, the dispossession of many Californios who were legally deprived of their land grants, and the growth of racial animosity toward the Chinese in particular. The major characteristics of the mining frontier, evident first in the California Gold Rush and repeated many times thereafter in similar "rushes" in Colorado, Montana, Idaho, South Dakota, and Arizona, were a lack of stable communities and a worsening of racial tensions.

THE POLITICS OF MANIFEST DESTINY

In three short years, from 1845 to 1848, the territory of the United States grew an incredible 70 percent and became a continental nation. This expansion and the concept of manifest destiny that justified it quickly became the dominant issues in national politics.

The "Young America" Movement

One source of the belief in manifest destiny was national pride—the conviction that American democracy was so superior it would lead inevitably to the expansion of the nation. The swift victory in the Mexican-American War and the "prize" of California gold seemed to confirm that conviction. European events in 1848 also served to foster American pride. In that year a series of democratic revolutions—in Italy, France, Germany, Hungary, and parts of the Austrian Empire—swept the Continent. Expansionists assumed that American democracy and manifest destiny were the models for these liberal revolutions. When Lajos Kossuth, the famed Hungarian revolutionary, visited the United States in 1851, he was given a hero's welcome, and Daniel Webster complacently assured him that "we shall rejoice to see our American model upon the lower Danube."

In an even more confident gesture, President Franklin Pierce dispatched Commodore Matthew Perry across the Pacific to Japan, a nation famous for its insularity and hostility to outsiders. The mission resulted in 1854 in a commercial treaty that opened Japan to American trade. Perry's feat caused a newspaper in tiny Olympia, Washington, to boast, "We shall have the boundless Pacific for a market in manifest destiny. We were born to command it."

But efforts closer to home by the Young America movement, as expansionist Democrats styled themselves, were more controversial. Victory in the Mexican-American War and the evident weakness of the

This Japanese painting shows Commodore Matthew Perry landing in Japan in 1854. The commercial treaty Perry signed with the Japanese government, which opened a formerly closed country to American trade, was viewed in the United States as another fruit of manifest destiny.

1844	Whigs reject President John Tyler's move to annex Texas and expel him from the Whig Party.
	Southern Democrats choose expansionist James K. Polk as their presidential candidate, passing over Martin Van Buren, who is against expansion.
	Liberty Party runs abolitionist James Birney for president, attracting northern antislavery Whigs.
1846	The Wilmot Proviso, proposing to ban slavery in the territories that might be gained in the Mexican-American War, splits both parties: southern Whigs and Democrats oppose the measure; northern Whigs and Democrats support it.
1848	The new Free-Soil Party runs northern Democrat Martin Van Buren for president, gaining 10 percent of the vote from abolitionists, antislavery Whigs, and some northern Democrats. This strong showing by a third party causes Democrat Lewis Cass to lose the electoral votes of New York and Pennsylvania, allowing the Whig Zachary Taylor to win.

Mexican government whetted the appetite of some southern expansionists for more territory. But most American politicians were cautious about further gains. When in the spring of 1848 Polk recommended American intervention in the civil war in the Mexican province of Yucatán, Congress rebuffed him. Senator John C. Calhoun, harking back to Polk's manipulation of Congress in 1846, cautioned, "I did hope that the experience of the Mexican War—that precipitate and rash measure which has cost the country so dearly in blood and treasure—would have taught the administration moderation and caution." In the winter of 1848, rumors swept Washington that Polk had offered Spain up to $100 million for Cuba (compared with the $15 million paid for Mexico's provinces of California and New Mexico). The nation was spared a raging political battle when Spain spurned all offers.

Thus the Mexican-American War was divisive even after it was won. A small group of expansionists, most from the South, wanted more, in spite of clear evidence that most Americans had had enough. Throughout the 1850s, these expansionists continued to covet Mexico, Central America, and Cuba. Adventures in these directions, all organized by Southerners intent on acquiring new lands for cotton, further inflamed the festering sectional differences of the 1850s that are discussed in Chapter 15.

The Wilmot Proviso

In 1846, almost all the northern members of the Whig Party opposed Democratic president James Polk's belligerent expansionism on antislavery grounds. Northern Whigs correctly feared that expansion would reopen the issue of slavery in the territories. "We appear...to be rushing upon perils headlong, and with our eyes all open," Daniel Webster warned in 1847. His remedy? "We want no extension of territory; we want no accession of new states. The country is already large enough." But the outpouring of enthusiasm for the Mexican-American War drowned Webster's words and convinced most Whig congressmen that they needed to vote military appropriations for the war in spite of their misgivings.

Ironically it was not the Whigs but a freshman Democratic congressman from Pennsylvania, David Wilmot, who opened the door to sectional controversy over expansion. In August 1846, only a few short months after the beginning of the Mexican-American War, Wilmot proposed, in an amendment to a military appropriations bill, that slavery be banned in all the territories acquired from Mexico. He was ready, Wilmot said, to "sustain the institutions of the South as they exist. But sir, the issue now presented is not whether slavery shall exist unmolested where it is now, but whether it shall be carried to new and distant regions, now free, where the footprint of a slave cannot be found." In the debate and voting that followed, something new and ominous occurred: southern Whigs joined southern Democrats to vote against the measure, while Northerners of both parties supported it. Sectional interest had triumphed over party loyalty. Wilmot's Proviso triggered the first breakdown of the national party system and reopened the debate about the place of slavery in the future of the nation.

The Wilmot Proviso was so controversial that it was deleted from the necessary military appropriations bills during the Mexican-American War. But in 1848, following the Treaty of Guadalupe Hidalgo, the question of the expansion of slavery could no longer be avoided or postponed. Antislavery advocates from the North argued with proslavery Southerners in a debate that was much more prolonged and more bitter than the Missouri Crisis of 1819. Civility quickly wore thin: threats were uttered and fistfights broke out on the floor of the House of Representatives. The Wilmot Proviso posed a fundamental challenge to both parties. Neither the Democrats nor the Whigs could take a strong stand on the amendment because neither party could get its northern and southern wings to agree. Decisive action, for or against, was a serious threat to party unity. Webster's fear that expansion would lead to sectional conflict had become a reality.

The Free-Soil Movement

Why did David Wilmot propose this controversial measure? Wilmot, a northern Democrat, was propelled not by ideology but by the pressure of practical politics. The dramatic rise of the Liberty Party, founded in 1840 by abolitionists, threatened to take votes away from both the Whig and the Democratic parties. The Liberty Party won 62,000 votes in the 1844 presidential election, all in the North. This was more than enough to deny victory to the Whig candidate, Henry Clay. Neither party could afford to ignore the strength of this third party.

The Liberty Party took an uncompromising stance against slavery. As articulated by Ohio's Salmon P. Chase, the party platform called for the "divorce of the federal government from slavery." The party proposed to prohibit the admission of slave states to the Union, end slavery in the District of Columbia, and abolish the interstate slave trade that was vital to the expansion of cotton growing into the Old Southwest (see Chapter 11). Liberty Party members also favored denying office to all slaveholders (a proposal that would have robbed all the southern states of their senators) and forbidding the use of slave labor on federal construction projects. In short, the party proposed to quickly strangle slavery. The popularity of this radical program among northern voters in 1844 was an indication of the moral fervor of abolitionism (see Chapter 13).

But Liberty Party doctrine was too uncompromising for the mass of northern voters, who immediately realized that the southern states would leave the Union before accepting it. Still, as the 1844 vote indicated, many Northerners opposed slavery. From this sentiment the Free-Soil Party was born. The free-soil argument was a calculated adjustment of abolitionist principles to practical politics. It shifted the focus from the question of the morality of slavery to the ways in which slavery posed a threat to northern expansion. The free-soil doctrine thus established a direct link between expansion, which most Americans supported, and sectional politics.

Free-soilers were willing to allow slavery to continue in the existing slave states because they supported the Union, not because they approved of slavery. They were unwilling, however, to allow the extension of slavery to new and unorganized territory. If the South were successful in extending slavery, they argued, northern farmers who moved west would find themselves competing at an economic disadvantage with large planters using slave labor. Free-soilers also insisted that the northern values of freedom and individualism would be destroyed if the slave-based southern labor system were allowed to spread. To free-soilers, the South was composed of little more than corrupt aristocrats, degraded slaves, and a large class of poor whites who were deprived of opportunity because they did not understand the value of honest labor.

Finally, many free-soilers really meant "antiblack" when they said "antislavery." They proposed to ban all African American people from the new territories (a step that four states—Indiana, Illinois, Iowa, and Oregon—took but did not always enforce). William Lloyd Garrison promptly denounced the free-soil doctrine as "whitemanism," a racist effort to make the territories white. There was much truth to his charge, but there was no denying that the free-soil doctrine was popular. Although abolitionists were making headway in their claim for moral equality regardless of skin color, most Northerners were unwilling to consider social equality for African Americans, free or slave. Banning all black people from the western territories seemed a simple solution.

Finally, the free-soil movement was a repudiation of the sectional compromise of 1820. If the Missouri Compromise line were carried westward to the Pacific Ocean, as Secretary of State James Buchanan proposed in 1848, much of present-day New Mexico and Arizona and the southern half of California would have been admitted as slave states, and everything to the north would have been free. Free-soilers opposed this arrangement. Their opposition in 1848 to the Missouri Compromise line indicated how influential antislavery feeling was becoming in the North.

The Election of 1848

A swirl of emotions—pride, expansionism, sectionalism, abolitionism, free-soil sentiment—surrounded the election of 1848. The Treaty of Guadalupe Hidalgo had been signed earlier in the year, and the vast northern Mexican provinces of New Mexico and California and the former

Republic of Texas had been incorporated into the United States. But the issues raised by the Wilmot Proviso remained to be resolved, and every candidate had to have an answer to the question of whether slavery should be admitted in the new territories.

Lewis Cass of Michigan, the Democratic nominee for president (Polk, in poor health, declined to run for a second term), proposed to apply the doctrine of popular sovereignty to the crucial slave–free issue. This democratic-sounding notion of leaving the decision to the citizens of each territory was based on the Jeffersonian faith in the common man's ability to vote both his own self-interest and the common good. In fact, however, popular sovereignty was an admission of the nation's failure to resolve sectional differences. It simply shifted decision making on the crucial issue of the expansion of slavery from national politicians to the members of territorial legislatures, who,

In 1848, the Whigs once again adopted the campaign strategy that had worked so successfully for them in the presidential election of 1840. They nominated a hero of the Mexican-American War, General Zachary Taylor, who ran on his military exploits. In this poster, every letter of Taylor's name is decorated with scenes from the recent war, which had seized the popular imagination in a way no previous conflict had done. Emphasizing Taylor's reputation as a national hero (and therefore above petty politics), the Whigs were able to evade the question of whether or not he favored the extension of slavery into the territories.

belonging to different parties, were in as much disagreement as members of Congress and just as unable to resolve it.

As Cass stated it, the doctrine of popular sovereignty was deliberately vague about when a territory would choose its status. Would it do so during the territorial stage? at the point of applying for statehood? Clearly, this question was crucial, for no slave owner would invest in new land if the territory could later be declared free, and no abolitionist would move to a territory that was destined to become a slave state. Cass hoped his ambiguity on this point would win him votes in both North and South. Even so, sectional differences ran so deep that the Democrats found it necessary to print two campaign biographies of Cass. The biography circulated in the North touted Cass's doctrine of popular sovereignty as the best way to keep slavery out of the territories; the biography in the South implied the opposite.

For their part, the Whigs passed over perennial candidate Henry Clay and turned once again to a war hero, General Zachary Taylor. Taylor, a Louisiana slaveholder, refused to take a position on the Wilmot Proviso, allowing both northern and southern voters to hope that he agreed with them. Privately, Taylor

opposed the expansion of slavery. In public, he evaded the issue by running as a war hero and a national leader who was above sectional politics.

The deliberate vagueness of the two major candidates displeased many northern voters. An uneasy mixture of disaffected Democrats (among them David Wilmot) and Whigs joined former Liberty Party voters to support the candidate of the Free-Soil Party, former president Martin Van Buren. Van Buren, angry at the Democratic Party for passing him over in 1844 and displeased with the growing southern dominance of the Democratic Party, ran as a spoiler. He knew he could not win the election, but he could divide the Democrats. In the end, Van Buren garnered 10 percent of the vote (all in the North). The vote for the Free-Soil Party cost Cass the electoral votes of New York and Pennsylvania, and General Taylor won the election with only 47 percent of the popular vote. This was the second election after 1840 that the Whigs had won by running a war hero who could duck hard questions by claiming to be above politics. Uncannily, history was to repeat itself: Taylor, like William Henry Harrison, died before his term was completed, and the chance he offered to maintain national unity—if ever it existed—was lost.

CHRONOLOGY

1609	First Spanish settlement in New Mexico	1833–34	Prince Maximilian and Karl Bodmer visit Plains Indians
1670s	British and French Canadians begin fur trade in western Canada	1834	Jason Lee establishes first mission in Oregon Country
1716	First Spanish settlements in Texas	1835	Texas revolts against Mexico
1769	First Spanish settlement in California	1836	Battles of the Alamo and San Jacinto
			Republic of Texas formed
1780s	New England ships begin sea otter trade in Pacific Northwest	1843–44	John C. Frémont maps trails to Oregon and California
1790	First American ship visits Hawaii	1844	Democrat James K. Polk elected president on an expansionist platform
1803	Louisiana Purchase		
1804–06	Lewis and Clark expedition	1845	Texas annexed to the United States as a slave state
1806	Russian-Californio trade begins		John O'Sullivan coins the phrase "manifest destiny"
1806–07	Zebulon Pike's expedition across the Great Plains to the Rocky Mountains		
		1846	Oregon question settled peacefully with Britain
1819–20	Stephen Long's expedition across the Great Plains		Mexican-American War begins
			Bear Flag Revolt in California
1821	Hudson's Bay Company gains dominance of western fur trade		Wilmot Proviso
	Mexico seizes independence from Spain	1847	Cayuse Wars begin in Oregon
			Americans win battles of Buena Vista, Veracruz, and Mexico City
	Santa Fé Trail opens, soon protected by U.S. military		
	Stephen F. Austin becomes first American empresario in Texas	1848	Treaty of Guadalupe Hidalgo
			Free-Soil Party captures 10 percent of the popular vote in the North
1824	First fur rendezvous sponsored by Rocky Mountain Fur Company		
	Hudson's Bay Company establishes Fort Vancouver in Oregon Country		General Zachary Taylor, a Whig, elected president
1830	Indian Removal Act moves eastern Indians to Indian Territory	1849	California Gold Rush

CONCLUSION

In the decade of the 1840s, westward expansion took many forms, from relatively peaceful settlement in Oregon, to war with Mexico over Texas, to the sheer overwhelming numbers of gold rushers who changed California forever. Most of these frontiers—in Oregon, New Mexico, and California—began as frontiers of inclusion in which a small number of Ameri-

cans were eager for trade, accommodation, and intermarriage with the original inhabitants. Texas, with its agricultural enclaves, was the exception to this pattern. Yet on every frontier, as the number of American settlers increased, so did the sentiment for exclusion, so that by 1850, whatever their origins, the far-flung American continental settlements were more similar than different and the success of manifest destiny seemed overwhelming.

The election of 1848, virtually a referendum on manifest destiny, yielded ironic results. James K. Polk, who presided over the unprecedented expansion, did not run for a second term, and thus the Democratic Party gained no electoral victory to match the military one. The electorate that had been so thrilled by the war news voted for a war hero—who led the antiexpansionist Whig Party. The election was decided by Martin Van Buren, the Free-Soil candidate who voiced the sentiments of the abolitionists, a reform group that had been insignificant just a few years before. The amazing expansion achieved by the Mexican-American War—America's manifest destiny—made the United States a continental nation but stirred up the issue that was to tear it apart. Sectional rivalries and fears now dominated every aspect of politics. Expansion, once a force for unity, now divided the nation into Northerners and Southerners, who could not agree on the community they shared—the federal Union.

REVIEW QUESTIONS

1. Define and discuss the concept of manifest destiny.
2. Trace the different ways in which the frontiers in Oregon, Texas, and California moved from frontiers of inclusion to frontiers of exclusion.
3. Take different sides (Whig and Democrat) and debate the issues raised by the Mexican-American War.
4. Referring back to Chapter 13, compare the positions of the Liberty Party and the Free-Soil Party. Examine the factors that made the free-soil doctrine politically acceptable to many, and abolitionism so controversial.

RECOMMENDED READING

Arnoldo De Leon, *The Tejano Community, 1836–1900* (1982). Traces the changing status of Tejanos after Texas came under the control of American Texans.

John Mack Faragher, *Women and Men on the Overland Trail* (1979). One of the first books to consider the experience of women on the journey west.

William Goetzman, *Exploration and Empire: The Explorer and the Scientist in the Winning of the American West* (1966). Considers the many government-sponsored explorations of the West.

Thomas R. Hietala, *Manifest Design: Anxious Aggrandizement in Late Jacksonian America* (1985). An interesting reassessment of manifest destiny from the perspective of party politics.

Julie Roy Jeffrey, *Converting the West: A Biography of Narcissa Whitman* (1991). Makes a clear connection between the missionary Whitman's evangelical upbringing and her failure to understand the culture of Oregon's Cayuse Indians.

Robert W. Johannsen, *To the Halls of the Montezumas: The Mexican War in the American Imagination* (1985). A lively book that explores the impact of the Mexican-American War on public opinion.

Paul D. Lack, *The Texas Revolutionary Experience: A Political and Social History, 1835–1836* (1992). A political and social history that stresses the chaotic and discordant nature of the Texas Revolt.

Janet Lecompte, *Pueblo, Hardscrabble, Greenhorn: The Upper Arkansas, 1832–1856* (1978). A social history that portrays the racial and ethnic diversity of the trading frontier.

Michael Morrison, *Slavery and the American West: The Eclipse of Manifest Destiny and the Coming of the Civil War* (1997). In a study of competing ideas over the future of the West, the author stresses the links between expansion and sectional disagreements.

Malcolm Rohrbough, *Days of Gold: The California Gold Rush and the American Nation* (1997). A lively history that emphasizes the effects of this "great American epic" on the national self-image.

David J. Weber, *The Mexican Frontier, 1821–1846: The American Southwest under Mexico* (1982). A fine study of the history of the Southwest before American conquest. The author is a leading borderlands historian.

Richard White, *"It's Your Misfortune and None of My Own": A History of the American West* (1991). A major reinterpretation that focuses on the history of the region itself rather than on the westward expansion of Americans. Pays much more attention to Spanish Mexicans and Indian peoples than earlier texts.

ADDITIONAL BIBLIOGRAPHY

Exploration, the Fur Trade, and Expansion

Jennifer S. H. Brown, *Strangers in Blood: Fur Trade Company Families in Indian Country* (1980)

William H. Goetzmann, *Army Exploration in the American West, 1803–1863* (1959)

William H. Goetzmann and William N. Goetzmann, *The West of the Imagination* (1986)

Norman A. Graebner, *Empire on the Pacific: A Study in American Continental Expansion* (1955)

LeRoy R. Hafen, ed., *The Mountain Men and the Fur Trade of the Far West*, 10 vols. (1968–72)

Reginald Horsman, *Race and Manifest Destiny* (1981)

Theodore J. Karaminski, *Fur Trade and Exploration: Opening of the Far Northwest, 1821–1852* (1983)

Patricia Nelson Limerick, *The Legacy of Conquest: The Unbroken Past of the Unbroken West* (1987)

Frederick Merk, *Manifest Destiny and Mission in American History: A Reinterpretation* (1963)

———, *History of the Westward Movement* (1978)

Dale Morgan, *Jedediah Smith and the Opening of the West* (1982)

Peter Nabakov, ed., *Native American Testimony: An Anthology of Indian and White Relations* (1978)

James P. Ronda, *Astoria and Empire* (1990)

Henry Nash Smith, *Virgin Land: The American West as Symbol and Myth* (1950)

Edward H. Spicer, *Cycles of Conquest: The Impact of Spain, Mexico, and the United States on the Indians of the Southwest, 1533–1960* (1981)

Robert A. Trennert, *Alternative to Extinction: Federal Indian Policy and the Beginnings of the Reservation System, 1846–1851* (1975)

Sylvia Van Kirk, *"Many Tender Ties": Women in Fur Trade Society in Western Canada, 1670–1870* (1980)

Albert K. Weinberg, *Manifest Destiny: A Study of Nationalist Expansionism in American History* (1957)

Peter Booth Wiley with Korogi Ichiro, *Yankees in the Land of the Gods: Commodore Perry and the Opening of Japan* (1990)

David J. Wishart, *The Fur Trade of the American West, 1807–1840: A Geographic Synthesis* (1979)

California and Oregon

John W. Caughey, *The California Gold Rush* (1975)

Malcolm Clark Jr., *Eden Seekers: The Settlement of Oregon, 1818–1862* (1981)

Douglas H. Daniels, *Pioneer Urbanites: A Social and Cultural History of Black San Francisco* (1980)

James R. Gibson, *Farming the Frontier: The Agricultural Opening of Oregon Country, 1786–1846* (1985)

Albert L. Hurtado, *Indian Survival on the California Frontier* (1988)

Julie Roy Jeffrey, *Frontier Women: Civilizing The West?, 1840–1860* (1998)

David Johnson, *Founding the Far West: California, Oregon, and Nevada, 1840–1890* (1992)

Alvin Josephy, *The Nez Perce and the Opening of the Northwest* (1965)

Rodman W. Paul, *California Gold: The Beginning of Mining in the Far West* (1974)

Leonard Pitt, *The Decline of the Californios: A Social History of the Spanish-Speaking Californians, 1846–1890* (1966)

James J. Rawls, *Indians of California: The Changing Image* (1984)

Kevin Starr, *Americans and the California Dream, 1850–1915* (1973)

John I. Unruh Jr., *The Plains Across: Overland Emigrants and the Trans-Mississippi West, 1840–1860* (1979)

Texas and the Mexican-American War

K. Jack Bauer, *The Mexican War, 1846–1848* (1974)

William C. Binkley, *The Texas Revolution* (1952)

Gene M. Brack, *Mexico Views Manifest Destiny* (1976)

Donald E. Chipman, *Spanish Texas, 1519–1821* (1992)

Seymour Conner and Odie Faulk, *North America Divided: The Mexican War, 1846–1848* (1971)

Arnoldo De Leon, *They Called Them Greasers: Anglo Attitudes toward Mexicans in Texas, 1821–1900* (1983)

John S. D. Eisenhower, *So Far from God: The U.S. War with Mexico 1846–1848* (1989)

Neil Harlow, *California Conquered: War and Peace on the Pacific, 1846–1850* (1982)

Ernest McPherson Lander Jr., *Reluctant Imperialist: Calhoun, South Carolina, and the Mexican War* (1980)

Timothy Matovina, *Tejano Religion and Ethnicity: San Antonio, 1921–1860* (1995)

Frederick Merk, *Slavery and the Annexation of Texas* (1972)

David Montejano, *Anglos and Mexicans in the Making of Texas, 1836–1986* (1987)

Chaplain W. Morrison, *Democratic Politics and Sectionalism: The Wilmot Proviso Controversy* (1967)

Stanley Noyes, *Los Comanches: The Horse People, 1751–1845* (1994)

David Pletcher, *The Diplomacy of Annexation: Texas, Oregon, and the Mexican War* (1973)

Joseph G. Raybeck, *Free Soil: The Election of 1848* (1970)

Andreas V. Reichstein, *Rise of the Lone Star: The Making of Texas* (1989)

John H. Schroeder, *Mr. Polk's War: American Opposition and Dissent, 1846–1848* (1971)

Joel H. Sibley, *The Shrine of Party: Congressional Voting Behavior, 1841–1852* (1967)

Otis A. Singletary, *The Mexican War* (1960)

Jésus F. de la Teja, *San Antonio de Béxar: A Community on New Spain's Northern Frontier* (1995)

Biography

Marquis James, *The Raven: The Story of Sam Houston* (1929)

Charles G. Sellers, *James K. Polk: Jacksonian, 1795–1843* (1957)

———, *James K. Polk: Continentalist, 1843–1846* (1966)

CHAPTER FIFTEEN

THE COMING CRISIS
THE 1850s

Frederick Douglass on the cover of an abolitionist song sheet published at Boston in 1845. The Granger Collection.

AMERICAN COMMUNITIES
Illinois Communities Debate Slavery

On seven occasions through the late summer and autumn of 1858, each at one of seven small Illinois towns—Ottawa, Freeport, Jonesboro, Charleston, Galesburg, Quincy, and Alton—thousands of Illinois farmers and townspeople put aside their daily routines and customary chores; climbed into carriages, farm wagons, carts, and conveyances of all sorts; and converged on the town green. Entertained by brass bands, pageantry, and vast quantities of food and local gossip, they waited impatiently for the main event, the chance to take part in the debate on the most urgent question of the day—slavery. Two Illinois politicians—Democratic senator Stephen A. Douglas and his Republican challenger, Springfield lawyer Abraham Lincoln, the principal figures in the debates—presented their views in three hours of closely reasoned argument. But they did not speak alone. Cheers, boos, groans, and shouted questions from active, engaged listeners punctuated all seven of the now famous confrontations between the two men. Although commonly referred to as the Lincoln-Douglas debates, these were really community events in which Illinois citizens—people who, like Americans everywhere, held varying political beliefs—took part. Some individuals were proslavery, some antislavery, and many were undecided, but all were agreed that democratic politics gave them the means to air their opinions and resolve their differences.

"The prairies are on fire," announced the *New York Evening Post* correspondent who covered the debates. "It is astonishing how deep an interest in politics this people take." The reason was clear: by 1858, the American nation was in deep political crisis. The decade-long effort to solve the problem of the future of slavery had failed. For most of this time Washington politicians trying to build broad national parties with policies acceptable to voters in both the North and the South had done their best not to talk about slavery. Thus, that the Lincoln-Douglas debates were devoted to one issue alone—slavery and the future of the Union—showed how serious matters had become.

Democrat Stephen Douglas was the leading Democratic contender for the 1860 presidential nomination, but before he could mount a campaign for national office he had first to win reelection to the Illinois seat he had held in the U.S. Senate for twelve years. His vote against allowing slavery in Kansas had alienated him from the strong southern wing of his own party and had put him in direct conflict with its top leader, President James Buchanan. Because the crisis of the Union was so severe and Douglas's role so pivotal, his reelection campaign clearly previewed the 1860 presidential election. For the sake of its future, the Republican Party had to field a strong opponent: it found its candidate in Abraham Lincoln.

Lincoln had represented Illinois in the House of Representatives in the 1840s but had lost political support in 1848 because he opposed the Mexican-American War. Developing a prosperous Springfield law practice, he had been an influential member of the Illinois Republican Party since its founding in 1856. Although he had entered political life as a Whig, Lincoln was radicalized by the issue of the extension of slavery. Even though his wife's family were Kentucky slave owners, Lincoln's commitment to freedom and his resistance to the spread of slavery had now become absolute: for him, freedom and Union were inseparable.

Much less well known than Douglas, Lincoln was the underdog in the 1858 Senate race and thus it was he who challenged Douglas to debate. As they squared off in the seven Illinois towns, Douglas and Lincoln were an amusing sight. Douglas was short (5 feet, 4 inches) and his build was very square; his nickname was "the Little Giant." Lincoln, on the other hand, was very tall (6 feet, 4 inches) and very thin. Both were eloquent and powerful speakers—and they had to be. The three-hour debates were held without amplification of any kind. Nevertheless, in every town, audiences of 10,000 to 15,000 listened attentively and responded vocally to each speaker's long and thought-packed arguments.

Douglas had many strengths going into the debates. He spoke for the Union, he claimed, pointing out that the Democratic Party was a national party whereas the Republican Party was only sectional. He repeatedly appealed to the racism of much of his audience with declarations such as, "I would not blot out the great inalienable rights of the white men for all the negroes that ever existed!" He repeatedly called his opponent a "Black Republican," implying that Lincoln and his party favored the social equality of whites and blacks, even race mixing.

Lincoln did *not* believe in the social equality of the races, but he did believe wholeheartedly that slavery was a moral wrong. Pledging the Republican Party to the "ultimate extinction" of slavery, Lincoln continually warned that Douglas's position would lead to the opposite result: the spread of slavery everywhere. Although in this argument Lincoln was addressing the northern fear of an expansionist "slave power," he strove at the

same time to present himself as a moderate. He did not favor the breakup of the Union, but he never wavered from his antislavery stance.

The first of the seven debates, held in Ottawa on Saturday, August 21, 1858, showed not only the seriousness but the exuberance of the democratic politics of the time. By early morning the town was jammed with people. The clouds of dust raised by carriages driving to Ottawa, one observer complained, turned the town into "a vast smoke house." By one o'clock the town square was filled to overflowing. At two o'clock, just as the debate was about to begin, the wooden awning over the speakers' platform collapsed under the weight of those sitting on it, delaying the start for half an hour. But then the debate got under way, enthralling an estimated 12,000 people. Ottawa, in northern Illinois, was pro-Republican, and the audience heckled Douglas unmercifully. At the second debate, a week later in Freeport, Douglas's use of the phrase "Black Republicans" drew angry shouts of "White, white" from the crowd. But as the debates moved south in the state, where Democrats predominated, the tables were turned, and Lincoln sometimes had to plead for a chance to be heard.

Although Douglas won the 1858 senatorial election in Illinois, the acclaim that Lincoln gained in the famous debates helped establish the Republicans' claim to be the only party capable of stopping the spread of slavery and made Lincoln himself a strong contender for the Republican presidential nomination in 1860. But the true winners of the Lincoln-Douglas debates were the people of Illinois who gathered peacefully to discuss the most serious issue of their time. The young German immigrant Carl Schurz, who attended the Quincy debate, was deeply impressed by its democratic character. He noted, "There was no end of cheering and shouting and jostling on the streets of Quincy that day. But in spite of the excitement created by the political contest, the crowds remained very good-natured, and the occasional jibes flung from one side to the other were uniformly received with a laugh." The Illinois people who participated in the community debates of 1858 showed the strong faith Americans held in their democratic institutions and the hope—finally shattered in the election of 1860—that a lasting political solution to the problem of slavery could be found.

Illinois

KEY TOPICS

- The failure of efforts by the Whigs and the Democrats to find a lasting political compromise on the issue of slavery

- The end of the Second American Party System and the rise of the Republican Party

- The secession of the southern states following the Republican Party victory in the election of 1860

AMERICA IN 1850

In 1850, after half a century of rapid growth and change, America was a very different nation from the republic of 1800. Geographic expansion, population increase, economic development, and the changes wrought by the market revolution had transformed the struggling new nation. Economically, culturally, and politically Americans had forged a strong sense of national identity.

Expansion and Growth

America was now a much larger nation than it had been in 1800. Through war and diplomacy, the country had grown to continental dimensions, more than tripling in size from 890,000 to 3 million square miles. Its population had increased enormously: from 5.3 million in 1800 to more than 23 million, 4 million of whom were African American slaves and 2 million new immigrants, largely from Germany and Ireland. Comprising just sixteen states in 1800, America in 1850 had thirty-one, and more than half of the population lived west of the Appalachians. America's cities had undergone the most rapid half-century of growth they were ever to experience.

America was also much richer: it is estimated that real per capita income doubled between 1800 and 1850, moving the nation decisively out of the "developing" category. Southern cotton, which had contributed so much to American economic growth, continued to be the nation's principal export, but it was no longer the major influence on the domestic economy. The growth of manufacturing in the Northeast and the rapid opening up of rich farmlands in the Midwest fostered the interdependence of these two regions, which was aided by the rapid growth and consolidation of railway links between them in the 1850s. The future of the United States as a manufacturing nation, second only to Britain, and as a major exporter of agricultural products was assured. Nevertheless, the development of manufacturing in the Northeast and the increased economic importance of the Midwest had serious domestic political implications. As the South's share of responsibility for economic growth waned, so did its political importance—at least in the eyes of many Northerners. Thus

the very success of the United States both in geographic expansion and economic development served to undermine the role of the slave South in national politics and to hasten the day of open conflict between it and the free-labor North and Midwest.

Cultural Life and Social Issues

By 1850 the first shock of the far-reaching social changes caused by the market revolution had been absorbed. The conflicting social impulses played out in the politics and reform movements of the Jacksonian period were gradually giving way to new middle-class values, institutions, and ideas. Newspapers, magazines, and communication improvements of all kinds created a national audience for American scholars and writers. Since the turn of the century, American writers had struggled to find distinctive American themes, and these efforts bore fruit in the 1850s in the burst of creative activity termed "the American Renaissance." During this decade, Henry Thoreau, Nathaniel Hawthorne, Walt Whitman, Herman Melville, Emily Dickinson, Frederick Douglass, and others wrote works of fiction and nonfiction that are considered American classics.

During the American Renaissance, American writers pioneered new literary forms. Nathaniel Hawthorne, in stories like "Young Goodman Brown" (1835), raised the short story to a distinctive American literary form. Poets like Walt Whitman and Emily Dickinson experimented with unrhymed and "off-rhyme" verse, Whitman (in *Leaves of Grass*, published in 1855) to celebrate the boisterous pleasures of everyday life in New York City, Dickinson (who lived as a recluse in Amherst, Massachusetts) to catch her every fleeting thought and feeling in scraps of poetry that were not published until after her death. Another recluse, Henry David Thoreau, published *Walden* in 1854. A pastoral celebration of his life at Walden Pond, in Concord, Massachusetts, the essay was also a searching meditation on the cost to the individual of the loss of contact with nature that was a consequence of the market revolution.

Indeed, most of the writers of the American Renaissance were social critics. In *The Scarlet Letter* (1850) and *The House of the Seven Gables* (1851), both set in Puritan New England in the colonial period, Nathaniel Hawthorne brilliantly explored the moral choices faced by individuals as they try to reconcile repressive social expectations with private desires. Hawthorne's friend Herman Melville, in his great work *Moby Dick* (1851), drew on his own personal experience to write about the lives of ordinary sailors on a whaling voyage, but the story had deeper meanings. Melville's novel of Captain Ahab's obsessive search for the white whale is a profound study of the nature of good and evil and a critique of American society in the 1850s. The strongest social critique, however, was Frederick Douglass's starkly simple autobiography, *Narrative of the Life of Frederick Douglass* (1845), which told of his brutal life as a slave.

The most successful American novel of the mid-nineteenth century was about the great issue of the day, slavery. In writing *Uncle Tom's Cabin*, Harriet Beecher Stowe combined the literary style of the then-popular women's domestic novels (discussed in Chapter 12) with vivid details of slavery culled from firsthand accounts by northern abolitionists and escaped slaves. Stowe, the daughter of the reforming clergyman Lyman Beecher,

had married a Congregational minister and was herself a member of the evangelical movement. She had long been active in antislavery work, and a new Fugitive Slave Law passed in 1850 impelled her to write a novel that would persuade everyone of the evils of slavery. She wrote every night at her kitchen table after putting her six children to bed, and, as she said later, the events of the novel came to her "with a vividness that could not be denied," making her feel like "an instrument of God."

Stowe's famous novel told a poignant story of the Christ-like slave Uncle Tom, who patiently endured the cruel treatment of an evil white overseer, Simon Legree. Published in 1851, it was a runaway best seller. More than 300,000 copies were sold in the first year, and within ten years the book had sold more than 2 million copies, becoming the all-time American best-seller in proportion to population. Turned into a play that remained popular throughout the nineteenth century, *Uncle Tom's Cabin* reached an even wider audience. Scenes from the novel such as that of Eliza carrying her son across the ice-choked Ohio River to freedom, Tom weeping for his children as he was sold south, and the death of little Eva are among the best-known passages in

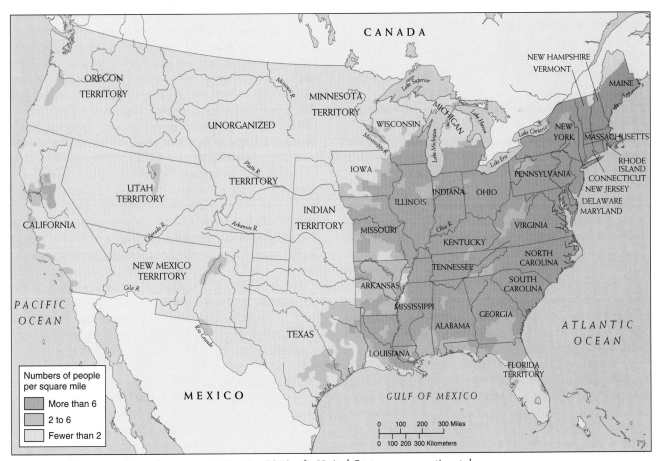

U.S. Population and Settlement, 1850   *By 1850, the United States was a continental nation. Its people, whom Thomas Jefferson had once thought would not reach the Mississippi River for forty generations, had not only passed the river but leapfrogged to the west coast. In comparison to the America of 1800 (see the map on p. 233) the growth was astounding.*

The Webbs, a free African American family, toured northern cities performing dramatic readings from Uncle Tom's Cabin. *An all-time best-seller, the novel outlasted the Civil War and, adapted into dramatic form, remained popular with theater audiences through the second half of the nineteenth century.*

all of American literature. *Uncle Tom's Cabin* was more than a heart-tugging story: it was a call to action. In 1863, when Harriet Beecher Stowe was introduced to Abraham Lincoln, the president remarked, "So you're the little woman who wrote the book that made this great war!"

Political Parties and Slavery

Stowe's novel clearly spoke to the growing concern of the American people. Slavery had long been a divisive issue in national politics. Until the 1840s, compromises had always been found, most notably in the Constitution itself (see Chapter 8) and in the Missouri Crisis of 1820 (see Chapter 9). But the struggle over the place of slavery in the vast new territories gained in the Mexican-American War gave rise to intractable new sectional arguments. The year 1850 opened to the most serious political crisis the United States had ever known. The struggle over the issue of slavery in the territories had begun in 1846 with the Wilmot Proviso and was still unresolved. Increasingly, both politicians and ordinary people began to consider the almost unthinkable possibility of disunion. As politician James Buchanan wrote to a friend early in the year, "The blessed Union of these states is now in greater danger than it has ever been since the adoption of the federal

Constitution." He feared that the two great national parties, the Whigs and the Democrats, would not be able to find a solution to the increasingly sectional division between North and South over slavery.

The Second American Party System forged in the great controversies of Andrew Jackson's presidency (see Chapter 10) was a national party system. In their need to mobilize great masses of recently enfranchised voters to elect a president every four years, politicians created organized party structures that overrode deeply rooted sectional differences. Politicians from all sections of the country cooperated because they knew their party could not succeed without national appeal. At a time when the ordinary person still had very strong sectional loyalties, the mass political party created a national community of like-minded voters. Yet by the election of 1848 sectional interests were eroding the political "glue" in both parties. Although each party still appeared united, sectional fissures already ran deep.

Political splits were preceded by divisions in other social institutions. Disagreements about slavery had already split the country's great religious organizations into northern and southern groups, the Presbyterians in 1837, the Methodists in 1844, and the Baptists in 1845. (Some of these splits turned out to be permanent. The Southern Baptist Convention, for example, is still a separate body.) Theodore Weld, the abolitionist leader, saw these splits as inevitable: "Events...have for years been silently but without a moment's pause, settling the basis of two great parties, the nucleus of one slavery, of the other, freedom." Indeed, the abolitionists had been posing this simple yet uncompromising choice between slavery or freedom since the 1830s. Moreover, they had been insisting on a compelling distinction: as Liberty Party spokesman Salmon P. Chase said, "Freedom is national; slavery only is local and sectional."

States' Rights and Slavery

But was freedom national and slavery sectional, or was it the other way around? Southern politicians took the latter view, as their foremost spokesman, South Carolina's John C. Calhoun, made ringingly clear throughout his long career.

In 1828 Calhoun had begun the protracted Nullification Crisis by asserting the constitutional right of states to "nullify" national laws that were harmful to their interests (see Chapter 10). Calhoun argued, as others have since, that the states' rights doctrine protected the legitimate rights of a minority in a democratic system governed by majority rule.

In 1847, Calhoun responded to the 1846 Wilmot Proviso with an elaboration of the states' rights argument. In spite of the apparent precedents of the Northwest Ordinance of 1787 and the Missouri Compromise, Calhoun argued that Congress did not have a constitutional right to prohibit slavery in the territories. The territories, he said, were the common property of all the states, north and south, and Congress could not discriminate against slave owners as they moved west. On the contrary, Calhoun argued, slave owners had a constitutional right to the protection of their property wherever they moved. Of course, Calhoun's legally correct description of African American slaves as property enraged abolitionists. But on behalf of the South, Calhoun was expressing the belief—and the fear—that his interpretation of the Constitution was the only protection for slave owners, whose right to own slaves (a fundamental right in southern eyes) was being attacked. Calhoun's position on the territories quickly became southern dogma: anything less than full access to the territories was unconstitutional. Slavery, Calhoun and other Southerners insisted, had to be national.

As Congressman Robert Toombs of Georgia put the case in 1850, there was very little room for compromise:

> I stand upon the great principle that the South has the right to an equal participation in the territories of the United States....She will divide with you if you wish it, but the right to enter all or divide I shall never surrender....Deprive us of this right and appropriate the common property to yourselves, it is then your government, not mine. Then I am its enemy....Give us our just rights, and we are ready...to stand by the Union....Refuse [them], and for one, I will strike for independence.

Northern Fears of "The Slave Power"

The words of Southerners like Calhoun and Toombs confirmed for many Northerners the warnings of antislavery leaders that they were endangered by a menacing "slave power." Liberty Party leader James Birney, in a speech in 1844, was the first to add this phrase to the nation's political vocabulary. "The slave power," Birney explained, was a group of aristocratic slave owners who not only dominated the political and social life of the South but conspired to control the federal government as well, posing a danger to free speech and free institutions throughout the nation.

Birney's "slave power" was a caricature of the influence slave owners wielded over southern politics and of the increasingly defensive and monolithic response of southern representatives in national politics after 1830 (see Chapter 11). The proslavery strategy of maintaining supremacy in the Senate by having at least as many slave as free states admitted to the Union (a plan that required slavery expansion) and of maintaining control, or at least veto power, over presidential nominees seemed, in southern eyes, to be nothing less

This strident poster warns that "the Slave Power" aims "to control the government of the nation, and make it subservient to its wicked designs." For good measure, the poster also appeals to nativist fears and to workers.

than ordinary self-defense. But to antislavery advocates, these actions looked like a conspiracy by sectional interests to control national politics. Birney's warnings about "the slave power" seemed in 1844 merely the overheated rhetoric of an extremist group of abolitionists. But the defensive southern political strategies of the 1850s were to convince an increasing number of northern voters that "the slave power" did in fact exist. Thus in northern eyes the South became a demonic monolith that threatened the national government.

Two Communities, Two Perspectives

Ironically, it was a common belief in expansion that made the arguments between Northerners and Southerners so irreconcilable. Southerners had been the strongest supporters of the Mexican-American War, and they still hoped to expand into Cuba, believing that the slave system must grow or wither. On the other hand, although many northern Whigs had opposed the Mexican-American War, most did so for antislavery reasons, not because they opposed expansion. The strong showing of the Free-Soil Party (which evolved out of the Liberty Party) in the election of 1848 (10 percent of the popular vote) was proof of that. Basically, both North and South believed in manifest destiny, but each on its own terms.

Similarly, both North and South used the language of basic rights and liberties in the debate over expansion. But Free-Soilers were speaking of personal liberty, whereas Southerners meant their right to own a particular kind of property (slaves) and to maintain a way of life based on the possession of that property. In defending its own rights, each side had taken measures that infringed on the rights of the other. Southerners pointed out that abolitionists had libeled slave owners as a class and that they had bombarded the South with unwanted literature, abused the right of petition to Congress, incited slaves to rebellion, and actively helped slaves to escape. For their part, Northerners accused slave owners of censorship of the mails; imposition of the "gag rule" (repealed in 1844), which prohibited any petition against slavery from being read to or discussed by Congress; suppression of free speech in the South; and, of course, of committing the moral wrong of enslaving others in the first place.

By 1850, North and South had created different communities. To antislavery Northerners, the South was an economic backwater dominated by a small slave-owning aristocracy that lived off the profits of forced labor and deprived poor whites of their democratic rights and the fruits of honest work. The slave system was not only immoral but a drag on the entire nation, for, in the words of Senator William Seward of New York, it subverted the "intelligence, vigor and energy" that were essential for national growth. In contrast, the dynamic and enterprising commercial North boasted a free labor ideology that offered economic opportunity to the common man and ensured his democratic rights (see Chapter 12).

Things looked very different through southern eyes. Far from being economically backward, the South, through its export of cotton, was, according to Southerners, the great engine of national economic growth from which the North benefited. Slavery was not only a blessing to an inferior race but the cornerstone of democracy, for it ensured the freedom and independence of all white men without entailing

the bitter class divisions that marked the North. Slave owners accused northern manufacturers of hypocrisy for practicing "wage slavery" without the paternal benevolence they claimed to bestow on their slaves. The North, James Henry Hammond of South Carolina charged, had eliminated the "name [of slavery], but not the thing," for "your whole hireling class of manual laborers and 'operatives'...are essentially slaves."

By the early 1850s, these vastly different visions of the North and the South—the result of many years of political controversy—had become fixed, and the chances of national reconciliation increasingly slim. Over the course of the decade, many Americans came to believe that the place of slavery in the nation's life had to be permanently settled. And they increasingly wondered whether their two sectional communities—one slave, one free—could continue to be part of a unitary national one.

THE COMPROMISE OF 1850

By 1850 the issue raised by the Wilmot Proviso—whether slavery should be extended to the new territories—could no longer be ignored. Overnight, the California Gold Rush had turned a remote frontier into a territory with a booming population. In 1849 both

In 1850, the three men who had long represented America's three major regions attempted to resolve the political crisis brought on by the applications of California and Utah for statehood. Henry Clay is speaking; John C. Calhoun stands third from right; and Daniel Webster is seated at the left with his head in his hand. Both Clay and Webster were ill, and Calhoun died before the compromise of 1850 was arranged by a younger group of politicians led by Stephen A. Douglas.

OVERVIEW

THE GREAT SECTIONAL COMPROMISES

Missouri Compromise	1820	Admits Missouri to the Union as a slave state and Maine as a free state; prohibits slavery in the rest of the Louisiana Purchase Territory north of 36°30'.
		Territory Covered: The entire territory of the Louisiana Purchase, exclusive of the state of Louisiana, which had been admitted to the Union in 1812.
Compromise of 1850	1850	Admits California to the Union as a free state, settles the borders of Texas (a slave state); sets no conditions concerning slavery for the rest of the territory acquired from Mexico.
		Territory Covered: The territory that had been part of Mexico before the end of the Mexican-American War and the Treaty of Guadalupe Hidalgo (1848): part of Texas, California, Utah Territory (now Utah, Nevada, and part of Colorado), and New Mexico Territory (now New Mexico and Arizona).

California and Utah applied for statehood. Should these territories be admitted as slave or free states? A simmering border war between Texas (a slave state) and New Mexico, which seemed likely to be a free state, had to be settled, as did the issue of the debts Texas had incurred as an independent republic. Closer to home, antislavery forces demanded the end of slavery in the District of Columbia, while slave owners complained that Northerners were refusing to return escaped slaves, as federal law mandated.

Debate and Compromise

The Compromise of 1850 was the final act in the political careers of the three aging men who in the public mind best represented America's sections: Westerner Henry Clay; Southerner John C. Calhoun; and Daniel Webster, spokesman for the North. It was sadly appropriate to the bitter sectional argument of 1850 that the three men contributed great words to the debate but that the compromise itself was enacted by younger men. Calhoun brought an aura of death with him to the Senate as he sat, shrouded in flannels, listening to the speech that he was too ill to read for himself. He died less than a month later, still insisting on the right of the South to secede if necessary to preserve its way of life. Daniel Webster claimed to speak "not as a Massachusetts man, nor as a Northern man, but as an American....I speak today for the preservation of the Union." He rejected southern claims that peaceable secession was possible or desirable and pleaded with abolitionists to compromise

enough to keep the South in the Union. Clay, claiming he had "never before risen to address any assemblage so oppressed, so appalled, and so anxious," argued eloquently for compromise, but left the Senate in ill health before his plea was answered.

On July 9, 1850, in the midst of the debate, President Zachary Taylor died of acute gastroenteritis, caused by a hasty snack of fruit and cold milk at a Fourth of July celebration. A bluff military man, Taylor had been prepared to follow Andrew Jackson's precedent during the Nullification Crisis of 1832 and simply demand that southern dissidents compromise. When Vice President Millard Fillmore assumed the presidency, however, he helped adjust the Compromise of 1850 to southern liking. Fillmore was a moderate northern Whig and more prosouthern than the southern-born Taylor had been. Moreover, although Clay had assembled all the necessary parts of the bargain, it was not he but members of a younger political generation, and in particular the rising young Democrat from Illinois, Stephen Douglas, who drove the Compromise of 1850 through Congress. The final product consisted of five separate bills (it had been impossible to obtain a majority for a comprehensive measure), embodying three separate compromises.

First, California was admitted as a free state, but the status of the remaining former Mexican possessions was left to be decided by popular sovereignty (a vote of the territory's inhabitants) when they applied for statehood. (Utah's application for statehood was not accepted until 1896 because of controversy over the Mormon practice of polygamy.) The result was, for the time being,

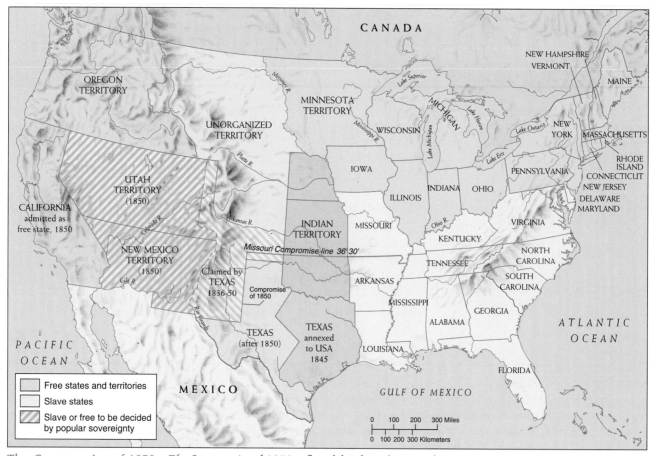

The Compromise of 1850   *The Compromise of 1850 reflected heightened sectional tensions by being even messier and more awkward than the Missouri Compromise of 1820. California was admitted as a free state, the borders of Texas were settled, and the status of the rest of the former Mexican territory was left to be decided later by popular sovereignty. No consistent majority voted for the five separate bills that made up the compromise.*

fifteen slave states and sixteen free states. Second, Texas (a slave state) was required to cede land to New Mexico Territory (free or slave status undecided). In return, the federal government assumed $10 million of debts Texas incurred before it became a state. Finally, the slave trade, but not slavery itself, was ended in the District of Columbia, but a stronger fugitive slave law was enacted.

Jubilation and relief greeted the news that compromise had been achieved. In Washington, where the anxiety and concern had been greatest, drunken crowds serenaded Congress, shouting, "The Union is saved!" That was certainly true for the moment, but analysis of the votes on the five bills that made up the compromise revealed no consistent majority. The sectional splits within each party that had existed before the compromise remained. Antislavery northern Whigs and proslavery southern Democrats, each the larger wing of their party, were the least willing to compromise. Southern Whigs and northern Democrats were the forces for moderation, but each group was dwindling in popular appeal as sectional animosities grew.

In the country as a whole, the feeling was that the problem of slavery in the territories had been solved. The *Philadelphia Pennsylvanian* was confident that "peace and tranquillity" had been ensured, and the *Louisville Journal* said that a weight seemed to have been lifted from the heart of America. But as former Liberty Party spokesman Salmon P. Chase, now a senator from Ohio, soberly noted, "The question of slavery in the territories has been avoided. It has not been settled." The most immediately inflammatory measure of the compromise was the Fugitive Slave Act.

The Fugitive Slave Act

From the early days of their movement, northern abolitionists had urged slaves to escape, promising assistance and support when they reached the North. Some free African Americans had offered far more than verbal support. Among them, Harriet Tubman, an escaped slave from Maryland, was one of the most famous. Tubman made nineteen return trips and brought almost 300 slaves to freedom, among them all the other members of her family. Northerners had long been appalled by professional slave catchers, who zealously seized African Americans in the North and took them south into slavery again. Most abhorrent in northern eyes was that captured black people were at the mercy of slave catchers because they had no legal right to defend themselves. In more than one case, a northern free African American was captured in his own community and helplessly shipped into slavery.

Solomon Northup was one such person. In his widely sold account *Twelve Years a Slave*, published in 1853, he told a harrowing tale of being kidnapped in Washington, the nation's capital, and shipped south. Northup spent twelve years as a slave before he was able to send a message to northern friends to bring the legal proof to free him. As a result of stories like Northup's and the very effective publicity generated by abolitionists, nine northern states passed personal liberty laws between 1842 and 1850, serving notice that they would not cooperate with federal recapture efforts. These northern laws enraged Southerners, who had long been convinced that all Northerners, not just abolitionists, were actively hindering efforts to reclaim their escaped slaves. At issue were two distinct definitions of "rights": Northerners were upset at the denial of legal and personal rights to escaped slaves; Southerners saw illegal infringement of their property rights. Southerners insisted that a strong federal law be part of the Compromise of 1850.

The Fugitive Slave Law, enacted in 1850, dramatically increased the power of slave owners to capture escaped slaves. The full authority of the federal government now supported slave owners, and although fugitives were guaranteed a hearing before a federal commissioner, they were not allowed to testify on their own behalf. Furthermore, the new law imposed federal penalties on citizens who protected or assisted fugitives, or who did not cooperate in their return. In Boston, the center of the abolitionist movement, reaction to the new law was fierce. When an escaped slave named Shadrach Minkins was seized in February 1851, a group of African American men broke into the courtroom, overwhelmed the federal marshals, seized Minkins, and sent him safely to Canada. Although the action had community support—a Massachusetts jury defiantly refused to convict the perpetrators—many people, including Daniel Webster and President Fillmore, condemned it as "mob rule."

The federal government responded with overwhelming force. In April 1851, 300 armed soldiers were mobilized to prevent the rescue of Thomas Sims, who was being shipped back into slavery. In the most famous case in Boston, a biracial group of armed abolitionists led by Unitarian clergyman Thomas Wentworth Higginson stormed the federal courthouse in 1854 in an attempt to save escaped slave Anthony Burns. The

rescue effort failed, and a federal deputy marshal was killed. President Pierce sent marines, cavalry, and artillery to Boston to reinforce the guard over Burns and ordered a federal ship to be ready to deliver the fugitive back into slavery. When the effort by defense lawyers to argue for Burns's freedom failed, Bostonians raised money to buy his freedom. But the U.S. attorney, ordered by the president to enforce the Fugitive Slave Law in all circumstances, blocked the purchase. The case was lost, and Burns was marched to the docks through streets lined with sorrowing abolitionists. Buildings were shrouded in black and draped with American flags hanging upside down, while bells tolled as if for a funeral.

The Burns case radicalized many Northerners. Conservative Whig George Hilliard wrote to a friend, "When it was all over, and I was left alone in my office, I put my face in my hands and wept. I could do nothing less." During the 1850s, 322 black fugitives were sent back into slavery; only 11 were declared free. Northern popular sentiment and the Fugitive Slave Law, rigorously enforced by the federal government, were increasingly at odds. The northern abolitionists who used force to rescue captured slaves were breaking the law, but they were winning the battle for public opinion.

In this volatile atmosphere, escaped African Americans wrote and lectured bravely on behalf of freedom. Frederick Douglass, the most famous and eloquent of the fugitive slaves, spoke out fearlessly in support of armed resistance. "The only way to make the Fugitive Slave Law a dead letter," he said in 1853, "is to make a half dozen or more dead kidnappers." Openly active in the underground network that helped slaves reach safety in Canada, Douglass himself had been constantly in danger of capture until his friends bought his freedom in 1847. Harriet Jacobs, who escaped to the North after seven years in hiding in the South, wrote bitterly in her *Incidents in the Life of a Slave Girl* (1861) that the Fugitive Slave Law made her feel that "I was, in fact, a slave in New York, as subject to slave laws as I had been in a slave state....I had been chased during half my life, and it seemed as if the chase was never to end." Threatened by owners who came north for her, Jacobs went into hiding again, until she was informed that friends had arranged her purchase: "A gentleman near me said, 'It's true; I have seen the bill of sale.' 'The bill of sale!' Those words struck me like a blow. So I was sold at last! A human being sold in the free city of New York!"

The Fugitive Slave Law brought home the reality of slavery to residents of the free states. In effect, this law made slavery national and forced northern communities to confront what that meant. Although most people were still unwilling to grant social equality to the free African Americans who lived in the northern states, more and more had come to believe that the institution of slavery was wrong. The strong northern reaction against the Fugitive Slave Law also had consequences in the South. As Democrat Cave Johnson of Tennessee warned, "If the fugitive slave bill is not enforced in the North, the moderate men of the South…will be overwhelmed by the 'fire-eaters,'" the extremists who favored immediate secession. Northern protests against the Fugitive Slave Law bred suspicion in the South and encouraged secessionist thinking. These new currents of public opinion were reflected in the election of 1852.

The Election of 1852

The first sign of the weakening of the national party system in 1852 was the difficulty both parties experienced at their nominating conventions. With long-time party leaders like Henry Clay now dead, William Seward of New York became the unofficial party head, much to the displeasure of southern Whigs. Seward preferred General Winfield Scott (a military hero like the party's previous two candidates) to the prosouthern Fillmore, and after fifty-two ballots, managed to get him nominated. Many southern Whigs were angered and alienated by the choice and either abstained during the voting, like Georgia's Alexander Stephens, or, like Robert Toombs, cast a protest vote for the Democratic candidate. Although southern Whigs were still elected to Congress, their loyalty to the national party was strained to the breaking point. The Whigs never again fielded a presidential candidate.

The Democrats had a wider variety of candidates: Lewis Cass of popular sovereignty fame; Stephen Douglas, architect of the Compromise of 1850; and James Buchanan, described as a "Northern man with Southern principles." Cass, Douglas, and Buchanan competed for forty-nine ballots, each strong enough to block the others but not strong enough to win. Finally the party turned to a handsome, affable nonentity, Franklin Pierce of New Hampshire, who was thought to have southern sympathies. Uniting on a platform pledging "faithful execution" of all parts of the Compromise of 1850, including the Fugitive Slave Law, Democrats polled well in the South and in the North. Most Democrats who had voted for the Free-Soil Party in 1848 voted for Pierce. So, in record numbers, did immigrant Irish and German voters, who were eligible for citizenship after three years' residence. The strong immigrant vote for Pierce was a sign of the strength of the Democratic machines in northern cities (see Chapter 13), and reformers complained, not for the last time, about widespread corruption and "vote buying" by urban ward bosses. Overall, however, "Genl. Apathy is the strongest candidate out here," as one Ohioan reported. Pierce easily won the 1852 election, 254 electoral votes to 42. Voter turnout was below 70 percent, lower than it had been since 1836.

"Young America": The Politics of Expansion

Pierce entered the White House in 1853 on a wave of good feeling. Massachusetts Whig Amos Lawrence reported, "Never since Washington has an administration commenced with the hearty [good]will of so large a portion of the country." This goodwill was soon strained by Pierce's support for the expansionist adventures of the "Young America" movement.

The "Young America" movement was a group within the Democratic Party whose members used manifest destiny to justify their desire for conquest of Central America and Cuba. Young America expansionists had glanced covetously southward since the end of the Mexican-American War. President Polk himself had wanted to buy Cuba and to intervene in Mexican politics but was rebuffed by Congress (see Chapter 14). During the Pierce administration, several private "filibusters" (from the Spanish filibustero, meaning an "adventurer" or "pirate") invaded Caribbean and Central American countries, usually with the declared intention of extending slave territory. The best-known of the filibusters, William Walker, was also the most improbable. Short, slight, and soft-spoken, Walker led not one but three invasions of Nicaragua. After the first invasion in 1855, Walker became ruler of the country and encouraged settlement by southern slave owners, but was unseated by a regional revolt in 1857. His subsequent efforts to regain control of the country failed, and on the last he was captured and executed by firing squad in Honduras.

The Pierce administration, not directly involved in the filibustering, was deeply involved in an effort to obtain Cuba. In 1854, Pierce authorized his minister to Spain, Pierre Soulé, to try to force the unwilling Spanish to sell Cuba for $130 million. Soulé met in Ostend, Belgium, with the American ministers to France and England, John Mason and James Buchanan, to compose the offer, which was a mixture of cajolements and threats. At first appealing to Spain to recognize the deep affinities between the Cubans and American Southerners that made them "one people with one destiny," the document went on to threaten to "wrest" Cuba from Spain if necessary. This amazing document, which became known as the Ostend Manifesto, was supposed to be secret but was soon leaked to the press. Deeply embarrassed, the Pierce administration was forced to repudiate it.

The complicity between the Pierce administration and proslavery expansionists was foolhardy and lost it the northern goodwill with which it had begun. The sectional crisis that preceded the Compromise of 1850 had made obvious the danger of reopening the territorial issue. Ironically, it was not the Young America expansionists but the prime mover of the Compromise of 1850 himself, Stephen A. Douglas, who reignited the sectional struggle over slavery expansion.

THE CRISIS OF THE NATIONAL PARTY SYSTEM

In 1854, Douglas introduced the Kansas-Nebraska Act, proposing to open those lands that had been the northern part of Indian Territory to American settlers under the principle of popular sovereignty. He thereby reopened the question of slavery in the territories. Douglas knew he was taking a political risk, but he believed he could satisfy both his expansionist aims and his presidential ambitions. He was wrong. Instead, he pushed the national party system into crisis, first killing the Whigs and then destroying the Democrats.

The Kansas-Nebraska Act

Until 1854, white Americans thought of Kansas only as a passageway to other places farther west. A part of Indian Territory, Kansas was peopled largely by tribes who had been moved from their original homes in the East. In the great Indian removals of the 1830s, these tribes had been promised the Kansas lands "as long as grass grows and water flows." The promise was broken in 1854, when prior treaties were ignored and the northern part of Indian Territory was thrown open to white settlement.

Stephen Douglas introduced the Kansas-Nebraska Act to further the construction of a transcontinental railroad, which he ardently supported as a way to foster American democracy and commerce. He wanted the rail line to terminate in Chicago, in his own state of Illinois, rather than in the rival St. Louis, but for that to happen, the land west of Iowa and Missouri had to be organized into territories (the first step toward statehood). To get Congress to agree to the organization of the territories, however, Douglas would need the votes of southern Democrats, who would be unwilling to support him unless the territories were open to slavery. Douglas also coveted his party's nomination for the presidency in 1856, and would need the continuing support of southern Democrats to secure it.

Douglas thought he was solving his problem by proposing that the status of slavery in the new

The Kansas-Nebraska Act, 1854   *The Kansas-Nebraska Act, proposed by Steven A. Douglas in 1854, opened the central and northern Great Plains to settlement. The act had two major faults: it robbed Indian peoples of half the territory guaranteed to them by treaty, and, because it repealed the Missouri Compromise Line, it opened up the lands to warring proslavery and antislavery factions.*

territories be governed by the principle of popular sovereignty. Democratic politicians had favored this democratic-sounding slogan, vague enough to appeal to both proslavery and antislavery voters, ever since 1848. Douglas thought Southerners would support his bill because of its popular sovereignty provision, and Northerners because it favored a northern route for the transcontinental railroad. Privately, Douglas believed that the topography of the Kansas-Nebraska region was unsuitable for slave agriculture and that the region's inhabitants would decide to enter the Union as free states. Douglas chose also to downplay the price he had to pay for southern support—by allowing the possibility of slavery in the new territories his bill in effect repealed the Missouri Compromise of 1820, which barred slavery north of latitude 36°30'.

The Kansas-Nebraska bill passed, but it badly strained the major political parties. Southern Whigs voted with southern Democrats in favor of the measure, northern Whigs rejected it absolutely, creating an irreconcilable split that left Whigs unable to field a presidential candidate in 1856. The damage to the Democratic Party was almost as great. In the congressional elections of 1854, northern Democrats lost two-thirds of their seats (a drop from ninety-one to twenty-five), giving the southern Democrats (who were solidly in favor of slavery extension) the dominant voice both in Congress and within the party.

Douglas had committed one of the greatest miscalculations in American political history. A storm of protest arose throughout the North. More than 300 large anti-Nebraska rallies occurred during congressional consideration of the bill, and the anger did not subside. Douglas, who confidently believed that "the people of the North will sustain the measure when they come to understand it," found himself shouted down more than once at public rallies when he tried to explain the bill. "I could travel from Boston to Chicago," he ruefully commented, "by the light of my own [burning] effigy."

The Kansas-Nebraska bill shifted a crucial sector of northern opinion: the wealthy merchants, bankers, and manufacturers (called "Cotton Whigs") who had economic ties with southern slave owners and had always disapproved of abolitionist activity. Convinced that the bill would encourage antislavery feeling in the North, Cotton Whigs urged southern politicians to vote against it, only to be ignored. Passage of the Kansas-Nebraska Act convinced many northern Whigs that compromise with the South was impossible. Even as sober a newspaper as the *New York Times* regarded the act as "part of this great scheme for extending and perpetuating the supremacy of the Slave Power." Joining the antislavery cause were some Cotton Whigs like manufacturer Amos Lawrence of Massachusetts, who had so

warmly welcomed the prospect of sectional peace at the beginning of the Pierce administration. Lawrence provided the financial backing for the first group of antislavery New Englanders who settled Kansas in 1854, and in gratitude they named their town for him.

In Kansas itself in 1854, hasty treaties were concluded with the Indian tribes who owned the land. Some, such as the Kickapoos, Shawnees, Sauks, and Foxes, agreed to relocate to small reservations. Others, like the Delawares, Weas, and Iowas, agreed to sell their lands to whites. Still others, such as the Cheyennes and Sioux, kept the western part of Kansas Territory (now Colorado)—until gold was discovered there in 1859. Once the treaties were signed, both proslavery and antislavery white settlers began to pour in, and the battle was on.

"Bleeding Kansas"

The first to claim land in Kansas were residents of nearby Missouri, itself a slave state. Egged on by Democratic senator David Atchison of Missouri (who took a leave of absence from Congress to lead them), Missourians took up land claims, established proslavery strongholds such as the towns of Leavenworth, Kickapoo, and Atchison, and repeatedly and blatantly swamped Kansas elections with Missouri votes. In 1855, in the second of several notoriously fraudulent elections, 6,307 ballots were cast in a territory that had fewer than 3,000 eligible voters. The rest of the votes—all proslavery—were cast by "border ruffians," as they proudly called themselves, from Missouri. These were frontiersmen, fond of boasting that they could "scream louder, jump higher, shoot closer, get drunker at night and wake up soberer in the morning than any man this side of the Rocky Mountains."

Northerners quickly responded, with the encouragement of sympathetic politicians. Free-Soil (antislavery) New Englanders were recruited to Kansas by the New England Emigrant Aid Society, founded by abolitionist Eli Thayer of Massachusetts. The first party of New Englanders arrived in the summer of 1854 and established the free-soil town of Lawrence. More than a thousand others had joined them by the following summer. Lawrence quickly blossomed from a town of tent homes to one of solid log cabins, a church, a sawmill, stores, and a stone foundation for what became the Free State Hotel, sponsored by the Emigrant Aid Society. These migrants were all free-soilers, and many were religious reformers as well. The contrast of values between them and the border ruffians was almost total. When nondrinking William Phillips stiffly refused a friendly offer of a drink from a Missourian, the border ruffian burst out, "That's just it! This thing of temperance and abolitionism and the Emigrant Aid Society are all the same kind of thing."

Kansas soon became a bloody battleground as the two factions struggled to secure the mandate of "popular sovereignty." Free-Soilers in Lawrence received shipments of heavy crates, innocuously marked "BOOKS" but actually containing Sharps repeating rifles, sent by eastern supporters. For their part, the border ruffians—already heavily armed, with Bowie knives in their boots, revolvers at their waists, rifles slung from their shoulders, and swords at their sides—called for reinforcements. David Atchison exhorted Alabamans: "Let your young men come forth to Missouri and Kansas! Let them come well armed!"

In the summer of 1856 these lethal preparations exploded into open warfare. First, proslavery forces burned and looted the town of Lawrence. The Free State Hotel, among other buildings, was burned to the ground. In retaliation, a grim old man named John Brown led his sons in a raid on the proslavery settlers of Pottawatomie Creek, killing five unarmed people. A wave of violence ensued. Armed bands roamed the countryside, and burnings and killings became commonplace. John Brown and his followers were just one of many bands of marauding murderers who were never arrested, never brought to trial, and never stopped from committing further violence. Peaceful residents of large sections of rural Kansas were repeatedly forced to flee to the safety of military forts when rumors of one or another armed band reached them.

This engraving shows "Border Ruffians" from Missouri lining up to vote for slavery in the Kickapoo, Kansas Territory election of 1855. The widespread practice of illegal voting and of open violence earned Kansas the dreadful nickname of "Bleeding Kansas."

The rest of the nation watched in horror as the residents of Kansas slaughtered each other in the pursuit of sectional goals. Americans' pride in their nation's great achievements was threatened by the endless violence in one small part—but a part that increasingly seemed to represent the divisions of the whole.

The Politics of Nativism

Meanwhile, sectional pressures continued to reshape national politics. The breakup of the Whig Party coincided with one of the strongest bursts of nativism, or anti-immigrant feeling, in American history, a reaction to the Democratic Party's success in capturing the support of the rapidly growing population of mostly Catholic foreign-born voters (see Chapter 13 and "Immigration and Community: The Changing Nature of Ethnicity in America, 1800–1860," p. 380).

Irish immigrants in particular voted Democratic, both in reaction to Whig hostility (as in Boston) and because of their own antiblack prejudices. Frequently in competition with free African Americans for low-paying jobs, Irish immigrants were more likely to share the attitudes of Southerners than those of abolitionists. Violent urban riots in which free African Americans were the scapegoats periodically erupted in northern cities such as Cincinnati (1829), Providence (1831), New York (1834), and Philadelphia (1834 and 1842).

The reformist and individualistic attitudes of many Whigs inclined them toward nativism and toward the new American Party, which formed in 1850 to give political expression to anti-immigrant feeling. Many Whigs disapproved of the new immigrants because they were poor, Catholic, and often disdainful of the temperance movement. The Catholic Church's opposition to the liberal European revolutions of 1848 also fueled anti-Catholic fears. If America's new Catholic immigrants opposed the revolutions in which other Americans took such pride (believing them to be modeled on the American example), how could the future of America's own democracy be ensured? Finally, nativist Whigs held immigration to be solely responsible for the increases in crime and the rising cost of relief for the poor that accompanied the rapid urban growth of the 1830s and 1840s.

Women reformers were as prone to nativism as men. As early as 1838, the influential Lydia Sigourney wrote in alarm in her *Letters to Mothers* about the "influx of untutored foreigners" that had made the United States "a repository for the waste and refuse of other nations." Sigourney urged women to organize an internal missionary movement that would carry the principles of middle-class American domesticity to the unenlightened foreigners.

Nativism drew former Whigs, especially young men in white-collar and skilled blue-collar

Cartoons like this one sought to couple concerns about temperance (suggested by the barrels of Irish whiskey and German lager beer) with nativist claims that immigrant voters were voting illegally (indicated by the struggle in the background).

occupations, to the new American Party. At the core of the party were several secret fraternal societies open only to native-born Protestants who pledged never to vote for a Catholic (on the grounds that all Catholics took their orders straight from the pope in Rome—a fear that was to be voiced again by Southern Baptists in 1960 when John F. Kennedy ran for president). When questioned about their beliefs, party members maintained secrecy by answering, "I know nothing"— Hence the popular name for American Party members, Know-Nothings. Few Know-Nothings were wealthy: most were workers or small farmers whose jobs or ways of life were threatened by the cheap labor and unfamiliar culture of the new immigrants.

Know-Nothings scored startling victories in northern state elections in 1854, winning control of the legislature in Massachusetts and polling 40 percent of the vote in Pennsylvania. No wonder one Pennsylvania Democrat reported, "Nearly everybody seems to have gone altogether deranged on Nativism." Although most of the new immigrants lived in the North, resentment and anger against them was national, and the American Party initially polled well in the South, attracting the votes of many former southern Whigs. But in the 1850s, no party could ignore slavery, and in 1855 the American Party split into northern (antislavery) and southern (proslavery) wings. Soon after this split, many people who had voted for the Know-Nothings shifted their support to another new party, one that combined many characteristics of the Whigs with a westward-looking, expansionist, free-soil policy. This was the Republican Party, founded in 1854.

The Republican Party and the Election of 1856

In 1854 a Massachusetts voter described the elections in his state in terms of "freedom, temperance, and Protestantism against slavery, rum, and Romanism," linking nativism with sectional politics. "Slavery, rum, and Romanism" were supposed to describe the national Democratic Party, whose supporters included southern slave owners and northern immigrant Catholics. "Freedom, temperance, and Protestantism," were meant to characterize the Republican Party. Many constituencies, however, found room in the new party. Its supporters included many former northern Whigs who opposed slavery absolutely, many Free-Soil Party supporters who opposed the expansion of slavery but were willing to tolerate it in the South, and many northern reformers concerned about temperance and Catholicism. The Republicans also attracted the economic core of the old Whig Party—the merchants and industrialists who wanted a strong national government to promote economic growth by supporting a protective tariff, transportation improvements, and cheap land for western farmers. In quieter times it would have taken this party a while to sort out all its differences and become a true political community. But because of the sectional crisis, the fledgling party nearly won its very first presidential election.

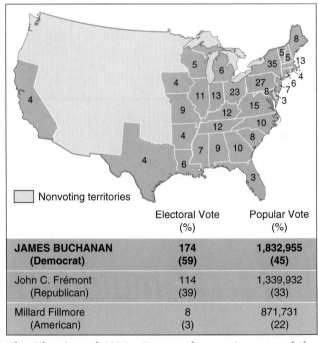

	Electoral Vote (%)	Popular Vote (%)
JAMES BUCHANAN (Democrat)	**174 (59)**	**1,832,955 (45)**
John C. Frémont (Republican)	114 (39)	1,339,932 (33)
Millard Fillmore (American)	8 (3)	871,731 (22)

The Election of 1856 *Because three parties contested the 1856 election, Democrat James Buchanan was a minority president. Although Buchanan alone had national support, Republican John Frémont won most of the free states, and Millard Fillmore of the American Party gained 40 percent of the vote in most of the slave states.*

The immediate question facing the nation in 1856 was which new party, the Know-Nothings or the Republicans, would emerge the stronger. But the more important question was whether the Democratic Party could hold together. The two strongest contenders for the Democratic nomination were President Pierce and Stephen A. Douglas. Douglas had proposed the Kansas-Nebraska Act and Pierce had actively supported it. Both men therefore had the support of the southern wing of the party. But it was precisely their support of this act that made Northerners oppose both of them. The Kansas-Nebraska Act's divisive effect on the Democratic Party now became clear: no one who had voted on the bill, either for or against, could satisfy both wings of the party. A compromise candidate was found in James Buchanan of Pennsylvania, the "Northern man with Southern principles." Luckily for him, he had been ambassador to Great Britain at the time of the Kansas-Nebraska Act and thus had not had to commit himself.

The election of 1856 appeared to be a three-way contest that pitted Buchanan against explorer John C. Frémont of the Republican Party and the American (Know-Nothing) Party's candidate, former president Millard Fillmore. In fact, the election was two separate contests, one in the North and one in the South. The southern race was between Buchanan and Fillmore. Frémont's name appeared on the ballot in only four southern states, all in the Upper South, and even there he polled almost no votes. Fillmore received strong support from many former southern Whigs. Although he carried only the state of Maryland, he attracted more than 40 percent of the vote in ten other slave states. Buchanan, though, won the electoral votes in all those states.

Frémont decisively defeated Buchanan in the North, winning eleven of sixteen free states. Nationwide he garnered 1.3 million votes to Buchanan's 1.8 million. Buchanan won the election with only 45

OVERVIEW

POLITICAL PARTIES SPLIT AND REALIGN

Whig Party	Ran its last presidential candidate in 1852. The candidate, General Winfield Scott, alienated many southern Whigs and the party was so split it could not field a candidate in 1856.
Democratic Party	Remained a national party through 1856, but Buchanan's actions as president made southern domination of the party so clear that many northern Democrats were alienated. Stephen Douglas, running as a northern Democrat in 1860, won 29 percent of the popular vote; John Breckinridge, running as a southern Democrat, won 18 percent.
Liberty Party	Antislavery party ran James G. Birney for president in 1844. He won 62,000 votes, largely from northern antislavery Whigs.
Free-Soil	Ran Martin Van Buren, former Democratic president, in 1848. Gained 10 percent of the popular vote, largely from Whigs but also from some northern Democrats.
American (Know-Nothing) Party	Nativist party made striking gains in 1854 congressional elections, attracting both northern and southern Whigs. In 1856, its presidential candidate Millard Fillmore won 21 percent of the popular vote.
Republican Party	Founded in 1854. Attracted many northern Whigs and northern Democrats. Presidential candidate John C. Frémont won 33 percent of the popular vote in 1856; in 1860 Abraham Lincoln won 40 percent and was elected in a four-way race.

percent of the popular vote because he was the only national candidate. His southern support, plus the electoral votes of Pennsylvania, New Jersey, Illinois, Indiana, and California gave him the victory. But the Republicans, after studying the election returns, claimed "victorious defeat," for they realized that in 1860 the addition of just two more northern states to their total would mean victory. Furthermore, the Republican Party had clearly defeated the American Party in the battle to win designation as a major party. These were grounds for great optimism—and for great concern, for the Republican Party was a sectional rather than a national party; it drew almost all its support from the North. Southerners viewed its very existence as an attack on their vital interests. Thus the rapid rise of the Republicans posed a growing threat to national unity.

The election of 1856 attracted one of the highest voter turnouts in American history—79 percent. Ordinary people had come to share the politicians' concern about the growing sectional rift. The combined popular vote for Buchanan and Fillmore (67 percent) showed that most voters, north and south, favored politicians who at least claimed to speak for national rather than sectional interests. The northern returns also showed something else. Northerners had decided that the threat posed by the expansion of slavery was greater than that posed by the new immigrants; although it never disappeared, nativism subsided. The Buchanan administration, however, proved unequal to the task of resolving the free versus slave issue, and the nation began an inexorable slide into civil war.

THE DIFFERENCES DEEPEN

In one dreadful week in 1856 the people of the United States heard, in quick succession, about the looting and burning of Lawrence, Kansas, about John Brown's retaliatory massacre at Pottawatomie, and about unprecedented violence on the Senate floor. In the last of these incidents, Senator Charles Sumner of Massachusetts suffered permanent injury in a vicious attack by Congressman Preston Brooks of South Carolina. Trapped at his desk, Sumner was helpless as Brooks beat him so hard with his cane that it broke. Blood streaming from his head, Sumner escaped only by wrenching loose his desk from the screws that held it to the floor. A few days earlier, Sumner had given an insulting antislavery speech entitled "The Crime against Kansas." Using the abusive, accusatory style favored by abolitionists, he had singled out for ridicule

Senator Andrew Butler of South Carolina, charging him with choosing "the harlot, slavery" as his mistress. Senator Butler was Preston Brooks's uncle; in Brooks's mind, he was simply avenging an intolerable affront to his uncle's honor. So far had the behavioral codes of North and South diverged that each man found his own action perfectly justifiable and the action of the other outrageous. Their attitudes were mirrored in their respective sections.

The *Dred Scott* Decision

Although James Buchanan firmly believed that he alone could hold together the nation so riven by hatred and violence, his self-confidence outran his abilities. When he entered the White House in March 1857 Buchanan was the oldest president (sixty-five) ever elected and a veteran of forty years of politics. Unfortunately, despite his experience, he was indecisive at moments that called for firm leadership. He was also so deeply indebted to the strong southern wing of the Democratic Party that he could not take the impartial actions necessary to heal "Bleeding Kansas." And his support for a momentous prosouthern decision by the Supreme Court further aggravated sectional differences.

In *Dred Scott v. Sandford*, decided on March 6, 1857, two days after James Buchanan was sworn in, a southern-dominated Supreme Court attempted—and failed—to solve the political controversy over slavery. Dred Scott had been a slave all his life. His owner, army surgeon John Emerson, had taken Scott on his military assignments during the 1830s to Illinois (a free state) and Wisconsin Territory (a free territory by the Missouri Compromise line). During that time Scott married another slave, Harriet, and their daughter Eliza was born in free territory. Emerson and the Scotts then returned to Missouri (a slave state) and there, in 1846, Dred Scott sued for his freedom and that of his wife and the daughter born in Wisconsin Territory (who as women had no legal standing of their own) on the grounds that residence in free lands had made them free. It took eleven years for the case to reach the Supreme Court, and by then its importance was obvious to everyone.

Chief Justice Roger B. Taney, of Maryland, seventy-nine years old, hard of hearing and failing of sight, insisted on reading his majority opinion in its entirety, a process that took four excruciating hours. Declaring the Missouri Compromise

SOUTHERN CHIVALRY_ ARGUMENT versus CLUB'S.

The beating of Senator Charles Sumner by Congressman Preston Brooks on the Senate floor horrified Northerners but won the approval of Southerners.

unconstitutional, Taney asserted that the federal government had no right to interfere with the free movement of property throughout the territories. Taney was in effect making John C. Calhoun's states' rights position, always considered an extremist southern position, the law of the land. He then dismissed the Dred Scott case on the grounds that only citizens could bring suits before federal courts and that black people—slave or free—were not citizens. With this bold judicial intervention into the most heated issue of the day, Taney intended to settle the controversy over the expansion of slavery once and for all. Instead, he enflamed the conflict.

The five southern members of the Supreme Court concurred in Taney's decision, as did one Northerner, Robert C. Grier. Historians have found that President-elect Buchanan had pressured Grier, a fellow Pennsylvanian, to support the majority. Two of the three other Northerners vigorously dissented, and the last voiced other objections. This was clearly a sectional decision, and the response to it was sectional. Southerners expressed great satisfaction and strong support for the Court. The *Louisville Democrat* said, "The decision is right...but whether or not [it is right], what this tribunal decides the Constitution to be, that it is; and all patriotic men will acquiesce." More bluntly, the *Georgia Constitutionalist* announced, "Southern opinion upon the subject of southern slavery...is now the supreme law of the land...and opposition to southern opinion upon this subject is now opposition to the Constitution, and morally treason against the Government."

Northerners disagreed. Few were quite so contemptuous as the *New York Tribune*, which declared that the decision was "entitled to just as much moral weight as would be the judgment of a majority of those congregated in any Washington bar-room." Still, many were so troubled by the Dred Scott decision that for the first time they found themselves seriously questioning the power of the Supreme Court to establish the "law of the land." Many northern legislatures denounced the decision. New York passed a resolution declaring that the Supreme Court had lost the confidence and respect of the people of that state and another refusing to allow slavery within its borders "in any form or under any pretense, or for any time, however short." New York Republicans also proposed an equal suffrage amendment for free African Americans, who were largely disenfranchised by a stringent property qualification for voting. But this was too liberal for the state's voters, who defeated it. This racist attitude was a bitter blow to free African Americans in the North. Frederick Douglass was so disheartened that he seriously considered emigrating to Haiti.

For the Republican Party, the Dred Scott decision represented a formidable challenge. By invalidating the Missouri Compromise, the decision

These sympathetic portraits of Harriet and Dred Scott and their daughters in 1857 helped to shape the northern reaction to the Supreme Court decision that denied the Scotts' claim for freedom. The infamous Dred Scott decision, which was intended to resolve the issue of slavery expansion, instead heightened angry feelings in both North and South.

swept away the free soil foundation of the party. But to directly challenge a Supreme Court decision was a weighty matter. The most sensational Republican counterattack—made by both Abraham Lincoln and William Seward—was the accusation that President Buchanan had conspired with the southern Supreme Court justices to subvert the American political system by withholding the decision until after the presidential election. Lincoln also raised the frightening possibility that "the next Dred Scott decision" would legalize slavery even in free states that abhorred it. President Buchanan's response to events in Kansas, including the drafting of a proslavery constitution, also stoked political antagonisms.

The Lecompton Constitution

In Kansas, the doctrine of popular sovereignty led to continuing civil strife and the political travesty of two territorial governments. The first election of officers to a territorial government in 1855 produced a lopsided proslavery outcome that was clearly the result of illegal voting by Missouri border ruffians. Free-soilers protested by forming their own government, giving Kansas both a proslavery territorial legislature in Lecompton and a free-soil government in Topeka. Because free-soil voters boycotted a June 1857 election for a convention to write a constitution for the territory once it reached statehood, the convention had a proslavery majority that wrote the proslavery Lecompton constitution and applied to Congress for admission to the Union under its terms. In the meantime, in October free-soil voters had participated in relatively honest elections for the territorial legislature, elections that returned a clear free-soil majority. Nevertheless, Buchanan, in the single most disastrous mistake of his administration, endorsed the proslavery constitution because he feared to lose the support of southern Democrats. It seemed that Kansas would enter the Union as a sixteenth slave state, making the number of slave and free states equal.

Unexpected congressional opposition came from none other than Stephen Douglas, author of the legislation that had begun the Kansas troubles in 1854. Now, in 1857, in what was surely the bravest step of his political career, Douglas opposed the Lecompton constitution on the grounds that it violated the principle of popular sovereignty. He insisted that the Lecompton constitution must be voted upon by Kansas voters in honest elections (as indeed Buchanan had initially promised). Douglas's decision was one of principle, but it was also motivated by the realization that a proslavery vote would never be accepted by the northern wing of the Democratic Party. Defying James Buchanan, his own president, Douglas voted with the majority in Congress in April 1858 to refuse admission to Kansas under the Lecompton constitution. In a new referendum, the people of Kansas also rejected the Lecompton constitution, 11,300 to 1,788. In 1859 Kansas held another constitutional convention, this one dominated by delegates from the new Republican Party. Kansas was finally admitted as a free state in January 1861.

The defeat of the Lecompton constitution did not come easily. There was more bloodshed in Kansas: sporadic ambushes and killings, including a mass shooting of nine free-soilers. And there was more violence in Congress: a free-for-all involving almost thirty congressmen broke out in the House late one night after an exchange of insults between Republicans and southern Democrats. There was conflict on still another level—the Democratic Party was breaking apart. Douglas had intended to preserve the Democrats as a national party, but instead he lost the support of the southern wing. Southerners reviled him, one claiming that Douglas was "stained with the dishonor of treachery without a parallel." Summing up these events, Congressman Alexander Stephens of Georgia wrote glumly to his brother: "All things here are tending my mind to the conclusion that the Union cannot and will not last long."

The Panic of 1857

Adding to the growing political tensions was the short but sharp depression of 1857 and 1858. Technology played a part. In August 1857, the failure of an Ohio investment house—the kind of event that had formerly taken weeks to be widely known—was the subject of a news story flashed immediately over telegraph wires to Wall Street and other financial markets. A wave of panic selling ensued, leading to business failures and slowdowns that threw thousands out of work. The major cause of the panic was a sharp but temporary downturn in agricultural exports to Britain, and recovery was well under way by early 1859. In the meantime, Republicans and some northern Democrats in Congress proposed to raise tariffs to help industries hurt by the depression but were outvoted by about half of northern Democrats and almost all southern representatives. The South had resisted protective tariffs since the 1820s (see Chapter 10), but now the opposition was regarded, in the bitter

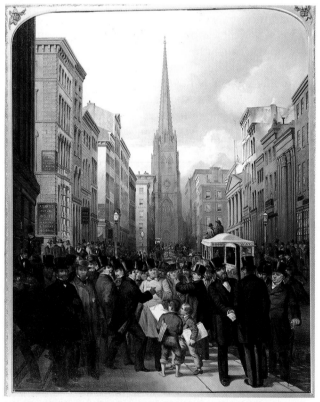

This painting by Charles G. Rosenberg and James H. Cafferty shows a worried crowd exchanging the latest news on Wall Street during the Panic of 1857. This was the first economic depression in which the telegraph played a part by carrying bad financial news in the West to New York much more rapidly than in the past.

words of one Republican, as yet another example of a Congress "shamelessly prostituted, in a base subserviency to the Slave Power."

Because it affected cotton exports less than northern exports, the Panic of 1857 was less harmful to the South than to the North. Southerners took this as proof of the superiority of their economic system to the free-labor system of the North, and some could not resist the chance to gloat. Senator James Henry Hammond of South Carolina drove home the point in his celebrated "King Cotton" speech of March 1858:

> When the abuse of credit had destroyed credit and annihilated confidence; when thousands of the strongest commercial houses in the world were coming down...when you came to a dead lock, and revolutions were threatened, what brought you up?...We have poured in upon you one million six hundred thousand bales of cotton just at the moment to save you from destruction....We have sold it for $65,000,000, and saved you.

It seemed that all matters of political discussion were being drawn into the sectional dispute. The next step toward disunion was an act of violence perpetrated by the grim abolitionist from Kansas, John Brown.

John Brown's Raid

In the heated political mood of the late 1850s, some improbable people became heroes. None was more improbable than John Brown, the self-appointed avenger who slaughtered unarmed proslavery men in Kansas in 1856. In 1859, Brown proposed a wild scheme to raid the South and start a general slave uprising. He believed, as did most northern abolitionists, that discontent among southern slaves was so great that such an uprising needed only a spark to get going. Significantly, free African Americans—among them Frederick Douglass—did not support Brown, thinking his first planned foray, to raid the federal arsenal at Harpers Ferry, Virginia, was doomed to failure. They were right. On October 16, 1859, Brown led a group of twenty-two white and African American men against the arsenal. However, he had made no provision for escape. Even more incredible, he had not notified the Virginia slaves whose uprising it was supposed to be. In less than a day the raid was over. Eight of Brown's men (including two of his sons) were dead, no slaves had joined the fight, and Brown himself was captured. Moving quickly to prevent a lynching by local mobs, the state of Virginia tried and convicted Brown, while he was still weak from the wounds of battle, of treason, murder, and fomenting insurrection.

Ludicrous in life, possibly insane, Brown was nevertheless a noble martyr. In his closing speech prior

JOHN BROWN AT HARPER'S FERRY.

In a contemporary engraving, John Brown and his followers are shown trapped inside the armory at Harper's Ferry in October 1859. Captured, tried, and executed, Brown was regarded as a martyr in the North and a terrorist in the South.

to sentencing, Brown was magnificently eloquent: "Now, if it is deemed necessary that I should forfeit my life for the furtherance of the end of justice, and mingle my blood further with the blood of my children and with the blood of millions in this slave country whose rights are disregarded by wicked, cruel, and unjust enactments, I say, let it be done."

Brown's death by hanging on December 2, 1859, was marked throughout northern communities with public rites of mourning not seen since the death of George Washington. Church bells tolled, buildings were draped in black, ministers preached sermons, prayer meetings were held, abolitionists issued eulogies. Ralph Waldo Emerson said that Brown would "make the gallows as glorious as the cross," and Henry David Thoreau called him "an angel of light." In a more militant frame of mind, abolitionist Wendell Phillips announced, "The lesson of the hour is insurrection." Naturally, not all Northerners supported Brown's action. Northern Democrats and conservative opinion generally repudiated him. In New York, for example, 20,000 merchants signed a petition for a public meeting designed to reassure the South of northern good intentions. But many people, while rejecting Brown's raid, did support the antislavery cause that he represented.

Brown's raid shocked the South because it aroused the greatest fear, that of slave rebellion. Southerners believed that northern abolitionists were provoking slave revolts, a suspicion apparently confirmed when documents captured at Harpers Ferry revealed that Brown had the financial support of half a dozen members of the northern elite. These "Secret Six"—Gerrit Smith, George Stearns, Franklin Sanborn, Thomas Wentworth Higginson, Theodore Parker, and Samuel Gridley Howe—had been willing to finance armed attacks on the slave system.

Even more shocking to Southerners than the raid itself was the extent of northern mourning for Brown's death. Although the Republican Party disavowed Brown's actions, Southerners simply did not believe the party's statements. Southerners wondered how they could stay in the Union in the face of "Northern insolence." The *Richmond Enquirer* reported, "The Harpers Ferry invasion has advanced the cause of disunion more than any other event that has happened since the formation of [the] government." The alarm in up-country South Carolina was so great that vigilance committees were formed in every district. Throughout the next year, these committees remained armed and ready to deal with strangers (they might be abolitionists) and any hint of slave revolt. This extreme defensiveness was not a good portent for the election year of 1860. Looking to the presidential race, Senator Robert Toombs of Georgia warned that the South would "never permit this Federal government to pass into the traitorous hands of the Black Republican party."

Talk of secession as the only possible response to the northern "insults" of the 1850s—the armed protests against the Fugitive Slave Law, the rejection of the Lecompton constitution, and now the support for John Brown's raid—was common throughout the South. Although the majority of Southerners probably rejected secession, the political passions of the election year fostered secessionist thinking.

THE SOUTH SECEDES

By 1860, sectional differences had caused one national party, the Whigs, to collapse. The second national party, the Democrats, stood on the brink of dissolution. Not only the politicians but ordinary people in both the North and the South were coming to believe there was no way to avoid what in 1858 William Seward (once a Whig, now a Republican) had called an "irrepressible conflict."

The Election of 1860

The split of the Democratic Party into northern and southern wings that had occurred during President Buchanan's tenure became official at the Democratic nominating conventions in 1860. The party convened first in Charleston, South Carolina, the center of seces-

sionist agitation. It was the worst possible location in which to attempt to reach unity. Although Stephen Douglas had the support of the plurality of delegates, he did not have the two-thirds majority necessary for nomination. As the price of their support, Southerners insisted that Douglas support a federal slave code—a guarantee that slavery would be protected in the territories. Douglas could not agree without violating his own belief in popular sovereignty and losing his northern support. After ten days, fifty-nine ballots, and two southern walkouts, the convention ended where it had begun: deadlocked. Northern supporters of Douglas were angry and bitter: "I never heard Abolitionists talk more uncharitably and rancorously of the people of the South than the Douglas men," one reporter wrote. "They say they do not care…where the South goes."

In June, the Democrats met again in Baltimore. The Douglasites, recognizing the need for a united party, were eager to compromise wherever they could, but most southern Democrats were not. More than a third of the delegates bolted. Later, holding a convention of their own, they nominated Buchanan's vice president John C. Breckinridge of Kentucky. The remaining two-thirds of the Democrats nominated Douglas, but everyone knew that a Republican victory was inevitable. To make matters worse, some southern Whigs joined with some border-state nativists to form the Constitutional Union Party, which nominated John Bell of Tennessee.

Republican strategy was built on the lessons of the 1856 "victorious defeat." The Republicans planned to carry all the states Frémont had won, plus Pennsylvania, Illinois, and Indiana. The two leading Republican contenders were Senator William H. Seward of New York and Abraham Lincoln of Illinois. Seward, the party's best-known figure, had enemies among party moderates, who thought he was too radical, and among nativists with whom he had clashed in the New York Whig Party. Lincoln, on the other hand, appeared new, impressive, more moderate than Seward, and certain to carry Illinois. Lincoln won the nomination on the third ballot.

The election of 1860 presented voters with one of the clearest choices in American history. On the key issue of slavery, Breckinridge supported its extension to the territories; Lincoln stood firmly for its exclusion. Douglas attempted to hold the middle ground with his principle of popular sovereignty; Bell vaguely favored compromise as well. The Republicans offered other platform planks designed to appeal to northern voters: a homestead act (free western lands), support for a transcontinental railroad, other internal improvements, and a higher tariff. Although they spoke clearly against the extension of slavery, Republicans sought to dispel their radical abolitionist image. The Republican platform condemned John Brown's raid as "the gravest of crimes," repeatedly denied that Republicans favored the social

$\mathcal{O}$ VERVIEW

THE IRREPRESSIBLE CONFLICT

Declaration of Independence	1776	Thomas Jefferson's denunciation of slavery deleted from the final version.
Northwest Ordinance	1787	Slavery prohibited in the Northwest Territory (north of the Ohio River).
Constitution	1787	Slavery unmentioned but acknowledged in Article I, section 2, counting three-fifths of all African Americans, slave and free, in a state's population, and in Article I, section 9, which barred Congress from prohibiting the international slave trade for twenty years.
Louisiana Purchase	1803	Louisiana admitted as a slave state in 1812; no decision about the rest of Louisiana Purchase.
Missouri Compromise	1820	Missouri admitted as a slave state, but slavery prohibited in Louisiana Purchase north of 36°30'.
Wilmot Proviso	1846	Proposal to prohibit slavery in territory that might be gained in Mexican-American War causes splits in national parties.
Compromise of 1850	1850	California admitted as free state; Texas (already admitted, 1845) is a slave state, the rest of Mexican Cession to be decided by popular sovereignty. Ends the slave trade in the District of Columbia but a stronger Fugitive Slave Law, leading to a number of violent recaptures, arouses northern antislavery opinion.
Kansas-Nebraska Act	1854	At the urging of Stephen A. Douglas, Congress opens Kansas and Nebraska Territories for settlement under popular sovereignty. Open warfare between proslavery and antislavery factions breaks out in Kansas.
Lecompton Constitution	1857	President James Buchanan's decision to admit Kansas to the Union with a proslavery constitution is defeated in Congress.
Dred Scott Decision	1857	The Supreme Court's denial of Dred Scott's case for freedom is welcomed in the South, condemned in the North.
John Brown's Raid and Execution	1859	Northern support for John Brown shocks the South.
Democratic Party Nominating Conventions	1860	The Democrats are unable to agree on a candidate; two candidates, one northern (Stephen A. Douglas) and one southern (John C. Breckinridge) split the party and the vote, thus allowing Republican Abraham Lincoln to win.

equality of black people, and strenuously affirmed that they sought to preserve the Union. In reality, Republicans simply did not believe the South would secede if Lincoln won. In this the Republicans were not alone; few Northerners believed southern threats—Southerners had threatened too many times before.

Breckinridge insisted that he and his supporters were loyal to the Union—as long as their needs

concerning slavery were met. The only candidate who spoke urgently and openly about the impending threat of secession was Douglas. Breaking with convention, Douglas campaigned personally, in both the North and, bravely, in the hostile South, warning of the danger of dissolution and presenting himself as the only truly national candidate. Realizing his own chances for election were slight, he told his private

This Republican Party poster for the election of 1860 combines the party's major themes: free land, free soil, opposition to "the Slave Power" (the slogan "Free Speech"), and higher tariffs. But above all was the message, "THE UNION MUST AND SHALL BE PRESERVED."

secretary, "Mr. Lincoln is the next President. We must try to save the Union. I will go South."

In accordance with tradition, Lincoln did not campaign for himself, but many other Republicans spoke for him. In an estimated 50,000 campaign speeches they built the image of "Honest Abe," the candidate who really had been born in a log cabin. The Republicans made a special effort, headed by Carl Schurz, to attract the German immigrant vote. They were successful with German Protestants but less so with Catholics, who were put off by the Republicans' lingering reputation for nativism. The general mood among the northern electorate was one of excitement and optimism. The Republicans were almost certain to win and to bring, because of their uncompromising opposition to the expansion of slavery, an end to the long sectional crisis. "I will vote the Republican ticket next Tuesday," wrote New York businessman and former Whig George Templeton Strong. "The only alternative is everlasting submission to the South." The Republicans did not campaign in the South; Breckinridge did not campaign in the North. Each side was therefore free to believe the worst about the other. All parties, North and South, campaigned with oratory, parades and rallies, free food and drink. Even in the face of looming crisis, this presidential campaign was the best entertainment of the day.

In spite of Breckinridge's protestations of loyalty to the Union, the mood in the Deep South was close to mass hysteria. Rumors of slave revolts—in Texas, Alabama, and South Carolina—swept the region, and vigilance committees sprang up to counter the supposed threat. Responding to the rumors, Alabaman Sarah R. Espy wrote in her diary, "The country is getting in a deplorable state owing to the depredations committed by the Abolitionist[s] especially in Texas; and the safety of the country depend[s] on who is elected to the presidency." Apparently, southern voters talked of little else, as another Alabaman, Benjamin F. Riley, recalled: "Little else was done this year, than discuss politics. Vast crowds would daily assemble at the places of popular resort, to canvass the questions at issue. Stump speaking was a daily occurrence. Men were swayed more by passion than by calm judgment."

In the South Carolina up-country, the question of secession dominated races for the state legislature. Candidates such as A. S. Wallace of York, who advocated "patriotic forbearance" if Lincoln won, were soundly defeated. The very passion and excitement of the election campaign moved Southerners toward extremism. Even the weather—the worst drought and heat wave the South had known for years—contributed to the tension.

The election of 1860 produced the second highest voter turnout in U.S. history (81.2 percent, topped only by 81.8 percent in 1876). The election turned out to be two regional contests: Breckinridge versus Bell in the South, Lincoln versus Douglas in the North. Breckinridge carried eleven slave states with 18 percent of the popular vote; Bell carried Virginia, Tennessee, and Kentucky with 13 percent of the popular vote. Lincoln won all eighteen of the free states (he split New Jersey with Douglas) and almost 40 percent of the popular vote. Douglas carried only Missouri, but gained nearly 30 percent of the popular vote. Lincoln's electoral vote total was overwhelming: 180 to a combined 123 for the other three candidates. But although Lincoln had won 54 percent of the vote in the northern states, his name had not even appeared on the ballot in ten southern states. The true winner of the 1860 election was sectionalism.

The South Leaves the Union

Charles Francis Adams, son and grandson of presidents, wrote in his diary on the day Lincoln was elected, "The great revolution has actually taken

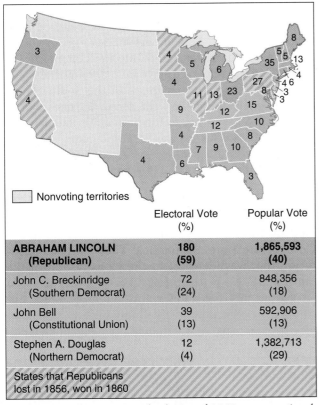

	Electoral Vote (%)	Popular Vote (%)
ABRAHAM LINCOLN (Republican)	**180 (59)**	**1,865,593 (40)**
John C. Breckinridge (Southern Democrat)	72 (24)	848,356 (18)
John Bell (Constitutional Union)	39 (13)	592,906 (13)
Stephen A. Douglas (Northern Democrat)	12 (4)	1,382,713 (29)

Nonvoting territories

States that Republicans lost in 1856, won in 1860

The Election of 1860   *The election of 1860 was a sectional election. Lincoln won no votes in the South, Breckinridge none in the North. The contest in the North was between Lincoln and Douglas, and although Lincoln swept the electoral vote, Douglas's popular vote was uncomfortably close. The large number of northern Democratic voters opposed to Lincoln was a source of political trouble for him during the Civil War.*

place.... The country has once and for all thrown off the domination of the Slaveholders." That was precisely what the South feared.

The results of the election shocked Southerners. They were humiliated and frightened by the prospect of becoming a permanent minority in a political system dominated by a party pledged to the elimination of slavery. In southern eyes the Republican triumph meant they would become unequal partners in the federal enterprise, their way of life (the slave system) existing on borrowed time. As a Georgia newspaper said ten days after Lincoln's election, "African slavery, though panoplied by the Federal Constitution, is doomed to a war of extermination. All the powers of a Government which has so long sheltered it will be turned to its destruction. The only hope for its preservation, therefore, is out of the Union." And Mary Boykin Chesnut, member of a well-connected South Carolina family, confided to her diary, "The die is cast—no more vain regrets—sad forebodings are useless. The stake is life or death."

The governors of South Carolina, Alabama, and Mississippi, each of whom had committed his state to

secession if Lincoln were elected, immediately issued calls for special state conventions. At the same time, calls went out to southern communities to form vigilance committees and volunteer militia companies. A visiting Northerner, Sereno Watson, wrote to his brother in amazement: "This people is apparently gone crazy. I do not know how to account for it & have no idea what might be the end of it. Union men, Douglas men, Breckinridge men are alike in their loud denunciation of submission to Lincoln's administration. There are of course those who think differently but they scarcely dare or are suffered to open their mouths." In the face of this frenzy, cooperationists (the term used for those opposed to immediate secession) were either intimidated into silence or simply left behind by the speed of events.

On December 20, 1860, a state convention in South Carolina, accompanied by all the hoopla and excitement of bands, fireworks displays, and huge rallies, voted unanimously to secede from the Union. James Buchanan, the lame-duck president (Lincoln would not be inaugurated until March), did nothing. In the weeks that followed, conventions in six other southern states (Mississippi, Florida, Alabama, Georgia, Louisiana, and Texas) followed suit, with the support, on average, of 80 percent of their delegates. Although there was genuine division of opinion in the South (especially in Georgia and Alabama, along customary up-country—low-country lines) none of the Deep South states held anywhere near the number of Unionists that Republicans had hoped. Throughout the South, secession occurred because Southerners no longer believed they had a choice. "Secession is a desperate remedy," acknowledged South Carolina's David Harris, "but of the two evils I do think it is the lesser."

In every state that seceded, the joyous scenes of South Carolina were repeated as the decisiveness of action replaced the long years of anxiety and tension. People danced in the streets, most believing the North had no choice but to accept secession peacefully. They ignored the fact that eight other slave states (Delaware, Maryland, Kentucky, Missouri, Virginia, North Carolina, Tennessee, and Arkansas) had not acted—though the latter four states would secede after war broke out. Just as Republicans had miscalculated in thinking southern threats a mere bluff, so secessionists now miscalculated in believing they would be able to leave the Union in peace.

The North's Political Options

What should the North do? Buchanan continued to do nothing. The decision thus rested with Abraham Lincoln, even before he officially became president. One possibility was compromise, and many proposals were suggested, ranging from full adoption of the Breckinridge campaign platform to reinstatement of the Missouri Compromise line. Lincoln cautiously refused them all, making it clear that he would not compromise on the extension of slavery, which was the South's key demand. He hoped, by appearing firm but moderate, to discourage additional southern states from seceding while giving pro-Union Southerners time to organize. He succeeded in his first aim, but not in the second. Lincoln and most of the Republican Party had seriously overestimated the strength of pro-Union sentiment in the South.

A second possibility, suggested by Horace Greeley of the *New York Tribune*, was to let the seven seceding states "go in peace." This is what many secessionists expected, but too many Northerners—including Lincoln himself—believed in the Union for this to happen. As Lincoln said, what was at stake was "the necessity of proving that popular government is not an absurdity. We must settle this question now, whether in a free government the minority have the right to break up the government whenever they choose." At stake was all the accumulated American pride in the federal government as a model for democracies the world over.

The third possibility was force, and this was the crux of the dilemma. Although he believed their action was wrong, Lincoln was loath to go to war to force the seceding states back into the Union. On the other hand, he refused to give up federal powers over military forts and customs posts in the South. These were precisely the powers the seceding states had to command if they were to function as an independent nation. A confrontation was bound to come. Abraham Lincoln, not for the last time, was prepared to wait for the other side to strike the first blow.

Establishment of the Confederacy

In February, delegates from the seven seceding states met in Montgomery, Alabama, and created the Confederate States of America. They wrote a constitution that was identical to the Constitution of the United States, with a few crucial exceptions: it strongly supported states' rights and made the abolition of slavery practically impossible. These two

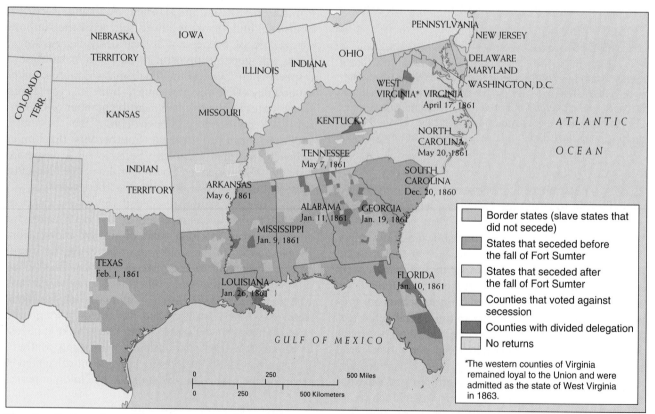

The South Secedes   *The southern states that would constitute the Confederacy seceded in two stages. The states of the Lower South seceded before Lincoln took office. Arkansas and three states of the Upper South—Virginia, North Carolina, and Tennessee—waited until after the South fired on Fort Sumter. And four border slave states—Delaware, Maryland, Kentucky and Missouri—chose not to secede. Every southern state (except South Carolina) was divided on the issue of secession, generally along up-country—low-country lines. In Virginia, this division was so extreme that West Virginia split off to become a separate nonslave state and was admitted to the Union in 1863.*

clauses did much to define the Confederate enterprise. It was difficult to avoid the conclusion that the structure of the new Confederacy had been decided by the southern dependence on slave labor. L. W. Spratt of South Carolina confessed as much in 1859: "We stand committed to the South, but we stand more vitally committed to the cause of slavery. It is, indeed, to be doubted whether the South [has] any cause apart from the institution which affects her." The South's entire defense of slavery was built on a commitment to individualism and decentralization: the rights of the slave owner over his slaves; the right of freedom claimed by all white men; and the rights of individual states versus the federal government. The military defense of the South, however, would require a strong central government. This was to be the South's basic dilemma throughout the Civil War.

The Montgomery convention passed over the fire-eaters—the men who had been the first to urge secession—and chose Jefferson Davis of Mississippi as president and Alexander Stephens of Georgia as vice president of the new nation. Both men were known as moderates. Davis, a slave owner who had been a general in the Mexican-American War and secretary of war in the Pierce administration, who was currently a senator from Mississippi, had expressed his own uncertainties by retaining his Senate seat for two weeks after Mississippi seceded. Stephens, a former leader in the Whig party, had been a cooperationist delegate to Georgia's convention, where he urged that secession not be undertaken hastily.

The choice of moderates was deliberate, for the strategy of the new Confederate state was to argue that secession was a normal, responsible, and expectable course of action, and nothing for the North to get upset about. This was the theme that President Jefferson Davis of the Confederate States of America struck in his Inaugural Address, delivered to a crowd of 10,000 from the steps of the State Capitol at Montgomery, Alabama on February 18, 1861. "We have changed the constituent parts," Davis said, "but not the system of our Government." Secession was a legal and peaceful step that, Davis said, quoting from the Declaration of Independence, "illustrates the American idea that governments rest on the consent of the governed...and that it is the right of the people to alter or abolish them at will whenever they become destructive of the ends for which they were established." After insisting that "a just perception of mutual interest [should] permit us peaceably to pursue our separate political [course]," Davis concluded, "Obstacles may retard, but they cannot long prevent, the progress of a movement sanctified by its justice and sustained by a virtuous

Abraham Lincoln's inauguration on March 4, 1861, *shown here in* Leslie's Illustrated Newspaper, *symbolized the state of the nation. As he took the oath to become president of a divided country, Lincoln stood before a Capitol building with a half-finished dome and was guarded by soldiers who feared a Confederate attack. Politicians had long been concerned about the dangers of sectionalism in American life. But most ordinary people had taken for granted the federal Union of states—and the ability of slave and nonslave states to coexist.*

people." This impressive inaugural prompted a deeply moved correspondent for the *New York Herald* to report, "God does not permit evil to be done with such earnest solemnity, such all-pervading trust in His Providence, as was exhibited by the whole people on that day."

Lincoln's Inauguration

The country as a whole waited to see what Abraham Lincoln would do, which at first appeared to be very little. In Springfield, Lincoln refused to issue public statements before his inaugural (although he sent many private messages to Congress and to key military officers), for fear of making a delicate situation worse. Similarly, during a twelve-day whistle-stopping rail-

CHRONOLOGY

1820	Missouri Compromise
1828–32	Nullification Crisis
1846	Wilmot Proviso
1848	Treaty of Guadalupe Hidalgo ends Mexican-American War Zachary Taylor elected president Free-Soil Party formed
1849	California and Utah seek admission to the Union as free states
1850	Compromise of 1850 California admitted as a free state American (Know-Nothing) Party formed Zachary Taylor dies, Millard Fillmore becomes president
1851	North reacts to Fugitive Slave Law Harriet Beecher Stowe's *Uncle Tom's Cabin* published
1852	Franklin Pierce elected president
1854	Ostend Manifesto Kansas-Nebraska Act Treaties with Indians in northern part of Indian Territory renegotiated Republican Party formed as Whig Party dissolves

1855	William Walker leads first filibustering expedition to Nicaragua
1856	Burning and looting of Lawrence, Kansas John Brown leads Pottawatomie massacre Attack on Senator Charles Sumner James Buchanan elected president
1857	Dred Scott decision President Buchanan accepts proslavery Lecompton constitution in Kansas Panic of 1857
1858	Congress rejects Lecompton constitution Lincoln-Douglas debates
1859	John Brown's raid on Harpers Ferry
1860	Four parties run presidential candidates Abraham Lincoln elected president South Carolina secedes from Union
1861	Six other Deep South states secede Confederate States of America formed Lincoln takes office

road trip east from Springfield, he was careful to say nothing controversial. Eastern intellectuals, already suspicious of a mere "prairie lawyer," were not impressed. Finally, hard evidence of an assassination plot forced Lincoln to abandon his whistle-stops at Harrisburg and, protected by Pinkerton detectives, to travel incognito into Washington "like a thief in the night," as he complained. These signs of moderation and caution did not appeal to an American public with a penchant for electing military heroes. Americans wanted leadership and action.

Lincoln continued, however, to offer nonbelligerent firmness and moderation. And at the end of his Inaugural Address on March 4, 1861, as he stood ringed by federal troops called out in case of a Confederate attack, the new president offered unexpected eloquence:

I am loath to close. We are not enemies, but friends. We must not be enemies. Though passion may have strained, it must not break our bonds of affection. The mystic chords of memory, stretching from every battlefield, and patriot grave, to every living heart and hearthstone, all over this broad land, will yet swell the chorus of the Union, when again touched, as surely they will be, by the better angels of our nature.

CONCLUSION

Americans had much to boast about in 1850. Their nation was vastly larger, richer, and more powerful than it had been in 1800. But the issue of slavery was slowly dividing the North and the South, two communities with similar origins and many common bonds. The following decade was marked by frantic efforts at political compromise, beginning with the Compromise of 1850, continuing with the Kansas-Nebraska Act of 1854, and culminating in the Supreme Court's 1859 decision in the Dred Scott case. Increasingly, the ordinary people of the two regions demanded resolution of the crisis. The two great parties of the Second American Party System, the Democrats and the Whigs, unable to find a solution, were destroyed. Two new sectional parties—the Republican Party and a southern party devoted to the defense of slavery—fought the 1860 election, but Southerners refused to accept the national verdict. Politics had failed: the issue of slavery was irreconcilable. The only remaining recourse was war. But although Americans were divided, they were still one people. That made the war, when it came, all the more terrible.

REVIEW QUESTIONS

1. What aspects of the remarkable economic development of the United States in the first half of the nineteenth century contributed to the sectional crisis of the 1850s?

2. How might the violent efforts by abolitionists to free escaped slaves who had been recaptured and the federal armed enforcement of the Fugitive Slave Act have been viewed differently by merchants (the so-called Cotton Whigs), Irish immigrants, and abolitionists?

3. Consider the course of events in "Bloody Kansas" from Douglas's Kansas-Nebraska Act to the Congressional rejection of the Lecompton constitution. Were these events the inevitable result of the political impasse in Washington, or could other decisions have been taken that would have changed the outcome?

4. The nativism of the 1850s that surfaced so strongly in the Know-Nothing Party was eclipsed by the crisis over slavery. But nativist sentiment has been a recurring theme in American politics. Discuss why it was strong in the 1850s and why it might have emerged periodically since then.

5. Evaluate the character and actions of John Brown. Was he the hero proclaimed by northern supporters or the terrorist condemned by the South?

6. Imagine that you lived in Illinois, home state to both Douglas and Lincoln, in 1860. How would you have voted in the presidential election, and why?

RECOMMENDED READING

William L. Barney, *The Secessionist Impulse: Alabama and Mississippi in 1860* (1974). Covers the election of 1860 and the subsequent conventions that led to secession.

Don E. Fehrenbacher, *The Dred Scott Case: Its Significance in American Law and Politics* (1978). A major study by the leading historian on this controversial decision.

Eric Foner, *Free Soil, Free Labor, Free Men: The Ideology of the Republican Party before the Civil War* (1970). A landmark effort that was among the first studies to focus on free labor ideology of the North and its importance in the political disputes of the 1850s.

Lacey K. Ford Jr., *Origins of Southern Radicalism: The South Carolina Upcountry, 1800–1860* (1988). One of a number of recent studies of the attitudes of upcountry farmers, who in South Carolina supported secession wholeheartedly.

Homan Hamilton, *Prologue to Conflict: The Crisis and Compromise of 1850* (1964). The standard source on the Compromise of 1850.

Bruce Levine, *Half Slave and Half Free: The Roots of the Civil War* (1992). Good survey of the contrasting attitudes of North and South.

Alice Nichols, *Bleeding Kansas* (1954). The standard source on the battles over Kansas.

David M. Potter, *The Impending Crisis, 1848-1861* (1976). A comprehensive account of the politics leading up to the Civil War.

Anne C. Rose, *Voices of the Marketplace: American Thought and Culture, 1830–1860* (1995). A new study that considers the effects of the concepts of Christianity, democracy, and capitalism on American cultural life.

Kenneth M. Stampp, *America in 1857: A Nation on the Brink* (1990). A study of the "crucial" year by a leading southern historian.

Albert J. Von Frank, *The Trials of Anthony Burns: Freedom and Slavery in Emerson's Boston* (1998). An eloquent study of the trial and the links between transcendentalist and abolitionist opinion.

ADDITIONAL BIBLIOGRAPHY

The Controversy over Slavery

Richard H. Abbott, *Cotton and Capital: Boston Businessmen and Antislavery Reform, 1854–1868* (1991)

Eugene Berwanger, *The Frontier against Slavery: Western Anti-Negro Prejudice and the Slavery Extension Controversy* (1967)

Stanley W. Campbell, *The Slave Catchers* (1970)

David B. Davis, *The Slave Power Conspiracy and the Paranoid Style* (1969)

W. Ehrlich, *They Have No Rights: Dred Scott's Struggle for Freedom* (1979)

P. Finkelman, *An Imperfect Union: Slavery, Freedom, and Comity* (1981)

C. C. Goen, *Broken Churches, Broken Nation* (1985)

Thomas F. Grossett, *Uncle Tom's Cabin and American Culture* (1985)

Joseph Herring, *The Enduring Indians of Kansas: A Century and a Half of Acculturation* (1990)

J. R. McKivigan, *The War against Proslavery Religion* (1984)

William Lee Miller, *Arguing About Slavery: The Great Battle in the United States Congress* (1996)

H. Craig Miner and William E. Unrau, *The End of Indian Kansas* (1978)

Thomas D. Morris, *Free Men All: The Personal Liberty Laws of the North, 1780–1861* (1974)

Allan Nevins, *The Ordeal of the Union*, vols. 1–2 (1947)

Roy Nichols, *The Disruption of American Democracy* (1948)

Joseph G. Rayback, *Free Soil: The Election of 1848* (1970)

J. Rossbach, *Ambivalent Conspirators: John Brown, the Secret Six and a Theory of Black Political Violence* (1982)

Thomas P. Slaughter, *Bloody Dawn: The Christiana Riots and Racial Violence in the Antebellum North* (1991)

Kenneth M. Stampp, *The Causes of the Civil War*, rev. ed. (1974)

Joanna L. Stratton, *Pioneer Women: Voices from the Kansas Frontier* (1981)

Gerald W. Wolff, *The Kansas-Nebraska Bill: Party, Section, and the Coming of the Civil War* (1977)

Bertram Wyatt-Brown, *Yankee Saints and Southern Sinners* (1985)

The Crisis of the National Party System

Thomas B. Alexander, *Sectional Stress and Party Strength* (1967)

Tyler Anbinder, *Nativism and Slavery: The Northern Know-Nothings and the Politics of the 1850s* (1992)

J. H. Baker, *Affairs of Party: The Political Culture of Northern Democrats in the Mid-Nineteenth Century* (1983)

F. J. Blue, *The Free Soilers: Third Party Politics* (1973)

G. B. Forgie, *Patricide in the House Divided* (1981)

Ronald Formisano, *The Birth of Mass Political Parties: Michigan, 1827–1861* (1971)

William E. Gienapp, *The Origins of the Republican Party, 1852–1856* (1987)

Michael Holt, *Forging a Majority: The Formation of the Republican Party in Pittsburgh, 1848–1860* (1969)

———, *The Political Crisis of the 1850's* (1978)

Thelma Jennings, *The Nashville Convention* (1980)

Robert W. Johannsen, *The Lincoln-Douglas Debates* (1965)

Paul Kleppner, *The Third Electoral System, 1853–1892: Parties, Voters, and Political Cultures* (1979)

John Mayfield, *Rehearsal for Republicanism: Free Soil and the Politics of Antislavery* (1980)

Richard Sewell, *Ballots for Freedom: Antislavery Politics in the United States, 1837–1865* (1976)

The South Secedes

William. L. Barney, *The Road to Secession* (1972)

Charles H. Brown, *Agents of Manifest Destiny: The Lives and Times of the Filibusters* (1980)

Steven A. Channing, *Crisis of Fear: Secession in South Carolina* (1970)

William J. Cooper, *The South and the Politics of Slavery* (1978)

Avery O. Craven, *The Growth of Southern Nationalism 1848–1861* (1953)

John Hope Franklin, *A Southern Odyssey: Travelers in the Antebellum North* (1976)

———, *The Militant South 1800–1861* (1956)

William W. Freehling, *The Road to Disunion*, vol. I: *Secessionists at Bay, 1776–1854* (1991)

William H. Goetzmann, *When the Eagle Screamed: The Romantic Horizon in American Diplomacy, 1800–1860* (1966)

Michael P. Johnson, *Toward a Patriarchal Republic: The Secession of Georgia* (1977)

———, *Secession and Conservatism in the Lower South: The Social and Ideological Bases of Secession in Georgia, 1860–1861* (1983)

Michael P. Johnson and James L. Roark, eds., *No Chariot Let Down: Charleston's Free People of Color on the Eve of the Civil War* (1984)

Robert E. May, *The Southern Dream of a Caribbean Empire, 1854–1861* (1973)

John McCardell, *The Idea of a Southern Nation: Southern Nationalists and Southern Nationalism, 1830–1861* (1979)

Rollin G. Osterweis, *Romanticism and Nationalism in the Old South* (1949)

David M. Potter, *The South and the Sectional Conflict* (1968)

Basil Rauch, *American Interest in Cuba* (1948)

William O. Scroggs, *Filibusters and Financiers: The Story of William Walker and His Associates* (1960)

K. M. Stampp, *And the War Came: The North and the Secession Crisis 1860–1861* (1950)

Joe A. Stout, *The Liberators: Filibustering Expeditions into Mexico, 1848–1862, and the Last Thrust of Manifest Destiny* (1973)

Ronald L. Takaki, *A Proslavery Crusade: The Agitation to Reopen the African Slave Trade* (1971)

J. Mills Thornton, *Politics and Power in a Slavery Society* (1978)

Eric H. Walter, *The Fire-Eaters* (1992)

C. Vann Woodward, *American Counterpoint: Slavery and Racism in the North–South Dialogue* (1971)

R. A. Wooster, *The Secession Conventions of the South* (1962)

Biography

K. J. Bauer, *Zachary Taylor: Soldier, Planter, Statesman of the Old Southwest* (1985)

D. H. Donald, *Charles Sumner and the Coming of the Civil War* (1960)

Donald E. Fehrenbacher, *Prelude to Greatness: Lincoln in the 1850's* (1962)

Joan Hedrick, *Harriet Beecher Stowe: A Life* (1994)

Robert W. Johannsen, *Stephen A. Douglas* (1973)

Stephen Oates, *To Purge This Land with Blood: A Biography of John Brown* (1970)

———, *With Malice toward None: A Life of Abraham Lincoln* (1977)

ℂHAPTER SIXTEEN

THE CIVIL WAR

1861–1865

Winslow Homer, *Near Andersonville*, 1865. Oil on canvas. Photograph by Armen Shamalian Photographers. The Newark Museum, Gift of the Corbin family in memory of their parents Hannah Stockton Corbin and Horace Kellogg Corbin.

AMERICAN COMMUNITIES
Mother Bickerdyke Connects Northern Communities to Their Boys at War

In May 1861 the Reverend Edward Beecher interrupted his customary Sunday service at Brick Congregational Church in Galesburg, Illinois, to read a disturbing letter to the congregation. Two months earlier, Galesburg had proudly sent 500 of its young men off to join the Union army. They had not yet been in battle. Yet, the letter reported, an alarming number were dying of diseases caused by inadequate food, medical care, and sanitation at the crowded military camp in Cairo, Illinois. Most army doctors were surgeons, trained to operate and amputate on the battlefield. They were not prepared to treat soldiers sick with dysentery, pneumonia, typhoid, measles—all serious, frequently fatal diseases that could often be cured with careful nursing. The letter writer, appalled by the squalor and misery he saw around him, complained of abuses by the army. The Union army, however, was overwhelmed with the task of readying recruits for battle and had made few provisions for their health when not in combat.

The shocked and grieving members of Beecher's congregation quickly decided to send not only supplies but one of their number to inspect the conditions at the Cairo camp and to take action. In spite of warnings from a veteran of the War of 1812 that army regulations excluded women from encampments, the congregation voted to send their most qualified member, Mary Ann Bickerdyke, a middle-aged widow who made her living as a "botanic physician." This simple gesture of community concern launched the remarkable Civil War career of "the Cyclone in Calico," who defied medical officers and generals alike in her unceasing efforts on behalf of ill, wounded, and convalescent Union soldiers.

"Mother" Bickerdyke, as she was called, let nothing stand in the way of helping her "boys." When she arrived in Cairo, she immediately set to work cleaning the hospital tents and the soldiers themselves and finding and cooking nourishing food for them. Ordered to leave by the hospital director, who resented her interference, she blandly continued her work. When he reported her to the commanding officer, General Benjamin Prentiss, she quickly convinced the general to let her stay. "I talked sense to him," she later said.

From a peacetime point of view, what Mother Bickerdyke was doing was not unusual. Every civilian hospital had a matron who made sure patients were supplied with clean bed linen and bandages and were fed the proper convalescent diet. But in the context of the war—the sheer number of soldiers, the constant need to set up new field hospitals and commandeer scarce food for an army on the move—it was unusual indeed and required an unusual person. A plain spoken, hardworking woman, totally unfazed by rank or tender masculine egos, Mother Bickerdyke single-mindedly devoted herself to what she called "the Lord's work." The ordinary soldiers loved her; wise generals supported her. Once, when an indignant officer's wife complained about Bickerdyke's rudeness, General William Tecumseh Sherman joked, "You've picked the one person around here who outranks me. If you want to lodge a complaint against her, you'll have to take it to President Lincoln."

By their actions, Mother Bickerdyke and others like her exposed the War Department's inability to meet the needs of the nation's first mass army. And like the Galesburg congregation, other communities all over the North rallied to make up for the department's shortcomings with supplies and assistance. The efforts of women on the local level—for example, to make clothing for men from their communities who had gone off to the war—quickly took on national dimensions. The Women's Central Association of Relief (WCAR), whose organizers were mostly reformers experienced in the abolitionist, temperance, and education movements, eventually had 7,000 chapters throughout the North. Its volunteers raised funds, made and collected a variety of items—food, clothes, medicine, bandages, and more than 250,000 quilts and comforters—and sent them to army camps and hospitals. Volunteers also provided meals, housing, and transportation to soldiers on furlough. All told, association chapters supplied an estimated $15 million worth of goods to the Union troops.

In June 1861, responding to requests by officials of the WCAR for formal recognition of the organization, President Abraham Lincoln created the United States Sanitary Commission and gave it the power to investigate and advise the Medical Bureau. Henry Bellows, a Unitarian clergyman, became president of the organization, and Frederick Law Olmsted, the author of influential books about the slaveholding South and later the designer of New York's Central Park, was named its executive secretary. The commission's more than 500 "sanitary inspectors" (usually men) instructed soldiers in such matters as water supply, placement of latrines, and safe cooking.

Although at first she worked independently and remained suspicious of all organizations (and even of

many other relief workers), in 1862 Mother Bickerdyke was persuaded to become an official agent of "the Sanitary," as it was known. The advantage to her was access to the commission's warehouses and the ability to order from them precisely what she needed. The advantage to the Sanitary was that Mother Bickerdyke was an unequaled fundraiser. In speaking tours throughout Illinois, she touched her female listeners with moving stories of wounded boys whom she had cared for as if they were her own sons. Her words to men were more forceful. It was a man's business to fight, she said. If he was too old or ill to fight with a gun, he should fight with his dollars. With the help of Bickerdyke's blunt appeals, the Sanitary raised $50 million for the Union war effort.

As the Civil War continued, Mother Bickerdyke became a key figure in the medical support for General Ulysses S. Grant's campaigns along the Mississippi River. She was with the army at Shiloh, and as Grant slowly fought his way to Vicksburg she set up convalescent hospitals in Memphis. Grant authorized her to commandeer any army wagons she needed to transport supplies. Between fifty and seventy "contrabands" (escaped former slaves) worked on her laundry crew. On the civilian side, the Sanitary Commission authorized her to draw on its supply depots in Memphis, Cairo, Chicago, and elsewhere. She was thus in a practical sense a vital "middlewoman" between the home front and the battlefield—and in a symbolic and emotional sense too, as a stand-in for all mothers who had sent their sons to war.

The Civil War was a community tragedy, ripping apart the nation's political fabric and producing more casualties than any other war in the nation's history. Yet in another sense, it was a community triumph. Local communities directly supported and sustained their soldiers on a massive scale in unprecedented ways. As national unity failed, the strength of local communities, symbolized by Mother Bickerdyke, endured.

Memphis

Key Topics

- The social and political changes created by the unprecedented nature and scale of the Civil War

- The major military campaigns of the war

- The central importance of the end of slavery to the war efforts of North and South

COMMUNITIES MOBILIZE FOR WAR

A neutral observer in March 1861 might have seen ominous similarities. Two nations—the United States of America (shorn of seven states in the Deep South) and the Confederate States of America—each blamed the other for the breakup of the Union. Two new presidents—Abraham Lincoln and Jefferson Davis—each faced the challenging task of building and maintaining national unity. Two regions—North and South—scorned each other and boasted of their own superiority. But the most basic similarity was not yet apparent: both sides were unprepared for the ordeal that lay ahead.

Fort Sumter: The War Begins

In their Inaugural Addresses, both Abraham Lincoln and Jefferson Davis prayed for peace but positioned themselves for war. Careful listeners to both addresses realized that the two men were on a collision course. Jefferson Davis claimed that the Confederacy would be forced to "appeal to arms...if...the integrity of our territory and jurisdiction [is] assailed." Lincoln said, "The power confided to me will be used to hold, occupy, and possess the property and places belonging to the government." One of those places, Fort Sumter, in South Carolina, was claimed by both sides.

Fort Sumter, a major federal military installation, sat on a granite island at the entrance to Charleston harbor. So long as it remained in Union hands, Charleston, the center of secessionist sentiment, would be immobilized. Realizing its military and symbolic importance, South Carolinians had begun demanding that the fort be turned over to them even before they seceded. Thus it was hardly surprising that Fort Sumter would provide President Lincoln with his first crisis.

With the fort dangerously low on supplies, Lincoln had to decide whether to abandon it or risk the fight that might ensue if he ordered it resupplied. In a process he would follow on many other occasions, Lincoln first hesitated, canvassed opinions of all kinds, and then took cautious and careful action (even as some of his cabinet urged more decisive steps). On April 6, Lincoln notified the governor of South Carolina that he was sending a relief force to the fort carrying only food and no military supplies. Now the decision rested with Jefferson Davis. Like Lincoln, Davis faced a divided cabinet; unlike Lincoln, however, he opted for decisive action. On April 10 he ordered General P. G. T. Beauregard to demand the surrender of Fort Sumter and to attack it if the garrison did not comply. On April 12, as Lincoln's relief force neared Charleston harbor, Beauregard opened fire. Two days later, the defenders surrendered and the Confederate Stars and Bars rose over Fort Sumter. The people of Charleston celebrated wildly. "I did not know," wrote Mary Boykin Chesnut in her diary, "that one could live such days of excitement."

The Call to Arms

Even before the attack on Fort Sumter, the Confederate Congress had authorized a volunteer army of 100,000 men to serve for twelve months. There was no difficulty finding volunteers. Men flocked to enlist, and their communities sent them off in ceremonies featuring bands, bonfires, and belligerent oratory. Most of that oratory, like Jefferson Davis's Inaugural Address (see Chapter 15), evoked the Revolutionary War and the right of free people to resist tyranny. In many places, the response to the hostilities at Fort Sumter was even more visceral. The first war circular, printed in Hickman County, Tennessee, trumpeted, "To Arms! Our Southern soil must be defended. We must not stop to ask who brought about war, who is at fault, but let us go and do battle...and then settle the question of who is to blame." Exhilarated by their own rapid mobilization, most Southerners believed that Unionists were cowards who would not be able to face up to southern bravery. "Just throw three or four shells among those blue-bellied Yankees," one North Carolinian boasted, "and they'll scatter like sheep." The cry of "On to Washington!" was raised throughout the South, and orators confidently predicted that the city would be captured and the war concluded within sixty days. For the early recruits, war was a patriotic adventure.

The "thunderclap of Sumter" startled the North into an angry response. The apathy and uncertainty that had prevailed since Lincoln's election disappeared, to be replaced by strong feelings of patriotism. On April 15, Lincoln issued a proclamation calling for 75,000 state militiamen to serve in the federal army for ninety days. Enlistment offices were swamped with so many enthusiastic volunteers that many men were sent home. Free African Americans, among the most eager to serve, were turned away: this was not yet a war for or by black people.

Public outpourings of patriotism were common. New Yorker George Templeton Strong recorded one example on April 18: "Went to the [City] Hall. The [Sixth] Massachusetts Regiment, which arrived here last night, was marching down on its way to Washington. Immense crowd; immense cheering. My eyes filled with tears, and I was half choked in sympathy with the contagious excitement. God be praised for the unity of feeling here! It is beyond, very far beyond, anything I hoped for."

The mobilization in Chester, Pennsylvania, was typical of the northern response to the outbreak of war. A patriotic rally was held at which a company of volunteers (the first of many from the region) calling themselves the "Union Blues" were mustered into the Ninth Regiment of Pennsylvania Volunteers amid cheers and band music. As they marched off to Washington (the gathering place for the Union army), companies of home guards were organized by the men who remained behind. Within a month, the women of Chester had organized a countywide system of war relief that sent a stream of clothing, blankets, bandages, and other supplies to the local troops and provided assistance to their families at home. Such relief organizations, some formally organized, some informal, emerged in every community, North and South, that sent soldiers off to the Civil War. These organizations not only played a vital role in supplying the troops but maintained the human, local link on which so many soldiers depended. In this sense, every American community accompanied its young men to war. And every American community stood to suffer terrible losses when its young men went into battle.

This patriotic painting shows the departure of New York's Seventh Regiment for Washington in mid-April of 1861. Stirring scenes like this occurred across the nation following "the thunderclap of Sumter" as communities mobilized for war.

George Hayward (1834–1872). *Departure of the Seventh Regiment*, N.Y.S.M., April 19, 1861. Pencil, watercolor, and gouache. M. and M. Karolik Collection, Courtesy, Museum of Fine Arts, Boston.

The Border States

The first secession, between December 20, 1860, and February 1, 1861, had taken seven Deep South states out of the Union. Now, in April, the firing on Fort Sumter and Lincoln's call for state militias forced the other southern states to take sides. Courted—and pressured—by both North and South, four states of the Upper South (Virginia, Arkansas, Tennessee, and North Carolina) joined the original seven in April and May 1861. Virginia's secession tipped the other three toward the Confederacy. The capital of the Confederacy was now moved to Richmond. This meant that the two capitals—Richmond and Washington—were less than 100 miles apart.

Still undecided was the loyalty of the northernmost tier of slave-owning states: Missouri, Kentucky, Maryland, and Delaware. Each controlled vital strategic assets. Missouri not only bordered the Mississippi River but controlled the routes to the west. Kentucky controlled the Ohio River. The main railroad link with the West ran through Maryland and the hill region of western Virginia (which split from Virginia to become the free state of West Virginia in 1863). Delaware controlled access to Philadelphia. Finally, were Maryland to secede, the nation's capital would be completely surrounded by Confederate territory.

Delaware was loyal to the Union (less than 2 percent of its population were slaves), but Maryland's loyalty was divided, as an ugly incident on April 19 showed. When the Sixth Massachusetts Regiment (the one Strong had cheered in New York) marched through Baltimore, a hostile crowd of 10,000 Southern sympathizers, carrying Confederate flags, pelted the troops with bricks, paving stones, and bullets. Finally, in desperation the troops fired on the crowd, killing twelve people and wounding others. In retaliation, Southern sympathizers burned the railroad bridges to the North and destroyed the telegraph line to Washington, cutting off communication between the capital and the rest of the Union for six days.

Lincoln's response was swift and stern. He stationed Union troops along Maryland's crucial railroads, declared martial law in Baltimore, and arrested the suspected ringleaders of the pro-Confederate mob and held them without trial. In July, he ordered the detention of thirty-two secessionist legislators and many sympathizers. Thus was Maryland's loyalty to the Union ensured.

In detaining the Baltimore agitators, Lincoln suspended the writ of habeas corpus, the constitutional requirement that authorities explain to a court their reasons for arresting someone. Chief Justice Roger B. Taney of the Supreme court ruled that the president had no right to do this, but Lincoln at first ignored him. Later Lincoln argued that the suspension of certain civil rights might be necessary to suppress rebellion. The arrests in Maryland were the first of a number of violations of basic civil rights during the war, all of which the president justified on the basis of national security.

Like Maryland, the loyalties of the other border states were also divided. Missouri was plagued by guerrilla battles (reminiscent of the prewar "Bleeding Kansas") throughout the war. In Kentucky, division took the form of a huge illegal trade with the Confederacy through neighboring Tennessee, to which Lincoln, determined to keep Kentucky in the Union, turned a blind eye. The conflicting loyalties of the border states were often mirrored within families. Kentucky senator John J. Crittenden had two sons who were major generals, one in the Union army and the other in the Confederate army. Such family divisions reached all the way to the White House: three brothers of Kentucky-born Mary Todd Lincoln, the president's wife, died fighting for the Confederacy.

That Delaware, Maryland, Missouri, and Kentucky chose to stay in the Union was a severe blow to the Confederacy. Among them, the four states could have added 45 percent to the white population and military manpower of the Confederacy and 80 percent to its manufacturing capacity. Almost as damaging, the decision of four slave states to stay in the Union punched a huge hole in the Confederate argument that the southern states were forced to secede to protect the right to own slaves.

The Battle of Bull Run

Once sides had been chosen and the initial flush of enthusiasm had passed, the nature of the war, and the mistaken notions about it, soon became clear. The event that shattered the illusions was the first battle of Bull Run, at Manassas Creek in Virginia in July 1861. Confident of a quick victory, a Union army of 35,000 men marched south, crying "On to Richmond!" So lighthearted and unprepared was the Washington community that the troops were accompanied not only by journalists but by a crowd of politicians and sightseers. At first the Union troops held their ground against the 25,000 Confederate troops commanded by General P. G. T. Beauregard (of Fort Sumter fame). But when 2,300 fresh Confederate troops arrived as reinforcements, the untrained northern troops broke ranks in an uncontrolled retreat that swept up the frightened sightseers as well. Soldiers and civilians alike retreated in disarray to Washington. Confederate Mary Boykin Chesnut recorded in her diary, "We might have walked into Washington any day for a week after Manassas, such was the consternation and confusion there." But the Confederates lacked the organization and the strength to follow the retreating Union troops and capture the capital.

Bull Run was sobering—and prophetic. The Civil War was the most lethal military conflict in American history, leaving a legacy of devastation on the battlefield and desolation at home. It claimed the lives of nearly 620,000 soldiers, more than the the First and Second World Wars combined. One out of every four soldiers who fought in the war never returned home.

The Relative Strengths of North and South

Overall, in terms of both population and productive capacity, the Union seemed to have a commanding edge over the Confederacy. The North had two and a half times the South's population (22 million to 9 million, of whom 3.5 million were slaves) and enjoyed an even greater advantage in industrial capacity (nine times that of the South). The North produced almost all of the nation's firearms (97 percent), had 71 percent of its railroad mileage, and produced 94 percent of its cloth and 90 percent of its footwear. The North seemed able to feed, clothe, arm, and transport all the soldiers it chose. These assets were ultimately to prove decisive: by the end of the war the Union had managed to field more than 2 million soldiers to the Confederacy's 800,000.

But in the short term the South had important assets to counter them.

The first was the nature of the struggle. For the South, this was a defensive war in which, as the early volunteers showed, the most basic principle of the defense of home and community united almost all white citizens, regardless of their views about slavery. The North would have to invade the South and then control it against guerrilla opposition to win. The parallels with the Revolutionary War were unmistakable. Most white Southerners were confident that the North, like Great Britain in its attempt to subdue the rebellious colonies, would turn out to be a lumbering giant against whom they could secure their independence.

Second, the military disparity was less extreme than it appeared. Although the North had manpower, its troops were mostly untrained. The professional federal army numbered only 16,000, and most of its experience had been gained in small Indian wars. Moreover, the South, because of its tradition of honor and belligerence (see Chapter 11), appeared to have an advantage in military leadership. More than a quarter of

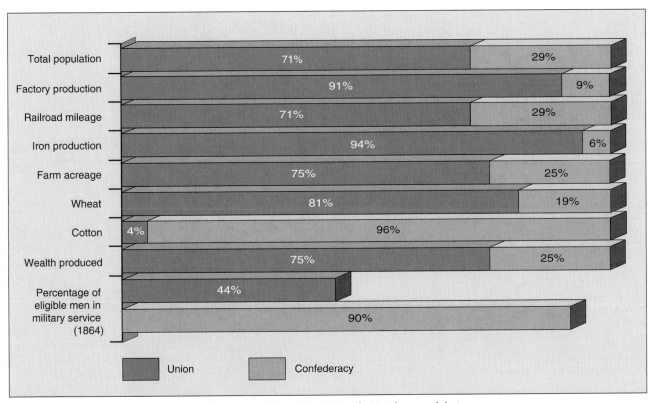

Comparative Resources, North and South, 1861   *By 1865, the North's overwhelming advantage in population, industrial strength, railroad mileage, agricultural productivity, and wealth had proved decisive in assuring victory. But initially these strengths made little difference in a struggle that began as a traditional war of maneuver in which the South held the defensive advantage. Only slowly did the Civil War become a modern war in which all of the resources of society, including the property and lives of civilians, were mobilized for battle.*

Source: *The Times Atlas of World History* (Maplewood, New Jersey: Hammond, 1978).

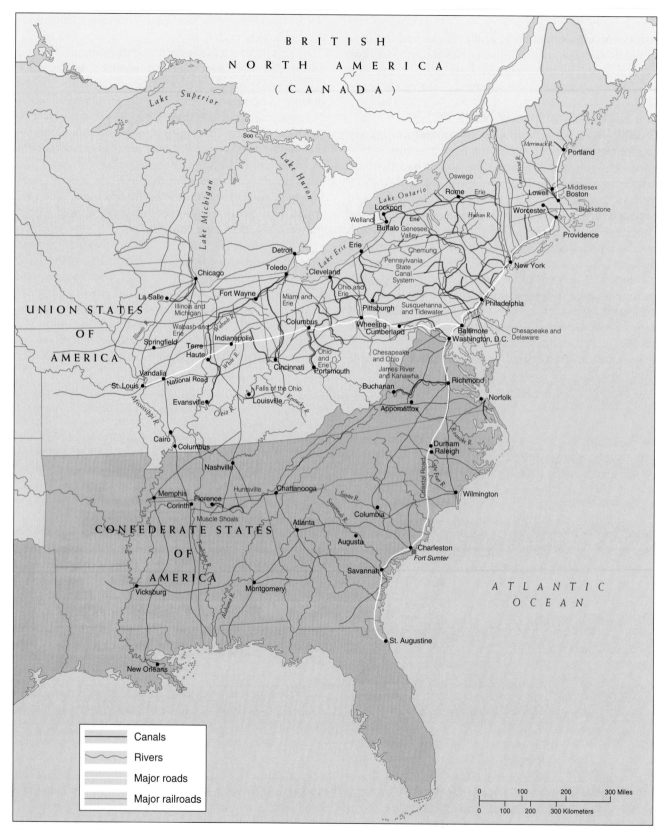

BRITISH
NORTH AMERICA
(CANADA)

UNION STATES
OF
AMERICA

CONFEDERATE STATES
OF
AMERICA

ATLANTIC
OCEAN

	Canals
	Rivers
	Major roads
	Major railroads

Comparative Transportation Systems, 1860   *Transportation systems were an important index of comparative strength: the North had almost three times the railroad mileage of the South. The relative lack of transportation hurt the Confederacy by hindering its ability to move troops and to distribute military and medical supplies.*

all the regular army officers chose to side with the South. The most notable was Robert E. Lee. Offered command of the Union army by President Lincoln, Lee hesitated but finally decided to follow his native state, Virginia, into the Confederacy, saying, "I have been unable to make up my mind to raise my hand against my native state, my relatives, my children, and my home."

Finally, the North's economic advantages, which were eventually decisive, initially seemed unimportant. The South could feed itself, and many soldiers brought their own weapons, uniforms, horses, and sometimes slaves when they enlisted. It was widely believed that slavery would work to the South's advantage, for slaves could continue to do the vital plantation work while their masters went off to war. But above all, the South had the weapon of cotton. "Cotton is King," James Henry Hammond had announced in 1858, at the height of the cotton boom that made the 1850s the most profitable decade in southern history. Because of the crucial role of southern cotton in industrialization, Hammond had declared, "The slaveholding South is now the controlling power of the world." Southerners were confident that the British and French need for southern cotton would soon bring those countries to recognize the Confederacy as a separate nation.

This aerial view of Washington shows the nation's capital during the Civil War as it underwent an abrupt transition from a small slave-owning community to the busy hub of the Union's war effort. Throughout the Civil War, the unfinished dome of the Capitol Building loomed over the city, its incompleteness symbolizing the divided state of the nation.

THE LINCOLN PRESIDENCY

The Civil War forced the federal government to assume powers unimaginable just a few years before. Abraham Lincoln took as his primary task to lead and unify the nation in his responsibility as commander in chief. He found the challenge almost insurmountable. Fortunately, the nation had found in Lincoln a man with the moral courage and the political skill to chart a course through the many conflicting currents of northern public opinion.

Lincoln as Party Leader and War President

Lincoln's first task as president was to assert control over his own cabinet. Because he had few national contacts outside the Republican Party, Lincoln chose to staff his cabinet with other Republicans, including, most unusually, several who had been his rivals for the presidential nomination. Secretary of State William

Seward, widely regarded as the leader of the Republican Party, at first expected to "manage" Lincoln as he had Zachary Taylor in 1848, but he soon became the president's willing partner. On the other hand, Treasury Secretary Salmon P. Chase, a staunch abolitionist, adamantly opposed concessions to the South and considered Lincoln too conciliatory. Chase, a key member of a group known as the Radical Republicans, remained a vocal and dangerous critic. That the Republican Party was a not-quite-jelled mix of former Whigs, abolitionists, moderate Free-Soilers, and even some prowar Democrats made Lincoln's task as party leader much more difficult than it might otherwise have been.

After the fall of Fort Sumter, military necessity prompted Lincoln to call up the state militias, order a naval blockade of the South, and vastly expand the military budget. Breaking with precedent, he took these actions without congressional sanction because Congress was not in session. Military necessity—the need to hold the border states—likewise prompted other early actions, such as the suspension of habeas corpus and the acceptance of Kentucky's ambiguous neutrality. Over howls of protest from abolitionists, the president also repudiated an unauthorized declaration issued by General John C. Frémont, military commander in Missouri, in August 1861 that would have freed Missouri's slaves, because he feared it would lead to the secession of Kentucky and Maryland.

Although James K. Polk had assumed responsibility for overall American military strategy during the

President Abraham Lincoln visits General George McClellan in 1862 after Antietam. Although as a young congressman Lincoln had objected to President James K. Polk's active participation in Mexican-American War strategy, he found himself taking a major role as commander in chief during the Civil War. His relationship with McClellan was especially difficult, for he could never convince the general to overcome his habitual caution.

Mexican-American War (see Chapter 14), Lincoln was the first president to act as commander in chief in both a practical and a symbolic way. He actively directed military policy, although he sometimes wondered whether he would ever find generals capable of carrying out his orders. Lincoln's involvement in military strategy sprang from his realization that a civil war presented problems different from those of a foreign war of conquest. Lincoln wanted above all to persuade the South to rejoin the Union, and his every military move was dictated by the hope of eventual reconciliation—hence his cautiousness, and his acute sense of the role of public opinion. Today we recognize Lincoln's exceptional abilities and eloquent language, but in his own time some of his most moving statements fell on deaf ears.

The War Department

The greatest expansion in government power during the war was in the War Department, which by early 1862 was faced with the unprecedented challenge of feeding, clothing, and arming 700,000 Union soldiers. Initially the government relied on the individual states to equip and supply their vastly expanded militias. States often contracted directly with textile mills and shoe factories to clothe their troops. In many northern cities volunteer groups sprang up to recruit regiments, buy them weapons, and send them to Washington. Other such community groups, like the one in Chester, Pennsylvania, focused on clothing and providing medical care to soldiers. By January 1862 the War Department, under the able direction of Edwin M.

Stanton, a former Democrat from Ohio, was able to perform many basic functions of procurement and supply without too much delay or corruption. But the size of the Union army and the complexity of fully supplying it demanded constant efforts at all levels—government, state, and community—throughout the war. Thus, in the matter of procurement and supply, as in mobilization, the battlefront was related to the home front on a scale that Americans had not previously experienced.

Taxes and the Greenback Dollar

Although Lincoln was an active commander in chief, he did not believe it was the job of the president to direct economic policy. This, he believed, was the task of Congress. In this important respect, the Civil War was fundamentally different from American wars of the twentieth century, during which executive control over economic policy was deemed essential. Yet the need for money for the vast war effort was pressing. Treasury Secretary Chase worked closely with Congress to develop ways to finance the war. They naturally turned to the nation's economic experts—private bankers, merchants, and managers of large businesses. With the help of Philadelphia financier Jay Cooke, the Treasury used patriotic appeals to sell war bonds to ordinary people in amounts as small as $50. Cooke sold $400 million in bonds, taking for himself what he considered a "fair commission." By the war's end, the United States had borrowed $2.6 billion for the war effort, the first example in American history of the mass financing of war. Additional sources of revenue were sales taxes and the first federal income tax (of 3 percent). Imposed in August 1861, the income tax affected only the affluent: anyone with an annual income under $800 was exempt.

Most radical of all was Chase's decision—which was authorized only after a bitter congressional fight—to print and distribute Treasury notes (paper money). Until then, the money in circulation had been a mixture of coins and state bank notes issued by 1,500 different state banks. The Legal Tender Act of February 1862 created a national currency, which, because of its color, was popularly known as the greenback. In 1863 Congress passed the National Bank Act, which prohibited state banks from issuing their own notes and forced them to apply for federal charters. Thus was the first uniform national currency created, at the expense of the independence that many state banks had prized. "These are extraordinary times, and extraordinary measures must be resorted to in order to save our Government and preserve our nationality," pleaded Congressman Elbridge G. Spaulding, sponsor of the legislation. Only through this appeal to wartime necessity were Spaulding and his allies able to overcome the opposition, for the switch to a national currency was widely recognized as a major step toward centralization of economic power in the hands of the federal government. Such a measure would have been unthinkable if southern Democrats had still been part of the national government. The absence of southern Democrats also made possible passage of a number of Republican economic measures not directly related to the war.

Politics and Economics: The Republican Platform

Although the debate over slavery had overshadowed everything else, in 1860 the Republican Party had campaigned on a comprehensive program of economic development. Once in office, Republicans quickly passed the Morrill Tariff Act (1861); by 1864, this and subsequent measures had raised tariffs to more than double their prewar rate. In 1862 and 1864, Congress created two federally chartered corporations to build a transcontinental railroad—the Union Pacific Railroad Company, to lay track westward from Omaha, and the Central Pacific, to lay track eastward from California—thus fulfilling the dreams of the many expansionists who believed America's economic future lay in trade with Asia across the Pacific Ocean. Two other measures, both passed in 1862, had long been sought by Westerners. The Homestead Act gave 160 acres of public land to any citizen who agreed to live on it for five years, improve it by building a house and cultivating some of the land, and pay a small fee. The Morrill Land Grant Act gave states public land that would allow them to finance land-grant colleges offering education to ordinary citizens in practical skills such as agriculture, engineering, and military science. Coupled with this act, the establishment of a federal Department of Agriculture in 1862 gave American farmers a big push toward modern commercial agriculture.

This package revealed the Whig origins of many Republicans, for in essence the measures amounted to an updated version of Henry Clay's American System of national economic development (see Chapter 9). They were to have a powerful nationalizing effect, connecting ordinary people to the federal government in new ways. As much as the extraordinary war measures, the enactment of the Republican program increased the role of the federal government in national life. Although many

of the executive war powers lapsed when the battles ended, the accumulation of strength by the federal government, which southern Democrats would have opposed had they been in Congress, was never reversed.

Diplomatic Objectives

To Secretary of State William Seward fell the job of making sure that Britain and France did not extend diplomatic recognition to the Confederacy. Although Southerners had been certain that King Cotton would gain them European support, they were wrong. British public opinion, which had strongly supported the abolition of slavery within the British Empire in the 1830s, would not now countenance the recognition of a new nation based on slavery. British cotton manufacturers found economic alternatives, first using up their backlog of southern cotton and then turning to Egypt and India for new supplies. In spite of Union protests, however, both Britain and France did allow Confederate vessels to use their ports, and British shipyards sold six ships to the Confederacy. But in 1863, when the Confederacy commissioned Britain's Laird shipyard to build two ironclad ships with pointed prows for ramming, the Union threatened war and the British government made sure that the Laird rams were never delivered. Seward had wanted to threaten Britain with war earlier, in 1861, when the prospect of diplomatic recognition for the Confederacy seemed most likely, but Lincoln had overruled him, cautioning, "One war at a time."

Nonbelligerence was also the Union response in 1863, when France took advantage of the Civil War to invade Mexico and install the Austrian archduke Maximilian as emperor. This was a serious violation of the Monroe Doctrine that could have led to war, but fearing that France might recognize the Confederacy or invade Texas, Seward had to content himself with refusing to recognize the new Mexican government. In the meantime he directed Union troops to gain a stronghold in Texas as soon as possible. In November, five months after the French marched into Mexico City, Union troops seized Brownsville, a town on the Texas-Mexico border, sending a clear signal to the French to go no further. In 1866, after the Civil War, strong diplomatic pressure from Seward convinced the French to withdraw from Mexico. The following year, the hapless Maximilian was captured and shot during a revolt led by a future Mexican president, Benito Juárez.

Although the goal of Seward's diplomacy—preventing recognition of the Confederacy by the European powers—was always clear, its achievement was uncertain for more than two years. Northern fears and southern hopes seesawed with the fortunes of battle. Not until the victories at Vicksburg and Gettysburg in July 1863 could Seward be reasonably confident of success.

Confederate President Jefferson Davis (in the largest chair) and his cabinet are shown meeting with Confederate general Robert E. Lee in this 1866 lithograph. Davis carefully selected his cabinet to represent the South's major states. Shown here, left to right, are Stephen R. Mallory, Judah P. Benjamin, Leroy P. Walker, Davis, Lee, John Reagan, Christopher Memminger, Alexander Stephens, and Robert Toombs.

THE CONFEDERACY

Lincoln faced a major challenge in keeping the North unified enough to win the war, but Jefferson Davis's challenge was even greater. He had to create a Confederate nation. The Confederate States of America was a loose grouping of eleven states, each believing strongly in states' rights. Yet in the Confederacy, as in the Union, the conduct of the war required central direction.

Jefferson Davis as President

Although Jefferson Davis had held national cabinet rank (as secretary of war under president Franklin Pierce), had experience as an administrator, and was a former military man (none of which was true of Abraham Lincoln), he was unable to hold the Confederacy together. Perhaps no one could have. Born, like Lincoln, in Kentucky, Davis ultimately settled in Mississippi, where he became a rich planter. Davis was thus a "cotton nabob" (one of the newly rich class of slave owners), and as such was as scorned by some members of the old southern aristocracy as was Abraham Lincoln by some members of the northern elite. Davis's problems, however, were as much structural as they were personal.

Davis's first cabinet of six men, appointed in February 1861, included a representative from each of the states of the first secession except Mississippi, which was represented by Davis himself. This careful attention to the equality of the states pointed to the fundamental problem that Davis was unable to overcome. For all of

its drama, secession was a conservative strategy for preserving the slavery-based social and political structure that existed in every southern state. A shared belief in states' rights—that is, in their own autonomy—was a poor basis on which to build a unified nation. Davis, who would have preferred to be a general rather than a president, lacked Lincoln's persuasive skills and political astuteness. Although he saw the need for unity, he was unable to impose it. Soon his autonomous style of leadership—he wanted to decide every detail himself—angered his generals, alienated cabinet members, and gave southern governors reason to resist his orders. By the second year of the war, when rich slave owners were refusing to give up their privileges for the war effort, Davis no longer had the public confidence and support he needed to coerce them. After the first flush of patriotism had passed, the Confederacy never lived up to its hope of becoming a unified nation.

Diplomatic Hopes

The failure of "cotton diplomacy" was a crushing blow. White Southerners were stunned that Britain and France would not recognize their claim to independence. Well into 1863, the South hoped that a decisive battlefield victory would change the minds of cautious Europeans. In the meantime, plantations continued to grow cotton, but the Confederacy withheld it from market, hoping that lack of raw material for their textile mills would lead the British and French to recognize the Confederacy. The British reacted indignantly, claiming that the withholding of cotton was economic blackmail and that to yield "would be ignominious beyond measure," as Lord Russell put it. Because British textile manufacturers found new sources of cotton, when the Confederacy ended the embargo in 1862 and began to ship its great surplus, the world price of cotton plunged. Then too, the Union naval blockade, weak at first, began to take effect. Cotton turned out to be not so powerful a diplomatic weapon after all.

The Sinews of War

Perhaps the greatest southern failure was in the area of finances. At first the Confederate government tried to raise money from the states, but governors refused to impose new taxes. By the time uniform taxes were levied in 1863, it was too late. Heavy borrowing and the printing of great sums of paper money produced runaway inflation (a ruinous rate of 9,000 percent by 1865, compared with 80 percent in the North). Inflation, in turn, caused incalculable damage to morale and prospects for unity.

After the initial surge of volunteers, enlistment in the military fell off, as it did in the North also. In April 1862, the Confederate Congress passed the first draft law in American history, and the Union Congress followed suit in March 1863. The southern law declared that all able-bodied men between eighteen and thirty-five were eligible for three years of military service. Purchase of substitutes was allowed, as in the North, but in the South the price was uncontrolled, rising eventually to $10,000 in Confederate money. The most disliked part of the draft law was a provision exempting one white man on each plantation with twenty or more slaves. This provision not only seemed to disprove the earlier claim that slavery freed white men to fight, but it aroused class resentments. A bitter phrase of the time complained, "It's a rich man's war but a poor man's fight."

Contradictions of Southern Nationalism

In the early days of the war, Jefferson Davis successfully mobilized feelings of regional identity and patriotism.

Many Southerners felt part of a beleaguered region that had been forced to resist northern tyranny. But most Southerners felt loyalty to their own state and local communities, not to a Confederate nation. The strong belief in states' rights and aristocratic privilege undermined the Confederate cause. Some Southern governors resisted potentially unifying actions such as moving militias outside their home states. Broader measures, such as general taxation, were widely evaded by rich and poor alike. The inequitable draft was only one of many things that convinced the ordinary people of the South that this was a war for privileged slave owners, not for them. With its leaders and citizens fearing (perhaps correctly) that centralization would destroy what was distinctively southern, the Confederacy was unable to mobilize the resources—financial, human, and otherwise—that might have prevented its destruction by northern armies.

THE FIGHTING THROUGH 1862

Just as political decisions were often driven by military necessity, the basic northern and southern military strategies were affected by political considerations as much as by military ones. The initial policy of limited war, thought to be the best route to ultimate reconcil-

The contrast between the hope and valor of these young southern volunteer soldiers, photographed shortly before the first battle of Bull Run, and the later advertisements for substitutes is marked. Southern exemptions for slave owners and lavish payment for substitutes increasingly bred resentment among the ordinary people of the South.

SUBSTITUTE NOTICES.

WANTED—A SUBSTITUTE for a conscript, to serve during the war. Any good man over the age of 35 years, not a resident of Virginia, or a foreigner, may hear of a good situation by calling at Mr. GEORGE BAGBY'S office, Shockoe Slip, to-day, between the hours of 9 and 11 A. M.   [jy 9—1t*]   A COUNTRYMAN.

WANTED—Two SUBSTITUTES—one for artillery, the other for infantry or cavalry service. Also, to sell, a trained, thoroughbred cavalry HORSE.   Apply to   DR. BROOCKS, Corner Main and 12th streets, or to

jy 9—3t*   T. T. BROOCKS,
Petersburg, Va.

WANTED—Immediately, a SUBSTITUTE. A man over 35 years old, or under 18, can get a good price by making immediate application to Room No. 50, Monument Hotel, or by addressing "J. W.," through Richmond P. O.   jy 9—1t*

WANTED—A SUBSTITUTE, to go into the 24th North Carolina State troops, for which a liberal price will be paid. Apply to me at Dispatch office this evening at 4 o'clock P. M.
jy 9—1t*   R. R. MOORE.

WANTED—A SUBSTITUTE, to go in a first-rate Georgia company of infantry, under the heroic Jackson. A gentleman whose health is impaired, will give a fair price for a substitute. Apply immediately at ROOM, No. 13, Post-Office Department, third story, between the hours of 10 and 3 o'clock.   jy 9—6t*

WANTED—Two SUBSTITUTES for the war. A good bonus will be given. None need apply except those exempt from Conscript. Apply to-day at   GEORGE I. HERRING'S,
jy 9—1t*   Grocery store, No. 56 Main st.

1861–62

1863

Overall Strategy of the Civil War

In 1861 General Winfield Scott, then the Union's general in chief, proposed the so-called Anaconda plan for subduing the South, which involved strangling it by a blockade at sea and control of the Mississippi rather than directly assaulting its territory. Important aspects of this plan—the blockade of the Confederate coast and the attempt to divide the Confederacy by controlling the Mississippi—became part of the Union's overall war strategy. Union leaders realized, however, that they could not win the war without conquering Confederate territory. The South's strategy was defensive. If its armies could hold out long enough for the North to tire of fighting, its independence would be secured.

By the end of 1862, the Union had captured the sea islands of South Carolina and Georgia and areas of North Carolina, Ulysses S. Grant had won important victories in Tennessee, and Admiral David Farragut had taken New Orleans and advanced up the Mississippi. But in the East, Union armies were consistently stymied by Robert E. Lee's Army of Northern Virginia.

The turning point of the war came in 1863 with General George Gordon Meade's defeat of Lee at Gettysburg (July 1–3) and Grant's capture of Vicksburg (July 4). These two great victories turned the tide in favor of the Union. The Confederates never again mounted a major offensive, and total Union control of the Mississippi exposed the Lower South to Union advance.

1864–65

In 1864–65, Grant (now in command of all the Union armies) and General William Tecumseh Sherman brought the war home to the South. Sherman's destructive "March to the Sea" divided the South's heartland, and Grant's hammering tactics kept Lee under constant pressure in northern Virginia. Finally, on April 9, 1865, Lee surrendered to Grant at Appomattox, thus ending the bloodiest war in the nation's history.

iation, ran into difficulties because of the public's impatience for victories. But victories, as the mounting slaughter made clear, were not easy to achieve.

The War in Northern Virginia

The initial northern strategy, dubbed by critics the Anaconda Plan (after the constricting snake), envisaged slowly squeezing the South with a blockade at sea and on the Mississippi River. Proposed by the general in chief, Winfield Scott, a native of Virginia, it avoided invasion and conquest in the hope that a strained South would recognize the inevitability of defeat and thus surrender. Lincoln accepted the basics of the plan, but public clamor for a fight pushed him to agree to the disastrous battle of Bull Run and then to a major buildup of Union troops in northern Virginia under General George B. McClellan.

Dashing in appearance, McClellan was extremely cautious in battle. In March 1862, after almost a year spent drilling the raw Union recruits and after repeated exhortations by an impatient Lincoln, McClellan committed 120,000 troops to what became known as the Peninsular campaign. The objective was to capture Richmond, the Confederate capital. McClellan had his troops and their supplies ferried from Washington to Fortress Monroe, near the mouth of the James River, in 400 ships, an effort that took three weeks. Inching up the James Peninsula toward Richmond, he tried to avoid battle, hoping his overwhelming numbers would convince the South to surrender. By June, McClellan's troops were close enough to Richmond to hear the church bells ringing—but not close enough for victory. In a series of battles known as the Seven Days, Robert E. Lee (who had just assumed command of the Confederacy's Army of Northern Virginia) boldly counterattacked, repeatedly catching McClellan off guard. Taking heavy losses as well as inflicting them, Lee drove McClellan back. In August, Lee routed another Union army, commanded by General John Pope, at the second battle of Bull Rull (Second Manassas). Lincoln, alarmed at the threat to Washington and disappointed by McClellan's inaction, ordered him to abandon the Peninsular campaign and return to the capital.

Jefferson Davis, like Abraham Lincoln, was an active commander in chief. And like Lincoln, he responded to a public that clamored for more action than a strictly defensive war entailed. After the Seven Days victories, Davis supported a Confederate attack on Maryland. At the same time, he issued a proclamation urging the people of Maryland to make a separate peace. But in the brutal battle of Antietam on September 17, 1862, which claimed more than 5,000 dead and 19,000 wounded, McClellan's army checked Lee's advance. Lee retreated to Virginia, inflicting terrible losses on northern troops at Fredricksburg when they

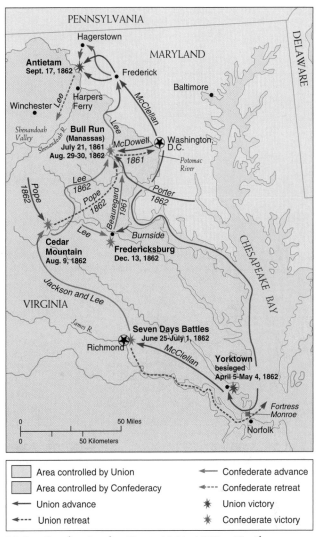

Major Battles in the East, 1861–1862   *Northern Virginia was the most crucial and the most constant theater of battle. The prizes were the two opposing capitals, Washington and Richmond, only 70 miles apart. By the summer of 1862, George B. McClellan, famously cautious, had achieved only stalemate in the Peninsular campaign. He did, however, turn back Robert E. Lee at Antietam in September.*

again made a thrust toward Richmond in December, 1862. The war in northern Virginia was stalemated: neither side was strong enough to win, but each was too strong to be defeated.

Shiloh and the War for the Mississippi

Although most public attention was focused on the fighting in Virginia, battles in Tennessee and along the Mississippi River proved to be the key to eventual Union victory. The rising military figure in the West was Ulysses S. Grant, who had once resigned from the service because of a drinking problem. Reenlisting as a colonel after the capture of Fort Sumter, Grant was promoted to brigadier general within two months. In February 1862

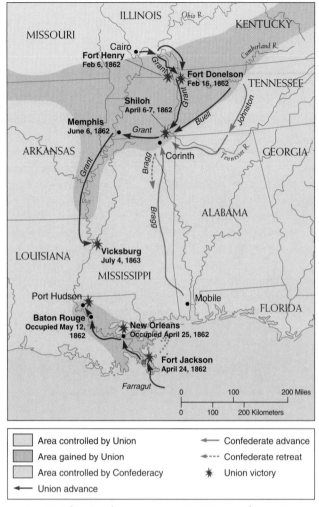

Area controlled by Union

Area gained by Union

Area controlled by Confederacy

← **Union advance**

← **Confederate advance**

◁--- **Confederate retreat**

✳ **Union victory**

Major Battles in the West, 1862–1863 *Ulysses S. Grant waged a mobile war, winning at Fort Henry and Fort Donelson in Tennessee in February 1862 and at Shiloh in April, and capturing Memphis in June. He then laid siege to Vicksburg, as Admiral David Farragut captured New Orleans and began to advance up the Mississippi River.*

Grant captured Fort Henry and Fort Donelson, on the Tennessee and Cumberland Rivers, establishing Union control of much of Tennessee and forcing Confederate troops to retreat into northern Mississippi.

Moving south with 28,000 men, Grant met a 40,000-man Confederate force commanded by General Albert Sidney Johnston at Shiloh Church in April. Seriously outnumbered on the first day, Grant's forces were reinforced by the arrival of 35,000 troops under the command of General Don Carlos Buell. After two days of bitter and bloody fighting in the rain, the Confederates withdrew. The losses on both sides were enormous: the North lost 13,000 men, the South 11,000, including General Johnston, who bled to death. McClellan's Peninsular campaign was already under way when Grant won at Shiloh, and Jefferson Davis,

concerned about the defense of Richmond, refused to reinforce the generals who were trying to stop Grant. Consequently, Union forces kept moving, capturing Memphis in June and beginning a campaign to eventually capture Vicksburg, "the Gibraltar of the Mississippi." Grant and other Union generals faced strong Confederate resistance, and progress was slow. Earlier that year, naval forces under Admiral David Farragut had captured New Orleans and then continued up the Mississippi River. By the end of 1862 it was clearly only a matter of time before the entire river would be in Union hands. Arkansas, Louisiana, and Texas would then be cut off from the rest of the Confederacy.

The War in the Trans-Mississippi West

Although only one western state, Texas, seceded from the Union, the Civil War was fought in small ways in many parts of the West. Southern hopes for the extension of slavery into the Southwest were reignited by the war. Texans mounted an attack on New Mexico, which they had long coveted, and kept their eyes on the larger prizes of Arizona and California. A Confederate force led by General Henry H. Sibley occupied Santa Fe and Albuquerque early in 1862 without resistance, thus posing a serious Confederate threat to the entire Southwest. Confederate hopes were dashed, however, by a ragtag group of 950 miners and adventurers organized into the first Colorado Volunteer Infantry Regiment. After an epic march of 400 miles from Denver, which was completed in thirteen days despite snow and high winds, the Colorado militia stopped the unsuspecting Confederate troops in the battle of Glorieta Pass on March 26–28, 1862. This dashing action, coupled with the efforts of California militias to safeguard Arizona and Utah from seizure by Confederate sympathizers, secured the Far West for the Union.

Other military action in the West was less decisive. The chronic fighting along the Kansas-Missouri border set a record for brutality when Confederate William Quantrill's Raiders made a predawn attack on Lawrence, Kansas, in August 1863, massacring 150 inhabitants and burning the town. Another civil war took place in Indian Territory, south of Kansas. The southern Indian tribes who had been removed there from the Old Southwest in the 1830s included many who were still bitter over the horrors of removal by federal troops and sympathized with the Confederacy. Furthermore, the Confederacy actively sought Indian support by offering Indian people representation in the Confederate Congress. Consequently, many Indians fought for the South, among them Stand Watie, who became a Confederate military officer. Union victories at Pea Ridge (in northwestern Arkansas) in 1862 and near Fort Gibson (in Indian Territory) in 1863 secured the area for the Union but did little to stop dissension among the Indian groups themselves. After the Civil War the victorious federal government used the tribes' wartime support for the Confederacy as a justification for demanding further land cessions.

Elsewhere in the West, other groups of Indians found themselves caught up in the wider war. An uprising by the Santee Sioux in Minnesota occurred in August 1862, just as McClellan conceded defeat in the Peninsular campaign in Virginia. Alarmed whites, certain that the uprising was a Confederate plot, ignored legitimate Sioux grievances and responded in kind to Sioux ferocity. In little more than a month, 500–800 white settlers and an even greater number of Sioux were killed. Thirty-eight Indians were hanged in a mass execution in Mankato on December 26, 1862, and subsequently all Sioux were expelled from Minnesota. In 1863, U.S. Army Colonel Kit Carson invaded Navajo country in Arizona in retaliation for Indian raids on U.S. troops. Eight thousand Navajos were forced on the brutal "Long Walk" to Bosque Redondo on the Pecos River in New Mexico, where they were held prisoner until a treaty between the United States and the Navajos was signed in 1868.

The hostilities in the West showed that no part of the country, and none of its inhabitants, could remain untouched by the Civil War.

The Naval War

The Union's naval blockade of the South, intended to cut off commerce between the Confederacy and the rest of the world, was initially unsuccessful. The U.S. Navy had only thirty-three ships with which to blockade 189 ports along 3,500 miles of coastline. Southern blockade runners evaded Union ships with ease: only an estimated one-eighth of all Confederate shipping was stopped in 1862. Moreover, the Confederacy licensed British-made privateers to strike at northern shipping. In a two-year period one such Confederate raider, the *Alabama*, destroyed sixty-nine Union

ships with cargoes valued at $6 million. Beginning in 1863, however, as the Union navy became larger, the blockade began to take effect. In 1864 a third of the blockade runners were captured, and in 1865 half of them. As a result, fewer and fewer supplies reached the South.

North and South also engaged in a brief duel featuring the revolutionary new technology of ironclading. The Confederacy refitted a scuttled Union vessel, the *Merrimac*, with iron plating and renamed it the *Virginia*. On March 8, 1862, as McClellan began his Peninsular campaign, the *Virginia* steamed out of Norfolk harbor to challenge the Union blockade. The iron plating protected the *Virginia* from the fire of the Union ships, which found themselves defenseless against its ram and

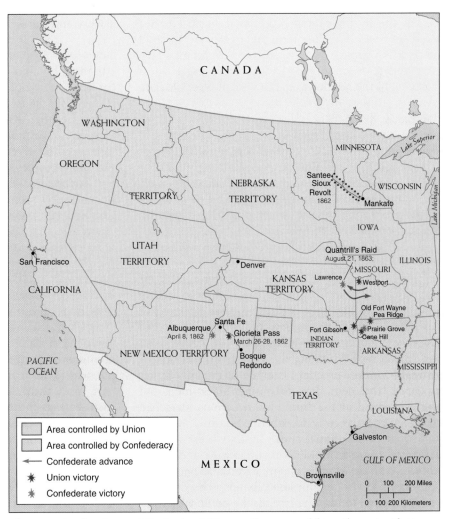

The War in the Trans-Mississippi West   *Far removed from the major theaters of battle, the Far West was nevertheless a rich prize in the Civil War. Battles in remote places like Glorieta Pass, New Mexico, were decisive in holding the Far West for the Union. The battles in Kansas and Indian Territory, however, arose primarily from prewar antagonisms and settled little.*

Source: Warren Beck and Ynez Haase, *Historical Atlas of the American West* (Norman: University of Oklahoma Press, 1989).

its powerful guns. Two Union ships went down, and the blockade seemed about to be broken. But the North had an experimental ironclad of its own, the *Monitor*, which was waiting for the *Merrimac* when it emerged from port on March 9. The *Monitor*, which looked like "an immense shingle floating on the water, with a gigantic cheese box rising from its center," was the ship of the future, for the "cheese box" was a revolving turret, a basic component of battleships to come. The historic duel between these first two ironclads was inconclusive, and primitive technology together with limited resources made them of little consequence for the rest of the war. But this brief duel prefigured the naval and land battles of the world wars of the twentieth century as much as did the massing of huge armies on the battlefield.

For the Union, the most successful naval operation in the first two years of the war was not the blockade but the seizing of exposed coastal areas. The Sea Islands of South Carolina were taken, as were some of the North Carolina islands and Fort Pulaski, which commanded the harbor of Savannah, Georgia. Most damaging to the South was the capture of New Orleans.

The Black Response

The capture of Port Royal in the South Carolina Sea Islands in 1861 was important for another reason. Whites fled at the Union advance, but 10,000 slaves greeted the troops with jubilation and shouts of gratitude. Union troops had unwittingly freed these slaves in advance of any official Union policy on the status of slaves in captured territory.

Early in the war, an irate Southerner who saw three of his slaves disappear behind Union lines at Fortress Monroe, Virginia, demanded the return of his property, citing the Fugitive Slave Law. The Union commander, Benjamin Butler, replied that the Fugitive Slave Law no longer applied and that the escaped slaves were "contraband of war." News of Butler's decision spread rapidly among the slaves in the region of Fortress Monroe. Two days later, eight runaway slaves appeared; the next day, fifty-nine black men and women arrived at the fort. Union commanders had found an effective way to rob the South of its basic workforce. The "contrabands," as they were known, were put to work building fortifications and doing other useful work in northern camps. Washington, D.C., became a refuge for contrabands, who crowded into the capital to join the free black people who lived there (at 9,000, they were one of the largest urban black populations outside the Confederacy). Many destitute contrabands received help from the Contraband Relief Association. Modeled on the Sanitary Commission, the association was founded by former slave Elizabeth Keckley, seamstress to Mary Todd Lincoln, the president's wife.

As Union troops drove deeper into the South, the black response grew. When Union General William Tecumseh Sherman marched his army through Georgia in 1864, 18,000 slaves—entire families, people of all ages—flocked to the Union lines. By the war's end, nearly a million black people, fully a quarter of all the slaves in the South, had "voted with their feet" for the Union.

THE DEATH OF SLAVERY

The overwhelming response of black slaves to the Union advance changed the nature of the war. As increasing numbers of slaves flocked to Union lines, the conclusion was unmistakable: the southern war to defend the slave system did not have the support of slaves themselves. Any northern policy that ignored the issue of slavery and the wishes of the slaves was unrealistic.

The Politics of Emancipation

Abraham Lincoln had always said that this was a war for the Union, not a war about slavery. In his Inaugural Address, he had promised to leave slavery untouched in the South. Although Lincoln personally abhorred slavery, his official policy was based on a realistic assessment of several factors. At first, he hoped to give pro-Union forces in the South a chance to consolidate and to prevent the outbreak of war. After the war began, he was impelled by the military necessity of holding the border states (Delaware, Maryland, Kentucky, and Missouri), where slavery was legal.

Finally, Lincoln was worried about unity in the North. Even within the Republican Party, before the war only a small group of abolitionists had favored freeing the slaves. Most Republicans were more concerned about the expansion of slavery than they were about the lives of slaves themselves. They did not favor the social equality of black people, whom they considered inferior. The free-soil movement, for example, was as often antiblack as it was antislave. For their part, most northern Democrats were openly antiblack. Irish workers in northern cities had rioted against free African Americans, with whom they often competed for jobs. There was also the question of what would become of slaves who were freed. Even the most fervent abolitionists had refused to face up to this issue. Finally, northern Democrats effectively played on racial fears in the 1862 congressional elections, warning that freed slaves would pour into northern cities and take jobs from white laborers.

Nevertheless, the necessities of war edged Lincoln toward a new position. In March 1862 he proposed that every state undertake gradual, compensated emancipation, after which former slaves would be resettled in Haiti and Panama (neither of which was under U.S. control). This unrealistic colonization scheme, as well as the reluctance of politicians in the border states to consider emancipation, doomed the proposal.

Radical Republicans chafed at Lincoln's conservative stance. In August 1862 Horace Greeley, editor of the *New York Tribune*, pressed the point in an open letter to the president: "On the face of this wide earth, Mr. President, there is not one disinterested, determined, intelligent champion of the Union cause who does not feel that all attempts to put down the Rebellion and at the same time uphold its inciting cause are preposterous and futile." Greeley's statement was incorrect, for many Northerners did not care what happened to the slaves but did care what happened to the Union. Lincoln's famous answer implicitly acknowledged the many shades of public opinion and cast his decision in terms of military necessity: "If I could save the Union without freeing any slave, I would do it; and if I could save it by freeing all the slaves, I would do it; and if I could do it by freeing some and leaving others alone, I would also do that. What I do about Slavery and the colored race, I do because I believe it helps to save this Union."

In fact, Lincoln had already made up his mind to issue an Emancipation Proclamation, and was simply waiting for the right moment. Following the Union victory at Antietam in September 1862, Lincoln issued a preliminary decree: unless the rebellious states returned to the Union by January 1, 1863, he would declare their slaves "forever free." Although Lincoln did not expect the Confederate states to surrender because of his proclamation, the decree increased the pressure on the South by directly linking the slave system to the war effort. Thus the freedom of black people became part of the struggle. Frederick Douglass, the voice of black America, wrote, "We shout for joy that we live to record this righteous decree."

On January 1, 1863, Lincoln duly issued the final Emancipation Proclamation, which turned out to be just as tortuous as his response to Greeley in August. The proclamation freed the slaves in the areas of rebellion—the areas the Union did not control—but specifically exempted slaves in the border states and in former Confederate areas conquered by the Union. Lincoln's purpose was to meet the abolitionist demand for a war against slavery while not losing the support of conservatives, especially in the border states. But the proclamation was so equivocal that Lincoln's own secretary of state, William Seward, remarked sarcastically, "We show our sympathy with slavery by emancipating slaves where we cannot reach them and holding them in bondage where we can set them free." And in Britain, where Lincoln had hoped to make a favorable impression on the public, government officials were more puzzled than impressed by the proclamation.

One group greeted the Emancipation Proclamation with open celebration. On New Year's Day, hundreds of African Americans gathered outside the White House and cheered the president. They called to him, as pastor Henry M. Turner recalled, that "if he would come out of that palace, they would hug him to death." Realizing the symbolic importance of the proclamation, free African Americans predicted that the news would encourage southern slaves either to flee to Union lines or refuse to work for their masters. Both of these things were already happening as African Americans seized on wartime changes to reshape white-black relations in the South. In one sense, then, the Emancipation Proclamation simply gave a name to a process already in motion.

Abolitionists set about moving Lincoln beyond his careful stance in the Emancipation Proclamation. Reformers such as Elizabeth Cady Stanton and Susan B. Anthony lobbied and petitioned for a constitutional amendment outlawing slavery. Lincoln agreed with them, and encouraged the Republican Party to support such an amendment in its 1864 election platform. Congress, at Lincoln's urging, approved and sent to the states a statement banning slavery throughout the United States. Quickly ratified by the Union states in 1865, the statement became the Thirteenth Amendment to the Constitution. (The southern states, being in a state of rebellion, could not vote.) Lincoln's firm support for this amendment is a good indicator of his true feelings about slavery when he was free of the kinds of military and political considerations taken into account in the Emancipation Proclamation.

Black Fighting Men

As part of the Emancipation Proclamation, Lincoln gave his support for the first time to the recruitment of black soldiers. Early in the war, eager black volunteers had been bitterly disappointed at being turned away. Many, like Robert Fitzgerald, a free African American from Pennsylvania, found other ways to serve the Union cause. Fitzgerald first drove a wagon and mule for the Quartermaster Corps, and later, in spite of persistent seasickness, he served in the Union navy. After the Emancipation Proclamation, however, Fitzgerald was able to do what he had wanted to do all along: be a soldier. He enlisted in the Fifth Massachusetts Cavalry, a regiment that, like all the units in which black soldiers served, was 100 percent African American but commanded by white officers. The most famous black regiment, the Fifty-fourth Massachusetts Colored Infantry, was commanded by abolitionist Robert Gould Shaw of Boston, who was killed in action along with half of his troops in a fruitless attack on Fort Wagner, South Carolina, in 1863. Thomas Wentworth Higginson, the Unitarian minister who had supported John Brown, led another of the first black regiments, the First South Carolina Volunteers.

In Fitzgerald's company of eighty-three men, half came from slave states and had run away to enlist; the other half came mostly from the North but also from Canada, the West Indies, and France. Other regiments had volunteers from Africa. The proportion of volunteers from the loyal border states (where slavery was still legal) was upwards of 25 percent—a lethal blow to the slave system in those states.

After a scant two months of training, Fitzgerald's company was sent on to Washington and thence to battle in northern Virginia. Uncertain of the reception they would receive in northern cities with their history of antiblack riots, Fitzgerald and his comrades were pleasantly surprised. "We are cheered in every town we pass through," he wrote in his diary. "I was surprised to see a great many white people weeping as the train moved South." White people had reason to cheer: black volunteers, eager and willing to fight, made up 10 percent of the Union army. Nearly 200,000 African Americans (one out of every five black males in the nation) served in the Union army or navy.

A fifth of them—37,000—died defending their own freedom and the Union.

Military service was something no black man could take lightly. He faced prejudice of several kinds. In the North, most white people believed that black people were inferior both in intelligence and in courage. Most army officers shared these opinions— but usually not those who had volunteered to lead black troops. Thus African American soldiers had to prove themselves in battle. The performance of black soldiers at Fort Wagner and in battles near Vicksburg, Mississippi, in 1863 helped to change the minds of the Union army command. In the battle of Milliken's Bend, untrained and poorly armed former slaves fought desperately—and successfully. "The bravery of the blacks...completely revolutionized the sentiment of the army with regard to the employment of negro troops," wrote Charles Dana, assistant secretary of war. "I heard prominent officers who formerly in private had sneered at the idea of negroes fighting express themselves after that as heartily in favor of it."

Among the Confederates, however, the feeling was very different. They hated and feared African American troops and threatened to treat any captured black soldier as an escaped slave subject to execution. On at least one occasion, the threats were carried out. In 1864 Confederate soldiers massacred 262 black soldiers at Fort Pillow, Tennessee, after they had surrendered. Although large-scale episodes such as this were rare (especially after President Lincoln threatened retaliation), smaller ones were not. On duty near Petersburg, Virginia, Robert Fitzgerald's company lost a picket to Confederate hatred: wounded in the leg, he was unable to escape from Confederate soldiers, who smashed his skull with their musket butts. Fitzgerald wrote in his diary, "Can such men eventually triumph? God forbid!"

Another extraordinary part of the story of the African American soldiers was their reception by black people in the South, who were overjoyed at the sight of armed black men, many of them former slaves themselves, wearing the uniform of the Union army. As his regiment entered Wilming-

When the family of Robert and Cornelia Fitzgerald posed for a group picture in the 1890s, Robert Fitzgerald proudly dressed in the Union Army uniform he had worn during the Civil War. Fitzgerald's pride in his war service, doubtless shared by many African American veterans, was an important family memory of the fight against slavery.

ton, North Carolina, one soldier wrote, "Men and women, old and young, were running throughout the streets, shouting and praising God. We could then truly see what we have been fighting for."

Robert Fitzgerald's own army career was brief. Just five months after he enlisted, he caught typhoid fever. Hearing of his illness, Fitzgerald's mother traveled from Pennsylvania and nursed him, probably saving his life. Eventually, 117 members of his regiment died of disease—and only 7 in battle. Eight months after he had enlisted, Fitzgerald was discharged for poor eyesight. His short military career nevertheless gave him, in the words of a granddaughter, the distinguished lawyer Pauli Murray, "a pride which would be felt throughout his family for the next century."

African American soldiers were not treated equally by the Union army. They were segregated in camp, given the worst jobs, and paid less than white soldiers ($10 a month rather than $13). Although they might not be able to do much about the other kinds of discrimination, the men of the Fifty-fourth Massachusetts found an unusual way to protest their unequal pay: they refused to accept it, preferring to serve the army for free until it decided to treat them as free men. The protest was effective; in June 1864 the War Department equalized the wages of black and white soldiers.

In other ways the army service of black men made a dent in northern white racism. Massachusetts, the state where abolitionist feeling was the strongest, went the furthest by enacting the first law forbidding discrimination against African Americans in public facilities. Some major cities, among them San Francisco, Cincinnati, Cleveland, and New York, desegregated their streetcars. Several states—Ohio, California, Illinois—repealed statutes that had barred black people from testifying in court or serving on juries. But above all, as Frederick Douglass acutely saw, military service permanently changed the status of African Americans. "Once let the black man get upon his person the brass letters, U.S., let him get an eagle on his button and a musket on his shoulder and bullets in his pocket," Douglass said, and "there is no power on earth that can deny that he has earned the right to citizenship."

THE FRONT LINES AND THE HOME FRONT

Civil War soldiers wrote millions of letters home, more proportionately than in any American war. Their letters and the ones they received in return were links between the front lines and the home front, between the soldiers and their home communities. They are a testament to the patriotism of both Union and Confederate troops, for the story they tell is frequently one of slaughter and horror.

The Toll of War

In spite of early hopes for what one might call a "brotherly" war, one that avoided excessive brutality, Civil War battles were appallingly deadly. One reason was technology: improved weapons, particularly modern rifles, had much greater range and accuracy than the muskets they replaced. The Mexican-American War had been fought with smooth-bore muskets, which were slow to reload and accurate only at short distances. As Ulysses Grant said, "At a distance of a few hundred yards, a man could fire at you all day [with a musket] without your finding out." The new Springfield and Enfield rifles were accurate for a quarter of a mile or more.

Civil War generals, however, were slow to adjust to this new reality. Almost all Union and Confederate generals remained committed to the conventional military doctrine of massed infantry offensives—the Jomini doctrine—that they had learned in their military classes at West Point. Part of this strategy had been to "soften up" a defensive line before an infantry assault, but now the range of the new rifles made artillery itself vulnerable to attack. As a result, generals relied less on "softening up" than on immense numbers of infantrymen, hoping that enough of them would survive the withering rifle fire to overwhelm the enemy line. Enormous casualties were a consequence of this basic strategy.

Medical ignorance was another factor in the casualty rate. Because the use of antiseptic procedures was in its infancy, men often died because minor wounds became infected. Gangrene was a common cause of death. Disease was an even more frequent killer, taking twice as many men as were lost in battle. The overcrowded and unsanitary conditions of many camps were breeding grounds for smallpox, dysentery, typhoid, pneumonia, and, in the summer, malaria. The devastating effect of disease was apparent, for example, in McClellan's Peninsular campaign. Among his 130,000 men, nearly a quarter of the unwounded were ill in July 1862. The knowledge that this situation could only deteriorate during August and September—the most disease-ridden months—was one of the reasons Lincoln decided to recall McClellan and his army.

Both North and South were completely unprepared to handle the supply and health needs of their large armies. Twenty-four hours after the battle of Shiloh, most of the wounded still lay on the field in the rain. Many died of exposure; some, unable to help themselves, drowned. Nor were the combatants prepared to deal with masses of war prisoners, as the shocking example of the Confederate prison camp of Andersonville in northern Georgia demonstrated. Andersonville was an open stockade with no shade or shelter erected early in 1864 to hold 10,000 northern prisoners, but by midsummer it held 33,000. During the worst weeks of that summer, 100 prisoners died of disease, exposure, or malnutrition each day.

Army Nurses

Many medical supplies that the armies were unable to provide were donated by the United States Sanitary Commission in the North, as described in the opening of this chapter, and by women's volunteer groups in the South. But in addition to supplies, there was also an urgent need for skilled nurses to care for wounded and convalescent soldiers. Nursing within a family context was widely considered to be women's work. Caring for sick family members was a key domestic responsibility for women, and most had considerable experience with it. But taking care of strange men in hospitals was another thing. There were strong objections that such work was "unseemly" for respectable women.

Under the pressure of wartime necessity, and over the objections of most army doctors—who resented the challenge to their authority from people no different than their daughters or wives—women became army nurses. Hospital nursing, previously considered a job only disreputable women would undertake, now became a suitable vocation for middle-class women. Under the leadership of veteran reformer Dorothea Dix of the asylum movement (see Chapter 13), and in cooperation with the Sanitary Commission (and with the vocal support of Mother Bickerdyke), by the war's end more than 3,000 northern women had worked as paid army nurses and many more as volunteers.

One of the volunteers was Ellen Ruggles Strong of New York, who, over her husband's objections, insisted on nursing in the Peninsular campaign of 1862. "The little woman has come out amazingly strong during these two months," George Templeton Strong wrote in his diary with a mixture of pride and condescension. "Have never given her credit for a tithe of the enterprise, pluck, discretion, and force of character that she has shown. God bless her." Other women organized other volunteer efforts outside the Sanitary Commission umbrella. Perhaps the best known was Clara Barton, who had been a government clerk before the war and consequently knew a number of influential members of Congress. Barton organized nursing and the distribution of medical supplies; she also used her congressional contacts to force reforms in army medical practice, of which she was very critical.

Southern women were also active in nursing and otherwise aiding soldiers, though the South never boasted a single large-scale organization like the Sanitary Commission. The women of Richmond volunteered when they found the war on their doorstep in the summer of 1862. During the Seven Days Battles, thousands of wounded poured into Richmond; many died in the streets because there was no room for them in hospitals. Richmond women first established informal "roadside hospitals" to meet the need, and their activities expanded from there. As in the North, middle-class women at first faced strong resistance from army doctors and even their own families, who believed that a field hospital was "no place for a refined lady." Kate Cumming of Mobile, who nursed in Corinth, Mississippi, after the Battle of Shiloh, faced down such reproofs, though she confided to her diary that nursing wounded men was very difficult: "Nothing that I had ever heard or read had given me the faintest idea of the horrors witnessed here." She and her companion nurses persisted and became an important part of the Confederate medical services. For southern women, who had been much less active in the public life of their communities than their northern reforming sisters, this Civil War activity marked an important break with prewar tradition.

Although women had made important advances, most army nurses and medical support staff were men. One volunteer nurse was the poet Walt Whitman, who visited wounded soldiers in the hospital in Washington, D.C. Horrified at the suffering he saw, Whitman also formed a deep admiration for the "incredible

Nurse Ann Bell shown preparing medicine for a wounded soldier. Prompted by the medical crisis of the war, women such as Bell and "Mother" Bickerdyke actively participated in the war effort as nurses.

dauntlessness" of the common soldier in the face of slaughter and privation. While never denying the senselessness of the slaughter, Whitman nevertheless found hope in the determined spirit of the common man and woman.

The Life of the Common Soldier

The conditions experienced by the eager young volunteers of the Union and Confederate armies included massive, terrifying, and bloody battles, apparently unending, with no sign of victory in sight. Soldiers suffered from the uncertainty of supply, which left troops, especially in the South, without uniforms, tents, and sometimes even food. They endured long marches over muddy, rutted roads while carrying packs weighing fifty or sixty pounds. Disease was rampant in their dirty, verminous, and unsanitary camps, and hospitals were so dreadful that more men left them dead than alive. Many soldiers had entered military service with unrealistic, even romantic ideas about warfare. The Mexican-American War had been short and glorious (or at least far enough away to seem so), and the Revolutionary War was even more shrouded in myth. Reality was thus a rude shock, and not all soldiers reacted as nobly as those glorified by Walt Whitman. Desertion was common: an estimated one of every nine Confederate soldiers and one of every seven Union soldiers deserted. Unauthorized absence was another problem. At Antietam, Robert E. Lee estimated that unauthorized absence reduced his strength by a third to a half.

Another widespread phenomenon was fraternization between the two sides. A southern private, for example, wrote about how he celebrated the Fourth of July after the Seven Days Battles in 1862: "There are blackberries in the fields so our boys and the Yanks made a bargain not to fire at each other, and went out in the field, leaving one man on each post with the arms, and gathered berries together and talked over the fight, and traded tobacco and coffee and newspapers as peacefully and kindly as if they had not been engaged for...seven days in butchering one another." In October 1861 a Louisiana man wrote to his brother-in-law: "You spoke as if you had some notion of volunteering. I advise you to stay at home." Once the initial patriotic fervor had waned, attitudes such as his were increasingly common, both on the battlefield and at home.

This painting helped to establish the reputation of the young artist Winslow Homer, for in it he broke with the tradition of heroic battle scenes and focused instead on the psychology of defeat. In a landscape devastated by battle, three disarmed Confederate prisoners of war await the decision of a Union general on their future. The prisoners, although bedraggled, appear psychologically undefeated, evoking an expression of sympathy from their captor.

The Metropolitan Museum of Art, Gift of Mrs. Frank B. Porter.

Wartime Politics

In the earliest days of the war, Northerners had joined together in support of the war effort. Democrat Stephen A. Douglas, Lincoln's defeated rival, paid a visit to the White House to offer Lincoln his support, then traveled home to Illinois, where he addressed a huge rally of Democrats in Chicago: "There can be no neutrals in this war, only patriots— or traitors!" Within a month, Douglas was dead at age forty-eight. The Democrats had lost the leadership of a broad-minded man who might have done much on behalf of northern unity. By 1862 Democrats had split into two factions: the War Democrats and the Peace Democrats, or Copperheads (from the poisonous snake).

Despite the split in the party in 1860 and the secession of the South, the Democratic Party remained a powerful force in northern politics. It had received 44 percent of the popular vote in the North in the 1860 election and its united opposition to the emancipation of slaves explains much of Lincoln's equivocal action on this issue. But the Peace Democrats went far beyond opposition to emancipation, denouncing the draft, martial law, and the high-handed actions of "King Abraham." Echoing old complaints against the Whigs, Peace Democrats appealed to the sympathies of western farmers by warning that agriculture was being hurt by the Republican Party's tariff and industrial policies. At the same time, they appealed to urban workers and immigrants with racist warnings that Republican policies would bring a flood of black workers into northern cities.

The leader of the Copperheads, Clement Vallandigham, a former Ohio congressman, advocated an armistice and a negotiated peace that would "look only to the welfare, peace and safety of the white race, without reference to the effect that settlement may have on the African." Western Democrats, he threatened, might form their own union with the South, excluding New England with its radical abolitionists and high-tariff industrialists.

At the time, long before Grant captured Vicksburg and gained control of the Mississippi River, Lincoln could not afford to take Vallandigham's threats lightly. Besides, he was convinced that some Peace Democrats were members of secret societies—the Knights of the Golden Circle and the Sons of Liberty—that had been conspiring with the Confederacy. In 1862, Lincoln proclaimed that all people who discouraged enlistments in the army or otherwise engaged in disloyal practices would be subject to martial law. In all, 13,000 people were arrested and imprisoned, including Vallandigham, who was exiled to the Confederacy. Lincoln rejected all protests, claiming that his arbitrary actions were necessary for national security.

Lincoln also faced challenges from the radical faction of his own party. As the war continued, the Radicals gained strength: it was they who pushed for emancipation in the early days of the war and for harsh treatment of the defeated South after it ended. The most troublesome Radical was Salmon P. Chase, who in December 1862 caused a cabinet crisis when he encouraged Senate Republicans to complain that Secretary of State William Seward was "lukewarm" in his support for emancipation. This Radical challenge was a portent of the party's difficulties after the war, which Lincoln did not live to see—or prevent.

Economic and Social Strains on the North

Wartime needs caused a surge in northern economic growth, but the gains were unequally distributed. Early in the war, some industries suffered: textile manufacturers could not get cotton, and shoe factories that had made cheap shoes for slaves were without a market. But other industries boomed—bootmaking, shipbuilding, and the manufacture of woolen goods such as blankets and uniforms, to give just three examples. Coal mining expanded, as did ironmaking, especially the manufacture of iron rails for railroads. Agricultural goods were in great demand, promoting further mechanization of farming. The McCormick brothers grew rich from sales of their reapers. Once scorned as a "metal grasshopper," the ungainly-looking McCormick reaper made hand harvesting of grain a thing of the past and led to great savings in manpower. Women, left to tend the family farm while the

men went to war, found that with mechanized equipment they could manage the demanding task of harvesting.

Meeting wartime needs enriched some people honestly, but speculators and profiteers also flourished, as they have in every war. By the end of the war, government contracts had exceeded $1 billion. Not all of this business was free from corruption. New wealth was evident in every northern city. Harper's Monthly reported that "the suddenly enriched contractors, speculators, and stock-jobbers...are spending money with a profusion never before witnessed in our country." Some people were appalled at the spectacle of wealth in the midst of wartime suffering. Still, some of the new wealth went to good causes. Of the more than $3 million raised by the female volunteers of the United States Sanitary Commission, some came from gala Sanitary Fairs designed to attract those with money to spend.

For most people, however, the war brought the day-to-day hardship of inflation. During the four years of the war, the North suffered an inflation rate of 80 percent, or nearly 15 percent a year. This annual rate, three times what is generally considered tolerable, did much to inflame social tensions. Wages rose only half as much as prices, and workers responded by joining unions and striking. Thirteen occupational groups, among them tailors, coal miners, and railroad engineers, formed unions during the Civil War. Manufacturers, bitterly opposed to unions, freely hired strikebreakers (many of whom were African Americans, women, or immigrants) and formed organizations of their own to prevent further unionization and to blacklist union organizers. Thus both capital and labor moved far beyond the small, localized confrontations of the early industrial period. The formation of large-scale organizations, fostered by wartime demand, laid the groundwork for the national battle between workers and manufacturers that would dominate the last part of the nineteenth century.

Another major source of social tension was conscription. The Union draft, introduced in March 1863, was based on the theory that the very threat of coercion would stimulate reenlistments and encourage volunteering. It soon became clear, however, that coercion, backed by federal marshals, was necessary to fill the ranks. Especially unpopular was a provision in the draft law that allowed the hiring of substitutes or the payment of a commutation fee of $300. The most likely source of substitutes was recent immigrants who had not yet filed for citizenship and were thus not yet eligible to be drafted. It is estimated that immigrants (some of whom were citizens) made up 20 percent of the Union army. Substitution had been accepted in all previous European and American wars. It was so common that President Lincoln, though overage, tried to set an example by paying for a substitute himself. The Democratic Party, however, made substitution an inflammatory issue.

Pointing out that $300 was almost a year's wages for an unskilled laborer, they denounced the draft law (88 percent of Democratic congressmen had voted against it). They appealed to popular resentment by calling it "aristocratic legislation" and to fear by running headlines such as "Three Hundred Dollars or Your Life."

As practiced in the local communities, conscription was indeed often marred by favoritism and prejudice. Local officials called up many more poor than rich men and selected a higher proportion of immigrants than nonimmigrants. In reality, however, only 7 percent of all men called to serve actually did so. About 25 percent hired a substitute, another 45 percent were exempted for "cause" (usually health reasons), and another 20–25 percent simply failed to report to the community draft office. Nevertheless, by 1863 many northern urban workers believed that the slogan "a rich man's war but a poor man's fight," though coined in the South, applied to them as well.

A black man is lynched during the New York City Draft Riots in July 1863. Free black people and their institutions were major victims of the worst rioting in American history until then. The riots were less a protest against the draft than an outburst of frustration over urban problems that had been festering for decades.

The New York City Draft Riots

In the spring of 1863 there were protests against the draft throughout the North. Riots and disturbances broke out in many cities, and several federal enrollment officers were killed. The greatest trouble occurred in New York City between July 13 and July 16, 1863, where a wave of working-class looting, fighting, and lynching claimed the lives of 105 people, many of them African American. The rioting, the worst up to that time in American history, was quelled only when five units of the U.S. Army were rushed from the battlefield at Gettysburg, where they had been fighting Confederates the week before.

The riots had several causes. Anger at the draft and racial prejudice were what most contemporaries saw. George Templeton Strong, a staunch Republican, believed that the "brutal, cowardly ruffianism and plunder" was instigated by Confederate agents stirring up "the rabble" of "the lowest Irish day laborers." From a historical perspective, however, the riots had less to do with the war than with the urban growth and tensions described in Chapter 13. The Civil War made urban problems worse and heightened the visible contrast between the lives of the rich and those of the poor.

These tensions exploded, but were not solved, during those hot days in the summer of 1863.

Ironically, African American men, a favorite target of the rioters' anger, were a major force in easing the national crisis over the draft. Though they had been barred from service until 1863, African American volunteers ultimately composed one-tenth of the Union army. Nearly 200,000 black soldiers filled the manpower gap that the controversial draft was meant to address.

The Failure of Southern Nationalism

The war brought even greater changes to the South. As in the North, war needs led to expansion and centralization of government control over the economy. In many cases, Jefferson Davis himself initiated government control (over railroads, shipping, and war production, for example), often in the face of protest or inaction by governors who favored states' rights. The expansion of government brought sudden urbanization, a new experience for the predominantly rural South. The population of Richmond, the Confederate capital, almost tripled, in large part because the Confederate bureaucracy grew to 70,000 people. Because of the need for military manpower, a good part of the Confederate bureaucracy consisted of women, who were referred to as "government girls." All of this—government control, urban growth, women in the paid workforce—was new to Southerners, and not all of it was welcomed.

Even more than in the North, the voracious need for soldiers fostered class antagonisms. When small yeoman farmers went off to war, their wives and families struggled to farm on their own, without the help of mechanization, which they could not afford, and without the help of slaves, which they had never owned. But wealthy men could be exempted from the draft if they had more than twenty slaves. Furthermore, many upper-class Southerners—at least 50,000—avoided military service by paying liberally ($5,000 and more) for substitutes. In the face of these inequities, desertions from the Confederate army soared. One Mississippi soldier spoke for many when he said that "he did not propose to fight for the rich men while they were at home having a good time." But the rich men, the South's traditional ruling class, paid little attention to such complaints.

Worst of all was the starvation. The North's blockade and the breakdown of the South's transportation system restricted the availability of food in the South, and these problems were vastly magnified by runaway inflation. Prices in the South rose by an unbelievable 9,000 percent. Speculation and hoarding by the rich made matters even worse. Women and children were left destitute, and a government-sponsored civilian relief program was soon diverted to meet the pressing needs of the military. Ordinary people suffered. "It is folly for a poor mother to call on the rich people about here," one woman wrote bitterly. "Their hearts are of steel; they would sooner throw what they have to spare to the dogs than give it to a starving child."

In the spring of 1863 food riots broke out in four Georgia cities (Atlanta among them) and in North Carolina. In Richmond, more than a thousand people, mostly women, broke into bakeries and snatched loaves of bread, crying "Bread! Bread! Our children are starving while the rich roll in wealth!" When the bread riot threatened to turn into general looting, Jefferson Davis himself appealed to the crowd to disperse—but found he had to threaten the rioters with gunfire before they would leave. A year later, Richmond stores sold eggs for $6 a dozen and butter for $25 a pound. One woman wept, "My God! How can I pay such prices? I have seven children; what shall I do?"

Increasingly, the ordinary people of the South, preoccupied with staying alive, refused to pay taxes, to provide food, or to serve in the army. Soldiers were drawn home by the desperation of their families as well as the discouraging course of the war. By January 1865 the desertion rate had climbed to 8 percent a month.

At the same time, the life of the southern ruling class was irrevocably altered by the changing nature of slavery. By the end of the war, one-quarter of all slaves had fled to the Union lines, and those who remained often stood in a different relationship to their owners. As white masters and overseers left to join the army, white women were left behind on the plantation to cope with shortages, grow crops, and manage the labor of slaves. Lacking the patriarchal authority of their husbands, white women found that white-black relationships shifted, sometimes drastically (as when slaves fled) and sometimes more subtly. Slaves increasingly made their own decisions about when and how they would work, and they refused to accept the punishments that would have accompanied this insubordination in prewar years. One black woman, implored by her mistress not to reveal the location of a trunk of money and silver plate when the invading Yankees arrived, looked her in the eye and said, "Mistress, I can't lie over that; you bought that silver plate when you sold my three children."

Peace movements in the South were motivated by a confused mixture of realism, war weariness, and the animosity of those who supported states' rights and opposed Jefferson Davis. The anti-Davis faction was led by his own vice president, Alexander Stephens, who early in 1864 suggested a negotiated peace. Peace sentiment was especially strong in North Carolina, where more than a hundred public meetings in support of negotiations were held in the summer of 1863. Davis would have none of it, and he commanded enough votes in the Confederate Congress to enforce his will and to suggest that peace sentiment was traitorous. The Confederacy, which lacked a two-party system, had no official way to consider alternatives. Thus the peace sentiment, which grew throughout 1864, flourished outside the political system in secret societies such as the Heroes of America and the Red Strings. As hopes of Confederate victory slipped away, conflict expanded beyond the battlefield to include the political struggles that southern civilians were fighting among themselves.

THE TIDE TURNS

As Lincoln's timing of the Emancipation Proclamation showed, by 1863 the nature of the war was changing. The proclamation freeing the slaves struck directly at the southern home front and the civilian workforce. That same year, the nature of the battlefield war changed as well. McClellan's notion of a limited war with modest battlefield casualties was gone forever. The Civil War became the first total war.

The Turning Point of 1863

In the summer of 1863 the moment finally arrived when the North could begin to hope for victory. But for the Union army the year opened with stalemate in the East and slow and costly progress in the West. For the South, 1863 represented its highest hopes for military success and for diplomatic recognition by Britain or France.

Attempting to break the stalemate in northern Virginia, General Joseph "Fighting Joe" Hooker and a

Union army of 130,000 men attacked a Confederate army half that size at Chancellorsville in May. In response, Robert E. Lee daringly divided his forces, sending General Thomas "Stonewall" Jackson and 30,000 men on a day-long flanking movement that caught the Union troops by surprise. Although Jackson was killed (shot by his own men by mistake), Chancellorsville was a great Confederate victory. However, Confederate losses were also great: 13,000 men, representing more than 20 percent of Lee's army (versus 17,000 Union men).

Though weakened, Lee moved to the attack. In June, in his second and most dangerous single thrust into Union territory, he moved north into Maryland and Pennsylvania. His purpose was as much political as military: he hoped that a great Confederate victory would lead Britain and France to intervene in the war and demand a negotiated peace. The ensuing battle of Gettysburg, July 1–3, 1863, was another horrible slaughter. On the last day, Lee sent 15,000 men, commanded by George Pickett, to attack the heavily defended Union center. The charge was suicidal. When the Union forces opened fire at 700 yards, one southern officer reported, "Pickett's division just seemed to melt away....Nothing but stragglers came back." The next day a Union officer reported, "I tried to ride over the field but could not, for dead and wounded lay too thick to guide a horse through them."

Pickett's Charge, one historian has written, was the perfect symbol of the entire Confederate war effort: "matchless valor, apparent initial success, and ultimate disaster." Lee retreated from the field, leaving more than one-third of his army behind—28,000 men killed, wounded, or missing. Union general George Meade elected not to pursue with his battered Union army (23,000 casualties). "We had them in our grasp," Lincoln said in bitter frustration. "We had only to stretch forth our arms and they were ours. And nothing I could say or do could make the Army move." Nevertheless, Lee's great gamble had failed; he never again mounted a major offensive.

The next day, July 4, 1863, Ulysses S. Grant took Vicksburg, Mississippi, after a costly siege. The combined news of Gettysburg and Vicksburg dissuaded Britain and France from recognizing the Confederacy and checked the northern peace movement. It also tightened the North's grip on the South, for the Union now controlled the entire Mississippi River. In November, Generals Grant and Sherman broke the Confederate hold on Chattanooga, Tennessee, thereby opening the way to Atlanta.

Grant and Sherman

In March 1864, President Lincoln called Grant east and appointed him general in chief of all the Union

The Turning Point: 1863   *In June, Lee boldly struck north into Maryland and Pennsylvania, hoping for a victory that would cause Britain and France to demand a negotiated peace on Confederate terms. Instead, he lost the hard-fought battle of Gettysburg, July 1–3. The very next day, Grant's long siege of Vicksburg succeeded. These two great Fourth of July victories turned the tide in favor of the Union. The Confederates never again mounted a major offensive. Total Union control of the Mississippi now exposed the Lower South to attack.*

forces. Lincoln's critics were appalled. Grant was an uncouth Westerner (like the president) and (unlike the president) was rumored to have a drinking problem. Lincoln replied that if he knew the general's brand of whiskey he would send a barrel of it to every commander in the Union army.

Grant devised a plan of strangulation and annihilation. While he took on Lee in northern Virginia, he sent General William Tecumseh Sherman to defeat Confederate general Joe Johnston's Army of Tennessee, which was defending the approach to Atlanta. Both Grant and Sherman exemplified the new kind of warfare. They aimed to inflict maximum damage on the fabric of southern life,

Sherman's Campaign in Georgia, 1864   Ulysses S. Grant and William Tecumseh Sherman, two like-minded generals, commanded the Union's armies in the final push to victory. While Grant hammered away at Lee in northern Virginia, Sherman captured Atlanta in September (a victory that may have been vital to Lincoln's reelection) and began his March to the Sea in November 1864.

The Final Battles in Virginia, 1864–1865   In the war's final phase early in 1865, Sherman closed one arm of a pincers by marching north from Savannah while Grant attacked Lee's last defensive positions in Petersburg and Richmond. Lee retreated from them on April 2 and surrendered at Appomattox Court House on April 9, 1865.

hoping that the South would choose to surrender rather than face total destruction. This decision to broaden the war so that it directly affected civilians was new in American military history and prefigured the total wars of the twentieth century.

In northern Virginia, Grant pursued a policy of destroying civilian supplies. He said he "regarded it as humane to both sides to protect the persons of those found at their homes, but to consume everything that could be used to support or supply armies." One of those supports was slaves. Grant welcomed fleeing slaves to Union lines and encouraged army efforts to put them to work or enlist them as soldiers. He also cooperated with the efforts of groups like the New England Freedmen's Aid Society, which sent northern volunteers (many of them women) into Union-occupied parts of the South to educate former slaves. (The Freedmen's Bureau, authorized by Congress in March 1865, continued this work into Reconstruction. One of the northern teachers who

went south in 1866 to work for the bureau was Robert Fitzgerald, the former soldier.) But the most famous example of the new strategy of total war was General Sherman's 1864 march through Georgia.

Sherman captured Atlanta on September 2, 1864, after outmaneuvering and outfighting Johnson and his successor, John Bell Hood. Atlanta lay in ruins as Sherman and his troops entered the city. With the rest of Georgia now vulnerable, gloom enveloped the South. "Since Atlanta I have felt as if all were dead within me, forever," Mary Boykin Chesnut wrote in her diary. "We are going to be wiped off the earth."

In November, Sherman set out to march the 285 miles to the coastal city of Savannah, living off the land and destroying everything in his path. His military purpose was to tighten the noose around Robert E. Lee's army in northern Virginia by cutting off Mississippi, Alabama, and Georgia from the rest of the Confederacy. But his second purpose, openly stated, was to "make war so terrible" to the people of the South, to "make them so sick of war that generations would pass away before they would again appeal to it." Accordingly, he told his men to seize, burn, or destroy everything in their path (but, significantly, not to harm civilians).

One Union soldier wrote to his father, "You can form no idea of the amount of property destroyed by us on this raid....A tornado 60 miles in width from Chattanooga to this place 290 miles away could not have done half the damage we did." A southern woman supplied the details: "The fields were trampled down and the road was lined with carcasses of horses, hogs and cattle that the invaders, unable either to consume or to carry with them, had wantonly shot down to starve our people and prevent them from making their crops. The stench in some places was unbearable." It was estimated that Sherman's army did $100 million worth of damage. "They say no living thing is found in Sherman's track," Mary Boykin Chesnut wrote, "only chimneys, like telegraph poles, to carry the news of [his] attack backwards."

Terrifying to white southern civilians, Sherman was initially hostile to black Southerners as well. In the interests of speed and efficiency, his army turned away many of the 18,000 slaves who flocked to it in Georgia, causing a number to be recaptured and reenslaved. This callous action caused such a scandal in Washington that Secretary of War Edwin Stanton arranged a special meeting in Georgia with Sherman and twenty African American ministers who spoke for the freed slaves. This meeting in itself was extraordinary: no one had ever asked slaves what they wanted. Equally extraordinary was Sherman's response in Special Field Order 15, issued in January 1865: he set aside more than 400,000 acres of Confederate land to be given to the freed slaves in forty-acre parcels. This was war of a kind that white Southerners had never imagined.

The 1864 Election

The war complicated the 1864 presidential election, aggravating the usual political factionalism. Public opinion about Lincoln and the conduct of the war had been on a roller coaster, soaring to great heights with news of Union victories and plunging during long periods of stalemate. Just as in the Mexican-American War, the "instant news" provided by the telegraph and special correspondents pulled people out of their daily lives and fixed their attention on the war. But the Civil War was much larger and much nearer. Almost everyone had a son or a father or a brother at the front, or knew someone in their community who did. The war news was personal.

Lincoln was renominated during a low period. Opposed by the Radicals, who thought he was too conciliatory toward the South, and by Republican conservatives, who disapproved of the Emancipation Proclamation, Lincoln had little support within his own party. Secretary of the Treasury Salmon P. Chase, a man of immense ego, went so far as to encourage his supporters to propose him, rather than Lincoln, as the party's nominee.

The Democrats had an appealing candidate: General George McClellan, a war hero (always a favorite with American voters) who was known to be sympathetic to the South, although he was unwilling to endorse the plank of the Democratic Party platform that proclaimed the war a failure and proposed an armistice to end it. Other Democrats played shamelessly on the racist fears of the urban

This striking photograph by Thomas C. Roche shows a dead Confederate soldier, killed at Petersburg on April 3, 1865, only six days before the surrender at Appomattox. The new medium of photography conveyed the horror of the war with a gruesome reality to the American public.

working class, accusing Republicans of being "negro-lovers" and warning that racial mixing lay ahead.

A deeply depressed Lincoln fully expected to lose the election. "I am going to be beaten," he told an army officer in August 1864, "and unless some great change takes place badly beaten." A great change did take place: Sherman captured Atlanta on September 2. Jubilation swept the North: some cities celebrated with 100-gun salutes. Lincoln won the election with 55 percent of the popular vote. Seventy-eight percent of the soldiers voted for him rather than for their former commander. The vote probably saved the Republican Party from extinction. Furthermore, the election was important evidence of northern support for Lincoln's policy of unconditional surrender for the South. There would be no negotiated peace; the war would continue.

In many ways, Lincoln's reelection was extraordinary. Ordinary people and war-weary soldiers had voted to continue a difficult and divisive conflict. This was the first time in American history that the people had been able to vote on whether they were willing to continue wartime hardships, and that 45 percent of the electorate voted against Lincoln suggests how severe those hardships were.

Nearing the End

As Sherman devastated the lower South, Grant was locked in struggle with Lee in northern Virginia.

Grant did not favor subtle strategies. He bluntly said, "The art of war is simple enough. Find out where your enemy is. Get at him as soon as you can. Strike at him as hard as you can, and keep moving on." Following this plan, Grant eventually hammered Lee into submission, but at enormous cost. Lee had learned the art of defensive warfare (his troops called him "the King of Spades" because he made them dig trenches so often), and he inflicted heavy losses on the Union army in a succession of bloody encounters in the spring and summer of 1864: almost 18,000 at the battle of the Wilderness, more than 8,000 at Spotsylvania, and 12,000 at Cold Harbor. At Cold Harbor, Union troops wrote their names and addresses on scraps of paper and pinned them to their backs, so certain were they of being killed or wounded in battle. Grim and terrible as Grant's strategy was, it proved effective. Rather than pulling back after his failed assaults, he kept moving South, finally settling in for a prolonged siege of Lee's forces at Petersburg. The North's great advantage in population finally began to tell. There were more Union soldiers to replace those lost in battle, but there were no more white Confederates.

In desperation, the South turned to what had hitherto been unthinkable: arming slaves to serve as soldiers in the Confederate army. As Jefferson Davis said in February 1865, "We are reduced to choosing whether the negroes shall fight for or against us."

But—and this was the bitter irony—the African American soldiers and their families would have to be promised freedom or they would desert to the Union at the first chance they had. Even though Davis's proposal had the support of General Robert E. Lee, the Confederate Congress balked at first. As one member said, the idea was "revolting to Southern sentiment, Southern pride, and Southern honor." Another candidly admitted, "If slaves make good soldiers our whole theory of slavery is wrong." Finally, on March 13, the Confederate Congress authorized a draft of black soldiers—without mentioning freedom. Although two regiments of African American soldiers were immediately organized in Richmond, it was too late. The South never had to

Abraham Lincoln toured Richmond, the Confederate capital, just hours after Jefferson Davis had fled. This photograph, taken April 4, 1865, shows Yankee cavalry horses in the foreground and the smoldering city in the background. It gives a sense of the devastation suffered by the South and the immense task of rebuilding and reconciliation that Lincoln would not live to accomplish.

publicly acknowledge the paradox of having to offer slaves freedom so that they would fight to defend slavery.

By the spring of 1865, public support for the war simply disintegrated in the South. Starvation, inflation, dissension, and the prospect of military defeat were too much. In February, Jefferson Davis sent his vice president, Alexander Stephens, to negotiate terms at a peace conference at Hampton Roads. Lincoln would not countenance anything less than full surrender, although he did offer gradual emancipation with compensation for slave owners. Davis, however, insisted on southern independence at all costs. Consequently, the Hampton Roads conference failed and southern resistance faded away. In March 1865, Mary Boykin Chesnut recorded in her diary: "I am sure our army is silently dispersing. Men are going the wrong way all the time. They slip by now with no songs nor shouts. They have given the thing up."

Lincoln's assassination, just days after Lee's surrender at Appomattox, was a stunning blow. This lithograph shows the elaborate funeral cortege in New York City on April 25, 1865, just one of the many ceremonies that marked Lincoln's final trip to Springfield, Illinois, his burying place.

Appomattox

Grant's hammering tactics worked—slowly. In the spring of 1865 Lee and his remaining troops, outnumbered two to one, still held Petersburg and Richmond. Starving, short of ammunition, and losing men in battle or to desertion every day, Lee retreated from Petersburg on April 2. The Confederate government fled Richmond, stripping and burning the city. Seven days later, Lee and his 25,000 troops surrendered to Grant at Appomattox Court House. Grant treated Lee with great respect and set a historic precedent by giving the Confederate troops parole. This meant they could not subsequently be prosecuted for treason. Grant then sent the starving army on its way with three days' rations for every man. Jefferson Davis, who had hoped to set up a new government in Texas, was captured in Georgia on May 10. The war was finally over.

Death of a President

Sensing that the war was near its end, Abraham Lincoln visited Grant's troops when Lee withdrew from Petersburg on April 2. Thus it was that Lincoln came to visit Richmond, and to sit briefly in Jefferson Davis's presidential office, soon after Davis had left it. As Lincoln walked the streets of the burned and pillaged city, black people poured out to see him

and surround him, shouting "Glory to God! Glory! Glory! Glory!" Lincoln in turn said to Admiral David Porter: "Thank God I have lived to see this. It seems to me that I have been dreaming a horrid dream for four years, and now the nightmare is gone." Lincoln had only the briefest time to savor the victory. On the night of April 14, President and Mrs. Lincoln went to Ford's Theater in Washington. There Lincoln was shot at point-blank range by John Wilkes Booth, a Confederate sympathizer. He died the next day. For the people of the Union, the joy of victory was muted by mourning for their great leader. After a week of observances in Washington, Lincoln's coffin was loaded on a funeral train that slowly carried him back to Springfield. All along the railroad route, day and night, in small towns and large, people gathered to see the train pass and to pay their last respects. At that moment, the Washington community and the larger Union community were one and the same.

The nation as a whole was left with Lincoln's vision for the coming peace, expressed in the unforgettable words of his Second Inaugural Address:

> With malice toward none, with charity for all, with firmness in the right as God gives us to see the right, let us strive on to finish the work we are in, to bind up the nation's wounds, to care for him who shall have borne the battle and for his widow and his orphan, to do all which may achieve and cherish a just and lasting peace among ourselves and with all nations.

CHRONOLOGY

1861 March: Morrill Tariff Act
April: Fort Sumter falls; war begins
April: Mobilization begins
April–May: Virginia, Arkansas, Tennessee, and North Carolina secede
June: United States Sanitary Commission established
July: First Battle of Bull Run

1862 February: Legal Tender Act
February: Battles of Fort Henry and Fort Donelson
March: Battle of Pea Ridge
March: Battle of the *Monitor* and the *Merrimack*
March–August: George B. McClellan's Peninsular campaign
March: Battle of Glorieta Pass
April: Battle of Shiloh
April: Confederate Conscription Act
April: David Farragut captures New Orleans
May: Homestead Act
June–July: Seven Days Battles
July: Pacific Railway Act
July: Morrill Land Grant Act
August: Santee Sioux Uprising, Minnesota
September: Battle of Antietam
December: Battle of Fredericksburg

1863 January: Emancipation Proclamation
February: National Bank Act

March: Draft introduced in the North
March: Colonel Kit Carson sends 8,000 Navajos on the "Long Walk" to Bosque Redondo, New Mexico Territory
April: Richmond bread riot
May: Battle of Chancellorsville
June: French occupy Mexico City
July: Battle of Gettysburg
July: Surrender of Vicksburg
July: New York City Draft Riots
November: Battle of Chattanooga
November: Union troops capture Brownsville, Texas

1864 March: Ulysses S. Grant becomes general in chief of Union forces
April: Fort Pillow massacre
May: Battle of the Wilderness
May: Battle of Spotsylvania
June: Battle of Cold Harbor
September: Atlanta falls
November: Abraham Lincoln reelected president
November–December: William Tecumseh Sherman's March to the Sea

1865 April: Richmond falls
April: Robert E. Lee surrenders at Appomattox
April: Lincoln assassinated
December: Thirteenth Amendment to the Constitution becomes law

CONCLUSION

In 1865, a divided people had been forcibly reunited by battle. Their nation, the United States of America, had been permanently changed by civil war. Devastating losses among the young men of the country—the greatest such losses the nation was ever to suffer—would affect not only their families but all of postwar society. Politically, the deepest irony of the Civil War was that only by fighting it had America become

completely a nation. For it was the war that broke down local isolation. Ordinary citizens in local communities, North and South, developed a national perspective as they sent their sons and brothers to be soldiers, their daughters to be nurses and teachers. Then, too, the federal government, vastly strengthened by wartime necessity, reached the lives of ordinary citizens more than ever before. The question now was whether this strengthened but divided national community, forged in battle, could create a just peace.

REVIEW QUESTIONS

1. At the outset of the Civil War, what were the relative advantages of the North and the South, and how did they affect the final outcome?
2. In the absence of the southern Democrats, in the early 1860s the new Republican Congress was able to pass a number of party measures with little opposition. What do these measures tell you about the historical roots of the Republican Party? More generally, how do you think we should view legislation passed in the absence of the customary opposition, debate, and compromise?
3. The greatest problem facing Jefferson Davis and the Confederacy was the need to develop a true feeling of nationalism. Can the failure of this effort be blamed on Davis's weakness as a leader alone, or are there other causes?
4. In what ways can it be said that the actions of African Americans, both slave and free, came to determine the course of the Civil War?
5. Wars always have unexpected consequences. List some of these consequences both for soldiers and for civilians in the North and in the South.
6. Today, Abraham Lincoln is considered one of our greatest presidents, but he did not enjoy such approval at the time. List some of the contemporary criticisms of Lincoln, and evaluate them.

RECOMMENDED READING

Nina Brown Baker, *Cyclone in Calico: The Story of Mary Ann Bickerdyke* (1952). Mother Bickerdyke's wartime career is told in homely detail.

Iver Bernstein, *The New York City Draft Riots* (1990). A social history that places the famous riots in the context of the nineteenth century's extraordinary urbanization.

Paul Escott, *After Secession: Jefferson Davis and the Failure of Confederate Nationalism* (1978). A thoughtful study of Davis's record as president of the Confederacy.

Drew Gilpin Faust, *Mothers of Invention: Women of the Slaveholding South in the American Civil War* (1996). A major study that considers the importance of gender at the white South's "moment of truth."

Alvin Josephy, *The Civil War in the West* (1992). A long-needed study, by a noted western historian, of the course of the war in the Trans-Mississippi West.

William Quentin Maxwell, *Lincoln's Fifth Wheel: The Political History of the United States Sanitary Commission* (1956). A useful study of the major northern volunteer organization.

James M. McPherson, *The Negro's Civil War: How American Negroes Felt and Acted during the War for the Union* (1965). One of the earliest documentary collections on African American activity in wartime.

———, *Battle Cry of Freedom: The Civil War Era* (1988). An acclaimed, highly readable synthesis of much scholarship on the war.

———, *The Atlas of the Civil War* (1994). Detailed battle diagrams with clear descriptions.

Pauli Murray, *Proud Shoes: The Story of an American Family* (1956). Murray tells the proud story of her African American family and her grandfather, Robert Fitzgerald.

Phillip Shaw Paludan, *"A People's Contest": The Union at War, 1861–1865* (1988). A largely successful social history of the North during the war.

ADDITIONAL BIBLIOGRAPHY

The Lincoln Presidency and the Northern Home Front

Richard Franklin Bensel, *Yankee Leviathan: The Origins of Central State Authority in America, 1859–1877* (1991)

David Donald, *Liberty and Union* (1978)

Eric Foner, *Politics and Ideology in the Age of the Civil War* (1980)

George M. Frederickson, *The Inner Civil War: Northern Intellectuals and the Crisis of the Union* (1965)

J. Matthew Gallman, *The North Fights the Civil War: The Home Front* (1994)

Ernest A. McKay, *The Civil War and New York City* (1990)

James M. McPhersen, *Abraham Lincoln and the Second American Revolution* (1990)

Mark E. Neely, *The Fate of Liberty: Abraham Lincoln and Civil Liberties* (1991)

Phillip Shaw Paludan, *The Presidency of Abraham Lincoln* (1994)

William E. Parrish, *Turbulent Partnership: Missouri and the Union, 1861–1865* (1963)

James Rawley, *The Politics of Union: Northern Politics during the Civil War* (1974)

Heather Cox Richardson, *The Greatest Nation of the Earth: Republican Economic Policies during the Civil War* (1997)

Anne C. Rose, *Victorian America and the Civil War* (1992)

Joel Sibley, *A Respectable Minority: The Democratic Party in the Civil War Era, 1860–1868* (1977)

Lewis P. Simpson, *Mind and the American Civil War* (1989)

John L. Thomas, ed., *Abraham Lincoln and the American Political Tradition* (1986)

Hans L. Trefousse, *The Radical Republicans* (1968)

Thomas H. O'Connor, *Civil War Boston: Homefront and Battlefield* (1997)

Bell I. Wiley, *The Life of Johnny Reb* (1943)

———, *The Life of Billy Yank* (1952)

Maris A. Vinovskis, ed., *Toward a Social History of the American Civil War: Exploratory Essays* (1990)

T. Harry Williams, *Lincoln and His Generals* (1952)

Gary Wills, *Lincoln at Gettysburg: Words that Remade America* (1992)

The Death of Slavery

Herman Belz, *A New Birth of Freedom: The Republican Party and Freedmen's Rights, 1861–1866* (1976)

Ira Berlin, et al., *Slaves No More: Three Essays on Emancipation and the Civil War* (1992)

Ira Berlin, et al., eds., *Freedom, A Documentary History of Emancipation, 1861–1867,* Series 1, Volume I: *The Destruction of Slavery* (1985)

———, et al., eds. *Freedom, A Documentary History of Emancipation, 1861–1867,* Series 1, Volume II: *The Wartime Genesis of Free Labor: The Upper South* (1993)

———, et al., eds. *Freedom, A Documentary History of Emancipation, 1861–1867,* Series 1, Volume III: *The Wartime Genesis of Free Labor: The Lower South* (1990)

———, et al., eds. *Freedom, A Documentary History of Emancipation, 1861–1867,* Series 2: *The Black Military Experience* (1988)

John Hope Franklin, *The Emancipation Proclamation* (1963)

Benjamin Quarles, *The Negro in the Civil War* (1953)

Willie Lee Rose, *Rehearsal for Reconstruction: The Port Royal Experiment* (1964)

The Confederacy and the Southern Home Front

Steven V. Ash, *When the Yankees Came: Conflict and Chaos in the Occupied South 1861–1865* (1995)

Daniel W. Crofts, *Reluctant Confederates: Upper South Unionists in the Secession Crisis* (1989)

William C. Davis, *"A Government of Our Own": The Making of the Confederacy* (1994)

Wayne K. Durrill, *War of Another Kind: A Southern Community in the Great Rebellion* (1990)

Clement Eaton, *A History of the Southern Confederacy* (1954)

Drew Gilpin Faust, *The Creation of Confederate Nationalism* (1988)

Robert M. Myers, ed., *The Children of Pride: A True Story of Georgia and the Civil War* (1972)

Phillip S. Paludan, *Victims: A True History of the Civil War* (1981)

George C. Rable, *Civil Wars: Women and the Crisis of Southern Nationalism* (1989)

———, *The Confederate Republic: A Revolution against Politics* (1994)

Charles W. Ramsdell, *Behind the Lines in the Southern Confederacy* (1944)

James L. Roark, *Masters without Slaves: Southern Planters in the Civil War and Reconstruction* (1978)

Daniel E. Sutherland, *Seasons of War: The Ordeal of a Confederate Community 1861–1865* (1995)

Emory M. Thomas, *The Confederate Nation, 1861–1865* (1979)

LeeAnn Whites, *The Civil War as a Crisis in Gender: Augusta, Georgia, 1860–1890* (1995)

Bell I. Wiley, *The Plain People of the Confederacy* (1943)

The Fighting

Michael Barton, *Good Men: The Character of Civil War Soldiers* (1981)

Ken Burns, *The Civil War* (1990)

Bruce Catton, *A Stillness at Appomattox* (1953)

Shelby Foote, *The Civil War: A Narrative,* 3 vols. (1958–1974)

Joseph T. Glatthaar, *Forged in Battle: The Civil War Alliance of Black Soldiers and White Officers* (1990)

———, *The March to the Sea and Beyond: Sherman's Troops in the Savannah and Carolinas Campaign* (1985)

Mark Grimsley, *The Hard Hand of War: Union Policy toward Southern Civilians, 1861–1865* (1995)

Edward Hagerman, *The American Civil War and the Origins of Modern Warfare* (1988)

Gerald F. Linderman, *Embattled Courage: The Experience of Combat in the American Civil War* (1987)

Reid Mitchell, *The Vacant Chair: The Northern Soldier Leaves Home* (1993)

Allan Nevins, *The War for the Union,* 4 vols. (1959–71)

Edwin S. Redkey, ed., *A Grand Army of Black Men: Letters from African-American Soldiers in the Union Army, 1861–1865* (1992)

Charles Royster, *The Destructive War: William Tecumseh Sherman, Stonewall Jackson, and the Americans* (1991)

Biography

William C. Davis, *Jefferson Davis: The Man and His Hour* (1991)

William S. Feeley, *Grant: A Biography* (1980)

Thomas E. Schott, *Alexander H. Stephens of Georgia: A Biography* (1988)

Stephen W. Sears, *George B. McClellan: The Young Napoleon* (1988)

Emory M. Thomas, *Robert E. Lee: A Biography* (1995)

CHAPTER SEVENTEEN

RECONSTRUCTION

1863–1877

AMERICAN COMMUNITIES
Hale County, Alabama: From Slavery to Freedom in a Black Belt Community

On a bright Saturday morning in May 1867, 4,000 former slaves eagerly streamed into the town of Greensboro, bustling seat of Hale County in west-central Alabama. They came to hear speeches from two delegates to a recent freedmen's convention in Mobile and to find out about the political status of black people under the Reconstruction Act just passed by Congress. Tensions mounted in the days following this unprecedented gathering as military authorities began supervising voter registration for elections to the upcoming constitutional convention that would rewrite the laws of Alabama. On June 13, John Orrick, a local white, confronted Alex Webb, a politically active freedman, on the streets of Greensboro. Webb had recently been appointed a voter registrar for the district. Orrick swore he would never be registered by a black man, and shot Webb dead. Hundreds of armed and angry freedmen formed a posse to search for Orrick, but failed to find him. Galvanized by Webb's murder, 500 local freedmen formed a chapter of the Union League, the Republican Party's organizational arm in the South. The chapter functioned as both a militia company and a forum to agitate for political rights.

Violent political encounters between black people and white people were common in southern communities in the wake of the Civil War. The war had destroyed slavery and the Confederacy, but left the political and economic status of newly emancipated African Americans unresolved. Communities throughout the south struggled over the meaning of freedom in ways that reflected their particular circumstances. The 4 million freed people constituted roughly one-third of the total southern population, but the black–white ratio in individual communities varied enormously. In some places the Union army had been a strong presence during the war, hastening the collapse of the slave system and encouraging experiments in free labor. Other areas remained relatively untouched by the fighting. In some areas small farms prevailed; in others, including Hale County, large plantations dominated economic and political life.

West-central Alabama had emerged as a fertile center of cotton production just two decades before the Civil War. There African Americans, as throughout the South's black belt, constituted more than three-quarters of the population. The region was virtually untouched by fighting until the very end of the Civil War. But with the arrival of federal troops in the spring of 1865, African Americans in Hale County, like their counterparts elsewhere, began to challenge the traditional organization of plantation labor.

One owner, Henry Watson, found that his entire workforce had deserted him at the end of 1865. "I am in the midst of a large and fertile cotton growing country," Watson wrote to a partner.

"Many plantations are entirely without labor, many plantations have insufficient labor, and upon none are the laborers doing their former accustomed work." Black women refused to work in the fields, preferring to stay home with their children and tend garden plots. Nor would male field hands do any work, such as caring for hogs, that did not directly increase their share of the cotton crop.

Above all, freed people wanted more autonomy. Overseers and owners thus grudgingly allowed them to work the land "in families," letting them choose their own supervisors and find their own provisions. The result was a shift from the gang labor characteristic of the antebellum period, in which large groups of slaves worked under the harsh and constant supervision of white overseers, to the sharecropping system, in which African American families worked small plots of land in exchange for a small share of the crop. This shift represented less of a victory for newly freed African Americans than a defeat for plantation owners, who resented even the limited economic independence it forced them to concede to their black workforce.

Only a small fraction—perhaps 15 percent—of African American families were fortunate enough to be able to buy land. The majority settled for some version of sharecropping, while others managed to rent land from owners, becoming tenant farmers. Still, planters throughout Hale County had to change the old routines of plantation labor. Local African Americans also organized politically. In 1866 Congress had passed the Civil Rights Act and sent the Fourteenth Amendment to the Constitution to the states for ratification; both promised full citizenship rights to former slaves. Hale County freedmen joined the Republican Party and local Union League chapters. They used their new political power to press for better labor contracts, demand greater autonomy for the black workforce, and agitate for the more radical goal of land confiscation and redistribution. "The colored people are very anxious to get land of their own to live upon independently; and they want money to buy stock to make crops," reported one black Union League organizer. "The only way to get these necessaries is to give our votes to the [Republican] party . . . making every effort possible to bring these blessings about by reconstructing the State." Two Hale County former slaves, Brister Reese and James K. Green, won election to the Alabama state legislature in 1869.

It was not long before these economic and political gains prompted a white counterattack. In the spring of 1868, the Ku Klux Klan—a secret organization devoted to terrorizing and intimidating African Americans and their white Republican allies—came to Hale County. Disguised in white sheets, armed with guns and whips, and making nighttime raids on horseback, Klansmen flogged, beat, and murdered freed people. They intimidated voters and silenced political activists. Planters used Klan terror to dissuade former slaves from leaving plantations or organizing for higher wages.

With the passage of the Ku Klux Klan Act in 1871, the federal government cracked down on the Klan, breaking its power temporarily in parts of the former Confederacy. But no serious effort was made to stop Klan terror in the west Alabama black belt, and planters there succeeded in reestablishing much of their social and political control.

The events in Hale County illustrate the struggles that beset communities throughout the South during the Reconstruction era after the Civil War. The destruction of slavery and the Confederacy forced African Americans and white people to renegotiate their old economic and political roles. These community battles both shaped and were shaped by the victorious and newly expansive federal government in Washington. In the end, Reconstruction was only partially successful. Not until the "Second Reconstruction" of the twentieth-century civil rights movement would the descendants of Hale County's African Americans begin to enjoy the full fruits of freedom—and even then not without challenge.

Greensboro

FREEDOM TO SLAVES!

Whereas, the President of the United States did, on the first day of the present month, issue his *Proclamation* declaring "that *all persons held as Slaves in certain designated States, and parts of States, are, and henceforward shall be free,"* and that the Executive Government of the United States, including the Military and Naval authorities thereof, would recognize and maintain the freedom of said persons. *And Whereas,* the county of *Frederick* is included in the territory designated by the Proclamation of the President, in which the *Slaves should become free,* I therefore hereby notify the citizens of the city of Winchester, and of said County, of said Proclamation, and of my intention to maintain and enforce the same.

I expect all citizens to yield a ready compliance with the Proclamation of the Chief Executive, and I admonish all persons disposed to resist its peaceful enforcement, that upon manifesting such disposition by acts, they will be regarded as rebels in arms against the lawful authority of the Federal Government and dealt with accordingly.

All persons liberated by said Proclamation are admonished to abstain from all violence, and immediately betake themselves to useful occupations.

The officers of this command are admonished and ordered to act in accordance with said proclamation and to yield their ready co-operation in its enforcement.

R. H. Milroy,
Brig. Gen'l Commanding.

Winchester Va.
Jan. 5th, 1863.

A Union commander notifies the citizens of Winchester, Virginia, of President Abraham Lincoln's Emancipation Proclamation. Union officers throughout the South had to improvise arrangements for dealing with African Americans who streamed into Union army camps. For many newly freed slaves, the call for taking up "useful occupations" meant serving the Union forces in their neighborhoods as laborers, cooks, spies, and soldiers.

mule" that would soon capture the imagination of African Americans throughout the South. Sherman's intent was not to revolutionize southern society but to relieve the demands placed on his army by the thousands of impoverished African Americans who followed his march to the sea. By the summer of 1865 some 40,000 freed people, eager to take advantage of the general's order, had been settled on 400,000 acres of "Sherman land."

Conflicts within the Republican Party prevented the development of a systematic land distribution program. Still, Lincoln and the Republican Congress supported other measures to aid the emancipated slaves. In March 1865 Congress established the Freedmen's Bureau. Along with providing food, clothing, and fuel to destitute former slaves, the bureau was charged with supervising and managing "all the abandoned lands in the South and the control of all subjects relating to refugees and freedmen." The act that established the bureau also stated that forty acres of abandoned or confiscated land could be leased to freed slaves or white Unionists, who would have an option to purchase after three years and "such title thereto as the United States can convey." To guarantee the end of slavery once the war ended, Republicans drafted the Thirteenth Amendment, declaring that "neither slavery nor involuntary servitude, except as a punishment for crime . . . , shall

exist within the United States." This amendment passed both houses of Congress by January 1865 and was ratified by the necessary three-fourths of the states on December 18, 1865—eight months after Lee's surrender.

At the time of Lincoln's assassination, his Reconstruction policy remained unsettled and incomplete. In its broad outlines the president's plans had seemed to favor a speedy restoration of the southern states to the Union and a minimum of federal intervention in their affairs. But with his death the specifics of postwar Reconstruction had to be hammered out by a new president, Andrew Johnson of Tennessee, a man whose personality, political background, and racist leanings put him at odds with the Republican-controlled Congress.

Andrew Johnson and Presidential Reconstruction

Andrew Johnson, a Democrat and former slaveholder, was a most unlikely successor to the martyred Lincoln. By trade a tailor, educated by his wife, Johnson overcame his impoverished background and served as state legislator, governor, and U.S. senator. Throughout his career Johnson had championed yeoman farmers and viewed the South's plantation aristocrats with contempt. He was the only southern member of the U.S. Senate to remain loyal to the Union, and he held the planter elite responsible for secession and defeat. In 1862 Lincoln appointed Johnson to the difficult post of military governor of Tennessee. There he successfully began wartime Reconstruction and cultivated Unionist support in the mountainous eastern districts of that state.

In 1864 the Republicans, in an appeal to northern and border state "War Democrats," nominated Johnson for vice president. But despite Johnson's success in Tennessee and in the 1864 campaign, many Radical Republicans distrusted him, and the hardscrabble Tennessean remained a political outsider in Republican circles. In the immediate aftermath of Lincoln's murder, however, Johnson appeared to side with those Radical Republicans who sought to treat the South as a conquered province. "Treason is a crime and must be made odious," Johnson declared. "Traitors must be impoverished. . . . They must not only be punished, but their social power must be destroyed." The new president also hinted at indicting prominent Confederate officials for treason, disfranchising them, and confiscating their property.

Such tough talk appealed to Republicans. But support for Johnson quickly faded as the new president's policies unfolded. Johnson defined Reconstruction as the province of the executive, not the legislative branch, and he planned to restore the Union as quickly as possible. He blamed individual Southerners—the planter elite—rather than entire states for leading the South down the disastrous road to secession. In line with this philosophy, Johnson outlined mild terms for reentry to the Union.

In the spring of 1865 Johnson granted amnesty and pardon, including restoration of property rights except slaves, to all Confederates who pledged loyalty to the Union and support for emancipation. Fourteen classes of Southerners, mostly major Confederate officials and wealthy landowners, were excluded. But these men could apply individually for presidential pardons. The power to pardon his former enemies—the Old South's planter elite—gratified Johnson and reinforced his class bias. It also helped win southern support for his lenient policies, for Johnson pardoned former Confederates liberally. In September 1865 Johnson granted an average of a hundred pardons a day, and during his tenure he pardoned roughly 90 percent of those who applied. Significantly, Johnson instituted this plan while Congress was not in session.

Johnson also appointed provisional governors for seven of the former Confederate states, requiring them to hold elections for state constitutional conventions. Participation in this political process was limited to white people who had been pardoned or who had taken a loyalty oath. Johnson also called on state conventions to repudiate secession, acknowledge the abolition of slavery, and void state debts incurred during the war. By the fall of 1865 ten of the eleven Confederate states claimed to have met Johnson's requirements to reenter the Union. On December 6, 1865, in his first annual message to Congress, the president declared the "restoration" of the Union virtually complete. But a serious division within the federal government was taking shape, for the Congress was not about to allow the president free rein in determining the conditions of southern readmission.

Andrew Johnson used the term "restoration" rather than "reconstruction." A lifelong Democrat with ambitions to be elected president on his own in 1868, Johnson hoped to build a new political coalition composed of northern Democrats, conservative Republicans, and southern Unionists. Firmly committed to white supremacy, he opposed political rights for the freedmen. In 1866, after Frederick Douglass and other black leaders had met with him to discuss black suffrage, Johnson told an aide: "Those damned sons of bitches thought they had me in a trap! I know that damned Douglass; he's just like any nigger, and he would sooner cut a white man's throat than not." Johnson's open sympathy for his fellow white Southerners, his antiblack bias, and his determination to control the course of Reconstruction placed him on a collision course with the powerful Radical wing of the Republican Party.

The Radical Republican Vision

Most Radicals were men whose careers had been shaped by the slavery controversy. At the core of their thinking lay a deep belief in equal political rights and equal economic opportunity, both guaranteed by a powerful national government. They argued that once free labor, universal education, and equal rights were implanted in the South, that region would be able to share in the North's material wealth, progress, and fluid social mobility. Representative George W. Julian of Indiana typified the Radical vision for the South. He called for elimination of the region's "large estates, widely scattered settlements, wasteful agriculture, popular ignorance, social degradation, the decline of manufactures, contempt for honest labor, and a pampered oligarchy." This process would allow Republicans to develop "small farms, thrifty tillage, free schools, social independence, flourishing manufactures and the arts, respect for honest labor, and equality of political rights."

In the Radicals' view, the power of the federal government would be central to the remaking of southern society, especially in guaranteeing civil rights and suffrage for freedmen. In the most far-reaching proposal, Representative Thaddeus Stevens of Pennsylvania called for the confiscation of 400 million acres belonging to the wealthiest 10 percent of Southerners, to be redistributed to black and white yeomen and northern land buyers. "The whole fabric of southern society must be changed," Stevens told Pennsylvania Republicans in September 1865, "and never can it be done if this opportunity is lost. How can republican institutions, free schools, free churches, free social intercourse exist in a mingled community of nabobs and serfs? If the South is ever to be made a safe republic let her lands be cultivated by the toil of the owners."

Northern Republicans were especially outraged by the stringent "black codes" passed by South Carolina, Mississippi, Louisiana, and other states. These were designed to restrict the freedom of the black labor force and keep freed people as close to slave status as possible. Laborers who left their jobs before contracts expired would forfeit wages already earned and be subject to arrest by any white citizen. Vagrancy, very broadly defined, was punishable by fines and involuntary plantation labor. Apprenticeship clauses obliged black children to work without pay for employers. Some states attempted to bar African Americans from land ownership. Other laws specifically denied African Americans equality with white people in civil rights, excluding them from juries and prohibiting interracial marriages.

The black codes underscored the unwillingness of white Southerners to accept the full meaning of freedom for African Americans. Mississippi's version contained a catchall section levying fines and possible imprisonment for any former slaves "committing riots, routs, affrays, trespasses, malicious mischief, cruel treatment to animals, seditious speeches, insulting gestures, language, or acts, or assaults on any person, disturbance of the peace, exercising the function of a minister of

This wood engraving appeared in Frank Leslie's Illustrated Newspaper, May 5, 1864. It depicted "vagrant" African Americans in New Orleans being rounded up by the Provost Guard, in compliance with Louisiana's restrictive "Black Code." These types of images helped raise concerns in the North about the treatment of recently freed slaves.

the Gospel without a license . . . vending spiritous or intoxicating liquors, or committing any other misdemeanor, the punishment of which is not specifically provided for by law."

The Radicals, although not a majority of their party, were joined by moderate Republicans as growing numbers of Northerners grew suspicious of white southern intransigence and the denial of political rights to freedmen. When the Thirty-ninth Congress convened in December 1865, the large Republican majority prevented the seating of the white Southerners elected to Congress under President Johnson's provisional state governments. Republicans also established the Joint Committee on Reconstruction. After hearing extensive testimony from a broad range of witnesses, it concluded that not only were old Confederates back in power in the South but that black codes and racial violence required increased protection for African Americans.

As a result, in the spring of 1866 Congress passed two important bills designed to aid African Americans. The landmark Civil Rights bill, which bestowed full citizenship on African Americans, overturned the 1857 Dred Scott decision and the black codes. It defined all persons born in the United States (except Indian peoples) as national citizens, and it enumerated various rights, including the rights to make and enforce contracts, to sue, to give evidence, and to buy and sell property. Under this bill, African Americans acquired "full and equal benefit of all laws and proceedings for the security of person and property as is enjoyed by white citizens."

Congress also voted to enlarge the scope of the Freedmen's Bureau, empowering it to build schools and pay teachers, and also to establish courts to prosecute those charged with depriving African Americans of their civil rights. The bureau achieved important, if limited, success in aiding African Americans. Bureau-run schools helped lay the foundation for southern public education. The bureau's network of courts allowed freed people to bring suits against white people in disputes involving violence, nonpayment of wages, or unfair division of crops. The very existence of courts hearing public testimony by African Americans provided an important psychological challenge to traditional notions of white racial domination.

An angry President Johnson vetoed both of these bills. In opposing the Civil Rights bill, Johnson denounced the assertion of national power to protect African American civil rights, claiming it was a "stride toward centralization, and the concentration of all legislative powers in the national Government." In the case of the Freedmen's Bureau, Johnson argued that Congress lacked jurisdiction over the eleven unrepresented southern states. But Johnson's intemperate attacks on the Radicals—he damned them as traitors unwilling to restore the Union—united moderate and Radical Republicans and they succeeded in overriding the vetoes. Congressional Republicans, led by the Radical faction, were now unified in challenging the president's power to direct Reconstruction and in using national authority to define and protect the rights of citizens.

In June 1866, fearful that the Civil Rights Act might be declared unconstitutional and eager to settle the basis for the seating of southern representatives, Congress passed the Fourteenth Amendment. The amendment defined national citizenship to include former slaves ("all persons born or naturalized in the United States") and prohibited the states from violating the privileges of citizens without due process of law. It also empowered Congress to reduce the representation of any state that denied the suffrage to males over twenty-one. Republicans adopted the Fourteenth Amendment as their platform for the 1866 congressional elections and suggested that southern states would have to ratify it as a condition of readmission. President Johnson, meanwhile, took to the stump in August to support conservative Democratic and Republican candidates. His unrestrained speeches often degenerated into harangues, alienating many voters and aiding the Republican cause.

For their part, the Republicans skillfully portrayed Johnson and northern Democrats as disloyal and white Southerners as unregenerate. Republicans began an effective campaign tradition known as "waving the bloody shirt"—reminding northern voters of the hundreds of thousands of Yankee soldiers left dead or maimed by the war. In the November 1866 elections, the Republicans increased their majority in both the House and the Senate and gained control of all the northern states. The stage was now set for a battle between the president and Congress. Was it to be Johnson's "restoration" or Congressional Reconstruction?

Congressional Reconstruction and the Impeachment Crisis

United against Johnson, Radical and moderate Republicans took control of Reconstruction early in 1867. In March Congress passed the First Reconstruction Act over Johnson's veto. This act divided the South into five military districts subject to martial law. To achieve restoration, southern states were first required to call new constitutional conventions, elected by universal manhood suffrage. Once these states had drafted new constitutions, guaranteed African American voting rights, and ratified the Fourteenth Amendment, they were eligible for readmission to the Union. Supplementary legislation, also passed over the president's veto, invalidated the provisional governments established by Johnson, empowered the military to administer voter registration, and required an oath of loyalty to the United States.

Congress also passed several laws aimed at limiting Johnson's power. One of these, the Tenure of Office Act, stipulated that any officeholder appointed by the president with the Senate's advice and consent could not be removed until the Senate had approved a successor. In this way, congressional leaders could protect Republi-

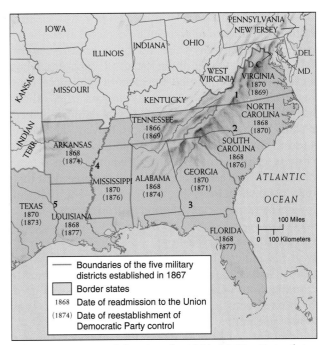

Reconstruction of the South, 1866–1877   *Dates for the readmission of former Confederate states to the Union and the return of Democrats to power varied according to the specific political situations in those states.*

cans, such as Secretary of War Edwin M. Stanton, entrusted with implementing Congressional Reconstruction. In August 1867, with Congress adjourned, Johnson suspended Stanton and appointed General Ulysses S. Grant interim secretary of war. This move enabled the president to remove generals in the field that he judged to be too radical and replace them with men who were sympathetic to his own views. It also served as a challenge to the Tenure of Office Act. In January 1868, when the Senate overruled Stanton's suspension, Grant broke openly with Johnson and vacated the office. Stanton resumed his position and barricaded himself in his office when Johnson attempted to remove him once again.

Outraged by Johnson's relentless obstructionism, and seizing upon his violation of the Tenure of Office Act as a pretext, Radical and moderate Republicans in the House of Representatives again joined forces and voted to impeach the president by a vote of 126 to 47 on February 24, 1868, charging him with eleven counts of high crimes and misdemeanors. To ensure the support of moderate Republicans, the articles of impeachment focused on violations of the Tenure of Office Act. The case against Johnson would have to be made on the basis of willful violation of the law. Left unstated were the Republicans' real reasons for wanting the president removed: Johnson's political views and his opposition to the Reconstruction Acts.

An influential group of moderate Senate Republicans feared the damage a conviction might do to the constitutional separation of powers. They also worried about the political and economic policies that might be pursued by Benjamin Wade, the president pro tem of the Senate and a leader of the Radical Republicans, who, because there was no vice president, would succeed to the presidency if Johnson were removed from office. Behind the scenes during his Senate trial, Johnson agreed to abide by the Reconstruction Acts. In May, the Senate voted 35 for conviction, 19 for acquittal—one vote shy of the two-thirds necessary for removal from office. Johnson's narrow acquittal established the precedent that only criminal actions by a president—not political disagreements—warranted removal from office.

The Election of 1868

By the summer of 1868, seven former Confederate states (Alabama, Arkansas, Florida, Louisiana, North Carolina, South Carolina, and Tennessee) had ratified the revised constitutions, elected Republican governments, and ratified the Fourteenth Amendment. They had thereby earned readmission to the Union. Though Georgia, Mississippi, Texas, and Virginia still awaited readmission, the presidential election of 1868 offered some hope that the Civil War's legacy of sectional hate and racial tension might finally ease.

Republicans nominated Ulysses S. Grant, the North's foremost military hero. An Ohio native, Grant had graduated from West Point in 1843, served in the Mexican War, and resigned from the army in 1854. Unhappy in civilian life, Grant received a second chance during the Civil War. He rose quickly to become commander in the western theater, and he later destroyed Lee's army in Virginia. Although his armies suffered terrible losses, Grant enjoyed tremendous popularity after the war, especially when he broke with Johnson. Totally lacking in political experience, Grant admitted after receiving the nomination that he had been forced into it in spite of himself: "I could not back down without leaving the contest for power for the next four years between mere trading politicians, the elevation of whom, no matter which party won, would lose to us, largely, the results of the costly war which we have gone through."

Significantly, at the very moment that the South was being forced to enfranchise former slaves as a prerequisite for readmission to the Union, the Republicans rejected a campaign plank endorsing black suffrage in the North. Their platform left "the question of suffrage in all the loyal States . . . to the people of those States." State referendums calling for black suffrage failed in eight northern states between 1865 and 1868, succeeding only in Iowa and Minnesota. The Democrats, determined to reverse Congressional Reconstruction, nominated Horatio Seymour, former governor of New York and a long-time foe of emancipation and supporter of states' rights. Democrats North and South exploited the race question to garner votes. Their platform blasted the Republicans for subjecting the nation "in time of profound peace, to military despotism and negro supremacy." The party sought "the abolition of the Freedmen's Bureau; and all political instrumentalities designed to secure negro supremacy."

Throughout the South, violence marked the electoral process. The Ku Klux Klan, founded as a Tennessee social club in 1866, emerged as a potent instrument of terror (see the opening of this chapter). In Louisiana, Arkansas, Georgia, and South Carolina the Klan threatened, whipped, and murdered black and white Republicans to prevent them from voting. This terrorism enabled the Democrats to carry Georgia and Louisiana, but it ultimately cost the Democrats votes in the North. In the final tally, Grant carried twenty-six of the thirty-four states for an electoral college victory of 214 to 80. But he received a popular majority of less than 53 percent, beating Seymour by only 306,000 votes. Significantly, more than 500,000 African American voters cast their ballots for Grant, demonstrating their overwhelming support for the Republican Party. The Republicans also retained large majorities in both houses of Congress.

In February 1869, Congress passed the Fifteenth Amendment, providing that "the right of citizens of the United States to vote shall not be denied or abridged . . . on account of race, color, or previous condition of servitude." Noticeably absent was language prohibiting the states from imposing educational, residential, or other qualifications for voting. Moderate Republicans feared that filling these discriminatory loopholes might make it difficult to obtain ratification for the amendment by the required three-quarters of the states. To enhance the chances of ratification, Congress required the three remaining unreconstructed states—Mississippi, Texas, and Virginia—to ratify both the Fourteenth and Fifteenth Amendments before readmission. They did so and rejoined the Union in early 1870. The Fifteenth Amendment was ratified in February 1870. In the narrow sense of simply readmitting the former Confederate states to the Union, Reconstruction was complete.

Woman Suffrage and Reconstruction

The battles over the political status of African Americans proved an important turning point for women as well. The Fourteenth and Fifteenth Amendments, which granted citizenship and the vote to freedmen, both inspired and frustrated women's rights activists. Many of these women had long been active in the abolitionist movement. During the war, they had actively supported the union cause through their work

OVERVIEW

RECONSTRUCTION AMENDMENTS TO THE CONSTITUTION, 1865–1870

Amendment and Date Passed by Congress	Main Provisions	Ratification Process (¾ of all states including ex-Confederate states required)
13 (January 1865)	Prohibited slavery in the United States	December 1865 (27 states, including 8 southern states)
14 (June 1866)	• Conferred national citizenship on all persons born or naturalized in the United States • Reduced state representation in Congress proportionally for any state disfranchising male citizens • Denied former Confederates the right to hold state or national office • Repudiated Confederate debt.	July 1868 (after Congress makes ratification a prerequisite for readmission of ex-Confederate states to the Union)
15 (February 1869)	Prohibited denial of suffrage because of race, color, or previous condition of servitude	March 1870 (ratification required for readmission of Virginia, Texas, Mississippi, and Georgia)

in the National Woman's Loyal League and the United States Sanitary Commission. Elizabeth Cady Stanton and Susan B. Anthony, two leaders with long involvement in both the antislavery and feminist movements, objected to the inclusion of the word "male" in the Fourteenth Amendment. "If that word 'male' be inserted," Stanton predicted in 1866, "it will take us a century at least to get it out."

Insisting that the causes of the African American vote and the women's vote were linked, Stanton, Anthony, and Lucy Stone founded the American Equal Rights Association in 1866. The group launched a series of lobbying and petition campaigns to remove racial and sexual restrictions on voting from state constitutions. In Kansas, for example, an old antislavery battlefield, the association vigorously supported two 1867 referendums that would have removed the words "male" and "white" from the state's constitution. But Kansas voters rejected both woman suffrage and black suffrage. Throughout the nation, the old abolitionist organizations and the Republican Party emphasized passage of the Fourteenth and Fifteenth Amendments and withdrew funds and support from the cause of woman suffrage. Disagreements over these amendments divided suffragists for decades.

The radical wing, led by Stanton and Anthony, opposed the Fifteenth Amendment, arguing that ratification would establish an "aristocracy of sex," enfranchising all men while leaving women without political privileges. In arguing for a Sixteenth Amendment that would secure the vote for women, they used racist and elitist appeals. They urged "American women of wealth, education, virtue, and refinement" to support the vote for women and oppose the Fifteenth Amendment "if you do not wish the lower orders of Chinese, Africans, Germans, and Irish, with their low ideas of womanhood to make laws for you and your daughters." Other women's rights activists, including Lucy Stone and Frederick Douglass, asserted that "this hour belongs to the Negro." They feared a debate over woman suffrage at the national level would jeopardize passage of the two amendments.

By 1869 woman suffragists had split into two competing organizations. The moderate American Woman Suffrage Association (AWSA), led by Lucy Stone, Julia Ward Howe, and Henry Blackwell, focused on achieving woman suffrage at the state level. It maintained close ties with the Republican Party and the old abolitionist networks, worked for the Fifteenth Amendment, and actively sought the support of men. The mor radical wing founded the all-female National Wo

Susan B. Anthony (1820–1906) and Elizabeth Cady Stanton (1815–1902), the two most influential leaders of the woman suffrage movement, ca. 1892. Anthony and Stanton broke with their longtime abolitionist allies after the Civil War when they opposed the Fifteenth Amendment. They argued that the doctrine of universal manhood suffrage it embodied would give constitutional authority to the claim that men were the social and political superiors of women. As founders of the militant National Woman Suffrage Association, Stanton and Anthony established an independent woman suffrage movement with a broader spectrum of goals for women's rights and drew millions of women into public life during the late nineteenth century.

Suffrage Association (NWSA). For the NWSA, the vote represented only one part of a broad spectrum of goals inherited from the Declaration of Sentiments manifesto adopted at the first women's rights convention held in 1848 at Seneca Falls, New York (see Chapter 13). Although women did not win the vote in this [...] did establish an independent suffrage move- [...] ally drew millions of women into polit- [...] in particular demonstrated that self- [...] mocratic participation in the public [...] for women's emancipation. Stanton [...] d the country, speaking to women's

audiences and inspiring the formation of suffrage societies. The NWSA's weekly magazine, *Revolution*, became a forum for feminist ideas on divorce laws, unequal pay, women's property rights, and marriage. The failure of woman suffrage after the Civil War was less a result of factional fighting than of the larger defeat of Radical Reconstruction and the ideal of expanded citizenship.

THE MEANING OF FREEDOM

For 4 million slaves, freedom arrived in various ways in different parts of the South. In many areas, slavery had collapsed long before Lee's surrender at Appomattox. In regions far removed from the presence of federal troops, African Americans did not learn of slavery's end until the spring of 1865. There were thousands of sharply contrasting stories, many of which revealed the need for freed slaves to confront their owners. One Virginia slave, hired out to another family during the war, had been working in the fields when a friend told her she was now free. "Is dat so?" she exclaimed. Dropping her hoe, she ran the seven miles to her old place, confronted her former mistress, and shouted, "I'se free! Yes, I'se free! Ain't got to work fo' you no mo'. You can't put me in yo' pocket now!" Her mistress burst into tears and ran into the house. That was all the former slave needed to see. But regardless of specific regional circumstances, the meaning of "freedom" would be contested for years to come.

The deep desire for independence from white control formed the underlying aspiration of newly freed slaves. For their part, most southern white people sought to restrict the boundaries of that independence. As individuals and as members of communities transformed by emancipation, former slaves struggled to establish economic, political, and cultural autonomy. They built on the twin pillars of slave culture—the family and the church—to consolidate and expand African American institutions and thereby laid the foundation for the modern African American community.

Emancipation greatly expanded the choices available to African Americans. It helped build confidence in their ability to effect change without deferring to white people. Freedom also meant greater uncertainty and risk. But the vast majority of African Americans were more than willing to take their chances. Many years later, one former Texas slave pondered the question "What I likes bes, to be slave or free?" She answered: "Well, it's dis way. In slavery I owns nothin' and never owns nothin'. In freedom I's own de home and raise de family. All dat cause me worryment and in slavery I has no worryment, but I takes de freedom."

Moving About

The first impulse of many emancipated slaves was to test their freedom. The simplest, most obvious way to do this involved leaving home. By walking off a plantation, coming and going without restraint or fear of punishment, African Americans could savor freedom. Throughout the summer and fall of 1865, observers in the South noted enormous numbers of freed people on the move. One former slave squatting in an abandoned tent outside Selma, Alabama, explained his feeling to a northern journalist: "I's want to be free man, cum when I please, and nobody say nuffin to me, nor order me roun'." When urged to stay on with the South Carolina family she had served for years as a cook, a slave woman replied firmly: "No, Miss, I must go. If I stay here I'll never know I am free."

Yet many who left their old neighborhoods returned soon afterward to seek work in the general vicinity, or even on the plantation they had left. Many wanted to separate themselves from former owners, but not from familial ties and friendships. Others moved away altogether, seeking jobs in nearby towns and cities. Many former slaves left predominantly white counties, where they felt more vulnerable and isolated, for new lives in the relative comfort of predominantly black communities. In most southern states, there was a significant population shift toward black belt plantation counties and towns after the war. Many African Americans, attracted by schools, churches, and fraternal societies as well as the army, preferred the city. Between 1865 and 1870, the African American population of the South's ten largest cities doubled, while the white population increased by only 10 percent.

Disgruntled planters had difficulty accepting African American independence. During slavery, they had expected obedience, submission, and loyalty from African Americans. Now many could not understand why so many former slaves wanted to leave despite urgent pleas to continue working at the old place. The deference and humility white people expected from African Americans could no longer be taken for granted. Indeed, many freed people went out of their way to reject the old subservience. Moving about freely was one way of doing this, as was refusing to tip one's hat to white people, ignoring former masters or mistresses in the streets, and refusing to step aside on sidewalks. After encountering an African American who would not step aside, Eliza Andrews, a Georgia plantation mistress, complained, "It is the first time in my life that I have ever had to give up the sidewalk to a man, much less to negroes!" When freed people staged parades, dances, and picnics to celebrate their new freedom, as they did, for example, when commemorating the Emancipation Proclamation, white people invariably condemned them angrily for "insolence," "outrageous spectacles," or "putting on airs."

The African American Family

Emancipation allowed freed people to strengthen family ties. For many former slaves, freedom meant the opportunity to reunite with long-lost family members. To track down relatives, freed people trekked to faraway places, put ads in newspapers, sought the help of Freedmen's Bureau agents, and questioned anyone who might have information about loved ones. Many thousands of family reunions, each with its own story, took place after the war. To William Curtis of Georgia, whose father had been sold to a Virginia planter, "that was the best thing about the war setting us free, he could come back to us." One North Carolina slave, who had seen his parents separated by sale, recalled many years later what for him had been the most significant aspect of freedom. "I has got thirteen great-gran' chilluns an' I know whar dey ever'one am. In slavery times dey'd have been on de block long time ago."

Thousands of African American couples who had lived together under slavery streamed to military and civilian authorities and demanded to be legally married. By 1870, the two-parent household was the norm for a large majority of African Americans. "In their eyes," a Freedmen's Bureau agent reported, "the work of emancipation was incomplete until the families which had been dispersed by slavery were reunited." For many freed people the attempt to find lost relatives dragged on for years. Searches often proved frustrating, exhausting, and ultimately disappointing. Some "reunions" ended painfully with the discovery that spouses had found new partners and started new families.

Emancipation brought changes to gender roles within the African American family as well. By serving in the Union army, African American men played a more direct role than women in the fight for freedom. In the political sphere, black men could now serve on juries, vote, and hold office; black women, like their white counterparts, could not. Freedmen's Bureau agents designated the husband as household head and established lower wage scales for women laborers. African American editors, preachers, and politicians regularly quoted the biblical injunction that wives submit to their husbands. African American men asserted their male authority, denied under slavery, by insisting their wives work at home instead of in the fields.

For years after 1865, southern planters complained about the scarcity of women and children available for field work. African American women generally wanted to devote more time than they had under slavery to caring for their children and to performing such domestic chores as cooking, sewing, gardening, and laundering. Yet African American women continued to work outside the home, engaging in seasonal field labor for wages or working a family rented plot. Most rural black families barely ek a living, and thus the labor of every family member was essential to survival. The key difference from slave times was that African American families themselves, not white masters and overseers, decided when and where women and children worked.

African American Churches and Schools

The creation of separate African American churches proved the most lasting and important element of the energetic institution building that went on in post-emancipation years. Before the Civil War, southern Protestant churches had relegated slaves and free African Americans to second-class membership. Black worshipers were required to sit in the back during services, they were denied any role in church governance, and they were excluded from Sunday schools. Even in larger cities, where all-black congregations sometimes built their own churches, the law required white pastors. In rural areas, slaves preferred their own preachers to the sermons of local white ministers who quoted Scripture to justify slavery and white supremacy. "That old white preachin' wasn't nothin'," former slave Nancy Williams recalled. "Old white preachers used to talk with their tongues without sayin' nothin', but Jesus told us slaves to talk with our hearts."

In communities around the South, African Americans now pooled their resources to buy land and build their own churches. Before these structures were completed, they might hold services in a railroad boxcar, where Atlanta's First Baptist Church began, or in an outdoor arbor, the original site of the First Baptist Church of Memphis. By late 1866 Charleston's African American community could boast of eleven churches in the city—five Methodist, two Presbyterian, two Episcopalian, one Baptist, and one Congregational. In rural areas, different denominations frequently shared the same church building. Churches became the center not only for religious life but for many other activities that defined the African American community: schools, picnics, festivals, and political meetings. They also helped spawn a host of organizations devoted to benevolence and mutual aid, such as burial societies, Masonic lodges, temperance clubs, and trade associations.

The church became the first social institution fully controlled by African Americans. In nearly every community ministers, respected for their speaking and organizational skills, were among the most influential leaders. By 1877 the great majority of black Southerners had withdrawn from white-dominated churches. In South Carolina, for example, only a few hundred black worshipers attended biracial churches, down from over 40,000 in the various Protestant denominations. Winning the allegiance of African American worshipers, among Methodists, the African Methodist

Episcopal Church, originally founded in 1816, gained ascendancy over white-dominated rivals. Black Baptist churches, with their decentralized and democratic structure and more emotional services, attracted the greatest number of freed people. By the end of Reconstruction the vast majority of African American Christians belonged to black Baptist or Methodist churches.

The rapid spread of schools reflected African Americans' thirst for self-improvement. Southern states had prohibited education for slaves. But many free black people managed to attend school, and a few slaves had been able to educate themselves. Still, over 90 percent of the South's adult African American population was illiterate in 1860. Access to education thus became a central part of the meaning of freedom. Freedmen's Bureau agents repeatedly expressed amazement at the number of makeshift classrooms organized by African Americans in rural areas. A bureau officer described these "wayside schools": "A negro riding on a loaded wagon, or sitting on a hack waiting for a train, or by the cabin door, is often seen, book in hand delving after the rudiments of knowledge. A group on the platform of a depot, after carefully conning an old spelling book, resolves itself into a class."

African American communities received important educational aid from outside organizations. By 1869 the Freedmen's Bureau was supervising nearly 3,000 schools serving over 150,000 students throughout the South. Over half the roughly 3,300 teachers in these schools were African Americans, many of whom had been free before the Civil War. Other teachers included dedicated northern white women, volunteers sponsored by the American Missionary Association (AMA). The bureau and the AMA also assisted in the founding of several black colleges, including Tougaloo, Hampton, and Fisk, designed to train black teachers. Black self-help proved crucial to the education effort. Throughout the South in 1865 and 1866, African Americans raised money to build schoolhouses, buy supplies, and pay teachers. Black artisans donated labor for construction, and black families offered room and board to teachers.

Land and Labor after Slavery

Most newly emancipated African Americans aspired to quit the plantations and to make new lives for themselves. Leaving the plantation was not as simple as walking off. Some freed people did find jobs in railroad building, mining, ranching, or construction work. Others raised subsistence crops and tended vegetable gardens as squatters. However, white planters tried to retain African Americans as permanent agricultural laborers. Restricting the employment of former slaves was an important goal of the black codes. For example, South Carolina legislation in 1865 provided that "no person of color shall pursue or practice the art, trade, or business of an artisan, mechanic, or shopkeeper, or any other trade employment, or business, besides that of husbandry, or that of a servant under contract for service or labor" without a special and costly permit.

The majority of African Americans hoped to become self-sufficient farmers. As *DeBow's Review* observed in 1869, the freedman showed "great anxiety to have his little home, with his horse, cow, and hogs, separate and apart from others." Many former slaves believed they were entitled to the land they had worked throughout their lives. General Oliver O. Howard, chief commissioner of the Freedmen's Bureau, observed that many "supposed that the Government [would] divide among them the lands of the conquered owners, and furnish them with all that might be necessary to begin life as an independent farmer." This perception was not merely a wishful fantasy. The Freedmen's Bureau Act of 1865 specifically required that abandoned land be leased for three years in forty-acre lots, with an option to buy. Frequent reference in the Congress and the press to the question of land distribution made the idea of "forty acres and a mule" not just a pipe dream but a matter of serious public debate.

Above all, African Americans sought economic autonomy, and ownership of land promised the most independence. "Give us our own land and we take care of ourselves," was how one former slave saw it. "But widout land, de ole massas can hire us or starve us, as dey please." At a Colored Convention in Montgomery, Alabama, in May 1867, delegates argued that the prop-erty now owned by planters had been "nearly all earned by the sweat of our brows, not theirs. It has been forfeited to the government by the treason of its owners, and is liable to be confiscated whenever the Republican Party demands it."

But by 1866 the federal government had already pulled back from the various wartime experiments involving the breaking up of large plantations and the leasing of small plots to individual families. President Johnson directed General Howard of the Freedmen's Bureau to evict tens of thousands of freed people settled on confiscated and abandoned land in southeastern Virginia, southern Louisiana, and the Georgia and South Carolina low country. These evictions created a deep sense of betrayal among African Americans. A former Mississippi slave, Merrimon Howard, bitterly noted that African Americans had been left with "no land, no house, not so much as a place to lay our head. . . . We were friends on the march, brothers on the battlefield, but in the peaceful pursuits of life it seems that we are strangers."

A variety of labor arrangements could be found in southern agriculture in the immediate postwar years. Each featured both advantages and disadvantages for planters and freed people. Writing in 1866, white planter Percy Roberts identified three distinct "systems of hire" for working the land: money wages, share wages, and sharecropping. Under both the money wage and share wage systems, planters contracted former slaves to work in large gangs, paying them either in

Leaving for Kansas, Harper's Weekly, May 17, 1879. *This drawing depicts a group of southern freedpeople on their way to Kansas. Black disillusionment following the end of Reconstruction led thousands of African Americans to migrate to Kansas, where they hoped to find the political rights, economic opportunities, and freedom from violence denied them in the South. Most of these "Exodusters" (after the biblical story of the Israelite Exodus from Egypt) lacked the capital or experience to establish themselves as independent farmers on the Great Plains. Yet few chose to go back to the South, where their former masters had returned to political and economic power.*

cash (money wage) or with a share of the crop that the workers divided among themselves (share wage). Freedmen's Bureau agents, who generally advocated the money wage arrangement, would often help freedmen negotiate labor contracts with planters. Planters tended to prefer the money wage system because it clearly defined laborers as hirelings and gave planters more direct control over the labor force—for example, by enabling them to discharge the hands they thought inefficient. Yet most planters were forced to adopt share wages at the insistence of black laborers who were adamantly opposed to serving as mere hirelings.

But both the money wage and share wage systems were unsatisfactory from the perspective of freed people. Both systems relied on the gang labor approach so reminiscent of slavery. And both systems often left African Americans at the mercy of unscrupulous planters who cheated them of their wages or fair

The Barrow Plantation, Oglethorpe County, Georgia, 1860 and 1881 (approx. 2,000 acres)   *These two maps, based on drawings from* Scribner's Monthly, *April 1881, show some of the changes brought by emancipation. In 1860 the plantation's entire black population lived in the communal slave quarters, right next to the white master's house. In 1881 black sharecropper and tenant families lived on individual plots, spread out across the land. The former slaves had also built their own school and church.*

shares. Above all, the deep desire for economic improvement and greater autonomy led many African Americans to press for an alternative. By the late 1860s, black people's resistance to working in gangs and their desire to establish independent homesteads forced planters into a compromise system, sharecropping, that emerged as the dominant form of working the land.

Under sharecropping arrangements, individual families contracted with landowners to be responsible for a specific plot. Large plantations were thus broken into family-sized farms. Generally, sharecropper families received one-third of the year's crop if the owner furnished implements, seed, and draft animals, or one-half if they provided their own supplies. African Americans preferred sharecropping to gang labor, as it allowed families to set their own hours and tasks and offered freedom from white supervision and control. For planters, the system stabilized the work force by requiring sharecroppers to remain until the harvest and to employ all family members. It also offered a way around the chronic shortage of cash and credit that plagued the postwar South. But as the *Southern Argus* of Selma, Alabama, editorialized, sharecropping was "an unwilling concession to the freedmen's desire to become a proprietor. . . . It is not a voluntary association from similarity of aims and interests." Freed people did not aspire to sharecropping. Owning land outright or tenant farming (renting land) were both more desirable. But though black sharecroppers clearly enjoyed more autonomy than in the past, the vast majority never achieved economic independence or land ownership. They remained a largely subordinate agricultural labor force.

Sharecropping came to dominate the southern agricultural economy and African American life in particular. By 1880 about 80 percent of the land in the black belt states—Mississippi, Alabama, and Georgia—had been divided into family-sized farms. Nearly three-quarters of black Southerners were sharecroppers. Through much of the black belt, family and community were one. Often several families worked adjoining parcels of land in common, pooling their labor in order to get by. Men usually oversaw crop production. Women went to the fields seasonally during planting or harvesting, but they mainly tended to household chores and child care. In addition, women frequently held jobs that might bring in cash, such as raising chickens or taking in laundry. The cotton harvest engaged all members of the community, from the oldest to the youngest. Cotton picking remained a difficult, labor-intensive task that took priority over all other work.

The Origins of African American Politics

Although the desire for autonomy had led African Americans to pursue their economic and religious goals largely apart from white people, inclusion rather than separation was the objective of early African American political activity. The greatest political activity by African Americans occurred in areas occupied by Union forces during the war. In 1865 and 1866, African Americans throughout the South organized scores of mass meetings, parades, and petitions that demanded civil equality and the right to vote. In the cities, the growing web of churches and fraternal societies helped bolster early efforts at political organization.

Hundreds of African American delegates, selected by local meetings or churches, attended statewide political conventions held throughout the South in 1865 and 1866. Previously free African Americans, as well as black ministers, artisans, and veterans of the Union army, tended to dominate these proceedings, setting a pattern that would hold throughout Reconstruction. Convention debates sometimes reflected the tensions within African American communities, such as friction between poorer former slaves and better-off free black people, or between lighter- and darker-skinned African Americans. But most of these state gatherings concentrated on passing resolutions on issues that united all African Americans. The central concerns were suffrage and equality before the law. Black Southerners firmly proclaimed their identification with the nation's history and republican traditions. The 1865 North Carolina freedmen's convention was typical in describing universal manhood suffrage as "an essential and inseparable element of self-government." It also praised the Declaration of Independence as "the broadest, the deepest, the most comprehensive and truthful definition of human freedom that was ever given to the world."

The passage of the First Reconstruction Act in 1867 encouraged even more political activity among African Americans. The military started registering the South's electorate, ultimately enrolling approximately 735,000 black and 635,000 white voters in the ten unreconstructed states. Five states—Alabama, Florida, Louisiana, Mississippi, and South Carolina—had black electoral majorities. Fewer than half the registered white voters participated in the elections for state constitutional conventions in 1867 and 1868. In contrast, four-fifths of the registered black voters cast ballots in these elections. Much of this new African American political activism was channeled through local Union League chapters throughout the South. However, as the fate of Alex Webb in Hale County, Alabama, again makes clear, few whites welcomed this activism.

Begun during the war as a northern, largely white middle-class patriotic club, the Union League now became the political voice of the former slaves. Union League chapters brought together local African Americans, soldiers, and Freedmen's Bureau agents to demand the vote and an end to legal discrimination

Electioneering at the South, Harper's Weekly, July 25, 1868. *Throughout the Reconstruction-era South, newly freed slaves took a keen interest in both local and national political affairs. The presence of women and children at these campaign gatherings illustrates the importance of contemporary political issues to the entire African American community.*

against African Americans. It brought out African American voters, instructed freedmen in the rights and duties of citizenship, and promoted Republican candidates. Not surprisingly, newly enfranchised freedmen voted Republican and formed the core of the Republican Party in the South.

In 1867 and 1868, the promise of Radical Reconstruction enlarged the scope of African American political participation and brought new leaders to the fore. Many were teachers, preachers, or others with useful skills, such as literacy. For most ordinary African Americans, politics was inseparable from economic issues, especially the land question. Grassroots political organizations frequently intervened in local disputes with planters over the terms of labor contracts. African American political groups closely followed the congressional debates over Reconstruction policy and agitated for land confiscation and distribution. Perhaps most important, politics was the only arena where black and white Southerners might engage each other on an equal basis. As the delegates to an Alabama convention asserted in 1867: "We claim exactly the same rights, privileges and immunities as are enjoyed by white men—we ask nothing more and will be content with nothing less. . . . The law no longer knows white nor black, but simply men, and consequently we are entitled to ride in public conveyances, hold office, sit on juries and do everything else which we have in the past been prevented from doing solely on the ground of color."

SOUTHERN POLITICS AND SOCIETY

By the summer of 1868, when the South had returned to the Union, the majority of Republicans believed the task of Reconstruction to be finished. Ultimately, they put their faith in a political solution to the problems facing the vanquished South. That meant nurturing a viable two-party system in the southern states, where no Republican Party had ever existed. If that could be accomplished, Republicans and Democrats would compete for votes, offices, and influence, just as they did in northern states. Most Republican congressmen were moderates, conceiving Reconstruction in limited terms. They rejected radical calls for confiscation and redistribution of land, as well as permanent military rule of the South. The Reconstruction Acts of 1867 and 1868 laid out the requirements for the readmission of southern states, along with the procedures for forming and electing new governments.

Yet over the next decade the political structure created in the southern states proved too restricted and fragile to sustain itself. Republicans had to employ radical means to protect their essentially conservative goals. To most southern whites the active participation of African Americans in politics seemed extremely dangerous. Federal troops were needed to protect Republican governments and their supporters from violent opposition. Congressional action to monitor southern elections and protect black voting rights became routine. Despite initial successes, southern Republicanism proved an unstable coalition of often conflicting elements, unable to sustain effective power for very long. By 1877, Democrats had regained political control of all the former Confederate states.

Southern Republicans

Three major groups composed the fledgling Republican coalition in the postwar South. African American voters made up a large majority of southern Republicans throughout the Reconstruction era. Yet African Americans outnumbered whites in only three southern states—South Carolina, Mississippi, and Louisiana. They made up roughly one-quarter of the population in Texas, Tennessee, and Arkansas, and between 40 and 50 percent in Virginia, North Carolina, Alabama, Florida, and Georgia. Thus, Republicans would have to attract white support to win elections and sustain power.

A second group consisted of white Northerners, derisively called "carpetbaggers" by native white Southerners. One Democratic congressman in 1871 said the term "applied to the office seeker from the North who came here seeking office by the negroes, by arraying their political passions and prejudices against the white people of the community." In fact, most carpet-baggers combined a desire for personal gain with a commitment to reform the "unprogressive" South by developing its material resources and introducing Yankee institutions such as free labor and free public schools. Most were veterans of the Union army who stayed in the South after the war. Others included Freedmen's Bureau agents and businessmen who had invested capital in cotton plantations and other enterprises.

Carpetbaggers tended to be well educated and from the middle class. Albert Morgan, for example, was an army veteran from Ohio who settled in Mississippi after the war. When he and his brother failed at running a cotton plantation and sawmill, Morgan became active in Republican politics as a way to earn a living. He won election to the state constitutional convention, became a power in the state legislature, and risked his life to keep the Republican organization alive in the Mississippi delta region. Although they made up a tiny percentage of the population, carpetbaggers played a disproportionately large role in southern politics. They won a large share of Reconstruction offices, particularly in Florida, South Carolina, and Louisiana and in areas with large African American constituencies.

The third major group of southern Republicans were the native whites pejoratively termed "scalawags." They had even more diverse backgrounds and motives than the northern-born Republicans. Some were prominent prewar Whigs who saw the Republican Party as their best chance to regain political influence. Others viewed the party as an agent of modernization and economic expansion. "Yankees and Yankee notions are just what we want in this country," argued Thomas Settle of North Carolina. "We want their capital to build factories and workshops. We want their intelligence, their energy and enterprise." Their greatest influence lay in the up-country strongholds of southern Unionism, such as eastern Tennessee, western North Carolina, and northern Alabama. Loyalists during the war, traditional enemies of the planter elite (most were small farmers), these white Southerners looked to the Republican Party for help in settling old scores and relief from debt and wartime devastation.

Deep contradictions strained the alliance of these three groups. Southern Republicans touted themselves as the "party of progress and civilization" and promised a new era of material progress for the region. Republican state conventions in 1867 and 1868 voiced support for internal improvements, public schools, debt relief, and railroad building. Yet few white Southerners identified with the political and economic aspirations of African Americans. Nearly every party convention split between "confiscation radicals" (generally African Americans) and moderate elements committed to white

control of the party and to economic development that offered more to outside investors than to impoverished African Americans and poor whites.

Reconstructing the States: A Mixed Record

With the old Confederate leaders barred from political participation, and with carpetbaggers and newly enfranchised African Americans representing many of the plantation districts, Republicans managed to dominate the ten southern constitutional conventions of 1867–69. Well-educated carpetbaggers usually chaired the important committees and drafted key provisions of the new constitutions. Most of the delegates were southern white Republicans. African Americans formed a majority of the conventions in Louisiana and South Carolina, but they were generally under-represented. In all, there were 258 African Americans among the 1,027 convention delegates at the ten conventions.

This poster, ca. 1880, honored seven prominent ex-slaves, including U.S. Senators Hiram R. Revels and Blanche K. Bruce, both representing Mississippi. In the center is Frederick Douglass. This poster was typical of many other Reconstruction-era prints celebrating the entry of African Americans into state and national legislatures.

Most of the conventions produced constitutions that expanded democracy and the public role of the state. The new documents guaranteed the political and civil rights of African Americans, and they abolished property qualifications for officeholding and jury service, as well as imprisonment for debt. They created the first state-funded systems of education in the South, to be administered by state commissioners. The new constitutions also mandated establishment of orphanages, penitentiaries, and homes for the insane. The changes wrought in the South's political landscape seemed quite radical to many. In 1868, only three years after the end of the war, Republicans came to power in most of the southern states. By 1869 new constitutions had been ratified in all the old Confederate states. "These constitutions and governments," one South Carolina Democratic newspaper vowed bitterly, "will last just as long as the bayonets which ushered them into being, shall keep them in existence, and not one day longer."

Republican governments in the South faced a continual crisis of legitimacy that limited their ability to legislate change. They had to balance reform against the need to gain acceptance, especially by white Southerners. Their achievements were thus mixed. In the realm of race relations there was a clear thrust toward equal rights and against discrimination. Republican legislatures followed up the federal Civil Rights Act of 1866 with various antidiscrimination clauses in new constitutions and laws prescribing harsh penalties for civil rights violations. While most African Americans supported autonomous African American churches, fraternal societies, and schools, they insisted that the state be color-blind. African Americans could now be employed in police forces and fire departments, serve on juries, school boards, and city councils, and hold public office at all levels of government.

Segregation, though, became the norm in public school systems. African American leaders often accepted segregation because they feared that insistence on integrated education would jeopardize funding for the new school systems. They generally agreed with Frederick Douglass that separate schools were "infinitely superior" to no schools at all. So while they opposed constitutional language requiring racial segregation in schools, most African Americans were less interested in the abstract ideal of integrated education than in ensuring educational opportunities for their children and employment for African American teachers. Many, in fact, believed all-black schools offered a better chance of securing these goals.

Patterns of discrimination persisted. Demands by African Americans to prohibit segregation in railroad cars, steamboats, theaters, and other public spaces revealed and heightened the divisions within the Republican Party. Moderate white Republicans feared such laws would only further alienate potential white supporters. But by the early 1870s, as black influence and assertiveness grew, laws guaranteeing equal access to transportation and public accommodation were passed in many states. By and large, though, such civil rights laws were difficult to enforce in local communities.

In economic matters, Republican governments failed to fulfill African Americans' hopes of obtaining land. Few former slaves possessed the cash to buy land in the open market, and they looked to the state for help. Republicans tried to weaken the plantation system and promote black ownership by raising taxes on land. Yet even when state governments seized land for nonpayment of taxes, the property was never used to help create black homesteads. In Mississippi, for example, 6 million acres, or about 20 percent of the land, had been forfeited by 1875. Yet virtually all of it found its way back to the original owners after they paid minimal penalties.

Republican leaders emphasized the "gospel of prosperity" as the key to improving the economic fortunes of all Southerners, black and white. Essentially, they envisioned promoting northern-style capitalist development—factories, large towns, and diversified agriculture—through state aid. Much Republican state lawmaking was devoted to encouraging railroad construction. Between 1868 and 1873 state legislatures passed hundreds of bills promoting railroads. Most of the government aid consisted not of direct cash subsidies but of official endorsements of a company's bonds. This government backing gave railroad companies credibility and helped them raise capital. In exchange, states received liens on railroads as security against defaults on payments to bondholders.

Between 1868 and 1872 the southern railroad system was rebuilt and over 3,000 new miles of track added, an increase of almost 40 percent. But in spite of all the new laws, it proved impossible to attract significant amounts of northern and European investment capital. The obsession with railroads drew resources from education and other programs. As in the North, it also opened the doors to widespread corruption and bribery of public officials. Finally, the frenzy of railroad promotion soon led to an overextension of credit and to many bankruptcies, saddling Republican governments with enormous debts. Railroad failures eroded public confidence in the Republicans' ability to govern. The "gospel of prosperity" ultimately failed to modernize the economy or solidify the Republican Party in the South.

White Resistance and "Redemption"

The emergence of a Republican Party in the reconstructed South brought two parties but not a two-party system to the region. The opponents of Reconstruction, the Democrats, refused to acknowledge Republi-

The Ku Klux Klan emerged as a potent political and social force during Reconstruction, terrorizing freedpeople and their white allies. An 1868 Klan warning threatens Louisiana governor Henry C. Warmoth with death. Warmoth, an Illinois-born "carpetbagger," was the state's first Republican governor. Two Alabama Klansmen, photographed in 1868, wear white hoods to protect their identities.

cans' right to participate in southern political life. In their view, the Republican Party, supported primarily by the votes of former slaves, was the partisan instrument of the northern Congress. Since Republicans controlled state governments, this denial of legitimacy meant, in effect, a rejection of state authority itself. In each state, Republicans were split between those who urged conciliation in an effort to gain white acceptance and those who emphasized consolidating the party under the protection of the military.

From 1870 to 1872 the Ku Klux Klan fought an ongoing terrorist campaign against Reconstruction governments and local leaders. Although not centrally organized, the Klan was a powerful presence in nearly every southern state. It acted as a kind of guerrilla military force in the service of the Democratic Party, the planter class, and all those who sought the restoration of white supremacy. Klansmen employed violence to intimidate African Americans and white Republicans, murdering innocent people, driving them from their homes, and destroying their property. Planters sometimes employed Klansmen to enforce labor discipline

by driving African Americans off plantations to deprive them of their harvest share.

In October 1870, after Republicans carried Laurens County in South Carolina, bands of white people drove 150 African Americans from their homes and murdered 13 black and white Republican activists. In March 1871, three African Americans were arrested in Meridian, Mississippi, for giving "incendiary" speeches. At their court hearing, Klansmen killed two of the defendants and the Republican judge, and thirty more African Americans were murdered in a day of rioting. The single bloodiest episode of Reconstruction era violence took place in Colfax, Louisiana, on Easter Sunday 1873. Nearly 100 African Americans were murdered after they failed to hold a besieged courthouse during a contested election. One former Confederate officer observed that the Klan's goal was "to defy the reconstructed State Governments, to treat them with contempt, and show that they have no real existence."

Southern Republicans looked to Washington for help. In 1870 and 1871 Congress passed three Enforcement Acts designed to counter racial terrorism.

These declared interference with voting a federal offense, provided for federal supervision of voting, and authorized the president to send the army and suspend the writ of habeas corpus in districts declared to be in a state of insurrection. The most sweeping measure was the Ku Klux Klan Act of April 1871, which made the violent infringement of civil and political rights a federal crime punishable by the national government. Attorney General Amos T. Akerman prosecuted hundreds of Klansmen in North Carolina and Mississippi. In October 1871 President Grant sent federal troops to occupy nine South Carolina counties and round up thousands of Klan members. By the election of 1872 the federal government's intervention had helped break the Klan and restore a semblance of law and order .

The Civil Rights Act of 1875 outlawed racial discrimination in theaters, hotels, railroads, and other public places. But the law proved more an assertion of principle than a direct federal intervention in southern affairs. Enforcement required African Americans to take their cases to the federal courts, a costly and time-consuming procedure.

As wartime idealism faded, northern Republicans became less inclined toward direct intervention in southern affairs. They had enough trouble retaining political control in the North. In 1874 the Democrats gained a majority in the House of Representatives for the first time since 1856. Key northern states also began to fall to the Democrats. Northern Republicans slowly abandoned the freedmen and their white allies in the South. Southern Democrats were also able to exploit a deepening fiscal crisis by blaming Republicans for excessive extension of public credit and the sharp increase in tax rates. Republican governments had indeed spent public money for new state school systems, orphanages, roads, and other internal improvements.

Gradually, conservative Democrats "redeemed" one state after another. Virginia and Tennessee led the way in 1869, North Carolina in 1870, Georgia in 1871, Texas in 1873, and Alabama and Arkansas in 1874. In Mississippi, white conservatives employed violence and intimidation to wrest control in 1875 and "redeemed" the state the following year. Republican infighting in Louisiana in 1873 and 1874 led to a series of contested election results, including bloody clashes between black militia and armed whites, and finally to "redemption" by the Democrats in 1877. Once these states returned to Democratic rule, African Americans faced obstacles to voting, more stringent controls on plantation labor, and deep cuts in social services.

Several Supreme Court rulings involving the Fourteenth and Fifteenth Amendments effectively constrained federal protection of African American civil rights. In the so-called Slaughterhouse cases of 1873, the Court issued its first ruling on the Fourteenth Amendment. The cases involved a Louisiana charter that gave a New Orleans meat-packing company a monopoly over the city's butchering business on the grounds of protecting public health. A rival group of butchers had sued, claiming the law violated the Fourteenth Amendment, which prohibited states from depriving any person of life, liberty, or property without due process of law. The Court held that the Fourteenth Amendment protected only the former slaves, not butchers, and that it protected only national citizenship rights, not the regulatory powers of states. The ruling in effect denied the original intent of the Fourteenth Amendment—to protect against state infringement of national citizenship rights as spelled out in the Bill of Rights.

Three other decisions curtailed federal protection of black civil rights. In *U.S. v. Reese* (1876) and *U.S. v. Cruikshank* (1876) the Court restricted congressional power to enforce the Ku Klux Klan Act. Future prosecution would depend on the states rather than on federal authorities. In these rulings the Court held that the Fourteenth Amendment extended the federal power to protect civil rights only in cases involving discrimination by states; discrimination by individuals or groups was not covered. The Court also ruled that the Fifteenth Amendment did not guarantee a citizen's right to vote; it only barred certain specific grounds for denying suffrage—"race, color, or previous condition of servitude." This interpretation opened the door for southern states to disfranchise African Americans for allegedly nonracial reasons. States back under Democratic control began to limit African American voting by passing laws restricting voter eligibility through poll taxes and property requirements.

Finally, in the 1883 Civil Rights Cases decision, the Court declared the Civil Rights Act of 1875 unconstitutional, holding that the Fourteenth Amendment gave Congress the power to outlaw discrimination by states, but not by private individuals. The majority opinion held that black people must no longer "be the special favorite of the laws." Together, these Supreme Court decisions marked the end of federal attempts to protect African American rights until well into the next century.

"King Cotton" and the Crop Lien System

The Republicans' vision of a "New South" remade along the lines of the northern economy failed to materialize. Instead, the South declined into the country's poorest agricultural region. Unlike midwestern and western farm towns burgeoning from trade in wheat, corn, and livestock, southern communities found themselves

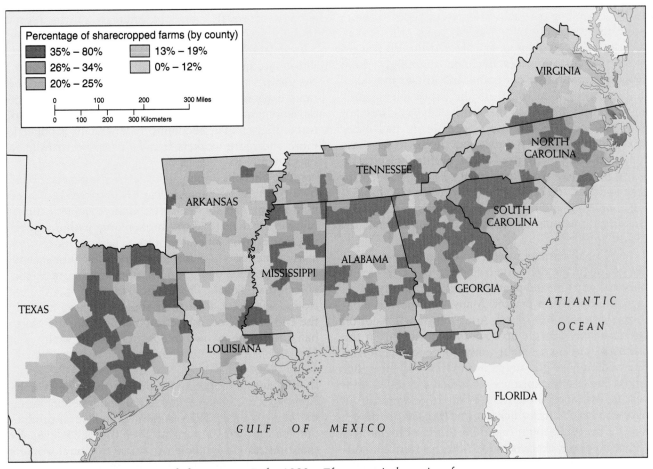

Southern Sharecropping and the Cotton Belt, 1880   *The economic depression of the 1870s forced increasing numbers of southern farmers, both white and black, into sharecropping arrangements. Sharecropping was most pervasive in the cotton belt regions of South Carolina, Georgia, Alabama, Mississippi, and east Texas.*

Percentage of sharecropped farms (by county)

- 35% – 80%
- 26% – 34%
- 20% – 25%
- 13% – 19%
- 0% – 12%

almost entirely dependent on the price of one commodity. Cotton growing had defined the economic life of large plantations in the coastal regions and black belt communities of the antebellum South. In the post–Civil War years "King Cotton" expanded its realm, as greater numbers of small white farmers found themselves forced to switch from subsistence crops to growing cotton for the market. The transition to cotton dependency developed unevenly, at different speeds in different parts of the South. Penetration by railroads, the availability of commercial fertilizers, and the opening up of new lands to cultivation were key factors in transforming communities from diversified, locally oriented farming to the market-oriented production of cotton.

The spread of the crop lien system as the South's main form of agricultural credit forced more and more farmers, both white and black, into cotton growing. This system developed because a chronic shortage of capital and banking institutions made local merchants and planters the sole source of credit. They advanced loans to small owners, sharecroppers, and tenant farmers only in exchange for a lien, or claim, on the year's cotton crop. Merchants and planters frequently charged exorbitant interest rates on advances, as well as marking up the prices of the goods they sold in their stores. Taking advantage of the high illiteracy rates among poor Southerners, landlords and merchants easily altered their books to inflate the figures. At the end of the year, sharecroppers and tenants found themselves deep in debt to stores (many owned by Northerners) for seed, supplies, and clothing. Despite hard work and even bountiful harvests, few small farmers could escape from heavy debt.

As more and more white and black farmers turned to cotton growing as the only way to obtain credit, expanding production depressed prices. Competition from new cotton centers in the world market, such as Egypt and India, accelerated the downward spiral. As cotton prices declined alarmingly, from roughly eleven cents per pound in 1875 to five cents in 1894, per capita wealth in the South fell steadily, equaling only one-third that of the East, Midwest, or West by the 1890s. Cotton dependency had other repercussions. The planters lacked capital to purchase the farm equipment needed to profitably cultivate wheat or corn, and their reliance on cheap labor kept them wedded to cotton. Planters persisted in employing hand labor and mule power. As soil depletion took its toll, crop outputs, or yields per acre, either remained steady or fell.

Small farmers caught up in a vicious cycle of low cotton prices, debt, and dwindling food crops found their old ideal of independence sacrificed to the cruel logic of the cotton market. Many must have sympathized with men like John F. Armstrong, a white cotton farmer in the Georgia up-country, who fled from the crushing burdens of debt, only to be captured and returned. "I just got tired of working for the other fellow," he grimly explained. "I worked and toiled from year to year and all the fruits of my labor went to the man who never struck a lick. . . . I never made anything."

By 1880, about one-third of the white farmers and nearly three-quarters of the African American farmers in the cotton states were sharecroppers or tenants. Of the roughly 1.1 million farms in the nine large cotton-planting states that year, sharecroppers worked 301,000 of them. Many former slaves and poor white people had tried subsistence farming in the undeveloped backcountry. Yet to obtain precious credit, most found themselves forced to produce cotton for market and thus became enmeshed in the debt-ridden crop lien system. In traditional cotton producing areas, especially the black belt, landless farmers growing cotton had replaced slaves growing cotton. In the up-country and newer areas of cultivation, cotton-dominated commercial agriculture, with landless tenants and sharecroppers as the main workforce, had replaced the more diversified subsistence economy of the antebellum era.

RECONSTRUCTING THE NORTH

Abraham Lincoln liked to cite his own rise as proof of the superiority of the northern system of "free labor" over slavery. "There is no permanent class of hired laborers amongst us," Lincoln asserted. "Twenty-five years ago, I was a hired laborer. The hired laborer of yesterday, labors on his own account today; and will hire others to labor for him tomorrow. Advancement—improvement in condition—is the order of things in a

society of equals." But the triumph of the North brought with it fundamental changes in the economy, labor relations, and politics that brought Lincoln's ideal vision into question. The spread of the factory system, the growth of large and powerful corporations, and the rapid expansion of capitalist enterprise all hastened the development of a large unskilled and routinized work force. Rather than becoming independent producers, more and more workers found themselves consigned permanently to wage labor.

The old Republican ideal of a society bound by a harmony of interests had become overshadowed by a grimmer reality of class conflict. A violent national railroad strike in 1877 was broken only with the direct intervention of federal troops. That conflict struck many Americans as a turning point. Northern society, like the society of the South, appeared more hierarchical than equal. That same year, the last federal troops withdrew from their southern posts, marking the end of the Reconstruction era. By then, the North had undergone its own "reconstruction" as well.

The Age of Capital

In the decade following Appomattox, the North's economy continued the industrial boom begun during the Civil War. By 1873, America's industrial production had grown 75 percent over the 1865 level. By that time, too, the number of nonagricultural workers in the North had surpassed the number of farmers. Between 1860 and 1880 the number of wage earners in manufacturing and construction more than doubled, from 2 million to over 4 million. Only Great Britain boasted a larger manufacturing economy than the United States. During the same period, nearly 3 million immigrants arrived in America, almost all of whom settled in the North and West.

The railroad business both symbolized and advanced the new industrial order. Shortly before the Civil War, enthusiasm mounted for a transcontinental line. Private companies took on the huge and expensive job of construction, but the federal government funded the project, providing the largest subsidy in American history. The Pacific Railway Act of 1862 granted the Union Pacific and the Central Pacific rights to a broad swath of land extending from Omaha, Nebraska, to Sacramento, California. An 1864 act bestowed a subsidy of $15,000 per mile of track laid over smooth plains country and varying larger amounts up to $48,000 per mile in the foothills and mountains of the Far West. The Union Pacific employed gangs of Irish American and African American workers to lay track heading west from Omaha, while the Central Pacific brought in more than 10,000 men from China to handle the difficult work in the Sierra Nevada mountain region.

Completion of the transcontinental railroad, May 10, 1869, as building crews for the Union Pacific and Central Pacific meet at Promontory Point, Utah. The two locomotive engineers salute each other, while the chief engineers for the two railroads shake hands. Construction had begun simultaneously from Omaha and Sacramento in 1863, with the help of generous subsidies from Congress. Work crews, consisting of thousands of ex-soldiers, Irish immigrants, and imported Chinese laborers, laid nearly 1,800 miles of new track.

On May 10, 1869, Leland Stanford, the former governor of California and president of the Central Pacific Railroad, traveled to Promontory Point in Utah Territory to hammer a ceremonial golden spike, marking the finish of the first transcontinental line. Other railroads went up with less fanfare. The Southern Pacific, chartered by the state of California, stretched from San Francisco to Los Angeles, and on through Arizona and New Mexico to connections with New Orleans. The Atchison, Topeka, and Santa Fe reached the Pacific in 1887 by way of a southerly route across the Rocky Mountains. The Great Northern, one of the few lines financed by private capital, extended west from St. Paul, Minnesota, to Washington's Puget Sound.

Railroads paved the way for the rapid settlement of the West, and both rural and urban areas grew dramatically over the next several decades. The combined population of Minnesota, the Dakotas, Nebraska, and Kansas, for example, jumped from 300,000 in 1860 to over 2 million in 1880. In the fifty years after 1870, the nation's railroad system expanded to more than a quarter million miles—more than all the rest of the world's railroad track combined.

Railroad corporations became America's first big businesses. Railroads required huge outlays of investment capital, and their growth increased the economic power of banks and investment houses centered in Wall Street. Bankers often gained seats on boards of directors, and their access to capital some-

times gave them the real control of lines. By the early 1870s the Pennsylvania Railroad stood as the nation's largest single company, with more than 20,000 employees. A new breed of aggressive entrepreneur sought to ease cutthroat competition by absorbing smaller companies and forming "pools" that set rates and divided the market. A small group of railroad executives, including Cornelius Vanderbilt, Jay Gould, Collis P. Huntington, and James J. Hill, amassed unheard-of fortunes. When he died in 1877, Vanderbilt left his son $100 million. By comparison, a decent annual wage for working a six-day week was around $350.

A growing number of Republican politicians maintained close connections with railroad interests. Railroad promoters, lawyers, and lobbyists became ubiquitous figures in Washington and state capitals, wielding enormous influence among lawmakers. "The galleries and lobbies of every legislature," one Republican leader noted, "are thronged with men seeking . . . an advantage." Railroads benefited enormously from government subsidies. Between 1862 and 1872 Congress alone awarded more than 100 million acres of public lands to railroad companies and provided them over $64 million in loans and tax incentives.

Some of the nation's most prominent politicians routinely accepted railroad largesse. Republican senator William M. Stewart of Nevada, a member of the Committee on Pacific Railroads, received a gift of 50,000 acres of land from the Central Pacific for his services. Senator Lyman Trumbull of Illinois took an annual retainer from the Illinois Central. The worst scandal of the Grant administration grew out of corruption involving railroad promotion. As a way of diverting funds for the building of the Union Pacific Railroad, an inner circle of Union Pacific stockholders created the dummy Crédit Mobilier construction company. In return for political favors, a group of prominent Republicans received stock in the company. When the scandal broke in 1872, it ruined Vice President Schuyler Colfax politically and led to the censure of two congressmen.

Other industries also boomed in this period, especially those engaged in extracting minerals and processing natural resources. Railroad growth stimulated expansion in the production of coal, iron, stone, and lumber, and these also received significant government aid. For example, under the National Mineral Act of 1866, mining companies received millions of acres of free public land. Oil refining enjoyed a huge expansion in the 1860s and 1870s. As with railroads, an early period of fierce competition soon gave way to concentration. By the late 1870s John D. Rockefeller's Standard Oil Company controlled almost 90 percent of the nation's oil-refining capacity. The production of pig iron tripled from 1 million tons in 1865 to 3 million tons in 1873. Between 1869 and 1879 both the capital investment and the number of workers in iron nearly doubled. Coal production shot up from 17 million tons in 1861 to 72 million tons in 1880. The size of individual ironworks and coal mines—measured by the number of employees and capital invested—also grew in these years, reflecting the expanding scale of industrial enterprise as a whole.

Liberal Republicans and the Election of 1872

With the rapid growth of large-scale, capital-intensive enterprises, Republicans increasingly identified with the interests of business rather than the rights of freedmen or the antebellum ideology of "free labor." The old Civil War–era Radicals had declined in influence. State Republican parties now organized themselves around the spoils of federal patronage rather than grand causes such as preserving the Union or ending slavery. Despite the Crédit Mobilier affair, Republicans had no monopoly on political scandal. In 1871 New York City newspapers reported the shocking story of how Democratic Party boss William M. Tweed and his friends had systematically stolen tens of millions from the city treasury. The "Tweed Ring" had received enormous bribes and kickbacks from city contractors and businessmen. Grotesquely caricatured by Thomas Nast's cartoons in *Harper's Weekly*, Tweed emerged as the preeminent national symbol of an

increasingly degraded and dishonest urban politics. But to many, the scandal represented only the most extreme case of the routine corruption that now plagued American political life.

By the end of President Grant's first term, a large number of disaffected Republicans sought an alternative. They were led by a small but influential number of intellectuals, professionals, businessmen, and reformers who articulated an ideology that helped reshape late-nineteenth-century politics. The Liberal Republicans, as they called themselves, shared several core values. First, they emphasized the doctrines of classical economics, stressing the law of supply and demand, free trade, defense of property rights, and individualism. They called for a return to limited government, arguing that bribery, scandal, and high taxes all flowed from excessive state interference in the economy.

Liberal Republicans were also suspicious of expanding democracy. "Universal suffrage," Charles Francis Adams Jr. wrote in 1869, "can only mean in plain English the government of ignorance and vice—it means a European, and especially Celtic, proletariat on the Atlantic coast, an African proletariat on the shores of the Gulf, and a Chinese proletariat on the Pacific." Liberal Republicans believed that politics ought to be the province of "the best men"—educated and well-to-do men like themselves, devoted to the "science of government." They proposed civil service reform as the best way to break the hold of party machines on patronage. Competitive examinations, they argued, were the best way to choose employees for government posts. At a time when only a very small fraction of Americans attended college, this requirement would severely restrict the pool of government workers.

Although most Liberal Republicans had enthusiastically supported abolition, the Union cause, and equal rights for freedmen, they now opposed continued federal intervention in the South. The national government had done all it could for the former slaves; they must now take care of themselves. "Root, Hog, or Die" was the harsh advice offered by Horace Greeley, editor of the *New York Tribune*. In the spring of 1872 a diverse collection of Liberal Republicans nominated Greeley to run for president. A longtime foe of the Democratic Party, Greeley nonetheless won that party's presidential nomination as well. He made a new policy for the South the center of his campaign against Grant. The "best men" of both sections, he argued, should support a more generous Reconstruction policy based on "universal amnesty and impartial suffrage." All Americans, Greeley urged, must put the Civil War behind them and "clasp hands across the bloody chasm."

Grant easily defeated Greeley, carrying every state in the North and winning 56 percent of the popular vote. Most Republicans were not willing to abandon the regular party organization, and "waving the bloody shirt" was still a potent vote-getter. But the 1872 election accelerated the trend toward federal abandonment of African American citizenship rights. The Liberal Republicans quickly faded as an organized political force. But their ideas helped define a growing conservative consciousness among the northern public. For the rest of the century, their political and economic views attracted a growing number of middle-class professionals and businessmen. This agenda included retreat from the ideal of racial justice, hostility toward trade unions, suspicion of working-class and immigrant political power, celebration of competitive individualism, and opposition to government intervention in economic affairs.

The Depression of 1873

In the fall of 1873 the postwar boom came to an abrupt halt as a severe financial panic triggered a deep economic depression. The collapse resulted from commercial overexpansion, especially speculative investing in the nation's railroad system. The investment banking house of Jay Cooke and Company failed in September 1873 when it found itself unable to market millions of dollars in Northern Pacific Railroad bonds. Soon other banks and brokerage houses, especially those dealing in railroad securities, caved in as well, and the New York Stock Exchange suspended operations. By 1876 half the nation's railroads had defaulted on their bonds. Over the next two years more than 100 banks folded and 18,000 businesses shut their doors. The depression that began in 1873 lasted sixty-five months—the longest economic contraction in the nation's history until then.

The human toll of the depression was enormous. As factories began to close across the nation, the unemployment rate soared to about 15 percent. In many cities the jobless rate was much higher; roughly one-quarter of New York City workers were unemployed in 1874. Many thousands of men took to the road in search of work, and the "tramp" emerged as a new and menacing figure on the social landscape. The

The Tramp, Harper's Weekly, *September 2, 1876. The depression that began in 1873 forced many thousands of unemployed workers to go "on the tramp" in search of jobs. Men wandered from town to town, walking or riding railroad cars, desperate for a chance to work for wages or simply for room and board. The "tramp" became a powerful symbol of the misery caused by industrial depression and, as in this drawing, an image that evoked fear and nervousness among the nation's middle class.*

Pennsylvania Bureau of Labor Statistics noted that never before had "so many of the working classes, skilled and unskilled . . . been moving from place to place seeking employment that was not to be had." Farmers were also hard hit by the depression. Agricultural output continued to grow, but prices and land values fell sharply. As prices for their crops fell, farmers had a more difficult time repaying their fixed loan obligations; many sank deeper into debt.

During the winter of 1873, New York labor leaders demanded to know what measures would be taken "to relieve the necessities of the 10,000 homeless and hungry men and women of our city whose urgent appeals have apparently been disregarded by our public servants." Mass meetings of workers in New York and other cities issued calls to government officials to create jobs through public works. But these appeals were rejected. Indeed, many business leaders and political figures denounced even meager efforts at charity. E. L. Godkin wrote in the Christmas 1875 issue of the *Nation* that "free soup must be prohibited, and all classes must learn that soup of any kind, beef or turtle, can be had only by being paid for." Men such as Godkin saw the depression as a natural, if painful, part of the business cycle, one that would allow only the strongest enterprises (and workers) to survive. They dismissed any attempts at government interference, in the form of either job creation or poor relief.

Increased tensions, sometimes violent, between labor and capital reinforced the feeling of many Americans that the nation was no longer immune from European-style class conflict. The depression of the 1870s prompted workers and farmers to question the old free-labor ideology that celebrated a harmony of interests in northern society. More people voiced anger at and distrust of large corporations that exercised great economic power from outside their communities. Businessmen and merchants, meanwhile, especially in large cities, became more conscious of their own class interests. New political organizations such as Chicago's Citizens' Association united businessmen in campaigns for fiscal conservatism and defense of property rights. In national politics, the persistent depression made the Republican Party, North and South, more vulnerable than ever.

The Electoral Crisis of 1876

With the economy mired in depression, Democrats looked forward to capturing the White House in 1876. New scandals plaguing the Grant administration also weakened the Republican Party. In 1875, a conspiracy surfaced between distillers and U.S. revenue agents to cheat the government out of millions in tax revenues. The government secured indictments against more than 200 members of this "Whiskey Ring," including Orville E. Babcock, Grant's private secretary. Though acquitted, thanks to Grant's intervention, Babcock resigned in disgrace. In 1876, Secretary of War William W. Belknap was impeached for receiving bribes for the sale of trading posts in Indian Territory, and he resigned to avoid conviction.

Though Grant himself was never implicated in any wrongdoing, Democrats hammered away at his administration's low standard of honesty in government. For president they nominated Governor Samuel J. Tilden of New York, who brought impeccable reform credentials to his candidacy. In 1871 he had helped expose and prosecute the "Tweed Ring" in New York City. As governor he had toppled the "Canal Ring," a graft-ridden scheme involving inflated contracts for repairs on the Erie Canal. In their platform, the Democrats linked the issue of corruption to an attack on Reconstruction policies. They blamed the Republicans for instituting "a corrupt centralism" that subjected southern states to "the rapacity of carpetbag tyrannies," riddled the national government "with incapacity, waste, and fraud," and "locked fast the prosperity of an industrious people in the paralysis of hard times."

Republican nominee Rutherford B. Hayes, governor of Ohio, also sought the high ground. As a lawyer in Cincinnati he had defended runaway slaves. Later he had distinguished himself as a general in the Union army. Republicans charged Tilden with disloyalty during the war, income tax evasion, and close relations with powerful railroad interests. Hayes promised, if elected, to support an efficient civil service system, to vigorously prosecute officials who betrayed the public trust, and to introduce a system of free universal education.

On an election day marred by widespread vote fraud and violent intimidation, Tilden received 250,000 more popular votes than Hayes. But Republicans refused to concede victory, challenging the vote totals in the electoral college. Tilden garnered 184 uncontested electoral votes, one shy of the majority required to win, while Hayes received 165. The problem centered in 20 disputed votes from Florida, Louisiana, South Carolina, and Oregon. In each of the three southern states two sets of electoral votes were returned. In Oregon, which Hayes had unquestionably carried, the Democratic governor replaced a disputed Republican elector with a Democrat.

The crisis was unprecedented. In January 1877 Congress moved to settle the deadlock, estab-

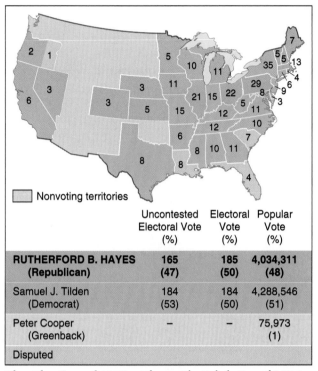

	Uncontested Electoral Vote (%)	Electoral Vote (%)	Popular Vote (%)
RUTHERFORD B. HAYES (Republican)	**165** **(47)**	**185** **(50)**	**4,034,311** **(48)**
Samuel J. Tilden (Democrat)	184 (53)	184 (50)	4,288,546 (51)
Peter Cooper (Greenback)	–	–	75,973 (1)
Disputed			

Nonvoting territories

The Election of 1876   *The presidential election of 1876 left the nation without a clear-cut winner.*

lishing an Electoral Commission composed of five senators, five representatives, and five Supreme Court justices; eight were Republicans and seven were Democrats. The commission voted along strict partisan lines to award all the contested electoral votes to Hayes. Outraged by this decision, Democratic congressmen threatened a filibuster to block Hayes's inauguration. Violence and stalemate were avoided when Democrats and Republicans struck a compromise in February. In return for Hayes's ascendance to the presidency, the Republicans promised to appropriate more money for Southern internal improvements, to appoint a Southerner to Hayes's cabinet, and to pursue a policy of noninterference ("home rule") in southern affairs.

Shortly after assuming office, Hayes ordered removal of the remaining federal troops in Louisiana and South Carolina. Without this military presence to sustain them, the Republican governors of those two states quickly lost power to Democrats. "Home rule" meant Republican abandonment of freed people, Radicals, carpetbaggers, and scalawags. It also effectively nullified the Fourteenth and Fifteenth Amendments and the Civil Rights Act of 1866. The "Compromise of 1877" completed repudiation of the idea, born during the Civil War and pursued during Congressional

Reconstruction, of a powerful federal government protecting the rights of all American citizens. As one black Louisianan lamented, "The whole South—every state in the South—had got into the hands of the very men that held us slaves." Other voices hailed this turning point in policy. "The negro," declared the *Nation*, "will disappear from the field of national politics. Henceforth, the nation, as a nation, will have nothing more to do with him."

CONCLUSION

Reconstruction succeeded in the limited political sense of reuniting a nation torn apart by civil war. The Radical Republican vision, emphasizing racial justice, equal civil and political rights guaranteed by the Fourteenth and Fifteenth Amendments, and a new southern economy organized around independent small farmers, never enjoyed the support of the majority of its party or the northern public. By 1877 the political force of these ideals was spent and the national retreat from them nearly complete.

The end of Reconstruction left the way open for the return of white domination in the South. The freed people's political and civil equality proved only temporary. It would take a "Second Reconstruction," the civil rights movement of the next century, to establish full black citizenship rights once and for all. The federal government's failure to pursue land reform left former slaves without the economic independence needed for full emancipation. Yet the newly autonomous black family, along with black-controlled churches, schools, and other social institutions, provided the foundations for the modern African American community. If the federal government was not yet fully committed to protecting equal rights in local communities, the Reconstruction era at least pointed to how that goal might be achieved.

Even as the federal government retreated from the defense of equal rights for black people, it took a more aggressive stance as the protector of business interests. The Hayes administration responded decisively to one of the worst outbreaks of class violence in American history by dispatching federal troops to several northern cities to break the Great Railroad Strike of 1877. In the aftermath of Reconstruction, the struggle between capital and labor had clearly replaced "the southern question" as the number one political issue of the day. "The overwhelming labor question has dwarfed all other questions into nothing," wrote an Ohio Republican. "We have home questions enough to occupy attention now."

CHRONOLOGY

1865	Freedmen's Bureau established
	Abraham Lincoln assassinated
	Andrew Johnson begins Presidential Reconstruction
	Black codes begin to be enacted in southern states
	Thirteenth Amendment ratified
1866	Civil Rights Act passed
	Congress approves Fourteenth Amendment
	Ku Klux Klan founded
1867	Reconstruction Acts, passed over President Johnson's veto, begin Congressional Reconstruction
	Tenure of Office Act
	Southern states call constitutional conventions
1868	President Johnson impeached by the House, but acquitted in Senate trial
	Fourteenth Amendment ratified
	Most southern states readmitted to Union
	Ulysses S. Grant elected president
1869	Congress approves Fifteenth Amendment
	Union Pacific and Central Pacific tracks meet at Promontory Point in Utah Territory
	Suffragists split into National Woman Suffrage Association and American Woman Suffrage Association
1870	Fifteenth Amendment ratified
1871	Ku Klux Klan Act passed
	"Tweed Ring" in New York City exposed
1872	Liberal Republicans break with Grant and Radicals, nominate Horace Greeley for president
	Crédit Mobilier scandal
	Grant reelected president
1873	Financial panic and beginning of economic depression
	Slaughterhouse cases
1874	Democrats gain control of House for first time since 1856
1875	Civil Rights Act
1876	Disputed election between Samuel Tilden and Rutherford B. Hayes
1877	Electoral Commission elects Hayes president
	President Hayes dispatches federal troops to break Great Railroad Strike and withdraws last remaining federal troops from the South

REVIEW QUESTIONS

1. How did various visions of a "reconstructed" South differ? How did these visions reflect the old political and social divisions that had led to the civil war?
2. What key changes did emancipation make in the political and economic status of African Americans? Discuss the expansion of citizenship rights in the post–Civil War years. To what extent did women share in the gains made by African Americans?
3. What role did such institutions as the family, the church, schools, and political parties play in the African American transition to freedom?
4. How did white Southerners attempt to limit the freedom of former slaves? How did these efforts succeed, and how did they fail?
5. Evaluate the achievements and failures of Reconstruction governments in the southern states.
6. What were the crucial economic changes occurring in the North and South during the Reconstruction era?

RECOMMENDED READING

Michael Les Benedict, *The Impeachment and Trial of Andrew Johnson* (1973). The best history of the impeachment crisis.

Laura F. Edwards, *Gendered Strife & Confusion: The Political Culture of Reconstruction* (1997). An ambitious analysis of how gender ideologies played a key role in shaping the party politics and social relations of the Reconstruction-era South.

Michael W. Fitzgerald, *The Union League Movement in the Deep South* (1989). Uses the Union League as a lens through which to examine race relations and the close connections between politics and economic change in the post–Civil War South.

Eric Foner, *Reconstruction: America's Unfinished Revolution, 1863–1877* (1988). The most comprehensive and thoroughly researched overview of the Reconstruction era.

William Gillette, *Retreat from Reconstruction: A Political History, 1867–1878* (1979). Covers the national political scene, with special attention to the abandonment of the ideal of racial equality.

Jacqueline Jones, *Labor of Love, Labor of Sorrow* (1985). Includes excellent material on the work and family lives of African American women in slavery and freedom.

Leon Litwack, *Been in the Storm So Long: The Aftermath of Slavery* (1979). A richly detailed analysis of the transition from slavery to freedom; excellent use of African American sources.

Michael Perman, *Emancipation and Reconstruction, 1862–1879* (1987). A short but very useful overview of Reconstruction, emphasizing racial issues and the end of slavery.

Edward Royce, *The Origins of Southern Sharecropping* (1993). A sophisticated, tightly argued work of historical sociology that explains how sharecropping emerged as the dominant form of agricultural labor in the post–Civil War South.

Mark W. Summers, *Railroads, Reconstruction, and the Gospel of Prosperity* (1984). The best study of the economic and political importance of railroad building in this era.

Allen W. Trelease, *White Terror: The Ku Klux Klan Conspiracy and Southern Reconstruction* (1971). The most complete account of Klan activity and the efforts to suppress it.

ADDITIONAL BIBLIOGRAPHY

The Politics of Reconstruction

Richard H. Abbott, *The Republican Party and the South, 1855–1877* (1986)

Herman Belz, *Emancipation and Equal Rights* (1978)

Michael Les Benedict, *A Compromise of Principle: Congressional Republicans and Reconstruction* (1974)

Michael Kent Curtis, *No State Shall Abridge: The Fourteenth Amendment and the Bill of Rights* (1990)

Ellen Carol DuBois, *Feminism and Suffrage* (1978)

Eric Foner, *Politics and Ideology in the Age of the Civil War* (1980)

William C. Harris, *With Charity for All: Lincoln and the Restoration of the Union* (1997)

Robert Kaczorowski, *The Politics of Judicial Interpretation: The Federal Courts, Department of Justice, and Civil Rights, 1866–1876* (1985)

James McPherson, *Ordeal by Fire: The Civil War and Reconstruction* (1982)

Kenneth M. Stampp, *The Era of Reconstruction, 1865–1877* (1965)

The Meaning of Freedom

Ira Berlin et al., eds., *Freedom: A Documentary History*, 3 vols. (1985–91)

W. E. B. Du Bois, *Black Reconstruction* (1935)

Barbara J. Fields, *Slavery and Freedom on the Middle Ground* (1985)

Eric Foner, *Freedom's Lawmakers: A Directory of Black Officeholders during Reconstruction* (1996)

Herbert G. Gutman, *The Black Family in Slavery and Freedom* (1976)

Thomas Holt, *Black over White: Negro Political Leadership in South Carolina during Reconstruction* (1977)

Lynda J. Morgan, *Emancipation in Virginia's Tobacco Belt* (1992)

Nell Irvin Painter, *Exodusters* (1977)

Howard N. Rabinowitz, *Race Relations in the Urban South, 1865–1890* (1978)

Roger L. Ransom and Richard Sutch, *One Kind of Freedom: The Economic Consequences of Emancipation* (1977)

Southern Politics and Society

Dan T. Carter, *When the War Was Over: The Failure of Self Reconstruction in the South, 1865–1877* (1985)

Richard N. Current, *Those Terrible Carpetbaggers* (1988)

Stephen Hahn, *The Roots of Southern Populism* (1983)

William C. Harris, *The Day of the Carpetbagger: Republican Reconstruction in Mississippi* (1979)

Michael S. Perman, *Reunion without Compromise: The South and Reconstruction, 1865–1868* (1973)

———, *The Road to Redemption: Southern Politics, 1868–1979* (1984)

Howard N. Rabinowitz, *The First New South, 1865–1920* (1991)

James Roark, *Masters without Slaves* (1977)

Jonathan M. Wiener, *Social Origins of the New South* (1978)

Reconstructing the North

Stephen Buechler, *The Transformation of the Woman Suffrage Movement* (1986)

Morton Keller, *Affairs of State* (1977)

James C. Mohr, ed., *Radical Republicans in the North* (1976)

David Montgomery, *Beyond Equality: Labor and the Radical Republicans, 1862–1872* (1967)

Keith I. Polakoff, *The Politics of Inertia: The Election of 1876 and the End of Reconstruction* (1973)

Mark W. Summers, *The Era of Good Stealings* (1993)

Margaret S. Thompson, *The "Spider Web": Congress and Lobbying in the Age of Grant* (1985)

C. Vann Woodward, *Reunion and Reaction: The Compromise of 1877 and the End of Reconstruction* (1956)

Biography

Fawn M. Brodie, *Thaddeus Stevens* (1959)

David Donald, *Charles Sumner and the Rights of Man* (1970)

Russell Duncan, *Freedom's Shore: Tunis Campbell and the Georgia Freedmen* (1986)

William S. McFeely, *Frederick Douglass* (1989)

———, *Grant: A Biography* (1981)

———, *Yankee Stepfather: General O. O. Howard and the Freedmen* (1968)

Hans L. Trefousse, *Andrew Johnson* (1989)

APPENDIX

THE DECLARATION OF INDEPENDENCE

When in the course of human events it becomes necessary for one people to dissolve the political bands which have connected them with another and to assume, among the powers of the earth, the separate and equal station to which the laws of nature and of nature's God entitle them, a decent respect to the opinions of mankind requires that they should declare the causes which impel them to the separation.

We hold these truths to be self-evident, that all men are created equal; that they are endowed by their Creator with certain unalienable rights; that among these are life, liberty, and the pursuit of happiness. That, to secure these rights, governments are instituted among men, deriving their just powers from the consent of the governed; that, whenever any form of government becomes destructive of these ends, it is the right of the people to alter or to abolish it, and to institute a new government, laying its foundation on such principles, and organizing its powers in such form, as to them shall seem most likely to effect their safety and happiness. Prudence, indeed, will dictate that governments long established should not be changed for light and transient causes; and, accordingly, all experience hath shown that mankind are more disposed to suffer, while evils are sufferable, than to right themselves by abolishing the forms to which they are accustomed. But when a long train of abuses and usurpations, pursuing invariably the same object, evinces a design to reduce them under absolute despotism, it is their right, it is their duty, to throw off such government and to provide new guards for their future security. Such has been the patient sufferance of these colonies, and such is now the necessity which constrains them to alter their former systems of government. The history of the present King of Great Britain is a history of repeated injuries and usurpations, all having, in direct object, the establishment of an absolute tyranny over these States. To prove this, let facts be submitted to a candid world:

He has refused his assent to laws the most wholesome and necessary for the public good.

He has forbidden his governors to pass laws of immediate and pressing importance, unless suspended in their operation till his assent should be obtained; and, when so suspended, he has utterly neglected to attend to them.

He has refused to pass other laws for the accommodation of large districts of people, unless those people would relinquish the right of representation in the legislature, a right inestimable to them and formidable to tyrants only.

He has called together legislative bodies at places unusual, uncomfortable, and distant from the depository of their public records, for the sole purpose of fatiguing them into compliance with his measures.

He has dissolved representative houses, repeatedly for opposing, with manly firmness, his invasions on the rights of the people.

He has refused, for a long time after such dissolutions, to cause others to be elected; whereby the legislative powers, incapable of annihilation, have returned to the people at large for their exercise; the state remaining, in the meantime, exposed to all the danger of invasion from without and convulsions within.

He has endeavored to prevent the population of these States; for that purpose, obstructing the laws for naturalization of foreigners, refusing to pass others to encourage their migration hither, and raising the conditions of new appropriations of lands.

He has obstructed the administration of justice by refusing his assent to laws for establishing judiciary powers.

He has made judges dependent on his will alone for the tenure of their offices and the amount and payment of their salaries.

He has erected a multitude of new offices and sent hither swarms of officers to harass our people and eat out their substance.

He has kept among us, in time of peace, standing armies, without the consent of our legislatures.

He has affected to render the military independent of, and superior to, the civil power.

He has combined with others to subject us to a jurisdiction foreign to our Constitution and unacknowledged by our laws, giving his assent to their acts of pretended legislation—

For quartering large bodies of armed troops among us;

For protecting them, by mock trial, from punishment for any murders which they should commit on the inhabitants of these States;

For cutting off our trade with all parts of the world;

For imposing taxes on us without our consent;

For depriving us, in many cases, of the benefit of trial by jury;

For transporting us beyond seas to be tried for pretended offences;

For abolishing the free system of English laws in a neighboring province, establishing therein an arbitrary government, and enlarging its boundaries, so as to render it at once an example and fit instrument for introducing the same absolute rule into these colonies;

For taking away our charters, abolishing our most valuable laws, and altering, fundamentally, the powers of our governments.

For suspending our own legislatures and declaring themselves invested with power to legislate for us in all cases whatsoever.

He has abdicated government here by declaring us out of his protection and waging war against us.

He has plundered our seas, ravaged our coasts, burnt our towns, and destroyed the lives of our people.

He is, at this time, transporting large armies of foreign mercenaries to complete the works of death, desolation, and tyranny already begun with circumstances of cruelty and perfidy scarcely paralleled in the most barbarous ages, and totally unworthy the head of a civilized nation.

He has constrained our fellow citizens, taken captive on the high seas, to bear arms against their country, to become the executioners of their friends and brethren, or to fall themselves by their hands.

He has excited domestic insurrections amongst us and has endeavored to bring on the inhabitants of our frontiers, the merciless Indian savages, whose known rule of warfare is an undistinguished destruction of all ages, sexes, and conditions.

In every stage of these oppressions, we have petitioned for redress in the most humble terms; our repeated petitions have been answered only by repeated injury. A prince whose character is thus marked by every act which may define a tyrant is unfit to be the ruler of a free people.

Nor have we been wanting in attention to our British brethren. We have warned them, from time to time, of attempts made by their legislature to extend an unwarrantable jurisdiction over us. We have reminded them of the circumstances of our emigration and settlement here. We have appealed to their native justice and magnanimity, and we have conjured them, by the ties of our common kindred,

to disavow these usurpations, which would inevitably interrupt our connections and correspondence. They, too, have been deaf to the voice of justice and consanguinity. We must, therefore, acquiesce in the necessity which denounces our separation, and hold them, as we hold the rest of mankind, enemies in war, in peace, friends.

We, therefore, the representatives of the United States of America, in general Congress assembled, appealing to the Supreme Judge of the world for the rectitude of our intentions, do, in the name and by the authority of the good people of these colonies, solemnly publish and declare, that these united colonies are, and of right ought to be, free and independent states: that they are absolved from all allegiance to the British Crown, and that all political connection between them and the state of Great Britain is, and ought to be, totally dissolved; and that, as free and independent states, they have full power to levy war, conclude peace, contract alliances, establish commerce, and to do all other acts and things which independent states may of right do. And, for the support of this declaration, with a firm reliance on the protection of Divine Providence, we mutually pledge to each other our lives, our fortunes, and our sacred honor.

THE CONSTITUTION OF THE UNITED STATES OF AMERICA

We the people of the United States, in order to form a more perfect union, establish justice, insure domestic tranquillity, provide for the common defense, promote the general welfare, and secure the blessings of liberty to ourselves and our posterity, do ordain and establish this Constitution for the United States of America.

Article I

Section 1. All legislative powers herein granted shall be vested in a Congress of the United States, which shall consist of a Senate and House of Representatives.

Section 2. 1. The House of Representatives shall be composed of members chosen every second year by the people of the several States, and the electors in each State shall have the qualifications requisite for electors of the most numerous branch of the State legislature.

2. No person shall be a representative who shall not have attained to the age of twenty-five years, and been seven years a citizen of the United States, and who shall not, when elected, be an inhabitant of that State in which he shall be chosen.

3. Representatives and direct taxes[1] shall be apportioned among the several States which may be included within this Union, according to their respective numbers, which shall be determined by adding to the whole number of free persons, including those bound to service for a term of years, and excluding Indians not taxed, three fifths of all other persons.[2] The actual enumeration shall be made within three years after the first meeting of the Congress of the United States, and within every subsequent term of ten years, in such manner as they shall by law direct. The number of representatives shall not exceed one for every thirty thousand, but each State shall have at least one representative; and until such enumeration shall be made, the State of New Hampshire shall be entitled to choose three, Massachusetts eight, Rhode Island and Providence Plantations one, Connecticut five, New York six, New Jersey four, Pennsylvania eight, Delaware one, Maryland six, Virginia ten, North Carolina five, South Carolina five, and Georgia three.

4. When vacancies happen in the representation from any State, the executive authority thereof shall issue writs of election to fill such vacancies.

5. The House of Representatives shall choose their speaker and other officers; and shall have the sole power of impeachment.

Section 3. 1. The Senate of the United States shall be composed of two senators from each State, chosen by the legislature thereof,[3] for six years; and each senator shall have one vote.

2. Immediately after they shall be assembled in consequence of the first election, they shall be divided as equally as may be into three classes. The seats of the senators of the first class shall be vacated at the expiration of the second year, of the second class at the expiration of the fourth year, and of the third class at the expiration of the sixth year, so that one third may be chosen every second year; and if vacancies happen by resignation, or otherwise, during the recess of the legislature of any State, the executive thereof may make temporary appointments until the next meeting of the legislature, which shall then fill such vacancies.[4]

3. No person shall be a senator who shall not have attained to the age of thirty years, and been nine years a citizen of the United States, and who shall not, when elected, be an inhabitant of that State for which he shall be chosen.

4. The Vice President of the United States shall be President of the Senate, but shall have no vote, unless they be equally divided.

5. The Senate shall choose their other officers, and also a president pro tempore, in the absence of the Vice President, or when he shall exercise the office of the President of the United States.

6. The Senate shall have the sole power to try all impeachments. When sitting for that purpose, they shall be on oath or affirmation. When the President of the United States is tried, the chief justice shall preside: and no person shall be convicted without the concurrence of two thirds of the members present.

7. Judgment in cases of impeachment shall not extend further than to removal from office, and disqualification to hold and enjoy any office of honor, trust or profit under the United States: but the party convicted shall nevertheless be liable and subject to indictment, trial, judgment and punishment, according to law.

Section 4. 1. The times, places, and manner of holding elections for senators and representatives, shall be prescribed in each State by the legislature thereof; but the Congress may at any time by law make or alter such regulations, except as to the places of choosing senators.

2. The Congress shall assemble at least once in every year, and such meeting shall be on the first Monday in December, unless they shall by law appoint a different day.

Section 5. 1. Each House shall be the judge of the elections, returns and qualifications of its own members, and a majority of each shall constitute a quorum to do business; but a smaller number may adjourn from day to day, and may be authorized to compel the attendance of absent members, in such manner, and under such penalties as each House may provide.

2. Each House may determine the rules of its proceedings, punish its members for disorderly behavior, and, with the concurrence of two thirds, expel a member.

3. Each House shall keep a journal of its proceedings, and from time to time publish the same, excepting such parts as may in their judgment require secrecy; and the yeas and nays of the members of either House on any ques-

---

[1]See the Sixteenth Amendment.
[2]See the Fourteenth Amendment.
[3]See the Seventeenth Amendment.

[4]See the Seventeenth Amendment.

tion shall, at the desire of one fifth of those present, be entered on the journal.

4. Neither House, during the session of Congress, shall, without the consent of the other, adjourn for more than three days, nor to any other place than that in which the two Houses shall be sitting.

Section 6. 1. The senators and representatives shall receive a compensation for their services, to be ascertained by law, and paid out of the Treasury of the United States. They shall in all cases, except treason, felony, and breach of the peace, be privileged from arrest during their attendance at the session of their respective Houses, and in going to and returning from the same; and for any speech or debate in either House, they shall not be questioned in any other place.

2. No senator or representative shall, during the time for which he was elected, be appointed to any civil office under the authority of the United States, which shall have been created, or the emoluments whereof shall have been increased, during such time; and no person holding any office under the United States shall be a member of either House during his continuance in office.

Section 7. 1. All bills for raising revenue shall originate in the House of Representatives; but the Senate may propose or concur with amendments as on other bills.

2. Every bill which shall have passed the House of Representatives and the Senate, shall, before it become a law, be presented to the President of the United States; If he approves he shall sign it, but if not he shall return it, with his objections, to that House in which it shall have originated, who shall enter the objections at large on their journal, and proceed to reconsider it. If after such reconsideration two thirds of that House shall agree to pass the bill, it shall be sent, together with the objections, to the other House, by which it shall likewise be reconsidered, and if approved by two thirds of that House, it shall become a law. But in all such cases the votes of both Houses shall be determined by yeas and nays, and the names of the persons voting for and against the bill shall be entered on the journal of each House respectively. If any bill shall not be returned by the President within ten days (Sundays excepted) after it shall have been presented to him, the same shall be a law, in like manner as if he had signed it, unless the Congress by their adjournment prevent its return, in which case it shall not be a law.

3. Every order, resolution, or vote to which the concurrence of the Senate and the House of Representatives may be necessary (except on a question of adjournment) shall be presented to the President of the United States; and before the same shall take effect, shall be approved by him, or being disapproved by him, shall be repassed by two thirds of the Senate and House of Representatives, according to the rules and limitations prescribed in the case of a bill.

Section 8. The Congress shall have the power

1. To lay and collect taxes, duties, imposts, and excises, to pay the debts and provide for the common defense and general welfare of the United States; but all duties, imposts, and excises shall be uniform throughout the United States.

2. To borrow money on the credit of the United States;

3. To regulate commerce with foreign nations, and among the several States, and with the Indian tribes;

4. To establish a uniform rule of naturalization, and uniform laws on the subject of bankruptcies throughout the United States;

5. To coin money, regulate the value thereof, and of foreign coin, and fix the standard of weights and measures;

6. To provide for the punishment of counterfeiting the securities and current coin of the United States;

7. To establish post offices and post roads;

8. To promote the progress of science and useful arts, by securing for limited times to authors and inventors the exclusive right to their respective writings and discoveries;

9. To constitute tribunals inferior to the Supreme Court;

10. To define and punish piracies and felonies committed on the high seas, and offenses against the law of nations;

11. To declare war, grant letters of marque and reprisal, and make rules concerning captures on land and water;

12. To raise and support armies, but no appropriation of money to that use shall be for a longer term than two years;

13. To provide and maintain a navy;

14. To make rules for the government and regulation of the land and naval forces;

15. To provide for calling forth the militia to execute the laws of the Union, suppress insurrections and repel invasions;

16. To provide for organizing, arming, and disciplining the militia, and for governing such part of them as may be employed in the service of the United States, reserving to the States respectively, the appointment of the officers, and the authority of training the militia according to the discipline prescribed by Congress;

17. To exercise exclusive legislation in all cases whatsoever, over such district (not exceeding ten miles square) as may, by cession of particular States, and the acceptance of Congress, become the seat of the government of the United States, and to exercise like authority over all places purchased by the consent of the legislature of the State in which the same shall be, for the erection of forts, magazines, arsenals, dockyards, and other needful buildings; and

18. To make all laws which shall be necessary and proper for carrying into execution the foregoing powers, and all other powers vested by this Constitution in the government of the United States, or any department or officer thereof.

Section 9. 1. The migration or importation of such persons as any of the States now existing shall think proper to admit, shall not be prohibited by the Congress prior to the year one thousand eight hundred and eight, but a tax or duty may be imposed on such importation, not exceeding ten dollars for each person.

2. The privilege of the writ of habeas corpus shall not be suspended, unless when in cases of rebellion or invasion the public safety may require it.

3. No bill of attainder or ex post facto law shall be passed.

4. No capitation, or other direct, tax shall be laid, unless in proportion to the census or enumeration hereinbefore directed to be taken.[5]

5. No tax or duty shall be laid on articles exported from any State.

6. No preference shall be given by any regulation of commerce or revenue to the ports of one State over those of another: nor shall vessels bound to, or from, one State be obliged to enter, clear, or pay duties in another.

7. No money shall be drawn from the treasury, but in consequence of appropriations made by law; and a regular statement and account of the receipts and expenditures of all public money shall be published from time to time.

8. No title of nobility shall be granted by the United States: and no person holding any office of profit or trust under them, shall, without the consent of the Congress, accept of any present, emolument, office, or title, of any kind whatever, from any king, price, or foreign State.

Section 10. 1. No State shall enter into any treaty, alliance, or confederation; grant letters of marque and reprisal; coin money; emit bills of credit; make any thing but gold and silver coin a tender in payment of debts; pass any bill of attainder, ex post facto law, or law impairing the obligation of contracts, or grant, any title of nobility.

2. No State shall, without the consent of the Congress, lay any imposts or duties on imports or exports, except what may be absolutely necessary for executing its inspection laws: and the net produce of all duties and imposts laid by any State on imports or exports, shall be for the use of the treasury of the United States; and all such laws shall be subject to the revision and control of the Congress.

3. No State shall, without the consent of the Congress, lay any duty of tonnage, keep troops, or ships of war in time of peace, enter into any agreement or compact with another State, or with a foreign power, or engage in war, unless actually invaded, or in such imminent danger as will not admit of delay.

Article II

Section 1. 1. The executive power shall be vested in a President of the United States of America. He shall hold his office during the term of four years, and, together with the Vice President, chosen for the same term, be elected, as follows:

2. Each State shall appoint, in such manner as the legislature thereof may direct, a number of electors, equal to the whole number of senators and representatives to which the State may be entitled in the Congress: but no senator or representative, or person holding any office of trust or profit under the United States, shall be appointed an elector.

The electors shall meet in their respective States, and vote by ballot for two persons, of whom one at least shall not be an inhabitant of the same State with themselves. And they shall make a list of all the persons voted for, and of the number of votes for each; which list they shall sign and certify, and transmit sealed to the seat of the government of the United States, directed to the president of the Senate. The president of the Senate shall, in the presence of the Senate and House of Representatives, open all the certificates, and the votes shall then be counted. The person having the greatest number of votes shall be the President, if such number be a majority of the whole number of electors appointed; and if there be more than one who have such majority, and have an equal number of votes, then the House of Representatives shall immediately choose by ballot one of them for President; and if no person have a majority, then from the five highest on the list the said House shall in like manner choose the President. But in choosing the President, the votes shall be taken by States, the representation from each State having one vote; a quorum for this purpose shall consist of a member or members from two thirds of the States, and a majority of all the States shall be necessary to a choice. In every case after the choice of the President, the person having the greatest number of votes of the electors shall be the Vice President. But if there should remain two or more who have equal votes, the Senate shall choose from them by ballot the Vice President.[6]

3. The Congress may determine the time of choosing the electors, and the day on which they shall give their votes; which day shall be the same throughout the United States.

4. No person except a natural born citizen, or a citizen of the United States, at the time of the adoption of this Constitution, shall be eligible to the office of President; neither shall any person be eligible to the office who shall not have attained to the age of thirty-five years, and been fourteen years a resident within the United States.

5. In case of the removal of the President from office, or of his death, resignation, or inability to discharge the powers and duties of the said office, the same shall devolve on the Vice President, and the congress may by law provide for the case of removal, death, resignation or inability, both of the President and Vice President, declaring what officer shall then act as President, and such officer shall act accordingly until the disability be removed, or a President shall be elected.

6. The President shall, at stated times, receive for his services a compensation which shall neither be increased nor diminished during the period for which he shall have been elected, and he shall not receive within that period any other emolument from the United States, or any of them.

7. Before he enter on the execution of his office, he shall take the following oath or affirmation:—"I do

---

[5]See the Sixteenth Amendment.

[6]Superseded by the Twelfth Amendment.

solemnly swear (or affirm) that I will faithfully execute the office of President of the United States, and will to the best of my ability, preserve, protect and defend the Constitution of the United States."

Section 2. 1. The President shall be commander in chief of the army and navy of the United States, and of the militia of the several States, when called into the actual service of the United States; he may require the opinion in writing, of the principal officer in each of the executive departments, upon any subject relating to the duties of their respective offices, and he shall have power to grant reprieves and pardons for offenses against the United States, except in cases of impeachment.

2. He shall have power, by and with the advice and consent of the Senate, to make treaties, provided two thirds of the senators present concur; and he shall nominate, and by and with the advice and consent of the Senate, shall appoint ambassadors, other public ministers and consuls, judges of the Supreme Court, and all other officers of the United States, whose appointments are not herein otherwise provided for, and which shall be established by law; but the Congress may by law vest the appointment of such inferior officers, as they think proper, in the President alone, in the courts of laws, or in the heads of departments.

3. The President shall have power to fill up all vacancies that may happen during the recess of the Senate, by granting commissions which shall expire at the end of their next session.

Section 3. He shall from time to time give to the Congress information of the state of the Union, and recommend to their consideration such measures as he shall judge necessary and expedient; he may, on extraordinary occasions, convene both Houses, or either of them, and in case of disagreement between them with respect to the time of adjournment, he may adjourn them to such time as he shall think proper; he shall receive ambassadors and other public ministers; he shall take care that the laws be faithfully executed, and shall commission all the officers of the United States.

Section 4. The President, Vice President, and all civil officers of the United States, shall be removed from office on impeachment for, and conviction of, treason, bribery, or other high crimes and misdemeanors.

Article III

Section 1. The judicial power of the United States shall be vested in one Supreme Court, and in such inferior courts as the Congress may from time to time ordain and establish. The judges, both of the Supreme and inferior courts, shall hold their offices during good behavior, and shall, at stated times, receive for their services, a compensation, which shall not be diminished during their continuance in office.

Section 2. 1. The judicial power shall extend to all cases, in law and equity, arising under this Constitution, the laws of the United States, and treaties made, or which shall be made, under their authority;—to all cases of admiralty and maritime jurisdiction;—to controversies to which the United States shall be a party;[7]—to controversies between two or more States;—between a State and citizens of another State;—between citizens of different States;—between citizens of the same State claiming lands under grants of different States, and between a State, or the citizens thereof, and foreign States, citizens or subjects.

2. In all cases affecting ambassadors, other public ministers and consuls, and those in which a State shall be party, the Supreme Court shall have original jurisdiction. In all the other cases before mentioned, the Supreme Court shall have appellate jurisdiction, both as to law and fact, with such exceptions, and under such regulations as the Congress shall make.

3. The trial of all crimes, except in cases of impeachment, shall be by jury; and such trial shall be held in the State where the said crimes shall have been committed; but when not committed within any State, the trial shall be such place or places as the congress may by law have directed.

Section 3. 1. Treason against the United States shall consist only in levying war against them, or in adhering to their enemies, giving them aid and comfort. No person shall be convicted of treason unless on the testimony of two witnesses to the same overt act, or on confession in open court.

2. The Congress shall have power to declare the punishment of treason, but no attainder of treason shall work corruption of blood, or forfeiture except during the life of the person attained.

Article IV

Section 1. Full faith and credit shall be given in each State to the public acts, records, and judicial proceedings of every other State. And the Congress may by general laws prescribe the manner in which such acts, records and proceedings shall be proved, and the effect thereof.

Section 2. 1. The citizens of each State shall be entitled to all privileges and immunities of citizens in the several States.[8]

2. A person charged in any State with treason, felony, or other crime, who shall flee from justice, and be found in another State, shall on demand of the executive authority of the State from which he fled, be delivered up to be removed to the State having jurisdiction of the crime.

3. No person held to service or labor in one State under the laws thereof, escaping into another, shall, in consequence of any law or regulation therein, be discharged from such service or labor, but shall be delivered up on claim of the party to whom such service or labor may be due.[9]

Section 3. 1. New States may be admitted by the Congress into this Union; but no new State shall be formed or erected within the jurisdiction of any other State, nor any State be formed by the junction of two or more States, or parts of States, without the consent of the legislatures of the States concerned as well as of the Congress.

---

[7]See the Eleventh Amendment.
[8]See the Fourteenth Amendment, Sec. 1.
[9]See the Thirteenth Amendment.

2. The Congress shall have power to dispose of and make all needful rules and regulations respecting the territory or other property belonging to the United States; and nothing in this Constitution shall be so construed as to prejudice any claims of the United States, or of any particular State.

Section 4. The United States shall guarantee to every State in this Union a republican form of government, and shall protect each of them against invasion; and on application of the legislature, or of the executive (when the legislature cannot be convened) against domestic violence.

Article V

The Congress, whenever two thirds of both Houses shall deem it necessary, shall propose amendments to this Constitution, or, on the application of the legislatures of two thirds of the several States, shall call a convention for proposing amendments, which in either case shall be valid to all intents and purposes, as part of this Constitution, when ratified by the legislatures of three fourths of the several States, or by conventions in three fourths thereof, as the one or the other mode of ratification may be proposed by the Congress; Provided that no amendment which may be made prior to the year one thousand eight hundred and eight shall in any manner affect the first and fourth clauses in the ninth section of the first article; and that no State, without its consent, shall be deprived of its equal suffrage in the Senate.

Article VI

1. All debts contracted and engagements entered into, before the adoption of this Constitution, shall be as valid against the United States under this Constitution, as under the Confederation.[10]

2. This Constitution, and the laws of the United States which shall be made in pursuance thereof; and all treaties made, or which shall be made, under the authority of the United States, shall be the supreme law of the land; and the judges in every State shall be bound thereby, any thing in the Constitution or laws of any State to the contrary notwithstanding.

3. The senators and representatives before mentioned, and the members of the several State legislatures, and all executive and judicial officers, both of the United States and of the several States, shall be bound by oath or affirmation to support this Constitution; but no religious test shall ever be required as a qualification to any office or public trust under the United States.

Article VII

The ratification of the conventions of nine States shall be sufficient for the establishment of this Constitution between the States so ratifying the same.

Done in Convention by the unanimous consent of the States present the seventeenth day of September in the year of our Lord one thousand seven hundred and eighty-

seven, and of the independence of the United States of America the twelfth. In witness whereof we have hereunto subscribed our names.

[Names omitted]

* * *

Articles in addition to, and amendment of, the Constitution of the United States of America, proposed by Congress, and ratified by the legislatures of the several States, pursuant to the fifth article of the original Constitution.

Amendment I [First ten amendments ratified December 15, 1791]

Congress shall make no law respecting an establishment of religion, or prohibiting the free exercise thereof; or abridging the freedom of speech, or of the press; or the right of the people peaceably to assemble, and to petition the government for a redress of grievances.

Amendment II

A well regulated militia, being necessary to the security of a free State, the right of the people to keep and bear arms, shall not be infringed.

Amendment III

No soldier shall, in time of peace be quartered in any house, without the consent of the owner, nor in time of war, but in a manner to be prescribed by law.

Amendment IV

The right of the people to be secure in their persons, houses, papers, and effects, against unreasonable searches and seizures, shall not be violated, and no warrants shall issue, but upon probable cause, supported by oath or affirmation, and particularly describing the place to be searched, and the persons or things to be seized.

Amendment V

No person shall be held to answer for a capital or otherwise infamous crime, unless on a presentment or indictment of a grand jury, except in cases arising in the land or naval forces, or in the militia, when in actual service in time of war or public danger; nor shall any person be subject for the same offense to be twice put in jeopardy of life or limb; nor shall be compelled in any criminal case to be a witness against himself, nor be deprived of life, liberty, or property, without due process of law; nor shall private property be taken for public use, without just compensation.

Amendment VI

In all criminal prosecutions, the accused shall enjoy the right to a speedy and public trial, by an impartial jury of the State and district wherein the crime shall have been committed, which district shall have been previously ascertained by law, and to be informed of the nature and cause of the accusation; to be confronted with the witnesses against him; to have compulsory process for obtaining witnesses in his favor, and to have the assistance of counsel for his defense.

---

[10]See the Fourteenth Amendment, Sec. 4.

Amendment VII

In suits at common law, where the value in controversy shall exceed twenty dollars, the right of trial by jury shall be preserved, and no fact tried by a jury shall be otherwise reexamined in any court of the United States, than according to the rules of the common law.

Amendment VIII

Excessive bail shall not be required, nor excessive fines imposed, nor cruel and unusual punishments inflicted.

Amendment IX

The enumeration in the Constitution of certain rights shall not be construed to deny or disparage others retained by the people.

Amendment X

The powers not delegated to the United States by the Constitution, nor prohibited by it to the States, are reserved to the States respectively, or to the people.

Amendment XI [January 8, 1798]

The judicial power of the United States shall not be construed to extend to any suit in law or equity, commended or prosecuted against one of the United States by citizens of another State, or by citizens or subjects of any foreign State.

Amendment XII [September 25, 1804]

The electors shall meet in their respective States, and vote by ballot for President and Vice President, one of whom, at least, shall not be an inhabitant of the same State with themselves; they shall name in their ballots the person voted for as President, and in distinct ballots, the person voted for as Vice President, and they shall make distinct lists of all persons voted for as President and of all persons voted for as Vice President, and of the number of votes for each, which lists they shall sign and certify, and transmit sealed to the seat of the government of the United States, directed to the President of the Senate;—The President of the Senate shall, in the presence of the Senate and House of Representatives, open all the certificates and the votes shall then be counted;—The person having the greatest number of votes for President, shall be the President, if such number be a majority of the whole number of electors appointed; and if no person have such majority, then from the persons having the highest numbers not exceeding three on the list of those voted for as President, the House of Representatives shall choose immediately, by ballot, the President. But in choosing the President, the votes shall be taken by States, the representation from each State having one vote; a quorum for this purpose shall consist of a member or members from two thirds of the States, and a majority of all the States shall be necessary to a choice. And if the House of Representatives shall not choose a President whenever the right of choice shall devolve upon them, before the fourth day of March next following, then the Vice President shall act as President, as in the case of the death or other constitutional disability of the President.

The person having the greatest number of votes as Vice President shall be the Vice President, if such number be a majority of the whole number of electors appointed, and if no person have a majority, then from the two highest numbers on the list, the Senate shall choose the Vice President; a quorum for the purpose shall consist of two thirds of the whole number of Senators, and a majority of the whole number shall be necessary to a choice. But no person constitutionally ineligible to the office of President shall be eligible to that of Vice President of the United States.

Amendment XIII [December 18, 1865]

Section 1. Neither slavery nor involuntary servitude, except as a punishment for crime whereof the party shall have been duly convicted, shall exist within the United States, or any place subject to their jurisdiction.

Section 2. Congress shall have power to enforce this article by appropriate legislation.

Amendment XIV [July 28, 1868]

Section 1. All persons born or naturalized in the United States, and subject to the jurisdiction thereof, are citizens of the United States and of the State wherein they reside. No State shall make or enforce any law which shall abridge the privileges or immunities of citizens of the United States; nor shall any State deprive any person of life, liberty, or property, without due process of law; nor deny to any person within its jurisdiction the equal protection of the laws.

Section 2. Representatives shall be apportioned among the several States according to their respective numbers, counting the whole number of persons in each State, excluding Indians not taxed. But when the right to vote at any election for the choice of electors for President and Vice President of the United States, representatives in Congress, the executive and judicial officers of a State, or the members of the legislature thereof, is denied to any of the male inhabitants of such State, being twenty-one years of age, and citizens of the United States, or in any way abridged, except for participating in rebellion, or other crime, the basis of representation there shall be reduced in the proportion which the number of such male citizens shall bear to the whole number of male citizens twenty-one years of age in such State.

Section 3. No person shall be a senator or representative in Congress, or elector of President and Vice President, or hold any office, civil or military, under the United States, or under any State, who having previously taken an oath, as a member of Congress, or as an officer of the United States, or as a member of any State legislature, or as an executive or judicial officer of any State, to support the Constitution of the United States, shall have engaged in insurrection or rebellion against the same, or given aid or comfort to the enemies thereof. But Congress may by a vote of two thirds of each House, remove such disability.

Section 4. The validity of the public debt of the United States, authorized by law, including debts incurred for payment of pensions and bounties for services in suppressing insurrection or rebellion; shall not be questioned.

But neither the United States nor any State shall assume or pay any debt or obligation incurred in aid of insurrection or rebellion against the United States, or any claim for the loss or emancipation of any slave; but all such debts, obligations, and claims shall be held illegal and void.

Section 5. The Congress shall have the power to enforce, by appropriate legislation, the provisions of this article.

Amendment XV [March 30, 1870]

Section 1. The right of citizens of the United States to vote shall not be denied or abridged by the United States or by any State on account of race, color, or previous condition of servitude.

Section 2. The Congress shall have power to enforce this article by appropriate legislation.

Amendment XVI [February 25, 1913]

The Congress shall have power to lay and collect taxes on incomes, from whatever source derived, without apportionment among the several States, and without regard to any census or enumeration.

Amendment XVII [May 31, 1913]

The Senate of the United States shall be composed of two senators from each State, elected by the people thereof, for six years; and each senator shall have one vote. The electors in each State shall have the qualifications requisite for electors of the most numerous branch of the State legislature.

When vacancies happen in the representation of any State in the Senate, the executive authority of such State shall issue writs of election to fill such vacancies: *Provided,* That the legislature of any State may empower the executive thereof to make temporary appointments until the people fill the vacancies by election as the legislature may direct.

This amendment shall not be so construed as to affect the election or term of any senator chosen before it becomes valid as part of the Constitution.

Amendment XVIII[11] [January 29, 1919]

After one year from the ratification of this article, the manufacture, sale, or transportation of intoxicating liquors within, the importation thereof into, or the exportation thereof from the United States and all territory subject to the jurisdiction thereof for beverage purposes is thereby prohibited.

The Congress and the several States shall have concurrent power to enforce this article by appropriate legislation.

This article shall be inoperative unless it shall have been ratified as an amendment to the Constitution by the legislatures of the several States, as provided in the constitution, within seven years from the date of the submission hereof to the States by Congress.

[11]Repealed by the Twenty-first Amendment.

Amendment XIX [August 26, 1920]

The right of citizens of the United States to vote shall not be denied or abridged by the United States or by any State on account of sex.

Congress shall have the power to enforce this article by appropriate legislation.

Amendment XX [January 23, 1933]

Section 1. The terms of the President and Vice President shall end at noon on the 20th day of January and the terms of Senators and Representatives at noon on the 3d day of January, of the years in which such terms would have ended if this article had not been ratified; and the terms of their successors shall then begin.

Section 2. The Congress shall assemble at least once in every year, and such meeting shall begin at noon on the 3d day of January, unless they shall by law appoint a different day.

Section 3. If, at the time fixed for the beginning of the term of President, the President-elect shall have died, the Vice President-elect shall become President. If a President shall not have been chosen before the time fixed for the beginning of his term, or if the President-elect shall have failed to qualify, then the Vice President-elect shall act as President until a President shall have qualified; and the Congress may by law provide for the case wherein neither a President-elect nor a Vice President-elect shall have qualified, declaring who shall then act as President, or the manner in which one who is to act shall be selected, and such person shall act accordingly until a President or Vice President shall have qualified.

Section 4. The Congress may by law provide for the case of the death of any of the persons from whom, the House of Representatives may choose a President whenever the right of choice shall have devolved upon them, and for the case of the death of any of the persons from whom the Senate may choose a Vice President whenever the right of choice shall have devolved upon them.

Section 5. Sections 1 and 2 shall take effect on the 15th day of October following the ratification of this article.

Section 6. This article shall be inoperative unless it shall have been ratified as an amendment to the Constitution by the legislatures of three-fourths of the several States within seven years from the date of its submission.

Amendment XXI [December 5, 1933]

Section 1. The Eighteenth Article of amendment to the Constitution of the United States is hereby repealed.

Section 2. The transportation or importation into any State, Territory, or possession of the United States for delivery or use therein of intoxicating liquors in violation of the laws thereof, is hereby prohibited.

Section 3. This article shall be inoperative unless it shall have been ratified as an amendment to the Constitution by conventions in the several States, as provided in the Constitution, within seven years from the date of the submission thereof to the States by the Congress.

Amendment XXII [*March 1, 1951*]

No person shall be elected to the office of the President more than twice, and no person who has held the office of President, or acted as President, for more than two years of a term to which some other person was elected President shall be elected to the office of the President more than once.

But this article shall not apply to any person holding the office of President when this article was proposed by the Congress, and shall not prevent any person who may be holding the office of President, or acting as President, during the term within which this article becomes operative from holding the office of President or acting as President during the remainder of such term.

This article shall be inoperative unless it shall have been ratified as an amendment to the Constitution by the legislatures of three-fourths of the several States within seven years from the date of its submission to the States by the Congress.

Amendment XXIII [*March 29, 1961*]

Section 1. The District constituting the seat of Government of the United States shall appoint in such manner as the Congress may direct.

A number of electors of President and Vice President equal to the whole number of Senators and Representatives in Congress to which the District would be entitled if it were a State, but in no event more than the least populous State; they shall be in addition to those appointed by the States, but they shall be considered, for the purposes of the election of President and Vice President, to be electors appointed by a State; and they shall meet in the District and perform such duties as provided by the twelfth article of amendment.

Section 2. The Congress shall have power to enforce this article by appropriate legislation.

Amendment XXIV [*January 23, 1964*]

Section 1. The right of citizens of the United States to vote in any primary or other election for President or Vice President, for electors for President or Vice President, or for Senator or Representative in Congress, shall not be denied or abridged by the United States or any State by reason of failure to pay any poll tax or other tax.

Section 2. The Congress shall have power to enforce this article by appropriate legislation.

Amendment XXV [*February 10, 1967*]

Section 1. In case of the removal of the President from office or of his death or resignation, the Vice President shall become President.

Section 2. Whenever there is a vacancy in the office of the Vice President, the President shall nominate a Vice President who shall take office upon confirmation by a majority of both Houses of Congress.

Section 3. Whenever the President transmits to the President pro tempore of the Senate and the Speaker of the House of Representatives his written declaration that he is unable to discharge the powers and duties of his office, and until he transmits to them a written declaration to the contrary, such powers and duties shall be discharged by the Vice President as Acting President.

Section 4. Whenever the Vice president and a majority of either the principal officers of the executive departments or of such other body as Congress may by law provide, transmit to the President pro tempore of the Senate and the Speaker of the House of Representatives their written declaration that the President is unable to discharge the powers and duties of his office, the Vice President shall immediately assume the powers and duties of the office as Acting President.

Thereafter, when the President transmits to the President pro tempore of the Senate and the Speaker of the House of Representatives his written declaration that no inability exists, he shall resume the powers and duties of his office unless the Vice President and a majority of either the principal officers of the executive departments or of such other body as Congress may by law provide, transmit within four days to the President pro tempore of the Senate and the Speaker of the House of Representatives their written declaration that the President is unable to discharge the powers and duties of his office. Thereupon Congress shall decide the issue, assembling within forty-eight hours for that purpose if not in session. If the Congress, within twenty-one days after receipt of the latter written declaration, or, if Congress is not in session, within twenty-one days after Congress is required to assemble, determines by two-thirds vote of both Houses that the President is unable to discharge the powers and duties of his office, the Vice President shall continue to discharge the same as Acting President; otherwise, the President shall resume the powers and duties of his office.

Amendment XXVI [*June 30, 1971*]

Section 1. The right of citizens of the United States who are eighteen years of age or older to vote shall not be denied or abridged by the United States or by any State on account of age.

Section 2. The Congress shall have power to enforce this article by appropriate legislation.

Amendment XXVII[12] [*May 7, 1992*]

No law, varying the compensation for services of the Senators and Representatives, shall take effect until an election of Representatives shall have intervened.

---

[12]James Madison proposed this amendment in 1789 together with the ten amendments that were adopted as the Bill of Rights, but it failed to win ratification at the time. Congress, however, had set no deadline for its ratification, and over the years—particularly in the 1980s and 1990s—many states voted to add it to the Constitution. With the ratification of Michigan in 1992 it passed the threshold of 3/4ths of the states required for adoption, but because the process took more than 200 years, its validity remains in doubt.

PRESIDENTS AND VICE PRESIDENTS

1. George Washington (1789)
   John Adams (1789)
2. John Adams (1797)
   Thomas Jefferson (1797)
3. Thomas Jefferson (1801)
   Aaron Burr (1801)
   George Clinton (1805)
4. James Madison (1809)
   George Clinton (1809)
   Elbridge Gerry (1813)
5. James Monroe (1817)
   Daniel D. Thompkins (1817)
6. John Quincy Adams (1825)
   John C. Calhoun (1825)
7. Andrew Jackson (1829)
   John C. Calhoun (1829)
   Martin Van Buren (1833)
8. Martin Van Buren (1837)
   Richard M. Johnson (1837)
9. William H. Harrison (1841)
   John Tyler (1841)
10. John Tyler (1841)
11. James K. Polk (1845)
    George M. Dallas (1845)
12. Zachary Taylor (1849)
    Millard Fillmore (1849)
13. Millard Fillmore (1850)
14. Franklin Pierce (1853)
    William R. King (1853)
15. James Buchanan (1857)
    John C. Breckinridge (1857)
16. Abraham Lincoln (1861)
    Hannibal Hamlin (1861)
    Andrew Johnson (1865)
17. Andrew Johnson (1865)
18. Ulysses S. Grant (1869)
    Schuyler Colfax (1869)
    Henry Wilson (1873)
19. Rutherford B. Hayes (1877)
    William A. Wheeler (1877)
20. James A. Garfield (1881)
    Chester A. Arthur (1881)
21. Chester A. Arthur (1881)
22. Grover Cleveland (1885)
    T. A. Hendricks (1885)

23. Benjamin Harrison (1889)
    Levi P. Morgan (1889)
24. Grover Cleveland (1893)
    Adlai E. Stevenson (1893)
25. William McKinley (1897)
    Garret A. Hobart (1897)
    Theodore Roosevelt (1901)
26. Theodore Roosevelt (1901)
    Charles Fairbanks (1905)
27. William H. Taft (1909)
    James S. Sherman (1909)
28. Woodrow Wilson (1913)
    Thomas R. Marshall (1913)
29. Warren G. Harding (1921)
    Calvin Coolidge (1921)
30. Calvin Coolidge (1923)
    Charles G. Dawes (1925)
31. Herbert C. Hoover (1929)
    Charles Curtis (1929)
32. Franklin D. Roosevelt (1933)
    John Nance Garner (1933)
    Henry A. Wallace (1941)
    Harry S. Truman (1945)
33. Harry S. Truman (1945)
    Alben W. Barkley (1949)
34. Dwight D. Eisenhower (1953)
    Richard M. Nixon (1953)
35. John F. Kennedy (1961)
    Lyndon B. Johnson (1961)
36. Lyndon B. Johnson (1963)
    Hubert H. Humphrey (1965)
37. Richard M. Nixon (1969)
    Spiro T. Agnew (1969)
    Gerald R. Ford (1973)
38. Gerald R. Ford (1974)
    Nelson A. Rockefeller (1974)
39. James E. Carter Jr. (1977)
    Walter F. Mondale (1977)
40. Ronald W. Reagan (1981)
    George H. Bush (1981)
41. George H. Bush (1989)
    James D. Quayle III (1989)
42. William J. Clinton (1993)
    Albert Gore (1993)

PRESIDENTIAL ELECTIONS

Year	Number of States	Candidates	Party	Popular Vote*	Electoral Vote[†]	Percentage of Popular Vote
1789	11	GEORGE WASHINGTON	No party designations		69	
		John Adams			34	
		Other Candidates			35	
1792	15	GEORGE WASHINGTON	No party designations		132	
		John Adams			77	
		George Clinton			50	
		Other Candidates			5	
1796	16	JOHN ADAMS	Federalist		71	
		Thomas Jefferson	Democratic-Republican		68	
		Thomas Pinckney	Federalist		59	
		Aaron Burr	Democratic-Republican		30	
		Other Candidates			48	
1800	16	THOMAS JEFFERSON	Democratic-Republican		73	
		Aaron Burr	Democratic-Republican		73	
		John Adams	Federalist		65	
		Charles C. Pinckney	Federalist		64	
		John Jay	Federalist		1	
1804	17	THOMAS JEFFERSON	Democratic-Republican		162	
		Charles C. Pinckney	Federalist		14	
1808	17	JAMES MADISON	Democratic-Republican		122	
		Charles C. Pinckney	Federalist		47	
		George Clinton	Democratic-Republican		6	
1812	18	JAMES MADISON	Democratic-Republican		128	
		DeWitt Clinton	Federalist		89	
1816	19	JAMES MONROE	Democratic-Republican		183	
		Rufus King	Federalist		34	
1820	24	JAMES MONROE	Democratic-Republican		231	
		John Quincy Adams	Democratic-Republican		1	
1824	24	JOHN QUINCY ADAMS	Democratic-Republican	108,740	84	30.5
		Andrew Jackson	Democratic-Republican	153,544	99	43.1
		William H. Crawford	Democratic-Republican	46,618	41	13.1
		Henry Clay	Democratic-Republican	47,136	37	13.2
1828	24	ANDREW JACKSON	Democrat	647,286	178	56.0
		John Quincy Adams	National-Republican	508,064	83	44.0
1832	24	ANDREW JACKSON	Democrat	687,502	219	55.0
		Henry Clay	National-Republican	530,189	49	42.4
		William Wirt	Anti-Masonic	} 33,108	7	} 2.6
		John Floyd	National-Republican		11	

*Percentage of popular vote given for any election year may not total 100 percent because candidates receiving less than 1 percent of the popular vote have been omitted.

[†]Prior to the passage of the Twelfth Amendment in 1904, the electoral college voted for two presidential candidates; the runner-up became Vice-President. Data from *Historical Statistics of the United States, Colonial Times to 1957* (1961), pp. 682–683, and *The World Almanac*.

PRESIDENTIAL ELECTIONS
(continued)

Year	Number of States	Candidates	Party	Popular Vote	Electoral Vote	Percentage of Popular Vote
1836	26	MARTIN VAN BUREN	Democrat	765,483	170	50.9
		William H. Harrison	Whig		73	
		Hugh L. White	Whig		26	
		Daniel Webster	Whig	739,795	14	49.1
		W. P. Mangum	Whig		11	
1840	26	WILLIAM H. HARRISON	Whig	1,274,624	234	53.1
		Martin Van Buren	Democrat	1,127,781	60	46.9
1844	26	JAMES K. POLK	Democrat	1,338,464	170	49.6
		Henry Clay	Whig	1,300,097	105	48.1
		James G. Birney	Liberty	62,300		2.3
1848	30	ZACHARY TAYLOR	Whig	1,360,967	163	47.4
		Lewis Cass	Democrat	1,222,342	127	42.5
		Martin Van Buren	Free-Soil	291,263		10.1
1852	31	FRANKLIN PIERCE	Democrat	1,601,117	254	50.9
		Winfield Scott	Whig	1,385,453	42	44.1
		John P. Hale	Free-Soil	155,825		5.0
1856	31	JAMES BUCHANAN	Democrat	1,832,955	174	45.3
		John C. Frémont	Republican	1,339,932	114	33.1
		Millard Fillmore	American ("Know Nothing")	871,731	8	21.6
1860	33	ABRAHAM LINCOLN	Republican	1,865,593	180	39.8
		Stephen A. Douglas	Democrat	1,382,713	12	29.5
		John C. Breckinridge	Democrat	848,356	72	18.1
		John Bell	Constitutional Union	592,906	39	12.6
1864	36	ABRAHAM LINCOLN	Republican	2,206,938	212	55.0
		George B. McClellan	Democrat	1,803,787	21	45.0
1868	37	ULYSSES S. GRANT	Republican	3,013,421	214	52.7
		Horatio Seymour	Democrat	2,706,829	80	47.3
1872	37	ULYSSES S. GRANT	Republican	3,596,745	286	55.6
		Horace Greeley	Democrat	2,843,446	*	43.9
1876	38	RUTHERFORD B. HAYES	Republican	4,036,572	185	48.0
		Samuel J. Tilden	Democrat	4,284,020	184	51.0
1880	38	JAMES A. GARFIELD	Republican	4,453,295	214	48.5
		Winfield S. Hancock	Democrat	4,414,082	155	48.1
		James B. Weaver	Greenback-Labor	308,578		3.4
1884	38	GROVER CLEVELAND	Democrat	4,879,507	219	48.5
		James G. Blaine	Republican	4,850,293	182	48.2
		Benjamin F. Butler	Greenback-Labor	175,370		1.8
		John P. St. John	Prohibition	150,369		1.5
1888	38	BENJAMIN HARRISON	Republican	5,447,129	233	47.9
		Grover Cleveland	Democrat	5,537,857	168	48.6
		Clinton B. Fisk	Prohibition	249,506		2.2
		Anson J. Streeter	Union Labor	146,935		1.3

*Because of the death of Greeley, Democratic electors scattered their votes.

PRESIDENTIAL ELECTIONS
(continued)

Year	Number of States	Candidates	Party	Popular Vote	Electoral Vote	Percentage of Popular Vote
1892	44	GROVER CLEVELAND	Democrat	5,555,426	277	46.1
		Benjamin Harrison	Republican	5,182,690	145	43.0
		James B. Weaver	People's	1,029,846	22	8.5
		John Bidwell	Prohibition	264,133		2.2
1896	45	WILLIAM MCKINLEY	Republican	7,102,246	271	51.1
		William J. Bryan	Democrat	6,492,559	176	47.7
1900	45	WILLIAM MCKINLEY	Republican	7,218,491	292	51.7
		William J. Bryan	Democrat; Populist	6,356,734	155	45.5
		John C. Woolley	Prohibition	208,914		1.5
1904	45	THEODORE ROOSEVELT	Republican	7,628,461	336	57.4
		Alton B. Parker	Democrat	5,084,223	140	37.6
		Eugene V. Debs	Socialist	402,283		3.0
		Silas C. Swallow	Prohibition	258,536		1.9
1908	46	WILLIAM H. TAFT	Republican	7,675,320	321	51.6
		William J. Bryan	Democrat	6,412,294	162	43.1
		Eugene V. Debs	Socialist	420,793		2.8
		Eugene W. Chafin	Prohibition	253,840		1.7
1912	48	WOODROW WILSON	Democrat	6,296,547	435	41.9
		Theodore Roosevelt	Progressive	4,118,571	88	27.4
		William H. Taft	Republican	3,486,720	8	23.2
		Eugene V. Debs	Socialist	900,672		6.0
		Eugene W. Chafin	Prohibition	206,275		1.4
1916	48	WOODROW WILSON	Democrat	9,127,695	277	49.4
		Charles E. Hughes	Republican	8,533,507	254	46.2
		A. L. Benson	Socialist	585,113		3.2
		J. Frank Hanly	Prohibition	220,506		1.2
1920	48	WARREN G. HARDING	Republican	16,143,407	404	60.4
		James M. Cox	Democrat	9,130,328	127	34.2
		Eugene V. Debs	Socialist	919,799		3.4
		P. P. Christensen	Farmer-Labor	265,411		1.0
1924	48	CALVIN COOLIDGE	Republican	15,718,211	382	54.0
		John W. Davis	Democrat	8,385,283	136	28.8
		Robert M. La Follette	Progressive	4,831,289	13	16.6
1928	48	HERBERT C. HOOVER	Republican	21,391,993	444	58.2
		Alfred E. Smith	Democrat	15,016,169	87	40.9
1932	48	FRANKLIN D. ROOSEVELT	Democrat	22,809,638	472	57.4
		Herbert C. Hoover	Republican	15,758,901	59	39.7
		Norman Thomas	Socialist	881,951		2.2
1936	48	FRANKLIN D. ROOSEVELT	Democrat	27,752,869	523	60.8
		Alfred M. Landon	Republican	16,674,665	8	36.5
		William Lemke	Union	882,479		1.9
1940	48	FRANKLIN D. ROOSEVELT	Democrat	27,307,819	449	54.8
		Wendell L. Willkie	Republican	22,321,018	82	44.8
1944	48	FRANKLIN D. ROOSEVELT	Democrat	25,606,585	432	53.5
		Thomas E. Dewey	Republican	22,014,745	99	46.0

PRESIDENTIAL ELECTIONS
(continued)

Year	Number of States	Candidates	Party	Popular Vote	Electoral Vote	Percentage of Popular Vote
1948	48	HARRY S. TRUMAN	Democrat	24,105,812	303	49.5
		Thomas E. Dewey	Republican	21,970,065	189	45.1
		J. Strom Thurmond	States' Rights	1,169,063	39	2.4
		Henry A. Wallace	Progressive	1,157,172		2.4
1952	48	DWIGHT D. EISENHOWER	Republican	33,936,234	442	55.1
		Adlai E. Stevenson	Democrat	27,314,992	89	44.4
1956	48	DWIGHT D. EISENHOWER	Republican	35,590,472	457[*]	57.6
		Adlai E. Stevenson	Democrat	26,022,752	73	42.1
1960	50	JOHN F. KENNEDY	Democrat	34,227,096	303[†]	49.9
		Richard M. Nixon	Republican	34,108,546	219	49.6
1964	50	LYNDON B. JOHNSON	Democrat	42,676,220	486	61.3
		Barry M. Goldwater	Republican	26,860,314	52	38.5
1968	50	RICHARD M. NIXON	Republican	31,785,480	301	43.4
		Hubert H. Humphrey	Democrat	31,275,165	191	42.7
		George C. Wallace	American Independent	9,906,473	46	13.5
1972	50	RICHARD M. NIXON[‡]	Republican	47,165,234	520	60.6
		George S. McGovern	Democrat	29,168,110	17	37.5
1976	50	JIMMY CARTER	Democrat	40,828,929	297	50.1
		Gerald R. Ford	Republican	39,148,940	240	47.9
		Eugene McCarthy	Independent	739,256		
1980	50	RONALD REAGAN	Republican	43,201,220	489	50.9
		Jimmy Carter	Democrat	34,913,332	49	41.2
		John B. Anderson	Independent	5,581,379		
1984	50	RONALD REAGAN	Republican	53,428,357	525	59.0
		Walter F. Mondale	Democrat	36,930,923	13	41.0
1988	50	GEORGE BUSH	Republican	48,901,046	426	53.4
		Michael Dukakis	Democrat	41,809,030	111	45.6
1992	50	BILL CLINTON	Democrat	43,728,275	370	43.2
		George Bush	Republican	38,167,416	168	37.7
		H. Ross Perot	United We Stand, America	19,237,247		19.0
1996	50	BILL CLINTON	Democrat	45,590,703	379	49.0
		Robert Dole	Republican	37,816,307	159	41.0
		H. Ross Perot	Reform	7,874,283		8.0

[*]Walter B. Jones received 1 electoral vote.

[†]Harry F. Byrd received 15 electoral votes.

[‡]Resigned August 9, 1974: Vice President Gerald R. Ford became President.

ADMISSION OF STATES INTO THE UNION

State	Date of Admission	State	Date of Admission
1. Delaware	December 7, 1787	26. Michigan	January 26, 1837
2. Pennsylvania	December 12, 1787	27. Florida	March 3, 1845
3. New Jersey	December 18, 1787	28. Texas	December 29, 1845
4. Georgia	January 2, 1788	29. Iowa	December 28, 1846
5. Connecticut	January 9, 1788	30. Wisconsin	May 29, 1848
6. Massachusetts	February 6, 1788	31. California	September 9, 1850
7. Maryland	April 28, 1788	32. Minnesota	May 11, 1858
8. South Carolina	May 23, 1788	33. Oregon	February 14, 1859
9. New Hampshire	June 21, 1788	34. Kansas	January 29, 1861
10. Virginia	June 25, 1788	35. West Virginia	June 20, 1863
11. New York	July 26, 1788	36. Nevada	October 31, 1864
12. North Carolina	November 21, 1789	37. Nebraska	March 1, 1867
13. Rhode Island	May 29, 1790	38. Colorado	August 1, 1876
14. Vermont	March 4, 1791	39. North Dakota	November 2, 1889
15. Kentucky	June 1, 1792	40. South Dakota	November 2, 1889
16. Tennessee	June 1, 1796	41. Montana	November 8, 1889
17. Ohio	March 1, 1803	42. Washington	November 11, 1889
18. Louisiana	April 30, 1812	43. Idaho	July 3, 1890
19. Indiana	December 11, 1816	44. Wyoming	July 10, 1890
20. Mississippi	December 10, 1817	45. Utah	January 4, 1896
21. Illinois	December 3, 1818	46. Oklahoma	November 16, 1907
22. Alabama	December 14, 1819	47. New Mexico	January 6, 1912
23. Maine	March 15, 1820	48. Arizona	February 14, 1912
24. Missouri	August 10, 1821	49. Alaska	January 3, 1959
25. Arkansas	June 15, 1836	50. Hawaii	August 21, 1959

DEMOGRAPHICS OF THE UNITED STATES

POPULATION GROWTH

Year	Population	Percent Increase
1630	4,600	
1640	26,600	478.3
1650	50,400	90.8
1660	75,100	49.0
1670	111,900	49.0
1680	151,500	35.4
1690	210,400	38.9
1700	250,900	19.2
1710	331,700	32.2
1720	466,200	40.5
1730	629,400	35.0
1740	905,600	43.9
1750	1,170,800	29.3
1760	1,593,600	36.1
1770	2,148,100	34.8
1780	2,780,400	29.4
1790	3,929,214	41.3
1800	5,308,483	35.1
1810	7,239,881	36.4
1820	9,638,453	33.1
1830	12,866,020	33.5
1840	17,069,453	32.7
1850	23,191,876	35.9
1860	31,443,321	35.6
1870	39,818,449	26.6
1880	50,155,783	26.0
1890	62,947,714	25.5
1900	75,994,575	20.7
1910	91,972,266	21.0
1920	105,710,620	14.9
1930	122,775,046	16.1
1940	131,669,275	7.2
1950	150,697,361	14.5
1960	179,323,175	19.0
1970	203,235,298	13.3
1980	226,545,805	11.5
1990	248,709,873	9.8
1996	265,557,000	6.8

Source: *Historical Statistics of the United States* (1975); *Statistical Abstract by the United States* (1991, 1997).
Note: Figures for 1630–1780 include British colonies within limits of present United States only; Native American population included only in 1930 and thereafter.

WORKFORCE

Year	Total Number Workers (1000s)	Farmers as % of Total	Women as % of Total	% Workers in Unions
1810	2,330	84	(NA)	(NA)
1840	5,660	75	(NA)	(NA)
1860	11,110	53	(NA)	(NA)
1870	12,506	53	15	(NA)
1880	17,392	52	15	(NA)
1890	23,318	43	17	(NA)
1900	29,073	40	18	3
1910	38,167	31	21	6
1920	41,614	26	21	12
1930	48,830	22	22	7
1940	53,011	17	24	27
1950	59,643	12	28	25
1960	69,877	8	32	26
1970	82,049	4	37	25
1980	108,544	3	42	23
1990	117,914	3	45	16
1995	124,900	3	46	15

Source: *Historical Statistics of the United States* (1975); *Statistical Abstract of the United States* (1991, 1996).

VITAL STATISTICS
(per thousands)

Year	Births	Deaths	Marriages	Divorces
1800	55	(NA)	(NA)	(NA)
1810	54.3	(NA)	(NA)	(NA)
1820	55.2	(NA)	(NA)	(NA)
1830	51.4	(NA)	(NA)	(NA)
1840	51.8	(NA)	(NA)	(NA)
1850	43.3	(NA)	(NA)	(NA)
1860	44.3	(NA)	(NA)	(NA)
1870	38.3	(NA)	9.6 (1867)	0.3 (1867)
1880	39.8	(NA)	9.1 (1875)	0.3 (1875)
1890	31.5	(NA)	9.0	0.5
1900	32.3	17.2	9.3	0.7
1910	30.1	14.7	10.3	0.9
1920	27.7	13.0	12.0	1.6
1930	21.3	11.3	9.2	1.6
1940	19.4	10.8	12.1	2.0
1950	24.1	9.6	11.1	2.6
1960	23.7	9.5	8.5	2.2
1970	18.4	9.5	10.6	3.5
1980	15.9	8.8	10.6	5.2
1990	16.7	8.6	9.8	4.7
1994	15.0	8.8	9.1	4.6

Source: *Historical Statistics of the United States* (1975); *Statistical Abstract of the United States* (1991, 1997).

RACIAL COMPOSITION OF THE POPULATION
(in thousands)

Year	White	Black	Indian	Hispanic	Asian
1790	3,172	757	(NA)	(NA)	(NA)
1800	4,306	1,002	(NA)	(NA)	(NA)
1820	7,867	1,772	(NA)	(NA)	(NA)
1840	14,196	2,874	(NA)	(NA)	(NA)
1860	26,923	4,442	(NA)	(NA)	(NA)
1880	43,403	6,581	(NA)	(NA)	(NA)
1900	66,809	8,834	(NA)	(NA)	(NA)
1910	81,732	9,828	(NA)	(NA)	(NA)
1920	94,821	10,463	(NA)	(NA)	(NA)
1930	110,287	11,891	(NA)	(NA)	(NA)
1940	118,215	12,866	(NA)	(NA)	(NA)
1950	134,942	15,042	(NA)	(NA)	(NA)
1960	158,832	18,872	(NA)	(NA)	(NA)
1970	178,098	22,581	(NA)	(NA)	(NA)
1980	194,713	26,683	1,420	14,609	3,729
1990	205,710	30,486	2,065	22,354	7,458
1996	219,749	30,503	2,288	28,269	9,743

Source: U.S. Bureau of the Census, *U.S. Census of Population: 1940*, vol. II, part 1, and vol. IV, part 1; *1950*, vol. II, part 1; *1960*, vol. I, part 1; *1970*, vol. I, part B; and *Current Population Reports*, P25-1095 and P25-1104; *Statistical Abstract of the United States* (1997); and unpublished data.

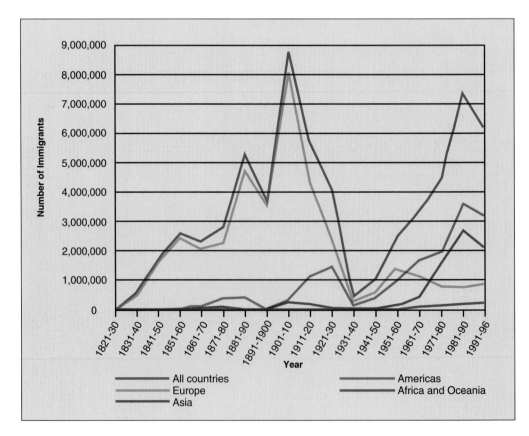

Immigration to the United States since 1820

Source: *Statistical Yearbook of the Immigration and Naturalization Service*, 1996.

PHOTO AND TEXT CREDITS

Chapter 1: Photos: Cahokia Mounds State Historic Site, xxxii (vols. I, II, A, B, C)/xlviii (combined edition); Jerry Jacka/Arizona State Museum, University of Arizona, 6; Denver Museum of Natural History, 7; American Museum of Natural History, 11; National Museum of the American Indian/Smithsonian Institution, 13; Helga Teiwes, Arizona State Museum, 13; David Hiser/David Muench Photography, Inc., 14; George Gerster/Comstock, 15; Rota/American Museum of Natural History, 20 Text: "Emergence Song" (excerpt) from William Brandon, *The Magic World: American Indian Songs and Poems.* Copyright © 1971 by William Brandon. Reprinted with the permission of William Morrow and Company, Inc., 5; Winnebago song, "This Newly Created World," from the Winnebago Medicine Rite as recorded in Raul Radin, *The Road to Life and Death: A Ritual Drama of the American Indians* (Bollinger Series V), p. 254. Copyright 1945 and © renewed 1972 by Princeton University Press. Reprinted with the permission of the publishers., 10

Chapter 2: Photos: The Granger Collection, 25; Art Resource, Musee Conde, Chantilly/Giraudon, Art Resource, NY, 29; From THE SHIP, AN ILLUSTRATED HISTORY by Bjorn Landstrom, Copyright © 1961 by Bokforlaget Forum AB. Used by permission of Doubleday, a division of Bantam Doubleday Dell Publishing Group, Inc., 31; The Granger Collection, 32; The British Library, 34; Library of Congress, 35; The British Library, 36; Jacques Le Moyne, "Rene de Loudonniere and Chief Athore," 1564, watercolor, The New York Public Library, NY, 41; Capitaine de la Nation, *Codex Canadienses*, artist Louis Nicolas, from the collection of Gilcrease Museum, Tulsa, OK, 42; The Bridgeman Art Library, 43; The Granger Collection, 44 Text: "The African, Indian and European Population of the Americas" from Colin McEvedy and Richard Jones, *Atlas of World Population History.* Copyright © 1978 by Colin McEvedy and Richard Jones. Reprinted with the permission of Penguin Putnam, Inc., 39

Chapter 3: Photos: Jerry Jacka Photography, 49; New York Public Library, 53; (left) "Princeton University Library," Manuscripts Division. Department of Rare Books and Special Collections. Princeton University Library, 55; Library of Congress, 55; Library of Congress, 56; Library of Congress, 60; The John Carter Brown Library, at Brown University, 61; The Fine Arts Museum of San Francisco, 62; The New York Historical Society, 65; The Historical Society of Pennsylvania, 66; Courtesy, American Antiquarian Society, 68

Chapter 4: Photos: The British Library, 73; Library of Congress, 77; The Bridgeman Art Library, 79; Library of Congress, 81; The Granger Collection, New York, 82; American Antiquarian Society, 83; The Maryland Historical Society, 85; Carolina Art Association/Gibbes Museum of Art, 86; Colonial Williamsburg Foundation, 90; The Philbrook Museum of Art, 91; Michael Holford/The Victoria and Albert Museum, 93; The Saint Louis Art Museum, 96; Virginia Museum of Fine Arts, 99 Text: "Estimated Number of Africans Imported to British North America," from R.C. Simmons, *The American Colonies: From Settlement to Independence* (London:Longman, 1976). Copyright © 1976 by R.C. Simmons. Reprinted with the permission of The Peters Fraser and Dunlop Group Limited, 80

Chapter 5: Photos: Colonial Williamsburg Foundation, 103; The Historical Society of Pennsylvania, 106; Jack W. Dykinga & Associates, 110; United States Geological Survey, 112; William Johnson/Stock, Boston, 113; Henry Glassie, Pattern in the Material Folk Culture of the Eastern United States, 114; (left) Courtesy, American Antiquarian Society, 118; Library of Congress, 118; Schalkwijk/Art Resource, NY, 121; American Antiquarian Society, 124; John Carter Brown Library, Brown University, 127 Text: "Distribution of Assessed Taxable Wealth in Eighteenth-Century Chester County, Pennsylvania," Copyright © 1968 by Peter N. Stearns. Reprinted with the permission of the publishers. 122; "Wealth Held by Richest 10 Percent of the Population: Northern and

Southern Colonies Compared, 1770," Copyright © by Princeton University Press, renewed 1993 by Jackson Turner Main. Reprinted with the permission of Princeton University Press, 122

Chapter 6: Photos: The Granger Collection, 132; National Gallery of Canada, 138; Treaty, dated 13 July 1765, between Sir William Johnson and representatives of the Delaware, Shawnee, and Mingo nations. On parchment, 16" x 24.5". Photo by Carmelo Guadagno. Photograph courtesy of National Museum of the American Indian/Smithsonian Institution. Neg. 39369, 140; Massachusetts Historical Society, 142; Museum of Fine Arts, Boston, 144; Library of Congress, 145; The Granger Collection, 146; Library of Congress, 147; Library of Congress, 149; Christie's Images, 150; Connecticut Historical Society, 154; The Granger Collection, 156; The Granger Collection, 158

Chapter 7: Photos: Sam Holland, South Carolina State House, 162; Anne S. K. Brown Military Collection, Brown University Library, 166; Museum of Fine Arts, Boston, 167; The Granger Collection, 168; (top) Gilbert Stuart. "The Mohawk Chief Joseph Brant," 1786. Oil on canvas, 30" x 25". New York State Historical Association, Cooperstown, NY, 172; The Bostonian Society/Old State House, 172; Library of Congress, 176; Data available from U.S. Geological Survey, EROS Data Center, Sioux Falls, SD, 181; Corbis-Bettmann, 185; Library of Congress, 186; Art Resource, NY, 189

Chapter 8: Photos: The Granger Collection, 193; Print and Picture Collection, The Free Library of Philadelphia, 197; Collection of The New York Historical Society, 200; "The Republican Court," 1861, by Daniel P. Huntington. Oil on canvas. Gift of the Crescent Boys' Club. Brooklyn Museum of Art, 201; Indiana Historical Society Library (negative no. C2584), 205; "General George Washington Reviewing the Western Army...," by Francis Kemmelmeyer, after 1794. Oil on paper backed with linen. Dimensions 18 1/8" x 23 1/8". Courtesy of Winterthur Museum, 206; Collection of The New York Historical Society, 210; The Granger Collection, 212; Pennsylvania Academy of the Fine Arts, 213; Library of Congress, 214; Courtesy of American Antiquarian Society, 216; Library Company of Philadelphia, 217 Text: "Housing Values," Copyright © 1985 by Social Science History Association. Reprinted with the permission of Duke University Press, 215

Immigration & Community, to 1800: Photos: The Granger Collection, 225; The Granger Collection, 226 Text: "The Ancestry of the British Colonial Population" from Thomas L. Purvis, "The European Ancestry of the United States Population" in *William and Mary Quarterly,* 61 (1984): 85–101. Copyright © 1984 by the Institute of Early American History and Culture. Reprinted with the permission of the publishers., 223

Chapter 9: Photos: Henry Ford Museum & Greenfield Village, 228; Friedrich H. von Kittlitz, A View of the Russian Capital, 1827, from F.P. Litke. Alaska and Polar Regions, Department, Elmer E. Rasmusen Library Rare books, University of Alaska, Fairbanks, 232; Launching of ship "Fame" from Becket's Shipyard, Essex, Massachusetts, 1802, oil on canvas, by George Ropes. Mark Sexton, Peabody Essex Museum, 236; top, Library of Congress, 237; Library of Congress, 237; Museum of Early Southern Decorative Arts, 238; Thomas Gilcrease Institute of American History and Art, 243; Field Musuem of Natural History, 245; Library of Congress, 245; Library of Congress, 249; Library of Congress, 250; The New York Historical Society, 253

Chapter 10: Photos: NationsBank, 261; Walters Art Gallery, 268; Library of Congress, 270; The Maryland Historical Society, 273; Munson-Williams-Proctor Institute, 275; Chicago Historical Society, 277; Museum of the City of New York, 282; Library of Congress, 285; "Collection of the

Boston Athenaeum," 289; New York Public Library, 290 Text: "The Impact of the Erie Canal on Household Textile Manufacture" from Arthur Harrison Cole, The American Wool Manufacture. Copyright 1926 by the President and Fellows of Harvard College. Reprinted with the permission of Harvard University Press, 274

Chapter 11: Photos: Chicago Historical Society, 294; Library of Congress, 298; Wilson S. Armistead, University of Michigan Press, 299; Library of Congress, 307; The Historic New Orleans Collection, 308; Sophia Smith Collection, Smith College, 309; Library of Congress, 310; American Numismatic Society of New York, (left and right), 311; Daughters of the Republic of Texas, Yanaguana Society Collection, 312; The Historic New Orleans Collection, 315; National Archives, 317; Library of Congress, 319

Chapter 12: Photos: American Textile History Museum, 324; Abby Aldrich Rockefeller Folk Art Center, Williamsburg, VA, 328; Museum of Fine Arts, Boston, 329; Library of Congress, 332; Rhode Island Historical Society, 333; James L. Amos, National Geographic Society, (top & bottom) 336; High-Pressure Steamboat Mayflower, 1855, color lithograph by N. Currier. The Bettmann Archive. Corbis-Bettmann, 338; Baker Library, Graduate School of Business Administration, Harvard University, 340; Musuem of Fine Arts, Boston, 343; Mathew Brady/Brown Brothers, 344; The New York Historical Society, 346; Library of Congress, 347

Chapter 13: Photos: The New York Historical Society, 351; The Granger Collection, 358; Library of Congress, 360; Zelsa P. Mackay Collection, Courtesy George Eastman House, 362; "Seabury Champlin's June 3, 1791 Certificate of Membership in NY Mechanic Society," Abraham Godwin, print. Courtesy Winterthur Museum, 363; Frank and Marie-Therese Wood Print Collections, The Picture Bank, 364; The Schlesinger Library, Radcliffe College, 367; Library of Congress, 369; Hannah Harrison, Hancock Shaker Village, 371; Library of Congress (left & right), 373; Sophia Smith Collection, Smith College, 374; Lynn Historical Society, 376

Immigration & Community, 1800–1860: Photos: Dover Publications, Inc., 383; Museum of the City of New York, 384

Chapter 14: Photos: San Jacinto Museum of History Association, 386; Walters Art Gallery, 390; Henry E. Huntington Library and Art Gallery, 395; American Antiquarian Society, 397; The Walters Art Gallery, Baltimore, 398; Art Resource, NY, 399; Brown University Library, 404; National Gallery of Art, 406; The New York Historical Society, 408; California State Library, 409; Bigelow Collection, Museum of Fine Arts, Boston, 410; Steven Laschever/Museum of American Political Life/University of Hartford, 413 Text: "Overland Emigration to Oregon, California, and Utah, 1840-1860" from John Unruh, Jr., The Plains Across: The Overland Emigrants and the Trans-Mississippi West, 1840-60. Copyright © 1979 by the Board of Trustees of the University of Illinois. Reprinted with the permission of the University of Illinois Press., 396; "California in the Gold Rush," from Warren A. Beck and Ynez D. Haase, Historical Atlas of California. Copyright © 1974 by the University of Oklahoma Press. Reprinted with the permission of the publishers., 407

Chapter 15: Photos: The Granger Collection, 417; Harriet Beecher Stowe Center, Hartford, CT, Stowe-Day Foundation, 422; Courtesy American Antiquarian Society, 423; Library of Congress, 424; The Granger Collection, 431; Corbis-Bettmann, 432; New York Public Library, 434; Library of Congress, 435; Museum of the City of New York, 436; The Granger Collection, 437; Library of Congress, 440; United States Senate, 443

Chapter 16: Photos: Armen Shamalian Photographers, Art Resource, NY, 447; Courtesy Museum of Fine Arts, Boston, 451; The Picture Bank, 455; Alexander Gardner, National Archives, 456; Library of Congress, 458; Valentine Museum Library, (left) 459; Library of Congress, 459; Reproduced from Pauli Murray, Proud Shoes: The Story of an American Family,

HarperCollins Publishers, Inc., 1987, 466; Center of Military History, U.S. Army, 468; The Metropolitan Museum of Art, 469; Culvery Pictures, Inc., 471; Thomas C. Roche, Library of Congress, 475; Army Military History Institute, 476; Library of Congress, 477

Chapter 17: Photos: The Metropolitan Museum of Art, 481; National Archives, 485; Chicago Historical Society, 486; The Granger Collection, 488; The Susan B. Anthony House, Rochester, NY, 492; The Picture Bank/Harper's Weekly, 495; Library of Congress, 498; Library of Congress, 499; The University of North Carolina, (left) 501; Rutherford B. Hayes Presidential Center, 501; The Granger Collection, New York, 505; The Picture Bank, Frank and Marie-Therese Wood Print Collection, 507

Chapter 18: Photos: Christie's Images, 513; National Anthropological Archives, 518; Marion Koogler McNay Art Museum, 519; Timothy O'Sullivan, Amon Carter Museum, 522; Witte Museum, 525; Harper's Weekly, 527; Nebraska State Historical Society, Solomon D. Butcher Collection, 531; Library of Congress, 532; The Metropolitan Museum of Art, 537; Library of Congress, 538; Photo courtesy of State Historical Society of Iowa, Iowa City, 541; Edward Truman/The Denver Public Library, Western History Collection, 542 Text: "Oklahoma Territory" from John W. Morrois, Charles R. Goins, and Edwin C. McReynolds, Historical Atlas of Oklahoma, Third Edition. Copyright © 1965, 1976, 1986 by the University of Oklahoma Press. Reprinted with the permission of the publishers., 515; History and the Land feature and "Ethnic Composition of North Dakota, 1900," from John R. Shortridge, "The Great Plains" in Mary Kupiec Cayton, Elliott J. Gorn, and Peter W. Williams, Encyclopedia of American Social History II. Copyright © 1993 by Charles Scribner's Sons. Reprinted with the permission of Scribner's, an imprint of Simon & Schuster Macmillan. 528–529

Chapter 19: Photos: The Granger Collection, 547; U.S. Department of the Interior, National Park Service, Edison National Historic Site, 551 Chicago Historical Society, 553; Color engraving by J. Keppler from Puck, February 23, 1881, Collection of The New York Historical Society, New York City, 554; The Denver Public Library, Western History Collection, 556; Museum of the City of New York, 563; National Archives, 565; Terra Museum of American Art, 568; The Granger Collection, 570; Rhode Island School of Design, 573 Text: "U.S. Economy, 1873-1900" from Bernard Bailyn et al., The Great Republic, Third Edition. Copyright © 1985 by D.D. Heath and Company. Reprinted with the permission of Houghton Mifflin Company., 557

Chapter 20: Photos: Vermont State House, 578; Sally Anderson-Bruce/Museum of American Political Life, 583; Library of Congress, 585; Library of Congress, 588; Library of Congress, 590; The Granger Collection, New York, 594; National Archives, 596; Library of Congress, 601; Library of Congress, 603; Library of Congress, 604

Chapter 21: Photos: San Diego Museum of Art, 609; Lewis W. Hine/George Eastman House, 614; Henry Street Settlement, 615; Museum of the City of New York, 618; The Toledo Museum of Art, 622; Brown Brothers, 624; UPI/Corbis-Bettmann, 626; Collection of The American Labor Museum, Botto House National Landmark, 629; Planned Parenthood ® Federation of America, Inc. At, 810 Seventh Avenue, New York, NY, 10019., 631; Schomburg Center for Research in Black Culture, 632; California Historical Society, 635; Theodore Roosevelt Collection, Harvard College Library/The Houghton Library, Harvard University, 636

Chapter 22: Photos: Corbis-Bettmann, 642; The Granger Collection, 646; Culver Pictures, Inc., 649; Wallace Kirkland Papers, Jane Addams Memorial Collection, Special Collections, The University Library, University of Illinois at Chicago, 651; The Granger Collection, 652; Library of Congress, 653; National Archives, 654; National Archives, 655; Virginia War Museum/War Memorial Museum of Virginia, 659; Library of Congress, 661; Stock Montage Inc./ Historial Pictures Collection, 665;

INDEX

Forest Management Act (1897), 536
Forests, national, 535–36
Fort Gibson, battle at (1863), 462
Fort Jackson, Treaty of (1814), 248, 250
Fort Laramie, Treaty of (1868), 519, 540
Fort McIntosh, Treaty of (1785), 182
Fort Pillow, Tennessee, massacre at (1863), 466
Fortress Monroe, Virginia, 464
Fort Stanwix, Treaty of (1768), 140
Fort Stanwix, Treaty of (1784), 182
Fort Wayne, Treaty of (1809), 246
"Forty–niners," 407, 408
Fosdick, Raymond, 661
Fossils, early American, 4
Foster, Andrew "Rube," 687
Foster, Hannah Webster, 218
Four Bears, Chief, 230
Four Corners, 14
Fourier, Charles, 370
Fourteen Points, 666
Fourteenth Amendment, 483, 489, 502, 509, 619, 854
Fox, Charles James, 152
Fox, George, 114
Fox, William, 682
Fox Indians, 107, 281–82
Foxwoods Casino, Connecticut, 962
France: *See also* New France; World War I; World War II; American Revolution and, 170–71, 177; British blockade of (1793–1794), 206–7; colonization by, 39–42; cotton diplomacy in Civil War and, 457; Franco-American alliance of 1778, 203; in French and Indian War, 135–41; French Resistance in World War II, 775–76; fur trade, 41–42, 53–54; immigration from, 222, 223–24; in Indochina, 837; Louisiana Purchase and, 239–41; Napoleonic Wars, 242, 248, 249; Reign of Terror, 203; revolution in, 203–4, 216, 236; sugar plantations, 76–77; XYZ affair, 209–10
Franciscan missionaries, 50, 52–53, 109, 110, 396
Franco, Francisco, 738, 751
Frankfurter, Felix, 723
Franklin, Ann Smith, 117
Franklin, Benjamin, 117, 118, 119, 121, 222; American culture and, 288; in American Revolution, 169, 170, 177; colonial newspapers and, 142; Constitutional Convention and, 197, 198; Declaration of Independence and, 158; on Great Awakening, 126; in House of Commons, 146; Hutchinson and, 150; Paxton Boys and, 140; Plan of Union, 135; *Poor Richard's Almanac*, 125; as Postmaster, 141, 156
Franklin, James, 142
Franklin Evans, or the Inebriate (Whitman), 360
Franz Ferdinand, Archduke, 650
Fraternal societies, 570
Fredericksburg, battle of (1862), 461
Freed, Alan, 828
Freedmen, 482–83, 487, 497
Freedmen's Bureau, 474, 486, 488, 494, 495
Freedmen's Bureau Act (1865), 495
Freedom Rides, 860–61
Freedom's Journal, 372
Freedom Summer (Mississippi, 1964), 867–68
Free labor, notion of, 341
Free silver issue, 593–94
Free-Soil Party, 412, 413, 423–24, 430–31, 433
Free speech, wartime restrictions on, 663
Free speech movement, 884
Frémont, John C., 390, 403, 404, 433, 455
French and Indian War, 135–41
French Canadian immigrants, 561
French crescent, 106, 111–12
French Revolution (1789), 203–4, 216, 236
Freneau, Philip, 213, 216
Freud, Sigmund, 688
Frick, Henry C., 591
Friedan, Betty, 823, 898

Friends of Oder, 208
Fries, John, 211
Frobisher, Martin, 45
Frontier heritage, 117–19
Frontiers, 137, 396, 520–28, 530–31; *See also* Westward expansion
Fruitlands, Massachusetts, 370
Fugitive Slave Act (1850), 426–28, 464
Fugitive slaves, 75, 91–92, 109, 308–9
Fugitives (scholarly group), 703
Fulbright, J. William, 844, 883
Fuller, Margaret, 347–48
Fulton, Robert, 275, 276
Fundamental Orders, 63
Fur trade, 41–42, 53–54, 106, 107, 231, 236, 389–90, 397

G

Gabrielson, Guy, 804
Gadsden, Christopher, 152, 153
Gadsden Purchase (1853), 406, 524
Gage, Thomas, 148, 152, 153, 155, 157
Gag rule, 319, 375
Galileo, 124
Gallatin, Albert, 210, 211
Gallaudet, Edward Miner, 344
Galloway, Joseph, 152
Galton, Francis, 620
Gambling, Indian tribes and, 961–63
Gandhi, Mohandas, 405, 856, 858
Gang labor system, 75
Gangster films, 739
Garfield, James A., 583, 584
Garment industry, 339, 556, 626
Garrison, William Lloyd, 318–19, 372–76, 412
Garvey, Marcus, 701, 868
Gary, Elbert, 657, 666
Gates, Horatio, 169, 174, 175, 178
Gavin, Anna Maria, 383
Gay Activist Alliance, 899
Gay Liberation Front (GLF), 899
Gay liberation movement, 899
Gay Men's Health Crisis, 966
Gay Pride marches, 899
Geeche dialect, 90
Gemeinschaft and *Gesellschaft*, 620
General Agreement on Tariffs and Trade (GATT), 793, 978–79
General Court of Massachusetts Bay Colony, 60, 62, 63, 112, 113
General Federation of Women's Clubs, 630, 669
General Land Revision Act (1891), 535
General Motors, 658, 677, 679, 715
General Society of Mechanics and Tradesmen, 344
General Trades Union of New York, 365
General Union for Promoting the Observance of the Christian Sabbath, 366
Generational conflict, 883–88
Genêt, Edmond, 203–4
Genocide of Spanish conquest, 35
Gente de razón, 120
Gentility, middle class and, 568–69
Geological surveys of West, 390, 537
George, David Lloyd, 666
George, Henry, 534, 587–88
George III of England, King, 143, 145, 151, 153, 156, 157, 175
Georgia: civil rights movement in, 858, 859; in Civil War, 474, 476; colony of, 74–75, 86, 155; slavery in, 74–75
Georgia Constitutionalist, 435
German immigrants, 224–26, 355, 358, 359, 363, 365, 380, 381, 384–85; culture of, 381
Germany: Berlin crisis (1948), 793–94; Nazis in, 751, 775–76; post-World War II division of, 790; reparations, 667, 690–91; reunification of, 972; World War I and, 650–52, 656–57; World War II and, 771–78

Geronimo, 520
Gettysburg, battle of (1863), 460, 473
Ghent, Treaty of (1814), 249
Ghettos, 625–26, 709
Ghost Dance, 541–42
Ghost towns, 523
Gibbons v. Ogden, 276
GI Bill of Rights (1944), 787, 807, 822, 825
Gibson, Charles Dana, 653
Gibson, Josh, 687
Gifford, Walter S., 721
GI Forum, 871
Gilbert, Humphrey, 44, 45
Gilded Age, 567–75
Gilder, George, 950
Gillespie, Dizzy, 852
Gillette, George, 873
Gingrich, Newt, 979–80
Ginsberg, Allen, 832–33
Girard, Stephen, 282, 330–31
Girls Friendly Societies, 593
Gish, Lillian, 752
Giton, Judith, 223–24
Gladden, Washington, 592
Glasnost, 955–56
Global warming trend, 6
Glorieta Pass, battle of (1862), 462
"Glorious Ninety-two," 148
Glorious Revolution, 66, 69
Gnadenhutten, massacre at (1782), 194
Godey's Lady's Book, 345
Godkin, E.L., 508, 606
Gold: in Black Hills, 519; California Gold Rush, 381, 382, 383–84, 395, 407, 408–10, 516, 522; search for in New World, 32–33, 36
Gold, Michael, 738
Goldman, Emma, 629, 631, 669
Gold Standard Act (1900), 595
Goldwater, Barry, 869, 949
Goldwyn, Samuel, 682
Gompers, Samuel, 559, 590, 596, 606, 627, 644, 658, 678
Gone with the Wind (Mitchell), 737
Gonzales, Corky, 901
Goodman, Andrew, 867
Goodman, Benny, 741
Goodman, Paul, 832
Good Neighbor Policy, 599–600
Gorbachev, Mikhail, 956–57, 971
Gordon, Richard, 823
Gordon, Thomas, 142
Gorman, Howard, 735
Gorton, Samuel, 63
Gospel of Wealth, The (Carnegie), 555
Gospel of work, 555
Gossip column, 684
Gould, Jay, 505, 550, 554
Government: *See also* Politics; balance of power in, 239; civil service reform, 506, 584–85, 799; colonial, 123; commission form of, 616; era of divided, 979–81; exploration of West sponsored by, 390; under Jefferson, 238–39; machinery of politics, 583–84; post–Civil War growth of, 581–83; post-revolutionary, formation of, 196–200; spoils system, 269–70, 584–85; in the twenties, 688–92; urban, structural reforms in, 616
Government-business partnership, 658
Graduated income tax, 636
Graduate studies, 571–72; *See also* Colleges and universities
Grady, Henry Woodfin, 564
Graham, Billy, 807, 931
Gramercy Park, New York City, 356–57
Gramm-Rudman Act (1985), 966–67
Grand Banks, fish in, 41–42
Grand Coulee Dam, 733
Grandfather clauses, 596

16; Open Door policy and, 601; reexport, 236, 242; Russian-Californio, 406–7; Santa Fé, 397; shipping, 235–37, 242, 243, 331; spice, 29; trade deficit with Great Britain (1784–1786), 187, 188; triangular, 98
Trade associations, expansion of national, 690
Trading monopolies, 95–97
"Trail of Tears," 281
Trans-Appalachian settlement, 231, 233–34
Transborder peoples, 986
Transcendentalism, 347–48
Transcendental meditation (TM), 934
Transcendental Wild Oats (Alcott), 370
Transcontinental Treaty (1819), 254
Trans-Mississippi West, 513–45; cattle industry in, 526–28; Civil War in, 462–63; ethnography of, 538–39; farming communities in, 529–33; frontier settlement, 520–26, 530–31; landscape of West, 536–39; legends of, 537–38; mining communities, 521, 522–23; Mormon settlements, 523–24; Native Americans and, 516–20, 539–45; Oklahoma Land Rush, 514–15; Southwest settlements, 524–26
Transportation: *See also* Railroads; agriculture in Old Northwest and, 276–77; American System and, 253–54; automobiles, 658, 679–80, 715–16, 759, 823; canals, 254, 262, 272, 273–75, 278, 279, 355, 636; steamboats, 275, 337, 338; mass transportation systems, 563; revolution, 271–79; roads, 254, 267, 271, 272–73, 278, 279, 822; slavery and growth of, 93; in South, 301; steamboats, 275, 337, 338; subways and trolleys, 563
Trans-Siberian Railway, 668
Travis, Joseph, 310
Travis, William, 387
Treason, 167
Treasury, Department of the, 581
Treatise on Domestic Economy (Beecher), 345
Trenchard, John, 142
Trench warfare, 656–57
Trenton, New Jersey, 169
Trescot, William Henry, 317
Tres Riches Heures, 29
Triangle Shirtwaist Company fire (1911), 626
Triangular trade, 98
Tribal council, 12
Tribal Government Tax Status Act (1983), 961
Triple Alliance (Central Powers), 650
Triple Entente (Allies), 650
Trist, Nicholas, 405
Trolleys, electric, 563
Trotter, William Monroe, 633, 667
Truman, Harry S.: atomic bomb and, 780–82; civil rights and, 851; Cold War and, 796–814; containment policy and, 791–96; election of 1948, 798–99; Fair Deal and, 799–800; Korean conflict and, 808–11; presidency, 796–814
Truman Doctrine, 791–92
Trumbull, John, 214, 216
Trumbull, Lyman, 505–6
Trustbusting, 633–34
Truth, Sojourner, 372, 373
Tsuzuki, Byron Takashi, 763
Tubb, Ernest, 766
Tuberculosis, 549, 611
Tubman, Harriet, 309, 310, 372, 426
Tugwell, Rexford G., 723, 728–29
Tukekas, Old Chief, 520
Tunney, Gene, 687
Turkey, post–World War II aid for, 791
Turnbull, Robert J., 309–10
Turner, Frederick Jackson, 392, 597
Turner, Henry M., 465
Turner, Nat, 296, 309, 310, 318, 372
Turner, Stansfield, 936
Turner Diaries (Pierce), 931
Tuscarora Indians, 68, 173

Tuskegee Institute, 571
Twain, Mark, 276, 604, 607
Tweed, William Marcy, 506, 584
"Tweed Ring," 508
Twelfth Amendment, 212
Twelve Years a Slave (Northup), 305, 427
Twenties, the, 673–707; African Americans in, 700–701; agriculture and ailing industries in, 681–82; automobile industry and, 679–80; bull market of, 717; cities and suburbanization in, 681; economy in, 688–92; election of 1928, 703–5, 707; feminism in, 697–98; foreign policy in, 691–92; government in, 688–92; immigration restrictions in, 693–94; intellectuals and alienation in, 701–3; Ku Klux Klan in, 694–95; mass culture, rise of, 675–76, 682–88; Mexican immigration in, 698–700; modern corporation and, 676–77; new morality in, 687–88; postwar prosperity in, 676–82; prohibition in, 692–93; religious fundamentalism in, 695–96; resistance to change in, 692–96; second industrial revolution in, 676; welfare capitalism and, 677–78
Twenty-First Amendment, 693
Two-income family, 805–7
Tydings, Millard E., 804
Tyler, John, 286, 287, 402, 403
Typhoid fever, 163, 563

U

U–2 incident (1960), 835
U–boats, 651, 655
Ulises criollo (Vasconcelos), 712
Uncle Tom's Cabin (Stowe), 375, 421–22
Underclass, 926–27
Underground Railroad, 309, 375
Underwood-Simmons Act (1913), 638
Unemployed Councils, 727
Unemployment: in depression of 1873, 507–8; financial collapse of 1893 and, 590; in Great Depression, 719–21, 744
Unidentified flying object (UFO) sightings, 808
Unification Church, 934
Union(s), 363–64; *See also* specific unions; African Americans in, 760; American Federation of Labor (AFL), 559, 627–28, 643, 644, 658, 694, 729; biracial cooperation in, 851; craft, 559; Industrial Workers of the World (IWW), 628, 630, 643, 644, 659, 669; mining industry, 523, 627; in New Deal coalition, 716; in 1970s, 919; in 1930s, 729; open shop, 627, 678; strikes in 1890s and, 591–92; in the twenties, 678, 682; women in, 588; in World War I, 658–59; in World War II, 760
Union Army, 451, 453, 464, 469, 470–71; *See also* Civil War
Union League, 482, 497–98
Union of Russian Workers, 669
Union Pacific Railroad Company, 457, 504, 554
United Automobile Workers (UAW), 715, 729, 759
United Fruit Company, 553, 646, 837
United Latin American Citizens (LULAC), 700
United Mine Workers, 627, 682, 729
United Nations (UN), 789–90, 809
U.S. Children's Bureau, 614, 636, 662, 762
U.S. Foreign Debt Commission, 691
U.S. Forest Service, 535, 536, 634
United States Industrial Commission, 595
U.S. Office of Education, 762
U.S. Patent Office, 533
U.S. Public Health Service, 662
U.S. Rubber Company, 760
United States Sanitary Commission, 449, 470, 491
U.S. Steel Corporation, 555, 564, 628, 658
U.S. v. Cruikshank, 502
United States v. John, 961
U.S. v. Reese, 502
United States v. Reynolds, 524

United States v. Wheeler, 874, 927, 961
Universal Doctrine of Human Rights, 789
Universal Negro Improvement Association, 701
Universal white manhood suffrage, 212–13, 263, 264–65, 266, 330
University of California at Berkeley, 884, 902
University of Mississippi, 862
University of Washington, 786–87
University of Wisconsin, 886
Up from Slavery (Washington), 632
Uprising of the 20,000, 625–26
Uptown, Chicago, Illinois, 879–80
Upward Bound, 889
Urban civilizations, Mesoamerican, 10–11
Urbanization. *See* Cities and towns
Urban Renewal Act, 879
Urbina, Rosa Maria, 990
Urey, Harold C., 796
Utah, 425; *See also* Mormonism; admission to Union, 425
Ute Indians, 8
Utopianism, 369–70, 579

V

Vallandigham, Clement, 470
Valley Forge, 163–64, 169
Van Buren, Martin, 262–63, 267, 268, 280, 284–87, 402, 413
Vance, Cyrus R., 936, 938, 940
Vandenberg, Arthur H., 791, 796
Vanderbilt, Cornelius, 505
Van Devanter, Wilis, 742
Van Kleeck, Mary, 660
Vardaman, James, 617
Vasconcelos, José, 712
Vaudeville, 573
Vaughn, Robert, 55
Veblen, Thorstein, 567
Venereal disease, campaign against, 661–62
Veramendi, Ursula, 400
Vergennes, Comte de, 170, 171, 177
Verrazano, Giovanni da, 42
Versailles peace conference (1918), 666
Versailles Treaty (1919), 667–68, 751
Vertical integration, 553, 555, 690
Vesey, Denmark, 309–10, 318
Vespucci, Amerigo, 33
Vessey, John, 953
Veterans Bureau, 582
Veterans of Foreign Wars, 887
Veto power, 201
Vice-admiralty courts, 146
Vicksburg, battle of (1863), 460, 473
Videocassette recorders (VCR), 963
Vietnam, Democratic Republic of, 905
Vietnam Veterans against the War, 887
Vietnam War, 881–83; African Americans in, 887, 897; air attacks, 882; antiwar movement, 883–88, 904; domestic agenda and, 880; domino theory and, 837; foundations for, 837–38; generational opposition to, 883–88; Johnson and, 881–83, 893; Kennedy and, 842; King and, 893–94; military in, 887–88, 905; My Lai Massacre, 905; Nixon and, 904–5; refugees at end of, 989; television and, 882; Tet Offensive (1968), 892–93; veterans of, 887, 888
Vigilantism, 195, 643–44, 663–64
Villa, Francisco "Pancho," 648–49
Vincennes, capture of (1779), 173
Virginia: American Revolution and reform in, 184–85; backcountry, 115; Bacon's Rebellion, 66, 68, 84; Civil War in northern, 461; colony of, 54, 98; Harpers Ferry raid, 437–38; House of Burgesses, 98, 147, 149; House of Delegates, 184; Jamestown colony, 54–55; John Smith's map of, 55; ratification of Constitution, 199–200; Roanoke colony, 26–27, 45; secession of, 452